I0815218

Large, Lasting, & Inevitable

Jorge Silvetti in Dialogues and Writings on Architecture as a Cultural Practice

PARK BOOKS

Contents

Foreword

BY NICOLÁS DELGADO ALCEGA

Jorge Silvetti's writings over the past six decades boldly and unapologetically address many issues afflicting our architectural culture today. They bring great cultural and social complexity to bear on architecture while remaining focused on the art of making buildings and cities. His candid writings have influenced the thinking of generations of architects and scholars and are a breath of fresh air in a world where politics often disguises itself as discourse, threatening the free inquiry that our universities have stood for throughout centuries.

Jorge is first and foremost an architect and a teacher. He has been in the trenches of American architectural education since the late sixties with a level of involvement that makes him a unique window into the rapidly changing decades that have unfolded since. Jorge understands architecture to be an art primarily focused on all those aspects of buildings that make them material culture. He can take a building, unpack the cultural and historical processes that shaped it, and explain why a particular architectural form gained significance at a specific moment of its lifetime. This ability has helped thousands of students understand why *they* marvel at certain works of architecture, and how this experience is influenced by their own contemporary cultural context. It has also given them the intellectual tools to free themselves from the shackling allure of those contemporary works that, despite their seductive novelty, contain no real substance. This book tracks how such a way of seeing architecture has developed throughout Jorge's life.

More than a traditional scholarly output, Jorge's writings stem from a deep-seated urge to contribute to contemporary conversations when he feels they lack clarity. The structure of this book emerged from the nature of his body of work. We began by carefully selecting Jorge's most representative and valuable writings. After organizing them chronologically, we identified five distinct stages of Jorge's intellectual journey, to which we have dedicated a section each.

The selection begins with Jorge's first published piece, "The Beauty of Shadows." This abstract and theoretically dense essay synthesizes the research that he was doing as a PhD student and organizes many of his early ideas about architecture. This essay is followed by a group of writings from Jorge's early teaching years that make sense of issues in the discourse of the mid-seventies in an almost didactic, if still opinionated, fashion. From these writings, the book moves on to more scholarly pieces that come out of Jorge's years of research in Sicily. These pieces reveal Jorge's distinct way of thinking about the relationship between architecture and history amid the unraveling of Postmodernism. Then, there are a series of pieces that begin around the time that Jorge becomes chair of the Department of Architecture at Harvard. These texts are squarely critical of the architectural discourse in the late nineties. They collect confident, assertive positions that seek to move the conversation away from an exhausted theory, frivolous trends, and the short-lived novelties that we are still jumping between in lieu of a real disciplinary project. The book ends with Jorge's latest pieces of writing. These are more reflective, whether they revisit topics closer to Jorge's own geographical origins or assess the ways in which guiding theories for the production of architecture like typology require repositioning.

To complete the book, we invited one interlocutor to read each grouping of Jorge's writings and join us in a dialogue to explore the world in which they emerged. If there is something I have learned about Jorge since I met him eight years ago, it's that he is a person for whom candid dialogue is an essential vehicle for exploration and reflection. His ability to leave a strong mark on so many generations of students doesn't just come from his peculiar ability to bring a broad range of cultural forces to bear on the explanation of an architectural event. It also comes from his genuine curiosity for the perspective of his interlocutors, even when he strongly disagrees with them, and his ability to integrate what he learns from these exchanges into his own theses.

Dialogues allowed us to include individuals from different generations who could interrogate in distinct ways the events we have revisited alongside Jorge. They unleashed a fluid process through which we were able to gather Jorge's perceptive first-person account of the developments within our discipline since Modernism began to lose its vitality. This resulted in distinct explorations of the contexts Jorge moved through, decanted on the basis of what feels most broadly useful about it all in the present.

However, the dialogues took us beyond revisiting this history. Nothing is simply an academic or documentary exercise for Jorge. He is interested in studying architecture so that he can design it; interested in looking into the past to fuel his thinking about what is going on in the present. The dialogues quickly became a space through which we debated, with the hindsight of Jorge's past experience, the issues that most concern us about architectural culture today. This turned the book on its head. The dialogues all of a sudden became the main thread of the book, enriched by the supporting selection of Jorge's past writings that gave rise to them.

Each section of the book is named after a physical place that Jorge engaged with during the time of the selected writings, and which revealed itself to be of particular relevance as we engaged in dialogue with our interlocutors. With Alfredo Thiermann we explored Jorge's experience at Berkeley during the late sixties. We discussed the evolving cultural and intellectual climate that was unfolding as the emergence of the computer, countercultural rock concerts, systems theory, and the Vietnam War converged. This allowed us to uncover how this eye for architecture as material culture consolidated in Jorge, and through what balance the designer and the intellectual in him coexist.

With Mark Lee, we discussed the shifts that Jorge saw at the Harvard Graduate School of Design from the departure of dean Josep Lluís Sert to that of dean Gerald M. McCue. We clarified how the "theory generation" that Jorge belongs to reopened the doors to a historical and culturally loaded reading of architecture using an original theoretical framework. This led us to delve into how one fosters a school of thought, as well as the relationship between our discipline and the institutions that nurture it.

Erika Naginski joined us in the third section of the book to explore Jorge's decade-long relationship with Sicily. She unpacked the passionate way in which Jorge has engaged with architectural history and historians themselves throughout his life. The dialogue produced a series of lasting lessons about the development of theories through which we, as architects, engage with the past and the way in which we make buildings from other buildings.

Elisa Silva then revisited Jorge's years as chair of the Department of Architecture at Harvard. We discussed how Jorge navigated a decade of disciplinary distraction driven by the definitive arrival of the personal computer and the exhaustion of the expired theories of the seventies and eighties. This led us to outline the needs in the world that demand architecture, and the ways in which they determine the field of operation of our discipline in practice, expanding our understanding of how architecture operates within its broader cultural and temporal context.

In the final section of the book, Nader Tehrani pushed us to review the cultural practice that Jorge and Rodolfo Machado built over the decades in Boston around the understanding that architecture *is* material culture. The conversation explored how many of the topics touched upon elsewhere in the book make their way to the design process itself, and why drawing was such an important aspect of Jorge and Rodolfo's work.

For Jorge, the act of designing buildings and cities serves as the guiding force that shapes the space he gives to all other academic and professional endeavors. No matter the depths of the world of theory that he has dived into, or the cultural complexity of the readings he enjoys formulating, his own journey has always been centered by the realities that come into play when one needs to make these large, inert, and functional objects that we require for the purpose of dwelling. We have much to gain by reflecting upon such a way of grounding a broad set of concerns and curiosities amid our current world of interdisciplinary thinking. There are so many urgent issues that demand our attention and creativity. But to address them tangibly, we must abandon the hang-ups that have us treading water. We must rewire the synaptic connections between inquiry, critique, and action within our discipline. This book is our way of fostering a conversation that can orient collective effort towards this process. Towards a profound way of thinking about architecture that is fueled by all of that *realism* that the world is sending our way.

Prologue

Buenos Aires: Twelve Scenes from My Youth

BY JORGE SILVETTI

Previous spread: At the time I was born (1942), Buenos Aires was in full mode of transformation into a world metropolis, keeping pace with architecture's changing styles. In this emblematic intersection of Arroyo, Esmeralda, and Juncal Streets, from left to right: the brand new Minner Apartments (1934), one of the earliest modern rationalist buildings in Argentina by Hungarian-born architect Jorge Kalnay; the eclectic Mihanovic Tower of 1928, topped with a "replica" of the Mausoleum of Halicarnassus, by Calvo, Jacobs y Giménez (the tallest building in South America until 1936); and the Palacio Estrugamou (1925, Eduardo Sauze y August Huguier), a luxury apartment building in the Beaux-Arts style typical of the exclusive neighborhoods of the city. All three buildings are in use to this day.

Somos nuestra memoria, somos ese quimérico museo de formas inconstantes, ese montón de espejos rotos.

—Jorge Luis Borges[1]

This prologue contrasts sharply with the genres of the rest of the book. Unlike the dialogues and essays that make up the bulk of the volume, this is a monologue in the first person focused on the formative years of my life in Argentina. Conceived as a prolegomenon to extensive discussions about topics and events associated with my intellectual, professional, and academic development since I left Argentina, I feared that it could easily fall into the traps of autobiography—a genre I purposely dismissed from the outset. Autobiography's misleading rhetoric of smooth, seamless, and totalizing discourse of recalled events in chronological order tends to suggest—with an inherent logic of causality—uncomfortable justifications or false prefigurations. Rather, I have chosen a cruder format, even if it is unable to sustain a narrative: fragments—those sharp, vivid standalone images, figures, and stories of my past that pop up with a power and honesty of their own. These fragments do not claim autonomy from their whole—a whole that nevertheless cannot be known or reconstructed—but they possess the innate force of everything that emerges on its own from memory; and like the ruins of an ancient building—found by chance—fragments have the indisputable capacity to act as evidence, which they are. While they are incomplete by nature, these fragments exist as fully comprehensible, eventful entities independent of context. This is why they can activate, without burden, the power of the reader's imagination. They are worthy of consideration not because they explain my life but rather because, from the distance of decades, they are the ones, as opposed to others, that choose to *emerge now*. I selected these fragments as they have come to me because if they have chosen to come, then it means they are significant forms of evidence that are valuable to the work I have been doing through this book.

These standalone fragments that follow nonetheless share a common denominator in my mind: clear, graphic images with the city as their backdrop. The city not merely because it is where they mostly took place, but also because it acts as the scenery of a play does, defining the character and tone of the events, their locations, or periods as I recall them. Some of them have a specific building or public space in the foreground. They are all inseparable from the actions that took place. I will preface what follows with some basic personal information.

I spent the first twenty-five years of my life in Buenos Aires, where I was born in 1942, with sporadic short-term displacements within its vast, flat geographic realm.[2] This city is the salient factor that defines who I still am eight decades later. Even if Buenos Aires shares generic characteristics with other metropolises, its urbanity in those years of my youth was remarkable, productive, and exemplary. I see the character of urban life during those years as having propelled me, a second-generation descendant of Italian immigrants, as well as my generation of peers. We all belonged to a very large urban middle class and became highly educated urban individuals. When I recall my infancy and youth, my memories are populated almost exclusively by the urban rather than the domestic scene.

So, here go my urban fragments.

Four scenes in mid-century Buenos Aires. I am eight years old. I begin there and then, with a few selected fragmentary memories, because it is a year full of images that emerge, persistently. Always.

SCENE 1 *I am with my mother in the waiting area of the music conservatory to pick up my sister, who has been enrolled there for two years. We can see her through the glass doors of one of the classrooms in her sol-fa lesson, singing the notes she reads while marking the tempo with repetitive, automaton-like movements of her right hand. The piano teacher sees us and comes to greet my mother and discuss my sister's progress. She explores my hands as she speaks. She grabs my fingers one at a time, stretching, pulling, and lifting them, and she concludes that they are wonderful, promising hands for piano playing. She asks me whether I want to learn to play, and I say yes. My mother agrees, and I start the following week, although she hides this from my father for a few months because she is unsure how he will take it. She needs to prepare him.*

I am performing in a student recital. I am playing Mozart's Sonata No. 11 in A Major K 331 at the auditorium of the Sociedad Científica Argentina, Buenos Aires, 1953.

Entering *the world of music* was the most consequential of all these mid-century events, I now recall. It was an entirely new world where, from day one, I played a very different role than the one I played in my daily life. While there was smooth continuity between home and school, stepping *into* and *up to* the conservatory—I had to climb a very long staircase to enter—immersed me in an experience of a different order.[3] Music was my first foreign language. I learned to express something of myself, not with words, but with my physical actions and my singing in the sol-fa lessons—with my limbs, my breathing, my eyes sometimes shut when confident, and my mind sensing rather than thinking.

It was also consequential that studying music afforded me my first serious aesthetic experience by playing the works of the great composers, almost from day one; by interpreting them, that is, by repeating what they had "said," filtered through my expressive self, as soon as I was able to read with my own eyes the entirely new and complex graphic language that sent directives to my brain on how to articulate each of my fingers to push down on the right keys. This is the first, fundamental formative experience for any music student. And it all happened under the rigorous one-on-one scrutiny of my idolized teacher.[4] She heard and assessed my playing, checked the correctness of every one of my bodily operations: the position of my wrists and fingers, never straight, but curved in a cusp, in the perfect French mode *comme il faut*, and pressuring keys only with their tips; my desirable "seating posture," vertical, straight up with lowered, relaxed shoulders; and my faithful delivery of the dynamics and rhythmic marks as indicated by the author, which she underlined for emphasis with her energetic pencil marks and comments on the scores, still visible in the yellowed music books that I conserve.

SCENE 2 *It is December 8, 1950, and I am experiencing wonder. I am seated among a cohort of impeccably well-dressed children in orderly, parallel rows divided by a central aisle. On the right side, girls with fancy long white dresses and caps of embroidered organza, tulle, and brocade. We, the boys, on the left in dark suits and ties, displaying our fancy right-arm bands of wide white silk ribbons tied up in a bow that ends in long tassels. We are in church, the main protagonists of the event in the central nave, amid marvelous scenery. Families, friends, and the public on the side naves are all focused on us. We are entranced, ready to receive a miraculous meal.*

Interior view of the altar and pulpit of the Iglesia de la Santa Cruz in Buenos Aires from the pews in the central nave.

It is our first communion, my earliest experience of something somewhat close to ecstasy, triggered by the ritualistic mise-en-scène that transformed the well-known dark church of my neighborhood into a space of wonder; into what I interpreted, after the shock of seeing it on that day so utterly changed, to be an anticipation of Heaven—which I now understand was the point of all that staging! The conjunction of live choral music with the organ resonating in the gigantic nave, the exuberant decor of white flowers, the dizzying incense being spilled on and all over us, and the sea of lit candles—enhanced by hidden electrical lights—metamorphosed the upward lift of the church's neo-Gothic architecture with a supernatural, celestial impulse.[5] There we all were, celebrating an abstract concept: purity, incarnated in what the priests called, without ever explaining, the incomprehensible notion of the Immaculate Conception of Mary. We were center stage, at our brightest, purest, and most chaste. It was a totalizing experience. I was transfixed.

SCENE 3 *I am in line with my family, waiting to enter an unusual building recently erected in one of the most exclusive neighborhoods of Buenos Aires. It is a house that does not look like any other house I have ever seen. It is also a museum—a replica of the house where our national hero, el General del Ejército de los Andes y Libertador de América, Don José de San Martín, died a century earlier. I am intrigued by the uniqueness of this house; it is an enshrined image that reinforces our hero's own. I inspect the contents of the house with genuine commotion, including all of the daily artifacts that General San Martín used. Soon, I return a second time, at my insistence, with my uncle's family.*

Above: The house in Grand Bourg, Paris, where General José de San Martín lived in exile.
Below: The enlarged replica of the house of General José de San Martín in Grand Bourg, Paris, built in the neighborhood of Palermo Chico, Buenos Aires, in 1946 for the celebration of the centenary of his death.

In 1950, all Argentinians were in a very special mood; a celebratory state of mind that lasted 365 days. It was the kind of hype that a boy of my age could fully feel, appreciate, and participate in. It was the centennial year of the death of General San Martín, also referred to more poetically as *El Santo de la Espada* in all communications and official documents that reminded us all of our duty to honor our superman at all times, everywhere: in schools, on the radio, in the large urban ornaments decorating main streets and public spaces, in the relentlessly recurrent acts of reverence and military might.

Amid the cheerful feast was this "house" of great popular impact that the government had recently inaugurated. It was a *brand new, exact replica* of the original house outside of Paris where San Martín spent the last years of his life in a self-imposed exile. This building, which housed a museum with corresponding furniture replicas, authentic memorabilia, and documents, became one of the main attractions for thousands of Argentinians who flocked to see the fraudulent "relic" during the yearlong celebration. The house had a more compelling effect on me than the military parades, publications, and public displays of patriotism to which we were all subjected.

However, what most persists in my mind today is the effect of the Spanish word *réplica* employed in all promotional material on our new national treasure. It was permanently installed in my incipient vocabulary, at an age incongruous with its charged meaning but absorbed within a context in which it carried a precisely paradoxical message: because it was an exact replica, it held the original's authority; it was authentic because its form matched, exactly, the original. And everybody rejoiced in such a condition, simply because for us in Argentina, it was, *of course*, amazing that we possessed *an exact replica* of the place where our national hero had lived so far away from us, because a replica of a remote cultural artifact has an entirely different value than one that exists in close proximity to the original.[6] We lived in a geographic location where all that seemed to matter was out of reach, only available to us in movies, then in the news, in the accounts of lucky travelers, and, of course, in the memories recited by our grandparents, relatives, and friends of the family that migrated to Argentina in search of a better life.[7] Within that frame of mind so shaped by representations, a replica that one could touch and inhabit looked perfectly legitimate. More importantly, when attached to a mythical narrative—the house of our unimpeachable secular *Saint*—the relic acquired the status of a reliquary and magic took over. So, fascinated, I came to regard this work of artifice, this imitation, as an authentic treasure.

My affective connection with this building and its aura was intense, and the fact that I was attached to a singular piece of French vernacular architecture reinforced that sentiment: it was different from all other houses in the city. A house I still see in passing every time I am in Buenos Aires, one that brings both a smile and a jolt in my heart as I remind myself of the disillusion that came later when I learned that while the replica was "faithful" as a figure, its *dimensions* were all augmented proportionally by a third of the original. The real one was a residence of very modest size, unsuited to operate as a public museum. As usual, with the passage of time childhood myths melt away.[8]

SCENE 4 *Any time, any day between 1942 and 1960, my home in Buenos Aires.*

Above: View of a street in San Isidro, Buenos Aires, made up of *casas chorizo*. Below: View of the main patio of a *casa chorizo* in Buenos Aires.

In this exercise in fragments, I want to introduce one of a purely intellectual nature, which depends on a generalization and which might, with reason, not be accepted by the reader as a veritable fragment. Yet it is a single fact, ever present in the years I'm evoking. It is my home, in two ways: as a representative instance of a generic building type with significant urban consequences for Buenos Aires, and conversely, as the singular, constant interior scene of my personal life.

My house was the typical middle-class house in mid-century Buenos Aires: a *casa chorizo*. This contraption produced by Italian immigrant masons at the turn of the century emerged as a building

Horacio Coppola's 1936 photograph of the undefined shoreline of Río de la Plata in Olivos, an adjacent locality to the north of Buenos Aires, which is visible on the horizon. Today this area is completely urbanized and continuous with the metropolitan area.

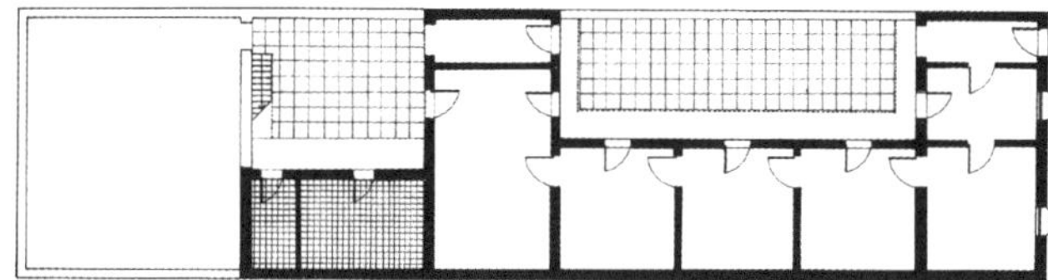

Generic plan of a *casa chorizo*.

type that would be the physical unit in the first major expansion of what had been, up until the latter half of the nineteenth century, a dormant Spanish colonial city.[9] The most synthetic and effective way to describe the type to an audience of architects is to say that it is a half of the classical Roman domus, cut along the axis of symmetry. Although its origin is Roman, its width is invariably ten Spanish *varas*, as established by the Laws of the Indies in the early sixteenth century regarding the foundation of cities by the Spanish Crown.[10]

In this mutilated domus, the remaining half atrium served as a formal open courtyard, usually covered by a *toldo*.[11] The other open space in the back—the half-sized inner peristyle of a domus—became the private, domestic multipurpose family patio, be it for drying clothes, growing a small vegetable garden or fruit trees, hosting a makeshift workshop, providing storage, or accommodating an eventual addition. The property line, coinciding with the original longitudinal axis of symmetry, was materialized by a thick masonry party wall, usually shared with an adjacent *casa chorizo*. Each *casa chorizo* is, of course, an exception to these generic rules, but overall there are a few constants that determine a very precise and clear way of occupying, aggregating, and flexibly using the type. Invariably, the first half patio is lined with porticos against the building's side, creating a covered exterior circulation.[12] Adjacent to this is an interior circulation, an enfilade connecting all the rooms of the house—one after the other, like a *ristra de chorizos*, hence the type's name and distinctive mode of use.[13] It is a unique and incomparable kind of house in which the idea of "privacy" is filtered and acted through the particular conventions and mores of society and each family.

The *casa chorizo* is an anachronistic collection of equal classical rooms, linked together like a chain, all approximately 4×4×4 meters. Yet, it has proven, to this day, to be infinitely pliable to the fluctuations and idiosyncrasies of a society that evolved rapidly through industrialization, immigration, and explosive urban growth. The type is *a string* of neutral spaces in which each generic room could acquire conventional or uniquely distinctive functions, sometimes even depending on the hour of the day; from openness to total privacy. Growing up, I saw rooms in many such houses that I had access to become a final home-within-a-home for grandparents and their vintage possessions, the daytime workshop of a spinster aunt who was a seamstress converted into a bedroom at night, a small but full-fledged appliance repair shop in the back patio, a temporary bedroom for a whole branch of distant family that had come from the countryside for an errand, and lately fully dedicated home offices or artist's studios.

My *casa chorizo* gave me a powerful model of what a house was and how it could be used. It is the kind of house in which more or less everyone I knew lived—certainly most of my extended family, friends, and many unknown people in my entire neighborhood in the Barrio Sur, which belonged to the then-huge Argentinian urban middle class. This predominantly one-story building adapted well to simple aggregation. One adjacent to the other and repeatable on all four sides of a square block. The type spread like oil in all directions across the city's uneventful topography. Buenos Aires lies on the eastern edge of an immense flat land that stretches from the foot of the Andes, slopes imperceptibly eastward, and finally slips quietly under the waters of the Río de la Plata, without a defined boundary mark. Indeed, the city and its metropolitan area have an undefined, vague border against the river. Perhaps because of this, Buenos Aires never resolved its face to the river and produced instead a surprisingly ambiguous, and at times indifferent relationship with its extensive waterfront.[14]

That was the Argentinian topography that I knew until I broadened my social group at the university, with colleagues that had similar interests but came from a wider spectrum of society, and I began to travel with them beyond the area within which my family had ventured. That was when I saw the Andes and snow for the first time. But it was too late: these were the "other landscapes" of the country. Argentina still is, for me, the abstract landscape of my youth, defined entirely by the absolute line of the horizon, which separates land from either sky or water.

Mourners lining up on Diagonal Norte (Avenida Presidente Roque Sáenz Peña) in downtown Buenos Aires in the winter of 1952 to pay their respects to Eva Perón at her wake.

SCENE 5 *It is Saturday, July 26, 1952. It is my debut concert, playing a piano sonatina by Clementi at the auditorium of the Biblioteca del Consejo de Mujeres.*[15] *I am standing on the left wing of the stage with fellow performers of various levels within the ranks, all unseen by the public. We are each waiting for our turn to go on stage, bow, sit at the piano, and give it our best. Most have done this before, my sister among them. Only two of us are debutants. My mind is blank during the performance until the applause shakes me up and it is over. In the end, we all bow alongside our teacher. When we return home after dinner, our neighbor is at the door and stops my father to whisper something into his ear.*

Most Argentinians of my generation undoubtedly remember that date, but due to another event, an event that became a before-and-after moment in everyone's life. Early in the evening, when clocks marked eight hours and twenty-five minutes—as would be repeated every day on the radio at that exact time for the rest of the year—the thirty-three-year-old wife of the president and strong idol of the masses had died. "Evita," as they called her, instantly became a mythical deity that still resonates with many in every corner of Argentina. "Eva Perón ha muerto, la República está de duelo..." were the first words we would hear at school, as spoken by our principal, every morning.

Already two years into music studies, the extended period of mourning introduced me, in excess, to *música sacra*, a genre previously unknown to me, creating a background of somber mood that was broadcast continuously by the state radio. For the grand finale after a fifteen-day-long wake, on the day of her interminable public burial, we heard a single, unforgettable piece all day long: the second movement of Chopin's Piano Sonata No. 2—the famous Funeral March—orchestrated and played by a military band and broadly amped up by the loudspeakers of our neighborhood's Unidad Básica Peronista.[16]

However, these rituals were not the only actions related to her death that had an impact on children. Orders came from above that on one of the days of the wake, school children should be bussed to the place where her embalmed corpse lay in view. And so we were. In our best clothes—perfectly ironed white uniforms and wearing black ties provided by the school—we boys entered through a faster

The Legislature of the City of Buenos Aires, which in 1952 was the seat of the Ministry of Labor, where Evita had held her desk, from where she dispensed her charities, and where her wake took place.

Mezzanine of the rotunda of the atlantes of the Legislature of the City of Buenos Aires, from where school children and the general public paid their respects to the corpse of Eva Perón lying on the ground floor.

line than that formed by the public.[17] People waited for hours, even days, in lines that extended for blocks covered in flowers. The building was, at the time, the seat of the Ministry of Labor, where Evita had held her desk and from where she dispensed her charities. It is an exquisite, eclectic early-twentieth-century building with a distinctive clock tower adjacent to the city's historic center, the Plaza de Mayo.[18]

We were led to the second floor, where we could observe the coffin from the balcony circling the beautiful central rotunda. It was a perfectly circular space, capped with a Roman hemispherical coffered dome, like the Roman Pantheon, and supported by unforgettable, frightening marble atlantes with balustrades between them that allowed us to peek down. A space like no other I had seen.

It was probably then that all my classmates saw their first dead person. Not me—I had already done that a month earlier! Another famous person had passed away, closer to me but less popular than Evita. Alberto Williams, the dean of Argentinian classical music, founder of the conservatory I attended, and a key figure in establishing an Argentinian school of composers, performers, and educators, had died on June 17. My piano teacher, one of his devoted disciples, invited her students and their families to pay their respects at his wake, so my sister and I went with my mother.

It was another building of note: the deceased's splendid house, a *petit hotel* (as they are still called in Buenos Aires) in the remote

Architect Amancio Williams, son of the famed musician, in the library of the house, depicted on the right, where he grew up, ca. 1970. It is in this room that his father's wake took place in 1952.

Maestro Alberto Williams in the garden of his house in Barrancas de Belgrano, Buenos Aires, designed by architect Alejandro Christophersen, ca. 1940.

neighborhood of Barrancas de Belgrano.[19] Built by Williams for his large family in 1910 and designed by the prominent Beaux-Arts-trained Argentinian architect Alejandro Christophersen, it was a two-story classical house sitting on a podium with an ample terrace with steps leading down into the exuberant garden that surrounded the building and other adjacent service facilities.[20] What remains more vivid in my mind, though, were the ground-floor interiors, lined with dark boiserie, a large curvilinear grand staircase, and the impressive library, some steps down, lined with bookshelves and French doors that opened to the terrace and garden beyond. There, in the open coffin, *el maestro* lay in peace next to his grand piano. This was a magnificent piece of architecture and within it lay an arresting staged scene—of a very different tone than Evita's—that registered in my mind in all its exceptionality.[21]

Serendipitously, I revisited the Williams mansion thirty-four years later, but in a different role and on another mission, when I organized an exhibit at Harvard of original drawings of the work of Amancio Williams, son of the musician and an elusive, exquisite, and extraordinary Argentinian architect. The show opened a year later, in 1987, at the Gund Hall Gallery, where the School of Design still operates, with Williams present as a Harvard guest.[22] He inherited the house and lived there with his family, until he moved out, retaining part of the ground floor as his studio and archive. I met him there on many occasions. The house and gardens were still as notable as I remembered, though I felt the size of the overall property had shrunk, and now I was able to appreciate Christophersen's mastery of the classical architectural vocabulary and his overall site planning more deeply.[23]

Doubling down, over decades, on this alternation of wakes and celebrations, more than fifty years later, in 2009 I returned to the building where Evita's funeral had taken place, now the seat of the City of Buenos Aires Legislature, as I had returned to maestro Williams's house to meet his son in 1986. This time, I was attending an international celebration, joining my fellow jury members in the ceremony in which we awarded the Pritzker Prize in Architecture to Peter Zumthor. I made sure I could spend some time in the rotunda. It was now functioning as a grand foyer between two major halls in this very significant public building in the city. The rotunda's magnificence was still manifest, and its quality more evident to my architect's eye, even if the atlantes did not scare me as they had before. Yet, the lively talk of a hundred excited architects and the public made it impossible to recall the solemnity with which the classical rotunda had lingered in my memory, where it was underlined by the echoes of muted whisperings and the faint sizzling of children's shoes rubbing on the marble floor, awestruck by what was hard to comprehend.

My first concert, my first corpses, my first palaces.

1954 BUENOS AIRES BY THE SEA

SCENE 6 *It is March 8, 1954. It is late summer in the Southern Hemisphere, and I, at twelve, am in Mar del Plata on vacation with my family. It is nighttime. We are all sitting in the enormous outdoor theater built for a special occasion on an immense esplanade along the central beaches. We can hear the surf when the crowd is silent and see the moon and the stars reflecting on the sea. The National Ballet is performing* Les Sylphides, *appropriately under bright moonlight, followed by a mixed program of classical and popular music, speeches, and presentations of movie stars and government figures.*[24] *We, those thousands sitting in the gigantic theater, are a part of something that is being closely observed by the entire planet.*

Poster announcing the first Festival Internacional Cinematográfico in Mar del Plata, 1954.

It is the inauguration of the first Festival Internacional del Cine.[25] Most of the Argentinians vacationing in this splendid beach city south of Buenos Aires are assiduous year-round weekly moviegoers and are waiting for the launch of this significant event. It is the first such festival in the continent, aiming to compete with Cannes and Venice, and it has everything it takes: a cash-rich country whose government is paying the bills; a large literate middle class adept to world cinema, served by a pervasive infrastructure of movie houses and a supportive press; and the stars from all over the world who had arrived and were ready to brighten this world-class cultural event. This was big for the country and an even bigger opportunity to show off for General Juan Domingo Perón, Argentina's president at the time.[26] This monumental event—in terms of urban dimension, crowd size, and international outreach—was something Buenos Aires had never offered us. I could sense, without comprehending it, the formidable display of power by both the political-military establishment and the international artistic crème de la crème of this most popular of arts. They were all mixed up on stage, smiling, chatting, and exciting the crowd, and I could see the sheer size of the entranced audience that filled the theater and lined the streets in wait to greet the stars.[27]

From the time I was six years old until I was eighteen, I lived a sort of double life each year, in sync with a substantial number of my fellow *porteños*.[28] During the summer, my family went to Mar del Plata. There was never a discussion about alternative sites for vacation. The only variable was my father's luck in business—at which he was terribly "unpredictable." This would determine the length and nature of our stay. Some years, it was a few weeks in a hotel; others, months in a rented chalet.[29] In Mar del Plata, in accordance with its uniqueness, we also changed and tried "other" things we would never do in Buenos Aires. For instance, we ate fish, which in Buenos Aires we would only have, against our taste, during Lent. We would practice sports we could not care less about in the big city, like roller skating or ping-pong. Conversely, we rarely played *fútbol* in Mar del Plata—it belonged to "normal" life. Mar del Plata allowed us to play out our fantasies, encouraged by watching adults do the same.

These metamorphoses that *porteños* experienced every year as they stepped on the sands of Mar del Plata were remarkable enough to deserve notice. However, what exalted and framed such peculiarities, and induced their eccentricity, was the unique man-made setting in which they occurred. This was not another version of Buenos Aires. This was a city that displayed what was probably the most remarkable piece of urban design built in the mid-century worldwide—in the short span of twenty years—by what was then one of the wealthiest countries in the world. This unmatched waterfront development began in the 1930s and acquired its identity when the then-reigning

Aerial view of the urban ensemble of Playa Bristol, with the twin buildings for the Casino and Hotel Provincial, and La Ramblas, designed by architect Alejandro Bustillo. Opened in 1939, it remains to this day the center of gravity of the city of Mar del Plata, the monumental gate to the beach and associated leisure facilities.

dean of Argentina's architecture, Alejandro Bustillo, became involved. In coordination with the city, Bustillo masterfully composed a monumental ensemble of public buildings of complex programmatic and topographical attributes, including hotels, entertainment venues, extensive sports infrastructure facilities, plazas and promenades. This became the city's new center of gravity, along which five kilometers of urban waterfront and a series of new parks still organize themselves. It thus transformed this formerly aristocratic beach city into a world-class vacation destination, genuinely inclusive for all social classes.

This centerpiece is made up of twin monumental buildings—the Casino and the Hotel Provincial—which create a grand gate to the beaches that is marked by two colossal statues of sea lions. It all sits on a spectacularly ample promenade called La Rambla. This, Bustillo's masterpiece, is still Mar del Plata's magnet and distinctive urbanistic icon. It is also—and very importantly—the waterfront that Buenos Aires never had.

While the then-remote location of Mar del Plata with respect to the developed world did not allow it to enter the set of international vacation destinations for which it was prepared by size, ambition, and quality of leisure offerings, in compensation it became the "Buenos Aires by the Sea", as I call it; where *porteños* of all classes moved to their corresponding neighborhoods. They went to villas, to owned or rented houses and apartments, to hotels of every category, or to the different labor union facilities built by the government shortly before. For a few months of the year, Mar del Plata was the alter ego of the

At left, I am walking in La Rambla of Playa Bristol, in the company of (from left to right) my mother, Catalina Malanca de Silvetti; my sister, Ana María Rosa; and my aunt, Rina Lida Malanca, 1951. The casino building is visible in the background.

metropolis four hundred kilometers to the north. It is still called, appropriately, even if today a bit nostalgically, *La Feliz*: The Happy One.

I have returned very recently after decades of absence. Only with such distance have I come to fully comprehend how I *lived* Mar del Plata as a phenomenon of wonder and a unique specimen of urbanity.

1956 THE "SHULE MITRE"

The "Shule Mitre", as it stands today. The first skylight-covered courtyard, flanked by classrooms on either side remains intact; beyond it, the former open court, now also topped with a skylight, stretches out. I stand between them, next to the bust of Bartolomé Mitre, a nineteenth century towering figure in Argentina's history.

SCENE 7 *It is one of the last days of October. We are in our third year of high school at Nacional nº 5 Bartolomé Mitre. It is the afternoon, and we are on a large covered patio during the long break, having a snack and chatting. Suddenly, a commotion breaks out among a small group of vociferous classmates, and some get into a physical fight. I'm astonished; they are all my friends.*

Our classroom was in the first courtyard. This was where the action took place. It was a wide rectangular patio covered by a skylight, a feature that in our minds marked our progress as we effectively moved up toward graduation. The first two years, we had been in classrooms located around the second, back courtyard,

Class picture of my fourth year of high school (*bachillerato*) at the Colegio Nacional nº 5, Barlolomé Mitre—"Shule" Mitre—1957. I am on the second row, seated on the far right. Sitting at the center is our beloved psychology professor R. Fuselli, whom we all asked to join us in the picture.

which, while covered by peripheral porticos, was open air and was shared with the student latrines, the laboratories, the natural history "museum," ancillary service offices, and storage facilities. Now, in our third year, we knew we would never have to return to the back!

The building was a quintessential *escuela sarmientina*,[30] which repeated the layout of the *casa chorizo*, but with its symmetry and size approximating a full Roman domus. Its two-story version was a typical arrangement for institutions. A familiar but more "whole" environment with which I would alternate daily for five years; half a domus at home, a whole one at school.

However, what was most peculiar about my high school was not the building or its curriculum but its social composition. Because of its urban location and easy access thanks to the well-developed subway system that the city had developed, it was the public school of choice for many families who were part of the second wave of middle-class Jews that had migrated to Argentina in huge numbers before, during, and after the Second World War.[31] They lived and worked around the school's area and in neighborhoods along one of the longest subway lines in the city's network.[32] The proportion of Jewish classmates—all first-generation Argentinians—was over 70 percent. After spending the first part of my education in the company of people called Escudero, Delgado, Bonafide, Serrano, and Sposito, I surprisingly joined a group composed of the likes of Trachtenberg,

Dvorkin, Kravietz, Smulewicz, and Levinas. This was a major surprise on my first day of class, and it ended up being truly transformative.

Since the turn of the century, Buenos Aires had been a melting pot of natives moving from rural areas to the rapidly industrializing metropolis and European immigrants. The greater majority from the latter group was Italian, as my four grandparents were, but there were also many republican Spanish immigrants exiled after the civil war, and other Europeans too. The progressive policies of different Argentinian governments in the late nineteenth century aimed to populate what was, and in many ways still is, an unpopulated territory. Growing up in a second-generation Italian family in Buenos Aires, it was customary for me to find others with my same pedigree, and because of our location in the city, we also interacted with our neighbors, whom we called *los turcos*: people of Syrian Lebanese origin that comprised a large part of an adjacent *barrio* along Jujuy Street, where they ran their typical houseware commerce, the *bazares*. But we had little if any interaction with *los rusos*, as Jews were called.[33] And now here I was, in a school whose operation came to a de facto halt for Rosh Hashanah and Yom Kippur. Jewish holidays were not acknowledged in the official calendar, but the school could neither advance with its curriculum nor close for the day as it should have, for lack of sufficient students. The sparse 30 percent that showed up, to which I belonged, enjoyed a special program for the day: we were asked to just "hang around," read, relax, chat—and don't tell anyone about it!

Many good things came from all this. One was the acquisition of a basic but rich vocabulary of words and expressions in Yiddish, the language that all my new friends spoke at home and at school, freely mixed with our shared Argentinian Spanish that was already mixed with *lunfardo*, which we all spoke.[34] Another good thing was the new food—the *varenikes*, *kreplach*, knishes, and gefilte fish, prepared by their *bobes,* which I got to taste and came to like at their homes when I visited, occasionally staying overnight. And then there was the daily dose of Jewish jokes. What continuously fascinated me was that this group of individuals were ostensibly the same as I was, but shared an intense "other life" into which they could switch, as on a whim or triggered by a word, and which established another discourse and reality—a discourse and a reality that I could not understand.

Otherwise, everything was normal: we liked the same movies; loved or hated the same soccer teams; discussed sex with the same curiosity, excitement, and uncertainties; and began to develop political tendencies together.

This was everyday life at "Shule Mitre", as we all called our school to the dismay of the staff. But one day, in the last weeks of October 1956, something unexpected revealed to me a fracture in this community with a violence that had never been evident until that moment.

The Suez Crisis had erupted, and the Jewish community among us became, shockingly, sharply divided. Agitated discussions, shouts, insults, and even punches followed. Some students asked to change their assigned seats in the classroom to avoid undesired adjacencies, and at one point two classmates and I had to separate two of our friends. It was well known to all of us that one of them, an outgoing, outspoken, and bright fellow with whom I was very close, belonged to a family whose parents were members of the Communist Party and did not support Israel's siding with the United Kingdom and France's invasion of Egypt, while the other friend was the son of a rabbi, ultrareligious, shy, very gentle, and also bright, suddenly passionate in his support of Israeli war actions and accusing the other of not being "a real Jew."

This was the first time I witnessed a division other than Peronists vs. Anti-Peronists. It was a fissure, an insurmountable crack among a group of people that to my eyes had been, until that time, extremely cohesive and tight.

1957 LANGUAGE, METAPHOR & *IL PENNELLO DIVINO*[35]

SCENE 8 *I am in the fourth year of high school. We are in the music room, a classic lecture hall with parallel rows of fixed wooden benches and writing ledgers stepping up. But we are not in music class. We are in our foreign language class: Italian. Those who, like me, had chosen Dante over Shakespeare formed a smaller group, and during foreign language class we had to meet in whatever room was available, leaving the primary daily classroom for the anglos. Mrs. Bender, the Italian teacher, announces the three best papers from the midterm assignment that we turned in the previous week. I wrote one of the three. She praises my writing and the choice of topic and adds some advice too: I need to follow proper academic protocols, which she outlines, regarding the attribution of the paper's final quote. I am not sure I understand what she means, but I sense it is not good. In any case, I am very happy with my paper.*

LE VITE
DE PIV ECCELLENTI ARCHITETTI, PITTORI, ET SCVLTORI ITALIANI, DA CIMABVE
INSINO A' TEMPI NOSTRI: DESCRITTE in lingua Toscana, da GIORGIO VASARI
Pittore Aretino. Con vna sua vtile
& neceſſaria introduzzione
a le arti loro.

IN FIRENZE
M D L.

The frontispiece of the first edition of Giorgio Vasari's *Le vite de più eccellenti architetti, pittori, et scultori italiani, da Cimabue insino a'tempi nostri*... (1550).

It was an essay in Italian on the life and work of Raffaello Sanzio of Urbino, a topic of my choice. Today, I cannot recall anything I wrote, but I have never forgotten the quotation I included at the end. It was something I had found in my readings during what became my first true literary experience, which has remained among my paradigms of literary writing.

I had been mesmerized by some of the reproductions of Raffaello's paintings, specifically the *Madonna della Sedia,* the *Sposalizio della Vergine,* and his self-portrait, all of which I had found in a book I had seen around the house—an unusual occurrence since there were no art books at home, only novels. I developed a great interest in the life of this artist of unmatched fame and a beautiful, angelical face, and his shocking and untimely death deeply affected my young sentiments. But more consequential, and beyond sentiments, was a short paragraph that confronted me with poetic language for the first time, which is why I will recall this episode. It was a quote from Vasari's *Le vite de' più eccellenti pittori, scultori, e architettori* (1550),[36] a source that I cannot recall how I came across it, nor could appreciate for its monumental importance at the time. The fragment is an emotive lamentation and glorification of Raffaello's quasi-supernatural talents and superhuman beauty upon his death, and I borrowed it without any second thought to be used in my Italian essay and produce what I thought was a very effective, grand, and tragic end. Vasari concludes his account of Raffaello's life at the moment of death with these powerful words and image: "Ben poteva la pittura, quando questo nobile artefice morì, morire anche ella che quando egli gli occhi chiuse, ella quasi cieca rimase."[37] My "attribution" consisted of a generic: "Si dice che ben poteva la pittura ... "[38]

Vasari's last sentence, with its intense pathos, rapturous alliteration, and poetic brilliance, reverberates in my ears with the same power when I recall it today. This was the first time I *sensed* metaphor, without even associating it with that strange term presented to me in Literature class. "La pittura ... ella quasi cieca rimase." Painting almost becoming blind! This was an explosion of words arranged in such a way, with such intent and tension, that it profoundly altered my way of reading and imagining what I read: there he was, dying, lying in bed, his eyelids slowly closing and his soul departing, while Painting, a profoundly sad and distraught lady, with her brushes and palette inactive by her side, observes disconsolately how the life of her favorite son vanishes, while her own eyes, blurred by tears and weakness, begin to falter.

This could probably be identified as the moment when I also intuited the possibility of what, I would later learn, was an allegory in literature. I guess this was the moment I finally learned how to read.

SCENE 9 *I'm at the school of architecture at the university, in the studio on the top floor of our building on Perú Street with my peers. Someone enters waving the latest issue of Architectural Review. As I see James Stirling's School of Engineering at Leicester University for the first time, something radical changes in the mind of the architect-in-progress that I am at the moment.*

University of Leicester Engineering Building, James Stirling and James Gowan (1959–1963).

I have seen many buildings in publications that have left an indelible impression on me and enhanced my appreciation of architecture,[39] but no other architectural image knocked me down like this inexplicable, seductive building did. It looked like nothing I had ever seen before. It was contradictory—implausible yet verisimilar, possible, and real. A building I could not decide whether it was beautiful (which I felt it was!) or ugly, as any reasonable modernist would have declared without doubt. It was a pile of oddly shaped, fragmentary volumes, each in a different material, juxtaposed in the most unlikely combination. It defied proportions, gravity, and conventions, yet it produced a delightful feeling of control and uncanny harmony. In addition, it was a masterclass in drawing ingenuity that embraced radical pragmatism and established axonometric projection as a definitive graphic creative tool. Until then, such a representational method had only appeared to us as a simplistic shortcut to clumsily convey three dimensions in two.

It was not only me. My entire circle of friends at school felt the same irresistible attraction, although I cannot be sure whether they were as entranced by it as I was. It opened new visions of architecture, yet I was unable to articulate how one could emulate something like that. Where do you start a design like that? It was undoubtedly the product of a design process we had never explored or even imagined possible. We did not even know where to turn to find such a road. This building will stay in my mind for years, even when the world of architecture has been able to produce many more striking, anti-modernist pieces of architecture. Nothing has had the power to shake my convictions about how architecture takes form as Leicester did.

The morning-after newspaper photographs of the events that took place during the Night of the Long Batons, July 29, 1966.

SCENE 10 *It is early evening on Friday, July 29, 1966, at the Facultad de Arquitectura y Urbanismo de la Universidad de Buenos Aires, in Los Galpones.*[41] *The atmosphere is tense; we are all on edge. We chat in small groups, not in class, but in the broad entry hallway and other public areas. Suddenly, a fully armed platoon of federal police forcefully enters our building, shouting, and proceeds to evacuate everyone: students, faculty, and staff. As we walk out in a single line with our arms up, we move fast between flanking lines of policemen who push and hit us on our heads, backs, and buttocks with their riot batons.*

I had recently been appointed as a teaching assistant in a *taller de composición arquitectónica* together with some of my friends, an academic position won in an open competition, as all academic ranks were back then.[42] The competition consisted of a public demonstration of our desk crit abilities when reviewing students' projects, assessed by a faculty jury. I was elated to be part of what was, to me, our school's best *taller*[43] at the moment, led by Manolo Borthagaray.[44]

We had done about three months of *taller* sessions since the beginning of the academic year, but on that night our primary concern was not teaching. It was what would happen to our school, our university, and our country. The political situation in Argentina had been deteriorating rapidly in the previous months, with open threats coming from far-right militant groups supported by the armed forces, the Catholic Church, and sectors of the press. A few weeks earlier, a group called Tacuara had shot a few rounds at our building and wounded one of our classmates. Since 1957, Argentina's public university system had been declared, by a constitutional amendment, to be autonomous from the government. Universities governed themselves through elected representatives of their three constituent bodies: faculty, alumni, and students. Public higher education blossomed in this period, excelling in many fields of study and research. In particular, the Universidad de Buenos Aires had achieved international preeminence in the most advanced areas of science, staying at the forefront of research in computation and astrophysics. The university had recently adopted a more advanced model of academics and research

Snapshot of the party celebrating my graduation from architecture school with my classmates. From left to right: Raquel Chocrón, Rodolfo Machado, Sylvia Duliztky, myself, Mario Zito, Eduardo Charosky, and El "Oso" Iturrieta.

that went beyond its purely academic and traditional scope, structuring and promoting research programs based on national and regional demands and involving the applied sciences, the humanities, and technology. This was a model for a contemporary university, in which its former modus operandi as an ivory tower had been challenged in terms of its reach but, at the same time, maintained institutionally. This allowed the university to safeguard the intellectual freedom that was, and still is, indispensable for academic work, and to protect itself from political interference.

However, the university's intellectual freedom was perceived by the current government as a seditious threat to national identity. The country had been struggling to reconstitute its democracy for nearly four decades. Its political system was initially established in the second part of the nineteenth century; the nascent, imperfect democracy catapulted Argentina to become one of the wealthiest and most promising countries in the world at the turn of the century. While the first decades of the twentieth century saw steady progress in the consolidation of the country's democratic form of government, this trend stopped in 1930, when the first of what would become a continuous series of military-led coups took place. Only a month before the night I am describing, these powerful groups had overthrown a short-lived, legitimately elected civil government, shut down the Parliament, and established a de facto military dictatorship. It was clear that public universities would be the next victim.

The police takeover on behalf of the government was repeated with varying degrees of violence in other schools, with those that were considered more suspicious receiving harsher treatment: Natural and Physical Sciences, Architecture and Urbanism, as well as Philosophy and Letters. In our school, we were only hit hard but not detained, unlike the scientific community, which suffered a grinding and bloody operation. More than two hundred of their faculty and students spent the night in jail, were interrogated and marked as "dangerous" in their security files. Because of the batons used by the police, the night of July 29, 1966, became known as the Noche de los Bastones Largos.

It was the end of my youth. From then on, "left" and "right" meant something more than political ideologies. With the resignation of over 70 percent of the university's faculty and authorities after the takeover, I devoted myself to finishing my exams, meeting with my former teachers and students in private homes or architecture offices to continue our intellectual relationships at all costs. I received my degree and license as an architect a few months after, on September 20, which was my father's birthday. Almost immediately, I began to plan my move abroad to either work or pursue a postgraduate degree, a plan that I had in mind, along with many of my friends, before the political crisis, but that acquired sudden urgency. I was ready to leave. I only needed to know where, what for, and how.

1967 FAREWELL TO BUENOS AIRES

Facing the camera, I am acting as a construction supervisor (jointly with Nucho Petchersky, not int the picture), on the jobsite of a stand at the annual Fair of the Sociedad Rural Argentina of 1966 (Buenos Aires), designed by Tony Diaz (behind me, on the right) and Jorge Erbin (turning his back to the camera).

SCENE 11 *It is noon on a sunny, late-autumn day, and Rodolfo [Machado] and I are sitting on the grass of the slope of Plaza San Martín, a beautiful park embedded in the heart of Buenos Aires. We are facing the broad expanse of Plaza Retiro below, with the Torre de los Ingleses at its center, the messiness of the city harbor and the barely visible river far beyond. Plaza San Martín is the only point in this flat city where, from the ground, one can have a long, uninterrupted view toward the water, gaining a faint sense, if not an actual view, of the shoreline and the horizon from a higher vantage point.*[45] *We are taking a break from work. The high noon sun is hitting us, and it is warm. I am finally very relaxed after several convulsive months of uncertainty, and we are mostly talking about concrete and practical things. In retrospect, this scene, with its unforgettable and "unfinished" long view, is the perfect backdrop for our conversation.*

I had graduated less than a year ago and was working for Francisco Bullrich and Alicia Cazzaniga.[46] It was a short-term job, assisting them with a set of construction drawings. In addition, along with three other friends, I had a freelance job with a construction firm, producing a large set of working drawings and documents for a massive public infrastructural project that included a new, long-span suspended bridge over the Paraná River. The four of us were colleagues in the same class, and we enjoyed the ease with which we got these short-term jobs. Unlike two of my closest friends, Nucho Petchersky and Rafael Viñoly, who had been appointed for permanent positions in one of Argentina's most exciting new young firms, I was fine with these *changas*.[47] They were well paid, and some of them offered unusual, challenging professional rewards like one I had taken months earlier when I was a construction supervisor/manager for a pavilion made of novel prefabricated elements, at a national fair in Buenos Aires.[48] Having decided to move on and go abroad soon, I needed to save money to survive there, where I would be self-supporting and live alone for the first time. All I knew was that my destination was the San Francisco Bay Area; I had already obtained a US work visa and secured a temporary place to stay with friends in Berkeley. Since my initial application to the architecture school there had failed due to my poor TOEFL scores, I was going to follow my school friend's advice: work in a local office—a job I still needed to find in person—and reapply for admission, which would also allow for an in-person interview. That was the plan.

As soon as Rodolfo had arrived a few minutes earlier, we delved into what was obsessing us: the utterly unclear details of our plans to emigrate, each of us heading in somewhat opposite directions. Remarkably, we did not discuss what would happen to our relationship, which had existed, progressed, and deepened for over two years and was about to be interrupted. Perhaps this was because it had never been spelled out, defined, or questioned; or rather because we lacked the language to discuss it. It existed as if suspended inside a cloud, where we were at the same time both the sole protagonists and the entire context, invisible to the rest of the world. In the Argentina of 1967, this was the happiest and, for us, the only way to exist as a couple. It was as if the continuity of our relationship did not factor into our plans, which might have been somewhat true since, in the wordless logic of "all of this just happens to us," we could not speculate about it. It did not help that in the local context it was unthinkable that our relationship could become public. Like most single men of our age, we still lived with our parents. But we spent most of our time together in our shared office, with six other young colleagues, partaking daily and enthusiastically in the stimulating cultural life of Buenos Aires. We kept going to the movies, concerts, exhibitions, and performances; dining out every night; and occasionally escaping together for short weekend trips.

In Buenos Aires, and this was one of its most perplexing contradictions, the artistic and ideological earthquakes of the sixties had taken hold and vibrated continuously through the decade with genuinely original manifestations that pulsated in synchrony with the frequencies of New York and London.[49] All of this in spite of the gloomy political situation, with the military government extending its tight grip, day after day, on all political and cultural manifestations, from powerful protests by parties and unions to gatherings of left-leaning, long-haired youths or those with "devious" inclinations. I belonged to the last two of these groups, though I prudently played a game of haircuts that were not-too-short, not-too-long. That said, I knew that somewhere in the State Intelligence Offices there was a file on me.[50] Still, as we saw it, our two years of being thus "together" were bliss.

Sitting on the grass that day, we mainly focused on Rodolfo's uncertainties. He was still searching for a concrete way to arrive at his desired destination: France. Although it was not the most attractive place to advance in the world of architecture, Paris existed in our minds as the model of urbanity and culture we wished to be a part of.

So we did not talk about "the future," although we kept saying, incongruously but wishfully, that we very much wanted to see each other as much as possible while we were apart—on two different continents! The conversation continued but began to peter out. Both of us were already lying on our backs on the grass, discreetly holding hands, until suddenly it was time to go: immediately, back to work, and soon, far away.

SCENE 12 *Four months later, on September 6, I am with my parents, my sister, Rodolfo, and other friends in the departure lounge of Ezeiza International Airport. The mood: emotionally charged, cheerful, and tense. A departure to a far-and-away place with a very vague return date in a remote place like Buenos Aires invariably convenes a large crowd. It is an important event which, I sense, I hope, marks the beginning of a transformative experience.*

The *bolso de viaje*—the classic Argentinian bag my friends gave me as a farewell present before my departure to the United States in September 1967. The bag was made in Argentina by Casa Lopez with calf leather and brass fittings, ca. 1967.

At that time, the type of airport security we endure today was non-existent, and we were all by the gate waiting for me to board. What I recall most vividly is carrying a beautiful leather bag, one of a pair that our closest friends had given Rodolfo and I as farewell presents—not too discreetly hinting at what had become obvious to them![51] I had loaded my bag with about thirty of the best issues of *Architectural Design*, my only magazine subscription, and a dozen books I wanted neither to part with nor check with the rest of the luggage. They were my treasure, a weighty load that cost me an excessive "tip" to be allowed on board. I still have the books, the magazines, and the bag.

I do not remember the actual moment of boarding and the emotional goodbyes nor any details of the long trip. I remember my landing in San Francisco and my friends Cata Gandelsonas and Juan Manuel Martin waiting for me.

Soon, Rodolfo and I would begin to share a new, insufficient mode of being together: a copious epistolary exchange of handwritten letters on thin airmail paper. In these handwritten words, besides reporting on our new lives and our astounding and incomparable discoveries in Paris and the Bay Area, we immediately, openly, and squarely addressed the what, when, and where of our future together and began planning it. We had not been able to spell this out when we were together in Buenos Aires, but putting it in writing, now at a distance from each other, was a very easy, precise, and effective task. It worked.

Technique, repetition, interpretation, rituals, performance; replicas, imitations, mise-en-scènes, sceneries; foreign languages, artistic languages, and ideological confrontation—all these elements emerge from the memories of my youth in Buenos Aires. Do these operations resonate within themselves or with other scenes from later in life? Do they connect with the designs and writings I have created? I believe so, but how? I am unable to answer these questions definitively, nor am I inclined to do so. I will continue pondering on these sympathies, alignments, and intersections over space and time whenever I reminisce about these shards of the past. Each time, they reflect back new insights, new images, fresh connections, and more memories. Like the fragments of Borges's broken mirrors, they are all I have, so I can only continue trying to make sense of them.

Jorge Silvetti
Boston, January 12, 2023

I would like to acknowledge the following individuals that have impacted decisively who I am as an intellectual and as an architect.

At some point in my life, chronologically: Severina Tognella de Diz, Horacio Baliero, Tony Diaz, Diana Agrest, Mario Gandelsonas, Tito Serebrinsky, George Baird, Colin Rowe, Rafael Moneo, Tarek Ashkar, Calvin Tsao, Nader Tehrani, Fares El-Dahdah, and Graciela Silvestri.

Throughout and always: Rodolfo Machado.

CINZANO
FRESCA PURA SABROSA
7up
Seven-Up

Previous page: Plaza San Martín, in the heart of the city, with its gentle slope at the time when Scene 11 takes place. The center of attention of this photograph of the mid-1960s, is the Kavanagh residential building of 1936, by Sanchez, Lagos y de la Torre, which became the tallest building in South America until 1947 and the first skyscraper with a concrete structure in the world. With its harmonious combination of European modernism with New York Art Deco style, it is still one of the most representative and symbolic images of the city.

Notes

1 "We are our memory, we are that chimerical museum of inconstant forms, that pile of broken mirrors." Jorge Luis Borges, "Cambridge," in *Elogio de la sombra* (Buenos Aires: Emecé, 1969).

2 Since leaving Argentina in 1967, I have lived in many other cities. The longest time has been in Boston, for almost five decades, alternating with regular stays in our cottage in Wellfleet, Cape Cod—which is double the time of my youth in Buenos Aires. Then there was the San Francisco Bay Area for seven years, Pittsburgh for two, Rome for one, and Palermo sporadically but often over a period of eleven years. These are all my cities, and I have something of them in me. However, throughout all of my time away since leaving Argentina, I have returned to Buenos Aires very often. It is the city I long for and the city that is home.

3 Conservatorio de Música de Buenos Aires, founded in 1893 by Alberto Williams, the self-declared creator of Argentinian musical nationalism, following similar trends in Europe at the time.

4 Severina Tognela de Diz, a pianist and teacher who was a disciple of Alberto Williams.

5 Iglesia de la Santa Cruz, an excellent and well-crafted Gothic Revival specimen of Norman-Gothic style, designed by the architect Edwin Merry and consecrated in 1894 for the community of Irish Passionist Fathers.

6 We were in Buenos Aires, at the very bottom of the map—in an unfair universe where the South was also at the lowest level in a hierarchy of worthiness, at a time when travel abroad was not yet available to most.

7 This motivation for immigration was called *hacer la América.*

8 This was a disillusion that was reinforced when, in parallel, the heroic figure of San Martín that we acquired and idolized in school was eroded by serious historians, and our esteem for his character was challenged. He was not the Liberator of the Americas, as we were told, or at least not the only one. He was perhaps, just perhaps, at most, second to Simón Bolívar in some versions.

9 Versions of these houses were the prevalent, typically narrow and deep urban dwellings that appeared in some cities of South America during the later nineteenth and early twentieth centuries. They were all variations resulting from limited formal combinations, the dimensional prescriptions of the Laws of the Indies,

and the cultural traditions of Mediterranean vernacular houses.

10 *Varas*: a Spanish measurement. Ten *varas*, the width of the colonial plot, is equivalent to 8.66 meters (28 feet, 4 inches).

11 *Toldo*: a movable canvas for rain and sun protection.

12 Sometimes the second patio would also have covered porticos, although not as ornate as in the first patio.

13 *Ristra de chorizos*: a string of linked sausages.

14 In his 1929 visit to Buenos Aires, Le Corbusier was ambivalently impressed: the city was filled with energy but at the same time displayed a formal monotony of aggregated *casas chorizo* that—thanks to the pragmatic Spanish design of the colonial urban grid—could be extended ad infinitum. A decade later, he commented that when he first visited Buenos Aires he called it "the city without hope" but was later compelled to admit it was one of the great capitals of the world.

15 Auditorio del Consejo de Mujeres (currently Teatro El Globo) in Plaza Libertad, Buenos Aires.

16 Unidad Básica Peronista was a community center operated by the Peronist Party to serve as a source of information, as a place to hold meetings or events, and, mostly, as center to engage in political proselytism. Each Unidad Básica covered and served a small area within a neighborhood in Buenos Aires, as well as in every other city and town in the country. Typically, it used loudspeakers to convey information, transmit music, and voice its support of the policies of the government.

17 It should be noted that my mother refused to send me to the event wearing a black tie, so the school gave me one before we parted.

18 The Palacio de la Legislatura de la Ciudad de Buenos Aires. Elegant and richly built, this distinctive public building was designed by the architect Héctor Ayerza, following the classical principles of French academicism, and opened in 1931. It has been the seat of the city government legislative branch, with the exception of the years of the first government of Juan Domingo Perón, when it was assigned to the Ministry of Labor.

19 The area had formerly been the outskirts of the city but was already at the time beginning to be engulfed by the ever-growing metropolis.

20 Alejandro Christophersen (1866–1946) was a prominent architect, born in Spain and educated in Belgium and France, who arrived and settled in Buenos Aires in 1888. He became one of the leading architects of his generation, authoring a number of very important civic, religious, and private commissions.

21 I had never visited another house like this until I worked in the architecture studio of OAM that was functioning in one of those *petit hotels* in the center of the city. The building was still untouched, but was shared by about a dozen architects occupying different rooms and floors.

22 Jorge Silvetti, "Aires de la Pampa," in *Amancio Williams*, ed. Jorge Silvetti and Gabriel Feld (project assistant) (New York, NY: Rizzoli; Cambridge, MA: Harvard University, Graduate School of Design, 1987), 5–9.

23 A true jewel in the city, demolished years later and replaced by a residential tower.

24 *Les Sylphides* is a non-narrative ballet made up of an assemblage of Chopin's piano pieces, orchestrated by Alexander Glazunov and choreographed by Fokine. It premiered in Paris in 1909.

25 Officially "Festival Internacional Cinematográfico" in Mar del Plata during 1954. The name was later changed to "*Festival Internacional del Cine—Mar del Plata*."

26 After a popular revolt supporting Perón took place in 1945, he was elected to office in 1946. He was deposed in 1955 by a military coup that involved armed struggle on the streets, air bombings of the Government Palace in Buenos Aires, and reverberations in other parts of the country which left more than three hundred dead. This became a recurrent (albeit not artistic!) "happening" that I was to witness throughout my remaining time in Argentina.

27 A great number of international movie luminaries attended in representation of their countries, some from the consecrated old guard—like Edward G. Robinson, Walter Pidgeon, and Mary Pickford—and others from the younger generation—like Errol Flynn and Joan Fontain, all from Hollywood. There were also recent prominent young European stars like Gina Lollobrigida, Jeanne Moreau, and Alberto Sordi.

28 From *puerto* (port), *porteños* refers to the people of the port. Since colonial times, this name has been given to those born or living permanently in Buenos Aires. Given the city's location and how the vast country was settled (mostly towards its north), Buenos Aires was the primary harbor connecting easily with the Atlantic and the world beyond well into the twentieth century.

29 A chalet was Mar del Plata's response to

Buenos Aires's *casa chorizo*: a hybrid of English and Californian cottage inspiration that sprung up early after the foundation of this new city. Free of the constraints of older Argentine cities tied to the dimensional and formal rules of the Laws of the Indies, it would not necessarily need to be squeezed into narrow lots or share party walls, so it could include small gardens in front and at the side, or be completely freestanding. More characteristically, it always had pitched roofs finished with French red tile (*teja Marsella*) and facades clad with local stone (*Piedra Mar del Plata*), cut into different rectangular sizes arranged in loose patterns that gave the chalets a distinctive look.

30 *Escuela sarmientina*: the building unit, literally as well as symbolically, of the public education system in Argentina, fundamentally shaped by the ideas and reforms of Domingo Faustino Sarmiento. Sarmiento was a prominent educator and President of Argentina in the last third of the nineteenth century. These schools played a crucial role in reducing illiteracy and promoting social cohesion by offering free, secular, and mandatory education to all children, irrespective of their social background. The *escuela sarmientina* became a symbol of progress and egalitarianism, significantly contributing to the cultural and intellectual development of Argentina. By the end of the nineteenth century, the country had one of the highest literacy rates in the world. See Eugenio Monjeau and Helena Rover, *La mala educación* (Buenos Aires: Sudamericana, 2017).

31 During the early to mid-twentieth century, Argentina received a second wave of Jewish immigration and Buenos Aires became one of the largest Jewish communities worldwide. Unlike the earlier wave at the turn of the century, which was more rural and dispersed across various regions, including the Pampa Húmeda and the Mesopotamia, this later migration was predominantly urban. Many settled in Buenos Aires and became integral to its cultural and economic fabric.

32 La Linea B of the metropolitan system of underground public transportation of Buenos Aires: from the old harbor of Puerto Madero to Chacarita, following along and under the long Calle Corrientes, until the large Cemetery of Chacarita. The Jewish community was mostly located from the Callao station until the end of the line. Recently, La Linea B was extended further west to Villa Urquiza.

33 This simplification applied to all nationalities or ethnicities present in the country: the Italians were called *tanos*; the Spaniards were *gallegos*; Muslims from the Middle East were *turcos*; Jews from all over, *rusos*; and the few Japanese, typically present in the dye and laundry business, were *chinos*!

34 The Castilian of Buenos Aires is different from the one spoken in the rest of the country, but it is shared by our neighbors across the Río de la Plata in Montevideo, the capital of Uruguay. *Lunfardo* is the argot of Buenos Aires.

35 Giorgio Vasari, *Le vite de' più eccellenti pittori, scultori, e architettori* (Italy: G. C. Sansoni, 1896).

36 Ibid.

37 The full quote read, "Fu data al corpo suo quella onorata sepoltura che tanto nobile spirito aveva meritato perché non fu nessuno artefice che dolendosi non piangesse et insieme alla sepoltura non l'accompagnasse. Dolse ancora sommamente la morte sua a tutta la corte del Papa, prima per avere egli avuto in vita uno officio di cubiculario et appresso per essere stato sì caro al Papa che la sua morte amaramente lo fece piagnere. O felice e beata anima, da che ogn'uomo volentieri ragiona di te e celebra i gesti tuoi et ammira ogni tuo disegno lasciato. Ben poteva la pittura, quando questo nobile artefice morì, morire anche ella che quando egli gli occhi chiuse, ella quasi cieca rimase."
In a very unpoetic English, "Well could painting, when this noble craftsman died, have also died, for when he closed his eyes, she remained almost blind."

38 *Si dice*: it is said.

39 For instance, Alvar Aalto's Säynätsalo Town Hall in Finland, BBPR's Torre Velasca in Milan, Aldo Rossi's drawings of the Modena Cemetery published in Controspazio, or the early stone and concrete house by Herzog and de Meuron in Tavole, Italy, come to mind.

40 Vasari, *Le vite*.

41 Los Galpones (the sheds) were an exhibition facility erected and used during the sesquicentennial celebrations of the independence of Argentina from Spain in 1960. They consisted of a very large, hangar-like metal building. Conceived as temporary, they were nonetheless refurbished soon after the exhibition was over, and given to the school of architecture and urbanism as its new main facility. The whole structure was an immense roof supported by large arched trusses of laminated wood. The trusses spanned high up and over all the rooms, studios, and

service spaces, which had their own independent substructures and roofs. By pure happenstance, this curious assemblage of small buildings inside a larger one coincided with one of the favorite design ideas in vogue at the time for flexible, light-construction institutional buildings. We were delighted with this very contemporary design, even if it was precarious in terms of its durability. It was a unique kind of space in Buenos Aires, and it housed the place where "the future of architecture" was being conceived and discussed.

42 The role of teaching assistant (*ayudante*) in the university system of Argentina held a very different academic rank at that time than it does in American institutions today. A teaching assistant, even though they might not have graduated yet, was responsible for carrying out the pedagogy of the *taller*, advising students, assigning tasks, and evaluating their work.

43 A *taller* was the most important and distinct pedagogical unit of the discipline of architecture. The model derived from the French Beaux-Arts system, but had been completely transformed by the massive nature of the Argentinian public university system at midcentury—our school of architecture had around five thousand students. It was (and still is) a sort of a "mini-school within the school," led by a distinguished professor. The professor is always a practitioner, generally with a very specific approach to architecture and the philosophy of work. *Talleres* were organized vertically. Students would select one after two years of general preparatory studies, where they would remain for the rest of their studies. Within the *taller*, they would concentrate on specific projects, following the design approaches and methods established by the head of the *taller*, in large sections of about thirty students, each led by an *ayudante*.

44 Juan Manuel Borthagaray, one of the founders of OAM (Organización de Arquitectura Moderna). This group represented an advanced, second-generation version of modernism in architecture. They worked together with the publishing house Nueva Visión and Agrupación Nueva Música, all in the same *petit hotel* on Cerrito Street in Buenos Aires.

45 Plaza San Martín is just one point in a long, notable slope that, for kilometers, borders the entire city's frontage to the river. Originally, it was the natural embankment separating the flat low shore ground with the equally flat human settlement on top, against which the river ebbed freely according to its relative volume. Given the shallowness of the river and the indefiniteness of a clear border, the low ground, prone to flooding, was slowly filled in with two harbors, electrical plants, water purification treatment plants, and other infrastructural buildings. Later this expanded to residential and industrial buildings, parks, and sports facilities, effectively making the frontage to the river even more difficult to understand and experience. Plaza San Martín's slope was, at the time, the only real, long view that still helped, if not to actually see the liquid horizon, at least to confidently confirm its existence and allow one to imagine it.

46 Bullrich and Cazzaniga were members of the famed group OAM (Organización de Arquitectura Moderna).

47 *Changa* is a term used in Argentina to describe temporary or occasional jobs often outside a person's main profession or vocation.

48 The firm was Manteola, Sánchez Gómez, Santos, and Solsona.

49 See Fernando García, *El Di Tella. Historia íntima de un fenómeno cultural* (Buenos Aires: Paidós, 2021). This is an excellent compendium of historical, journalistic, and institutional documents; interviews with the protagonists; and the author's insights into the artistic and cultural life of Buenos Aires in the sixties, focusing on its emblematic institution: the Instituto Di Tella.

50 I am referring to the Servicio de Inteligencia de Estado (SIDE). During my year of obligatory military service (1964–1965), after three months of tough boot-camp training, I was assigned to a clerical job at the Ministry of War in downtown Buenos Aires for the rest of my service. I was confidentially informed by a friendly non-commissioned officer that there was a file with my profile as "a suspect of engaging in leftist political activities and suspicious sexual behavior" in the army's intelligence office, with "no action recommended at the time." It was obvious that I had been under observation for some time.

51 By then, Rodolfo had obtained a fellowship from the French government and was set to depart for Paris two months after I did.

Berkeley

Architecture: The Question of Method

WITH ALFREDO THIERMANN

Previous spread: On May 20, 1969, student demonstrations associated with the People's Park dispute are tear-gassed by the National Guard on Sproul Plaza at the UC Berkeley campus on the order of then-Governor Ronald Reagan.

1. Times of Cultural Awakening

ALFREDO THIERMANN Jorge, I have found it very interesting to dig into this archaeology of your past. As usual with history, there are many echoes with the present.

JORGE SILVETTI And yet it's not the same, right? History never repeats itself.

AT As the old adage says, "History rhymes but it does not repeat."

JS Everything is full of resonances. In the end, we are all the same people, made up of the same matter. However, contrary to what many think today, societies move at a different pace than our lives, just like the seasons of the year move at yet another pace. Each one of these phenomena has a distinct inertia, which is beautiful and with which we must work patiently. Life operates on different timescales, making each new collision in the present unique. This has always fascinated me.

Claude Lévi-Strauss's *Tristes tropiques* offers one of the great metaphors that has remained with me since my youth.[1] Lévi-Strauss was interested in the different rhythms of change that can be read through linguistics, anthropology, and geology. In *Tristes tropiques*, he describes walking through a sierra in France when he was young and encountering a face of the mountain where the terrain had slid, revealing a series of misaligned strata. Along the two sides of the fracture, he saw millions of years' worth of shells and plants of different geological systems that had never coexisted, but suddenly, in that moment, they appeared next to one another.

AT Were you reading Lévi-Strauss in Argentina before coming to the United States?

JS Yes, but I don't really know why. When I came here, I read some of his more scientific books, but the genre of *Tristes tropiques* is one that I have always loved: travel books that are part autobiography, part intellectual voyage. Goethe's *Italian Journey* also belongs to this genre and is perhaps the book that has taught me the most.[2]

NICOLÁS DELGADO ALCEGA The seeds of your relational, cross-scalar way of looking at culture were planted early.[3]

AT I want to know more about what motivated you to embark on your journey to the United States, but I am curious to learn about your upbringing first. What part of Buenos Aires did you grow up in?

JS I grew up in Barrio Sur, a middle-class neighborhood that was close to the city center.

AT Was it an urban environment? Were you a city animal?

JS I was certainly born into city life, having lived it for my first twenty-five years! I walked ten blocks to school on my own starting when I was around ten years old. I often stopped along the way to pick up some friends, and when it rained, my mother gave me money to take the underground. There was no school bus!

AT Did this have anything to do with your interest in architecture?

JS No, I honestly had no idea what architecture was. My most developed interest was music, since I began playing the piano when I was eight years old. However, it was tacitly assumed within the social context of my family that while this interest was laudable and supported, it could not really become an acceptable career.

Architecture and urbanism were relatively new careers that had come out of engineering. When I was in high school, I thought engineering was the most interesting choice out of the more traditional options like law, medicine, and agronomy. I had a friend who was a couple of years older and already in architecture school. He told me about his experience: that students drew and painted and discussed how people lived to come up with ways to improve their lives. It was a very simple introduction but it sounded good.

I ended up enrolling in architecture, which back then had a very structured and traditional pedagogy. I still remember the first two years of mathematics. The teacher, who was French, wore white gloves to handle the piece of chalk she used to demonstrate theorems on the board and worried about the elegance with which we did our proofs!

AT This was at the Universidad de Buenos Aires (UBA) in the 1960s, right? UBA is famous for being a massive public university, and I imagine there must have been hundreds of students in architecture.

JS Just in architecture there were about five thousand. It was very different from the American university model. We were divided into shifts, and after spending half a day at the school, we went home or to a friend's house that had a good space to work in. But I shouldn't forget the most important difference of all: it was a public institution, so it was totally free! It was open to all, and there was no selection process during admissions. We just had to enroll and pass an intensive two-month preparatory summer course.

AT Yes, this is very similar to the experience I had at the Universidad de Chile. Is this where you met Rodolfo [Machado]?

JS Yes, I met Rodolfo at the school. There were all these small cliques, and at the beginning Rodolfo and I were on totally different wavelengths. We were introduced toward the end of our course of studies by two young professors that had a small practice, with whom we became close friends. They assembled a group of five or six advanced students to work together on competitions.

Another difference from the American model is that the university in Buenos Aires back then did not have a campus. The schools were spread throughout the city, and you traveled across neighborhoods to attend conferences at other departments or eat with friends from different fields. *College was an urban experience.* Architecture in particular operated in two different buildings separated by a twenty-minute bus ride.

AT Studying like this creates a very different relationship with the city.

JS Absolutely. There weren't even cafeterias. You ate out in a restaurant or café of your choice. Buenos Aires was very similar to Paris in terms of café culture. My friends and I walked from school to the theater to watch movies before dinner at least three times a week!

AT I've heard very similar recounts about Chile, but perhaps Argentina was always more cosmopolitan because it was always looking across the Atlantic toward Europe. Relative to Europe, Chile is more in the backyard of the Southern Cone.

JS You have the Andes on your east, so looking toward Europe is impossible!

AT [*laughs*] This perhaps gives credence to the cliché that Chileans are more melancholic, whereas Argentinians have a broader cultural horizon.

JS Our cultural horizon was definitely more oriented toward Europe than the United States. American culture didn't stick yet, and few people spoke English. Television was not such a strong influence; only Hollywood had a big impact.

AT Those that could speak another language spoke French.

JS Yes, they spoke French but also many spoke Italian. There was an immense migration from Italy to Argentina—including my entire family—so you heard Italian everywhere on the streets.

AT Jorge Luis Borges is famous for having been able to write all his work without leaving Argentinian libraries. Argentina at one point had the monopoly over the translation of knowledge into Spanish, in part because of the situation with Franco in Spain.

JS Exactly! Rafael Moneo once corroborated this to me. He told me that practically all the literature translated into Spanish—whether scientific, literary, or architectural—arrived in Spain via Buenos Aires. Some of my professors were the founders of Editorial Nueva Visión, which in the sixties published not only everything "architectural" but also all books on design and contemporary art—Nikolaus Pevsner, Rudolf Wittkower, Bruno Zevi, Giulio Carlo Argan, Wilhelm Worringer, and so forth.[4] This is also because Argentina is primarily a literary society. The visual arts are important but not like in Brazil or Mexico. Argentina is, still, a country of readers.

AT Did you feel closer to certain discourses through this active literary culture when you started to plan your departure for the United States? Did your relationship to architecture develop from literature or literary criticism?

JS I don't think so. Perhaps this was the problem of polytechnic schools back then.[5] They were very endogamic. Even though I spent so much time at the movies and was always reading literature, I didn't connect these to architecture *at all* until much later. Maybe painting was the exception because of its historical and practical relationships with architecture, which the twentieth century had reconceived.[6]

AT But it was precisely the 1960s when other disciplines began to strongly influence architecture in universities.

JS Yes, though we were not totally aware of it, many of us at school were trying to find ways to understand certain questions about architecture that profession-oriented education couldn't answer. The great cultural asset of an urban, dispersed university campus was not helpful in this sense. It precluded the possibility of a more fluid disciplinary interaction that college campuses offer naturally.

Modernism had dried up. It was inspiring, but it felt exhausted, frustrated, and unsuccessful. The "new" was Team 10, Archigram, Cedric Price, and Yona Friedman. More than being exciting experiments that helped us imagine the actual architecture and city of the future, they were invitations to open our minds and search for new knowledge. We felt that these figures were breaking down some barriers to talk about architecture in novel ways.

Enough time had passed since the postwar rebuilding of Europe that it was possible to evaluate what had happened. Conversations were emerging about the reconstruction of Warsaw and Rotterdam, and "the city" was coming back to the center of the conversation both theoretically and pragmatically. The city was the new important reference for architecture, and it was no longer understood as Le Corbusier's Ville Radieuse, which had been completely discredited at that point. Discussing how to intervene in the existing city became *the* hot topic.

The British were very much ahead in this regard. They had overcome Le Corbusier and were doing interesting experiments in the public sector through institutions like the London County Council. They were doing impressive housing projects that addressed the complexity of the city through an entanglement of architecture, urbanism, and landscape architecture. For us, members of Team 10 like Alison and Peter Smithson were at the head of these developments, opening up new doors of thinking without abandoning the modernist tradition.[7] My enthusiasm for all of this is what called me abroad. Originally, I actually wanted to go to London to work with them.

AT You wanted to go work with the Smithsons?

JS Well, with someone good there! Or in the public sector. I wanted to live in London and participate in some of the projects being developed by the London County Council or some of the architects that had visibility at that time.

AT Why didn't you go?

JS I didn't feel like going there without a concrete job offer. One of my teachers reached out to Monica Pidgeon, the extraordinary director of the British journal *Architectural Design*, which was the only magazine I subscribed to. He asked her to recommend me for a job, and even though she was cordial, nothing concrete came out of it.

The changes that were going on within architecture were part of a greater cultural atmosphere of transformation that our daily life was being bombarded with in Buenos Aires. In music there were the Beatles and Agrupación Nueva Música.[8] In the visual arts, there was the impact of Pop art and the beginnings of Conceptualism. This was creating an artistic revolution that had international resonance. There were "happenings" going on all over the city, particularly at the internationally famous Instituto di Tella.[9] We were also being exposed to an explosion of new cinema from Europe: François Truffaut, Luchino Visconti, Ingmar Bergman, Joseph Losey, and Jean-Luc Godard.

These were the new cultural scenes proliferating worldwide in architecture, technology, and the visual arts. Even though London didn't pan out for me, Rodolfo, other colleagues, and I were determined to go out and explore these forces. We were at the right moment in our lives to pack up and experience them firsthand, so we did! It just so happened that I ended up in Berkeley, California, rather than London because some friends who were there got me excited about what was going on at the College of Environmental Design.

AT I imagine the political situation had something to do with your departure as well. It must have been a difficult reality to avoid during those years in Argentina.

JS Totally. Everything was completely politicized. I had been very active in politics since high school, which was common in Latin America. One of the first issues I remember protesting against, during my last year of high school, was the government's attempt to undermine the secular nature of education. This is perhaps something I would be less alarmed by today, but back then it was a real affront to a country that presented itself to the world as a very laic democracy. Coming from a progressive and anticlerical family, I was propelled to join "the struggle."

I was later an elected delegate at the student center of UBA and participated in a lot of the discussions that happened there. However, by the time we were finishing our degrees in the mid-'60s, the situation had become really somber. It was the beginning of a series of right-wing military dictatorships, Peronist revolts, and failed democratic governments.[10]

When I left Argentina in 1967, it was the right moment to go. I left in a bit of a rush, but by then I was focused on going to graduate school at the University of California, Berkeley. I decided to push my departure forward because the political situation kept deteriorating and my friends urged me to move fast. I told everyone—my parents in particular—that I would be back in two years or, if I stayed to get some experience, maybe a bit longer. But I never came back.

AT Never?

JS No, because everything in Argentina continued to get worse. I would visit of course, and held onto the idea of returning for a while, but within a decade Argentina was controlled by a military junta that kidnapped, tortured, and assassinated thousands of people. It was scary to be on the streets, especially if you were young, "lefty," and—God forbid—gay! I was also already at the Harvard Graduate School of Design at that point.

I once got detained at the airport for a random search on my way back to see my parents. Nothing happened in the end, but after hours of being interrogated and investigated, I walked out of there thinking to myself, "As soon as I am back in the States, I'll begin the process for American citizenship. I'm not coming back."

2. From Systems Theory to Structuralism

NDA What was happening at Berkeley that excited you to go there?

JS At that point, everyone in our circle was interested in finding a new methodology for the design process. This is where we thought the opportunities were to move beyond the limits of modernism that still stood, even if we approached the subject with the same positivism of modernism, assuming that there existed such a thing as a correct methodology for design.

UC Berkeley was then the most advanced center for architecture, planning, and landscape research in the United States. It was also one of the most prominent research universities in the world. Its architecture school was engaging a fresh group of international faculty members and participating in the methodological discussion that was flourishing in Europe, particularly in England. Notably, the school had even been renamed the College of Environmental Design. It's hard to grasp from today's perspective, but this was a radical move by the leading faculty, particularly Gerald M. McCue, the chair of architecture at the time who would later become dean of the Harvard Graduate School of Design.[11]

The college was full of professors coming from the modernist tradition who called themselves design methodologists: Christopher Alexander, Horst Rittel, natural scientist Richard L. Meier, and so forth. These people were pushing something different than the older-generation modernists. They were trying to apply new ideas from the world of systems theory and cybernetics to optimize the design process. Systems theory saw everything as an interconnected web of variables constantly influencing one another. Theoretically all you had to do was figure out how to properly describe all relevant variables of a system, and the doors to produce better solutions would spread wide open.

I was super enthusiastic about Christopher Alexander's work, particularly his *Notes on the Synthesis of Form*.[12] I read it before leaving Buenos Aires, and it surely pushed me toward Berkeley. Different from his later work, it was profound and philosophical. Although I don't care much about it now, back then his very rational understanding of the design process appealed to me, particularly since it was written intelligently. The book indicated a path to follow and a goal to aspire to, following his description of how the design process worked. It impressed upon me how deeply one could think about architecture.

When I got into UC Berkeley I went straight to work with computers. This went on for more than two years, and lasted until I got too tired of punching cards until three o'clock in the morning in Fortran, only to then go to the central computer in a university basement, stand in line, get my cards read, and have my programs tested.[13] Systems theory and cybernetics were spreading throughout the university at that time. It was the next great promise of the future, and at first I got very interested in it as a way to understand how architecture worked.

Everything suddenly seemed explainable—life, death, and the world beyond too! This was obviously enabled by the concurrent opening up to interdisciplinarity mentioned earlier. The design college had recently hired a sociologist, William Russell Ellis, who ended up being one of my PhD advisors.

AT I would like to hear more about how you think this relates to your later interest in typological thinking. Systems theory attempts to go beyond the idea of the singular object, and thus the idea of the author, like similar theories of typology that emerged in the 1960s. Even if these are different points of view, both theoretical frameworks aim at understanding how a sequence—or a genealogy—takes a specific form in opposition to focusing on individual authors.

JS Believing in systems theory for a while really helped. Of course, we were not able to model a perfect system to then produce new, perfect solutions for architecture. We didn't find *the best* methodology for architecture either. All of this was so naive in retrospect! But there's nothing wrong with thinking that everything is part of a complex interdependent system. To some degree I still have this idea stuck in my head.

The problem is that any model of society that we try to construct is then itself influenced culturally, and this elusive term *culture* is harder to calculate for with quantitative parameters. This is something that many thought was not true back then, and it is exactly why Christopher Alexander became such a disappointment for me. He was already working on *A Pattern Language*, which I really disliked.[14] He applied a hyper-empirical approach, whereby one could statistically register all the patterns that converge on an architectural event. This in itself was not bad. However, Alexander thought that by doing so he could develop a conclusive dictionary of solutions with which to answer any demand from clients. I'm oversimplifying, of course. But at that point I discovered it was all kind of flat, and despite Alexander's claims, this approach didn't do justice to the larger artistic and cultural forces dynamically at play in the design process.

AT He approached the matter in a completely positivist way.

JS Exactly. I heard him speak on several occasions, and he refused to acknowledge the relevance of culture to architecture. He would toss aside the questions and get back to describing how a statistical study of 12,300 occurrences of a similar physical event had distilled a pattern that determined the right place to locate the street number at the door of a house. This was a way of thinking so contrary to my being that it completely repulsed me.

AT From what you have said about your experience in Buenos Aires, I get the sense that going to Berkeley was also associated with a wish for a less professionalizing education. Is that correct?

JS I got this message very clearly from my Berkeley friends. They told me I could study whatever I wanted, which I had never imagined possible. In Argentina there were no postgraduate degrees, and doctorates were only for fields like the sciences, philosophy, and letters. The idea of a master's degree for a professional discipline was something strange to me, and I got very excited when I understood how graduate studies worked in the United States.

AT When I arrived at Princeton University from Chile, all I wanted to do was take classes in the German and philosophy departments. I took only one studio, because I felt I had already learned what I needed to learn from architecture in that way. I spent all my time going to history and philosophy seminars. It was fantastic. I didn't have the slightest desire to sit down and draw.

JS Same with me. I did not take a single studio at Berkeley. You probably learned architecture in the canonical sense through the studio format in Chile much better than you would have in the United States, anyway.

AT Yes. I've been thinking a lot about this topic lately, especially since I began teaching under this system. When you approximate architecture for the first time at the master's level, having studied another discipline before, the way you build yourself up as an architect is extremely different.

JS That was a great surprise for me. For how expansive the breadth of knowledge you can acquire may be, this education can be very limiting. I now realize how lucky I was to have acquired a solid knowledge of architecture in Argentina, even if under a single perspective. I did six years and twenty-six mandatory courses! We did very serious projects, studied building technology and statics—which came in handy with systems theory—and I got my license directly upon graduation because I was prepared to build. We also stayed up with everything that was going on in architecture, at least as much as was possible in the '60s from that remote place at the bottom of the globe. Then, I had all the time in the world to expand beyond this first experience.

This is a discussion I keep having with colleagues, despite everything we've seen at Harvard. Some people want the core program of the MArch I degree to speak to every issue.[15] For me, the core program must do exactly the opposite. It must speak architecture first and in the strictest of senses.[16]

AT Falling into a philosophy or literature course with your roots very anchored in your own discipline felt innovative for me. But it was my clear expertise in architecture that allowed me to bring another perspective and take away something from the rest.

JS My reasons to avoid design studios at Berkeley were similar to yours, but I also just thought they were very weak. I used the time to complement my experience with the opportunities that the traditional Latin American university didn't offer.

You can imagine that in my case this feeling was exacerbated by the era we were in. The youth revolution at Berkeley was real, it was happening at all levels and all around me. It was inescapable. Berkeley's ethos then was "Make your own curriculum and be free." People would go around with long hair, bring dogs to class, smoke marijuana while professors lectured—all those kinds of things. Everyone *really* did whatever they wanted. For people that were coming into the school without a strong architectural framework, this pedagogical experiment was disastrous.

NDA You landed straight into another very politically charged environment at Berkeley in 1967.

JS Absolutely. I remember that when I arrived in the United States, my friends picked me up at the airport and, as a prank, dropped me off in front of Berkeley's Sproul Plaza while they parked. This was where protests happened every day at noon. I found myself standing there alone, with my tucked-in shirt and my perfect Argentinian military crew cut, staring at a Mao Zedong poster the size of a building! In the meantime, a guy with hair down to his waist, wearing nothing other

Group carrying a "Free Speech" banner through Sather Gate in Sproul Plaza, UC Berkeley, ca. 1965.

than a tiny thong, walked by me, books in hand, dog following him, on his way to class. I had never even seen a man with long hair in my life!

At that point, I *was* accustomed to the tear gas and water cannons that came with protesting in Argentina, but Berkeley was a very different situation in terms of the clarity of aims and methods of action. There was a tremendous amount of political activity going on that really challenged the system and asked for freedom. Freedoms that were very palpable, by the way, even if many were kind of self-centered. A big part of it was about freedom of speech, but in the end, it was about the freedom to be yourself, whether it had to do with identity, gender, race, or political views. People were bringing out into the open things that were considered truly taboo to a degree that someone today couldn't imagine. Being gay and feeling for the first time that I could be myself in the open, all the time, and everywhere I went fueled my enthusiasm and energy for everything I did. The coalescence of the sexual revolution, experimentation with drugs, and the continuous immersion in rock and roll were really explosive and positive for me.

Then, in the background, there was of course the cruel and unpopular war in Vietnam, which went on for years, taking the lives of thousands of young people drafted to "serve their country." This was met with huge resistance from young people. However, at Berkeley there was this strange mix of serious discussion, violent confrontation, *and* flower power. People started the day demonstrating and physically confronting the police and ended it smoking a joint, kissing each other, getting laid, and drinking cheap wine while watching the sunset on the Pacific!

I remember after the first big demonstration at People's Park everyone arrived at the building of the College of Environmental Design full of energy. Some people kept repeating, "We have to do something, we have to do something!" So all of a sudden, a group of classmates decided to start lifting the asphalt from the professors' parking spots to plant daisies and pansies. I remember Rodolfo and I looking at each other and saying, "What the hell is this?" They went from protesting the Vietnam War to putting flowers all over the parking lot.

In Buenos Aires everything had been a bit more ominous and serious. There was no time off for weed and wine at the end of the day, and the military was the aggressor itself. We all knew someone who had been killed, kidnapped, or imprisoned.

NDA I wonder how you compare this experience to the political struggles we see today within American universities. Even though there is less mass protest and open confrontation, there is a great deal of political activism going on. There is a lot of sentiment against the status quo across the political spectrum. However, instead of a desire for unadulterated freedom, there are calls to order. There is limited consensus on what the order should be but rather implicit agreement that a new definition of right-versus-wrong should be established and aggressively policed. Liberal institutions like universities are really struggling to handle this, and their mishandling is affecting their ability to pursue their statutory objectives, like education and the pursuit of truth.

JS Of everything that was going on back then, I think the free-speech movement was the most consistent and resounding. Historically, freedom of speech in Argentina had been sporadic. As children during the first Peronist regime, people of my generation were advised by our parents to avoid saying certain things outside the home, particularly in school. As teenagers, while our opinions brewed, we were advised to avoid getting involved in politics. During one particular period of a military regime, some words were even forbidden.

By comparison, I thought of Berkeley as a place that was tremendously open and free. Despite this, I saw people actively fighting for freedom of speech, which I thought was an incredible phenomenon. The possibility of being free to say and, by extension, to do whatever you wanted at the university was really something that was acquired with a lot of energy. There was no call to "cancel" anything in the demands that students were making. I think perhaps it is time to reflect on this again. The values that were being fought for back then seem to have been taken for granted.

NDA Yes, now we are the first to silence one another in the name of freedom. We justify our urge to censor by framing it as a way of protecting the most vulnerable. We are convinced that the values behind our actions are on the right side of history, with a renewed positivist conviction. However, it's easy to become the opposite of what we think we stand for. As someone that saw firsthand revolution and the total collapse of democratic order in Venezuela, I worry about this slippery slope. You can't fight hate with hate and expect the outcome to be anything other than a simple transfer of raw power between classes.

JS I think a big difference is that back then the threat to values like free speech came from outside the university. Today, it seems to be coming from within, which is frightening and wrong, in my opinion. You know, we used to live right around the corner from People's Park, which in the spring of 1969 became an intense hotspot of confrontation between students and the university, the latter of which was supported by local police. The university wanted to build student dorms on the land. Students and neighbors refused, because they thought it should be a free-speech area that was not policed in the same way as Sproul Plaza at the heart of the campus. The daily confrontations between students and authorities became extremely violent, and eventually Ronald Reagan, then-governor of California, ordered the National Guard to occupy the campus and establish a curfew for two weeks.

More than a hundred people were hospitalized during one of the demonstrations, and a bystander watching from a roof died from a police gunshot. Another was totally blinded. During those days, Rodolfo and I couldn't even retreat to our apartment because it was always full of tear gas from the protests! Defending a space in the university for political or intellectual disagreement was hard-fought. People died and went to jail for these values.

AT Political turmoil seemed to follow you around.

JS Indeed. I have to say it was a very politically charged period all over. The other parallel momentous event was the student revolution of May '68 in France. Rodolfo left for Paris several weeks after I arrived in Berkeley in 1967, so he got to experience the strikes and street action that brought Paris to a total standstill. These events really shook the politics and culture of Europe, and even managed to bring down the government of Charles de Gaulle.

It was interesting to be exposed to both movements. In Paris people also strove to utilize art for political protest in novel ways that were distinct from the American flower-power approach.

AT What was Rodolfo doing in Paris?

JS He received a scholarship from the French government to study urbanism at the Centre de Recherche d'Urbanisme (CRU) and took classes of his choice at the École Pratique des Hautes Études. However, he ended up auditing the seminar of none other than Roland Barthes. He very quickly got involved in the world of French structuralism, literary criticism, and semiotics.

Throughout the year that we were separated, our exchanges revealed to me the differences between the intellectual and political climates of Berkeley and Paris. I kept working on my interest in computers, but what Rodolfo was sharing contributed to my growing skepticism of this work. Whereas in Berkeley everything was explained rationally through systems theory, in France everything—and I mean *everything*—was interpreted through the lens of language. So I started to read a lot on linguistics and then anthropology. When Rodolfo arrived in California he definitively contaminated me with what he had been exposed to. I owe the biggest intellectual shift in my career to him.

It became clear to me that aside from the healthy and transformative "liberation" I had experienced in Berkeley, the content of what was occupying me was not true to my roots in the continental intellectual tradition. Seeing the world from a scientific approach was driving me crazy! I had forced myself into it, encouraged by friends who were excited about this line of work. I could not avoid being curious about computers when they were a totally new thing, and everybody was raving about what they promised.

At that point, I was a research assistant for a professor in the field of cybernetics, and he was a good guy who was paying me for my work, which I continued for a while out of loyalty. However, in the meantime, I picked up a minor in anthropology and took courses in rhetoric and comparative literature.

AT How did Rodolfo interpret the situation at Berkeley when he arrived?

JS Rodolfo stormed my life in more than one way when he arrived. He had a better sense of the transformative events unfolding in the cultural revolution that California was at the forefront of. He was curious in different ways than I was and discovered things like the Cockettes and John Waters. At the time, Rodolfo had a more profound sensibility to interpret those cultural phenomena. He pushed me to overcome my resistance to what I thought was just another group of flower children getting stoned in public.

NDA Who were the Cockettes?

JS The Cockettes were a group of young males, mostly, that lived in a commune in Haight-Ashbury, a stronghold of the counterculture movement in San Francisco. They had a vigorous stance in terms of sexual and gender identity, which they put into a show they performed every weekend at midnight during the early '70s. The Cockettes were something phenomenal that had never been seen. In these experimental spectacles, they explored the relationship between the physical presentation of a person and their personality, identity, or gender. They were fascinating, and it was really inspiring to see them at that time. The Cockettes stood out against many other radical manifestations taking place, which were typically more au contraire and relied heavily on verbal messaging. They put on a purely visual and aesthetic experience, behaving on the stage exactly as they did off it, which gave the whole thing an entrancing realism.

The context in which the shows happened was also important. They were played on weekends as midnight sessions at the Palace, a small movie house in San Francisco's Chinatown to which otherwise only Chinese people went, because the movies were in Mandarin. The Palace was a true expression of urban multiculturalism and diversity. It was set in a part of the city that intersected Chinatown, the

Still from Steven Arnold's film *Luminous Procuress* (1971) depicting the Cockettes.

Italian neighborhood of North Beach, the hottest and most popular gay bars, the tourist stripteases, and the drag nightclubs. Everything converged and overlapped in a casual way.

The Cockettes were never understood by critics and were extremely mismanaged, because they were not really artists. They were ... I honestly don't know what they were. A nonprofessional group of performers of a new, powerful genre. Perhaps we could tentatively describe them as living allegories of another way of life. They were stoned all day, dressing up in these unbelievably suggestive, exuberant, and unsettling ways, and they danced and sang in a mostly improvisational mode. They were these kinds of angels amid this unique moment in time.

Sadly, most of the Cockettes died very young during the AIDS epidemic, which is, of course, the first big pandemic this country went through, in the 1980s. Most people have forgotten or totally ignored it because they thought it did not threaten them. Only a small group of people remembers it very well, myself included.

NDA And what about John Waters?

JS I was very impacted by his independent film *Pink Flamingos*, which opened in San Francisco in 1972 and made a big splash. I believe it was John Waters's first film, and it was a very intelligent "exercise in bad taste," as the movie was advertised.[17] It was about a group of mean, horrendous people with terrible taste, at the center of which was a drag queen called Divine.

The characters of the film exhibited these extreme and foul behaviors, literally eating dog shit on-screen. It was both repulsive and fascinating, because it really freed you from some of your most ingrained hang-ups. There was nothing less "filmworthy" or further from propriety, and yet there it was, in public. You didn't want to do anything that the characters did on screen, but at some moments you were mesmerized by their actions thanks to Waters's skills as a filmmaker.

Pink Flamingos was also a very strong and refreshing statement on the difference between taste, fashion, and style—another one of these things made clear to me by Rodolfo's sensibility and acute visual perception. We usually confuse these things, but I think they're important to understand. The taste of the movie was intentionally and consistently bad; the fashion that was created for it was quite extraordinary and imaginative; and the style was perfectly coherent, engaging, and repulsive. *Pink Flamingos* then brought this all together into a cinematographic language of total verisimilitude! I had never seen anything like that film.

NDA It's really a revelation for me to hear you talk about this moment, because it's not something I naturally associate with architects from your generation. Perhaps this is because the most important production of architects tends to be out of sync with their youth, unlike the average rock star or performer. We associate an architect's lived experience with the zeitgeist of later periods. Your intellectual and creative identity was shaped while these events were taking place in the late '60s, but you are called to build in the decades around the turn of the millennium.

JS It's true. I believe we developed a consistent, even if not clearly articulated, understanding of the underlying politics at the heart of all these new experiences in art, architecture, cinema, sex, rock and roll, and fashion. All of these converged with specific topics we were discussing in architecture, such as Robert Venturi's and Aldo Rossi's ideas about the vernacular. You have to see these debates within this larger context, because they were equally destabilizing, and they opened up fresh paths for architectural theory and practice.

NDA I see the attitude of your generation in all of this: the rejection of rigid canons or dogmatic positions; the fascination with complex readings of any and every aspect of architecture; the conviction that a meaningful criticism of society could be effected through architecture; the unfettered enthusiasm for the power of art and creativity; and in the case of some, the delirious cult of idiosyncratic personal expression.

JS There was this "realism" to all of these new experiences. They were true epiphanies that we felt in flesh and spirit. Each one of these events felt like we had uncovered something about how things *really* worked. One step at a time, without any difficulty, a new picture of reality began to feel obvious and indisputable. This is the time I began to use the phrase "Let's call things by their proper name" as a preface to any comment, particularly when I began teaching studio courses.

All of this also relates to the reason the vernacular became so important to me, and why I conflated Rossi and Venturi's ideas at the time. I was focusing on how both architects convincingly exposed the facts of the vernacular rather than considering the profound differences in their interpretations of the city. I saw the vernacular as the key to realigning architecture to the reality we were discovering. And this realization had the same political value for me as many of the other liberations that I was experiencing in my thinking and life.

NDA Only you would invite us to place Aldo Rossi and Mick Jagger on the same scene, Jorge!

The crowd at the 1969 Altamont Speedway Free Festival outside Tracy, CA, attended by approximately 300,000 people. Photograph: Bill Owens for Associated Press.

Stragglers and trash the day after the tragic and emblematic Altamont Speedway Free Festival in 1969.

JS Well, yes! It was the time of music, particularly in California. We were all fascinated by Bob Dylan—I still am—as well as the stars of the moment: Creedence Clearwater Revival, Procol Harum, Jimmy Hendrix, and the Rolling Stones, which I was totally in love with. Rodolfo and I were habitués of all the massive concerts at Winterland and the Fillmore. Rodolfo actually attended the history-making Altamont concert in December 1969, which was a dramatic epitome of the late '60s. It was one of the biggest concerts ever. There were about 300,000 people, and everyone was there: Santana, Jefferson Airplane, and the Grateful Dead, who had to withdraw from their stage appearance due to the violent climate developing in the audience. But the Rolling Stones performed nonetheless, with Mick Jagger driving everyone crazy in an act that was final in more than one way. Altamont was the prelude to the 1970s—a completely new era. The concert got out of control. The security provided by the Hells Angels—this gang of guys riding Harley Davidsons—was a fiasco, and people wound up dead. It felt like a change of direction for everything, much like People's Park did. The whole experiment of the '60s began to look somewhat grim and lacking in clear objectives. We began to sense the bitter taste of the new politics ahead of us.

Those pictures of Altamont after the concert really give you a sense of what this moment felt like: a scaffolding that was barely standing, presiding over a field of debris that would hang around us for another decade while we sorted it all out. The Summer of Love was over. I stayed home because I had a paper due! But Rodolfo's emotional and shocking account upon his return is still vivid in my mind.

3. Architecture as Material Culture

NDA I see how all these situations you confronted motivate you to pursue anthropology at Berkeley. You were being bombarded with correlated transformations in art, urban culture, identity, and politics.

JS Yes. In fact, when I decided to do a PhD at Berkeley, I only selected one designer as an advisor: Donald Olsen, who was perfectly versant in both architecture and Popperian philosophy. My two other advisors were the sociologist William Russell Ellis, as I mentioned earlier, and William A. Shack, a professor in the anthropology department.

AT How far did you get in your excursion with doctoral studies?

JS I did all of the requirements for the program, including the coursework and the minor, which I did in anthropology. I also took some elective courses, always outside of the design college, and took the qualifying exams after the third year.

AT Did you have an idea at that point of what your dissertation was going to be?

JS I wasn't expected to have made the decision at that point, so the focus wasn't fully fixed. But "The Beauty of Shadows" is the best condensation of those three years of expansive research and intellectual exploration leading up to the dissertation. It probably contains about 70 percent of the topics I was looking into.[18]

When I first approached William Shack, I told him that I really wanted to understand how buildings are produced and how they function as elements in the material culture of societies. I was interested in how buildings were expressions of a whole community, not just their individual builders. Shack was a complete outsider to our field, but he decided to advise me because of a genuine interest in what was, at that point, a messy project! I was able to convey what I wanted to him, even if I articulated it with a poor image. I told him, "I want to be able to make buildings speak to me."

Shack was a true scholar. He was the person that taught me the fundamentals of anthropology and initiated me into urban anthropology as a path of research. William Russell Ellis then was the person that helped me bridge these interests in the social sciences and architecture. He had been brought to the College of Environmental Design because of his scholarly interest in the relation between sociology and design. Donald Olsen, for his part, was someone with whom I could discuss architecture at a very high level, because he belonged squarely within the discipline but was very well educated in a wider sense. Put together, they were quite a productive trio.

NDA Understanding architecture as material culture is something of an obsession for you. Our conversations over the past three years have made me realize that, whether explicitly stated or not, this preoccupation is always at the root of what you do, whether it's writing, teaching, researching, discussing, or designing architecture. The allusions you've made to systems theory, structuralism, and typology all converge for me as tools for this work.

For you, architecture is first and foremost a specific type of material culture that is present in all societies and deals with the making of buildings. It should be understood as such, and any further definition we may want to give to the term must cohere with this cultural understanding. I know you despise oversimplifications, but is this accurate?

JS Yes, I do! But it is accurate, and what you have interpreted as a personal obsession touches inadvertently on the major effect that such obsession has in my work. When I observe, talk about, or design architecture, I am thinking from the perspective of the larger system of material culture to which it belongs. This is what brings me to the city, because it is the unit that most synthetically represents the system.[19]

AT Since you brought it up, I want us to talk a bit about "The Beauty of Shadows." How did this essay come about?

JS The essay came out of a symposium at Princeton in 1974 and associated activities during that semester related to architectural theory.[20] The event was organized by my friend Diana Agrest, who was teaching there. I did not participate in the symposium itself, but Diana asked George Baird, myself, and others to prepare a lecture that accompanied the semester's series. That became the seed for "The Beauty of Shadows." This was actually my first lecture for a public that I did not know and in a major American university. I didn't have the intention to publish the contents of the lecture at that time, since I had my eyes on writing my dissertation. However, it drew some attention. Michael Graves, who was in the audience, congratulated me effusively and even asked me for copies of some of the slides I had shown. I was very encouraged!

The symposium was really the first of its kind. Diana invited people that represented a sort of new generation in architecture, including Rodolfo, Mario Gandelsonas, Peter Eisenman, Anthony Vidler, and some others. Diana also invited Manfredo Tafuri, whom I believe was in the United States for the first time thanks to an invitation from MIT.

Mario Gandelsonas, who is another close friend from Argentina and Diana's husband, was one of the three original editors of *Oppositions*, the influential and original architectural journal that was taking shape at just around that time and that established the general tone of architectural discourse of the following decades in the United States.

The first issue of *Oppositions* was about to come out. Along with the other editors, Mario asked me to write the lecture in article form, which I worked a lot on with Joan Oackman, an editor they gave me. In the end, the article appeared in *Oppositions* 9, dated 1977. It took a while to get published, but the written and edited version of my 1974 lecture was ready about a year after I delivered it at Princeton. Each issue of *Oppositions* would take quite a bit of time to produce, which may come as no surprise to you, Nicolás! In fact, issue 9 was released in 1977, even though the article had already been circulating in a prepublication format.

AT One of the things I find fascinating in "The Beauty of Shadows" is your critique of Tafuri. I can't think of anything I have read from those years that confronts him so directly, and yet at the same time, it is a very Tafurian article.

JS In fact, mounting a response to Tafuri is what allowed me to organize all of my thoughts at the time. Being very young, I did this without knowing what I was getting myself into. I had met him personally, and despite how interesting his work was, he was not yet so important. Later he became a sort of god, which made me feel that I had so much courage back then!

AT I was going to say, it takes guts to stand up to Tafuri!

My interpretation of your argument is the following: Tafuri's work, at least in those years, suggested that history is essentially a critical practice, even a critical *destructive* practice. By this, he meant that architectural history has to be in a critical and almost confrontational position vis-à-vis the conditions of practice per se and not be a palette of solutions with the weight of history for contemporary problems. Thus, the medium for a critical project understood this way is obviously the written word because, in theory, it is independent of the laws of capital. For Tafuri, at least at that stage, a professional practice could never aspire to have that independence and autonomy. I think what you try to suggest in the essay is that you *can* use architecture as a critical tool; that the potential to be "critical from within" is possible and must be enacted using the language of architecture itself. This is how one could interpret, for example, some of Jean-Luc Godard's films from that time: the film is a critical commentary on how to make a film.

JS Yes, that was the time when metalanguage reigned in academia, and if you could handle it properly, then you could get ahead in the game. I think some arguments in the article were pretty original at the time. Much of the broader theoretical and philosophical foundations were not, obviously. The article leans a lot on Roland's Barthes's *The Pleasure of the Text* and *Mythologies* and Tafuri's *Theories and History of Architecture*, and his lecture in Diana's symposium.[21] These are still very relevant texts today, by the way.

I think what my article contributed was that some concepts in this literature could be reinterpreted, even altered, for architecture. "Criticism from within" is the idea that architecture has the capacity to be in itself critical without escaping its larger social responsibility of making buildings. However, this quality exists in a dynamic, dialectical relationship with architecture's role in our human need of mythification. Criticism and mythification are essential in any culture. Barthes explains how this works in society very well, as part of his criticism of consumer culture. The author can do whatever he wants, but once the product is placed in the world, it is uncontrollable. Things mythify themselves by nature or else quickly disappear.

For this reason, the kind of criticism that can happen within architecture is always short-lived; it cannot escape this act of consumption. In architecture, this can be done through the use of images and forms in space. However, even if the critical attitude is one of the strongest engines that fuels creativity, the critiques themselves eventually lose their effect as apparitions. The examples in the article concentrate on the ways in which the vocabulary of architecture is used for the purpose of commentary, because it is most easily apprehensible in that format. But the idea transcends beyond the visuality of architecture. During certain historical periods, we can find examples of this critical attitude applied to programmatic and circulatory arrangements, for instance. By the way, I think a lot of this has become common knowledge today, even to the point of being invisible. This is the case for many of the positive contributions of postmodernism.

NDA Your article accepts that architecture's most fundamental role is that of a cultural product that validates a set of collectively held beliefs—what you call "myths"—even if embedded with minor critiques or propositions within. Architecture manifests the status quo more strongly than the opinion of any individual involved in the making. The dialectic you propose is between short-lived individual positions and slow-moving, widely held cultural conventions that are prerequisites to the making of architecture.

JS Well put! The dialectical aspect is essential, because it is what allows culture to change. It is what makes architecture rich and diverse but also what makes it elusive. I think this is an important reality to understand if one is an architect. The Barthes quote that I use in the article and that inspired its title feels more relevant than ever from where I stand today. Barthes argues that "to want a text (an art, a painting) without a shadow, without the 'dominant ideology' . . . is to want a text without fecundity, without productivity, a sterile text."[22] So, to want to stand on any one side of the dialectic in a pursuit for purity is to want to operate outside the bounds of cultural production—a futile pursuit in my view.

The discussions I'm having with friends right now revolve around this issue. I sense that many feel a profound desire to step outside the messiness and ambiguity of culture in this moment when everything feels contaminated. But I do not believe this is productive nor, sincerely, even possible. That said, I don't think this is a conversation we can sort out in today's polarized climate.

NDA This is why several people I have discussed this article with recently find it so refreshing. There is a lot of talk in schools of architecture about an architecture of resistance, an architecture that is critical and operates against the socioeconomic conventions of society. This is something that tends to be poorly formulated, precisely because of the desire for a pure alternative. If the attempt is to dismantle the most ingrained conventions of society through architecture, the result is more likely to be the destruction of our knowledge base as architects rather than of societal systems themselves. Architecture doesn't take apart systems; it merely proposes ways in which these systems *could be* slightly reformed to make life better for its constituents.

JS This extremist attitude is also encouraged by the long hangover of the avant-garde mentality that has been discredited in aesthetic and philosophical circles since the 1970s but that the architecture world remains stuck on. Upholding the avant-garde as a constant modus operandi is a self-destructive approach.[23]

AT This is basically the rupture that Manfredo Tafuri experiences with American architecture, right? For several years Tafuri engaged actively with the architectural discourse in the United States, but he ended up becoming quite bitter about it. In *The Ashes of Jefferson*, he famously defined the architecture being made in New York in the 1970s, as it related to ideas of the avant-garde, as "pure play."[24]

JS Yes, Tafuri was very negative during that period, and there is a degree to which he is absolutely correct.

AT I agree. However, since you were coming "from within" architecture, in your essay you try to give some nuance to that argument. This is one of the aspects I find interesting about "The Beauty of Shadows." Beyond that, the essay also expresses a fascination for understanding the relationship between architecture and language that—

JS Which has its limits, by the way. It was very useful to look at architecture through the lens of linguistics, but not everything crosses over. We express ourselves through buildings in a different way than we do through words. Each way in which we communicate—be it writing, painting, architecture, or music—has its own constitutive constraints and potentials.

Nowadays we are in the late stages of breaking down ossified disciplinary boundaries, a process that began when I was young. The contamination can be very productive, but we shouldn't lose sight of the fact that there are concrete ways in which one kind of cultural product has to be different from another because of the social conventions it is called to respond to and the medium through which it does so.

AT I can definitely see some implicit comments on your appreciation of the work of the so-called "Five Architects" in the article, too, but there is also the whole question of the vernacular. It is not mentioned explicitly, but in the final lines of the article you introduce the term *typology*.

JS Yes, well a strong analogy can be made between language and vernacular architecture, which itself is always made up of organically evolving social conventions. The vernacular is a concept through which to describe the social, programmatic, material, and technological conventions in a given society that determine how buildings are made. It contains all those buildings that are built prototypically and represent a condition "before architecture."[25] Capital-*A* architecture for me is not an elite class; it is just buildings that are designed with a certain self-awareness about the conventions through which they are made and the ways in which these conventions make up a language that can be used creatively.

I left the discussion of the vernacular and typology out of the article, even if they were both present in my work at the time, because

Sea Ranch Condominium 1, the first building erected in Sea Ranch in 1965, comprising ten residential units. This pioneering development, designed by MLTW (C. Moore, D. Lyndon, W. Turnbull Jr., and R. Whitaker), became a model for the principles used to control all future construction in the area following local building traditions.

it would have become too long. I tried to write a separate essay on the topic but realized that it was quite complicated and that I was not prepared to take it on seriously. It required going deeper into the realm of aesthetics and sociology. The essay was about how architectural forms and styles transform in vernacular building traditions, which was tied to concerns I had about how modernist language was undergoing a much-needed transformation of its own. I also wanted to say certain things about the Five Architects, one of whom I thought represented a degradation of style entering the terrain of kitsch. But then I realized that this would have made me too many enemies!

AT One of the interesting things about the history of the concept of typology is that it usually emerges in times when the discipline of architecture has to define its boundaries against external forces. The period in which you were at Berkeley was also marked by a suspicion of authorship, if not a crisis of the author altogether. The work of Christopher Alexander is symptomatic of this, I think. He took what he developed in *Notes on the Synthesis of Form* into the world of cybernetics and convinced himself that we can suspend our judgment, design an objective procedure, and let the computer decide what the right solution is.

How conscious were you about this issue of authorship back then? You reflect a lot on the productive capacity of critical theory in the article.

JS This conversation was more present in continental circles, especially around French structuralism. Poststructuralism and deconstruction as applied to language and writing inevitably lead to an intelligent attack on authorship. The idea is that all the structure in the background of language speaks by itself and is uncontrollable as it guides the author. I was never entirely sold on that idea. I thought these ideas were contradicted by the very "authorship" demonstrated by some of the writers advancing them, not least of which Barthes himself, who is inseparable from his unique form of writing.

Living in California, Sea Ranch was one of the more productive expressions of the discussion about the vernacular and authorship within architecture at the time. We discovered it in Argentina right before leaving for the United States, and it really impressed us when we visited. It was the first project I had seen that seriously sought to interpret vernacular architecture in a way that went beyond the imitative approach that people in the West Coast were used to. Led by Charles Moore, the architects used the rural wooden sheds characteristic of the area to produce an architecture with its own sense of modernity. They dealt with the dramatic topography and landscape in a totally novel way, following the rugged coastline with pitched shingle roofs. The project developed a whole set of rules that turned into a proper architectural style that people still adhere to.

You know, for all I remember of the heated discussions of the 1970s and '80s about the death of the poet and the end of the painter and of painting itself, none of it bore out, as we can see and read today.

AT Obviously.

JS But it *was* very strong. Particularly in the arts, which were more flexible than architecture at the time. The idea that painting was over after Abstract Expressionism, which had been discredited by Pop art, had an enormous ripple effect. Art was suddenly an installation, an ephemeral object, a performance on the street, a smart sentence intelligently etched onto the right material support, and so on. It was kind of like the "study whatever you want" model at Berkeley. At the beginning it seemed fascinating, but it was unsustainable. As a lapsus of time it was productive, but you couldn't really take it anywhere in itself. It became disconcerting.

NDA Once you can do anything, you find yourself with the problem of having to figure out what to do.

JS As always. Particularly as an architect, there is always the time when you are called upon to produce those construction documents!

I do think that the discussions being had today around vernacular architecture and the return to typology have this critical attitude you have described, Alfredo. They are attached to a general call to order. I think paying attention to the social conventions that affect architecture again is fundamental if we want to rebuild out of the current disaster that architecture schools have become: you find yourself in a design review, and after hours of discussion, not a single word has been uttered about architecture!

AT It's interesting that from systems theory, you end up very close to ideas of type and typology. Perhaps this arc is not too different from what we saw happen more recently with parametricism, which could be interpreted as a natural outcome of systems theory being understood as a totally positivistic form of technological heroism. The reasons why ideas of type might be relevant today are perhaps not very different from why they felt relevant to you, and others, back then.

JS That's a great example, and I'm convinced this is the case. Parametricism … What a bummer!

This is why, when I was invited to do Eduard Sekler's memorial lecture at the GSD in 2017, I took the invitation to discuss something of theoretical and historical relevance as an opportunity to wrap up what I had been thinking about typology over the last decade.[26] The lecture laid out preliminary reflections that I had elaborated through several courses about typology, introducing fresh perspectives and concepts that I think allowed us to go beyond the stalemate that we've been suspended in since the late '70s. The last good piece written about the topic was Rafael Moneo's *On Typology*, but it dates back to 1978.[27] Everything that happened later is less useful. It all falls apart, with one of the most embarrassing moments being of course the *Deconstructivist Architecture* show at the Museum of Modern Art in 1988, which demonstrated the intellectual poverty and theoretical exhaustion we had arrived at.

A repositioning of typology that opens up doors to new theoretical paths is past due.[28]

AT Knowing a bit about how you have been teaching this topic recently, I have to agree that typology as an idea has been very unstable across history. The same word has been used to refer to very different topics, from Quatremere de Quincy in the eighteenth century to Gottfried Semper in the nineteenth and the German Werkbund in the early twentieth, which used the term as a way to stand against consumer culture, and all the way to Rossi, later in the twentieth century, who turned it into a reflection about collective memory.

JS As Moneo put it so well, typology is a term that constantly resemanticizes itself.[29]

AT Do you think that there is a way of thinking about typology in this genealogy that is more relevant today? Or do you see the need to redefine the concept altogether?

JS I haven't thought about this "genealogically," let's say, but perhaps it *is* time to do away with the term *typology* altogether and come up with something else that conceptualizes the cultural and technical conventions imbued in the architecture of any social group. I am working on advancing the discourse about type by folding in conventions, myths, and critique.

I think we have to take the last moment in which the terms are really operative and intelligently discussed. This was the opposition between Venturi and Rossi, two contemporaries who understood typology and its relationship to the city differently. While Venturi interpreted typology for the American city, Rossi did so for the historical European city. One saw it from the perspective of popular culture, and the other of collective memory. As seductive, insightful, and poetic as both proposals were, they led to dead ends.

AT This parallel has an important political dimension as well. Rossi points at the European medieval, premodern, and arguably precapitalist city as the source of the vernacular tradition he tried to revitalize. Venturi, meanwhile, was celebrating American popular culture in the absence of planning and thus with an implicit acceptance of neoliberalism.

JS Well, Denise Scott Brown would disagree with that! As for Rossi, I think what he had going for himself was that his understanding of typology was based on European vernacular architecture, which operates in the Braudelian *longue durée*. It is much easier to identify and work with that than with the American twentieth-century vernacular of consumer culture.

4. Scholarship and the Architect

AT I'm curious, why didn't you complete your PhD? There was clearly so much material to work on that you had, and still have, strong opinions about.

JS Well, by the time I delivered the lecture at Princeton, Rodolfo and I were already teaching at Carnegie Mellon University in Pittsburgh. It was after the symposium at Princeton that we first began to have doubts about completing the work for our PhDs. I had a kind of epiphany that I was making the wrong choice.

We had passed our qualification exams at Berkeley, but suddenly we began to wonder whether it made sense to spend the next three years of our lives writing a three-hundred-page dissertation for a committee. We wanted to communicate our ideas through architecture, through the project, with the intellectual equipment we developed during our years in Berkeley. After all, that's the substance of what I was saying in "The Beauty of Shadows"! We felt that we had achieved a lot of what we had intended, which was not to write a book but rather to better understand how architecture and the design process worked so we could get down to it. Also, we were already doing projects, and with some success, too!

This devolved into somewhat of a personal crisis. I was quickly convinced of this change of direction, but I wanted to do it in the least painful way for my committee and myself. We were actually the first guinea pigs of the PhD program at the College of Environmental Design, and we didn't want to ruin the relationships we built over three years of collaboration with our committee members. I also had the difficult task of appeasing my friends. They were perplexed about my inexplicable abandonment of what they thought of as a very promising, desirable, and even enviable career opportunity in academia. I was aborting it halfway through, all in exchange for a more mundane professional path.

Everything ended well though. The incomplete PhD experience helped us understand who we were as designers. It allowed us to keep doing what we had always done with another level of confidence and a profound understanding of how architecture worked as a cultural practice.[30] When the "The Beauty of Shadows" article took its final form, I was certain that a PhD was not for me. After the article came out, I felt that I had already said everything I wanted to say at that point.

NDA The article essentially declares that it's the last article worth writing. When I first read it, I got the sense that you were articulating a theoretical position that explained what you wanted to go out and do, abandoning the very medium, writing, that allowed you to arrive at your conclusions.

JS In a way you're right, Nicolás. As you mentioned, Alfredo, from an academic perspective the article is dense and could have become an entire book. Each paragraph could have been expanded into a chapter, and that is what I needed to do if I wanted to develop the arguments in the article within the context of an American university. Every proposition had to be dissected in a scholarly and methodical exposition. But, although I was still attracted to the content, bibliography, and manner of thinking, I felt that if I continued along the PhD path, it would impede my almost opposite creative impulse to take the road of design.

I was honestly convinced at that point, after all our research, that Rodolfo and I had figured out architecture once and for all! This gave us a very powerful, albeit naive, sense of security that was propelled by our unbound passion for architecture, which had been put on hold for years. A passion for drawing, for designing, for building buildings, and, yes, cities too. Of course, I can say now that I was wrong to think that we had unlocked the mysteries of architecture, but I was absolutely right about the passion part of the epiphany. It has never left me and is the real engine of everything I do. I kept a foot in academia but redefined my profile, never looking back on this decision with regret. This was the mindset with which I went on to Harvard in 1975 and began teaching my studio and theory courses there. At that point we became confident that the path we had taken was in fact more honest and genuine. We didn't need to become scholars and write books in order to convey everything we had clarified about architecture.

AT What motivated the move to the East Coast? Was there a more exciting intellectual environment? Did the Institute for Architecture and Urban Studies in New York play a role?

JS We began looking for teaching jobs after our qualifying exams, which was a natural move back then if you wanted to make some money while continuing to do academic research and begin practicing. I am not sure how viable this model is today, by the way. This decision was also encouraged by the consequences of the 1973 oil crisis, a serious market crash, and a worldwide recession, which coincided with our departure from Berkeley. Work in the profession was scarce.

I applied to a lot of schools. I was very interested in Cooper Union in New York, and talked with John Hejduk to see if he would give me a job. He was quite taken by my House in Cuernavaca—for which his Wall House was one of my inspirations—but told me there were no openings at the school. In the end, I got interviews at two other places: Cornell University and Carnegie Mellon.

Cornell was one of the great architecture schools at the time, and it was where I really wanted to go because I had become fascinated by Colin Rowe's writings. The school also had the allure of Oswald Mathias Ungers, who had recently become dean. There was a lot of buzz about what he was doing. Carnegie Mellon, on the other hand, I had no clue about. I had applied on the advice of friends from New York and Peter Eisenman, whom I had met at that point. I didn't even know where Pittsburgh was on the map, but after receiving firm offers from both schools, I ended up opting for Carnegie Mellon to the surprise of everyone around me.

AT What led you to make this decision?

JS First and foremost, when I went to Cornell for the interview, I found a horrendous collegial atmosphere! I was just there for a couple of days, but it was enough to see how the animosity between Rowe and Ungers had spilled over and contaminated the entire school. There were two separate factions that couldn't even speak to one another. Door slamming in the corridors was usual, and any time you spoke to someone from one faction, they would tell you terrible things about the other.

I was interested in Rowe, but also Ungers. The constant interrogation from people there about what side of the line I was on made me feel that, if I taught there, I'd end up in a bind that might jeopardize my progress in academia. There was also the fact that when I visited in April, it was still snowing heavily! Never having lived outside a city, the idea of small-town life in the middle of nowhere with freezing-cold weather in the spring was quite unattractive.

The visit to Carnegie Mellon went the other way around. I had heard a lot of bad things about Pittsburgh: that it was unhealthy, polluted, and full of poverty due to the masses of laborers living along the rivers, close to the steel mills that characterized this industrial city until the middle of the century. However, these turned out to be clichés from previous decades. The steel mills had been moved out of the heart of the city, which was celebrating what people called the "Pittsburgh Renaissance." A truly spectacular city had been revealed now that the curtain of pollution had been drawn.

I can recall particularly my first arrival in Pittsburgh. From the airport, you had to go through a tunnel that cut through some hills that blocked the view of the city, and all of a sudden, when you exited the tunnel, a view of downtown suddenly opened up in a 180-degree panorama, flanked by the Allegheny and Monongahela Rivers, which converged at the tip of the city to make the robust Ohio River. Entering Pittsburgh was an amazing theatricalization of the American city!

The interview and presentations at Carnegie Mellon went well, and I got the sense that there was a real opportunity at the school. Even though there were good faculty, not that much was going on. However, there was an eagerness to make something happen that resonated well with the upbeat atmosphere of the Pittsburgh Renaissance that everybody kept talking about. I had my head loaded with ideas at that time, and going to Carnegie Mellon put me in a situation that rewarded all kinds of pedagogical experiments that I wanted to do! Pittsburgh was rich in urban historic buildings and abandoned industrial complexes, which I used as laboratories to look into conservation and reuse. I also worked on making public space a part of the education of the architect, which was novel at the time.

Going to Pittsburgh turned out to be a very productive experience. In teaching and in design work, Rodolfo and I got so much done. During the first year in Pittsburgh, Rodolfo worked at IKF Architects, and his first project as designer in charge was immediately picked up by *Progressive Architecture*. It was a project for the reuse of a cluster of independent buildings packed within a city block in downtown Pittsburgh through the insertion of a covered galleria. *Progressive Architecture* used his conceptual drawings for the cover of the magazine and titled it "The Pittsburgh Follies." We were on a roll!

NDA Your experience in Buenos Aires and San Francisco both marked your understanding of architecture and the city in important ways. In Buenos Aires, you grew up surrounded by a well-developed urban environment and culture. In San Francisco, you experienced the city's ability to accommodate a variety of subcultures side by side in an enriching way. Did Pittsburgh also leave a mark?

JS Well, now that you put it that way, I want to add something to your characterization of the context I grew up in. Although we lived in Buenos Aires, we vacationed every summer in Mar del Plata, which had a crucial impact on the formation of my urban experience. Mar del Plata was a city designed for leisure at a large scale, where *all* the social classes of Buenos Aires vacationed. It had remarkable urban design, public infrastructure, and landscape features, which were developed during the middle of the century. There are few places like Mar del Plata from that period in the Western world. The people of

Aerial view of the city of Pittsburgh. The foreground shows the Three Rivers Point and Downtown Pittsburgh, while in the background lies the educational and cultural center of Oakland. Photograph: Dustin McGrew.

Rodolfo Machado and Jorge Silvetti with the Fountain House model in their home in Pittsburgh, 1975.

Buenos Aires really inhabited two major urban centers, four hundred kilometers from one another, where they had everything they needed delivered at the highest level of design.

As for Pittsburgh, we don't always remember this, but it was one of the richest cities in the world at the turn of the twentieth century and a true melting pot of nationalities and ethnicities. This left behind a very interesting city from an architectural and urban perspective. Pittsburgh is in an impressive geographical setting, because it is at the confluence of many bodies of water, and is surrounded by an unbelievable amount of bridges. Infrastructure has an important presence on the urban landscape and as such is understood as part of the domain of architecture, whether it is the railroad and train stations that played a crucial role in the identity of the city or the imposing structures of the decommissioned steel mills that still stand over downtown like great monuments. The way infrastructure defines the character of the city is something I saw in a different light when I was in Pittsburgh.

Pittsburgh was very rich in a time when American industrial entrepreneurs were incredibly philanthropic. There was an understanding that creating public institutions and making buildings to house and represent them was the way to give back to the city. All of this was very novel to me. I didn't know anything about these American traditions of wealth transfer, but I found it fascinating how conscious the city was about the role that architecture played in the urban environment. Architecture in Pittsburgh during this period was the main tool through which the city defined the perception of itself, with a paradoxical mix of innocence and audacity.

The resulting environment is what encouraged me to work like crazy during those two years. Downtown Pittsburgh is flanked by the Oakland neighborhood on the west, and the city has this dual nature where on one side there is money and on the other there is intellect. Oakland is an extraordinary accumulation of institutional monuments: a Renaissance palazzo for the Pittsburgh Athletic Association, a classical temple for the Mellon Institute, a recreation of the Mausoleum at Halicarnassus—one of the Seven Wonders of the Ancient World—for the Soldiers and Sailors Memorial Hall, the exotic Syria Mosque for the headquarters of the Shriners, and so on.

Nothing is what it was supposed to be stylistically, because it was all an invention of its own time. The Cathedral of Learning is one of the best examples of this: a forty-story tower at the University of Pittsburgh containing classrooms and administrative offices built in the Gothic style around the same time as the Chicago Tribune Tower Competition. Like everything else in this town, the building is remarkable in terms of the quality of its construction and detailing, complete with stained glass and anything else one would liken to

Gothic cathedrals. The most perplexing aspect of the tower is that it has thirty-seven spaces called the "Nationality Rooms," because their decor and appointment reflects different cultures and nationalities. They were in fact funded by people from the communities they alluded to, given how diverse and rich in immigrants Pittsburgh was in the late nineteenth century. They are Chinese, Austrian, Israeli, Indian, Turkish, Swiss, Syrian-Lebanese, and anything else you can imagine. This tells you something about the spirit of this town and its fondness for architecture, exoticism, and the elaborate interpretations of culture at play.

There is also the Carnegie Museum of Art, one of Andrew Carnegie's great contributions to the city, because of both its architecture and its important collection of art. It is one of the few museums in the world that has preserved to this day its Architectural Hall: a collection of casts of buildings and building components that were considered canonical. You can see how architecture was learned and exhibited at that time, through copies and fragments of architecture.

NDA Did the Carnegie Mellon campus also play a role in this urban ensemble?

JS Carnegie Mellon University started off as a technical school that Andrew Carnegie founded for the children of the workers at his steel mills. The campus was designed by Henry Hornbostel, an architect whose contribution to Pittsburgh was very important. He was also the architect of the Williamsburg Bridge and the Hell's Gate Bridge, both in New York. Hornbostel's project for the school was an original piece of campus design, one of a kind in this country. The mall that organizes the campus terminates on one side with the College of Fine Arts, and on the other with today's College of Electrical and Computer Engineering, which used to house the campus's powerhouse and still has a tower that used to let smoke out of its top. All the buildings on the original campus were finished with glazed terra-cotta bricks, and they used Guastavino vaults in the most elegant ways.

The architecture department where I worked was lodged within the grand, Beaux-Arts-style College of Fine Arts. It was in the same building that housed the drama, music, and painting departments, which I found to be an amazing company for architecture! The building itself was a textbook of architecture as it was understood at the time it was built. The main facade facing the mall had four large niches flanking the entrance, each displaying different architectural styles. The first thing you found on the pavement of the ground floor when you entered were plans of buildings. I've never seen a more intelligent use of the floor in a school of architecture! You walked into the plan

The Hall of Architecture at the Carnegie Museum of Art in Pittsburgh, PA. The hall was built as part of the large expansion of the museum undertaken by Andrew Carnegie to "bring the world" to the people of Pittsburgh, in 1904.

Entrance lobby to the College of Fine Arts building at Carnegie Mellon University, designed by Henry Hornbostel in 1904. In the foreground, an inlaid plan of the Basilica of St. Peter's in Rome can be seen on the floor. Photograph: Bruce Coleman.

of St. Peter's Basilica, then the Parthenon, Chartres Cathedral, Hagia Sophia, and so on. And when you looked up into the Guastavino vaults, they were all decorated with frescoed views of these buildings and portraits of their architects.

NDA In one of your essays, you raise the idea that the object that architecture represents is architecture itself.[31] You say this in opposition to portraiture, let's say, where the object of representation is a person. Did the College of Fine Arts building influence this broader conclusion about architecture? The way it plays out in Hornbostel's building is very obvious, of course. However, it is obvious even in the styles of late-nineteenth-century architecture that you described as characterizing Pittsburgh. The architecture of one time seeks to "represent" an architecture of another. Gothic, Greek, or Renaissance architectural elements are used to imply something totally different than what they did at another point in time. They manifest an original image of how this society perceived itself at present.

JS Yes. Those are the creative forces that inform so-called historicism and eclecticism in architecture. In my opinion, the importance of these developments in architecture in the nineteenth century has to do with their corrosive role. They contribute to the demythification of the formal styles explained by historians and ideologues as the exclusive products of specific historical-cultural conditions. In their seemingly simplistic, superficial lightness, these eclectic minds performed a historical resemanticization, making any style reusable in other spatiotemporal contexts.

In effect, these architects realized and made palpable the inevitable disconnection with the presumed original architecture and its symbolic or allegorical meanings. The nineteenth century, so often trivialized by later critics, in fact inaugurated a process of slow moving "deconstruction." It established the foundations that would support the sharp and near-fatal blows inflicted to the modernist foundations of architecture by postmodern criticism in the late twentieth century.

There is much to think about here in relation to disputes about architecture and monuments today. Beaux-Arts architecture should warn those that so assiduously look for the deep roots of sociocultural malaises in the forms, styles, or spatial organizations of Western architecture without acknowledging—or worse, ignoring—the historicity of it all. Yes, cultural symbols have an expiration date! Always! And yes, historicism and eclecticism were not just the whimsical product of white European patriarchal dilettante men having a good time at a gentlemen's club. Some of these figures were more like cultural terrorists that cleared the way to a more open architecture. They had allegiances neither to nostalgic ideals of dead historical periods nor to

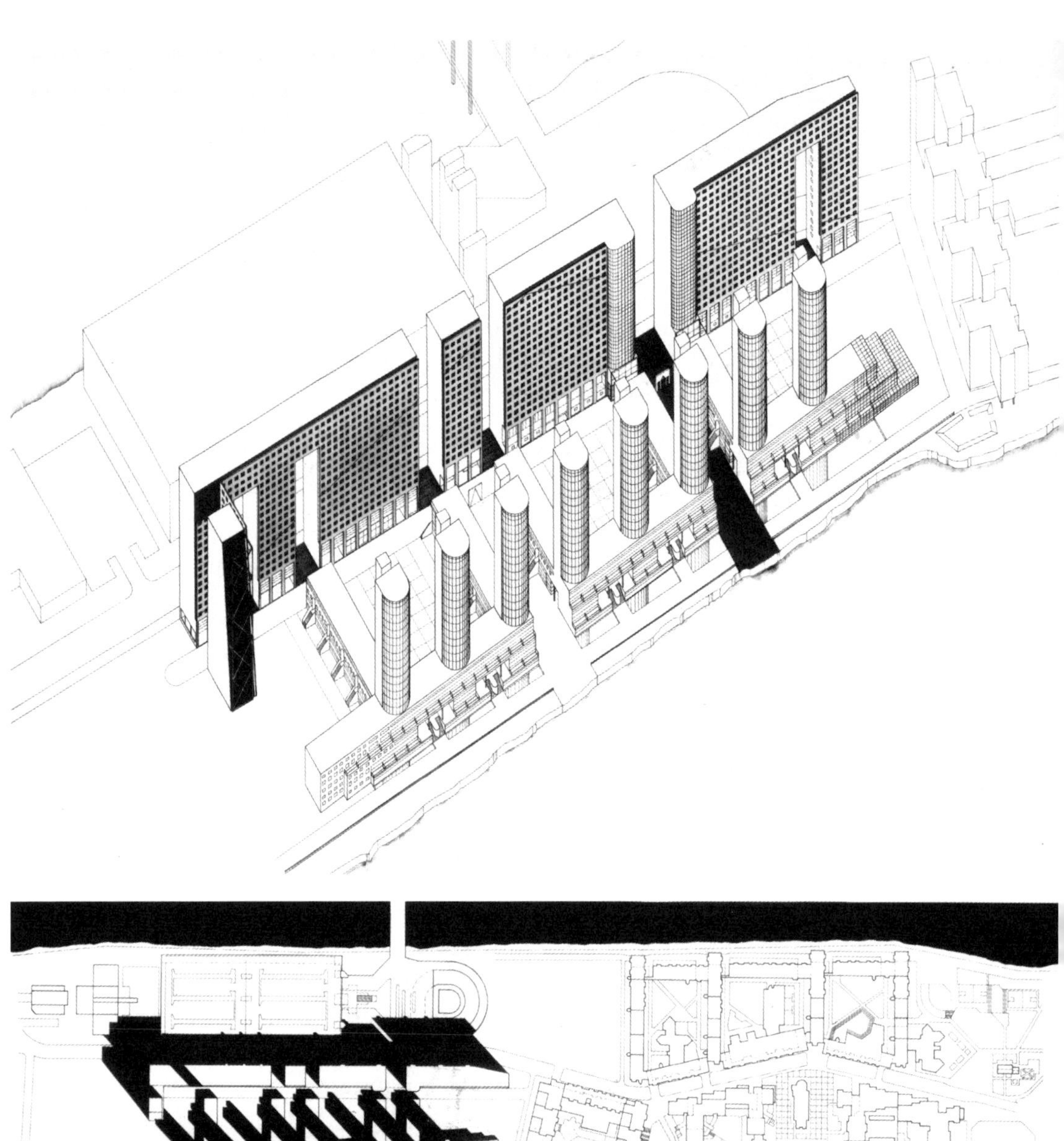

Axonometric and site plan of the Roosevelt Island Housing Competition project, designed in 1975 by Rodolfo Machado, Jorge Silvetti, Diana Agrest, and Mario Gandelsonas.

the positivist moralisms of modernism but rather only to the freedom of form and art.

AT We should end with a discussion of some of the projects you and Rodolfo developed during these years in Berkeley and Pittsburgh. As I read "The Beauty of Shadows," I tried to register how a form of "criticism from within" registered in the work that was contemporary to the article. However, I am now also thinking about ways in which your particular understanding of architecture's role in the city took form in projects.

One of the projects that I was happy to discover was your proposal for La Villette in Paris. I didn't know you had participated in the competition.

JS Yes, and we took the second prize. But it was the first competition in the '70s. The one that Bernard Tschumi won and got built happened in the '80s.

AT What I read in the competition entry is an intention to insert urban elements into the park. I see less invention and more references to the formal language of the city of Paris. The elements are typologically categorized and then redeployed at the scale of the site in an entirely different way.

JS To understand that competition entry you need to see another project that Rodolfo and I did during that period with Diana Agrest and Mario Gandelsonas.

AT The Roosevelt Island Housing Competition?

JS Yes, which is earlier and is the first project in which we really play with the idea of breaking down Manhattan typologically and redeploying it at the scale of the site. If you want, it is a miniaturization of Manhattan on Roosevelt Island, as if it were a distorted mirror of the city. It has the architecture of traditional townhouses and freestanding towers, as well as great slabs that serve as a background to the housing complex.

This was a competition organized by the city and sponsored by MoMA, so it generated a lot of discussion and produced an important collection of projects at the time.

AT It's interesting that you put the entry for La Villette as a sort of specimen within the same genealogy as the Roosevelt Island competition. They both deal with a formal analysis of the city that is then used to produce systematic architectural interventions that somewhat merge into the existing urban environment. They are absolutely not about singular interventions or formal exuberance.

JS There is a third project that we did with Diana and Mario during this period that also corresponds to this genealogy, as you've called it. It was another housing project for a competition organized by the French government. I don't think it was ever published but it was wonderful because we naively thought, "OK, this project will prove once and for all that the *only* approach to architecture that can be taken is a typological one." [*laughs*]

NDA This idea of the Roosevelt Island project as a mirror of the city across the river is very clear in relation to your description of Pittsburgh. The typological analysis doesn't lead to an authorless, nostalgic expansion of the city according to static rules. The language embedded in the city is used to manifest a new idea of what New York is through this monumental architectural intervention. This is an architecture that operates from within an existing cultural condition to propose a reform. It uses an available language to create an original proposition of what life in the city could be. You don't fantasize about a world where our cultural or social contract can be conceived *ex novo*, from the outside, as the cultural purists of our age aggressively demand.

JS Which brings us back to Barthes's quote from which the title for "The Beauty of Shadows" derives. Reforming culture is always a messy, imperfect process that requires getting your hands dirty with things *as they are*. This is especially true when you are dealing with a kind of material culture like architecture, which is so tightly bound by all kinds of constraints: social conventions, the relative slowness of the building process, and the permanence of its products vis-à-vis the velocity at which society changes.

NDA Your contribution has to be swallowed by the larger social contract so it can become mythified. This implies that it needs to be transformed in order to conform to other conditions that remain stable. That said, architecture has to represent our values, which are rarely in line with preexisting social conventions. But should this be architecture's constant aim? Or are there moments when architecture should try to pivot culture in a new direction and others when it should simply reinforce the status quo?

JS Again, the "facts" of architecture—buildings—are slow moving and long lived. The timeline of buildings cannot be adjusted to coincide one-to-one with social changes, particularly ideological or political ones. I don't think that we can define precisely the way in which the design process should respond to change. This depends on our understanding of change, of history, and of ethics, as well as the intelligence with which we can operate at the time.

Culturally, architecture is extremely risky! The risks of working with natural laws can be major, but they are knowable and eventually preventable. The risks of operating in culture cannot be addressed with scientific, technical, or political knowledge alone. I think that in architecture, these risks need to be faced with designers' personal understanding of the cultural processes they are subject to and the ways these relate to architectural form. I thought that we had come up with the only valid approach to architecture when we did the housing project in France, but I have come to believe that there are no techniques or formulas for design that can guarantee success when it comes to architecture's role in culture.

Notes

1 Claude Lévi-Strauss, *Tristes tropiques*, trans. John Weightman and Doreen Weightman (London: Penguin, 2012), 55–56.

2 J. W. Goethe, *Italian Journey, 1786–1788*, trans. Elizabeth Mayer (London: Penguin Books, 1992).

3 See Jorge Silvetti and Erika Naginski, "Architecture: The Reconception of History," in this volume, 215–271.

4 Editorial Nueva Visión was founded by Tomas Maldonado, Alfredo Hlito, and Carlos A. Mendez Mosquera in 1951. Maldonado was its director until 1954. The editorial committee included J. M. Borthagaray, F. Bullrich. Grisetti, J. Goldemberg, and later H. Baliero J. E. Bailey.

5 See Jorge Silvetti and Nader Tehrani, "Architecture: The Making of a Practice," in this volume, 369–412.

6 See Jorge Silvetti and Elisa Silva, "Architecture: The Purview of the Social," in this volume, 299–339.

7 See Jorge Silvetti and Mark Lee, "Architecture: The Emergence of Discourse," in this volume, 117–166.

8 Agrupación Nueva Música was an important musical group created in 1937 by J. C. Paz, a composer, writer, critic, and theoretician of modern music. It remained active for decades and was influential in the promotion of the most advanced musical work in the Argentinian context.

9 See Fernando García, *El Di Tella. Historia íntima de un fenómeno cultural* (Buenos Aires: Paidós, 2021).

10 Peronism was the dominant political movement in Argentina during the second half of the twentieth century, created by General Juan Domingo Perón.

11 See Silvetti and Lee, "Architecture: The Emergence of Discourse," *op. cit.*

12 Christopher Alexander, *Notes on the Synthesis of Form* (Cambridge, MA: Harvard University Press, 1964).

13 Fortran is a programming language that was first developed by IBM in the 1950s.

14 Christopher Alexander, A *Pattern Language: Towns, Buildings, Construction* (New York, NY: Oxford University Press, 1977).

15 The core program makes up the first year and a half or two years of study for MArch I students, who do not hold a previous professional degree in architecture, and many of which have no previous experience in the field of architecture.

16 See Silvetti and Lee, "Architecture: The Emergence of Discourse," *op. cit.*

17 John Waters, *Pink Flamingos* (Dreamland and New Line Cinema, 1972), 92 min. *Pink Flamingos* was the first and most famous of Waters' countercultural Trash Trilogy. The subsequent films of the trilogy are *Female Trouble* (1974) and *Desperate Living* (1977).

18 Jorge Silvetti, "The Beauty of Shadows," *Oppositions*, no. 9 (1977): 43–61.

19 See Silvetti and Lee, "Architecture: The Reconception of History," *op. cit.*

20 "Practice, Theory and Politics in Architecture," Princeton University's School of Architecture, Princeton, 1974. The symposium was an event that set the tone for the public programs during the semester that followed at the school, one of which was the lecture delivered by Jorge Silvetti that led to "The Beauty of Shadows."

21 Roland Barthes, *Le Plaisir du Texte* (Paris: Seuil, 1973).
Roland Barthes, *Mythologies* (Paris: Seuil, 1957).
Manfredo Tafuri, *Teorie e storia dell'architettura* (Bari: Laterza, 1968).

22 Roland Barthes, "The Death of the Author," in *Image, Music, Text*, trans. Stephen Heath (London: Fontana, 1977).

23 See Silvetti and Lee, "Architecture: The Emergence of Discourse," *op. cit.*

24 Manfredo Tafuri, "Les cendres de Jefferson / The Ashes of Jefferson," *L'Architecture d'aujourd'hui*, no. 186 (1976): 53.

25 See Silvetti and Lee, "Architecture: The Reconception of History," *op. cit.*

26 For an edited transcript of the lecture, see Jorge Silvetti, "TYPE: Architecture's Elusive Obsession and the Rituals of an Impasse," in this volume, 427–444.

27 Rafael Moneo, "On Typology," *Oppositions*, no. 13 (1978): 22–45.

28 See Silvetti and Lee, "Architecture: The Reconception of History," *op. cit.*

29 Moneo, "On Typology".

30 See Silvetti and Tehrani, "Architecture: The Making of a Practice," *op. cit.*

31 Jorge Silvetti, "Representation and Creativity in Architecture: The Pregnant Moment," in *Representation and Architecture*, ed. Ömer Akin and Eleanor F. Weinel (Silver Spring, MD: Information Dynamics, Inc., 1982): 159–184.

The Beauty of Shadows

JORGE SILVETTI, 1977

"There is nothing more essential for a society than to classify its own languages," wrote Roland Barthes in 1966.[1] This imperative seems to underlie much theoretical work of the present decade in the fields of literature, music, and particularly in architecture. What follows is an attempt to discuss and reaffirm the validity of contemporary inquiries that focus their attention on architecture as language: that is, architecture as a specific ideological practice concerned with the production of cultural symbols; architecture understood or "read" as a "text," as material that supports a signification which includes but goes beyond the functions it involves. Specifically, this essay seeks to contribute to such classificatory tasks by concentrating on one mode of architectural discourse of which we have become recently aware: architecture as a discourse critical of itself. Such a discourse does not itself make use of language, but instead places itself at the very moment of producing an architectural

Fig. 1 Hans Holbein the Younger. *The Ambassadors*, 1533. Oil on panel, 81 ½" x 82 ½". National Gallery, London. Reprinted from H. A. Schmid, *Hans Holbein der Jüngere* (Basel: Tafelband, 1945)

object, aiming through this at a critical reading of the system of architecture. The idea of "criticism from within" is not a new notion, and indeed it has been equated at times with the very notion of art. What is new, however, is the possibility of defining it more clearly by using new conceptual tools. As defined, this type of criticism seems to differ from other more conventional and well-established types of criticism by virtue of the instruments it uses. We shall see later that its identity depends on many other characteristics that include the type of "effects" it produces as well as its relationship with theory. For the moment, we need only make clear that the "realm" of criticism has traditionally been divided between two opposing modes: one that tries to evaluate the degree of "fitness" or "non-fitness" of a solution to a particular architectural question and another that attempts to see both the question and that solution as parts of a larger historical, cultural, or ideological process. The former, typical of architectural journals and chronicles, is mainly concerned to "evaluate facts"; it is in the end trapped within its own ideological perspective. This kind of critical discourse constitutes in most cases an obstacle for theory, and should perhaps be better termed "technical" or "evaluative" criticism. The latter is related more to historical and scholarly endeavors and has theory, to which it is a prolegomenon and constant check, as its final aim. This is indeed the only discourse that can safely claim the name of criticism in that it enjoys the more "comfortable" situation of being distanced from the act of making.[2]

Undoubtedly, the third type of critical discourse which I am introducing here, and which I shall call "criticism from within," does not appear to have the same conceptual clarity as these two traditional forms, particularly in its relation to theory and ideology. By placing itself within the act of making and by not using the instruments of language but those of architecture itself, it becomes compromised by the ideological nature of all objects produced by culture; but, at the same time, paradoxically, the very identification of this type of criticism depends on the fact that these same objects possess the capacity to expose certain meanings of the work that are otherwise obscured by ideological veils.

One might expect that among the copious writings that have appeared in the last decade which have attempted a description and explanation of architecture as language, attention would have been given to this third type of criticism if only because it is itself, as a criticism of architecture, one of the many discourses of language itself. Following the logic of the analogy between architecture and language (and noting that important contributions on this area of theory have concentrated heavily on the problems of theory versus ideology), the parallel contains the possibility of making, or at least proposing, the existence of such a criticism in architecture. But few have analyzed this notion of criticism, while many have abused the usage of the term.

Manfredo Tafuri has recently attempted to evaluate the historical significance of internal criticism, particularly for the present time.[3] In his writings, Tafuri takes a rather pessimistic view both of the historical and the cultural value of an attitude that concerns itself with the problem of language—"the return to language," he writes, "is a proof of failure"[4]—an attitude to which "criticism from within" belongs, and especially of the critical intentions that he sees as pervading the objects of present production. And yet, one of the central conclusions that emerge from his argument is that there are no fundamental differences between such architects as Aldo Rossi, James Stirling, Peter Eisenman, Robert Venturi, since they "all return to language." One may suspect that such frustration might well be a typical initial reaction to a work of criticism of such stature and originality that it shatters hitherto unchallenged systems of ordering and classifying and subverts our previously held values, rearranging what is known according to a more enlightened conceptual framework and thus transforming the object of analysis into a new, unexpected reality.

Nonetheless, such classifications as Tafuri's, which polarize the objects of analysis into categories that are too broad, thus erasing significant differences, or into trivial labeling systems as in the case of the originally amusing but by now boring chromatic grouping into "the whites," "the grays," and "the silvers" (a taxonomy which has retarded any serious understanding of the problem of architecture as language), are in the end still frustrating in themselves. Further treatment of the subject seems warranted, if for no other reason than because there has been no systematic discussion of the nature of "criticism from within" and its relation to a more general "return to language." As yet I do not know what mechanisms and operations it uses or how it differs from other types of work on language. Indeed, to test and evaluate Tafuri's macroscopic, global view it is indispensable to shift attention to the internal workings of language and to possess a clear model of its structure. I will begin my discussion at a microscopic, yet generalizable level, describing certain mechanisms and operations, which I hope will later enable me to establish the role that such "criticism from within" might play today in the development of architecture in its relation to theory, criticism, and ideology.

I would like for the purpose of my analysis to follow an opposite path to Tafuri and start with a general characterization of the common traits shared by most contemporary production concerned with architecture as language, ending with a more particularized

Fig. 2 Palazzo del Te, Mantova, Italy. Giulio Romano, c. 1530.

Fig. 3 Cartuja de Granada, detail of sacristy. Francisco de Hurtado and Francisco de Acero, 1732–1780.

Fig. 4 Choir of the Church of Santo Stefano, Florence. Bernardo Buontalenti, 1536–1608. Detail of stair.

2

3

4

analysis that is intended to help differentiate what is "criticism from within" from what is not.

Let us begin by assuming that the "return to language" has indeed occurred (a trend that seems to characterize the seventies, as has been said, but which also can be traced back to Kahn and even to the early Johnson). That is, this "return to language" is marked by an unusual degree of self-consciousness in architecture, which starts with the recognition that architecture, like any other cultural product, can be studied as a system of signification, establishing different levels, accumulating layers of meaning and sense, and constituting one of the many symbolic spheres instituted by society. As a consciousness of itself, architecture can only, and only willingly, operate with the known: its past, immediate or distant, and the existent world. It is, then, a work of reflection, essentially anti-utopian, one which automatically establishes a basis for criticism since criticism is a speculative reflection on the known.

It is undoubtedly for this reason that on so many occasions we hear the analogy drawn between the present moment and that of Mannerism, that "universal malaise", as Colin Rowe called it, that appeared in Italy during the Cinquecento.[5] This is probably because, for the first time since the twenties, we find ourselves looking back on the Modern Movement itself from a real historical perspective. Its "classicism" has by now been experienced, its effects sensed, and its postulates questioned; yet with all this nothing seems to have appeared to replace it. Like the Mannerist architect we can only manipulate the known. Such is, in my view, all that can be said in general terms about the state of architecture today.

But as soon as we begin to scrutinize these modern "manners" and their mechanisms for the production of meaning, we realize that the conscious reference either to past architectures or to contemporary realities can be established and expounded in many forms (some of them of antagonistic character), so that self-consciousness and the "return to language" are not sufficient categorizations upon which to reject or accept them; that there might be specific differentiations, much more useful than Tafuri's universalist label, to be made between Charles Moore's "wit" and Aldo Rossi's "silence"; that, in short, as a parallel to the general treatment we need to establish with clarity: (1) how operations on language work; (2) what their relations to theory and ideology are; (3) what their historic-cultural status is.

What then is it possible to do with an established code, or how can we operate on it? Without risking much, we could say that it is only possible either to transform it or to reproduce it. By transformation we mean those operations performed on the elements of a given existent code which depart from the original, normative, or canonical usage of the code by distorting, regrouping, reassembling, or in general altering it in such a way that it *maintains its reference to the original, while tending to produce a new meaning*. (For the purposes of our discussion, we need not enter into the problem of reproduction.)[6] From this very general point of view, the Renaissance becomes a transformation of Antiquity, Mannerism of Quattrocento architecture, Neo-Classicism of Classicism, eclecticism of the past as a whole, etc. We might usefully illustrate these transformational operations by means of an analogy with the classical figures of rhetoric. We can see, for example, the "hyperboles" to which the architect-monk submitted the classical code in the Cartuja de Granada, the "paradox" which Bernardo Buontalenti presents to us in the stair of the choir of Santo Stefano in Florence, the "ironies" in Giulio Romano's Palazzo del Te, the "metaphors" of most of the work of Charles Moore, the "ellipses" of Fascist architecture, of Robert Venturi, and of Aldo Rossi.[7] All these examples exhibit the same general characteristics: they all operate with known architectural codes, and they all re-deploy these codes by effecting some easily perceivable changes. Yet all the resulting effects are different; for while in one case we might be induced to smile with a certain condescension, in another we are puzzled by what seems an impossible mistake, and in another we might even need to close our eyes to imagine what is not there. An almost endless list could be compiled for the purpose of showing how powerful rhetoric can be in assisting a theoretical and hence systematic classification of these architectural operations, and for demonstrating the similar structure of production of meaning of most of man's products. My interest here is to concentrate on specific effects produced by some of these transformations. For this, it is enough to say that rhetoric is a *metalanguage*, a discourse built on another discourse. As we will see later, this concept that comes out of logic and semiotics provides us with a tool that will help us understand and delimit the problems posed at the beginning of this paper in relation to "criticism from within."

To begin with, it is clear that much of what is produced today in architecture consists of a discourse that comments on other already constituted architectural discourses: that is, the very special case of metalanguage in which both discourses belong to the same practice; architecture commenting on architecture, architecture "speaking" of itself. One way to clarify the concept of metalanguage in relation to our subject is to classify the range of possible object-languages; that is to say, the codes or elements that can be referred to or commented on by the metalanguage. For example, the metalanguage may refer to or comment on *the formal codes*; it may also refer to the functional codes, that is, the set of systematized, normalized functions (the program) and the uses they promote. Because they are the most conscious codes of modern architecture, both of these seem to have been rather thoroughly explored. But it is also possible to conceive of a commentary on the rhetorical codes themselves, and on the moral codes. In reality, these commentaries seem to concentrate on *elements of the codes*. This can be illustrated by the example of the column. The column has undoubtedly been one of the most significant elements of architecture, and as such it has become one of the favorite elements of architectural language, attracting commentaries of metalinguistic nature, as illustrated by the Désert de Retz by François Barbier of 1771, the inverted half-shaft column of the William Henry Seward Memorial by Hornbostel & Wood of 1929, and by Adolf Loos's Chicago Tribune competition entry of 1923. These examples all refer, on the first reading, not to the body of referents peculiar to the classical code, but to the element itself or to the code itself (in this case the column, in its denotative state). Thus, these examples refer not to the supposed contents of classical architecture (beauty, the human body, proportions, etc.) but to the classical element, column; that is to say, all these examples (each of them a fully constituted significant system of signified/signifier) contain in themselves another significant system previously constituted (i.e., the classical column). In most of these cases the metalinguistic operation is constituted by a simple change of scale or the substitution of a different function for the original one. Again, it is interesting to note that all of these displacements do not produce the same effect. In some cases, a certain surplus of meaning appears beyond the simple commentary, and in some cases this "beyond" approaches a dimension of *criticism*. The famous triglyphs of Giulio Romano might serve to further the analysis. The heresy perpetrated by Giulio Romano against the classical language seems to be more than a heresy, more than a trivial game: in it we find it extremely difficult to experience the principles of humanism. We are forced to refer back to architecture itself, since the disordered order within the order disturbs us. There is no change of scale, no inversion, no second stage; we are confronted with a wall conceived *within* a canon. However, if only one triglyph were loose, we would not see it; it would be an accident. It is precisely the insistent and systematic disorder within the order which disorders the old one, and which forbids us to experience the transparent effect of what it should have been—something classic. Giulio Romano thus invents, in a single heretical gesture, a new meaning—perhaps proving that the impossible is possible—by showing up the conventionality of the classical code. The operation is one of altering syntactic relationships. The rhetorical figure is irony, and its effect can be interpreted as critical. It is only at the end of this process of deciphering that we turn back to the original referent (beauty, the human body, proportions, etc.) in order to sense the strength of the new effect; but now we accept the reference only after demythifying it. This results in a de-naturalization of the code that has been interrogated. The object-language is thus questioned *in its own terms*. Indeed, this is an apparently trivial detail if considered by itself. It is only as part of the spirit that pervades the entire work that we can establish its place in a more complex system of critical meanings. Giulio Romano's building acquires a startling power when we discover that a similar attack has been carried at all levels, intentionally profaning the integrity of all the iconographic, compositional, structural codes of the classical language.

Shocking at first, the object impatiently unfolds before us a universe of meanings hitherto hidden from us; and our initial feeling of disturbance gives way to a pleasurable sensation of intellectual complicity between the architect and ourselves after we have, not without effort, succeeded in disclosing the building's arcane messages. The object appears as a revelation, not of sacred but of heretical nature because it confronts us with a subversive meaning whose opaque effect proposes and obliges us to perform a certain intellectual task of deciphering. The object cannot

5

6

7

8

be consumed, but must be interpreted; indeed, we must wander along the same path that the architect followed; we must work with it.

Although we cannot place ourselves at the same comfortable distance with the present that we are able to do with the Italian Cinquecento, perhaps it is possible, tentatively, to propose a similar reading of some recent architecture. We can recognize in some works of Charles Moore, for example, the same type of transformations to which we have alluded. Kresge College *re-presents* the known and all too familiar in a disjointed, unexpected, disturbing manner, and we can apply our previous remarks in relation to the effects of the "criticism from within" to describe what we are told through these buildings.

The effectiveness of such "criticism from within," however, does not necessarily depend

Fig. 5 Palazzata di Messina, Rome, competition entry. A. Libera, M. Ridolfi, M. Fagiolo, architects, 1931. Courtesy the author.

Fig. 6 Elementary School, Broni, Pavia, Italy. Aldo Rossi, architect, 1969–1970. Detail, courtyard. Reprint from *Oppositions*, no. 3 (May 1974).

Fig. 7 Kresge College, Santa Cruz, CA. Charles Moore and William Turnbull, architects, 1974. Photograph by Morley Baer.

Fig. 8 Vanna Venturi house, Philadelphia. Venturi and Rauch, Architects, 1963. Photograph by Rollin R. La France.

on such ironic manipulations of architectural codes. Rather, the critical effect depends on a subversion of known meanings and on the production of knowledge itself;[8] and to that end no rhetorical operation, per se, can offer guarantees. Lévi-Strauss, commenting on Duchamp's "ready mades," expresses eloquently the complex mixture of operations and effects in these types of works: "You then accomplish a new distribution between the signifier and the signified, a distribution that was in the realm of the possible but was not openly effected [in the primitive condition of the object]. You make then, in one sense, a work of learning, discovering in that object latent properties that were not perceived in the initial context; a poet does this each time he uses a word or turns a phrase in an unusual manner."[9] It is this test, and not the simple manipulation of known codes, which the work of "criticism from within" must pass. Thus, works like those of Rossi and Graves that are neither ironic nor paradoxical nonetheless impose on us an *oeuvre de connaissance*, make us discover latent properties, and open to us a poetic dimension. And, recalling Barthes, we may use and interpret the notion of "anamorphism" as a metaphor that can help us to circumscribe even more precisely this still evasive notion of "criticism from within."[10] In fact, anamorphism expresses almost literally the mechanism, effects, and dilemmas of this type of criticism. For example, the techniques used widely in painting during the sixteenth century and illustrated here by the "skull" depicted at the bottom of Holbein the Younger's *The Ambassadors* can be read in two different ways. We can see them as tricks, games, diversions; but it is also possible to read in them a much more subversive content than can be apprehended if we concentrate only on the technique of distortion employed. In this case, it is necessary to understand the implications of perspective as "symbolic form" (in Panofsky's sense) to see that the technique of anamorphism effects also a criticism of a mode of representation, making explicit the illusion of perspective and producing, if only for a moment, a condensed knowledge that must be unraveled by the beholder.

We can, then, base our understanding of the nature of "criticism from within" on this constellation of attributes, and this, in turn, helps us to differentiate it from other types of transformation. This distinction is important because there exists another possibility of transformation, which is opposed to criticism, an understanding of which should help us in the task of clarifying contemporary productions. If we analyze, for instance, some current architectures that abound in historical allusions and quotations, we find that neither the operations nor the effects produced belong to the category of criticism described, in spite of sharing with it a certain self-consciousness and transformational character. In these cases the material that supports meaning is not substantially altered in order to bring out any latent properties; rather, it is strategically marked—simply "quoted"—with the resulting effect of veiling, covering, wrapping as it were, the original sign in a new meaning. It tends to emphasize features of the already known, seeking an external, larger association. It seeks a connotation. And paradoxically, in the cases of historical quotation, it denies the history contained in it by erasing the contingencies by which it is or was determined; by denying history it naturalizes the object. It is a process of mythification of the known.[11] As such, this type of transformation is often found in the architecture of mass consumption, where nothing could be more alien to its aim than the deciphering activity which characterizes "criticism from within." But it is also, and at a more profound level, at the root of many of the present attempts to consciously work with architecture as language. Examples could be listed endlessly, but suffice it to say that it is probably the effect sought after by most of the iconographers of the present, so-called "populist" tendencies. For it is not history in its most profound sense that is the desired object of exploration, exposition, and unraveling, but rather the immediate, uncritical, almost urgent rapport between the architecture and the beholder.

Thus, in terms of mechanisms of transformation, we can differentiate clearly between "criticism from within" and mythification. "Criticism from within" is a signifying system in which the content is in itself a signifying system; that is to say, the form and the content of the original object are both, in turn, the content of another form (the transformed object). Mythification, conversely, institutes a new signifying system in which its form remains almost untransformed, but by subtle accents, a new content covers the object. The respective effects can also be seen as dichotomous: criticism generates opaqueness, intrigue, questioning, subversion; mythification generates transparency, complacency, naturalization, and conformism.

Using this reading, one cannot any longer group the members of the New York "Five"

9 10 11 12 13

together simply on the basis of their use of similar superficial elements. Of all of them, only John Hejduk and Michael Graves seem to achieve the effects produced by critical operations. Hejduk does so by elevating certain architectural components to the category of signs of themselves, and by virtue of this, he achieves an architecture almost devoid of any metaphorical or representative value except that of itself; plans and facades become the vehicles for unprecedented discoveries, while the myths of function and structure are dissipated by poetry. Graves, on the other hand, concentrates insistently on the metaphorical dimensions of architecture and thereby

Figs. 9–10 Désert de Retz, France. Francois Barbier, architect, 1771.
Figs. 11–12 William Henry Seward Memorial, Seward, AK. Henry Hornbostel and Eric Fisher Wood, architects, 1929.
Fig. 13 Chicago Tribune, competition entry. Adolf Loos, architect, 1923.

brings about a completely new reading of all the elements implicated (columns, walls, ceilings, colors, etc.), and as a result his architecture yields as surplus an enrichment of a vocabulary and mechanisms that were deemed exhausted. In both cases, our reading of the early work of Le Corbusier and of general architectural notions is both demythified and enriched.

We see then that the "return to language" deserves more than the merely perfunctory treatment which discards it altogether as senseless. In rather schematic fashion, we have been able to establish the existence of at least two opposite effects resulting from different ways of constructing the architectural discourse that reflects upon itself: the possibility of criticism and that of mythification. This analysis suggests other levels of investigation. As both criticism and myth produce a certain type of knowledge—criticism by digging into the object itself in a relentless search for fundamental meaning, mythification by re-presenting the object as a confirmation of our previous knowledge and then by naturalizing it—we must ask what kind of relations this very special type of criticism "from within" establishes with theory and ideology, what its locations are in regard to these two realms of human knowledge. We might even ask whether, indeed, this type of "production of knowledge" deserves the label of criticism. The consideration of this question seems imperative, since, as we said at the beginning, we are confronted with an apparently blatant contradiction: we assume that an object produced by culture (and as such marked by ideology) also has the capacity to present a critique of itself (and as such to contribute to theoretical knowledge). But, at the risk of constructing a tautology, it is this paradox itself that constitutes its own explanation and is the foundation of its own richness and uniqueness. For it is senseless to ask of this "criticism from within" a guarantee that it will discover some "truth" of scientific nature. As a discourse it can only be read through the object in which it is rooted and not through language, which manipulates concepts that are organized logically and provides the "matter" that science and theory transform. As criticism contained in an object (whether a painting, a sculpture, a work of architecture), it proposes itself to us as a totality, which cannot be reproduced or tested as a scientific or theoretical proposition. Once it has appeared, its own critical nature is compromised by its very object-nature, and it cannot escape the destiny that our culture reserves for its objects: its critical meaning becomes consumable after its operations are discovered. It is possible to transform these operations into techniques, or into normative principles (as, for example, in the efforts of Venturi to institutionalize irony), and *l'enfant terrible* becomes a desired connotation with time. This condition thus defines the difference between this type of criticism and the criticism involved in the production of scientific or theoretical knowledge: while both are subversive at the beginning, one becomes the object of consumption, the other, of systematic knowledge. "Criticism from within" is, then, a short-lived phenomenon in the continuum of knowledge, its initial power being recoverable only through exegesis and archaeology, although never to be experienced again with its own original vigor and authority. But this limitation only serves to clarify its role, not to suggest that it should be dismissed. Because of this specific and unique condition, there is a liberating effect: not being able to exercise the power of "truth," criticism from within institutes in its place the domain of art as poetry. The consequences of acknowledging its dependence on and its contradictory, ambiguous relationship with ideology becomes its force.

It is especially at such a time of questioning as the present that the mass of ideological formations cracks, that "criticism from within" penetrates the solidity of mythical constructions with the aim of exposing the multiplicity of meanings that lie hidden in it. Perhaps what is most promising about this type of criticism is precisely the awareness that we will not gain from it access to objective, scientific knowledge (a task that returns to the discipline where it belongs: history), but rather that through it we may aim at unfolding the imaginary-symbolic universe that architecture simultaneously proposes and represses. The clear objective of such criticism should be the production of a kind of "qualified" knowledge, even if short-lived, which will emerge as an "apparition" against a background of transparent myths. It should not be expected that the effects of a theory will be achieved. However, the poetical dimension which finds in this criticism its natural realm in the present moment may be rediscovered. And perhaps through the exercise of this criticism it will be possible to produce the "subtle subversion" that Barthes suggests as a possible solution to the contradictions of art;[12] that is to say, the subversion that does not accept the play with opposites that are merely accomplices within the same structure (i.e., the endless oscillation between formalism and functionalism), but one that seeks another term beyond the game of oppositions, a term not of synthesis but of an eccentricity that frustrates false oppositions. Therefore, one cannot conclude with Tafuri that "behind this laborious digging into architecture's own existence, there is a constant fear of an authentic critical process."[13] Both "criticism from within" as well as the criticism of theory and history have, de facto, a precisely delimited field of action, so that it is not necessary to engage in a discussion as to which criticism is "authentic." "Authentic" is too loaded a term to be useful in defining the boundaries of different practices. But if the possibilities of inquiry offered by historical criticism are not the same as those offered by the work of art, the distinction between them does not preclude their dialectical relationship. History aims at scientific explanation, and it has, consequently, an undeniable lead in the field of knowledge. It helps the artist to establish and become conscious of his own location. This consciousness has consequences for the artist's work, although these consequences are not automatic. But conversely, the artist's products provide the material for theory, and theory must wait for their appearance; for no matter how advanced a structural model of society theory might possess, it cannot forecast and depict the artistic products that that structure will produce.

Our inquiry into the nature of "criticism from within" cannot, however, be concluded here. In addressing the questions of its place in the sphere of knowledge, we found that some aspects of it are neither explained by a description of its internal mechanisms nor by its relationships with theory and ideology; more specifically, we implied that there is some temporal aspect to "criticism from within." It seems, then, that in order to understand the paradoxical nature of this criticism, we need to consider its relation with both of its coordinates: not only the structural, which we have just touched upon, but also the historical-cultural, which we will consider next.

As the concept of "criticism from within," or even the general notion of transformation implies, its operation requires the existence of well established codes on which to work. It is not, then, surprising that throughout history its appearance has been rather discreet and sporadic. In this context we might re-invoke the analogy of contemporary architecture to that of Mannerism, an architecture that responded to the "very human desire to impair perfection when once it has been achieved."[14] Mannerist architecture was, like the works of today, essentially a reflective task, a critical experimentation with Classicism, which effected the subversive dismembering of the classical language through the heretical and revealing work of Giulio Romano, Michelangelo, Serlio, and the like, at the same time as it unfolded an unexpected treasure from which the classical language could re-emerge renovated and ready for its most fulfilling moment, pregnant with a seemingly inexhaustible richness.

This sporadic nature of "criticism from within," which appears as it were as an irregular necessity of history, forms its principal historical differentiation from other types of transformational work, and specifically from that type we have defined as its opposite: mythification. Mythification appears as a continuum in history; it is the most basic, rudimentary, and unavoidable manner of signifying of any object of the material culture. The prevailing forces in architectural ideologies, throughout history, are those that try to "naturalize" the cultural constructs of architecture, to justify and rationalize it through mythification. The forms of objects are thus constantly wrapped and veiled with secondary meanings, establishing chains which can only be interrupted momentarily by the reversing act of criticism. But it is important, since we are testing these arguments against the historical coordinate, to differentiate within mythification the existence of two different and opposed modes of effecting the naturalization of historical contingencies, two clear and typical forms that correspond to two very well-differentiated historical moments: one (and this applies specifically to recent history) is the avant-garde moment, and the other, the moments that correspond to crisis or disbelief. Firstly, mythification (which attempts to achieve a particular transformation in men's consciousness—that of transforming the contingencies of the cultural and the historical into the natural) acquires in the avant-garde a positive value insofar as it is a genuine act of creation and insofar as it represents an intentional break with the past, placing the language in question within new terms and establishing its own parameters of production and criticism. Since no artistic movement can precede a general change in the historical determinants, the ideological work of the avant-garde—its mythification—consists precisely in making intelligible these determinants within a new ideological discourse; thus, for example, the aesthetics of the machine is a mythification, a naturalization of the historical *contingencies* of the machine itself, which does not explain it but rather borrows it uncritically, yet which, however, performs the role of establishing an iconography that symbolizes a positive utopia that is historically correct and forward looking. Now, this discourse that tells us about a new reality, that makes that reality legible and intelligible, is, because of its ideological nature, a distortion of those historical determinants. But although this fact is proven by time, it does not provide an automatic knowledge of what has been falsified; this is the work of criticism.

Secondly, in periods of disbelief, such as that which began in the late fifties and culminated during the sixties, mythification acquires the role of a cynical accomplice because it has nothing to propose and yet it continues to mimic the gestures of creation. At this point, there is only one positive option as to what to do with the "classic" language, and that is to demythify it. This act, together with theoretical work, can close a historical period. The counterpart of this proposition is—if I may be permitted the term—the mythification of myth, and as such it represents a reactionary force. It invariably implies a degradation of what is being transformed.

The type of mythification that is of interest for an analysis of the present moment then, is that which converts an already established architectural language into the material support of a sign which connotes what has already been sanctioned, approved, and digested by the system of architecture; that is to say, not into a language that connotes itself, but into one that seeks as a unique objective to signify the value that the system has acquired already in history. Hence, in many cases, the uses of the International Style, rationalism, "Corbusianism," etc. do not necessarily imply an intent to continue the tasks set forth in the heroic period of modern architecture or an attempt to realize the program of the avant-garde; rather, the style is often selected because of the connotations of "art" and "modernity" that it carries, and finally because it permits the architect to play safely within architecture.[15]

At this point it might be of help to introduce a more specific nomenclature, one that might serve to differentiate even further and with more precision the possibilities of work with language. These are the notions of "criticism" and "commentary" as elaborated by Michel Foucault in *The Order of Things*: "Since the classical age, commentary and criticism have been in profound opposition. By speaking of language in terms of representation and truth, criticism judges it and profanes it. Now as language in the irruption of its being, and questioning it as to its secret, commentary halts before the precipice of the original text, and assumes the impossible and endless task of repeating its own birth within itself: it sacralizes language. These two ways by which language establishes a relation with itself were now to enter into a rivalry from which we have not yet emerged—and which may even be sharpening as time passes."[16] For, to interrogate a language as to what, how, and why it represents, as criticism does, is to begin to disturb it at the very point where the ideological operation takes place; it is indeed to attempt to "profane" its inner sanctum and to judge its truth. Commentary, on the other hand, reproduces language, represents it with no other intention than to sanction its truth. And without attempting to generalize these two notions for the history of architecture, Foucault's categories are useful in separating present productions precisely and in regulating the use of the two terms which are loosely used in architecture today.

It is possible now to respond with more clarity to some of the questions that were posed at the beginning. We know it is possible to discern two types of discourse that are based on transformations of existing architectural codes, and that they are opposed in their mechanisms and in their effects. While one—criticism—attempts a reading of architecture in depth, unfolding the latent layers of meaning, the other—mythification—slides on the surface of the veils with which it has covered architecture. We have found that, historically, this seemingly simple duality is in fact a more complex, asymmetrical cultural phenomenon, since it is possible to sketch for the latter two opposing pictures, corresponding to two different historical moments, and for the former a sporadic appearance.[17] What our analysis has also yielded is the conviction that the critical reflection of language upon itself, "criticism from within," although sporadic, appears as an inevitable part of the architect's endeavor, in turn part of a more general phenomenon of a "return to language." Hence, as such, the phenomenon implies neither advancement nor regression. It is a historical reality, a common background against which we find ourselves working today. Within it, the searches, means, and objectives, which are marked by the subject and its contingencies, can be as varied as in any historical moment. Of course, it is not only possible but necessary that the theoretical/historical criticism that analyzes these phenomena be carried out with different focuses and at different scales. Thus the general view that Tafuri offers is more than necessary: it is indispensable to talk about the "return to language" and to try to disentangle the historical meaning that such an attitude, as a whole, might have as opposed to other historical possibilities, contemporary, past, or hypothetical. But such a view, when expounded in disregard of the meaning of the nuances and eccentricities that the historical material offers, might become unconstructive if not informed dialectically by an internal analysis of such an attitude toward architecture. Tafuri's principal theoretical objective justifies his level of generalization because in his analysis he seeks to oppose the architect

Fig. 14 Crooks House, Fort Wayne, IN. Michael Graves, architect, 1976.
Fig. 15 Bye House. John Hejduk, architect, 1972.

14

15

as a "producer" to the architect as an "expert in language";[18] however, his analysis of these two categories, which might have important theoretical consequences, is not altogether convincing because of his ambiguous use of the concept of "production." It is confusing because both types of work imply the "production" of something and as such both are historically and theoretically relevant; both operate upon and transform a given material by using and manipulating determinate means of production; both are related to ideology as well as to technique. Therefore, if it is true that a critic may find that some of the products of some of the "experts in language" have no cultural or historical relevance, obviously the same may be found for some of the producer's products, so that it is simply incorrect to try to establish the supremacy or importance of one over the other. Tafuri may consider that the work of certain contemporary architects is, in the end, irrelevant, but to generalize in such a way as to say that "the return to language [in this moment] is a proof of failure" obscures this fundamental principle: the production of "building" and the production of "meaning" are both parts of the production of architecture. Of course Tafuri would agree with this, but he seems to imply that the problem of the language of architecture ("as a system of communication . . . ") should be left aside, to "happen" as it were, and that it is more important to concentrate on the nature of "building construction in reality."[19]

But what is building construction in reality? It does not stop at the moment when all economic, managerial, and political problems have been taken into account. The building still has to be created, and at that moment, whether the agent involved is an architect, a planner, a politician, a builder, or a layman does not matter: the whole problem of architecture as language, architecture as symbol, architecture as material culture, starts all over again; the dialectical process between creativity and history is again put into motion; and however uncultivated or underdeveloped the agent is, the problem of the transformation of a language is posed.

It therefore seems that this consciousness about "language" which characterizes the present moment, these attempts at a real criticism "from within," are a positive step. To extend Tafuri's own parable of the magician,[20] an understanding of the position where the architect-critic places himself might help us to understand more fully "the tricks of the magician" since these tricks can only be explained from both vantage points; from "behind the scene" (as Tafuri would want it) one sees the *techniques* of the tricks, and from the "seat in the audience" one sees the way in which the trick is delivered and the effects it produces. Both positions are needed to explain the magician and his tricks. If this is true, then there is no way by which we can escape our involvement with language. And regardless of whether or not one agrees with the view that the architect may be a "producer," such a view is not an "either/or" option when considered in relation to architecture as language.

It is important now to move a step forward, to change the level of discourse and enlarge the focus as it were, in order to establish the place of the "concern for language" and specifically of "criticism from within" within the system of production. We should recall that we started our work by assuming that what characterizes architecture today is its capacity to be studied as a system of significations that establishes different levels and layers of meanings and sense and constitutes one of the symbolic spheres instituted by society. If our assumption was correct, we can further conclude that architecture defines its place and role in the spheres of the production of knowledge and the production of meaning, as well as in the technical production of artifacts, as being within the social practices, and that as such it can be regarded mainly as a technical-ideological practice insofar as it transforms both matter and man's consciousness and utilizes both techniques and human relations. But within the realm of the production of meaning and knowledge—that with which we have been specifically concerned in our analysis of "criticism from within"—it is necessary to establish with certainty what role and place this criticism occupies, its extensions and limits.

For it is clear, as has already been implied in our discussion of the multi-layered nature of the phenomena of meaning in architecture, that this aspect of "criticism from within" cannot be the only discourse proposed by architecture. This peculiar discourse, as is obvious to many and disturbing to most, concerns mainly the most hermetic level of meaning that architecture can articulate. What may be read in this architecture of "criticism from within" pertains only to the closed domain of architecture itself as a discipline, and requires a trained reader, one who knows the symbolic universe proposed and instituted by it, and one whose intimate knowledge of the universe of, for instance, classical and modern architecture enables him to decipher the depth of the critical messages of Giulio Romano and John Hejduk respectively. Thus, this "hermetic" language of "criticism from within" must be understood and used as an internal disciplinary mechanism, whose social value is delimited by the boundaries that any specialized language establishes in society. It is pointless, then, to argue about "elitism" or "hermeticism" as the socially and politically undesirable results of these internal elaborations, since they are by their very nature "hermetic" and "elitist" in their relations with the collective realm. However, that they are only as hermetic as any internal criticism of any contemporary discipline is a fact that we can easily test, for example, by attempting to decipher the communications among physicists. But if we can refrain from discarding physics for its seemingly "hermetic" quality, we should at the same time demand that its products have a more positive collective value. This also goes for architecture where the issue seems even more pressing because of the unavoidable impingement of its products upon the public realm. So there should be no controversy over whether architecture language should deal with one *or* the other. The two discourses, the hermetic and the collective, seem to define the two poles of the scale of possible discourses that architecture is capable of handling. Considering these terms as dichotomic and exclusive is an error that seems to explain much of the confusion and poverty pervading architectural discussion today—confusion insofar as there is no awareness that architecture operates, communicates, and speaks at many levels as a polyphonic composition, and poverty, as a consequence, because most seem to want to suppress this potential richness in favor of a monochord discourse which "speaks" solely the language of "the people" or of "the elite," as if such a thing were possible. It is only after establishing with clarity the place and limits of "criticism from within" in the system of production as an inescapable, indispensable, "elitist" language that we can assess more thoroughly and correctly some of the architecture produced today. If there is something to be questioned in architecture, it is not its preoccupation with language, which is a concern that it can rightfully display and dutifully respond to; rather, it should be questioned on its lack of articulation between the internal, speculative discourse implied by the return to language and the domain of architecture as a collective discourse.

At this point we return to the problem of Mannerism. It was precisely a moment of profound moral and intellectual crisis that produced the reflective attitude, the "signifying consciousness" and critical mind of the Mannerist artist of the sixteenth century. This chapter of history has been thoroughly explained, but what is important to note is that the magnificent Baroque explosion that followed it could only have happened after Mannerism demonstrated to what limits the classical language of architecture could be extended. The excesses and heresies of Mannerism cleared the way for the majestic and sure moves of the Baroque architect, opening the path to one of the most successful chapters in the history of architecture, when the bonds between a political and social program (the Counter Reformation) and an artistic program (based on the rhetoric of persuasion) seem to have been stronger than they are today. The optimistic conclusion that might be drawn from this analogy as far as our own future is concerned is not necessarily convincing, and one can only wish it were true. But we believe that one must, at the least, accept the necessity of this reflective moment, when architecture turns into itself to recognize its signifying nature and to search for its limits, as indispensable for any future. The period that followed the heroic years of the Modern Movement did not produce much knowledge about its own nature, but rather a pragmatic, over-optimistic and simplified application of its universalist principles. Slowly it withdrew into the most banal forms of consumerism, undoubtedly as a result of this uncritical application of its principles. Whereas some serious theoretical and historical criticism was produced, the practice of architecture proceeded with blind confidence in its language and its ethical codes, and culminated in stagnation and in premature failure.

As often with historical parallels, their value lies not so much in the points where coincidence occurs, but rather where the analogy no longer holds; indeed, it is at the moment when a difference appears that we can begin to gain knowledge. For this reason, the analogy between Mannerism and the present can only be stretched so far. The two moments in fact derived from two very different methodological commitments, each consciously established: the classical view was *typological*, the modern view was *programmatic*. The former furnished a symbol to be operated upon, the latter supposedly furnished a set of social demands from which

Fig. 16 Hans Holbein the Younger. Detail of *The Ambassadors*, 1533.

a form could be derived if reason and the spirit of the age were invoked. It is beyond the scope of this paper to analyze further the contradictions inherent in this last distinction, but some observations are possible. The tenets of modern architecture, simplified to pure formulae, continued to champion the programmatic approach at the same time that they generated architectural typologies, rooted in culture in the deepest sense, and instituted in practice but unacknowledged as such. This fact prevented and even forbade any conscious attempt to investigate the language of architecture "from within." The trap of the "form/function" ideology which reappeared, renovated and transformed into all the variants that characterized the dispersion of architecture during the sixties—"systems analysis," behaviorism, planning, "problem solving techniques," etc.—prevented any consideration of architecture as a fact of culture. (In this country, the work of Kahn stands out as a powerful reaction to it, although his work had to be wrapped in obscure and metaphysical rationalization.)

It is tempting to think, then, that a reconsideration of the implications of a typological approach in architecture today might suggest a possible articulation between those two unavoidable discourses that architecture must institute. For if we look at the problem of a typology of architecture as not just functional recipes or formal dictionaries, but rather as an ever changing, symbolic discourse articulated by culture as a whole and from which we can nurture our search, it becomes clear that it is *only* with a *conscious* "return to language" that we can successfully operate upon, transform, and invent *from architecture*. For this reason this approach, and the consciousness that arises from it, can establish the basis for a new type of creativity, one that allows us to depart from a collective intelligibility and to accept consciously the notion of transformation as a means of operation, thus dissipating the anguish that results from either "scientific" demands or from the myth of the genius. It seems possible, then, to find place for both internal speculation and social responsibility, "criticism from within" and "collective myths," the two inescapable voices that are uttered through architecture. This new consciousness does not stop with the memory of the type, but begins with it only to forget it at the moment of poetic transformation. It furnishes us with the conceptual foundations upon which it is possible to reestablish an intelligent discussion about representation and iconography in architecture, two subjects that have been denied or treated obliquely by modern architecture. Finally, such a typological approach to architecture, which recognizes the multiplicity of meanings of the built world, also affords the possibility of accepting and incorporating the ever present and unresolvable contradictions between myth and critique, the two substances that inform the space in which we inescapably act.

If these very tentative conclusions seem to pose more questions than answers, and to cast some doubt upon the exactitude of some of the previous speculations, at least this last fact of the double, paradoxical nature of architecture together with all its implications, seems to be undisputable. Through asserting this fact, we have attempted to erase the remaining traces of the false dilemma of "scientific versus intuitive" that still haunts us. Neither pure fact nor pure myth, architecture must unashamedly depict its ambiguous nature. It seems appropriate to recall Barthes in closing: "There are those who want a text (an art, a painting) without a shadow, without the 'dominant ideology'; but this is to want a text without fecundity, without productivity, a sterile text . . . . The text needs its shadows; this shadow is *a bit* of ideology, *a bit* of representation, *a bit* of subject: ghosts, pockets, traces, necessary clouds: subversion must produce its own chiaroscuro."

Notes

1 Roland Barthes, *Critique et verité* (Paris: Editions du Seuil, 1966), 45. Translation by the author.

2 For a substantive discussion on the concept of ideology and its implications for architecture, see Diana Agrest and Mario Gandelsonas, "Semiotics and Architecture: Ideological Consumption or Theoretical Work," *Oppositions*, no. 1 (September 1973): 93–100; see also Mario Gandelsonas, "Linguistica nell'architettura," *Casabella* no. 374 (February 1973): 17–31.

3 Manfredo Tafuri, "L'Architecture dans le Boudoir," *Oppositions*, no. 3 (May 1974): 37–62; Manfredo Tafuri, *Teoria e storia dell'architettura* (Bari: Laterza, 1971), ch. 3.

4 Tafuri, "L'Architecture dans le Boudoir," 55.

5 Colin Rowe, "Mannerism and Modern Architecture," *Architectural Review* (May 1950) 292: "that universal 'malaise' which in the arts, while retaining the externals of classical correctness, was obliged at the same time to disrupt the inner core of classical coherence."

6 I leave aside the general problem of which reproduction and transformation are part: a larger system that includes the invention of a code. In the context of this article I will avoid a discussion of invention as well as reproduction and the problems they pose for theory.

7 Hyperbole: rhetorical figure that consists of an exaggeration of the terms. Anacoluthon: rupture in the syntactic structure. Ellipsis: grammatical figure which consists of suppressing unnecessary elements as far as intelligibility can be maintained. Irony or antiphrasis: rhetorical figure that consists of expressing the contrary of the meaning intended (it is a connotation): "irony goes together with a sentiment of superiority."
Metaphor: rhetorical figure of substitution of one term for another both of different classes. The term present in the sentence stands for the one that is meant but is absent. Based on association. Paradox: rhetorical operation that consists of presenting a meaning contrary to common sense. Absurd and shocking affirmation at first, it should conform to reality after analysis.
These definitions, which are a sample of rhetorical figures and operations, have been taken from Henri Morier, *Dictionnaire de poétique et de rhétorique*, and Roland Barthes, "L'ancienne réthorique," *Communications* 16 (Paris: Editions du Seuil, 1970). It is interesting to note that at different times in history, architects and artists were well versed in the arts of rhetoric, which they tried consciously to apply to their work. See, for instance, Giulio Carlo Argan, "La retorica e l'arte barocca" and "Retorica e architettura," in *Studi e note. Dal Bramante al Canova* (Rome: Mario Bulzoni Editore, 1970).

8 We talk about subversion in very precise terms, as the discourse whose purpose or effect is to unveil the fallacies of another well-established ideological discourse. In that sense, Galileo's theories were as subversive in their moment as Marcel Duchamp's work on its own. The efficiency of subversion is diverse, and we will see later the differences of effects between the type of Galilean subversion (science) and that of art.

9 Georges Charbonnier, *Entretiens avec Claude Lévi-Strauss* (Paris: René Julliard et Librairie Plon, 1961). Translation by the author.

10 Barthes, *Critique et verité*, 64.

11 For a suggestive treatment of the idea of myth and mythification in present western society, see Roland Barthes, *Mythologies* (Paris: Editions du Seuil, 1957).

12 Roland Barthes, *Le plaisir du texte* (Paris: Editions du Seuil, 1973).

13 Manfredo Tafuri, *Teorie e storia dell'architettura* (Bari: Laterza, 1970), p. 161.

14 Rowe, "Mannerism and Modern Architecture," 292.

15 Although it would be possible to trace this process of degradation back into history, probably to the moment in which the notions of progress and change became active in history, it seems peculiar and characteristic of our present times, a result of the structural changes in society that have occurred in this century, which shifted the emphasis from us to consumption, from aesthetic contemplation to stylistic degradation. Degradation and consumption: these two words in this context recall the modern notion of kitsch—the operation which entails an uncritical debasement of the work of art, oriented toward an easy consumption. It takes very little effort to discover that the definition of kitsch applies to what we have been discussing in terms of mythification in architecture, and only the classic content that the artistic elite has attached to the notion of kitsch to defend its own lesser works has so far prevented us from seeing the parallel. It is only a matter of how inclusive one wants this notion to be. And, if we only take into account the type of operations involved in it, we might surprisingly find that kitsch is not only a reproduction of Mona Lisa on a towel, but also much of the present exquisite architecture.

16 Michel Foucault, *The Order of Things* (New York, NY: Vintage Books, 1973), 81.

17 And while this theoretical model seems to account for both Mannerism and the present, we need at this point further discussion and clarification because of the immediately apparent contradictions that a comparison with other views of the same problem produces. Particularly for its historical importance and the brilliance of its arguments, Colin Rowe's "Mannerism and Modern Architecture" needs to be discussed in this light. Rowe's contention that it is possible to understand not only some of the products of the early Modern Movement, but also the "mental climate" that produced them by drawing a parallel between this time and that of Mannerism, is at least in opposition to what has been said here about the avant-garde, insofar as it is a period of positive ideological impetus, while Mannerism is one of critical reflection. I believe it is not a case of two opposing tenets, but rather one of different focus: in my view what characterizes a "Mannerist" period is the absence of any attempt to produce new codes and rather to operate with them (as in Rowe's words: "it demands an orthodoxy within whose framework it might be heretical") in a critical fashion, which in turn eliminates the heroic period of the Modern Movement as the candidate for the Mannerist label (it was

mainly concerned with a new codification). It is also true that some of Rowe's arguments and parallels help us to understand unequivocally at what levels modern architecture was still dependent on a pre-existing order, and that modern architecture does not represent a total break with its past. The divergence in interpretation seems to arise from the fact that Rowe's impeccable characterization of Mannerism seems not to include the notion of criticism that is central in the present argument. While my present use of the term "criticism" seems to imply a degree of consciousness and intention on the part of the artist that might indeed be consciously manifest neither in the late Cinquecento architect nor in the present one, the actual effect produced by these operations on the codes of architecture in both cases belongs unquestionably, in my view, to the category of "criticism from within" as characterized so far. And this differs widely from the effect produced by early modern architecture. It seems that the work of deciphering proposed by these works of the heroic period had to do with discovering the new relationships between form and content, trying to match the symbols with their intended meanings, whereas today this interpretative task concentrates on the questioning of the nature of those bonds. In the end, as we will see later, what is important is not how far the analogy can be carried between two historical periods, but rather what type of knowledge its use might produce, and in this respect, Rowe's discussion of modern architecture continues to be a model of anti-empirical criticism, that type of criticism that relentlessly unfolds the object of analysis, uncovering its hidden meanings, and which, by its implacable scholarly precision, transforms that object into a treasure of knowledge.

18 Tafuri, "L'Architecture dans le Boudoir," 57.

19 Ibid.

20 Ibid. "We can only answer that, wishing to discover the tricks of a magician, it is often better to observe him from behind the scenes rather than to continue to stare at him from a seat in the audience."

Harvard

Architecture: The Emergence of Discourse

WITH MARK LEE

Previous spread: Gund Hall's studio space at the Harvard Graduate School of Design. Viewed from the topmost, fifth "tray," the space is a unified, common working area shared by all design disciplines. This was a novel concept promoted by Dean J. L. Sert and designed by architect John Andrews. Gund Hall opened in 1972 on the Harvard campus.

1. The GSD After Josep Lluís Sert

MARK LEE Jorge, I'd like to start by asking you to share the experience of your arrival at the Harvard Graduate School of Design (GSD) in the mid-1970s. The GSD has a long history characterized by periods many are familiar with: the Walter Gropius and Joseph Hudnut years, the Josep Lluís Sert era, and the contemporary period that started with Gerald M. McCue and Henry N. Cobb. Perhaps lesser known are the transitional periods between the regimes, which are significant moments in the history of the school. You arrived during the years of Maurice D. Kilbridge's deanship after the long tenure of Josep Lluís Sert, correct? This is a pivotal moment for the school that rarely gets discussed.

JORGE SILVETTI Yes, and it's time to do it! I came to Harvard a few years after Sert had stepped down and lived through the intense and at times agitated period that followed. So perhaps for good reasons the last fifty years of the school's history have not been spoken about so much. It could be confusing to look at them without enough hindsight. Walter Gropius's arrival at Harvard as dean of the GSD and the spread of modernism in the United States from there is well documented. The same is true of Josep Lluís Sert's deanship, but after that, the story becomes very vague and murky. Some important questions remain unanswered. Now that I have stepped away from the school and half a century has passed since Sert's days, I feel that I have the distance to attempt a critical assessment of this period.

I recognize some may consider that I'm probably not the right person to historicize this transitional moment because of my direct involvement with the events that took place. There is also the fact that I was a junior faculty member when this story began to unfold, so much of the specific politics and many administrative questions were opaque to me. However, I feel confident that I can sketch out with accuracy the crisis that unfolded after Sert's departure based on what I witnessed and experienced firsthand. In the end, it all happened in the open and was widely discussed; sometimes in the corridors, sometimes in the press. To do this though, we need to first bring in some context that can help make sense of the story.

Lately I've found it useful to look back at a place I encountered upon my arrival to the Boston area that was both a unique locus in the world and also representative of the times: Harvard Square. In the history of this microcosm, we can trace some of the important social and disciplinary changes that were happening at the time of my arrival from Pittsburgh in the fall of 1975. Harvard Square was a sort of civic center that acted as a counterpart to the academic centrality of the adjacent campus. It was a distinctive, secular alternate environment *fuori le mura*, in a way that it no longer is. It was an authentic "urban hub" full of life, action, and interaction. In a time when printed newspapers, journals, and magazines were the principal way to find out what was going on, Out of Town News—the kiosk that is now a "historically preserved structure" in the triangular traffic island—was vital. You found *Le Monde*, *El País*, *L'Espresso*, and *Der Spiegel* side by side, and you might have run into Julia Child or some Noble Prize laureate! Leafing through any one of them—which was permitted without paying, by the way—often led to casual coffee breaks at the popular nearby Café Algiers with bystanders who saw you reading in their native tongue.

ML It sounds like it was a "crossroads of the world" type of place, a cross between the local Cambridge community and the international world that the university brought in.

JS Harvard Square was a lively, international environment in the middle of Cambridge. Whether at the Brattle Theater, the Casablanca Club, or Café Pamplona—a tiny spot with amazing sandwiches that Rafael Moneo made very popular among the GSD crowd during his chairmanship a decade later because he refused to go elsewhere for lunch—everyone showed up there at one point or another. There was an atmosphere of opening up, which was beginning to pervade architecture as well.

At Harvard Square, the presence of the design world was marked by Design Research (D/R), probably the first significant designer "lifestyle" store in this country. One of the founders of D/R, Ben Thompson, was a former chair of the Department of Architecture at Harvard and had been one of the seven young architects that started The Architect's Collaborative (TAC) with Walter Gropius. This was a period in which architecture was not very responsive to the demands of everyday life. Ben and his wife, Jane Fiske McCullough, leaned into the idea that design should play into the enjoyment of the everyday, that it should engage beauty, fun, and the pleasures of lived experience. This was pivotal in several ways.

ML It is not widely known that Ben Thompson collaborated with Gropius on the design of a chair for Thonet along with his architectural projects.

View of Harvard Square with the Out of Town News kiosk at the center, ca. 1960–1969.

The Design Research Headquarters building in the heart of Harvard Square, Benjamin Thompson and Jane Fiske McCullough (1966–1969).

JS Yes. Thompson was also involved in the restoration of Boston's decrepit Faneuil Hall warehouses, turning them into a marketplace that, from an urban perspective, became an integrated part of the city fabric. This was during the rise of the shopping mall, by the way. They did the same with D/R. The shop was within a building complex they developed that connected Brattle and Mount Auburn streets with a narrow public passageway. The complex also housed TAC, the Sert Office, the pioneering architecture supplies and copying store Charrette, and the Harvest, the best restaurant back then, which was also designed and run by Ben Thompson. It was a real contemporary design hub in Harvard Square.

D/R was an emporium that made all aspects of everyday life a subject of design, from furniture all the way down to silverware, fabrics, and clothing. They created the market for designed objects in the United States that is ubiquitous today, and Jane brought Armi Ratia's Marimekko brand to the United States. Marimekko is the quintessential expression of how D/R was part of a turning point in the design scene. It was a clothing and fabric company that embraced the industrial manufacturing process in the modernist tradition. However, it used fabric as an expressive canvas in transgressive ways. Marimekko popularized the idea that design in the fashion world went beyond haute couture. Its impact was huge; even Jackie Kennedy wore Marimekko on the cover of *Sports Illustrated*.

ML In the twenty-five years of its existence, D/R was responsible for introducing and promoting the designs of Alvar Aalto, Arne Jacobsen, and Joe Colombo to the American public.

JS The D/R concept came from the modernist idea of *Gesamtkunstwerk* and the Bauhaus, but its application was truly adapted to the American postwar social reality. Industrially designed chairs were not priced like works of art. They were truly manufactured, priced, marketed, and sold in line with the greater democratization of access to consumer goods that was taking place in this country. This gives you a sense of what was going on with the design world. TAC had already been pretty novel with its conception of shared authorship. But now you had architects trying to have an impact on the city through a lifestyle store just off Harvard Square.

NICOLÁS DELGADO ALCEGA The modernist tradition was alive, but its inheritors were less ideologically defensive than the designers of the first generation. I can see it in the concept of D/R and also in this desire to weave new programs into the existing urban fabric, whether it be Faneuil Hall or the building by Thompson's office on Brattle Street.

JS Well, this takes me to one last element of Harvard Square that has recently clarified for me certain questions about this moment in the history of the modern movement: Sert's Holyoke Center, which was completed in 1960 and is now known as the Smith Campus Center.

The Holyoke Center tends to be overlooked, particularly after its recent renovation, but it is Sert's most important contribution to a new "urbanity" for the Harvard campus. It is a quintessential Team 10 building, cloaked in the vocabulary of modernism but very sophisticated in its treatment of the ground plane. Sert used an open-air *passage* or *galleria*—later enclosed and air-conditioned—fronted with commercial activity and offices like those in most European cities. The building collected people from the houses along the Charles River and delivered them on axis to one of the gates of Harvard Yard. If you look at the plan and the volumetric massing of the building, you notice tall office blocks that are recessed to create a new plaza and a two-story volume on the ground that prolongs the internal galleria out onto the plaza and aligns it perfectly with one of the main entrances of the Yard across Massachusetts Avenue. Sert's highly orchestrated organization of program, building volumes, and alignment of axes with a context are unthinkable in an urban building by Le Corbusier! He created a veritable plaza between the building, the Yard, and the town center that reconfigured the larger Harvard Square.

Sert did something similar when he built the Harvard Science Center in 1972. The figure of the ground plan and its programs are organized so that the building creates a perfect urban transition—literally a pivot—between Harvard Yard and the rotated urban grid of northern Cambridge, which collide at that point. Today we would call this urban design technique very "contextual," although back then it could only be described as a-modern. The massing above remains closer to modernist conventions, but the overall footprint of the complex gives a sense of how a new approach to the city, inconceivable to architects of Le Corbusier's generation, had seeped into the modern canon.

ML It's interesting to compare these buildings with the first two projects Sert did in Cambridge: his own courtyard house in 1958 and the Center for the Study of World Religions in 1960.

JS It hadn't occurred to me to compare them. In a way these projects exist more on their own, rather than as campus projects, particularly his house. However, they both display a new way of articulating building volumes in relation to open or public spaces. In this sense they share the site-specificity of the other campus projects. I think the projects that Sert did within the microcosm of the university in his years as dean tell you more clearly what he was trying to do with

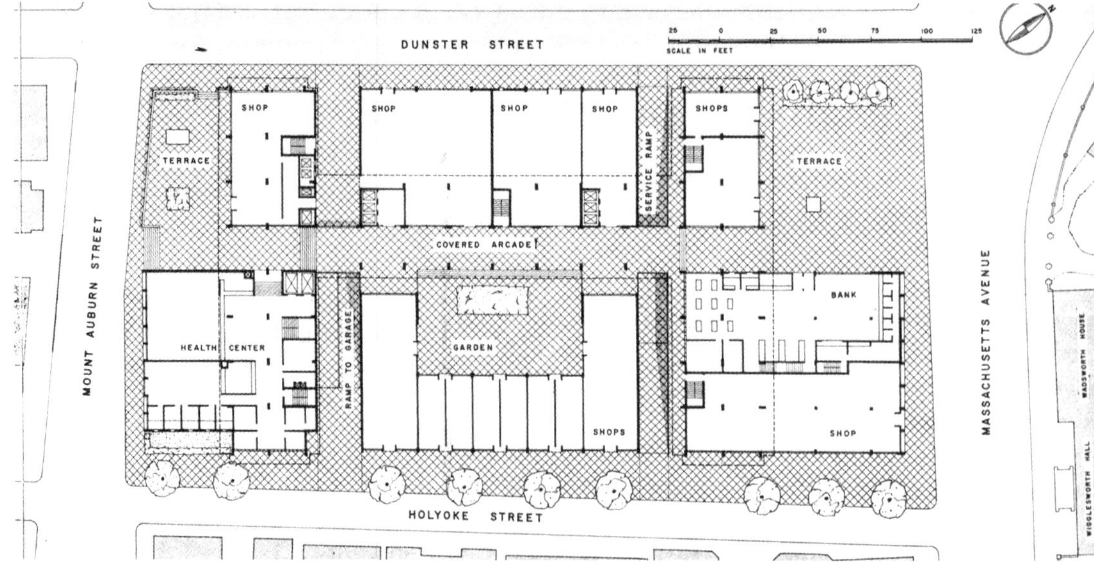

Plan of the Holyoke Center, Sert, Jackson and Associates (1966).

Model of the Harvard Science Center, Sert, Jackson and Associates (1973).

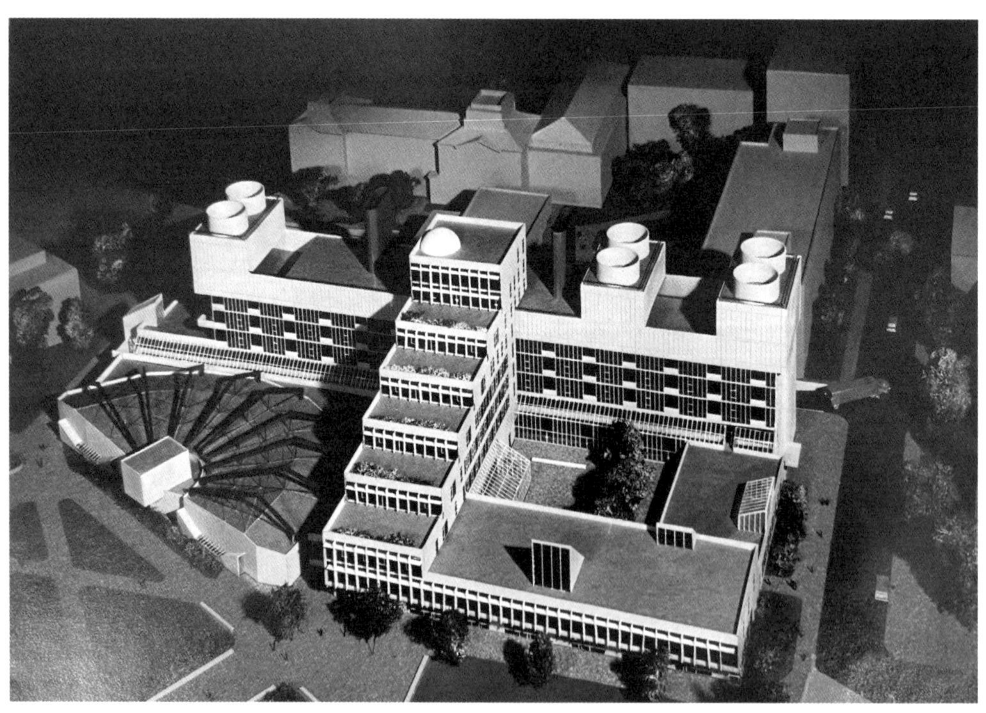

modern architecture and the city. Besides the Holyoke Center and the Science Center, the third project that completes this story is the student housing complex Peabody Terrace, from 1964. The low wings that create courtyards open to the river and the towers that loosely received porch-like balconies are yet again moves that indicate a transitional moment that is often overlooked. It made a big impression on Rodolfo [Machado] and me, as well as on our circle of classmates in Argentina, including Rafael Viñoly, who later authored some important housing projects in Buenos Aires that I know were inspired by Peabody Terrace. In this complex, you see how Sert is looking at the history of Georgian building types along the Charles River and attempting to reconcile them with a new density and typology: the high-rise. Fifty years later, when we did the One Western Avenue graduate dorms across the river, Rodolfo took a lot from Sert's approach.

While Sert completed these three projects separately and at different times, it was as if he always had a sense of the totality within which he was working on each project. I say all of this to illustrate that the years of Sert's deanship are an incredibly rich moment that we tend to overlook and in which there are real pedagogical and disciplinary transformations taking place. Even though I arrived at the GSD soon after Sert had retired, his presence and impact still reverberated in the new Gund Hall that he inaugurated and, of course, in all the built legacy that he contributed to the area. There was an invigorated idea of modernism being tested on the Harvard campus back then, with bare concrete used emphatically and daringly in important new buildings to challenge the red Georgian brick architecture. Gund Hall and Le Corbusier's Carpenter Center are a part of this story.

ML The way you talk about Peabody Terrace reminds me of your background in Argentina, and the presence of people like Antoni Bonet i Castellana or even, in your education, Juan Kurchan and Jorge Ferrari Hardoy. *That* group of modernists.

JS Yes, they belong to the same generation. I actually brought the Hardoy archive to the GSD when I became chair. I truly admire Sert, but in the United States, scholars and others in the field still emphasize Le Corbusier. This happens for all the good reasons, but when you look at Sert's buildings and how they work—how they engage history through very clear architectural moves—you find something that's missing from Le Corbusier's.

ML He is definitely underappreciated as an architect in this country and, to a certain degree, even in Spain.

JS Sert was one of the principal figures from that second generation who was able to effect a revision to some of the most consolidated dogmas of the early modern movement. He surfaced the need to deal with the city more successfully than the early modernists had, particularly in relation to existing cities. He was also instrumental in developing the tools for implementing this. Sert invented the term and discipline of *urban design* and developed a world-famous program at Harvard on how to intervene within the existing city.

ML Do you think this predilection for the urban scale started earlier?

JS His participation in CIAM congresses seems to indicate that. He was there to proclaim the end of CIAM in the 1959 Otterloo congress with others of his generation. However, most of his intellectual contributions were already present in the book that he coauthored with Ernesto N. Rogers and others after CIAM 8 in 1951: *The Heart of the City: Towards the Humanisation of Urban Life*.[1]

The book is still a good read because it outlines the beginnings of postmodern thinking in architecture. In a way, we all come from this congress. This tends to be overlooked because it marks a shift that attempts to redirect the modern tradition in a remarkable way, all without creating a rupture by establishing continuity with the vocabulary of capital-*M*, capital-*A* Modern Architecture. Starting in the '80s, the term *postmodern* was used almost exclusively to indicate the rejection of the modern "style," as it was reconceived in the United States. However, the first significant departure is best dated by *The Heart of the City*. The book opens with historian Sigfried Giedion, the president of CIAM and a big supporter of the modernist attitude toward history, saying that it is time to deal with people if we want cities to continue aggregating human life. And for this, we needed history.

ML Sert in fact brought both Sigfried Giedion and Eduard Sekler to teach at the GSD.

JS Then we have to remember that he ran a huge practice! Nobody compares them, but in many ways he was much more complete than Gropius. Gropius was not really a practitioner in the sense that Sert was. In the end, this became a problem because Sert treated the GSD and his office interchangeably. Everyone teaching at the GSD had worked or was still working in his office, and this gave the school a certain inbred constitution that I encountered when I arrived.

ML Fumihiko Maki gave an unusually autobiographical lecture a few years ago at the GSD, where he spoke about his time as a student at the school.[2] He said that there was a group of students at the GSD that

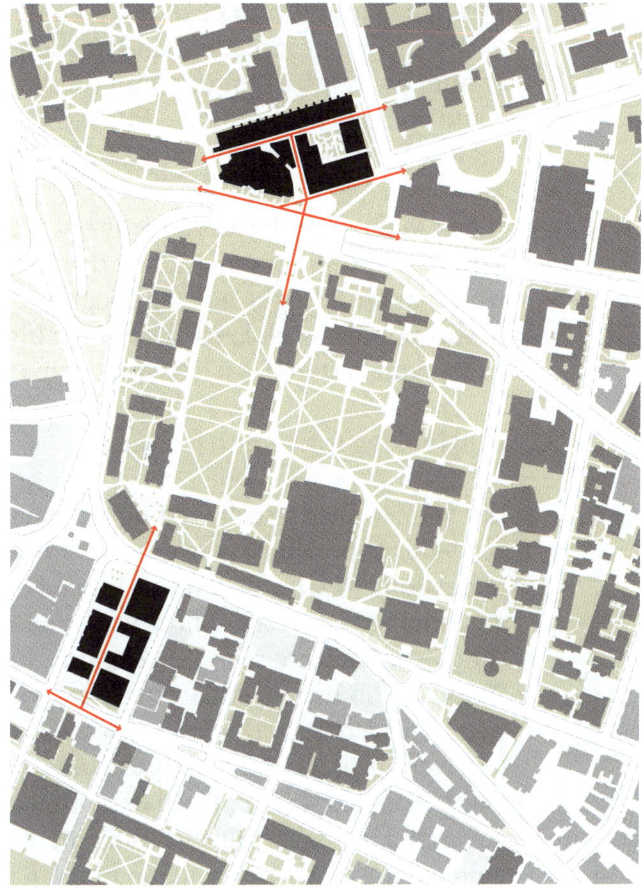

Site plan of the Harvard Yard, showing the Holyoke Center on the south and the Harvard Science Center on the north. Red lines and arrows show the capacity of these two new buildings to articulate the pedestrian circulation of the old campus yard with the surrounding urban context of the city of Cambridge.

Section through the "studio trays" of Gund Hall, designed by John Andrews (1967–1972).

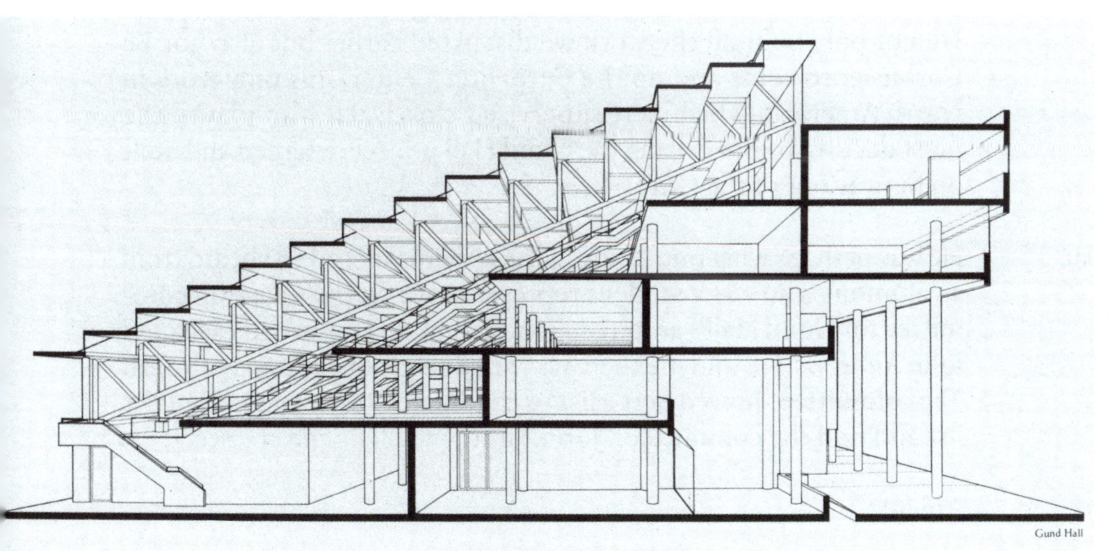

Sert liked and a group he didn't. And that you didn't want to be part of this second group! Maki said he was glad that Sert was supportive of him, but felt bad for the ones on the other side of the fence. One could imagine a student like Michael Graves, who bore a resentment against Sert and what he stood for, being on the other side.

JS When Maki came, he was already old, and perhaps that made his lecture very autobiographical, but this happens to everybody. Look at what I'm doing right now! So begin to prepare for when you come to this point too, because it's only in hindsight that it becomes easier to explain things—when you begin to see the whole arc.

ML I am looking forward to it! [*laughs*]

JS But yes, Sert had a really strong personality. Now that I've had more academic experience, I see that he didn't leave space for anybody else to blossom, which is a common type of leadership in figures with such a strong presence. The school was something of a one-man show, although there were some exceptions, like Jerzy Sołtan or Shadrach Woods, who were both from Team 10. However, Sołtan's practice was nonexistent at this point. Woods, on the other hand, was very involved in practicing in Europe and Africa, but with his untimely death Harvard was deprived of a potential credible successor.

Sert was a charming, intelligent, cultivated, and persuasive architect. This personality made him friends with all the administrators who came and went at Harvard. I saw it in the few engagements I had with him, even if he was retired. The kind of position that Sert had at the university as dean doesn't exist anymore, because both universities and the practice of architecture have changed. Sert had incredible power over the architecture that got done on the campus. He not only built all the work we discussed earlier but also got Le Corbusier to come and do the Carpenter Center—his only work in North America—which Sert supervised closely. He also played the most decisive role in getting the Gund Hall project designed and built on his way out of the GSD.

ML He was perhaps what one would call a "superdean" today. I heard from an alumnus who was a student representative on the selection committee for Gund Hall's architect—the group that eventually selected John Andrews. He told me there was not a single discussion with Sert. The committee showed Sert a list of candidates, but he discarded the list and told the committee, "John Andrews will be the architect."

JS Amen!

2. The GSD Under Gerald M. McCue

ML We've spoken about the university and Harvard Square, but what was the atmosphere at Gund Hall when you arrived? Who was there? I'd like to hear your account of what was going on at the school with Maurice D. Kilbridge's arrival as dean of the GSD. This wasn't a bright moment in the GSD's history.

JS Nothing captured better what the GSD was like after the move from Robinson Hall to Gund Hall than Ada Louis Huxtable's article about it in the *New York Times*.[3] Huxtable was a formidable critic. She always said what had to be said with a punch and could unpack with clarity the good, the bad, and the complicated in any architectural endeavor. She described the merits of Andrews's project for a school with the "environmental oneness" that Sert demanded. But she also mentioned the conflict and territoriality this generated among faculty and departments at the school.

The building had barely opened, but Huxtable hit the nail on the head when she called it "a place for extroverts." I was coming from Carnegie Mellon, which had a typical Beaux-Arts building with architectural fragments collected on the exterior, notable names inscribed on lintels, and halls of room after room with interchangeable uses—not unlike McKim, Mead & White's Robinson Hall at Harvard. Gund Hall was something entirely different.

From an urban perspective, it operates in a similar way as the projects by Sert at Harvard, engaging the street with its giant portico. The interior then achieved the all-encompassing studio environment that Sert wanted, using what were very contemporary building technologies at that point. In these regards, Gund Hall felt like a very powerful project at the time.

However, Gund Hall was an unbearable place to work! It was fun, social, and you could always see what everyone was doing. But it was impossible to concentrate! And the main problem was acoustic. As a student, I would not have been able to design anything there.

ML Did you ever see one of the famous truss races in Gund Hall? Where students would climb on the trusses and race from the first to the fifth tray while they charetted on their projects in the middle of the night?

JS I lived in a small apartment a block away from Gund during my first year at Harvard and worked out of my small office at the GSD until late, so I saw a lot of truss races at night! And the awards ceremonies. The races would scare me to death! But they go to show the problem that the trays still have to this day: there is no visual privacy.

I had a terrible reaction to the building when I arrived, particularly because I was coming from Carnegie Mellon. I was used to having four students per room and walking in and out of the hall to do desk crits with each. At Harvard the noise was disastrous. Final presentations were cacophonous, and on an average day there was always a plethora of radios playing music against one another. You would often see people screaming and throwing things at each other across trays out of frustration with this situation.

Peace on the trays at the GSD was achieved by a sudden miracle performed from Japan that changed the atmosphere of the space completely, and which had nothing to do with architecture: the invention of the Sony Walkman! Within six months of its release, Gund became a very pleasant, peaceful, and friendly environment. Everyone carried one around and listened to their own music, creating an auditory privacy screen that allowed them to focus without becoming alienated from their surroundings. After that, Gund became a very calm and silent place. A miracle on Quincy Street!

ML Another fine example in which architecture is not the only solution to the problem!

JS But to go back to your question about Kilbridge. After calling the school a place of unrest, irresolution, and bad vibes, Huxtable ended her article with reference to the drama surrounding the new dean. Kilbridge was not the successor one would expect after Sert. But there were two factors that played a role in his appointment: the first was that the school was not very well regarded by the new university administration. Not knowing the details, in traditional academic terms, I suppose this was because of this inbred constitution of the faculty, mostly made up of unremarkable modernists that had been followers of Sert. The second was a lack of quality in the production of scholarship, which is how universities still measure the output of their schools.

This was also the beginning of the trend of giving leadership positions within institutions to managerial types, who in theory are better equipped to handle a school's finances and make it run more efficiently. Sert, Gropius, and Joseph Hudnut were all fundamentally architects tuned into their times and grounded in the humanities. Kilbridge was a mathematician who had taught at the Harvard Business School, specializing in quantitative economics. He was brought in to start a world-class planning school focused on quantitative planning and to manage architects and their "funny" ways of thinking.

By consequence, Kilbridge didn't have a very high opinion of what was done at the school. Believe it or not, the dean of the GSD went around in public saying that the faculty in the architecture department were impossible and that "architects stop thinking at the age of 30," as the press reported at a conference he gave in Seattle.[4] This attitude, of course, caused a scandal when it made its way to the Harvard and Boston papers and was the welcoming salute I received when I arrived at the GSD.

ML This is a prescient tale of how administrative structures in universities across the country have evolved over the last fifty years.

JS Yes, this is a phenomenon that has somewhat followed us to this day. The tensions this created were then amplified by another scandal in the architecture scene of the Northeast regarding the visiting committee. The year before I arrived, one of the highly confidential reports to the president, produced by the visiting committee on their annual review of the school, was leaked directly to the press. The contents were devastating, particularly for the architecture department. It is now known that Philip Johnson, a member of the committee, leaked the report because he was so appalled by what he saw happening at the school.

This didn't bode well for Kilbridge, who was already acting in very un-dean-like ways, smearing his own faculty in public and trying to change disciplines by twisting faculty members' arms. At that point the planning department was having trouble with the dean as well, and faculty went public requesting his resignation over the fact that he was trying to make planning an appendix to the field of economics.

When I arrived Kilbridge was still dean, but the university was already trying to find a way to fix the issues of the school, which he was clearly in no position to do. The atmosphere was really noxious.

ML You didn't feel welcome.

JS Not really. Shortly after arriving, Rodolfo and I won our first Progressive Architecture award for Fountain House, which back then was quite prestigious, and also very notable because it was awarded to two young unknown arrivals from Argentina. No one else on the faculty was getting them. I remember that I went to a faculty meeting around that time, and the assistant chair of the department told me, "Well, I suppose we have to congratulate you, Jorge, but this is not the kind of work that we do at Harvard."

Museum cardboard model of the Fountain House, Rodolfo Machado and Jorge Silvetti (1974–1975). Model maker: Stephen Wierzwosky.

Just like that! In front of the whole faculty body. You can imagine how I felt as the newest, youngest member of the faculty, with no friends around.

ML This was George Anselevicius?

JS No, no. George was an outsider and much nicer, but by then he had announced his resignation. This was the beginning of a reshuffling that lasted for a few years, with the retreat and replacement of the old guard of the school. Kilbridge also resigned within a matter of years.

NDA Why did you decide to go from Carnegie Mellon to Harvard if this was the environment at the GSD?

JS We never thought of Pittsburgh as a permanent place, even if we had a fantastic experience. Like any young person, I wanted to go to New York. But then a call came out for a position at Harvard, where I did not know anybody. But I applied for the job and got it, and it was Harvard, so I took it...

ML What was the faculty-selection process like back then at the GSD? What did they look for in a junior faculty?

JS When I went in for my interview, the committee was composed of Jerzy Sołtan, the only person I had heard about, because of his participation in the CIAM congress in Otterloo; Joan E. Goody, a local architect; and Donald L. Stull, an architect with a distinguished practice in Boston. Of the whole committee, Jerzy was the one who somewhat understood where I was coming from intellectually, with my interests in French structuralism and the relationship between architecture and anthropology. The others were mostly impressed by our experimental design work.

Jerzy was this very educated European architect who went to Paris and worked with Le Corbusier after the war. He had participated in CIAM for a while until Sert brought him to the GSD. He didn't practice much, but he was the liveliest person at the school, always there talking with students and very much loved by everyone. He always painted and drew, like Le Corbusier, but he had that handicap of having been "touched" by him. As a second-generation modernist, somehow he was never able to shake this off.

Jerzy didn't necessarily understand everything that I was interested in, but he picked up that I would bring something fresh and valuable to the school, perhaps because of his more continental approach. I believe he played a big role in getting me hired. He then went on to be very supportive of me while he was at the school.

ML Let's go back to Team 10 for a minute then. I know you were also responsible for bringing the Alison and Peter Smithson archive to the GSD. Was the culture of Team 10 quite present at the GSD when you arrived?

JS Yes, yes. But that was much later, when I was chair. I'm an archive nut!

ML What was your own position in relation to Team 10? Did you find resonances with them, even if they belonged to a generation of modernist architects that faced a moment of transition earlier than yours?

JS When I came to the United States, I introduced myself as a product of Team 10. This was my strongest influence leaving Argentina, and the PhD I was pursuing at Berkeley had to do with clarifying and articulating more consistently the line of thinking that had derived from their approach. My only subscription back then was to *Architectural Design*, a big promoter of those ideas that was published in London, and a lot of my Argentinian professors were fans of Team 10.

Just to give you a sense: when I came to the United States, one of the few books I brought with me was a Spanish version of the *Team 10 Primer*—my English was horrible![5] I remember going to Jerzy Sołtan during my first semester and asking him to sign my copy. When he saw the book, he immediately asked me, "When was this published?" I told him I didn't know, but that I had gotten it at a bookstore in Buenos Aires. Well, he did some research, and it turns out it was a pirated translation made in Argentina! That was my arrival at Harvard, with my little third-world luggage that I had hauled all those years since I left Buenos Aires. [*laughs*]

But the thinking from the earlier days of Team 10 was not there when I arrived at the GSD. Even if most faculty were disciples of Sert, people in the architecture department were not talking seriously about Team 10. There was only some continuity within the urban design program.

ML It's great to hear that you considered yourself part of this Team 10 lineage when you arrived; I've always been curious about that relation.

JS Yes. I started more on the side of the Smithsons, and then slowly moved toward Rogers and the Italians, of course!

ML You've mentioned your affinity with the polemics of Aldo Rossi and the Tendenza generation on architecture and the city across the Atlantic. Could you elaborate on that?

JS These were all fantastic polemics, which are so vivid in my mind. To some extent, I feel that I am a product of them, just like I am of Le

Corbusier. People think I'm crazy when I say this, but that is really the beginning of my relationship with architecture.

From Team 10's interest in the city comes Colin Rowe, for me. You could say they have nothing to do with one another, but for both Rodolfo and me, this is just a continuation of our thinking. In a way this lineage is part of the reason we are so different from the post-modernists that we were sometimes thrown in with, like Michael Graves. Michael was intellectually and artistically remarkable, but he had a very different way of thinking about architecture and the city. Still today, I think I remain closer to the continental influences that were a part of my education than the American ones. But I do, you know, have a little "Venturi" side too! [*laughs*]

ML So what was the zeitgeist at the school when you first arrived? Who were the design forces and what was the work like? Were people doing brutalist work?

JS The two figures in the spotlight of the moment at the GSD were Gerhard Kallmann and Michael McKinnell, also European modernists. Without being an established professional office, they entered the open international competition for Boston City Hall in 1962. Even though they did not have any odds stacked in their favor, they won and built it! These were the things that happened during those times, which hardly ever happened again.

ML That was the year before Le Corbusier's Carpenter Center was completed at Harvard.

JS Exactly. City Hall became the project of the moment, and everyone talked about how Le Corbusier—in his La Tourette version—had finally crossed the Atlantic. It definitely made an impression on me as a student in Argentina, even if I later came to see many of the limits that still make the promise of tearing the building down an appealing mayoral campaign platform!

Kallmann and McKinnell were peculiar people. They were very much into themselves when I met them, perhaps affected by this overnight global success that came with Boston City Hall. They seemed bitter because their practice had not taken off, and I have to say they were not very fond of me, particularly McKinnell. But frankly, they didn't get along with anybody. They came across as very dogmatic at the time, but they were also excellent teachers, especially Kallmann. Being with them in reviews was always stimulating.

NDA What about architectural historians? Did they teach history at all at the GSD?

JS Eduard Sekler was all that the GSD had in terms of history. He was a first-class historian, with an impeccable pedigree: a student of Rudolf Wittkower, and an assistant of Sigfried Giedion. However, his office was at the Carpenter Center, and he split his academic obligations between the GSD and Harvard College. Since Sekler was the only one teaching at the GSD, the school had, effectively, half a historian, so to speak.[6]

ML Stanislaus von Moos once told me that when he was working with Sekler, he invited Robert Venturi and Denise Scott Brown to lecture, and he was not allowed to bring them into Gund Hall. They had to give the lecture at the Carpenter Center, and he was even chastised afterward for having invited them.

JS The GSD at that time never could have invited Venturi and Scott Brown. Right after my interview with the search committee, I was told I had to go meet Professor Tom Stifter, whom I had never heard of, for a chat. I walked into one of these offices that faces Quincy Street, and his first question was, "What do you have to do with the institute in New York?" He was of course referring to the Institute of Architecture and Urban Studies (IAUS) and, by extension, Peter Eisenman. It was instantly clear to me that he was a powerful figure at the GSD and paranoid that I might be part of Eisenman's cohort coming to infiltrate the school! That was the atmosphere. You can imagine what happened when I brought Eisenman for a discussion in my first seminar on architectural theory that same year.

NDA Of course you did.

JS It caused a lot of talk. It was one of those "Why did we hire this guy?" moments. But the old guard had to swallow the pill. It was all Jerzy's doing!

NDA Did you become very associated with the IAUS?

JS Rodolfo and I benefited immensely from direct contact with the activity and vibrancy of the institute. And we were big supporters of it. We went down to New York often and partook in their programs, which at that point were like nothing else that had been seen in the United States. They really brought everyone to talk there: Aldo Rossi, Manfredo Tafuri, Joseph Rykwert, you name it.

However, Rodolfo and I were on the outer circle, which was a sort of blessing because we escaped the cultural and political frays and the ideological polarizations that the institute ended up generating. The institute was more closely associated with "the Whites," the schools that they taught in—Princeton, Cooper Union, and Cornell—and the strong Corbusian connotations of their architecture. It was a place to confront the positions of "the Grays," who taught instead at Yale and UPenn. We were always very careful about the degree to which we were involved in this discourse, and the GSD was luckily never part of it.

At that point, we began feeling comfortable with the idea that one didn't *have* to live in New York at some point, and eventually became very enthusiastic and stimulated by the two situations we had at the Rhode Island School of Design (RISD) and Harvard.[7] These appeared to be real opportunities to have a personal, individual impact on an institution and to be part of a very different set of activities. The whole polemic between the Grays and the Whites was not something we were very interested in.

That said, the institute worked *so well* because, as a cultural figure, Eisenman and the other leading figures he brought in[8] were capable of stirring continuous debate and brought the most remarkable or promising figures in architecture at the time to the institute. This, to me, is his greatest contribution. He knew how to stir the pot, connecting with the international intellectual forefront and causing a lot of trouble. It made people think and talk about architecture in fresh, inspiring ways.

Eisenman also brought ideas from linguistics in architecture from an American perspective, through thinkers like Noam Chomsky. This became very productive as a perspective from which to understand architecture at the time. I'm referring to Eisenman's idea that we can understand architecture by unveiling its "deep structure" in the same way as Chomsky proposed ought to be done with language. However, in my opinion this path exhausted itself very quickly. Eisenman later moved from Chomsky to Jacques Derrida, who actually had some clashes with him.

This moment also bred a second generation of people interested in architectural theory that completely detached themselves from practice. They became interested in a much more pure, abstract theory and increasingly separated the discourse from a focus on the production of architecture, which made it lose relevance for the education of an architect. In some ways, weak threads of this tradition still survive to this day.

ML Did you feel very intellectually lonely at the GSD? It seems to me that you did not find as much affinity with the design work that was going on at Yale and Princeton or in Philadelphia as you did with the theory, which was not very present at Harvard.

JS At the beginning, yes. I was very disappointed when I arrived. With everything going on, I spent a lot of time thinking about leaving after

From left to right: Peter Eisenman, Mario Gandelsonas, Jorge Silvetti, Ms. Tafuri, Manfredo Tafuri, and Rodolfo Machado on the balcony of the Institute for Architecture and Urban Studies in New York City, 1975.

the end of the year. It would have been easy, given how I was not yet settled. However, two things changed.

The first was a major development at the GSD. In the middle of my first spring term at the GSD in 1976, the chair of the Department of Architecture resigned unexpectedly, and rumors about who was to replace him began to circulate. The second was that in that same spring, Rodolfo was hired by RISD, effective fall of the same year. With his arrival, I was in Providence often, engaging in a very different architectural sphere. Our joint design work regained intensity, undoubtedly energized by being in the same place and having received much publicity from our Progressive Architecture award. We kept doing competitions and experimental projects, and all of a sudden like-minded students at both schools started sticking to us, which was very invigorating.

With changes in the making at the GSD, I decided to stay put for a while and see what would happen with the arrival of the new chair, Gerald McCue. I knew him because he had been the chair of the architecture department at Berkeley during my time there, and I had a lot of respect for what he had done. There was a lot of hope that he would change things, and he did indeed! With McCue the GSD began to open up, and everything became brighter and more promising. But the start was messy and ugly!

The president of the university invited McCue to come in as chair of the Department of Architecture. Presidents don't usually get involved in this type of selection, so there were a lot of rumors that he was getting tested to become dean. This was already presumed, because he was also concurrently appointed as an associate dean. Within a couple of years it was confirmed: Kilbridge resigned and McCue went on to be the dean of the school from 1980 until 1992.

Academia is a cruel institution when it comes to remembering those that have given it service, but it's under McCue that the GSD turned around to become the school we know today. We owe him much of it even though there is hardly any talk about his transformational tenure as the dean whose changes produced, single-handedly, today's GSD. The GSD then was full of Sert's followers left to their own accord, sheltered in the sense of security that being a Harvard professor gave them, and very protective of one another. McCue gave the school a drastic cleanup! Even though there were not that many tenured positions back then, this still required courage and stamina. Too many heads had to roll and entrenched habits had to be challenged, so it seemed violent at times! You heard a lot of door slamming and screaming down the hallways. But within a couple of years he was able to diversify the schools of thought present at the GSD in a very refreshing way.

NDA What did this diversification look like?

JS Both with Sert or Gropius, the GSD was an outpost of whatever was happening with European modernism from which Americans partook in these discussions. It was a place of exchange with England, Italy, France, and Germany.

McCue came from California and had never been involved with the architecture culture of the East Coast. That said, he was very well informed. He knew that a significant new force moving everything in architecture was the IAUS in New York and that competing schools were well ahead in their involvement with this scene.

McCue's arrival produced very ebullient times. I remember that the second year after I was at the school, one of my MArch II students was Thom Mayne, with whom I ended up becoming good friends. At the GSD, he was a student of Oswald Mathias Ungers, Stanley Tigerman, and Colin Rowe—a cast of figures unimaginable at the GSD before McCue. The school renewed a lot of its appeal very quickly, and a lot of interesting conversations were going on. When Thom Mayne arrived at the GSD he certainly made himself noticed!

ML Thom told me he was rejected twice from the MArch II program and that he came to Cambridge without an invitation, stormed into McCue's office, and intercepted him to get some answers as to why he had not been accepted.

JS I can see that! I know him well and . . . it makes sense, he very well could have done that. He thrived at the GSD and was *extremely* comfortable here. He loved it. By the time he arrived, the school was already very different from what I first encountered. Colin Rowe was one of the important figures that McCue had started courting outside the IAUS during this period, inviting him to lectures and to join reviews.

Colin had been the first person in the '40s who dared to connect classicism with modern architecture. In 1947 he published "The Mathematics of the Ideal Villa," in which he developed a series of dialectics between Palladio's and Le Corbusier's work.[9] This had a great impact, first in England, then in the United States.

ML He wrote that article when he was twenty-seven years old.

JS Yes, and he followed it with "Mannerism and Modern Architecture," after he moved to the US.[10] Colin participated in a remarkable episode at the University of Texas at Austin in which an international and heterogeneous group of architects, theoreticians, artists, and historians referred to as "The Texas Rangers" created a new curriculum in architecture for American academia. This reverberated in schools across the country as the participants dispersed throughout them. Colin went to Cornell, where he had a profound impact on its program and created a veritable new center of gravity for architecture, which had transformational and lasting effects in all major schools of architecture. From Cornell, Colin also gained a lot of traction as a fresh, incisive, and inspiring architectural critic in the American context, writing two other canonical pieces: "Transparency: Literal and Phenomenal," with painter and Texas Ranger Robert Slutzky, who was then associated with Cooper Union, and his 1975 introduction to *Five Architects*.[11]

For obvious reasons, the old guard at Harvard remained very suspicious of him and his associations. Needless to say, I was elated with his presence! I had been attracted to Cornell because of Colin, but had regretfully rejected the offer to teach there because of the ugly politics I found when I visited on my way out of Berkeley.[12] McCue soon began serious talks about bringing Colin to the GSD, which I knew Colin also entertained with great interest. But this never happened because the opposition by the senior faculty to bringing in a character like him was too strong.

ML I can only imagine how very different history would be if Colin Rowe had come to the GSD.

JS I would have been delighted if he had come. I got to know him well at this time, and we became longtime friends. He stayed with Rodolfo and me many of the times he visited Boston thereafter. That said, a lot of Colin's former students came to teach at the GSD during McCue's years. They had a great impact on the school, particularly Fred Koetter. He was a brilliant pedagogue and later became dean at Yale. Colin and Fred wrote *Collage City* while he was at the GSD, and it certainly influenced what was happening in the school.[13]

However, the most important draw that McCue made was to have Henry N. Cobb—Harry—succeed him as chair of the Department of Architecture. McCue held both positions, chair and dean, for several years after Kilbridge resigned, but when he began the search, he did so very openly, consulting everyone at the school. I was a junior faculty, but McCue trusted me, I guess, so he always asked me what I thought about a lot of things. And I told him I thought bringing Harry was a really bad idea! I mean, with so much going on in architecture, why did we need a corporate architect, which was then my preconception of what he represented. Harry was still dealing with the aftermath of the Hancock Tower's curtain-wall problems, he spoke *really* slowly, and did not impress me at all!

This tells you how prejudiced we can be of someone we barely even know, as was my case with Harry. It shows you how unintentional but inevitably divisive lines can be drawn when intellectual battles rage as they did back then. By the end of Harry's tenure in 1990 I was in awe of the results of his actions and the skills with which he transformed the department and the school itself. Perhaps this is something to think about now that we are in the midst of such intense culture wars.

ML In many ways this marked the beginning of a new era for the GSD.

JS The combination of McCue and Cobb was explosive. Many other people played a role in the transformation of the school, but they were the ones who enabled the GSD to change. And this is because they were the right types in the right position to do it. This duo had not only the correct instincts but also the power to do what had to be done. McCue had the reputation of having been a transformative figure that put UC Berkeley on the architectural map, and Cobb was an established architect. Both of them were also open, always sharing their thoughts and allowing the faculty to engage along the way. They acted selflessly and never competed with their faculty.

NDA It's interesting that you say this about Cobb. Perhaps because I've never gone down into the history, but I've certainly felt he was part of the stale, corporate-leaning past of the school.

JS Harry was certainly a New England WASP coming back from the corporate architecture world in New York, but he put his whole heart into making a better department. In a moment when we were all trying to give the school a sorely lacking theoretical base, he had a lot to contribute.

I worked with Harry on a lot of initiatives that can give you a sense of the kind of figure he was. For instance, Harry was the one who led the complete rehauling of the core program. He charged Kallmann and McKinnell with the conception and organization of the third semester, which dealt with the fabric of the building, from structure to building systems to the ornamental program. It was a brilliant assignment, perfectly suited to their best intellectual and professional attributes, and they did it very, very well. They also did it in a better mood, because they started getting work around that time and became a lot friendlier!

We then added a fourth semester to the core sequence, devoting it entirely to an assignment dealing directly with the city through a housing project. I ended up as the coordinator of this for a decade. There were five sections, led by four GSD senior instructors and one yearly visitor: Fred Koetter, Michael Dennis, and I always taught it, together with someone from the urban design department, like Peter

Rowe. Many times the visiting critic was from ETH Zürich—for many years we had Mario Campi—but they also came from Japan and other American universities.

This was one of the new forms of engagement with the school introduced by McCue that changed the GSD in drastic ways. He basically conceived the idea of systematically bringing in visiting critics from abroad at a time when this was much more complicated than it is today. And it worked. The program really flourished, particularly the relationship with ETH Zürich.

This structure for the core program stuck around for quite a while. Today layers and layers of change have made it unrecognizable in terms of its original intent, which is not an uncommon phenomenon. For me, it is still unclear what the next strong pedagogical objective of the core sequence will be at the GSD. I have, however, become a firm believer that the core program is the soul of the program.

ML Cobb once told me that when he took over, he had the impression that there was not enough rigor at the school, so he played a role in bringing in a lot of those students of Colin Rowe from Cornell who you alluded to earlier: Dennis and Koetter, as well as Ralph Lerner.

JS Yes, Ralph was a big draw that Harry made, but he was from Cooper Union, not Cornell. He brought him in to teach visual studies and drawing, although he also taught studios.

ML Harry said he came across Ralph at a review at the University of Virginia that Jacque Robertson invited him to, after which he offered him a job.

JS Yes, Ralph was one of John Hejduk's best "products." He was a very gifted, precise, and effective teacher. He was also well-versed in architectural history and modernism.

ML He went on to become dean at Princeton. Harry told me that after he hired Ralph, Jacque, who was dean at UVA, called him and said, "You Yankees, we invite you for dinner and you steal our silverware!"

JS Yes, yes. That was a good acquisition for the GSD, even if the result of some deviousness!

Harry was also largely responsible for promoting the development of a strong architectural history and theory program. He created a new senior chair in history and conducted a search that brought in Howard Burns. This was transformative for the school.[14] You can see my preconceptions proved wrong again and again! In the search for rigor you described, Harry also put me to work on the draft of a thesis program for architecture, which did not exist back then. He also made some major contributions to the school more widely, getting involved with changes to the landscape department, based on his experience in the profession.

NDA It seems to me that both McCue and Cobb trusted you greatly. Why do you think that was? I suppose you were just one amid many junior faculty at the school, who usually do not get consulted on the kinds of decisions you have alluded to.

JS I think that the people who pushed for me from the very beginning, like Jerzy Sołtan, always saw me as a Trojan horse. In retrospect, I am not sure if that's the most comfortable position in which to find oneself as a young faculty member, but it certainly was exciting and motivating! I guess it was a way for them to bring a new generation of ideas to the school, which other faculty were very skeptical of. And it was true, to some degree. Of course, as more and more new people were brought in, there were others that they brought to bear on these changes. In one way or another, Cobb always included the architecture faculty in discussions about new ideas. He was always transparent regarding his intentions and goals, even when he had to follow confidentiality protocols.

There was also the fact that McCue knew me from Berkeley. Rodolfo and I were some of the first guinea pigs of the PhD program that he had created there. Actually, when we dropped out of the program, McCue was already at Harvard, so we broached the issue very delicately, and he understood our decision completely.

During these early days, I got to work on a lot of these interesting initiatives that had an impact on the pedagogy and curriculum of the school. McCue and Cobb even involved me, together with Carl Steinitz from landscape architecture, in a committee that formulated the conceptual framework for the new Master of Design program, a novel type of postgraduate program in the United States, which launched in 1985. This was during Harry's last year as chair.

I also had the chance to run my own experiments. As soon as he arrived, McCue entrusted me to teach a theory course as part of his desire to engage what was going on in this new world of architectural theory, which was being born at that time. He understood from Jerzy's advice that I was the most qualified person to do it, given my understanding of what was brewing in this emerging field. K. Michael Hays, who took the class as an active auditor shortly after his arrival at MIT for his PhD, later did some research and told me that this was the first required theory course within an architecture program in the country. However, this caused some mumbling from other, older factions of the school that were pretty upset about changes in general.

So Sekler was asked—by the old guard, I later learned—to come to my lectures and hear what I was saying! You can imagine this was quite intimidating. Fortunately, Sekler liked what he heard, and actually sat in on all my classes. We became close friends in the most collegial of ways: by attending each other's classes, as I did his lectures at the Carpenter Center!

I think that, fundamentally, McCue and Cobb were open-minded, and they liked my ideas and attitude. I guess from their position, they saw something in my personal academic project that aligned with what they had in mind for the school. They saw that my participation could help bring forth these changes, even if I was not a tenured faculty back then.

ML The more I know about McCue, the more work I find that he did behind the scenes. He did planning work for Sea Ranch before Charles Moore, Lawrence Halprin, and the rest of that group. He was organizing Erich Mendelsohn shows during his time at Berkeley. His reputation as more of a corporate architect is certainly an underestimation.

JS When I first met him as a student at Berkeley, it was my first academic experience in America, so I had nothing to compare him to as a dean. I thought all deans might be like this. But he was a doer. He basically invented the College of Environmental Design—and the name for it too! Now it feels a bit dated, but at the time it was revolutionary. He also brought Christopher Alexander to Berkeley. In spite of my disappointment with Alexander and his work, bringing him into the faculty at that time was a bold and intelligent move.[15]

ML So *he* brought Alexander?

JS Yes, I'm pretty sure he did. And he gathered all these Germans that were trying to figure out the best scientific methodology through which to design architecture.

ML A very strong group of students came up during Cobb's chairmanship, as well as during Rafael Moneo's subsequent chairmanship. I get the impression that during Harry's time, there was a greater diversity of positions, whereas during Moneo's everything seemed more ... not homogenous, but certainly more specific in sensibility. There was a big Spanish presence, but also many young practices like Herzog & de Meuron or Eduardo Souto de Moura. That said, Moneo also brought some of what was happening in California to the GSD, like Morphosis or Frank Israel. There was an ethos of the GSD as a crossroads of the world. I remember Jacques [Herzog] and Pierre [de Meuron] said they became friends with Eduardo not in Europe but rather through their teaching at the GSD. And I think this is something that continues with Mack Scogin's chair later on.

JS Moneo delivered the internationalism that McCue was after and a fresh and powerful one at that. There was zero modernist nostalgia, which the GSD was prone to when I arrived. He cemented the connection with Europe that had begun with Gropius but completely *aggiornata!* Moneo was young, not yet as big an architect as he became, but he had made connections everywhere and really knew *everything* that was being built by architects across the world at that time. The department under Moneo was definitely more monolithic, not so much because of who he brought in, but because he had a clearer, more rigorous vision about pedagogy. He gave substance, depth, and breadth to the program. This is really what he adds to the changes made by McCue and Cobb.

Then it's also true that Moneo only invited people that he thought were truly good architects, in the conservative sense of what that means. And to that point, there is no one I know that is better than him at spotting talent in young people. When Jacques and Pierre came here, they were kids of sorts. All they had to show was basically the Stone House in northern Italy—which was a knockout—and look at what they've become! I now see Moneo as the chair that really inaugurated a new era for the school, which each subsequent chair then made his or her own contributions to, whether it was Mack Scogin, myself, Toshiko Mori, or Scott Cohen.

3. Schools of Thought and Common Projects

ML I want to know more about what was happening in the larger academic context across the country in the mid-'70s, during McCue's early years at the GSD. I've read your earlier account on Cornell and the falling out between Colin Rowe and Oswald Mathias Ungers, but what about other schools?[16] You have César Pelli at Yale and James Stewart Polshek at Columbia, right? It seems like the rest of East Coast schools were under the helm of corporate figures like Cobb and McCue.

JS Correct, but they were an interesting subcategory of corporate, because they were genuinely interested in academic development. The only schools that had a different kind of leadership were Cooper Union—with John Hedjuk—and RISD, both of which offered professional undergraduate degrees. I think something ought to be said about RISD, because it tends to get sidelined, but the school had a big impact on American pedagogy. The generation of architects produced by the school during this period is incredible. It's impressive how many deans in the last decade can be traced back to those RISD days.

RISD began to boil while Harvard was still dealing with the Sert aftermath. After his arrival, Rodolfo quickly became chair of the architecture department in 1978. He was probably the youngest chairman ever, and not having a big research university behind him gave him a broad ability to make changes. He was able to bring in a much broader range of visitors than if he had been at a research university. Being in a position to compare how the GSD and RISD embarked on a process of intense change, I was able to see what the institutional differences allowed its leaders to do. I've always said the GSD is like a battleship. It doesn't sink, it certainly has the power to stay on its course, and it has an important impact. But the GSD is much harder to steer in a new direction. At RISD, as an arts and design school, there was much more space to experiment with pedagogy.

As an unintended but inevitable consequence of having Rodolfo at RISD and myself at the GSD, there was a lot of back-and-forth between the schools. A de facto sharing of resources came with this. For instance, at Harvard it was hard to get visiting critics to come teach because of the slowness and complexity of administrative procedures related to residence requirements. There was a lot of interest, but teaching required you to commit to stay all semester. So a lot of people actually started coming because they got two invitations that made the offer more palatable: one from the GSD and one from RISD. However, this was not a coordinated policy; it was more opportunistic than planned, since we were inevitably knowledgeable of what was going on in each school. But it created an exchange that both schools benefited from in different ways and made the local architectural scene much more vibrant.

ML RISD is part of a history of smaller avant-garde schools—like Cooper Union, SCI-Arc, or the AA—that were outsiders but eventually moved to the center of larger schools. You could even say that Gropius importing the pedagogy of the Bauhaus to Harvard started this trend.

You've critiqued the various iterations of the avant-garde as a movement and its retreat into academia. While I am sympathetic to the necessity of an avant-garde at various moments in history, it is contingent upon the specific context that gives rise to it. And this means it needs to have an expiration date. It shouldn't continue perpetually. Once an avant-garde approach has done its job, it should go away. When it doesn't, we start to get into perpetual revolutions which ultimately do not achieve anything.

I think these models from small, experimental schools always had contentious relationships with the larger research universities that they migrated to. Their precepts were either watered down or found themselves in a fight against the platform that supported them. For me there is a key difference between avant-garde or marginal models that grow into becoming established institutions versus those that try to graft themselves onto existing ones.

JS Yes! Although I always feel that aligning with the marginal is better than with the avant-garde. The main problem here is that architects have not yet historicized the avant-garde. This is because for the most part, they don't know any history! Historians and critics have already positioned the avant-garde as an episodic movement of the past. As you said, the avant-garde attitude has an expiration date, and we cannot continue to make it a program of life anymore. While the actual onset of the demise of the avant-garde can be detected in the postwar period, for practical and symbolic reasons let's agree on a date: more or less when the Soviet Union and its empire collapsed in the 1990s. Finito! Kaput!

The failure of the avant-garde is not in its left-leaning tendencies, by the way. It's in the fact that it presupposes a very specific approach toward history that is coherent only with a moment in time and does not admit continuity. There was an urge to produce a change that was shared by a majority, and it was incompatible with the continuity of history. This makes sense if we think of the great drama, urgency, and tragedy that existed for everyone to see during the First and Second World Wars. The violence promoted a "suspension of belief" in history, in the processes that had brought us to that point.

However, this is evidently not an attitude or a demeanor that can be continuous. It particularly cannot be developed in slow-moving academies on semesterly schedules year after year! Already in the American architectural scene of the early '60s, the avant-garde approach had become totally unproductive. As we know today, very few architects emerged from this period with work that had a lasting contribution, because what drove them was something that had already run its course. I think what made schools like RISD, Cooper Union, and Pratt relevant, though, was the fact that they came from a different institutional tradition than the Anglo-Saxon research university. They were all trade schools and, in that sense, better equipped to deal with the relationships between art, architecture, and society, which continue to be so problematic at places like Harvard.

ML They're closer to the German academic tradition in which architecture departments reside either in technical schools, like ETH Zürich, or in art schools, like the Akademie der Künste.

JS Exactly. European countries also have the polytechnic model, which works pretty well in places like Spain and Italy. This is also true in much of Latin America. My school in Buenos Aires belonged to that lineage.

NDA Each of these schools—whether a trade school, an art school, or a research university—seems to have had a distinct architectural ecosystem. With a few notable exceptions, the ideological stances of schools today seem much less pronounced.

JS More so than today, schools coalesced around a shared set of values that were represented in their leaders. We could say that under Sert there was such a thing as "the Harvard School"; under Hedjuk, "the Cooper School"; and under Colin Rowe, "the Cornell School." Nowadays we don't really have that.

Due to conditions beyond architecture, we have shifted toward a desire for diversity of positions and perspectives within any one institution. There is no discussion that this political intention is good and desirable. However, this approach to the pedagogy of a cultural practice requires a profound, previously acquired understanding of the dynamics of that practice's philosophical, discursive and operative mechanisms. It also requires knowledge of how these are founded on sociocultural habits, conventions, and deep-rooted aspirations, as well as the means by which such deep structures can be altered or transformed. We seem to have jumped over all this process, and have instead assumed that we have a well formed, solid practice of design. This has led us to approach issues directly at their operative level, simply transferring our individual political and ideological interpretations to the process of design. As if this, magically, would then carry over into the larger practice of design, transmitting and realizing all our good intentions.

This is static and dogmatic. It is, sadly, naive as well. More importantly, it fails to address the inherent tensions that exist between diversity, personal freedom, and equality, which emerge when we put them all to work together. These are tensions that should not be appeased, in my view, but rather fed and exploited to the benefit of the practice itself. The pulse of these tensions could change the constitutive apparatus of the practice of design at the proper depth. This is the way architecture changes, which is what we learn from its history.

A cultural practice like architecture depends a lot on shared values. It requires a minimum of consensus on how we understand reality—how we interpret what is going on, how a material practice works—so that we can manifest a vision in space, form, and figure.

ML Rafael Moneo also lamented the loss of a shared project among architects. He talked about how, during the interwar years, architects around the world were united by the project of modernism. There was a clear and direct isomorphism between modernism and what was happening in the world that made everyone coalesce around its vision. I think today everything is more about individualistic directions, and this makes sense if we go back to the parallels we were drawing between Moneo's and Cobb's years at the GSD.

Today I see schools less as vehicles to reinforce one single position and more as places to evaluate multiple positions through discussions with people from different backgrounds, geographies, and so forth. They are places where knowledge is not just transferred but also produced.

JS I think we need to treat these questions with a lot of care today. It is time to begin looking again for some sort of internally consistent architectural values that give institutions an identity and to start to produce true diversity *in between* schools of thought. We now know that without enough internal coherence, you cannot advance anything—certainly not a curriculum or a pedagogic vision.

NDA Everything becomes simply a daily exercise in tolerance.

JS That's a wonderful way to put it! A big myth that reigns today is that when a school has a clear position, with a coherent system of beliefs and shared sociocultural values, and subscribes to a set of formal principles—this means it is indoctrinating. I can say from experience that when this was more the norm, as it was in my student days in Argentina, we were not indoctrinated or forced into anything! Instead, we learned in a serious and methodical way how to consistently produce good architecture. From there, we each went on to develop our own way of doing architecture. All the students that did Hedjuk's nine-square-grid program had their own distinct evolution. There are a lot of great architects that came out of that school and are doing novel, personal, and distinctive work today. Think of Tod Williams, Billie Tsien, Elizabeth Diller, or Toshiko Mori.

There is this fear in the air that if you commit to spending some time working in the atelier of an experienced artist, then this will kill your creativity and suppress your identity. But maybe it's because we forget Picasso learned to draw the human body from Roman statues. Or that Le Corbusier had a canonical Beaux-Arts education. I don't think the problem is where we've been poking around for the last decade. There is a difference between being dogmatized and entering a contract between teachers and students for a couple of years in which a set of principles will be consistently delivered. We cannot judge the quality of what a person has done if we have no fundamental base against which to measure it.

I am not advocating for a return to the past. History doesn't repeat itself. But we may benefit from measuring our approach against more traditional teaching models and from evaluating their successes and failures.

ML This idea of the common project in academia is also about a common history. During the digital boom twenty years ago, there was an obsession around the "project of the new." I remember having a discussion back then with a young architect on his work, which had been designed with the latest digital tools. I suggested that it would be interesting to look at the parallels between his work and that of Erich Mendelsohn or Pier Luigi Nervi, which shared similar sensibilities. But I was surprised to find that he felt insulted by my suggestion, because he thought I was accusing him of being unoriginal. This blew my mind completely.

I think having a shared history, and being able to agree whether one is working from or against it, is part of that common ground you're describing.

JS If you talk to Moneo nowadays, he is no longer interested in these debates. Not because they are wrong or overly politicized. There is just no reference that we can agree upon from which to build up a conversation. We come up with the cultural references that support the ideas we already have and that we want architecture to move toward.

When I wrote "Representation and Creativity in Architecture: The Pregnant Moment," the article really clarified for me that architecture comes from architecture.[17] It sounds a bit tautological, but works of architecture acquire meaning by virtue of other architectures, whether by allusion, opposition, imitation, or absence. And this is necessarily selective. When we design something, we choose to "belong" to some architectures and not others. At a historical scale, this process of selection is then what we call the Western canon; a loose, ever-changing set of buildings that we can collectively agree represent us at a given moment.

NDA Something similar could be said of smaller intellectual and cultural traditions, say that of a school of thought or an institution.

JS Today you could contest that. You could choose not to identify with a prevalent cultural tradition or refuse to reform it. This is the whole discussion we are having. But you are not really escaping the core human need for something of the sort, for a cultural consensus that allows forms to acquire a shared meaning. Only then do you have a language with which to express yourself, with which to peacefully disagree with others. I am of the position that you cannot escape the culture you are part of, even if you belong to a marginalized sector of it. You can only reshape it by speaking its own language and layer new strains onto it.

NDA Many discussions lately feel like they aren't discussions at all. Everybody has already decided what they think and what they are going to do before they sit down to talk. The conversations become political lip service from opposing parties that are mainly at the same table out of brutally pragmatic interests, like carrying around an Ivy League badge. This is the only thing that makes them treat each other with a minimum of manners.

I had a wonderful experience at the GSD as a student because the diversity of approaches truly expanded the horizons of my thinking; it allowed me to measure the strengths and weaknesses of all the positions out there. But for me it was useful because it was a post-professional degree. I was already coming from somewhere very specific. I always wondered how one could get any fundamentals across to someone new to architecture in such a chaotic intellectual environment. It's really hard to get away with statements like "This is how you draw a floor plan" on the trays right now.

In a way this conversation has made me think that if with Sert there was a "you like it or you hate it" pedagogical model, then McCue begins this diversification, the opening up of positions. And it seems to me like this somehow continuously expands through Cobb, Moneo, Scogin, yourself, and even Toshiko Mori being chair. I think today we find ourselves at a moment in which the tension between the two poles—delivering fundamentals and fostering debate—have become quite high, perhaps at the expense of the former.

ML I think this goes back to the discussion about research universities versus vocational schools. One responsibility of a school is to train someone to serve the profession. The other is to create a place for discourse and research that could benefit the profession in a different way. The school tries to feed the profession from the top and bottom at the same time. I think an understanding that both of these need to exist is essential. Certainly there are moments in history when the best work is done in the field and others when the best work is done in academia. This is a back-and-forth that has to do with the times. So understanding what the times are is important in striking this balance.

JS That's true. I remember that in the '80s every single big office came from New York or Chicago to look for students at the school, and the GSD organized two-day job fairs that occupied the ground floor of Gund Hall with small tables, and reps from major American offices were looking to interview and hire! Many times they would make them offers to drop out of graduate school and go straight to work for them. This was because the university was producing things of interest to practice but also because of economic cycles and how that determined what the profession needed from us as a school.

ML I feel that some of the discussions we had earlier about the IAUS and the generation that came after it have to do with this issue of a balance between the two poles. The discourse becomes disconnected from the practice. And that is a problem.

JS The new theory that emerged around that time, in the early '70s, was pushed forward by a cohort of architects that were all interested in practice. Even if we were teaching, lecturing, and writing papers, what we wanted most was to design buildings. This changed. We were trying to explain how architecture worked with "the project" in mind and thinking about the production of architecture. The discussion was made up of people like Michael Graves or Fred Koetter, and certainly Rodolfo and me; all people committed to practice. Even Eisenman, who was at the forefront of all of this, held a practice and was committed to showing his theoretical project as such, at least at the beginning. I must confess that the way he was approaching practice was not convincing as a model. However, he was using drawings as the main research tool in a truly experimental way that intelligently engaged the discussion about how architecture works. He managed to build a few real buildings, a process that always teaches you something about architecture, even if that something is what not to do within your line of experimentation.

ML I can see some parallels. I mean, if you look at Gropius's generation, they were all trained in a traditional way, and they wanted to get rid of history. Fast-forward fifty years to Bernard Tschumi's generation, and they are also trained within a tradition, and they want to reinvent everything. There is a sort of cyclicity between generations of architects trained with a strong focus on fundamentals and the need to go beyond them and the architects trained by this cohort with more interest in the boundaries of architecture than the fundamentals themselves.

I don't think that a lot of people in architecture schools really care about buildings today. They are interested but in their own way.

JS I agree with you. Unfortunately some people are not interested, because they never had the opportunity to deal with making buildings. I think if they had practiced a few years, this would be different. Or if schools would invest more in the development of pedagogical models that deal with the well-understood process of designing and producing buildings. They were never exposed to a set of design fundamentals that can be extracted from the conventions around which a culture is structured at a given moment.

But part of the reason why there is a lack of fundamentals in core programs nowadays comes from the fact that nobody can agree on them. For many people, fundamentals shouldn't even exist. I wish them good luck with that!

ML The Swiss are especially obsessed with strong fundamentals, to the degree that it becomes suffocating. From a place like ETH Zürich, you come to appreciate the United States, because things can get a bit moralistic and risk becoming essentialist at some point. I think exposure to different cultures and mindsets is always important.

JS Just to be clear, I am not promoting "suffocating" or "moralistic" fundamentals. I am referring mostly to what we would call nowadays techniques of design. Those tools that allow us to communicate directly through architecture about basic performative aspects of architectural forms. But by the way, schools in the United States have in fact become "moralistic" in the recent past. However, their moralism is based more on factors external to architecture. It is much more about social and ideological issues, which creates very confusing and unproductive conversations for students, I would say.

ML Jorge, what you said about traditional teaching reminded me of Martha Graham Dance Company. She focused on modern dance but insisted on recruiting classically trained dancers; classical training was a prerequisite for modernity.

I think the question of how a school instills a position is also a question of when the position is instilled in the curriculum. I have seen many schools during moments of transition, when they need to put in place a position or identity very quickly, and they tend to frontload this into the first semester as an indoctrination. I much prefer models that do not privilege positions over fundamentals. I think the core studios can be seen as a way of instilling fundamentals, and the more ideological or experimental aspects can be sharpened and tested at the level of the option studios, when students have had the chance to develop criteria with which to evaluate a novel proposition.

JS As someone who has spent his life teaching at the graduate level, I think that an undergraduate degree in architecture works better as a first professional degree. Graduate students entering the MArch I, especially the ones we get at Harvard, who are particularly brilliant, have this immediate urge to *express* themselves as *individuals*, to be critical. But most do not know what to be critical about *within architecture* yet, so they are critical *of it* from a humanistic, technical, political, or general cultural perspective.

I remember a lot of discussions in the core with students who were not interested in doing the "basic" exercises we assigned, even though they had no training in architecture whatsoever. This led to a very elaborate discussion built on very shaky ground. People come to graduate school with certain expectations about what they will be able to produce from the start, but the truth is that at the graduate level we still have to deal with very basic principles when you arrive into the core program.

I don't think we can—nor should—deal with problems of self-expression in the core. If it is indeed "the core" of a discipline, then there is no place for individual expression and "feelings" as the focus of the work. To put it another way, even though personal expressions and emotion inevitably show up somehow in anything that an individual produces, when they do appear in the core, they should not be the focus of discussion. They should be peripheral. We come back to language: if you can't speak it, you cannot express your truest self to others. I don't think there is anything inherently problematic about this. In the end, it's a pretty practical problem.

ML This reminds me of an old adage: You ask undergraduate students to jump, and they say, "How high?" You ask graduate students to jump, and they say, "Why?"

There is a very different mentality and mindset.

4. Architecture in the Research University

NDA I think that a big part of what we have been discussing so far is related to the fact that a lot of faculty are not interested in teaching fundamentals and the system doesn't particularly incentivize them to. It seems to me that the junior faculty that rise are those who put their energy into producing more "advanced" contributions, if not also fatuous and irrelevant ones, to the intellectual ecosystem of the school, and not those who are concerned with being good teachers.

JS Yes, but this is not a problem exclusive to the GSD. Research universities require a certain type of research output from young faculty so they can move up the ladder. Broadly speaking, design is not considered to be in the research category. This may vary of course, depending on the understanding of design between those at the helm of the architecture school and the university.

Here, again, I have to bring in Jerry McCue and Harry Cobb, since they made contributions to this particular aspect of higher-education politics. They fiercely argued with the university, which at the time was led by Derek Bok, a lawyer with great management skills, and persuaded his administration about what a unique contribution architects are to the university as a whole. They made them see how technical, artistic, social, and cultural questions resided in creative design work.

More than a policy, this created an understanding between the school and the university, which was then advanced and truly well-managed by the following administrative team: President Neil Rudenstine, an English Renaissance literature scholar, and Dean Peter Rowe, an architect and urban designer. This progress was, however, set back by later interpretations during the short-lived, unfortunate presidency of Larry Summers, a brilliant economist, and Dean Alan Altshuler, a distinguished transportation planner. It is unclear where the consensus has stood during the current and preceding administration, because there have been very few cases of promotion to tenure of internal architecture design faculty since.

ML Oftentimes what you give to the school is not what the school values. No matter how well-intentioned the individuals are, when they come together as an institution, the incentive system makes it so that the institution focuses on taking care of its own interests. The institution elevates you for what additive value you bring to it, not necessarily for the service you provide.

JS Indeed! Let's also not lie to ourselves. What defines the excellence of universities like Harvard or MIT is research, not teaching. We are very interested in and committed to teaching at the GSD, but in these big universities, it's really secondary. To complicate things even more, in our school the trend in the last two decades has been to have fewer and fewer senior faculty involved in the core program. This responsibility is left to younger faculty.

As anyone with experience will agree, teaching the core program is a much more demanding and involved activity than teaching advanced courses. Then, on top of that service that is left to junior faculty, the university expects and demands all this research output to merit promotion. All of this makes it very challenging for junior faculty to practice and become the seasoned designers we want teaching our students. If we add how the profession has evolved in this country and how intensive running a practice has become ... Let's just say it's not an easy track to embark on nowadays.

ML I think this question also comes from comparing the situation to the old-world model, in which one first became a successful architect in a city and received a professorship afterward as a form of recognition. There was a direct correspondence between the values of academia and practice.

JS Yes, it's more typical in Europe, or even South America, for recognized practitioners to be actively sought after by schools and to have a chair at a university. When I was in school in Buenos Aires, I could not conceive of having professors that did not practice. *All my teachers had practices*, and their practices and their buildings were intrinsically an important part of the life of the school. In these systems, faculty generally do not have the salaries that are comparable with American universities, but on the other hand they have these real practices, big or small, that make up for it. This allows them to be accessible to schools with limited funding.

NDA Of course, this is the opposite of what we see in the United States now, where many architects that want to develop an interesting practice decide to teach with the assumption that it will help them achieve that goal.

JS Yes, that is what makes young, talented, and motivated designers think that they may be able to create a distinctive practice by working full-time at the university, supporting their outside work with the salaries. I think this is a fantasy, because the demands of the university do not leave room to really develop a practice, even if it pays decently.

ML In a way, Jorge, you are the end of a certain generation.

JS Yes, I would say that too.

ML The model of being an equally recognized professor and practitioner is something I don't think happens again after you. At least not in the way we know it.

JS Perhaps, and it's sad because I get a lot of students who come to me and say, "I want to do what you did." As much as I want to encourage them, I don't really think it's possible, so there is no advice I can give that might help produce that model. I'm not even sure how we did it, although I can see how many things converged to allow it. Today, this is not a problem of talent nor strength. Both the demands of the university and of practice have escalated, and I think this is the most valid and simple explanation. I've seen the modest stack of drawings that was needed to build Gund Hall. Today you may need as many drawings, spec books, consultants, and insurances just to renovate a kitchen!

ML You've talked about the '70s and how commissions came to you because of your affiliations with the university. You didn't have to go out looking for work.

JS No, we were able to develop our practice in spite of being affiliated with a university! Though what did help was that we spoke the same language as cultural institutions, which facilitated getting work from them. We knew the language and had shared interests with that world. We had little luck with commercial work, on the other hand. They tend not to trust architects who do not fit their idea of what a "full-time professional" is. Developers said, "Why are you wasting your time over there at the university? You should be doing more work for us." Some thought we were not serious because we were affiliated with the university!

This brings us back to the difference between research universities and polytechnics. In the polytechnic model, teachers are there *because* they are presumed to be talented practitioners and thinkers, not necessarily outstanding scholars or scientists. In addition, being an architect *and* a professor at a European university carries a certain cachet, a certain added prestige and value, which is almost the opposite in the US.

All the years that I worked as an architect in Italy, nobody ever referred to me as an architect. In Italy, people always use your titles to address you—doctor, lawyer—unless you are a professor. In my case, instead of calling me *architetto*, they always called me *professore*, even clients that we had paid commissions with.

ML The exchange rate between academic and professional respect is very direct in those environments. During my first teaching job in Europe, people came to me because I was in academia. When I came back to the US, I had to prove to people I knew how to build *despite* being related to the university. Being a professor actually cast more doubt on my ability than it confirmed.

These two worlds are moving further and further apart from one another, which is troubling. I often think that among twentieth-century models, this drift between academia and the profession in the American model is critical. One has to deal with the professionalization of the academic field, as we discussed earlier, with the stringent evaluation models and demand for more quantifiable achievements. This puts the discipline of architecture in a context in which its less measurable qualities, especially what it is expected to contribute to society, are undermined.

JS More than twentieth-century models, I think this comes from the Anglo-Saxon conception of the university. I don't have too much experience with British academia, but it seems more similar to the American one. During my visits to Cambridge, it didn't seem there were as many practitioners involved as in, say, Milan, Rome, Zurich, Tokyo, or Madrid. When Harry Cobb stepped down from the chairmanship of the GSD in 1985, the extraordinary Gropius Lecture he delivered was all about the importance and uniqueness of what architecture departments were doing inside American research universities. It was an extraordinary lesson for the university. This question is as relevant today as it was back then.

I think people commonly misconstrue the differences between scholarly and professional disciplines and, subsequently, the role that research plays in either one. In the case of the philosopher, the historian, or the scientist, the core outcome of their work is scholarship itself. Whereas for the doctor or the architect, the outcome is much more mundane or practical. Those disciplines are grounded in the sciences and humanities and have their own theoretical problems, but these are all means to their ultimate end. In the case of architecture, while theory, speculation, and scholarship are indispensable to practice during an educational process, it is the design of buildings and cities that matters the most. This means that it can never be evaluated with the same metrics used in the sciences or the humanities.

The structure of Harvard schools is a clear example of this, when compared with other universities. At Harvard, professional schools are entities with a high degree of autonomy, and each is run like a small college. Unlike other schools of architecture in the United States, the GSD does its own admissions, fundraising, administration, and so on.

I suppose this institutional body of a college plus a series of autonomous graduate schools, which is by now quite old, came from the understanding that what professional disciplines do is different from the scholarship that happens at Harvard College. The college is where a foundational liberal-arts education is delivered to undergraduates, but it's also where PhDs in those corresponding fields are pursued. Pure scholarship and sciences are centralized within it.

The professional schools then organize themselves according to their own specific aims. But given that their mandate is not just to educate professionals but also to advance the fields themselves, the question remains: what should we consider as research in these disciplines?

In the case of architecture, the answer to this question is always complicated because of its dual relationship with the building sciences and technology on one side and culture, society, and ideology on the other. I've seen six presidents come and go, and, with the exception of Neil Rudenstine, when they arrive they all immediately ask, "What are you all doing in the design school? Where are your books and scholarly papers? Where is the real research?"

ML This is the eternal question that our discipline will be asked in a research university.

JS It's very hard to judge what we call "design" by conventional academic standards, because it's not an objective scientific product. The studio teaching and inquiry method is something completely incomprehensible as an academic activity for university bureaucrats and other academicians. However, as the world has become more complex, there's been interest from other professional schools at the university about the way we teach and design architecture. Even the business school discovered not long ago that we were doing something right in terms of a method through which to tackle problems with a great degree of complexity. It came, understandably, when they discovered the value of "good design" in business and began to scrutinize what makes a design good. They found themselves talking to industrial, fashion, graphic, and architectural designers, and they saw that designers, particularly architects, take on complicated challenges. They are usually "defined" by poor or incomplete data, heterogeneous constraints, and often contradictory demands with the expectation to produce a cohesive and synthetic solution. Compare that to the way, say, an economist usually opens a paper outlining up-front dozens of assumptions that peel away all the complexity of reality so a theoretical outcome can be credibly realized.

That said, architectural inquiry remains too messy of an affair for the university to understand how to evaluate the production of the school, develop strict hiring policies, and give merits to its members. The idea that you can do research through design remains hard to grasp.

NDA I'm always impressed by the roster of people that you brought to the GSD or helped promote to tenure during your chairmanship between 1995 and 2002. People like Antoine Picon, Alejandro Aravena, Preston Scott Cohen, Mónica Ponce de León, Sarah M. Whiting, and Nader Tehrani. Based on the challenges you described about evaluating the merit of architects in academia, what priorities drove *your* decisions in that position? What long-term impacts do you think this has had on the school?

JS I can answer this question, but it takes me back to some larger issues about how the school works. First, the GSD is a school where chairs have historically held a considerable amount of academic power. This changed over the last decade, and most decisional power went to the office of the dean. Before that, it was the chairs who had a much stronger voice in faculty appointments. Administratively the system has not really changed, and in the end it was and still is the senior faculty who approve major decisions regarding faculty appointments and promotions. But let's say that, somehow, "once upon a time," the voice of the chairs was uttered with more volume and was heard more attentively by the senior faculty than it is now.

It was expected that you were responsive to objections from the dean, but this rarely happened. Decisions about departmental chairs were thus very careful and deliberate, at least since I have been at the school. I think this system worked quite well given the diversity of disciplines and degrees offered at the GSD.

This decisional power of the chairmanship also translated to something even more important: the tenure process. I say this because in the end, it is the tenured faculty who can really change schools. Junior faculty are not the ones who get to make decisions about the direction the school takes. It is, quite simply, an issue of power. In that sense, what had a lasting impact for the GSD was not the faculty I invited to teach. It's the people I advocated strongly in favor of, and occasionally against, in the tenure process.

The tenure process is a delicate issue, especially today. The way this works at Harvard and most American research universities is a much-discussed topic, and I am not really certain of what direction it is going. But it looks as though it is about to change, perhaps drastically. Whatever way it changes, it is going to define a new higher-education system for the United States.

NDA What are your concerns?

JS The tenure process is not perfect, and I am well aware of that. It is not always fair. This is particularly true in a field like architecture, due to the issues we have discussed regarding qualitative evaluations according to pre-established standards.

That said, the rigor with which the tenure process still proceeds is rather respectable and stringent. The university that I have known throughout my life and all that is good about it has to do with the tenure system, with carefully and slowly evaluating faculty with very high standards of measure and then giving them the freedom within the grounds of the university to express and articulate their beliefs and ideas in their teaching and research. This is a system that supports an intellectual's pursuits independently of what the marketplace or public opinion wants at any one moment in time. It allows them to pursue what should be important projects, the implications of which go beyond the immediate and which are thus hard to develop under alternative conditions, say, in a professional environment.

That said, these privileges of the tenure system at research universities are precisely what makes them unable to rapidly change in the face of emergent social or political priorities that they are inevitably a part of. This is much of what is being debated currently: how to change the tenure process so it is more accommodating of social demands in the present. But, to what extent should changing social and cultural demands produce changes within the university? How do universities decide what to change in view of a new context? At present it seems to me that these questions are not being asked because, for some reason, just the demand for change from students and the outside world seem to suffice as justification to make changes.

I don't have a solution for the issue of what should happen to tenureship. I can't say that I agree with the way it is being handled. But I do think universities are one of the institutions in this country that remain exceptional at a global level. To be extreme, I believe they are probably the only American institution that still has no match at an international scale. And the system of tenure has something to do with this.

I have a feeling the changes will be for the worse. At the same time, the university has never been a static institution, and in that sense change is expected. It will be what we want it to be right now. Time will tell the impact this will have on research, scholarship, and innovation. If we happen to have erred in our judgment, those contributions will shift over into the hands of a different kind of institution. This is the way culture works. Who knows, architecture might find itself flourishing in new types of trade or technical schools again.

NDA I think something that everyone agrees on is how volatile public opinion is right now. Every event asks you to stand on one side of a line or another. What we pay attention to also shifts very quickly, if we take a long view. Today we are alarmed by one issue and want all the institutions in our society to address it, and tomorrow it's the next issue. We all feel a degree of discontent with the status quo. Trust in institutions in the United States is at an all-time low. As we've discussed on other occasions, we have also become pretty good at activism, at mobilizing support and developing leverage to challenge structures of power.

I was wondering as you reflected on the tenure system, what are the institutions that we don't want to change as we try to change everything else? In any reform or improvement process, we pick out the most critical issues that we want to improve and decide what we want to leave as it is so that the machine does not fall apart. When we shake everything at once, we tend to end up with everything falling to the ground. At least that is my personal experience. It's only worthwhile if we fundamentally believe there is nothing worth saving.

JS I could buy that metaphor! Yes, everything is being shaken up at once. Your image is an accurate description of what I saw happening during my last years before retirement throughout the field of higher education, Harvard included. The environment has been destroyed, and I'm tempted to add that it has become destructive! Faculty are scared to speak their minds. Language is controlled and censored. Individuals are judged before the facts are studied.

It may sound extreme and exaggerated, but frankly, it isn't. You just have to look at the situation closely to see it. I have always avoided the word "crisis" to discuss difficult situations in academia, but today it is probably an adequate term.

The amount of problems and controversies that have piled up and are being handled concurrently has never been seen before: from the outrageous cost of education to the pursuit of diversity, the control of language, and the myriad of hot political, social, and cultural issues on the table. And I don't see any sort of organized agenda through which these issues are being discussed academically. I see a haphazard implementation of policies through highly predetermined processes that reveal a questionable understanding of how culture and society work. I am not trying to say that the issues of concern are wrong. However, the way they are being handled, weaving political links to fuse them all into a monolith, makes them an impenetrable mass that cannot be dealt with through a dispassionate, measured, and intelligent discussion.

Not surprisingly, never in the history of higher education has there been such a large turnaround of university administrators.[18] The staggering and unusual number of current vacancies in university presidencies is a clear indication of some trouble. The monster has become unwieldy, not at the level of conventional managerial issues but rather at the purely ideological and political level. It is sad, and from my South American perspective, I am inevitably reminded of experiences that go to show how damaging this type of political climate is to the institution of the university.

Notes

1 *The Heart of the City: Towards the Humanisation of Urban Life*, ed. J. Tyrwhitt, J. L. Sert, and E. N. Rogers (London: Lund, Humphries, 1952).
2 Fumihiko Maki, "Grounded Visionaries: The Harvard Campaign for the GSD," posted December 19, 2014, by Harvard GSD, YouTube, https://www.youtube.com/watch?v=qw3RYNQCXdo.
3 Ada Louise Huxtable, "New Harvard Hall: Drama and Questions," *The New York Times*, November 8, 1972, 52.
4 See Charles E. Shepard, "Kilbridge Won't Go Away," *The Harvard Crimson*, March 13, 1976, https://www.thecrimson.com/article/1976/3/13/kilbridge-wont-go-away-pmaurice-d/.
See also Charles E. Shepard, "Not Simply Another Release," *The Harvard Crimson*, April 17, 1976, https://www.thecrimson.com/article/1976/4/17/not-simply-another-release-pthe-news/.
5 Alison Smithson and Team 10, *Team 10 Primer* (Cambridge, MA: MIT Press, 1968).
6 For more, refer to Jorge Silvetti and Erika Naginski, "Architecture: The Reconception of History", in this volume, 215–271.
7 Rodolfo Machado joined RISD in 1976 and remained until 1986. He was head of its Department of Architecture from 1978 until 1986.
8 Among them: Kenneth Frampton, Tony Vidler, and Mario Gandelsonas.
9 Colin Rowe, "The Mathematics of the Ideal Villa," in *The Mathematics of the Ideal Villa, and Other Essays* (Cambridge, MA: MIT Press, 1976).
10 Colin Rowe, "Mannerism and Modern Architecture," in *The Mathematics of the Ideal Villa, and Other Essays* (Cambridge, MA: MIT Press, 1976).
11 Colin Rowe and Robert Slutzky, "Transparency: Literal and Phenomenal," in *The Mathematics of the Ideal Villa, and Other Essays* (Cambridge, MA: MIT Press, 1976). Colin Rowe, introduction to *Five Architects: Eisenman, Graves, Gwathmey, Hejduk, Meier* (New York, NY: Oxford University Press, 1975).
12 See Jorge Silvetti and Alfredo Thiermann, "Architecture: The Question of Method," in this volume, 49–96.
13 Colin Rowe and Fred Koetter, *Collage City* (Cambridge, CA: MIT Press, 1978).
14 See Silvetti and Naginski, "Architecture: The Reconception of History".
15 For more, refer to Silvetti and Thiermann, "Architecture: The Question of Method".
16 See Silvetti and Thiermann, "Architecture: The Question of Method".
17 Jorge Silvetti, "Representation and Creativity in Architecture: The Pregnant Moment," in *Representation and Architecture*, ed. Ömer Akin and Eleanor F. Weinel (Silver Spring, MD: Information Dynamics, Inc., 1982): 159–184.
18 When this conversation took place in 2022, there were eleven university presidencies in Massachusetts alone that were vacant or near vacancy. This trend was also reflected across Ivy League schools. See: Kate Selig, "With a Large Number of College Presidents Stepping Down, Vacancies May Open Door for More Diverse Leaders," *The Boston Globe*, July 6, 2022, https://www.bostonglobe.com/2022/07/05/metro/with-large-number-college-presidents-stepping-down-it-could-be-perfect-time-diversify/.

1

2

On Realism in Architecture

JORGE SILVETTI, 1978

The aim of this paper is to contribute to current discussions concerning the characterization of the present state of architecture. It also attempts to dispel some misconceptions about a term which has pervaded current literature: *Post-Modernism*. Post-Modernism announces itself as a beginning, a recuperation, or an end, depending on the emphasis or the persuasion of the critic, and establishes itself always as an antithesis or an opposite to Modern Architecture. It also assumes that it characterizes the present moment, and that as an historical event, it has no precedent. Antithetical positions such as those of Robert Venturi and Aldo Rossi are used as examples of Post-Modernism.[1] If it is true that the present is rich in positions, that there are proposals that displace or remove many of the notions and concepts that had been firmly installed by Modern Architecture, it is also possible to see the present moment as the logical result of tendencies and lines of thought that possess a long, rich, and suggestive pedigree.

What will be suggested here through a specific analysis is a general theoretical proposition which contends that the elements that comprise a historical period (its ideology, its theories, its icons, its forms and images) do not move, change or evolve with the same velocity—that while images might persist, the ideas which originally supported those images might have been replaced; or, more importantly for our case, that figurative and formal changes do not correspond directly to ideological development. This proposition, which should be taken as a speculative hypothesis, can help us to criticize and refocus the all too easy, empiricist and immediate conclusion that sees in current tendencies a definite break from the immediate past. While indeed architecture may portray a new outward appearance, it might be more important to notice that its preoccupation with specific ideological effects is not new.

Criticism seems to deal with two necessary scales: the small and immediate, concerned with facts that are "new" and which are invariably presented as such, and the large, which allows one to see how, in the end, history is "short" and made up of a few ideas and principles which transform and recombine themselves in its course. It is important, I believe, to take this latter perspective and scale now, in an attempt to understand more lucidly where we are, from where we come, and where we might possibly move.

Such a task can be modelled or attacked from a variety of perspectives, each of which, as a result of the limitations of criticism, will always be partial. Here, no claim is made to the contrary. I propose to focus on the figurative characteristics of architecture as depicted by both Modern Architecture and contemporary movements, and in dealing with the latter,

3

4

I will restrict myself to what appears to me to be two paradigmatic cases in the development of contemporary ideas, those of Venturi and Rossi. The choice of the figurative level of architecture is not casual. It is through architectural facts as visual entities and the way in which they present themselves to our senses and minds, that I believe we enact one of the most important entries into the world of ideas and thought that lie hidden in them. When words fade away, when the *zeitgeist* disappears, there is always the ineffable fact of architecture that is reiterated as a visual, permanent reality and which is "read" by us.

Within this perspective I will restrict myself to a most salient fact of contemporary tendencies which in my view makes the figurative aspect of architecture an unavoidable issue for criticism today: the reappearance of the notions of *architectural type* and *architectural typology*. The recovery and use of such notions may be seen and evaluated with respect to such contemporary concepts in art criticism as *realism* and *verisimilitude*, and together I hope they will begin to clarify and differentiate the diverse manners in which typology is presented, the diversity of figurative devices employed, and finally the disparate theories that have resulted from typology. This will also serve to establish with some certainty what is new and what is not, and by so doing will assert the richness of Modern architectural thought, which still defies the many death sentences to which it has been condemned.

> PHAEDRUS: On that point, Socrates, I have heard one who is to be an orator does not need to know what is really just, but what would seem just to the multitude who are to pass judgement, and not what is really good or noble, but what will seem to be so: for they say persuasion comes from what seems to be true, not from the truth.
>
> Passage from Plato's *Phaedrus*

To begin with, we might note that in the course of architectural history, it is possible and necessary to insist that very few moments can be identified as moments of "pure invention," in which it is possible to point to a real "rupture" where ideological mutations have produced a genuine figurative revolution. Within the scope of this article it is necessary to insist that Modern Architecture produced such a thing. This fact, that for the present detractors of Modern Architecture constitutes its sin and for its advocates its most rich and fruitful quality, will not be evaluated here for its virtues or its villainy. We shall note it here as a fact of history, incontrovertible, and as such, extraordinary. In spite of "Post-Modernism," the emergence of Modern Architecture is an inescapable reference point; after it, architecture is not, and cannot be, thought of in the same way as before its appearance. From this viewpoint, and corroborating what Modern architects and their buildings said, it is necessary to state once again the fact that one of the most striking characteristics of Modern Architecture is its refusal to deal with the

5

Fig. 1 Raphael, *The Marriage of the Virgin*, 1504, Pinacoteca di Brera, Milan.
Fig. 2 Claude Monet, *Palazzo da Mula, Venice*, 1846, National Gallery of Art, Washington, DC, Chester Dale Collection.
Fig. 3 Rene Magritte, *La Reproduction Interdite* (Not to be Reproduced), 1937, Museum Boijmans Van Beuningen, Rotterdam, E. F. W. James Collection.
Fig. 4 Jackson Pollock, *Echo*, 1951, Museum of Modern Art, New York, NY, acquired through the Lille P. Bliss Bequest and the Mr. and Mrs. David Rockefeller Fund.
Fig. 5 John Salt, *Riviera 2*, 1969, OK Harris Gallery, New York, NY.

past as a figurative resource. We need to say little about this refusal since it is Modern Architecture's most commonly agreed-upon attribute, and both theoreticians and propagators of Modern Architecture have insisted upon such a figurative rupture.[2] What has not been discussed enough, however, is how it is possible to define conceptually such a rupture; that is, within a general history, how it is possible to describe and classify a figurative change of such importance, how to relate it with more general and perdurable ideas in the history of art, what relationships such change establishes with other conceptualizations, and what operations of meaning are involved.

To do this, we need to digress for a moment and to examine some fundamental problems that exist between art and knowledge, and reality and its representation. If art in general is a form of knowledge, then architecture does not escape a similar formulation. Art critics, anthropologists, and philosophers have discussed and elaborated profusely in this respect, and it is not my intention to review their assertions and dissentions. Rather, I would like to emphasize that such knowledge is different from scientific knowledge, and that as with any type of knowledge, its problem lies in its relations to "reality": how it interprets reality and explains it, and how it reflects reality in its work (we might say, more accurately, "represents" it in its work). Each building, each drawing, each writing carries a vision of reality; this ideological condition makes it a testimony to an interpretation of reality. The problem of reality and of the "real," this involvement with a "reality" that is unavoidable in art, has been and is one of the most crucial issues in all figurative art, and at the same time it is one of the most arduous problems to disentangle in art history, theory and criticism. For a layman attempting to discover what "realism" in art is, the task is difficult, painful, and at times confusing. Because even if at the beginning one finds a direct reference to an artistic movement specifically related to the literature and painting of mid-nineteenth century, one soon becomes aware that the more notions of realism and representation are investigated, the more critics and historians find them elusive; and thus, depending on the critic's lenses, not only is "impressionism" realist (it attempts to represent reality the way our senses perceive it), "abstract expressionism" realist (it attempts to investigate and represent the reality of painting itself), but also realist is the Renaissance (is not the attempt to represent reality scientifically through the mathematical laws of perspective a realist enterprise?), and certainly, surrealism, pop-art and contemporary super-realism can qualify (Figs. 1–5).

As early as 1921, Roman Jakobson had already warned us about the difficulties and multiple meanings that the notion of "realism" in art had, and the fatal consequences its misuse had for art criticism:

> Classicists, sentimentalists, the romanticists to a certain extent, even "realists" of the nineteenth century, the modernists to a large degree, and finally the

6

7

> futurists, expressionists, and their like have more than once steadfastly proclaimed faithfulness to reality, maximum verisimilitude—in other words, realism, as the guiding motto of their artistic program.[3]

Probably "realism" is one of those terms we should not try to define. It might be enough to notice that such controversy and ambiguity express clearly art's continuous struggle with reality and that this struggle acquires many forms and interpretations. But I believe that by speculating about this problem and posing similar questions to architecture, we could contribute to a clarification of the nature of both the modern figurative rupture and of "return to history."

What, then is the "real" with which architecture establishes its relationships? It is possible to search for it in architectural theories and writings, which naturally contain in an immediate way possible representations of this reality. But this task we leave outside the scope of this paper. What we want to tackle seems more arduous, since we are asking a more specific question: with what "real", does architecture establish figurative relations? The difficulty is obvious; the usage of words such as "realism," "figuration," and "representation" immediately produces a certain discomfort in critics, many of whom still believe that architecture (together with music) is one of those arts in which representation does not take place. This is an old problem, but one which is easy to address. And leaving aside the problem of drawings (which present a much more complicated structure, since in our view they are representations of a representation), we would like to concentrate on the other product of architecture, its buildings. As with all material on the other products of culture, buildings cannot escape their signifying nature. Today we know that neither a word nor a functional object, nor an image, not even the minimum gesture, can be considered "neutral," or lacking intention or meaning. The problem of "form" always implies a relation to a referent (which might or might not exist in empirical reality) which is "represented." The difficulty in considering architecture as "representing" something arises from a too-restricted conception of representation and figuration in which only the so-called "visual arts" (painting, sculpture, cinema, etc.) are included simply because their thematic relation with the visual reality of life is direct. In the case of architecture (and in music also), the problem becomes more complicated because the process of representation historically can be seen (at the figurative level) as a kind of "tautology" in which what is represented and the ensuing knowledge initially *is architecture itself*. Until Modern Architecture (and since the Renaissance at least), the "real of architecture" was found always in its own history, which in turn provided a sufficient proof of truth. To be sure, that "real" is always selective and ideologically tinted; as in the case of the Renaissance, which "invented" a new architecture by selecting as its "reality" what it believed to be the architecture of

8

Fig. 6 Torre Velasca, Milan, L. B. Belgiojoso, E. Peressuti, and E. N. Rogers, 1957.
Fig. 7 House in Zattere, Venice, Ignazio Gardella, 1958.
Fig. 8 Alton West 9, Roehampton Estate, London County Council, 1958.

Rome, yet having the programmatic aim only of producing and restoring its grandeur.

Thus, architecture has posed itself as a figurative enterprise, a "real" of architectural substance (or at least of "building" substance) which necessarily refers to its own history; and it is due to this particular persistence of history as a figurative repository that the appearance of Modern Architecture, in its most radical expressions, about Modern Architecture is the *change in the "real" with which it operates*. Reality, as the object of representation is depicted by the use of elements found outside architecture—in technology, in aircraft and ocean liners, in the vocabulary of the new art—and as such it is incorporated as the new referent.

The problem could be left here, perfunctorily stated. We could say that the present moment is but a quick return to the past as the object of representation. But we would not have said much. The problem still remains—how to characterize the present diverse manifestations of history as the new "real" and in turn, how to clarify the concept of "realism" as a critical category. It seems pertinent, then, to discuss and clarify the effect of those different appropriations of the "real," what are the ideological strategies that support these appropriations, and finally what these contemporary "returns" might mean in their differences from the pre-Modern uses of history.

We are confronted with a problem as old as Western thought, for we are questioning among other things the relationships and nature of a type of knowledge to reality, its mode of exposition, its effects and its proof of "truth." It does not seem inappropriate to recall Plato and Aristotle, who in their *Gorgias* and *Phaedrus*, and *Rhetorics* and *Poetics* respectively, established the basis for consequent Western thought about the problem of the nature of representation. In the writings of both we find a concept that has served philosophical discourses, as well as epistemology and art criticism, up to the present day: that of *verisimilitude*, which reverberates still in the thought of such contemporaries as Karl Popper, Ernst Gombrich and Roland Barthes.[4]

Verisimilitude for Plato and Aristotle and for subsequent rhetoricians, is a concept which dismisses definitely what was thought to be the constitutive property of language and words: the direct reference to the real. Verisimilitude is the property of the text to produce an effect of reality, a reality which might or might not be historically or scientifically possible: it is the capacity a text has to "make believe" that that which is said is directly related to a real fact. To do so, it employs rhetorical mechanisms sufficiently strong and elaborate so as to produce such an effect. Plato sadly says, "In the courts, in fact, people do not bother to say the truth, but to persuade, and persuasion depends on verisimilitude." Wittier, Aristotle comments, "An impossible verisimilitude is preferable to a possible unverisimilitude."[5] Modern philosophy and criticism have elaborated the concept beyond that of forensic discourses (which was the primary subject of rhetorics in antiquity) to epistemological discussion on the nature

Fig. 9 Illustration from *Townscape*, Gordon Cullen, 1961.
Figs. 10–11 "Don't" and "Do" sketches for the rehabilitation of the English Canals, Gordon Cullen, 1949.

10

9

11

of scientific knowledge, to literary criticism and all types of narratives (i.e., cinema) as well as to the visual arts. This concept is a critical instrument with which it is possible to discuss the nature of some logical propositions, to define precisely the concept of mathematical probability (as in Popper's discussion), and to analyze also the nature of "realism" in the arts, with the accompanying notions of fiction, illusion, artifice, mimesis, and their attempts to create the "effect of reality."[6]

With the help of this concept of verisimilitude, we know that signs are not servants of the referent, but of their own internal laws; as a consequence, representation depends not on the "truth" (truth is not an artistic problem) but rather on that which is represented, on the efficiency with which such representation makes its appearance as a plausible real, and on the mechanisms used to make such effects possible.

I propose that with this concept we could begin to sort out and classify some of the different modes of producing architecture in this century, in so far as how they operate in relation to their object of representation: that is, how the "real" has been codified and presented, and correspondingly, what has been the performance and destiny of these modes of production with respect to their convincing and persuasive qualities. Modern Architecture of the heroic period was one of those rare cases of invention of a new verisimilitude; it replaced another architecture whose foundations of truth and credibility lay in history. As if the possibilities of such "realism" had been exhausted by the preceding paroxysm of eclecticism, revivalisms, etc., architecture joined ranks with the generalized figurative rupture that occurred in all the arts, from literature, painting, to music (where even that seemingly eternal "truth," the "natural" scale, lost its authority).

It was a true reversal, since the idea of verisimilitude in the arts had been, up to that moment, one of truthful, "truthlike" representation of the existent, and in that extraordinary time of the first decades of this century, the represented in architecture in deed was not there, but rather, in a new and final aim: a new society, a new man, a new physical reality. As does any utopian attempt, architecture represents fragments of a future reality, but unlike past architectural utopias, we are now confronted with fragments which are not the products of a recombination of hitherto known architectural elements. The verisimilitude of previous utopias had operated with the expected, still the solid and sure foundation of a verisimilitude. The startling novelty is that Modern Architecture, realistic in the sense that it uses as figurative source for representation something existent (but non-architectural), disregards what might be socially and collectively believable and plausible as its rhetorical basis of persuasion. Thus the terms of the verisimilitude operation are inverted, inasmuch as the representation of "reality" and its effects is not based on an *a priori* knowledge of what, as architecture, is socially believable or not, but rather on the "truth" in which the artist believes, since it will become the focus that will make that reality evident when Man is, by the sole potent presence of architecture, transformed.

It is a complex and contradictory verisimilitude, for if, on the one hand, as a truly *avant-garde* movement, it does not accept society's expectation as the source of its persuasion, on the other it believes that forms themselves will transform those expectations, and that persuasion will result.

In architecture, the reversal takes the form of a double—literal and metaphorical—loss of the center: the former expressed by the demotion of symmetry (the most evident victim of the new figurative strategy), and the latter by the displacement of figurative elements from their hitherto undisputed core where architectural substance reigned, to the periphery where nonarchitectural elements abound. Besides the incorporation of foreign icons as figurative devices (technology, vernacular languages, etc.), another primal element of abstract character comes to replace the authority of history in its role of persuading the generating element of design, aided by an all too rational procedure, function will logically produce buildings so self-evident that their truth will be incontestable.

A possible explanation from the point of view of verisimilitude as to why Modern Architecture began to be attacked in the postwar period and when the first deviations appeared will be discussed later. What we need to note here is that in the decade of the fifties, in Europe as well as in America, we witnessed the reappearance of the traditional idea of verisimilitude, a return to the logic of persuasion based on an elaboration of what is commonly "believable." The two most clear, substantial, solid and influential figurative changes occurred in Italy and England during this decade. In the former, corresponding to the aesthetic movement in literature and movies of "neo-realism," the problem of historical continuity is posed, the incorporation of contextual mimesis and popular motives is effected, and the turning to "common knowledge" as a resource for architectural persuasion becomes active. Architecture does not become "more" involved with representation, since it always is, but the "real" represented and the verisimilitude sought after are easier and more concrete. The "reality" predicated by Rogers's Torre Velasca and by Gardella's house in the Zattere (Figs. 6–7), although derived from very different lines of thought, are conscious efforts to install architecture with a figurative program that is more "realist" and more intelligible as a collective discourse.

In England, a similar concern with a more "believable" architecture took place, and by this we imply more specifically the search for believability and a figurative rhetoric where the image represented is more clearly understood. When praising Roehampton (Fig. 8), Pevsner talks about "roofs of gentle pitch, . . . winding streets, architecture at ease" and then chastises Leslie Martin, responsible for the last part of the project, because in his design "there is less variety in the architecture and more *unitè* as it were, and this instinctive refusal to compromise with sentimentality has created a conflict . . . "[7] In its concern for effectiveness a technique is invented, spelled out and prescribed through the pages of the *Architectural Review*: Townscape, which makes even more explicit the mechanisms of verisimilitude (Fig. 9).

In this technique of "do" and "don't" we are confronted with an almost paradigmatic prescription whose immediate aim is a verisimilitude based on common knowledge and which resolves itself exclusively at the most pure level of architectural representation: drawing (Figs. 10, 11). Presented by De Wolfe in a memorable piece in 1949, Townscape is the alternative to the French tradition of thinking (Le Corbusier) and to orthodox Romanticism (Frank Lloyd Wright); its main ingredient is character ("significant differentiation"), its main political aim a "democracy of things," its sensibility an "understanding of differences," and its artistic label "superrealism." And as if preannouncing the "do what you feel" techniques of the '60s in this country, De Wolfe outlines the main characteristics of that visual philosophy[8] as

> . . . a dislike which amounts to an inability to see wholes or principles and an incapacity for handling theory; but on the other hand a passionate preoccupation with independent details, parts, or persons, an urge to help them fulfill themselves, achieve their own freedom; and thus, by mutual differentiation, achieve a higher organization.[9]

He then goes on to propose "precedent" as the sole base for civic design, and to use as a model to be followed the "greatest contribution (of England) to civil organization: the common law."[10]

In this period we witness, in both cases, a complete change in the sources of the real

12

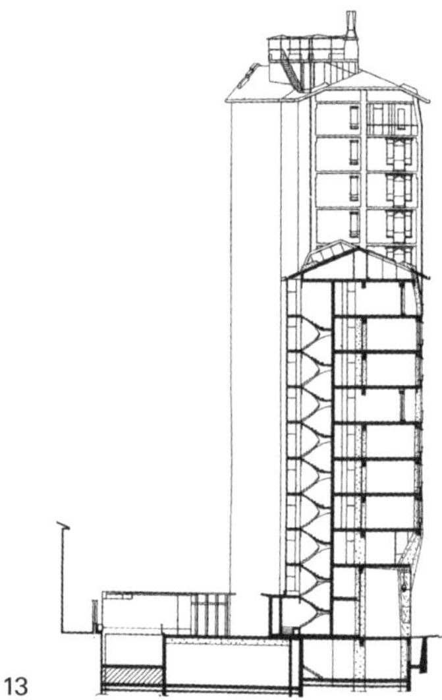

13

of architecture, history, and "city as is," and the reappearance of a verisimilitude based on a direct appeal to common knowledge and a rejection of a programmatic, promising but yet non-existent real.

I would like to suggest that if the term "Post-Modernism" has any value (and I am not sure that it has), its little history would begin with that decade of profound changes in architecture which can be detected through these figurative shifts. At the same time, we should note that the intentions and manifest theories of all this architecture continued to establish their ties with Modern Architecture, and that that variety of polemics depended on *zeitgeist* arguments to justify those changes. The fact remains incontestable that a break of important consequences occurred at the figurative level, and understanding this break is essential in assessing the present moment.

Besides the reintroduction of history and the picturesque as figurative devices, which could only have been momentary, a more substantial alteration in architectural thought had occurred. And if the figurative moves were all too clear and noticeable for critics and designers to generate an unusual and animated debate at the time, the most profound ideological shifts that took place seem to have passed unnoticed. Neither Banham nor Rogers (the two most conspicuous and interesting critics who engaged in a heated polemic about "neo-liberty" through the pages of *Architectural Review* and *Casabella*) seemed to be able to avoid the trap of the *zeitgeist* argument. In attacking the *torinese* and *milanese* architecture of the fifties, Banham used the argument that

> . . . the only conceivable justification for reviving anything in the arts is that the reviver finds himself culturally in a position analogous to that of the time he seeks to revive.[11]

This argument allowed him to discard neo-liberty for not being in accordance with

> . . . the domestic revolution that began with electric cookers, vacuum cleaners, the telephone, the gramophone and all those other mechanized aides to gracious living that are still invading the home, and have permanently altered the nature of domestic life and the meaning of domestic architecture.[12]

In responding to the "caretaker of frigidaires," Rogers attempted a defense of Banham's victims, and he saw in the new figurative attempts of the Italian scene of the day, the true interpretation of Modern Architecture ideals, as a

> . . . continuous revolution, that is to say, as the continuous development of the principles of adhering to the changing content of life.[13]

But the "changing content of life" is almost a truism (and indeed this argument could also, and paradoxically, very well be the one to

Figs. 12–14 Office and Apartment Building, Turin, L. B. Belgiojoso, E. Peressutti, and E. N. Rogers, 1959.
Fig. 15 Seagram Building, New York City, Mies van der Rohe and Philip Johnson, 1954-58.

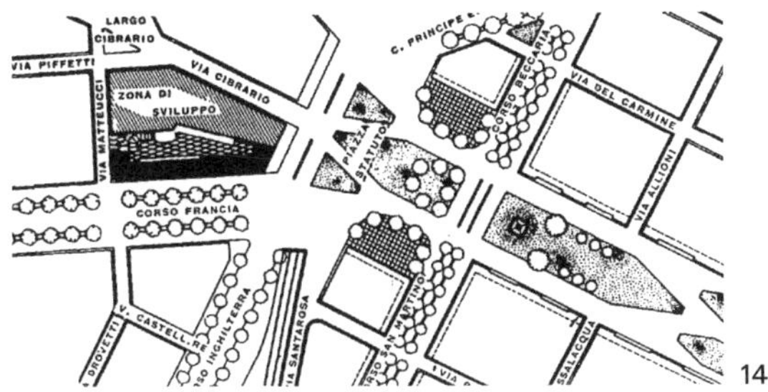

14

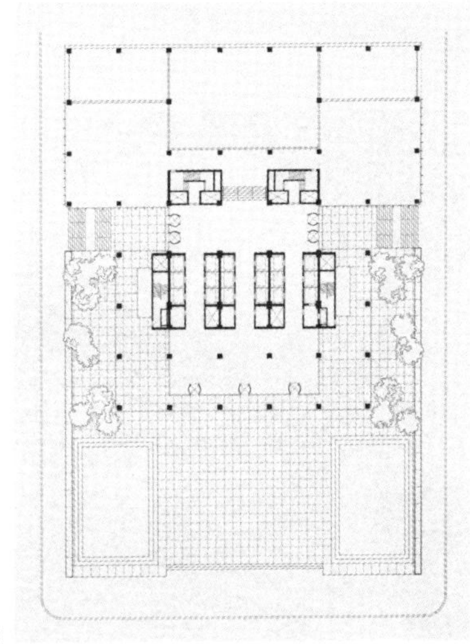
15

substantiate the "accordance with, the electric cookers, etc." and which the "caretaker of frigidaires" needs), and it offers help neither in seeing the beginning of a shift concerning the kind of reality that architecture will engage in nor in detecting the profound change in our state of mind that such a shift will produce, a state of mind which will flourish unchecked into our present time: the persistent, relentless and sometimes paralyzing "self-consciousness" to which architecture has turned. It is our perspective of twenty years that allows us to see the vicious circle in which such polemics engage, still too rooted in that all-pervasive, undefinable and always attractive idea of the "spirit of the age."

A simple look at what happened with the English "townscape" and with the Italian "neo-liberty" in the fifties reveals to us the sources of this departure from Modern Architecture: there was a problem between the figurative program and the social aims of Modern Architecture, a problem that in the history of art, politics, and in general, of all ideological practices, invariably produces a transformation of the language in question (be it words, paintings or buildings). We are beginning to see that such changes inevitably resort to specific rhetorical devices in their search for correction and persuasion. I propose that we understand such rhetorical changes as a search for a new strategy of verisimilitude, which in this particular case implied that in order to make architecture believable, the "effect of reality" had to be based on the known. This choice seems quite simple today: if the abstract, hermetic, figurative propositions of Modern Architecture fail to move and transform man, or, more prosaically, just do not seem to engage the beholder in its arcane discourse, and if those propositions rely heavily on the introduction into architectural language of elements foreign to it, the only apparent possibility is to close that door, after which one is left inside with the only pertinent elements: namely architectural elements whose proof and verification in practice can only be derived from history. But once this is said, the choices are still not self-evident. That it seems obviously logical and consistent that England resorted to the Picturesque and Italy to a more intellectual and abstract interpretation of its urban traditions can partially explain these choices (Figs. 12–14). But the phenomena is quite generalized and pervasive; besides our two beleaguered examples, in America, Mies turned to symmetry (Fig. 15), Gropius to "localisms" of dubious taste (Fig. 16), the Soviet Union (after successfully crushing the *avant-garde* of the twenties) turned unashamedly to classicism (Fig. 17), and in most places where Modern Architecture had established a foothold, incipient "vernacular" movements appeared.

Are we then to interpret the Modern Movement as a parenthesis in the history of architecture, as many present critics argue, with the aspiration of seeing a continuity with the various traditions, be they classic, local, vernacular, etc? I simply believe we cannot. The figurative shift, the rhetorical operations involved, the "new" reality represented, and

Fig. 16 University of Baghdad, The Architects Collaborative, Inc, 1959.
Fig. 17 Administrative Building, Moscow, M. Posokhin, 1949–1950.

16

17

the attempt to reinstate an orthodox verisimilitude are not the innocent result of a restored "continuity." Indeed, they are the result, as Colin Rowe says, of "the lapse into consciousness" and "the end of innocence."[14] In my view, this indicates a profound ideological mutation that is indeed new in the history of architecture. For the first time the architect chooses *"history"* as a whole, as an alternative. History, as the repository of forms has been separated from the continuum of time by that rebel, the Modern Movement, and as such it affords the designer a distance that never before existed. Before Modern Architecture, the use of history was not a problem to be discussed, it was the way architecture operated, and the only possible quarrels might have been about "what history" to choose; but its authority was not discussed. History had never been consciously "used," but naturally "assumed." That detachment has been produced by Modern Architecture, and things will never be the same. Before it, rhetorical operations were performed on the classical language of architecture, which was based on precedent, and on the classical or historical codes. After it, *"history" becomes a rhetorical operation per se*. All of this has given architecture a consciousness of itself and of its cultural origins that did not exist before. And if such consciousness has the positive effect of producing a criticism that results in the clear identification of architecture as a social discourse and of the mechanisms of communication and meaning that architecture must know in order to engage in such dialogue, it might also serve to divest architecture of any ideal when that consciousness and detachment (and the knowledge they produce) result in cynical manipulation to assure consumption of architectural signs.

And it is among these auguries and perils that this new verisimilitude of "history" begins its course of many strategies and effects, of which the most conspicuous tendencies of today are its inheritors.

It would be too adventurous to attempt an exhaustive classification of these tendencies, but within the limits of our subject it is acceptable to address our problem to two lines of thought and production: on the one hand, at architecture which corresponds loosely to the label of "populist," and on the other, the more European-based, so-called "neo-rationalists."[15] The choice is not innocent. Both serve the argument because, paradoxically as it might seem, both share some positive attitudes and features with respect to "representation;" both can be characterized by the use of "history;" both are "realist" in the sense of attempting to "represent" consciously such history with figurative devices; and for both the problem of the verisimilitude of architecture is almost obsessive. But this is where the similarities end.

For the neo-rationalist, represented by the Italian *tendenza*[16] and by Aldo Rossi as their foremost exponent, the recovery of history is essential. But it is viewed not as a repository of styles or as a possibility of order and intelligibility. Architecture is thus understood as discipline, in the quasi-academic sense of the word. (And indeed the *tendenza*'s program includes the production of a treatise of architectural composition[17].) As Scolari points out, a distinctive feature of the *tendenza* is that by acting as a critique of the regressive utopias of the immediate past (Archigram, Superstudio, Archizoom, etc.), this architecture is tautological in the sense that it closes in upon itself and declares its autonomy.[18] It does not deny the knowledge of politics and economics that it sees as necessary to an understanding of the place of architecture and its determinants, but it denies the possibilities of translating this information into architectural form. For these reasons architectural autonomy should be understood as a disciplinary autonomy, that is to say, as a specific and independent body of knowledge, theories, and techniques, and not as an "independent" social practice detached from and unrelated to all other elements that comprise the socio-political reality at a given moment, as many critics have misinterpreted this term to imply.

This particular relation to history and to the idea of discipline allows the *tendenza* to conceive of the idea of "progress" as "clarification of the discipline" instead of seeing it as "change."[19] Thus, logically, an architecture so established and defined implies the production of knowledge about itself. And if the rapidity with which an architectural proposition spreads is a measure of its clarity, one should conclude that the precision of Rossi's forms and the clarity of his principles are successful. But it might also be that his precision and clarity can be easily and quickly reduced to formulas and stencils, which seems also to be the case.

A different case of success seems to characterize the figurative attempt of the other line, the "populist," which resorts to a type of "realism" in which the idea and use of "history" acquire a unique dimension. History here is understood in its widest sense, certainly not as the "history" of a discipline, but as the sum total of culture's products, a view allowing for a permissiveness in which any idea of discipline disappears under the exuberant stimuli that the environment as a whole provides. The fatality of the "world as is," as a fact, is turned into its virtue, in the indisputable and inevitable empirical evidence to be followed rather than to be corrected. Its proof is not the history of architecture, but the "history" of life and things: hence, there could not be anything more alien to this thought than the notion of a disciplinary autonomy. Its *modus operandi* does not arise from the internal consistency of an architectural language and its possible operations, but from the dynamics of the consumption of symbols. To leave no doubts, Venturi asserts this fact by using as an example one of the most perishable products of our culture, one which also becomes a source of inspiration for him: ". . . The tempo of our economy encourages that changeable and disposable environmental decoration known as advertising art."[20] Its success finally seems to be guaranteed by the extreme facility with which the combination of both an unlimited resource of symbols and the disregard for a precise discipline for their incorporation into buildings can be adopted.

It appears, then, that we are indeed confronted with two types of "realism." The verisimilitude of the first attempt is to be derived logically and "naturally" from the internal consistency of architecture as "construction" (in Rossi's usage of the word), and based on a required, specific and limited knowledge on one hand, and on founding its "truth" and "reality" on the experience of the city by the beholder on the other. The verisimilitude of the second type is to be derived from the already "proven" and "believable" nature that the objects of consumption have in the market. And as a consequence, the neo-rationalists aim at a verisimilitude based not on the contingencies of history but on society's memory of it, in the perdurable—an "atemporal" history as it were, where architectural facts acquire their value as a contribution to the "construction" of the city and culture: the Gothic cathedral, the Renaissance palazzo, the Neo-Classic library or prison, and the Modern *seidlungen*, from this perspective, have not "time" but "presence" and are valid only for their consistency with both their articulation with the urban scene they produce, transform, and make intelligible, and with their own internal logic. On the contrary, the populists' verisimilitude is born out of the value of contingency: "this, here and now" appears to be its driving force, and Venturi is explicit about it:

> The short run is what our clients have largely retained us architects for. Architectural theories of the short-run tend toward the idealization and generalization of expediency.[21]

This idea of a "short run" architecture, the "tempo" of the American environment, the "architecture of expediency," reveals a very specific and original perception of the city, and a completely different focus for the sources of representation, realism and verisimilitude.[22]

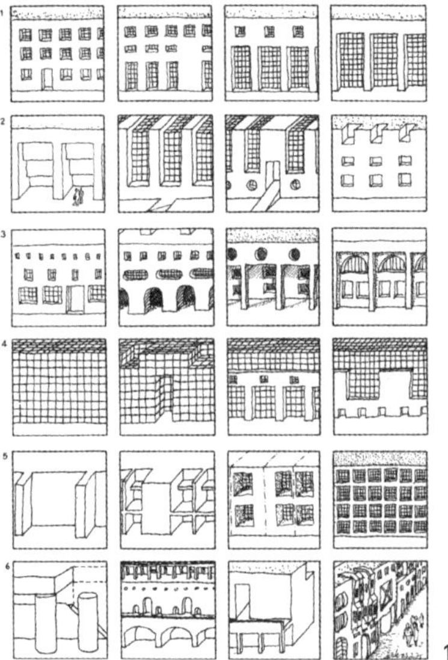

18

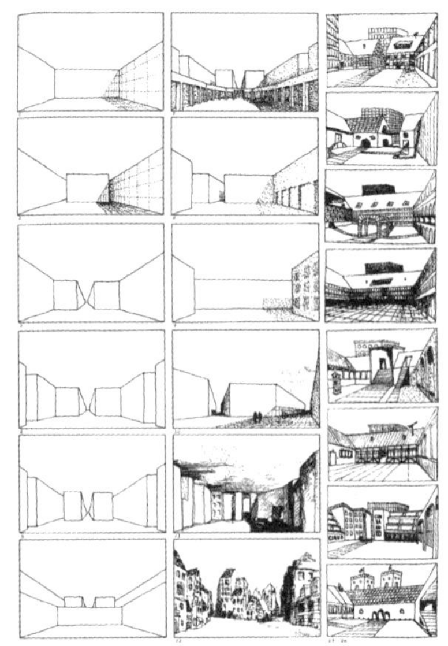

19

It may appear at first sight that the sources of these diverse kinds of verisimilitude are in fact quite similar, since both are based in some way on what the city provides, and their differences might be attributable to the unavoidable differences between European and American cities. But the differences go beyond the readily available sources of precedents into more substantive matters, and reveal two strongly different ideological and cultural aspirations. In our case, they clearly correspond to some specific categories of verisimilitude that have been established in art and literary criticism.[23] On the one hand, there is the idea of verisimilitudes as it still comes from Plato and Aristotle: the relations between the text or the figurative work with other, more diffuse and general "text," which is called "public opinion" and "common sense" (*doxa*). Here the verisimilitude, the effect of reality, is not based on truth or fact but rather on what the public believes to be "truth" regardless of its qualifications. It is common sense (*doxa*), common law, common knowledge. As defined by Aristotle, it deals with the techniques, in the forensic discourse, that appeal to the audience in order to convince and which are based on the sentiments, emotions and "knowledge" of the audience.[24] On the other hand, there is a level of "verisimilitude" strategy where the effect of reality is more relative, since within it there is multiplicity of subcases; its multiplicity is the result of a relationship established not with public opinion, but rather with the rules of the "genre" in question. Thus an epic, a tragedy, a comedy, a "conversation piece," "still life," etc., conform to their own reality if the rules of the genre are respected. As such this is a much more modern discovery, and its "effect" is that of engaging an audience or a beholder in the reality of the work, and it requires only—but importantly—that the rules of the genre are shared and that the work be consistent with them in its exposition.[25]

The applicability to our subject seems evident and immediate: in the works of the neo-rationalists we see that their rhetorical efforts are geared toward the establishment of a verisimilitude based on the purity and congruence of the "genre." This explains the notion of autonomy and the search for the "discipline," although the latter is probably reduced to the selection of genre. The populist choice, all too obvious, is linked to the Aristotelian notion of "common knowledge," "public opinion," etc., that what "people" think is true.

In short, I believe that it is possible to establish from a critical, theoretical point of view a fundamental difference in relation to the types of architecture produced today: on the one hand, there are architectures that concern themselves exclusively with the problem of the authenticity and logic of the "genre," and on the other, architectures that concern themselves with the problem of "public opinion." Both will necessarily produce divergent discourses because their "reals" are diverse. But, both are consciously engaged with one or another idea of verisimilitude.

And it is in relation to these two possible approaches to the problem of representation and verisimilitude (namely the "genre" and

Figs. 18–20. Typological and Morphological Classifications, Robert Krier, 1975.

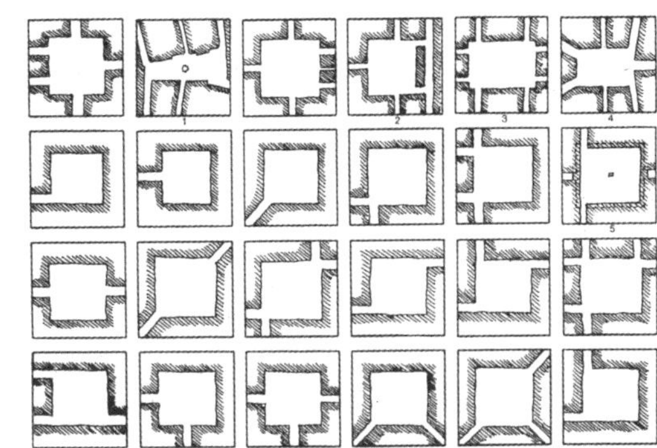

20

"common knowledge") in architecture that it is possible to clarify the two different uses that these approaches make of a concept of long and complex tradition in the history of architecture: both tendencies reflect in their thinking and sources a concern for the *concept of type* and that of *architectural typology*. It is not an over-generalization to say today the theoretical concept of typology pervades, consciously or unconsciously, almost all architectural thought, and that the variety of interpretations and uses make it necessary to establish clearly these differences and nuances.

The type relates to verisimilitude because the idea of "type" implies, first of all, a minimum level of intelligibility for forms based on the architect's and beholders' experience, which in turn will make architecture "believable." Almost all current tendencies base their critique of Modern Architecture on some sort of typological consciousness, which implies a definition of the real in some sort of typological manner. For the Italian *tendenza* it implies the reintroduction of history and an important acknowledgement that in design it is not possible to begin from zero since that would imply an "isolation from reality."[26] The idea of type also serves to reintroduce critically the idea of "monument" from the perspective of "realism." Scolari says:

> the image of the monument is, perhaps, what everybody can grasp more easily, and it is because of this that we will use its realism as an indication of simplicity.[27]

For them the "monumentalist" choice implies a search for the perfection of the type which is explicitly equated with "classicism."[28] The notion of type (together with its companion, urban morphology) is used as a source of realism by the Krier brothers, who more explicitly attack the figurative program of Modern Architecture as abstract and unintelligible and as the cause of the destruction of urban centers (Figs. 18–20). The base for "verisimilitude" is even more clearly stated in Ungers' "typological" method, which is not so much a search of architectural "mimesis" with past architectures or contexts but rather a search to "represent" metaphorically the *process* by which the city is built. Once the types are established (a catalogue of suitable types for the conditions), a simple combination, which indeed could be random, assures the "production of the city" with a resulting image that reproduces the construction of the city itself (Figs. 21–22). In all cases, verisimilitude is understood as discipline and in accordance with the laws of the "genre," be it the city, a context, etc. In all these cases the idea of type is recognized as the "foundation of architecture." When talking about the *tendenza* Scolari defines a typological method not as a historic method of observation, classification, and comparison, but rather as the very possibility of operation.[29] For them, both concepts of type and typology have their roots in the Enlightenment, and the constant references to Quatremere de Quincy and to the work of G. C. Argan (as the one who retrieved it in the fifties) establish the theoretical parameters

21

22

of its definition and understanding.[30] As is already well known, Quatremere de Quincy's argument is based on the differences between model and type.[31] Type becomes an abstraction, a principle that begins as a starting point. This then explains the possibility of transformation and change, and the structural interpretation of type as "genre".

In the theoretical and methodological discourse of the populists, the concept of type is apparently not so explicitly used, but most of their preferred terminology can easily be read in terms of the traditional discussion of type and model, type and character, and type and symbol, as will be shown later. Venturi's assertion that

> basic to the argument for the decorated shed is the assumption that symbolism is essential in architecture and that the model from a previous time or from the existing city is part of the source material, and the replication of elements is part of the design method of this architecture; that is, architecture that depends on association in the perception of it depends on association in the creation of it[32]

is quintessentially typological, and in the same text, it is suggestive that Venturi makes extensive use of Colquhoun's "Typology and Design Method" in his discussion of association and symbolism in architecture.[33] It is suggestive because the idea of type in this Anglo-Saxon interpretation does not correspond with that of the tradition of Enlightenment. Both Colquhoun's article and the use that Venturi makes of it point out clearly the other distinct direction or focus the issue of typology has received and which directly reflects a concern also with the problem of realism and verisimilitude. Here we have a purely iconographic interpretation and use of the idea of type. From this perspective, type is far from being an abstraction or a rational principle. Rather, it is the cultural icon that appears and circulates in society that is made identifiable, and becomes, in turn, the "represented symbol" (Figs. 23, 24).

The argument on behalf of this notion of type could be structurally similar to that of the neo-rationalist, since both base an assurance of future success on the past success of the type, but their foci are diametrically opposite. For the former it is a principle; for the latter, an icon. And their differences could well be illustrated by the two types of aesthetic "realism" that illustrate their discussion. For Rossi and the *tendenza* the most evocative images are those of De Chirico's metaphysical realities, and for Venturi it is Andy Warhol's pop-art realism (Figs. 25, 26).

For the first, the type represents the rational, "universal," non-individual, classical form, and for the other the concrete, idiosyncratic and temporal icon. For the *tendenza* the type is the instrument to decodify, distill or abstract a principle that then becomes the foundation of a realism. The effect of its verisimilitude is rooted in the collective memory that the principle represented would evoke. For the

Figs. 21–22 A vocabulary: Thirteen alternatives for the three-story single block with constant base, Oswald Mathais Ungers, Hans Kollhoff, and Thomas Will, 1977.
Fig. 23 Fountain for the Piazza d'Italia, New Orleans, Charles Moore, 1975.
Fig. 24 Brandt-Johnson House, Vail, CO, Venturi and Rauch, 1977.

23

24

populist the realism of its products is achieved by an almost literal and mimetic representation of a form, the product of the contingencies of a particular environmental condition, and the effect of its verisimilitude is an almost automatic consequence. As with most cases in the history of architecture in which one can synthesize the work of an architect by looking closely at the handling of a single element, we might attempt a summation of what has been said so far by comparing the figurative strategies that some of the foremost exponents of these tendencies follow in the design of that perennial condenser of architectural thought and theory: the column. In Rossi's case, the four round columns of the Gallaratese (Figs. 27, 28) make explicit the process of abstraction of a typical element and its further monumentalization. Its attributes are here represented as an almost platonic "idea" of a column, which includes both its intrinsic essences and its role in the construction of the architecture. The appearance of the four columns in the continuum of the sidewalk arcades and their particular configuration and placement in the building didactically explain the richness and complexity of the notion of type in this tradition. On one level these columns are exposed as architectural elements in themselves; further, they are subordinated to an architectural type of a larger order (*aedicula*), which is itself presented in its pure state; finally, the columns acquire another layer of significance as they become the "event," or focus of an even larger type, the arcaded block. The verisimilitude of all this systematic and "disciplined" layering of types comes purely from their autonomous tautological assertion (a column, is a column, is a column . . .) and from the impeccable manner in which the rules of a particular urban "genre" are effected.

The column in Venturi's addition to the Oberlin College Art Museum (Fig. 29) depicts paradigmatically the other view. A sense of urgency and immediacy pervades the object in a disconcerting manner, as if it wishes not to transcend its ephemeral quality. A column, in this case, is an Ionic column, with all the implications that such a "statement" has in a "post-modern" era. Here the architect's endeavor is not engaged in the exposition of a logical operation or of a principle; rather, the operation of iconic replica dissipates any possibility of typological abstraction, bringing the object closer to the idea of model. Whereas the Gallaratese's columns are a necessity, once the rules of the genre are accepted, the wooden ionic column of Oberlin is purely contingent and whimsical. But what further differentiates their respective uses of a similar element is the specific manner in which both architects enact through rhetorical operations the effect of "estrangement." In both cases the real has been distorted, and distance exists between it and the objects of representation, for neither Venturi's nor Rossi's columns are, in the end, typical. The choice of material, the column's specific location in the building, its framing, and its distortion of proportions bring Venturi close to the artistic operations of pop-art, specifically the art of Oldenburg and Warhol (and probably

Fig. 25 Giorgio de Chirico, *The Soothsayer's Recompense*, 1913, Philadelphia Museum of Art, The Louise and Walter Arensberg Collection.
Fig. 26 Andy Warhol, *Four Campbell Soup Cans*, 1962, Mr. and Mrs. Leo Castelli Collection.

25

26

precariously far from architecture and into the realm of a parody of the discipline), with the collateral effects of irony and joke. Rossi, by divesting the columns of any possible immediate connotation, and by operating a change in proportions, leans more towards the type of estrangement from the real produced by surrealist operations and metaphysical art, with their oneiric effects of remoteness and bewilderment. By effecting such estrangement, both operate within the common traits of contemporary and modern sensibility: self-consciousness, heresy, and paradox.

If these characteristic examples of current work in architecture can be labeled realistic because of the conscious concern with representation of a reality, and if they also reintroduce rhetorical strategies (such as verisimilitude in their different possibilities) of long standing in the history of art, can we conclude that the new element that differentiates them from the past is their manifest or latent use of the notion of type? Certainly it could be argued successfully that such a notion establishes a definitive distance from the methodological aims of Modern Architecture, but as intimated earlier, this notion itself has a long and animated history that needs to be recalled and matched against these tendencies in order to establish their status today.

The pedigree of the idea of type in the history of architecture has recently been exposed by Anthony Vidler, and when taking the necessary perspective that includes both pedigree as well as contemporary interpretations it is possible to see that we can describe the present predicaments as almost logical consequences of the history of that idea.[34] For there has always been a struggle in the history of architecture between the seemingly contradictory elements that have been associated with the concepts of type, specifically between the implications of type as "rational type" and type as "character," which directly or indirectly contributed to the vicissitudes of architectural theory for a century and a half and which in turn help to explain the vicissitudes of Modern Architecture. Because, from the point of view of typology, functionalism is the logical consequence of Durand's construct and of operations that destroy the notion of character, with all its implication of allegory, individuality, idiosyncrasy, and finally with its most perdurable result: the picturesque.

It is also possible to see Modern Architecture as the resolution of Durand's conflicts. Because Modern Architecture (and we think of Le Corbusier specifically) had the power reserved only for those unique artistic moves which allowed the inherent contradictions of a basic idea to coexist creatively even if founded on fragile premises: by not resorting to history, the contradiction between character and rationality is left aside, and re-elaborated in a new language. Le Corbusier synthesized both by something which may be called "rational character" as a result of the preeminence of function: this gives the "reason" *and* the form; it is logical, disciplined *and* expressive of the particularity of each contingency (the program). That the bind was tenuous, we know well, but its inventiveness, promise, and power

Fig. 27 Facade; Housing Unit at Gallaratese, Milan, Aldo Rossi, 1970.
Fig. 28 View of the Portico, Housing Unit at Gallaratese, Milan, Aldo Rossi, 1970.

27 28

as a generative idea have hardly been surpassed. The history of what happened after the heroic period of Modern Architecture, as Gandelsonas has outlined well (although from a different perspective),[35] is a renewed split between those contradictions. Thus, the critique of Modern Architecture that appeared in the fifties can be explained as the re-emergence of the idea of character in its picturesque format in England, and its symbolic and allegorical versions in Italy.

The criticism that the reintroduction of the notion of type has effected on Modern Architecture is probably the most valuable since the postwar era because it does not resort to peripheral explanations of its problems (such as sociology, behaviorism, economics or systems theory), but rather goes to the heart of the matter by immersing itself in "architectural substance." Argan, Colquhoun, Rossi and others all discuss the shortcomings of a vision that negates history in all its possible versions: it is not possible to start from zero, it is not possible to establish communication if some sort of collective memory is not invoked through architecture.

But in the reintroduction of type into architecture, an old and too familiar rift seems to have surfaced again, this time with seemingly intense virulence. It is historically naive, however, to expect a return to a polemic that seems to have stopped before Modern Architecture appeared. It has been intimated earlier in this paper that the existence of Modern Architecture cannot be wished away, that the present moment is its product as much as that of the conscious renewal of older ideas. It should be expected that such an equation would yield such complexity and some novelty. And in regard to the incorporation of history, the search for verisimilitude, and the reintroduction of the notion of typology, the changes can tentatively be outlined. Thus, the transposition of some European "realist strategies" of the fifties to the American scene of the seventies can be seen in the work of Venturi and Moore (two of the most influential personages of that tendency who profess a particular devotion to Italy, where they spent enough of their maturing years at the time when those propositions were advanced and could not have passed unnoticed). Hejduk's remark, that Venturi comes from Gardella, is a poignant and incisive synthesis of such kinship.[36] However, their pedigree is also a product of the parallel English townscape movement, which paradoxically appears in America as an affirmation of the sin that triggered Gordon Cullen's attack: the street signs and their malefic impact in the environment. The populists borrow from Cullen's technique that rendition of a reality of happiness and casualness, in which architecture somehow disappears, and the people, street furniture, color and all symbols of "joy" provide a persuasive account of an all too untroubled life, here improved and up-dated with pop-art collage (Fig. 30). But this marriage of two opposite approaches to realism is also the source of its strength. Whereas Gardella's mimesis was too tinted with academic connotations and intellectual interpretations, and Cullen's images too devoid of any architectural

Fig. 29 Column, Oberlin College Museum of Art Addition, Venturi and Rauch, 1976.
Fig. 30 A Bill-Ding-Board for the National Football Hall of Fame Competition, Venturi and Rauch, with the assistance of Gerod Clark, 1967.

29

30

commitment, Venturi's and Moore's propositions depict both an idea of "building" of empirical immediacy, of quasi-literal historical attachment (as if the urgent task in America was to build a history), and the very representation of the life that it will produce. As verisimilitude of common knowledge it synthesizes the best of both.

The Italian *tendenza* (and in the neo-rationalists in general) a similar transformation is apparent in some of the ideas on which their architecture is based. The notion of architectural typology is enriched on two fronts: on the one hand it cannot be separated from its dialectical counterpart of urban morphology (as expounded by Rossi's *L'architettura della città*)[37] and on the other it extends the concept of architectural type beyond the limits of the academic view of the Enlightenment to include all building types that "construct" the city (as expounded through research work[38]). This proposition allows the neo-rationalists to consider as subjects of architecture both the exceptional (the monument) and the plain (the fabric), enlarging architectural concerns in a comprehensive theory. Thus, in both cases, these realist attempts could be considered "inclusive" (a term usually associated with populists' tendencies in America alone) although in quite different manners, differentiated by the ways in which they propose, interpret, and deal with the idea of type.

We can now leave our analysis; it has provided us with some elements that allow us to assess the historical status of these current tendencies and to reaffirm some theoretical points. Throughout, our intention has been to focus on the figurative aspects of architecture, and inevitably we have had to consider the thought, ideas or ideological constructs that sustained them. Thus, when looking at current tendencies through these two exemplary cases, we are clearly presented with a seemingly contradictory set of ideas and architectures. Because, if on the one hand the reintroduction of history as a figurative device appears as a return to the pre-modern era (i.e. the quotations of Venturi or Moore, the Krier brothers' revival of Sitte's strategies, Rossi's insistence on typological methods, etc.) and as the inevitable outcome of a prolonged and at times belligerent critique of Modern Architecture, on the other hand, it is precisely in these two disparate attempts at inclusiveness that the legacy of Modern Architecture makes these tendencies unmistakably "modern"—they can only be explained as the product of a persistent conviction that the hitherto unfulfilled promise of justice, freedom, and democracy that Modern Architecture was to deliver to society must still be maintained and attempted.

This contradiction results from the fact that the figurative rupture with Modern Architecture effected during the fifties (and which culminates today as proposed in this text) was dependent on one of its most important programmatic tenets. In itself this only helps to reinforce the notion that the relations between thought, ideology, and form are not simple or direct. But more importantly,

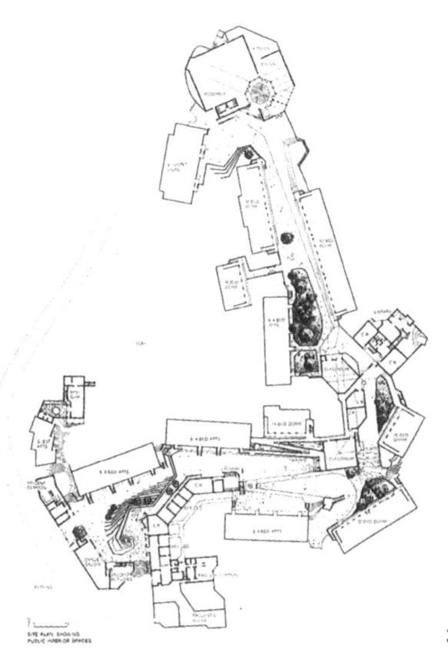

31

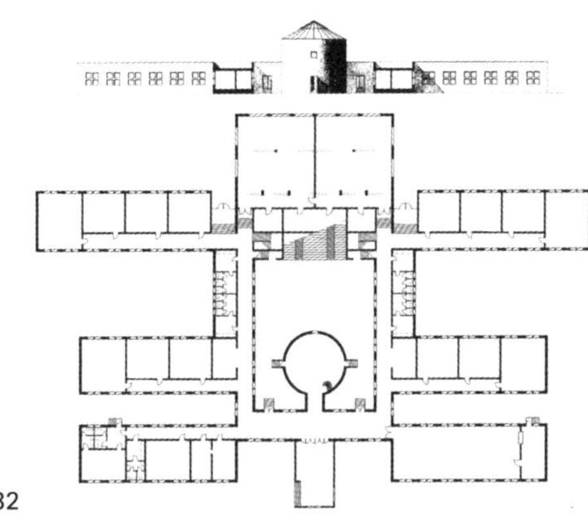

32

Fig. 31 Kresge College, University of California at Santa Cruz, Charles Moore, 1974.
Fig. 32 Elementary School at Fagnano Olona, Aldo Rossi, 1977.

it helps us to see that we are, at best, in a mixed period which cannot be treated either as a "beginning" or as an "end" of an era, but rather as a culmination of a process that has unmistakably characterized the discipline since the appearance of Modern Architecture. Since Modern Architecture's historical inception, the task of architecture appears to have been marked continuously by the necessity of refining, adjusting and reproposing the apparently inexhaustible resource of ideas that Modern Architecture presented. As with any new, truly revolutionary rupture, Modern Architecture condensed a wealth of new, disparate, sometimes contradictory ideas that took over the world in a resounding avalanche of formal and ideological possibilities. The loosening up of the figurative boundaries allowed and promoted the stampede of attempts that followed. For is it not possible, by taking those tenets one at a time, to order and classify almost all of the ensuing trends, tendencies, polemics and positions?[39] As if there were no more minds, nor cultural contexts invested with that heroic power that prevailed in the early decades that would allow for the same impetus, the whole period from the post-war up to the present seemed to have attempted to develop *in extenso* some of those original tenets, one by one, (and most of the time, quite ironically), as a reaction to Modern Architecture. And as most of these attempts seem to have discarded themselves, either by exhausting the original ideas, or by ending up in tragic ridicule, or by establishing themselves as endeavors independent from architecture, it is possible to see in the present tendencies (as they belong to that whole atmosphere that Tafuri calls "a return to language") that we have been left with some bare bones of what might very well constitute the real architectural "stuff" of Modern Architecture's problem: how to focus accurately the inquiry into the language of architecture in order to produce a collective discourse capable of addressing society at large, and producing, representing, and generating the physical manifestation of the resolution to the dilemma of modern society: namely, the contradiction between the law and individual freedom.

That the ideological premises and ideals of these two contemporary tendencies seem to have settled figuratively on the two extremes that Modern Architecture promised to conciliate, the populists' "representing" individual freedom and the neo-traditionalist displaying the preeminence of the law (Figs. 31, 32) is only a measure of the importance and of the complexity of the problem that Modern Architecture posed for itself and which continues to be central and unresolved in any contemporary proposition. As Rafael Moneo says ". . . [this is] an era in which every side thinks they are defending the same positions."[40] Indeed, Rossi recently expressed to an American audience that the aim of his projects is to produce "total freedom"[41] by which he implies that only by making architecture independent and autonomous, concerned only with its own internal substance and laws, can the ideal of freedom be returned clearly and unmistakably to its own domain,

Fig. 33 Frontispiece of Learning from Las Vegas, Robert Venturi, Denise Scott Brown, and Stephen Izenour, 1972.
Fig. 34 Drawing for the Competition of the new Central Business District, Florence, drawing by Aldo Rossi.

33

34

supposedly that of political action and civic exercise. For the populists instead, the idea of freedom must be metaphorically represented in iconographic terms, thus investing the building with the mythical power of inducing such freedom by its contiguity with everyday life.

Thus it seems to me that the products of these two current tendencies must be taken for what they are: at present the two most poignant and distinct artistic representations in architecture of a certain reality that insists on an old, perhaps worn-out, yet still unfulfilled aspiration of modern society. No more, but no less. And in reinterpreting an old dream they display, in a paradigmatic, exemplary way the possibilities at either end of the figurative spectrum that Modern Architecture involuntarily generated. Are they not the possibilities resulting from keeping the figurative repertoire open (that possibility that we still owe to Le Corbusier, the Constructivists, the Futurists) that allows in turn both the indiscriminate use of consumption symbols and the reintroduction of history (this time as just another possibility) as an alternative, in the name of architecture?

We might reassert more convincingly, as a by-product of our specific analysis, that an iconographic critique of architecture still holds one of the most important keys to the interpretation of architectural thought today. If the most profound philosophical and political aspirations articulated by Modern Architecture still haunt current tendencies, if they are interpreted, criticized and reproposed in disparate figurative propositions, this only reinforces the particular role that architecture plays with the ideological practices of society, in particular in the realm of art. By labeling them "realists," we are trying to stress the inescapable bond between an ideological knowledge of reality and its representation through diverse figurative mechanisms. If an orthodox verisimilitude in its various manners becomes once again the rhetorical tool of persuasion, it only alludes more convincingly to the validity of the argument that the primary task of architecture today seems to be that of elaborating an effective, plausible collective discourse, a task inherited directly from Modern Architecture. That the two extremes in this spectrum seem to indicate two modes of structuring architectural discourse in terms of cultural strategies (one an architecture of "genre" the other an architecture of "common knowledge"), makes explicit both the range of possibilities of verisimilitude in architecture and the still unresolved status in which architectural language finds itself today.

We are, then, operating with some fundamental fragments of ideologies, some modern and some not, which appear somehow independent from one another in the course of history, which evolve and displace themselves through time at different speeds, and which produce, at different moments of contact, diverse manifestations of architecture:

1. a socio-cultural aspiration that remains, in spite of its historical and political adjustments, a driving force since modern times;

2. a figurative operation produced by Modern Architecture that allowed for the loosening and opening up of the boundaries and substance of architectural representation, permitting in turn the seemingly endless trials of how to depict figuratively that socio-cultural aim;

3. the re-introduction, manifest or latent, of an enriched and invigorated architectural notion, *type* (and its consequent method), that is truly, at a theoretical and operational level, the most important element in this contemporary picture, and which by itself might be the most important "counter-idea" to some of Modern Architecture's fundamental tenets that seem by now to have been definitively dismissed.

The present moment seems to accommodate these premises. And it is possible that the results are the product of an adjustment of the old socio-cultural ideals and utopias to the sometimes discouraging realizations of the actual conditions of contemporary society we have come to accept with some disillusion. Thus, the old egalitarian "reality" that Modern Architecture represented in its grand schemes has been transformed by the new understanding of democracy: either the realities of the market of this society which stubbornly did not wither away and which are idealized through architecture, or the renewed, hopeful, yet always tragic representation of exemplary civic life in its passage from ideal principles to the empirical reality (Figs. 33, 34).

Notes

1 I would like to thank Jeffrey Katz, a student of the Harvard Graduate School of Design second professional degree masters program, for his assistance in preparing some bibliographical notes and illustrations for this article, but most importantly for being a most supportive reader and commentator of the different versions of this article.

Less precise but more substantial acknowledgement should be made to Professors Alan Colquhoun and Colin Rowe. It would be impossible to pinpoint with the exactitude of a quotation their contribution to this article, but it is to their profound efforts to restore the area of the iconography of architecture as a serious theoretical issue that the inspiration of this article is greatly indebted.

In this article I will focus specifically on the productions of these two architects. Besides being, undoubtedly, two of the most prominent figures in architecture today, insofar as they generate the most heated and passionate polemics, both represent within the theoretical context of this article two truly extreme positions of what I believe is the field of possibilities of a certain idea of architecture.

2 I certainly agree with contemporary criticism, chiefly Charles Jencks's, in that the idea of "Modern Architecture" is a deceiving one, as it is made up of a conglomerate of ideas, conceptions, and forms, most of the time contradictory among themselves, that resist (in a strict historical sense), such a generalized label. Yet, it seems to me that for the scope and focus of this article, we can still refer to some absolutely basic, elemental, fundamental notions that characterize that peculiar moment in the history of architecture, and which will always make us recognize, in their rich variety, its products as essentially "modern."

3 Roman Jakobson, "On Realism in Art," in Ladislav Matejka and Krystyna Pomorska, *Readings in Russian Poetics: Formalist and Structuralist Views* (Cambridge, MA: MIT Press, 1971), 39.

4 For a discussion on the history of the term *verisimilitude* and the confusion arising from its sometimes ambiguous usage in classical philosophy (particularly in relation to the term *probability*), see Karl Popper, *Conjectures and Refutations* (Harper Torchbooks, 1968), Chapter X; "Truth, Rationality, and the Growth of Knowledge," especially section three, "Truth and Content: Verisimilitude Versus Probability," and in the same book, "Addenda; Some Technical Notes." It seems that the usage of the term in English translations of classical philosophy is erratic. We are taking Popper's differentiation to correct some widely used translations of Plato and Aristotle in the light of the more consistent usage in Latin (*verisimilis*), French (*vraisemblance*), Spanish (*verosimilitud*), Italian (*verisimilitude*) and German (*wahrscheinlich*) translations, when it unmistakably means "similar to the truth," (Greek *eoikota tois etumoisi*).

5 Both quotes from "Le Vraisembleable," *Communications* 11 (Paris: Editions du Seuil, 1968).

6 Karl Popper, *op. cit.*; Roman Jakobson, *op. cit.* See also "Le Vraisembleable," in *Communications* 11, and Roland Barthes, "L'Anciene rhetorique," *Communications* 16 (Paris: Editions du Seuil, 1970).

7 Nicolaus Pevsner, "Roehampton: LCC Housing and the Picturesque Tradition," *Architectural Review* (July 1959): 35.

8 T de Wolfe is a pseudonym of a well-known architectural critic of the times.

9 T de Wolfe, "Townscape: Plea for an English Architecture founded on the true rock of Sir Uvedale Price," *Architectural Review*, (December 1949): 362.

10 T de Wolfe, *op. cit.*, 362.

11 Reyner Banham, "Neoliberty: The Italian Retreat from Modern Architecture," *Architectural Review* (April 1959): 235.

12 Reyner Banham, *op. cit.*, 235.

13 Ernesto Rogers, "The Evolution of Architecture: An Answer to the Caretaker of Frigidaires," *Casabella* (June 1959).

14 Colin Rowe, "Neo-Classicism and Modern Architecture," in *The Mathematics of the Ideal Villa and Other Essays* (Cambridge, MA: MIT Press, 1976), 131.

15 The precision, boundaries and general appropriateness of labels such as "populism" and "neo-rationalism" can indeed be argued. Yet, they seem to have been too widely accepted and established by the press and readers for us to attempt such a discussion, and, within the scope of the paper, they serve clearly to identify two important tendencies in the contemporary architectural scene. As we will see later, they also serve comfortably as labels for the political and social "realities" that those tendencies attempt to represent through architecture.

16 *Tendenza*: Italian, literally "trend" (not in the pejorative sense). A term accepted and much preferred by most of the protagonists of the also called "neo-rationalism" in Italy. See Massimo Scolari, "Avan-guardia e Nuova Architetture", in *Architettura razionale*, XV Triennale di Milano. Sezione Internazzionale di Architettura, Franco Angeli, Editor (Milano, 1973).

17 Ibid., 185.

18 Ibid., 158–159.

19 Ibid., 170.

20 Robert Venturi, Denise Scott Brown, and Steven Izenour, *Learning from Las Vegas* (Cambridge, MA: MIT Press, 1970), 81.

21 Ibid. 85.

22 In this sense (and paradoxically), the work of Venturi, Moore and their followers seems to be more in the line of Modern Architecture, by re-peating the Corbusian operation of opening architectural language to external codes, although we must grant that all this new openness is done with a certain degree of perversity or irony that is not found in Modern Architecture.

23 Tzvetan Todorov, Introduction to "Le Vraisembleable", in *Communications* 11 (Paris: Editions du Seuil, 1968).

24 It is not casual that a rhetoric of "common knowledge" as a serious technique of structuring discourse has been recovered first in our era by the art of advertisement. It is not coincidence that designers such as Venturi, Scott Brown, Moore, etc, are so fond of advertisement and city signs.

It is important to remark however, that architecture, (and particularly the work of all the protagonists of these tendencies), bring a complex practice in which building, icons and writings are involved, the written speculations that accompany the figurative proposals belong to Todorov's most elaborate case, (see note 23), in which the product belongs to a given category of verisimilitude but explanations of it attempt to present it as a truthful representation of reality.

25 For a discussion of the term and a systematic classification, see: Oswald Ducrot and Tzvetan Todorov, "Genres Litteraires," in *Dictionaire Encyclopedique des sciences du Langage* (Paris: Editions du Seuil, 1972).

26 Massimo Scolari, *op. cit.*, 155.

27 Ibid., 185. "L'imagine def monumenta forse quella che tutti piu facilmente rienscono a cogliere, e propria per questa suo realisma lo useremo qui coma indicazione di semplicita" (translated by the author in the text).

28 Ibid., 185.

29 Ibid., 182.

30 Quatremere de Quincy defines "type" in his contributions to the *Encyclopedie Methodique*, *Architecture*, volume 3, part II (Paris, 1825). Giulio Carlo Argan *Progetto e Destina*, "Sull Concerto de Tipologia Architettonica," Il Saggiatore de Alberto Mondadore Editore (Milano, 1965). See also Giulio Carlo Argan, "On the Typology of Architecture," *Architectural Design* (December 1963).

31 Quatremere de Quincy, *op. cit.* See English translation in "Type," *Oppositions* 8 (Spring 1977).

32 Venturi, Scott Brown, Izenour, *op. cit.*, 88.

33 Alan Colquhoun, "Typology and Design Method," published first in *Arena*, June 1967, and then in *Perspecta* 12, 1969, and in George Baird and Charles Jencks, eds., *Meaning in Architecture* (New York: George Braziller, 1970).

34 Anthony Vidler, "The Idea of Type," *Oppositions* 8 (Spring 1977).

35 Mario Gandelsonas, "Neo-Functionalism", *Oppositions* 5 (New York, Summer 1976).

36 Remarks by John Hejduk during the *Harvard Architectural Review* Forum at Sanders Theatre, Harvard University, October 1977.

37 Aldo Rossi, *L'Architettura della città*, Marsilio, editor, s.p.a., (Padova, 1966).

38 See the work of the Istituto de Storia Dell'Architettura dell Istituto Universitario di Architettura di Venezia, especially Aymonino and others; *La Città di Padova*, Officina Edizione (Rome, 1970); *Le Città Capitali del XIX Secolo Parigi e Vienna*, by Aymonino, Fabbri, Villa Officina Edizione (Rome, 1975); and Aymonino's *Lo Studio dei Fenomeni Urbani*, Officina Edizione (Rome, 1977).

39 For instance during the fifties, while effecting a departure, designers were still trying to perfect Modern Architecture, this time its whole ideology of rationalism and *zeitgeist* reduced to the area of construction, the new materials and their expression (indeed this is the common denominator of all architectural discourses of that time, be it neo-liberty, Brasilia, Mies, etc.). Later, the appearance of the idea of "research" in architecture was the ultimate stage of the notion of rationality and scientization, already contained in some of the manifestos of the twenties, which ends somewhat in the scientifically naïve dreams of people like Christopher Alexander, tinted then with a hyper-functionalist ideology. The same pedigree could be established even more directly with the updated version of the technological utopias and the strategy of *tabula rasa* in another extreme dead end, best exemplified by the "cities" of Archigram. In the same track, other endeavors seem to have had better luck establishing themselves independently from architecture after being for a while the direct offsprings of Modern Architecture, chiefly city planning.

40 Rafael Moneo, "Aldo Rossi: The Idea of Architecture and the Modena Cemetery," *Oppositions* 5 (Summer 1976). The complete quote, which is also to the point, reads: "We are now in an area in which every side thinks they are defending the same positions. The anti-autonomists vindicate the vicarious role of architecture in the consolidation of the environment and refer control to the exercise of ideological power: architecture is a simple game and as such to understand it as an autonomous closed discipline, can be on occasion better, insofar as it is less equivocal. On the other hand, for the autonomists, it is precisely through architecture that society can express its civic and public manifestation. The genuine value of the autonomy of architecture is that it allows for an expression of society in which architecture is an indispensable instrument for the production of the framework necessary to civil life."

41 Aldo Rossi, lecture on his own work given on April 13, 1978, at the Graduate School of Design, Harvard University.

Fig. 1 The Production of Meaning in Architecture: collage of projects by Machado and Silvetti

The Presence of the Past

RODOLFO MACHADO AND
JORGE SILVETTI, 1980

The current controversy about the "presence of the past" in architecture needs clarification, as there are many interpretations that confuse some current stylistic manifestations with more fundamental issues of what is the production of architecture. All this controversy is related to figurative choices, where "the presence of the past" can be checked literally. However, most of these literal figurative changes resemble in tone and in modes and effects the typical avant-garde operation of "inversion" as an opposition to what had previously happened. As most of Modern Architecture's ideological tenets seemed to have been exhausted in the '60s, the continuity of the "modern" stand had to resort blatantly to history in order to assure continuity. These manifestations contain all the avant-garde ingredients; and as such they contain also its quick self-demise, as they soon become the prey of modern society's most peculiar trait: the consumption of symbols.

Against these literal, avant-garde operations, we would like to present a more solid premise. Rather than attempting a critique through inversion with its consequences of shock, controversy, and alienation of both artist and public, and the assured final, quick collapse into kitsch, we would like to see a critique of the present state of architecture based on the more solid and general notions about the production of forms, the production of meaning. From this perspective, the idea of the "presence of the past" is at its foundations and it is an inevitable beginning: for we are what we know, and forms come from forms. The act of production is then, inevitably, one of transformation of the known, and it is only through this that mutations may occur, and eventual novelty result.

Our stand is then not "stylistic"; for better or worse, the present problems cannot be solved as a matter of style. We would like to discuss through our projects more fundamental principles, independent of style, against which architectural performance should be checked, a test that only history can substantiate. Thus the controversy about modern architecture is suspended, and whatever in it is valuable is incorporated into our own "historical resources."

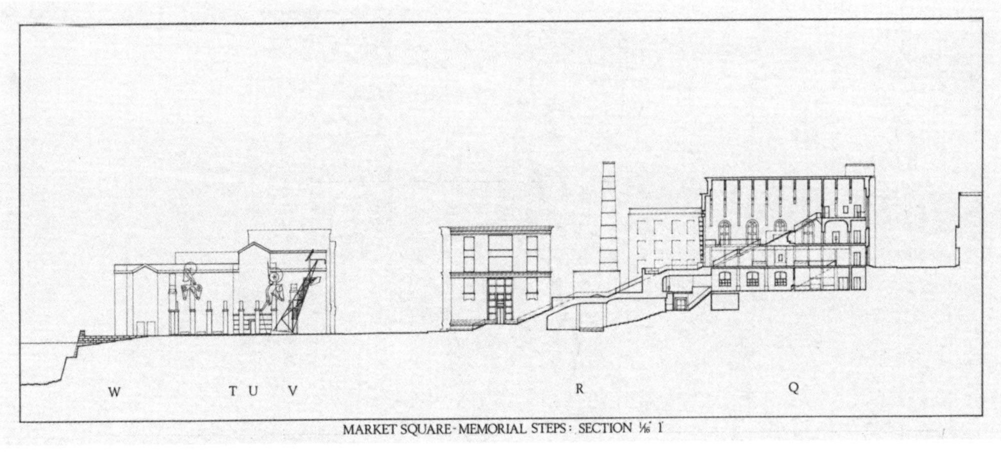

Fig. 2 The Steps of Providence, 1979: Market Square, Memorial Steps.

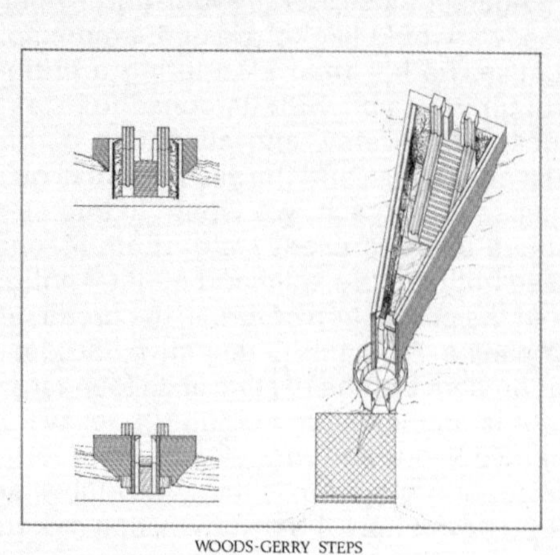

3

Fig. 3 The Steps of Providence, 1979: Woods-Gerry Steps.
Fig. 4 The Steps of Providence, 1979: general plan.
Figs. 5–8 The Steps of Providence, 1979: facade, Waterman Street Entrance and the Pool, the Garden Steps, Frazier Terrace.

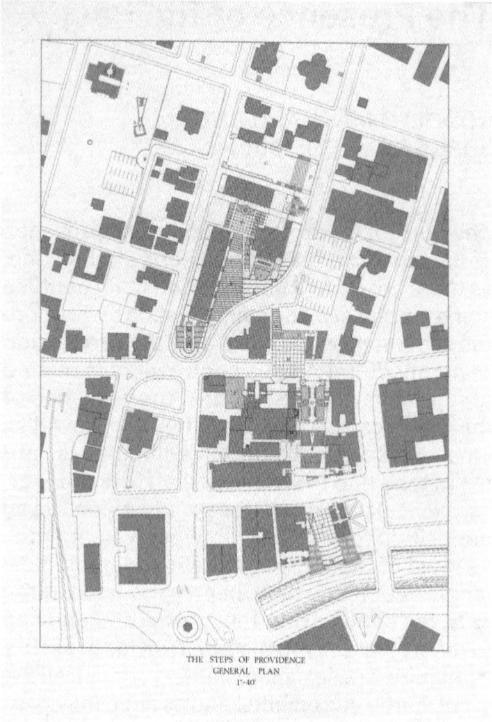

THE STEPS OF PROVIDENCE
GENERAL PLAN
1"=40'

4

5

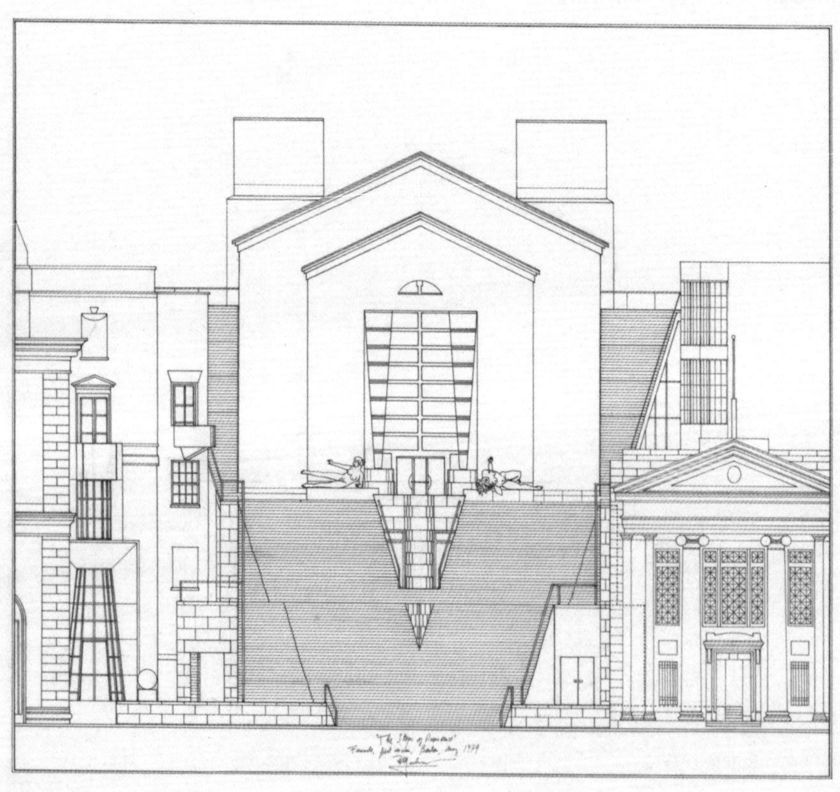

6

THE GARDEN STEPS

7

WATERMAN STREET ENTRANCE and THE POOL

8

FRAZIER TERRACE

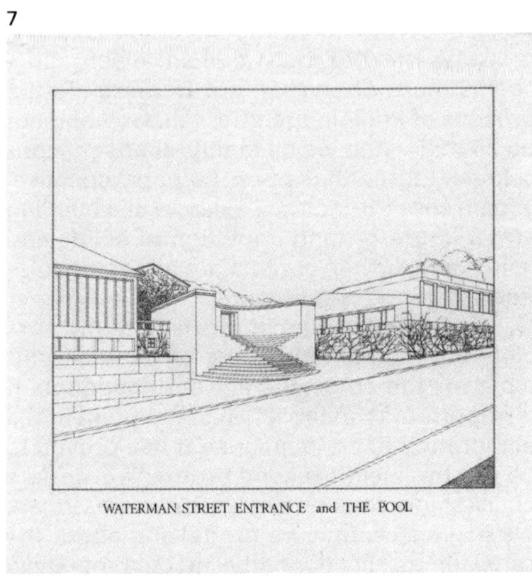

1

2

Representation and Creativity in Architecture: The Pregnant Moment

JORGE SILVETTI, 1982

Not too long ago, a few years at most, a serious discussion addressing itself critically, whether positively or negatively, to some of the issues that I am about to present here would probably have been inconceivable, if not unacceptable, to the greater part of the architectural world. Times are changing, and that there have emerged several special issues of architectural journals and conferences of some importance devoted enthusiastically to the discussion of such things as drawings, models and representation in general is, in itself, significant. It is clear that we want to know, and we certainly know more now than in the recent past, about *how* things architectural are represented and about what qualities each instance of representation depicts. We can—and some have—explore the *who*, the agents of representation, the subjects that generate them and the subjects that receive them. We have also dealt with a pragmatic issue of the utmost importance which has primarily to do with the final efficacy of the message —*the how*. We can—and others have—concern ourselves with the technical issues of the manufacture of an architectural representation, the *with what*, what means can be used, what problems are involved in it.

Classical communication theory deals with just about all these elements of the act of communication including, for example, the problems of the protagonist (the addressor and the addressee) thus dealing with matters of personal expression and emotivity, of decodification and persuasion; the problems of the techniques of representation appear; and again the reflection on the used code itself and of the poetic, artistic and ideological issues connected with the specific message itself.

Yet, although it is a subject that has gained popularity quite recently, very little has been accomplished in the way of describing *the nature of the phenomenon of representation itself, its structure, its place among cultural phenomena* and, what to us is more important now, *its status within the discipline of architecture*. That is not to say that what I have outlined above is of less importance, for I do not see how knowledge can advance if every time we discuss a subject we withdraw to the generally elusive matter of fundamental essences or of the nature of things, of precise definitions, of etymologies and histories. This, if it is always the prerequisite of any elaboration, seems more often than not to dissipate the process of knowledge. After all, we need not do all that when we all tacitly, almost unconsciously, agree that a two-point perspective, a foam core 1/8-inch scale model of a building and a figure-ground depiction of solids and voids in the urban context are all representations of things architectural.

At the same time, if this is not only possible but recommendable as a general principle for the advancement of knowledge, it is important to establish at some point in the elaboration of an idea, once it has proven to be worthy, insightful and productive, certain checkpoints and certain new directives where we make sure that we are talking about the same things, that our partial models somehow refer to some common phenomenon. And it is important in the truly dialectical process of theory to adjust the objectives of our inquiry as new knowledge is gathered in response to those most insightful questions of *how*, *who* and *with what*. Any science and any theory must have a clearly defined object of inquiry, and every science and theory refines, redefines and adjusts such an object according to the knowledge that has already been gained.

In light of this I should probably talk about that most philosophical and slightly pretentious question of *what*, even though what I have to say now is merely speculation and not new theory (for I want to speak as an architect not as a theoretician), a digression rather than a deliberation, an enumeration of attributes rather than a continuous discourse, ideological not scientific. It is a reply to those who have their doubts about this subject. It will, hopefully, turn some things upside down, in order to perhaps find that somehow things begin to finally look right; for we might find some answers to the poverty of architecture today by talking about representation, and we may realize that we need to subvert some current empirical categories that are entrenched in current thought and which are in the way of architecture.

The general problem of representation is one of the oldest of philosophical issues and indeed at times one has the impression that philosophers have always and only been talking about it either explicitly or implicitly. Plato and Aristotle discuss things like verisimilitude, rhetoric, truth, art, poetics and thus inaugurate the western tradition with its concerns for representation. St. Augustine and later Thomas Aquinas focused on the notion of sign, how it represents and thus, how the world is organized. The utopias of the Renaissance are representations of life and the first serious controversies between

Fig. 1 Caravaggio, *Canestro di Frutta*.
Fig. 2 La Scala production of Donizetti's *Poliuto*.
Fig. 3 Newspaper clipping.
Fig. 4 da Vinci, *Mona Lisa*.
Fig. 5 Mantegna, *Saint Sebastian*.

3

17-Year-Old Wins Our Mona Lisa Look-Alike Contest

. . . And a Free Trip To Paris for Two

Norma Pirkle really has something to smile about — she's the happy winner of our exciting Mona Lisa look-alike contest.

"Oh, no! I just can't believe it. I've never won anything before," exclaimed Norma in her Oxnard, Calif., home.

The 17-year-old high school student has won a fabulous all-expenses-paid vacation for two to Paris, France, for a fun-filled week of sight-seeing.

And, of course, she'll also visit the Louvre, the famed museum where the Leonardo da Vinci painting hangs. "I'm going to take my mother with me to Paris," said Norma.

"My friends are really going to be excited for me when they hear about this.

"I entered The ENQUIRER's contest after a friend told me I looked like Mona Lisa. So we took some pictures and sent them in.

"I didn't think about it much after that . . . I didn't want to get my hopes up too high. You can imagine how excited I am with the good news!

"And my mother is as excited as I am since we've never gone on many vacations. I'm not sure yet what we'll see while we're in Paris. I do know we'll see the real Mona Lisa. We'll probably leave during spring vacation so I don't miss any school."

MONA LISA

WINNER: Teenager Norma Pirkle

4

5

theology and science involve, in the end, implications of representation. The Bishop Berkeley introduces some disconcerting thoughts about reality and the self—that is, whether reality is not just a representation itself—and Descartes assures us about such reality by proposing a very successful, systematic representation of it; and we could go on through history to Nietzsche, Marx, the philosophical implications introduced by Freud and arrive at all the philosophies that spring from the social sciences to see that representation is a central subject, be it approached now from the subject of ideology, from the unconscious, from interpretation and hermeneutics or from the subject of language.

What I would like to turn to now, however, is far less sophisticated intellectually, certainly less intricate in manner and indeed more modest in content, for I am not prepared to deal with this subject in such depth. I will refer to just some aspects of the nature of representation that are not currently of popular interest in spite of their being quite apparent and sometimes even trivial, and which I believe may suggest ways to help in the building of a theory of representation of architecture (while remaining aloof to the fact that things labeled trivial or too apparent are usually victims of some ideological categorization which effaces their meaning). And to start with the most trivial, let us recall the dictionary which states among other things that to "represent is to present again." And in our everyday language:

- figure 1, a "still life," is a representation of a basket, fruits and leaves.
- A theatrical performance, a representation of a play, and in turn, the play a representation of a plot, a story (Fig. 2).
- And the newspaper clip of figure 3, a representation of a photograph, which in turn represents a woman, who at the time of the photograph was re-presenting the painting of another woman who lived about 500 years ago, painted (represented) by Leonardo, a painting which in turn has become objectified and which as a painting represents certain ideals of beauty, of art, of femininity (Figs. 3 and 4).

We notice then, as soon as we suspend the illusion, that a complex array of elements, combinations of elements, operations and problems contained and coexisting within a simple act of representation emerge. For instance we find that:

- there are phenomena such as likeness, verisimilitude and mimesis which present special and complex issues of their own;
- time and space are distorted and often forced to reappear in different media;
- in order to reappear a trick of sorts must be affected, that representation has something to do with illusion;
- a representation could become in its turn the represented of another representation, in a theoretically endless chain;
- a representation can acquire in culture a certain status that inverts the process, and that, instead of just representing its model which existed prior to it, can "produce" a new thing that did not exist before—that is, it can invent itself (take for example all of the connotations and symbolic meanings that a painting like the Mona Lisa has come to represent in its history) thus making the image, the painting, a thing in itself with a "life" and influential qualities of its own.

We could digress in this fashion almost endlessly—a type of speculation that is always fruitful and productive, but which I cannot attempt here. At the risk of losing some richness, then, let us reduce all of this to one simple yet paradoxical aspect of representation from which all the others seem to derive, which is that: A representation, whether a play, a painting, a drawing, a text, etc., something that supposedly presents something again (re-presents), *in order to be a representation must occur through a change of substance*, take place in a different form or matter. A piece of reality, a history, a personality can be translated into the words of a text, some graphisms on a page, some sounds—that is, language, which is part of yet a much more complicated matter, that of literary matter, with its special rules, syntax, symbols, rhythms, style, which are themselves specifically literary. A person, with the history, character, flesh, smells, thoughts, passions, weaknesses and a "time," can become an illusion made out of canvas, and a mixture of pigments applied with a certain technique and style, and a myth (Fig. 5).

All of this brings us to that curious problem that is built into the very nature of representation, which is an innate impossibility, an inevitable madness: because, in its most general yet most profound aspect, what is it that representation wants to depict? We could review the history of art and find innumerable reasons, the most sophisticated and insightful interpretations, the most profound motives and the most diverse and at times opposing aims as to what art does and for what; but in the end, the kernel of all art is a relentless and delirious desire to bring to us again (or represent) the real.

At a conference two years ago at this University I addressed the problem of "Realism in Architecture," and only tangentially touched upon the problem I am beginning to outline now. We realized then that a term like "realism" was elusive because, as Jakobson warned already in 1921,

> Classicists, sentimentalists, the romanticists to a certain extent, even "realists" of the nineteenth century, the modernists to a large degree, and finally the futurists, expressionists, and their like have more than once steadfastly proclaimed faithfulness to reality . . .[1]

At this conclusion most critics and artists are beginning to arrive in this moment of history when we have become acutely aware of the wickedness of words and labels; aware that useful labels such as "classic," "romantic," "realist," "abstract," "concrete," "expressionist," "impressionist," "surrealist," etc., all describe eloquently a certain aim, ideology and rhetoric; but that these labels conceal the very same common struggle, the same madness, that of presenting the real again in another substance. For as soon as we accept this fact, we are confronted with its contradiction.

I let Roland Barthes, in his poignant manner, underline the nature of this contradiction, which is the force, the energy of representation. In talking about literature specifically, which can then be extended to all arts, he says:

> From ancient times to the efforts of our avant-garde, literature has been concerned to represent something. What? I will put it crudely: the real. The real is not representable, and it is because men ceaselessly try to represent it by words that there is a history of literature. *That the real is not representable, but only demonstrable, can be said in several ways: either we can define it, with Lacan, as the* impossible, *that which is unattainable and escapes discourse, or in topological terms we observe that a pluri-dimensional order (the real) cannot be made to coincide with a unidimensional order (language).* Now, it is precisely this topological impossibility that literature rejects and to which it never submits. Though there is no parallelism between language and the real, men will not take sides, and it is this refusal, perhaps as old as language itself, which produces, in an incessant commotion, literature. We can imagine a history of literature, or better, say, of productions of language, which would be the history of certain (often abberant) verbal *expedients* men have used to reduce, tame, deny, or, on the contrary, to assume what is *always* a delirium, i.e., the fundamental inadequation of language and the real. I said a moment ago, apropos of knowledge,

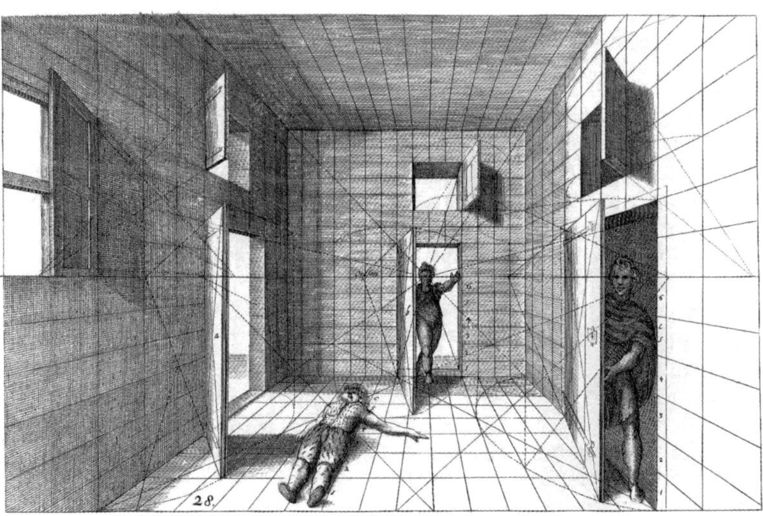

Fig. 6 Plate #28 from *Perspective*, Jan Vredeman de Vries, 1604.

7

8

> that literature is categorically realist, in that it never has anything but the real as its object of desire; and I shall say now, without contradicting myself—because I am here using the word in its familiar acceptation—that literature is quite as stubbornly unrealistic; it considers sane its desire for the impossible.[2]

What is then the value, the role, the status of this insanity? Why this persistence? Why does it not ever go away? Of course, there are and always will be those who have already answered these questions negatively, those who have wished representation away, no matter how close they seem to come and seem to share our common endeavor, those who appear sometimes paternalistically "understanding" of the madness of our attempts at representation, who in our specific field of architecture would at best accord secondary status to these aspects of architecture, and at worst dismiss them altogether as useless, futile and childish. And then, there are those of us who insist, reiterate and attempt to keep alive this supreme insanity, this obsession. And in spite of all the new talk, all of the good things we have been hearing and saying let us not forget that according to the current social and ideological organization of our discipline, the status of representation (specifically, drawings and models) is lower than that of the only thing that supposedly matters, which is, of course, the BUILDING. Indeed, we are reminded, representation is second class, and to put too much effort on it is to endanger the solidity of the apparatus upon which architecture relies, or upon which it thinks it relies.

Fortunately, we hear other voices, voices detached, outside the making, who observe and tell us what all of this might be about. Immediately, I would like to recall here the speculations of anthropology, which engages directly these matters when studying the meaning of the cultural products and the structure of the mind. For to be detached, as the anthropologist should be, helps to see a more general picture in which culture and its products (myth, magic, science and art) all become significant, without any implications of status, not one more important than the other, seeing them all as different and interdependent modes of representation of reality which are indispensable. I would like to introduce a particular contribution by Claude Lévi-Strauss to the specific subject of interest here. After delineating the nature of structural similarities, and opposed modalities of science and magic, he takes a detour in his argument (presented in the *The Savage Mind*) to devote some pages to some aspects of art. And his first observation is that the work of art appears always as what he calls a REDUCED MODEL.

Taking as an example Francois Cluet's portrait of Elizabeth of Austria, specifically the lace collar of her dress, he asks and contends,

> What is the virtue of reduction either of scale or in the number of properties? . . . The intrinsic value of a small-scale model is that it compensates for the renunciation of sensible dimensions by the acquisition of intelligible dimensions.[3]

What interests us in all this is that in the process of representation there is a reduction, a loss of some qualities or attributes and then that there is a choice, a preference for others which, by being chosen, occupy "more space" as it were, the space of the missing attributes, and become more apparent, marked and insightful; that whatever gains in knowledge we may acquire in this process become the support of general ideas, tendencies and movements of the spirit and of the mind, because modes of representation, which are reduced models on one level by necessity of the change of substance, become unavoidably and paradoxically universal models of explanations that constitute "symbolic forms" in themselves which give reason, sustain and support an epoch and a culture—in short, give to a society at a given time a way of representing itself, of knowing itself, of keeping itself together through the power of these reduced models without which culture would be impossible. One might recall Panofsky's "Perspective as Symbolic Form," in which he addresses this issue introducing and expounding upon the notion of perspective in general as a symbolic form of western society at a given time.

A look at perspective, in fact, may yield some interesting insights about this difficult problem of representation in architecture. With perspective, a system that leaves aside many attributes of real space, we have a reduced model of reality that permits us to study depth, to measure and manipulate relationships between objects in space, to place them and to establish hierarchies. Particularly,

Fig. 7 Antonello da Messina, *San Gerolamo nello Studio* (1430–1479).
Fig. 8 Albrecht Dürer, *Saint Jerome*.
Fig. 9 Giuseppe Galli Bibiena, *Scene from a theatrical performance on the occasion of the nuptials of the Prince Elector of Bavaria*, Architectural and Perspective Designs, 1740.
Fig. 10 Jean-Francois Niceron, *Pyramidal anamorphosis*, *Thaumaturgus Opticus*, Rome, 1646.
Fig. 11 Le Corbusier, *Plan Voisin*, 1925.

9

11

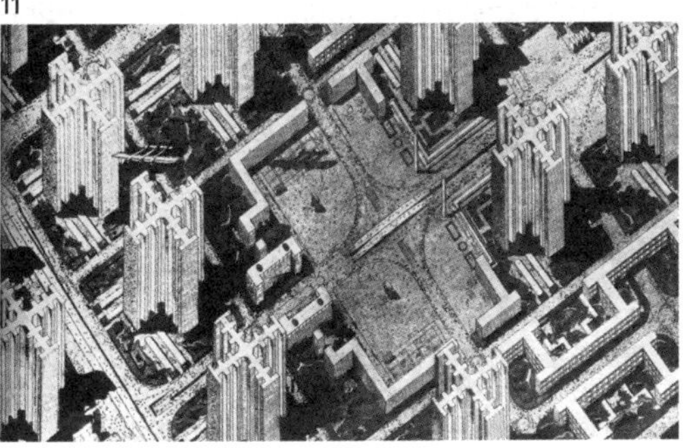

10

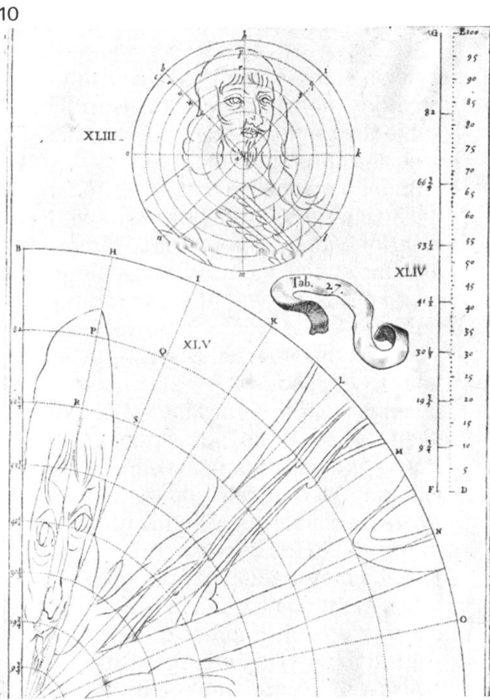

with one-point perspective we establish a hierarchy, a classification and an order without which the conception of Architecture advanced by Alberti and the rest of the Renaissance theoreticians could not have been developed (Fig. 6).

With this type of perspective which finally puts us in the center of the world from where everything is viewed, analyzed, measured and known, the ideological apparatus of humanism encounters its most felicitous symbolic form. One-point perspective casts aside the fact that it is rarely a reality, that the same object which it depicts exists independently of us, that what we see is indeed a curvilinear projection on our retina, a sensible world where straight lines are unknown, and indeed hardly exist—a myriad of "facts" that have been put aside, obliterated, negated, effaced, in order to establish a certain intelligible dimension which supports one of the few major shifts in the history of seeing, conceiving and knowing reality. And yet it is important to know that for all its irresistible power overriding the whole of western culture, its intrinsic contradiction allows for slight variations that individual personalities and cultures require to express their own identities and "view of the world." So, Panofsky addresses the duality of perspective:

> It is accordingly only a matter of course that . . . (Italy) . . . interpreted the meaning of perspective quite differently from the North: *there*—to speak very generally —its objective significance was felt to be more important, *here* (the North) its subjective significance . . . Antonello da Messina constructs St. Jerome's study with far distance (so that, like almost all Italian interiors, it is at bottom rather an exterior with the front surface removed): also the space begins with the picture plane or rather *behind* it and the sight point is almost exactly in the middle. Dürer, on the other hand, shows us—and he is by no means the first to do so—a genuine interior, into which we ourselves seem to have been drawn because the floor appears to come forward until it is under our own feet and the distance; expressed in terms of actual measurement, would not come to more than about a meter and a half; the position of the sight point, quite far off center, strengthens the impression of a representation determined not by the objective law of the architecture but by the subjective standpoint of the spectator who is just entering—a representation which owes to precisely this perspective arrangement a large part of its peculiarly "intimate" effect.[4] (Figs. 7–8).

And certainly it has not been the only, nor the best, for as soon as the one-point perspective begins to suffer its shortcomings and contradictions if nothing else than within perspective itself, the two-point perspective comes to reject the more seductive idea of center and begins to select other possibilities in which we begin to slide and move through the illusion of space in the surface of the picture plane, to wander in the space of illusion toward what is now a space that escapes to the sides, which begins to introduce a more disconcerting, yet more accurate idea of infinitum than one-point perspective (Fig. 9). To allow for this, perspective must itself, as a truly intellectual and scientific construct, effect its own parallel criticism through its own language, through that demystifying technique of anamorphism, where if on the one hand its effect appears as a simple game at an intellectual level, on the other, it constitutes a devastating critique of its own illusion (Fig. 10).

If one-point perspective has allowed us to produce the architecture of the Renaissance, the two-point contributes the more pragmatic idea of continuity of the Baroque without which the modern idea of urban design would be unthinkable, with its tools of continuity and persuasion as expressed by the arresting blurring of the visual arts that takes place in the Baroque, where the central point is not so important as the persuasive effect of images; and finally space escapes altogether, detached forever from the viewer, in the axonometric (Fig. 11). The sensible dimension of the cone of vision (that of the spectator) is discarded in favor of the sensible dimension of the real infinitude, social and physical, of space and by the realization of a universe in which we are not alone. Without it, many modern ideas of city and their corresponding social models of socialism, equality and total democracy would not have found their physical expression.

This is, somehow a brief, quite violent and too simplistic history of perspective, a method of representation with diverse modes from which architecture has thought about itself. In each instance we have reduced[4] the world of reality to a few attributes while obscuring others; perspective *has lied* (as far as facts and truth are concerned) but it has also *produced*

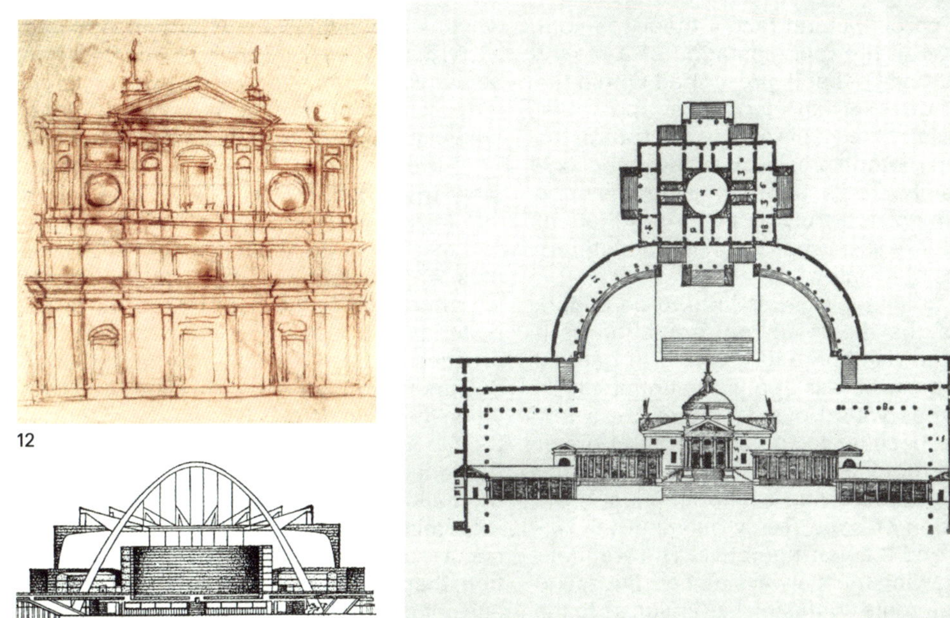

12

13

14

Fig. 12 Michelangelo, *San Lorenzo, Facade Project*.
Fig. 13 Le Corbusier, *Palais des Soviets*, 1931.
Fig. 14 Palladio, *Villa Trissino*.

meaning. It is indeed a remarkable fact of history; and we could extend the analysis to other modes of two-dimensional depictions of space (i.e. Pompeiian, Byzantine, Late Middle Ages, etc.) and their relationships to the corresponding architectures.

What I think I am trying to say with these brief, schematic and partial examples, is that what constitutes the fault of representation—its impossibility, its deception, its wickedness, its untruthfulness—what constitutes its deficiency in its depiction of reality (a lie that passes as reality through illusion—what a sin!) as opposed to science, which is also a representation of reality but which is always alert to its deceptions through the use of different methodological checkpoints through logic and constant critique and finally conscious confession of its limitations—that all of this unreliable, unrelenting activity of architecture encouraged by this mad obsession with an impossibility—is the source of a virtue; that without this impossibility, these partializations, this delirium, there would be no art, no architecture, and more importantly, as a result there would not exist the myths that literature, painting and architecture all produce and which are the types of knowledge indispensable for a society to exist, the types of knowledge that order the chaos of reality, that restrict yet illuminate perception, that conceal in order to discover new realities that reduce in order to depict positive aspirations.

I think it is best now to bring together all of these arguments specifically in relation to Architecture; for although the temptation to talk about all the arts collectively is always great (and it is always seductive to find commonalities, correspondences, etc., among all of them) structurally and historically they are, in the end, different. Again, if the translation between reality and representation is impossible because the respective substances are different, so also is an exact parallelism among the arts. Each art is characterized by the substance and matter it handles and manipulates and finally it is what it is because of this fact.

So, what are the products of architecture and where should we place representation? One would be tempted to say buildings, which is true; but, for reasons that I hope will become clear at the end, I would like to propose that the products of architecture are not just buildings, but also drawings and models, and writings, each of them a mode of representation of a reality with which architecture is engaged, each of them with some similar concerns, but each somehow keeping a certain degree of independence and autonomy from the other.

The architectural text, a theory, is concerned with the representation of a reality, an ideal reality, that is prescribed within the context of a certain ideological apparatus. The tense of the text is always the future, the tone and rhetoric prescriptive, the mood, one of certainty. *De Re Aedifictoria* and *Vers une Architecture* are truly as much products of architecture as any building; they are literary illusions of a reality.

Of drawings there is little to be added. Most of the theory of representation as it applies to painting and drawing in general can be more or less applied to architectural drawing as well. However, there are a few that are peculiar to the architectural drawing as a representation. Unlike painting, the architectural drawing cannot engage in the discussion or controversy between the figurative and the non-figurative. The architectural drawing must always be figurative, and from this some confusion has arisen as to the impact that some manifestations of the modern movement in art have had on architectural drawings.

Also, unlike the depiction of space and architecture in painting, an architectural drawing, by definition, *precedes the building*, and in fact we have many architectural drawings that for certain contingencies of history have never resulted in a building, but to which we still pay the same reverence as we do to buildings, three examples of which might be the facade of San Lorenzo, designed and rendered but, of course, never built by Michelangelo; the Villa Trissino by Palladio; and the Palace of the Soviets by Le Corbusier (Figs. 12, 13, 14). We do not need more than the drawings to know why these buildings are important, although we wish they had been built. This could, again, be a trivial observation as long as we harbor the prejudice which attaches a lower status to drawings among the products of architecture.

I would like to propose another seemingly trivial fact that I hope will be turned into insight in the context of this discussion and that is that architects do not build buildings. Architects draw. That is all we do, and we return thus to the issue of substance and materiality of a practice, which defines the practice itself; the task of the architect, as designer and conceiver of a building, ends when the drawing is finished (or by extension the model, the final presentation, in general the reduced model prior to the execution of the building). The implication of this simple fact being that CREATIVITY in architecture occurs only at the moment of representation, that moment full of partialities, delirium and concealments—that artistic moment. It is by the movements of the hand guided by the eyes that look into the vastness of the mind that architecture is produced. We imagine (the first representation occurring within the mind itself) and we draw (the second representation, a physical manifestation which is extracted from the mind).

Finally, the building appears: the world of illusion, of deceit and utopia contained in the representations of the mind and of the hand suddenly comes to an end. Here we have at last, the tangible reality, the fact, the proof. Or is this indeed the case? It seems that really what we see in a building and our experience of it depend once again on a certain kind of representation, or rather it seems that the only

Fig. 15 Baldassare Peruzzi, imaginary street in an ancient city, for tragic scene.

Fig. 16 Le Corbusier, L'Esprit Nouveau Pavilion, 1925.

way to decode it, to understand the building is to represent—a representation that may or may not coincide with that of the architect, and which somehow puts everybody into the process of creation again.

In a building we act, in both the most general sense of the word and in its theatrical sense as well. The final form of a building, conceived and created through words and drawings, depends on scenes imagined, predicted and staged by the architect and which wait to be re-enacted and re-presented even in spite of what we are told to the contrary—that we live in times of change, of mobility, of pluralistic life styles and of a myriad of choices, which should result in more free buildings, more flexible and accommodating, more unprecise and generally more neutral in style and form (and of less quality I should perhaps add). There is no way in which our imagination and creativity can escape this form of representation which is very precise, this form of specific illusion, the paradigmatic form of representation: the theatrical stage where a play is to take place.

It is in this sense that the last piece of FACT, that incorruptible ingredient in the creation of architecture which many minds still find to be the only piece of the process that escapes illusion and representation, that sacred and limpid thing called the PROGRAM, succumbs to representation. Because finally, since different matters cannot be translated into other matters, a set of words (a program) cannot be expected to produce architectural forms, and the way that finally a program is incorporated into the design is through images that are closer to theater than any other type of representation. The program then turns into a narrative, a play, a story, a plot, displayed most of the time as discrete tableau in which we see the scenes. Indeed this part of representation is very complex in architecture because it spans across both the moment of creation in the architect's mind, and the act of decoding and experiencing a building by the beholder.

Until not long ago, architects used to do sets for the theatre and the relationship between the two practices was a happy, almost natural one. It is still our model, the safest model of proceeding in relation to the program, and we use it all the time although in a highly repressed, subconscious way. It is the most elusive of all the types of representation we use, but it is the one that most vividly articulates the building as a reality. It is not written, not drawn, but finally it is the one that persists and is re-enacted and reinterpreted. Since it cannot operate with the precision of a theatrical representation, where all is calculated, necessary and sufficient, it finally has to depend on architecture itself, on the elements and history of the discipline from which it emerges to become believable, plausible, real.

It is this image of the theatre which will finally help us to define in a general way the nature of representation. This return to the theatre, as a mode of thought and of imagination I am proposing, certainly serves as a most powerful critique of the horrors that the architecture of the recent past has produced in our cities. The space of the theatre is always a positive "void," full of meaning, where everything is indispensable and significant. It is the opposite of the left-over and could be the model for both the public realm where true civic life can take place once again (Fig. 15), and for the private world where the domestic tableau can be enacted (Fig. 16). From the experience of the theatre, the representation *par excellence*, we might extract our final concept: following Roland Barthes again, when referring to Diderot, he imagines the classics to have said,

> to discourse (to represent), is to depict the tableau one has in one's mind . . . the tableau (pictorial, theatrical, literary) is a pure cut-out segment with clearly defined edges, irreversible and incorruptible: everything that surrounds it is banished into nothingness, remaining unnamed, while everything that it admits within its field is promoted into essence, into light, into view.[5]

This theatrical notion of the tableau then extends and strengthens that complex activity we call Architecture: in the words, in the drawings, in the buildings. The tableau, the imagined stage, constitutes the most powerful tool of the creator (Fig. 16). For it is there, by reasons of exclusions and inclusions, that the impossible depiction of true life can be yet reduced once more through representation to a few chosen instants of which also Barthes comments:

> In order to tell a story, the painter . . . has only an instant at his disposal, the instant he is going to immobilize on the

> canvas, and he must thus choose it well, assuring it in advance of the greatest possible yield of meaning and pleasure. Necessarily total, this instant will be artificial (unreal . . .) a hieroglyph in which can be read at a single glance . . . . the present, the past and the future; that is, the historical meaning of the represented action. This crucial instant, totally concrete and totally abstract, is what Lessing subsequently calls the PREGNANT MOMENT.[6]

Representation is a subject much more important in architecture than we have been led to believe. That it is not subservient to anything, because of its untranslatable substances, makes each of its instances an independent creative act. Unlike any of the other arts, the architectural representation at once must relate definitively to the final work, the building, and most clearly must also represent *a priori* what does not yet exist. Thus architecture exists, as a creative moment only in representations, and we can only be sure of those representations. For all its wickedness, partiality and untruthfulness, paradoxically, the tableau is the only thing we can be sure of, because of our inability to predict the future, because in all three modes of representation of architecture, the reality depicted has not yet arrived.

I think all of this might sound subversive and disturbing, perhaps scandalous; but then so is art, and perhaps all I have been trying to accomplish here is to somehow instill just a little more courage and a little more respect for the creative moments of architecture, to help remove the wasted energies that we put today into the fears of inexactitude, imprecision and uncertainty, fears of misplaced built feelings, and naive hopes of scientific method and technological truth, and to put those energies back without shame and with lots of pleasure into cultivating the imagination and creativity and the moment of representation, the pregnant moment, a moment without which architecture could not exist.

Notes

1 "On Realism in Art," in Ladislav Matejka and Krystyna Pomorske, *Readings in Russian Peotics: Formalists and Structuralist Views* (Cambridge, MA: MIT Press, 1971).

2 Roland Barthes, Lecture in Inauguration of the Chair of Literary Semiology, College de France, January 7, 1977. Published in *October*, no. 8 (Spring 1979): 3–16.

3 Claude Lévi-Strauss, *The Savage Mind* (Chicago, IL: University of Chicago Press, 1966), 22, 24.

4 Erwin Panofsky, "Perspective as Symbolic Form" from *Vortage der Bibliothek Warburd*, 1924–25 (Leipzig and Berlin: The Kulturwissenschaftliche Bibliothek Warburg, 1924–25): 258–330.

5 Roland Barthes, "Diderot, Brecht, Eisenstein," in *Image, Music, Text* (New York, NY: Hill & Wang, 1977).

6 Ibid.

Perspective and the Envious Longing for the Renaissance

JORGE SILVETTI, 1984

To discuss the use of perspective methods of representation of space in the process of architectural design today confronts us immediately, and inevitably, with a most substantial and profound (albeit mostly unacknowledged) issue in architectural theory, one that deals with the relationships between techniques of representation on one side, and ideology, creativity and the constraints that such techniques may impose on the language of architecture on the other. In addition, and as with most theoretical issues, it will confront us eventually with the problem of defining the specificity of architecture today, a very promising subject which, however, does not seem to find the echo that it deserves in the field of theory. On the one hand, perspective drawing is trivialized in the current, general debate (which seems to concentrate on the most superficial and banal aspects of contemporary architecture such as "historical styles" vs "modern style") and it becomes yet another stylistic issue. On the other hand, perspective drawing cannot resonate at the level that it deserves in the most serious theoretical debates because the most enthusiastic and productive efforts in theory and criticism in architecture have been devoted almost in their entirety to issues pertaining to the product, its effects and performance, and its relations with other cultural phenomena (such as ideology, language, literature, modernism and avant-gardism, etc.) rather than on an explanation and description of the moment of production of architecture. Besides the inherent difficulties deriving from the nature of the problem that will necessarily include a discussion about "the subject" that designs, it is understandable that the concentration has been on the product, because the habits and tendencies of architectural theory have been heavily influenced by historical research and by theories that are rooted mostly in iconographic or hermeneutic studies, or in theories derived from social studies, psychology or, simply, politics. This ample, rich and fertile tradition from which the ever-incipient architectural theory sprung has ultimately given us, in the best cases, a potent and devastating critique of ideology and a demystification of ideological notions such as "function," "nature," "solution," etc. Or at worst, we might say that we have been distracted by irritating tautologies supported by the kind of statistical trivia which characterize most of the behavioral studies. But whether good or bad, theoretical work has always established uncomfortable relationships with that opaque and seemingly impenetrable instance which is the moment of production and of creativity a problem that has been compounded even more by the tendency inherent in our architectural culture to instrumentalize theory into formulae that presumably would help to produce better buildings.

It is against this context that we must re-discuss perspective. A rather unstructured and somewhat improvised discussion about it indeed exists today, mostly in schools of architecture, which acknowledges its relevance, but which tends to orient itself rather quickly in the direction of the ideological ramifications and implications that have always been associated with perspective from the tradition of architectural history and iconographical studies. These biases are understandable, if we consider that those studies and conceptualizations, which bring together a mode of representation of space with the whole formal and ideological apparatus of an epoch, are perhaps the most powerful, synthetic and convincing constructs that architectural theory has produced. I believe that we all agree by now about the power to condense information of the most varied sources and natures that any mode of representation of space has.

But it is precisely because of this (by now an almost-unconscious awareness) that we are sometimes immersed in heated discussions about the appropriateness or not of perspective representation in the process of design. In the most "enlightened" circles today, it is more common than not to hear that utilizing perspective in the production of architecture is "wrong," that our conceptions of space are "different," that it is "historicist," etc., One even hears of "schools" that forbid its use. Undoubtedly, it is important to maintain a clear distance from the ideological implications that perspective once had and not to fall prey to a nostalgic temptation to imagine that the utilization of perspective will restore the positive qualities of classical architecture. But conversely, to deny its possible use because of past ideological associations is not to understand the complexity and the multiplicity of factors that coexist in the process of design and their mutual and dynamic relationships. Moreover, it is also to maintain a deterministic view of the process of design that has characterized most of the "methodologies" of the recent past that have been criticized by the very same critics.

To understand all this we must first remind ourselves about the characteristics of the relationships between the means of production and the product. We know that any practice is determined to a considerable degree by its means of production, by the techniques employed and by the nature of the matter that is being elaborated and transformed, be it agricultural production or film, be it a craftsman's object or a philosopher's theoretical construct. In that sense we know, as architects, that every element that enters into the production of architecture, in the process, influences and limits its resulting product, from the type of pen, pencil, paper, to financial resources, in one way or another and in various degrees. However, because most of these things are only mechanical or material influences, they do not seem to be the focus of attention of theory since they do not appear to be tied to ideology in any way, but rather to available resources or technological possibilities; but the modes of representation are tied to ideology, and so is the intensity of the theoreticians' and practitioners' concerns. It is not so much the recognition that the use of perspective (or any other type of representation) affects the product that is at issue as the fear that a particular type of product is going to result: namely a product that may be associated with past architectures. This naive and overdeterministic view is the typical, simplistic way of thinking about "process" that characterizes architectural thought in our century. Indeed, that multiplicity of elements which intervene in the process of design establish dynamic and ever-changing relationships which cannot be described by using all-embracing, deterministic models.

Thus, if we have come to accept the notion that the means of production and the techniques of production influence the product; and if we also know through history that in the field of the visual arts, and in particular in architecture, all the intervening elements might acquire symbolic value irrespective of their original or functional role, and that particularly technological or scientific discoveries have been favorite vehicles for symbolic representation, then we might also be willing to accept the fact that such a process of symbolization may become obsolete, irrelevant, and reverse itself or become inactive

1

2

Figs. 1–2 Jorge Silvetti: House in Pergusa, Sicily, 1982. Perspective.

leaving, thus, those elements free from symbolic and rhetorical tasks and able to return unencumbered to perform their original, functional roles, which in all likelihood may still be required.

This active, dynamic and unstable relationship between technique and symbol seems particularly clear in the case of perspective, which by now, and for a long time, has ceased to carry any of its original symbolic meaning. Certainly, a lot has happened since the days of Brunelleschi to our culture, to our society, to our understanding and conceptualization of space, and to art, for us to pretend that perspective representation still stands for the tenets of Humanism. And yet, unlike painting where the issue of representation of space was (or is?) *the issue*, and a reiteration of illusionistic, Renaissance-like perspective may not add anything to its history and evolution, in architecture the representation of space is a *means* to an end and not its substance; and the "discovery" of perspective, irrespective of the ideological connotations that it acquired at the time of its inception, formalized a technique of representation that has become indispensable ever since. For one must ask the obvious but somehow repressed question: what is wrong with representing the object, the space as it actually seems to appear to the viewer when it is inscribed in his cone of vision? Which generates other not so obvious questions such as: Is that a restricting technical device or may it rather complement others? May symbolism find another place in the rich output of architecture (perhaps in the building as experienced by the beholder rather than in its representation)?

Our art may have changed, its boundaries contracted or expanded over the centuries, and our concerns shifted one way or another, but we are still among many other constants, dealing with *visual material* of a three dimensional nature, and hence with spatial phenomena that *is to be seen*; and because of that, and because the project comes before the object exists, the anticipated test of its visual and spatial performances has become part of the process of design; in that moment, perspective still plays an irreplaceable role.

The paradox is that in the current attempts to "deconstruct" or "decompose" our culture and its products (of which perspective representation is an easy target), and in the parallel and determined struggle to find at all costs

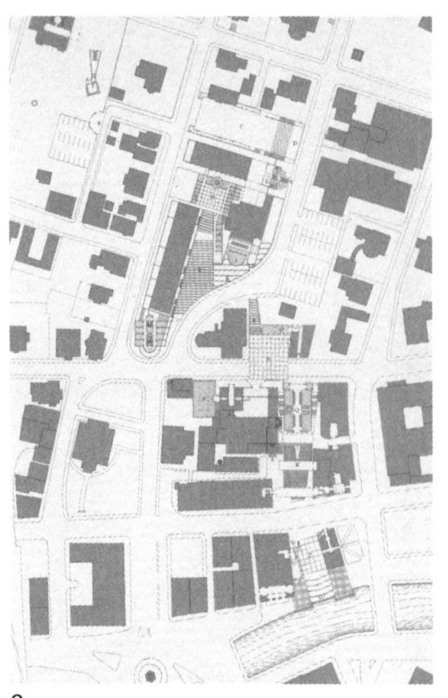

3

4

a symbolic form for our times and architecture, some critics fall into an even more profound "cultural trap" of "Renaissance envy" when unconsciously they long to replicate the overall *cultural format* of the Renaissance, a very unique format where an ideology, a conception of space, an architectural language, a newly defined practice (architecture), and a political structure all coincided and found their best, most felicitous and synthetic symbol in the newly "discovered" technique of illusionistic representation of three dimensional space in two dimensions.

It is this particular, startling and unique condition of convergence of all those factors on a technique of accurate representation that corresponds to the scientific understanding of the laws of optics (which in spite of its imperfections is still today the simplest and most accurate way of representing space figuratively) and which depicts reality "photographically," that we must understand *is* profoundly unique and peculiar to the Renaissance and may not be repeated again. This understanding will leave, then, perspective as such: as a privileged *technique of representation* of space that was discovered once, that still serves successfully to investigate some important spatial conditions in the process of design, although it may have no relevance anymore for the artistic and symbolic representation of space.

Moreover, and at a more general level, we must acknowledge that this is a stubborn problem that cannot fade away easily, because it is indeed difficult to separate in our minds two such different practices (architectural drawings from artistic practices such as drawing and painting) which share so many concrete, specific and determining components and which even at the outset of their modern history shared even the subject matter, namely the "scientific" and illusionistic representation of space. So the fact remains today that architectural drawings are the indispensable tool of the architect (in fact, they are what still defines the architect vis-a-vis a builder, or other related endeavors), they are by definition *figurative* and concerned with the representation of three dimensions in two (by many different techniques), and painting and drawing are not necessarily so. And is this difference (and the parallel insecurity that some contemporary "progressive" architects may feel when they see themselves still representing space illusionistically while painting is not concerned with it anymore) that generates that longing for the lost literal connection with painting and the consequent apprehension. I am convinced that the inability to articulate this understanding is what exists at the roots of many conceptual confusions in theory and criticism in architecture today.

At a time when so many of the traditional artistic practices are being questions in terms of their specificities and integrities, and their boundaries are being retraced, we may be faced with the necessity of finding a particular place for those drawings that are concerned with the investigation and depiction of space, and which may indeed constitute a new practice (and for which the old word "scenographia" may have to be revived with its full meaning and history).

The correct conceptual separation between idea, symbol and technique has been a constant problem of modernity and a source of confusion as has been its uneasy relation with representation. We are the inheritors of this problem together with modernity's enthusiasm with a conscious and obedient response to *its own* defined *zeitgeist*. It is a legacy that is beginning to embarrass us, because more often than not in modern times we have tended to confuse the depiction of space in two dimensions with something else, be it the building proper, or a symbol, or an idea. And of course, the possibilities of relations among all those things exist and occur,

Fig. 3 Rodolfo Machado and Jorge Silvetti, "The Steps of Providence." General plan, 1978.
Fig. 4 Perspective of Memorial Hall, Memorial Steps and lower plaza, 1978–1979.
Fig. 5 Perspective of Frazier-Terrace, 1978.
Fig. 6 Perspective of Garden Steps, 1978.
Fig. 7 Machado/Silvetti with Schwartz/Silver: Pioneer Square, 1980.

but these is not a single type of relationship that is indispensable, inherent or that should be active at all times.

It is with this "cool" understanding that there are techniques, there are ideas, there are symbolic processes which we may not control entirely, and uncontrollable; and that all these things establish relationships among themselves that are complex, dynamic, ever changing, and with no perpetual hierarchical order over time, space and cultures; it is with this awareness that we have accepted

8

Fig. 8 Rodolfo Machado, Urban Scenes, 1980. Gate/Arcade/Square/Street.
Fig. 9 Jorge Silvetti, House in Pergusa, Sicily, 1982.
Site Plan
1. Entrance gate
2. Garden
3. Ramp
4. Parking lot
5. By-road
Entrance
Veduta del Soggiorno

and used perspective methods of representation of space in our projects. For us it is an indispensable technique as much as axonometric of sketches are. And at different moments in our work it has served different purposes, always technical, sometimes ideologically loaded. We have selected some perspective drawings from a variety of our projects to illustrate different instances of its use.

In both "The Steps of Providence" and the "Pioneer Square" projects the use of perspective is straightforward, serving both as a device that helps solve an idea previously defined and as a means of description of the project. In the Providence project the overriding idea was that of re-reading a physical context that had reached a spatial "impasse" which did not seem to be resolved by conventional urban design techniques. Thus, in opening the core of the city block for public use, we established a new axis/promenade that corresponds to a programmatic narrative. And in so doing, we created a sequential and fragmented itinerary made out of "stations" that resolve and present particular urban conditions (programmatic requirements, iconographic themes, and individual character). The movement along this broken line is what first demanded its exploration by means of perspective. In "Pioneer Square" the synthesis of programmatic requirements, urban conditions and formal site constraints led us to propose the idea of conceiving the space as a theatre (both literally and metaphorically, depending on the specific use given to the space), and the resolution of its centerpiece, the Stage/Greenhouse required perspective verification.

In "Urban Scenes," however, the use of perspective is not just a technical device to investigate a condition or an idea, but a device to underline the idea itself (a tissue of objects). These drawings were not conceived in plan and in section, but rather, they were always perspectives illustrating the precise performance of a typological method that would produce an "urban effect" when utilized in the un-hierarchical, endless, traditional American grid-iron city (which, by the way, is today generally represented in axonometrics).

In the Hotel in San Juan Capistrano, and in the house in Pergusa, perspective became both a means to resolve a particular condition (a "picturesque" requirement by the City of San Juan Capistrano, in the case of the hotel, and site conditions in the house), and at this point in our work, perspective became in itself a figurative theme. In these two projects, given that the collision of two grids became a convenient device to deal with peculiar site conditions, we tried to find an alternative to the

9

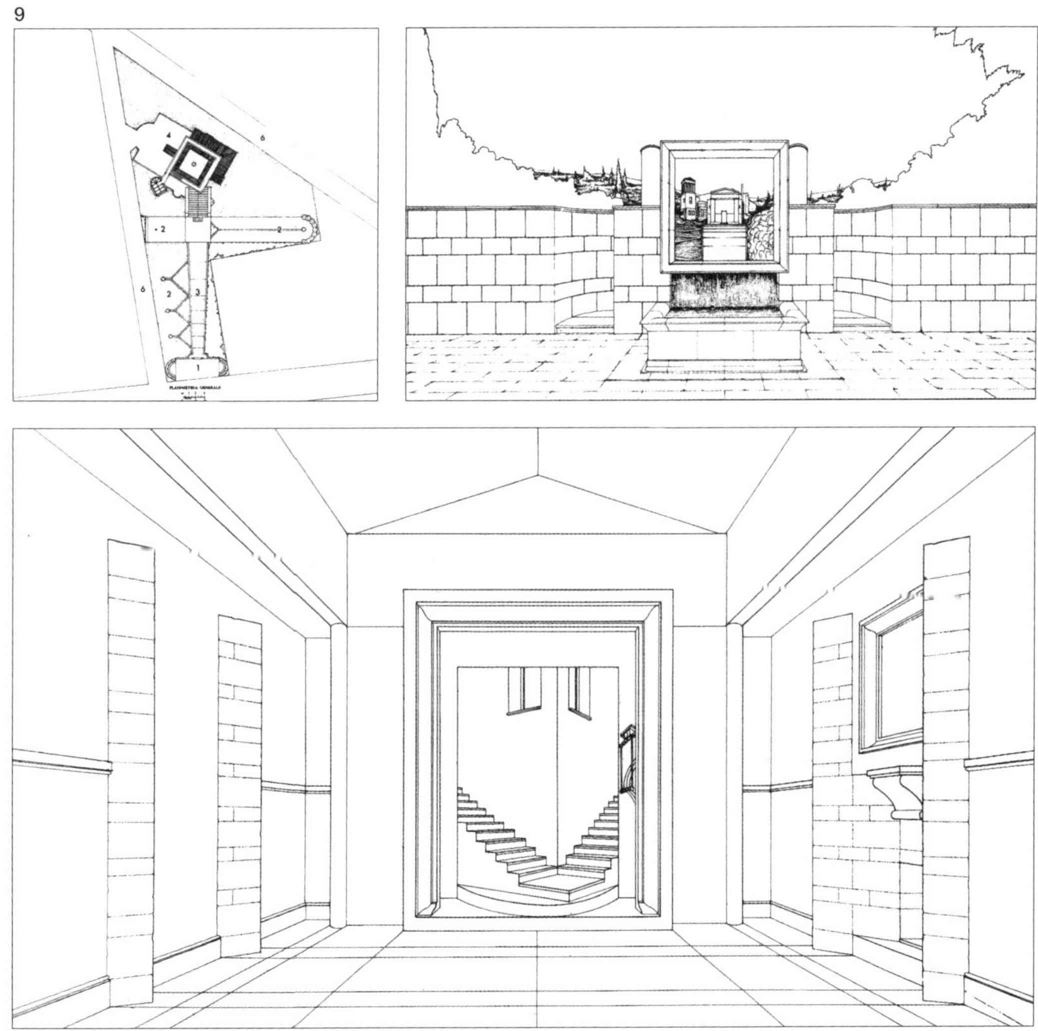

Fig. 10 Rodolfo Machado and Jorge Silvetti, Hotel in San Juan Capistrano, 1982. Lobby.
Fig. 11 Rodolfo Machado and Jorge Silvetti, Taberna Ancipitis Formae, 1983. Interior View.

10

11

two typical ways of "solving" this problem: on the one hand, the technique of "poche" that hides the problem and, on the other, the technique of resolving the collision two dimensionally, by composing the plan with cubist transparencies and ignoring the spatial result (this latter being a typical example of the confusion that I talked about before that exists among architectural drawings, painting and the representation of space). We chose to *show* the collision and made of it one of the figurative themes (very much in the sense of a Bibiena stage set). In both cases "frames" are used to "present" the perspective, isolating it and acknowledging it as an intentional figurative element. This is a step beyond the mere use of the technique to resolve a problem. By now perspective has become so pervasive a method in our projects that is represented in three dimensions as it should appear in two, reestablishing in the space an imaginary picture plane with the aid of the frames. In Pergusa, also the same basic perspective conditions (and frame), serves us to present two opposite scenes.

In "Taberna Ancipitis Formae" besides accomplishing in the interior what it does in Pergusa, perspective serves to establish the "ancipitis" conditions of duality by presenting one of the cranial cubes in a one-point, frontal perspective condition corresponding to the one-eyed cyclops (from whose eye, by the way, it is possible to look into the head and see the theatrical collision of the two cubes/cranea), and in a two-point perspective an oblique presentation of the two-eyed giant.

In all these last three projects, perspective is more than a technique, as it becomes an object of representation. As if to demonstrate that complexity I had been discussing before, we reversed the role of perspective from one of two dimensional representation of three dimensions into a representation by means of a three dimensional building of a two dimensional technique. In so doing we might be reiterating all the possible richness of a technique as far as we are aware of it, from pure mechanical device that helps us to design a building to figurative element that can be represented in the building; perhaps in doing so we convey a particular contemporary meaning, and make perspective act as a symbolic synthesis of this moment. But perhaps not, because, of course, we are not entirely aware of it and we know we cannot presume that we can control that aspect of technique. What we have always been interested in is resolving "architectural problems" and resolving them architecturally. For this we generate ideas, use techniques to aim at the objectives generated by the ideas, and experiment with the architectural language that we deem appropriate for the case. In this process, perspective has always helped us in different roles, and it has always been devoid of any sentimental value.

Sicily

Architecture: The Reconception of History

WITH ERIKA NAGINSKI

Previous spread: View of the eighteenth-century Palazzo Sant'Elia in Caltagirone, Sicily, designed by Natale Bonaiuto. The building presents its unusual one-bay-wide facade crowned by the family's coat of arms facing the Ponte di San Francesco.

1. The Strata of Culture

ERIKA NAGINSKI Let's explore the importance of Sicily for you. Sicily is a place that clearly shaped your understanding of architecture's relationship to history. Can you discuss what brought you to Sicily in the first place and what urban contexts you encountered there? I'm referring to Palermo and Caltagirone, which inspired your 1992 article "Interactive Realms: The Bridge of San Francesco and the Palazzo Sant'Elia."[1]

JORGE SILVETTI It's true that Sicily is a place that significantly impacted my work and thinking about the history of architecture. To this day, it remains a point of reference, because it allowed me to profoundly grasp the ways an architectural canon is formed and how it evolves. A canon is not monolithic, but rather it is varied according to geography, history, and culture. In Sicily, I learned how architectural conventions are transferred between cultures and altered along the way, a testament to art's capacity to be semantically transformed. I was also able to research cultural phenomena involving marginality and multiculturalism across large spans of time.

Rodolfo [Machado] and I worked for almost eleven years in Sicily, beginning in the early '80s. I took Harvard students there, taught at the University of Palermo, and worked on design projects for the island while in Boston year-round. In the end, nothing was ever built! However, I am glad we took on these projects. They allowed us to explore many complex architectural and urban issues we were interested in, which were not present or imaginable in our American commissions. In a way, our role as outsiders invigorated our ability to propose all sorts of things. That said, I'm not sure I've ever told you that the beginning of my interest in the history of architecture and Sicily are actually serendipitously intertwined.

EN How so?

JS When I was in architecture school in Buenos Aires, the history of architecture was taught differently than in the United States. The Universidad de Buenos Aires is based on a mass-educational system, which means that there are hundreds of students in a single class. When I was a student, there were formal evening lectures you could attend—even if no one checked—and then you had three-hour weekly sessions in small groups called *trabajos prácticos*. Led by a teaching assistant, these sessions were dedicated to drawing and analyzing buildings.

The first building I was assigned to analyze was the Temple of Apollo at Didyma,[2] which is one of the largest Hellenistic temples ever built. This is not the building's only peculiarity. It is completely atypical because *it has no roof*. Instead of the usual cella, the interior is a large courtyard that houses a smaller conventional temple. This most anomalous of Ionic examples is the way I discovered ancient Greek architecture, just to give you an idea! All of the buildings I was assigned afterwards were also oddities, probably because of my teaching assistant's interests. The second building was San Giovanni degli Eremiti in Palermo,[3] and this is where I came across Sicily and its Norman-Arab architecture. It was my first experience with Romanesque architecture, and what an idiosyncratic example of the Romanesque! This is how I began to learn about architecture's history: beyond the confines of the Western world, looking at eccentric instances of canonical periods. I wasn't very conscious of this at the time. I just loved buildings and was interested in studying how they came to be.

My first real encounter with Sicily, though, happened by chance when I was already living in the US. Rodolfo and I were in the midst of rediscovering history more seriously because of the rising influence in architectural circles of postmodernism, French structuralism, design methodology, and systems research.[4] These trends and my studies in linguistics and anthropology at UC Berkeley were driving me toward history in a more academic way. Then, in the summer of 1971, we took a trip to Europe with two close Argentinian friends, Diana Agrest and Mario Gandelsonas, who were teaching at Princeton University School of Architecture and the Institute for Architecture and Urban Studies of New York.

Rodolfo and I did our own sort of Grand Tour, and toward the end of the trip, when we met up with Diana and Mario in Rome, we changed plans for the remaining month and decided to go to Tunisia. We made our way down to Naples, and from there sailed to Tunis. However, we stopped over in Palermo for a few days to change boats. I was entranced by Palermo and its architecture. I found it both bizarre and enchanting, but I didn't think about it again for years. I kept traveling to Italy but mostly to Rome, Tuscany, and the Veneto region, places most would consider the "real" sources for architecture. Then, in 1982, I was invited to teach in Sicily, and this journey, which continued until 1993, had a profound and lasting effect on my work.

I was invited to the Università degli Studi di Palermo as a visiting professor during the summer of 1982. At that moment I was already thinking about my future at Harvard. Things were going well, but I was coming to the end of my contract and uncertain about what the

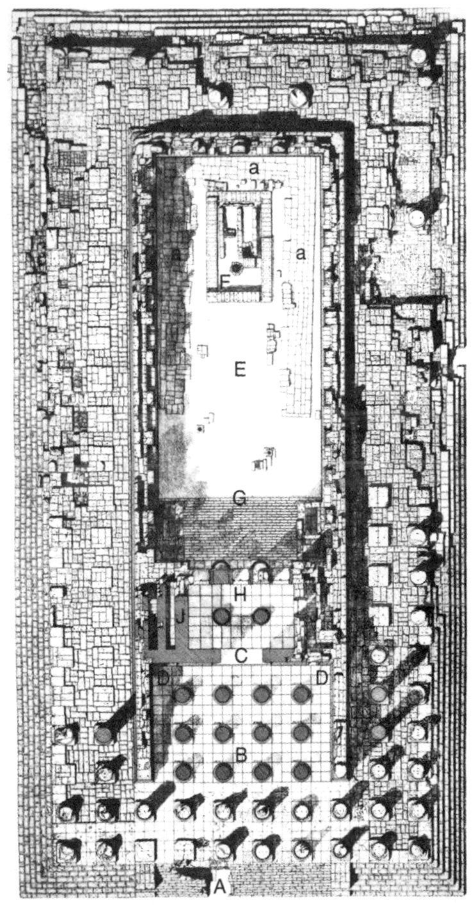

Temple of Apollo at Didyma, Ionia, Turkey. Cross-section of the temple's unroofed cella with the cult statue of Apollo within the *naiskos* (reconstruction after A. Thomas, 1873) and archaeological plan of its ruins as uncovered between 1906 and 1913.

The signing of the agreement between the Harvard GSD and the City of Caltagirone that launched the five-year research project "Architecture and the Urban Environments of Sicily." From left to right: Architect Leonardo Foderà, Professor Leonardo Urbani, Jorge Silvetti, Senator Salvatore Parisi (speaking), Mayor Giacomo De Caro, Harvard GSD Dean Gerald M. McCue, and Professor and Architect Pasquale Culotta.

View of the north elevation of the Cathedral of the Holy Nativity of Mary in Syracuse, Sicily. The church is built on the ruins of the Greek temple of Athena built in the fifth century B.C. The temple's Doric columns are visibly embedded in the north wall.

Graduate School of Design (GSD) was going to do with me. So I had been actively expanding my network and was being courted by other schools. I developed academic and professional ties in Italy and Spain and had taught at the ETH Zürich, where I was invited by different professors, such as Mario Campi, Bernhard Höesli, and Dolf Schnebli. When I received the invitation from Palermo, the idea of returning to Sicily for an extended period was irresistible, even if I did not know much about their school of architecture. So for two years, I taught in Palermo during the late spring and summer, as well as on short visits during the academic year in order to follow up with thesis students.

My participation as a visiting professor in Palermo, which I conducted in the fairly good Italian I learned in high school, was well received and inspired curiosity among the architecture and urban planning faculty with whom I developed strong relationships. Together we conceived of an ambitious research project, described and illustrated in the publications *Architectural and Urban Environments of Sicily*, which included the article you mentioned.[5] The project was officially launched in 1988 and ran until 1993. It was enthusiastically supported by Gerald M. McCue, the then-dean of the GSD. He was interested in defining the kind of scholarship that should be developed in an architecture school. This was in response to the ever-present demands of Harvard, who saw what we did as architects as completely alien to the scholarship produced by a research university. The Sicily project represented an opportunity for McCue to address this.

The project had three main institutional partners: the Harvard GSD, where it was situated and where I was the principal investigator; the University of Palermo, which had different academic units in design, design technology, and urbanism; and a consortium of municipalities in the Val di Noto region, led by the city of Caltagirone, which provided most of the financial support. It was the first collaborative research project of its kind at the GSD.

FN What specifically about Sicily caught your attention when you went back? What encounters with architecture and the city captured you in such a way that a casual stint as a visiting professor in Palermo turned into over a decade of work on the island?

JS Well, when I got to Sicily, I immediately felt that people were enthusiastic about working with me. People at all levels generously engaged me in the history of their city, something I still find wonderful. In any town, locals know their history and art well, and they are eager to tell you about it. This allowed for an intense immersion in the richness of people's stories as I navigated the buildings, streets, and piazze. What was peculiar about this experience was that nothing was as it first appeared, and further explanation was always needed to understand each anomaly. For example, a building historically originated in the Catalonian Renaissance, not just the Italian Renaissance. Or a building was doubtlessly Romanesque, but it had strange-looking pink domes because of its Islamic influences, as in the churches of San Giovanni degli Eremiti and San Cataldo.

I went to sleep every night with endless questions about the buildings that piqued my interest. I began to try to decipher what I had seen. I started by observing the formal operations of each building, but then I felt that I had to immerse myself in their historical and cultural contexts. I wanted to clarify the particular conditions and processes that led to their striking features, so I began to do my own version of research, addressing "things" I was attracted to without the use of explanation from the theoretical framework I was handling back then. As soon as I fit a "thing" somewhere, an additional excess or oddity surfaced that I couldn't account for. I did this out of curiosity as a designer, but soon enough, I was moving toward a more conventional path of historical research.

What anchored my research was the palpable physical and spatial fact that Sicily is essentially a roadblock in the middle of the Mediterranean. Sicily has been influenced by a great many cultures that confronted each other across time on this piece of land, and whose presence can still be felt. The island has continuously found itself in a position that is central yet marginal to other cultures, folding in influences from across the Mediterranean world. As seen from the outside, Sicily is simply the recipient of the cultural influences that have circumstantially converged there. But as seen from within, Sicily has a strong identity that swallows what it comes into contact with and makes it its own. This continues to be fascinating for me. Sicily presents itself as a form of creative "cannibalism," which we can find in other places and periods as well.[6]

Nothing summarizes what fascinates me about the history of Sicilian architecture better than the Cathedral of Syracuse.[7] It is a building that is hard to date, because it has been modified countless times during the long period in which Syracuse was one of the most important cities in the Mediterranean. The Baroque church that stands today is the most recent layer erected over the first known building on the site: the Doric Temple of Athena, built in the fifth century B.C. The robust Doric colonnades are still visible, embedded in the church's perimeter wall and nave. From a purely functional perspective, the building was most likely first a Greek temple erected over a prehistoric sacred site. It was later converted into a church by the Byzantines, into a mosque by the Arabs, then reverted to a space for Norman Christian rites, and, eventually, it was transformed into a Baroque cathedral. The same building has accommodated successive waves of political and spiritual conquerors for over twenty-five centuries. It is really remarkable, and the accumulation of cultural meanings and situations is visible in the architecture. It is yet another reminder of the agility buildings have to reconcile changing symbolic content.

I cannot succinctly explain Sicily's history better than this. It is a land where the Greeks and Phoenicians collided. Palermo is a sister to Carthage, Beirut, Biblos, and Tyros! Sicily is the granary of Rome. It is an island where the Elymians built an inexplicably perfect Doric Temple (albeit never finished). It is a place where the Romans built Greek theaters in brick rather than stone, as seen in Taormina. It is where late Roman houses display some of the most striking mosaic floors in the Mediterranean, which were the prologue to the later expanded craft that characterizes the art of the Byzantines. This island is where barbarian kingdoms of Norwegian origin erected European Romanesque cathedrals, such as the Cathedral of Cefalù, whose towers recall the defensive structures built by the Arabs during their centuries of occupation. The story continues all the way down to the Baroque edifices, which were built by architects who trained under Roman masters of the period and were embellished with colored marble intaglio that the Jesuit order found aesthetic inspiration for in the local Norman-Byzantine figural mosaic tradition. Should I say more?

These are the circumstances with which architecture in Sicily negotiates. The island's location allowed for a much richer and less linear story than that associated with ancient Greece or Rome. Architecture in Sicily is always a product of traditions contaminating each other in complex and exciting ways over time. This is what attracted me to working in Sicily and why I think it is particularly relevant today. I spent a lot of time at UC Berkeley—which you know well, Erika—thinking theoretically about how cultural processes unfold and what this means for architecture. However, the time I spent in Sicily provided a veritable education in how this all plays out over the long arc of time. There my engagement with the material evidence of centuries of cultural encounters gave me the conviction that cultural practices interact and evolve in any given society in a very dynamic way. This coincided with my experience in Argentina, which is yet another peripheral location that came into contact with the canons of Western culture and has interacted with them ever since. Sicily made it clear that these places don't produce minor versions of those canons, but rather they generate distinct renditions that are contaminated by the circumstances that converge in each place and sometimes lead to radical inventions.

EN I know you might resist what I'm about to say, Jorge, but I've realized there are certain patterns of thought that mark the ways in which you construct arguments in your writings. I would like to take a moment and analyze these patterns, because I think they are related to how you think about architecture's history.

JS Alright, give it to me! [*laughs*]

EN These are patterns of thought I sensed when we coordinated, in the spring of 2016, my seminar on ruins and your studio on Jesuit missions and the Guaraní territory in Argentina, Paraguay, and Brazil.[8] They came into more focus when I reacquainted myself with your article "The Bridge and the Palazzo: Urban Interventions and Social Representation" in preparation for our conversation.[9]

There are certain rhetorical strategies you like to use. I'll evoke a term that I probably shouldn't; you often begin with an appeal to the collective *habitus* provided by architecture without further explanation. You refer to broad principles, such as the need to embrace the humanity of architecture, or our innate desire for architecture. After that, you take the reader through a set of images stratified by time. Then, you come to a revelation or an "aha" moment. In the case of "The Bridge of San Francesco and the Palazzo Sant'Elia," this moment appears when you figure out that the entire building was reoriented to correspond to the transformation of the urban plan, discovered simply by identifying a few holes where the owner's crest was originally anchored. You do this again in your essay in the publication on the Guaraní studios, when you describe the moment that your studio actually stumbled on the ruins of the Jesuit mission in Candelaria.[10]

You enjoy this kind of narrative suspense, this way of proceeding, quite a bit! It reminds me of Manfredo Tafuri's ploy in *Interpreting the Renaissance*, in his chapter on architectural competitions under Pope Leo X.[11] He reveals that an unattributed elevation drawing of a church is surely Raphael's competition entry for the facade of the Basilica of San Lorenzo in Florence because of one small line that connects the design to the dimensions of the narthex of the extant basilica.

JS I'm beginning to feel as if I'm laying on the couch of a shrink! I'm not sure if this is good or bad, but I like how you describe my strategy of engagement. Rhetorical techniques can surely open the door to the ways of a mind, but now I'm going to push back. [*laughs*]

EN You should! And by the way, I don't think this is a strategy that is *a priori* or calculated.

JS No, no. Honestly, your description surprises me. My training as a scholar is not very solid. I don't like doing that kind of work very often, so I don't consider myself in possession of a research method, a consistent type of writing, or a recurrent way of presenting an argument. But I see clearly that this hypothesis of yours is a plausible way of looking at my writings and storytelling. What you describe as my revelations are something that I cannot counter, really.

EN That is why they interest me, not simply as a way to understand you, but the mind of the architect more generally: how an architect might look at history or how the eye of a designer structures knowledge and understanding.

JS I must acknowledge that what you call the "aha" moment in the design process is something I always look forward to. Sometimes it takes a long time, but I always know it's coming. You start articulating formal and material arrangements as an answer to this or that issue, and all of a sudden, there is this moment when a huge leap happens. Everything becomes clear, coherent, and solid. Suddenly, you have a project.

EN Maybe this is why you are drawn to Claude Lévi-Strauss's evocation of disrupted geological strata in his book *Tristes tropiques*, which we've talked about on numerous occasions.[12] Lines of rock and sediment collapse and collide, visualizing radical juxtapositions of places, contexts, and times.

Lévi-Strauss poetically relates the experience of coming across the line of contact between different strata inscribed on a plateau to making the collision of geological temporalities materially legible. This line goes on to symbolize, for him, the relationship between things that are inconsistent with one another yet make sense together; they coexist seamlessly in the present for the first time. I think he calls it "an image of knowledge."[13]

JS Yes, that's exactly the point!

EN There's a reason, then, why your essays are often structured this way, as layered or stratified.

JS I think I am beginning to understand what you're saying. I had never thought about this. It's a very interesting take, and knowing you, I'm sure you detected it with great seriousness. [*laughs*]

EN You start with what you call the "prehistoric," or on other occasions—for instance, in your lecture in honor of Eduard Sekler—the "prediscursive."[14] These, for you, are the elements of a site that are interpretable purely through their formal or material condition without the presence of textual evidence. Then, you often turn to a layering of what happened over time using plans. You like to decipher a building by stratifying it, particularly if that stratification does not always occur strictly from bottom to top, as it usually does in archaeology.

JS I am definitely a plan person in the sense that I see the plan as containing information exclusive to architecture. The visual is crucial to our understanding of architecture, but the visual is also a general kind of content shared by many disciplines and practices from art history to land surveying. The plan, however, does not respond to any real visual experience. It is an invention to describe what cannot be seen, which is nonetheless central to architectural making.

EN You privilege the plan, but you also privilege architectural elements embedded within it. Some things are obvious to you which are not obvious to everyone else. For example, in your Sekler lecture, the way you described the campaniles of three cathedrals—Cefalù, Monreale, and Palermo—then traced them back to Arab fortress architecture was breathtaking.[15] You were able to point out the origin or meaning of an architectural element even if it was lodged within a larger arrangement dependent on a much broader set of influences.

JS Those three churches are a good example, because getting to know Palermo turned my linear understanding of history on its side, literally! I was accustomed to the kind of archaeological inquiry you describe, in which we apprehend architectural events by identifying horizontal layers that usually belong to successive historical periods. When I started to look at the architectural remnants of Arab culture in Palermo, I found a different reality. Historic buildings that still stand and are often still in use are composites that require detective work to pull elements apart and then piece them together. The city is not layered and buried under each successive intervention. It is, rather, a collection of montages or collages. The diversity of sources becomes a single visual composition in which the simple, prismatic, and low defensive towers of the Arabs were integrated into, rather than submerged within, an urban fabric produced over time.

The natural landscape of Sicily also has this quality, in which geological strata are displayed on the surface of features rather than simply buried below. On top of this stratified ground, you have ancient features like cemeteries or roads carved into the rock that are vivid presences. When experienced for the first time with an archaeologist who walks you through them, these are things that leave an indelible impression.[16]

EN You turn to archeological and historical material to shed light on how an architectural event occurred. However, you also look closely at what the architectural event itself tells you, and in doing so you come up with original readings. This is definitely an aspect of your modus operandi, and I think it is really interesting because it verges on an obsession.

JS It is an obsession! Because I was so involved with the emergence of theoretical discourse in the late twentieth century, there was a moment at the turn of the millennium when I was profoundly disappointed with this discourse and its consequences, and so I swerved away. So I see this "prediscursive" approach as a kind of therapy. The reconsideration of theory also happened right around the time we began the Getty Villa project, which led to twelve years of working with the best of the best in archaeology and art history—people who were really good at looking at objects in their own ways.

I also had direct experience with excavations in Sicily. I often stayed in Sicily with a friend who was a member of the team of archaeologists at the famous dig where the Phoenician statue of a charioteer was discovered on the island of Mozia in 1979.[17] We would talk all day about archaeology, and she brought me along to these sites that were hard to reach and not really open to the public at the time.

EN Yes, I couldn't help but notice a certain remove in the texts about Sicily, as if your preoccupation with a kind of typological appraisal of Sicilian architecture could take you away from the intense world of theory in American architecture schools. Typology is something that we should discuss in this context because I wonder if in your mind, in the retinue of texts generated by postmodernism on the topic, typology risked simply becoming an image. It was an obligatory diagram. Whereas I think for you, typology functions differently.

JS I entirely agree.

EN For you, this involves the architect making connections between disparate aspects of architecture, reading typology not as definitive or fixed (into an image), but instead as a palimpsest in constant motion, appearing and reappearing under different guises in and through time. Something that strikes me about your attitude toward architecture is that it always registers the passage of time. Maybe this is what sparks your dialogue with architectural historians such as Howard Burns or Eduard Sekler or your conversations with the conceptions of typology put forth by Giulio Carlo Argan and Rafael Moneo.[18] Buildings are not simply intended to be fixed diagrammatically into a given formal arrangement. They also evolve temporally, changing arrangements and receiving new marks that transform the meanings we assign to its symbols.

JS Amen!

This takes me back to my fascination with geology. I cannot really claim to know geology as a science, but I understand how geological phenomena work, how they manifest themselves in space and time. Geology deals with something physical, which operates at a time scale that is different from our own, not unlike architecture. Its objects of study seem fixed, but they are nevertheless always changing. That is why I always think about the passage in *Tristes tropiques* you mentioned earlier.

EN As I think about what you accomplished in your Sekler lecture using the example of the three churches in Palermo, I can't help but compare this to Erwin Panofsky's *Gothic Architecture and Scholasticism*.[19] Panofsky tracked the development of Gothic churches in relation to the structures of scholasticism, as if each edifice were a step in a continuous progression of trial and error, even though in his account this unfolds in fits and starts—and even though this may or may not correspond to what actually happened! By contrast, James Ackerman resisted such cohesion in the Renaissance context. In response to Rudolf Wittkower's philosophically motivated diagram of the ideal Palladian villa, Ackerman posits a fundamental plurality and social complexity.[20] There is still an animated debate over whether chronology offers clear, inexorable architectural progressions. What struck me about your take on the three churches is that you also embrace the resistance of this premise.

JS You think I embrace that there is no progress?

EN No, you embrace that history does not move in a seamless or linear fashion even though there is chronology. You embrace that there is hybridity. That in Sicily, architecture does not just proceed from Norman, to Byzantine, to Islamic. It's actually Norman *and* Byzantine *and* Islamic. And, furthermore, that this hybridity is what animates the so-called vernacular, right?

JS Yes! Well put. This is why I question the idea that there is such a thing as progress in culture. It's something that has been deeply ingrained in me since I was young but became explicit when I was at UC Berkeley diving into anthropological studies.

We are all exactly the same in terms of makeup. Our brain hasn't changed that much. What changes are the circumstances we come across in our environment and how we interpret those circumstances to produce things. Some of these changes are new; specific areas of knowledge *do* make progress. The perfecting of the steam engine or Schoenbergian thinking about the structure of music, for example, are forms of progress. But it's not as if their creators are more intelligent than people who lived five hundred years ago. We may be at a different moment of development in some regards. Maybe we have more sophisticated technologies or more advanced understandings of the possibilities open to Western music, but as for the rest, it's all fairly horizontal.

If I had my own architecture school, I would introduce a bit of anthropology, especially the intellectual part. And why not music too, at least the principles of harmony and counterpoint. These are useful and illuminating for an architect! The forms of music—the sonata, the theme with variations, and so forth—are perennial structures that continually evolve. They get distorted, transformed, and at times are revolutionized and reinvented, but they continue to refer to some basic parameters that persist on another time scale. They are indomitable structures that do not progress, but rather become more firmly, richly, and solidly constituted after each round of transformation. They are marvelous examples of music's ineffable nature as a paradigm of cultural practice.

Lastly, I would have to add some linguistics. When I studied it at UC Berkeley, linguistics helped me in many ways. Of particular relevance to our conversation is how I came to understand how arbitrary yet historically crucial the relationship between symbols and their putative contents actually is. This understanding is essential for assessing how buildings perform when culture changes around them.

EN Let's discuss what motivated "The Bridge of San Francesco and the Palazzo Sant'Elia" in a more focused way. I think it can help us to explore *how* you see architecture being affected by changing cultural conventions. Can you describe your initial encounter with Caltagirone as well as the seminars you led there? What made you focus your research on the particular juncture between these two urban elements?

Your article aims to solve the mystery surrounding a palazzo that on one hand exhibits the ambition to visibly occupy an entire urban block and announce its public presence, yet on the other hand retains its main facade on its narrowest corner—one that lacks a main entrance stair and other elements of a conventional grand entry sequence. You describe how you were able to uncover the story of the bridge adjacent to the palazzo through archival means or "textual" material—as we have been referring to—because, as a public infrastructural work, it is well documented historically. However, when it came to the private palazzo, you were forced to look only at material evidence to understand the development of the building, which corresponds to your anthropological interests. Can you describe how these two methods of analysis helped you conquer the puzzle posed by the relationship between these structures?

JS Within the larger Sicilian research project we developed, the Val di Noto region was represented by the city of Caltagirone, which had secured an important part of the funding. So we conducted three or four option studios there. Rodolfo led one on urban design. Over the summer, I took students to Caltagirone to make physical surveys of the architecture, which was a great experience. This act of measuring was very important from a pedagogical point of view, and it was also very enjoyable. The Harvard GSD students lived in the city for weeks at a time to the knowledge of everyone there.

The San Francesco Bridge didn't grow on me as much, honestly. It was the Palazzo Sant'Elia which struck me as such an odd building. Despite its enormous size, when you walked toward it at street level, it presented itself as a single-bay, three-story Baroque facade, perfectly framed by the single arch bridge above!

EN Yes, it makes no sense.

JS And yet, this corner bay is the principal facade today. The building sits at one of the points at which the nineteenth-century city meets the old city, and two streets that frame the triangular site of the building converge right where the passage under the bridge is located. Because of the way its sides open out from the corner following the direction of the streets, the view from under the bridge is a living version of one of those striking, Baroque two-point perspectives by the Bibienas! Then, if you walk over the bridge, as opposed to under, you see the one-bay facade again, but you only see its top composition above the giant architectural order of the first two stories. All of these oddities encouraged me to focus a large part of the research on this building. I couldn't resist understanding it more thoroughly.

Throughout this summer of intense surveying, I was able to figure out certain details having to do with how the building had changed in relation to infrastructural developments that had affected the way religious processions moved through the urban environment. The lack of archival evidence made the story of the building opaque to many historians. By learning about the larger context of which it had been a part, however, and looking at the object in front of me with the eyes of a designer, I was able to understand why the architects had made certain decisions about the way it presented itself to the street at various moments in time.

We discovered that the palazzo had not been developed in a single move. It was the result of a series of acquisitions made by a family that rose in status and wanted to expand their house. When you look at the plan, you can see how the palazzo begins to grow, since you can trace the lots of the older houses contained within it as well as many of their original walls. Because of this, the interior is completely confusing; it doesn't follow the logic of a Renaissance or Baroque plan. It is an agglomeration of incongruous spaces with facades that pull them together into an odd triangular block.

Then there was a change in the city when they built the bridge right next to the palazzo, which is one story lower than the bridge, because it was essential to the proper functioning of the urban environment. The bridge worked so well that the large procession was rerouted through it, no longer passing in front of the original main facade of the palazzo on the street below. It was a marvelous moment when we were able to piece it all together, because there was such suspense about the architectural chaos we had in front of us. All of a sudden there was that "aha" moment you mentioned. We understood that the building *wanted* to be seen but the infrastructural changes and subsequent changes in the ritual paths through the city didn't allow for this visibility any longer. So the location of the main facade of the building needed to change to the most unlikely position in which its topmost story faced the procession once again.

Today I would not be so exclusionary as to say that this was something only an architect could have discovered, but I would still note the fact that no historian—and there were many local ones involved—ever thought about the palazzo this way. This had me bragging with some pride for some time that I saw this because I was an architect, and that my historical reconstruction of events and its conclusions were irrefutable. I ended up arguing with a local historian, because while he could not really disagree with me, he thought that my argument was so unhistorical, pragmatic, and simplistic that it made it untenable.

NICOLÁS DELGADO ALCEGA What do you mean by "unhistorical"?

JS Ask *him*! I suppose by "unhistorical" he meant that such a consequential change in decor—which paradoxically involved the minimal physical change of the location of the family crest from the original facade to the new one—was caused by adjustments to the changing urban configuration that surrounded it. There was no sufficient hard proof, such as documents or written evidence. I arrived at my conclusion by logical inferences based on unsupported assumptions. This was true, but it did not take away from the validity of my hypothesis, which shed light in a plausible way on an architectural mystery.

I feel more at home with the approach of the anthropologist or archeologist than that of the historian. I become engaged with artifacts and spend time observing, thinking about, and enjoying them very much. I cannot spend as much time sitting in a library looking for a revelation through writing. I suppose it is a personality trait more than a deliberate choice. But that is the way I research: with the eye of the designer, which gives me that extra push to promote creativity and the capacity for inference. This puts me in the shoes of the maker and helps me produce hypotheses.

Then I can understand these architectural histories and share my understanding with others, all the while remaining confident that the strength of my approach resides more in the verisimilitude of the proposition than in the hard proof of documents. That said, I am well aware of the inherent fragility of this approach's validity. I am convinced, though, of its indisputable value for explaining the architecture at hand. My comfort with this research method has to do with my absolute conviction as a designer that there is never one single solution to an architectural problem. Rather, there is always a range of solutions: good, excellent, brilliant, and awesome, to make the list short! When we are researching an artifact in front of us, this range allows us to speculate about its raison d'être as a design problem. In the end, my experience in Caltagirone verified all of this for me. It showed me how differently an architect looks at history than a historian does.

EN Exactly. I love this idea. It brings us back to the "pre-textual" reading you undertake. You realize the architecture wants to speak, it wants to announce its presence. But you don't demonstrate this through historical evidence. You actually find material traces in the original facade, the holes in the wall that correspond to the crest that was moved to the new facade on the corner where it would once again be seen during the religious procession. You recover the intent behind the design of the building by means of that moment of revelation, in which you are able to connect the dots of what happened just by reading the material traces offered by the building itself. I think this example says a great deal about the eye of the architect, particularly when it is cast toward the past. The project in Caltagirone is an exemplary model.

Another thing that struck me about "The Bridge of San Francesco and the Palazzo Sant'Elia" was the reference to the perspectives of the Bibiena family. I was so happy to see that! It elicits the scenographic dimension, paying heed to the city as a lived environment where processional routes determine its logic and where we conduct our everyday lives. How are certain urban design parameters mapped onto the customs of collective life? I want to touch on this because my sense is that you and Rodolfo both have a particular understanding of the relationship between architecture and urban-design, one in which scenography, or the way the city stages itself to accommodate and represent urban life, seems important.

I'm not always a fan of Pierre Bourdieu, but in his wonderful postface to Panofsky's *Gothic Cathedrals and Scholasticism*, he states that the way scholasticism applies to large cathedrals is actually an example of habitus—a means of understanding architecture through collective life—which is comparable to what is happening in your own analysis.[21]

JS I'd like to read Bourdieu on that topic.

EN The postface was in the back of my mind as I read your article. The role of processions in the early modern period and the ways in which they inscribe passages through the city with meaning is very striking. I've worked on this topic with regard to the Church of Sainte-Geneviève in Paris and the ongoing processions of Sainte Geneviève's miraculous relics during the Enlightenment period, as France moved toward revolution. These reclamations of public space testify to the scenographic quality of urban design and architecture as much as to the needs of people. I want to hear your thoughts about this. How did your experience in Sicily affect your understanding of architecture's relationship to urban design? Its relationship to public space and religious or civic ritual?

JS I was going to say that the topic of habitus is explicitly all about such processions, and my understanding of this really started in Sicily. Once you spend time in Sicily, in every town, no matter how small, you come across *big* processions. The first time this happened to me was in Palermo during one of the major ones: the Procession of Santa Rosalia.[22] They bring out these Baroque chariots, two-stories high and completely gilded. Palermo is a concentric Phoenician city, but it was the Spaniards in the sixteenth century who cut two perpendicular streets through its center, like the Roman Cardo and Decumanus. You understand these urban interventions when you see the processions: symbolic rites built around the idea of transporting something sacred—and, I would add, magic—across the city in monstrous chariots. Every town has its patron saint, and processions are organized to transport the symbol or relics of that saint from one end of town to the other. People celebrate their patron saint and the next day return the relics to the religious edifice in which they are kept and revered. In Palermo, the Procession of Santa Rosalia begins at the Palace of the Normans, at the foot of the Via del Cassaro, and ends in La Kalsa, the neighborhood on the waterfront still called by its original Arabic name. The procession gives measure to the city, and through the protective company of its patron saint, it claims the Christian power of the Norman kings over the Arab community.

This tradition in these parts of the Mediterranean stems from the Greeks and Phoenicians, who celebrated the summer harvests with processions and offerings. The city is calibrated and designed

Two representations of the feast of Santa Rosalia in Palermo.

Right: *Festa religiosa di Santa Rosalia a Palermo*, Mattei Pasquale (1850–1874), Appartamento Storico di Palazzo Reale, Napoli.

Below: A photograph of the feast in 1974.

around this type of spatialized ritual experience. This is clear in Baroque Sicily, where urban design and living traditions like processions are inextricably linked. But this is also more largely a feature of the Mediterranean. I have talked at length about this topic with colleagues; with Anita Berrizbeitia about Italian processions and their relationship to the landscape; with Raphael Moneo in regard to how this plays out in Spain, particularly in Andalucia—another land of processions!

EN When you revealed the readjustment of the palazzo toward the bridge, this didn't just lead to a rumination on its reorganization as a Renaissance and Baroque typology, or even to the function of facades more generally. It led to an understanding of the role of architecture in reconstituting an entire spatial milieu according to evolving rituals or to an urban function larger than itself.[23] As you put it: "The interplay between buildings, public spaces, and urban infrastructure holds a major key to understanding civic representation."[24] The scenographic dimension in this case, informed as it is by Baroque planning and the rebuilding of the city after the disastrous earthquake in Sicily, makes this palpable. One of the reasons I was fascinated by your essay—and this conversation confirms it—is that it reveals that the interplay of architecture in the city and the development of its infrastructure is crucial to your work with Rodolfo. You are uniquely equipped to think about it.

JS Part of what distinguished us early on in our careers was that we were making inroads with projects that saw architecture as inseparable from the city. We were getting important awards for projects like the Steps of Providence precisely because of this. And when the American Academy of Arts and Letters created its Award in Architecture in 1991, we were the first recipients, and we were given a citation that recognized this distinctive aspect of our creative work. It was quite rewarding. You've identified precisely what we were vehemently pushing at that time, when the issue of how the interdependence between urban form and architectural typology worked in practice was still not widely understood.

2. The Ruin and the Creative Process

EN Let's turn to the relationship between design and archaeology, which is in many ways related to your experience in Caltagirone. I have certain ideas about the subject.

JS Of course you do.

EN They are different from yours. Tell me why you think that representational practices related to a discipline like archaeology are so formative for young architects? This will allow us to consider the relevance of the past to an architect. Tell me about maps. Tell me about measure.

JS I think my fascination with these practices stems from the direct human experience that's involved. You are confronted with material culture and usually lack written documents or any other source to explain what you are seeing. Essentially you must make those things speak to you, without intermediaries. In some cases, and particularly if you are an architect and already know about the type of artifact or structure you are dealing with, there may be analogues that can orient you toward an interpretation. Otherwise, there is no language between yourself and the ruins.

The next step is to represent these ruins, because you need to record them. You need to create visual documents, which are interpretations that allow for in-depth study. For architects, making these drawings is a means to trigger the imagination, because it is in the nature of archaeological artifacts to be incomplete, fragmentary, or altered. To come to a sort of resolution with the ruin, you have to first represent what exists in a very incomplete state. Then, even if you are not representing the ruin reconstructed, as Renaissance architects might have, you still need to interpret what the whole would have looked like; what it could have been rather than what it can become. You do this to understand what you are seeing in order to document it correctly, in order to address all the ambiguities that emerge as the ruins slowly come out of the ground. This is crucial to the practice of both architecture and archaeology.

This is why I think it is a valuable experience for architects to work at an archaeological excavation. It is one instance in which you reverse your thinking and operational process. The drawn record of the ruin becomes the result of a process instead of an initial representation of something that does not yet exist. The making of architecture, being what it is, always requires the architect to engage in a preliminary and mediating act through representational practice. Every time you have to design something, that thing has to exist in another medium first, which is the drawing. In archaeological excavations, the ruins of buildings become givens; they are the drivers of an inquiry that demands a hypothetical visual reconstruction.

In order to imagine a ruin's original appearance, you draw using your projective capacity as a designer, keeping one foot on the physical evidence of the ruin. And I think this is good. The process of drawing is not initially tied to your imagination, but quickly you find yourself completing what you have just surveyed with the use of your own creativity. An experience of this kind forces you to measure and be absolutely accurate but also to use your capacity to interpret what is in front of you in a novel way. This is particularly true if you are dealing with ruins that time has altered repeatedly.

You begin to sort out what is a wall as opposed to the foundation, or where the floor is as opposed to where the doors and windows are. This leads you to discern the types of spaces you are looking at, whether they are open-air spaces, patios, or interiors. You deduce some of these things based on the kind of floor covering, on the wear and tear of different surfaces, and so on. Drawing a ruin that is in the process of being uncovered is not unlike the creative experience of the architect—it's just cranking it up in reverse gear!

EN Jorge, you are saying something that I have thought about a great deal: that retrospection and projection are inexorably tied.

JS Absolutely.

EN You are speaking to the ways in which representation as you survey, look at maps, and try to figure out where a patio might be—is the polar opposite of what you have called "the Rossi effect," in which architectural form is reduced to pure figure, as if it were floating in the ether.

JS Yes, architectural form is everything but immaterial. Taking my students to do surveys in the field in Caltagirone definitely exposed them to this tradition of studying objects carefully and closely, even if we were not exactly drawing ruins. I think it definitely gave them access to a different way of looking at how architectural form is generated. I have to say, it was one of the most successful courses I ever taught at the GSD. The students were enthralled. They spent most of the summer measuring the bridge and the palazzo's walls.

Harvard GSD Students surveying Palazzo Sant'Elia and the Bridge of San Francesco in Caltagirone, a pedagogical component of the "Architecture and the Urban Environments of Sicily" research project.

You know, Erika, when Nicolás was a student in one of the last typology seminars I taught, the summer was coming around, and he came to my office to discuss what he was thinking of doing over the break. He was pondering whether to go to Harvard's Archaeological Exploration of Sardis, in Turkey. To which I said, "Yes! Do that!" [*laughs*]

NDA And I did!

EN You did?

JS Working for at least one season in an archeological dig is still probably more important for an architecture student than being an intern in an architecture office for a summer.

EN That's amazing.

NDA Yes, even though it was definitely different from what I had expected. I went in with some naive expectations based on my imagination of Henri Labrouste winning the Grand Prix and traveling to Rome to measure monuments for four years from the comfort of the Villa Medici!

My partner Ginevra and I spent months hiking across an agricultural landscape, which had been radically reshaped by the ancient city buried beneath it, to survey ongoing excavation plots. We would set up stations over Lydian and Roman ruins, shoot laser points across mountains, and manually triangulate the position of every piece of rubble on a wall in order to draw it in excruciating detail on grid paper as it emerged from the ground. Something that became evident to me during this experience is the fragility of the relationship between form and meaning, to which you alluded, Jorge. I came to understand that in the end, as designers, we are giving form to buildings and cities in a way that embeds them with a certain meaning and makes an agglomeration of mundane materials represent something to society in a legible way.

One time, the archaeologists sent us for days to measure the rubble walls of late Roman houses built atop what they thought was the palace of Croesus.[25] We made a carefully surveyed drawing in which every little piece of rubble that was used to build the wall was precisely documented. We were able to read all of this complex architectural and historical information in it. However, as soon as we were done, they started taking the wall apart, because they had another ten centuries to research below it. In a second, the late Roman wall became a totally mundane pile of rocks! All because of a simple formal reconfiguration.

EN I think if you read Aloïs Riegl's "The Modern Cult of Monuments," you would see that he might have questioned this kind of treatment of ruins.[26]

NDA Totally, but it was an amazing, vivid experience. The rocks could no longer communicate anything to us because they had lost their formal arrangement. It made me realize how delicate the process in which we embed material culture with meaning, and sometimes sacred meaning, actually is.

EN I guess what we like about ruins—and maybe that is what you're pointing toward—is that they are so far removed from us but still evocatively legible.

NDA They leave enough space for our imagination to complete them, enough room for us to creatively interpret what those traces mean for us now and what we can do with them as a consequence.

EN And then there is that point when they are not legible anymore. When ruins are not even there anymore. Jorge, tell us more about this direct relationship with the ruin in your case.

JS I cannot deny that my relationship with ruins is purely born ... I don't even know what word to use. My affinity for archaeology comes from a sensibility, and frankly an affect. This is because I am an architect, and by circumstance I have been in close contact with archaeologists and archaeological sites. When I say "sensibility", I mean that in archaeology I have a tendency to appreciate, to *feel* the wear of buildings, the nicks and dents, the fading colors of paint, the wear of floor ceramics, stones, or wood. In general, the perfect look of new buildings does not please me.

As for the affective component, I think the emotional relationship with ruins and what they represent belongs to a broader Western cultural tradition that looks at them in a certain way, that values them precisely because of their ruinous, fragmentary, and incomplete condition. I feel that my connection to archaeology and the ruin is not primarily intellectual. Yes, I have a background in anthropology, which is close to archaeology and is tasked with making artifacts talk to you without the help of texts. The anthropologist's goal is to interpret all manifestations of a given culture, particularly those that are not in written form, such as rituals, social relations, family structures, buildings, utensils, and so on. But I guess what I am trying to say is that this only enhances what anyone interested in art and history feels when they see a ruin: the aggregate of meanings and interpretations across centuries that make them such a fertile source of inspiration. I speak of Western culture, by the way, because I think the ruin—although it is improper to use this term transculturally, and I should say, the "ruinous," damaged, or partially collapsed building—means something very different in other cultural lineages.

EN That is the thing about archaeology. There is an emotional relationship to ruins, surely, but we also have a very particular way of reading ruins based on the way we read images. However, the truth is that archaeology and ruins have chased you throughout your life.

JS Yes, always, always. [*laughs*]

EN Even when we did the studio on the Guaraní territory! You called the ruins of the Jesuit mission that you and the participants found in the jungle at the edge of Candelaria in Argentina an "uninvited guest." But I don't think it was uninvited at all. I think that you invited the ruins as part of your…

JS They come to me! I love that idea. We are acknowledging our affection for ruins and the acts through which we invest them with meaning, with imagined former and future lives. And now you are also investing ruins with movement, with actual active life, through which they chase crazy architects who fall in love with them!

EN They do.

As you suggested, the relationship between architecture and archaeology has its own history, and one of its pivotal moments is a period of great interest to you, namely the Baroque. The historiographic component of this relationship, in which archaeology is a kind of imaginative arena for architecture, is fascinating. I'd like to hear your thoughts on this as well as how you would position your own archaeological experience in relation to this history.

JS Of course, the idea of using archaeological experience as the foundation from which to generate new architecture takes us as far back as Raphael and Palladio. But it isn't until after the Enlightenment and the consolidation of typological thinking that the importance of the ruin to the creative moment in architecture becomes central. The creative moment always needs to start from something that is already architecture. Whether you want to or not, in the end you will have to draw something related to actual buildings.

This reminds me of the extraordinary MoMA show on Henri Labrouste curated by Barry Bergdoll and his team about ten years ago.[27] It was perhaps the best architecture exhibition I had ever seen. It presented the impact of the Grand Tour on Labrouste clearly and beautifully. They displayed all the revelatory documents—particularly his own drawings and renderings—connecting his intense experiences in Paestum and his encounter with the Basilica with his most original, influential, and paradigmatic work: the Bibliothèque Sainte-Geneviève in Paris.

Ruins of the Candelaria Mission near Posadas, Argentina, surveyed by Harvard GSD students as part of the Territorio Guaraní III option studio during the spring of 2015.

At the Bibliothèque Sainte-Geneviève, Labrouste draws from the Basilica, an anomalous Doric temple with a row of columns running across the center of its axis, as inspiration to work with a new building technology, steel construction, in a masonry structure. He exposed this innovation at the exact point where the Greek anomaly is most acute, or, in other words, at the longitudinal central axes of the plan along which the line of cast iron columns is placed. The site then forced Labrouste to position the rectangular plan with its long side facing the square, so he had to rethink the entire orientation of the temple facade and the circulation sequence. The whole anomaly of the original Greek temple, rendered in svelte metal forms, becomes secondary and more ornamental. The rotated temple metamorphoses into a new type of public building: the public library. The nineteenth century is one of the historical periods in which architecture and archaeology are closely tied, and it is key to understanding how the architectural mind thinks in relation to form-making and, specifically, how the process of symbolization works.

EN Maybe we can address this link by turning to where you discuss this topic in your Sekler lecture. Even though I understand what you are doing in the lecture, and it makes sense to me, I'm still a bit unsure about how your argument is structured. You describe a transition from what you term as a "preconscious discourse" in architecture, which lasted through the Enlightenment to today's overly self-conscious discourse. Archaeology plays a significant role in this transition. One of the things that has always intrigued me is how discursive and self-conscious the invention of the concept of type was during the Enlightenment, surely more so than in the Renaissance.

JS Well, I'm sure you are right. I was just trying to underline how totally and completely self-conscious the architectural discourse of the '70s became.

EN Yes, you're surely correct. But it's interesting that type is an Enlightenment idea developed by the very people you mention in your lecture, such as A. C. Quatremère de Quincy, who were obsessed with archaeological questions. For me, type is a discursive or methodological approach that, during the Enlightenment, was theorized on the basis of concrete material evidence. I wonder what you think about that, because I'm not sure the trajectory that you described in dialectical terms in your lecture can be characterized in this way. Yet I do find it interesting that in the arc that you drew between the Enlightenment and the present, we lose ... let's call it archaeology, right?

JS I had never thought of it that way, but that's a good way to put it. I have read the draft for your new book and have been to your recent lectures about that moment during the Enlightenment when archaeology played a fundamental role in the production of architecture. However, I hadn't put it all together in relation to this discussion about typology. I think what you are trying to pin down is the moment when typology becomes disconnected from archaeological remnants, from the material ruins that typological thinking feeds off of, correct?

NDA Maybe what you were calling the self-conscious discourse of the '70s in your Sekler lecture was actually a moment in which theories like typology were no longer judged against a form of concrete architectural evidence out in the world.

EN Exactly. To be a good architect in the eighteenth century, you had to actually survey, depict, and reconstruct an ancient site.

JS Right, which was the original idea of the Rome Prize for architects.

EN That is why Robert Adam goes to document Diocletian's Palace in Split.

JS Diocletian's Palace ... What a beautiful set of drawings Adam produced!

EN Indeed, and this is a context that is compelling because in that moment, type and archeological knowledge were interdependent.

NDA During this period, the balance between, on the one hand, existing architectural evidence and, on the other, a way of theorizing it that allows for architectural reinvention is a wonderful case study for us today. Typological theories allowed these architects to seize on an architectural logic embedded in ruins and use it in original ways to address the unique problems and pressures that their time posed. They produced an architecture that was grounded on the knowledge of an existing tradition, but in the end looked nothing like the originals to which they were referring. Typology during the Enlightenment is the manifestation of a mature modern eye that developed after the Renaissance and through which these designers interpreted the past. Your example of the Bibliothèque Sainte-Geneviève, even if dated somewhat later, is a case in point, Jorge.

I think today there is a chaotic search for something that can be as grounding as the classical ruin was during the Enlightenment. But since what this search yields is actually most often extra-architectural, it just ends up generating a series of new problems that need to be addressed without really paving a path for architectural resolutions. Perhaps the best analogue we have today to the ruin during the Enlightenment is the Modernist fixation on contemporary building technology, which is already dated.

JS If we agree that archaeology and typology cease to cohabitate after the Enlightenment, then that would explain why typology as a concept becomes incapable of handling the relationship between fragment and whole. It becomes exclusively about the production of an idealized whole, climaxing with the Rossi effect.

3. The Hereafter of Typology

EN Why don't you tell us more about your view of this so-called Rossi effect?

JS What I mean by "the Rossi effect" is the epidemic spread of Aldo Rossi's iconography in the US, which in my view had a horrific impact on American architecture. I always say that the journey European architecture takes when it travels across the Atlantic drastically and invariably metamorphoses it into something else. This effect in itself is healthy, promising, and culturally inevitable, but sometimes the results are deplorable!

Robert Stern described this spread to me as "Rancho Rossi Architecture" at one point. Although cruel, I think his characterization is on point. The translation of Rossi's work was poor and vacuous. To be fair, this was partly due to historical circumstances I witnessed with my own eyes. Rossi became popular in the US before anyone had read a single word of his writings. I had read him many years earlier in Spanish, but the English translation of *The Architecture of the City* was published much, much later.[28] The fascination with his work was purely figural. It was all about those magnetic images of the San Cataldo Cemetery in Modena, the Monumento ai Caduti in Como, and the Fagnano Olona Elementary School in Varese. This figural reception created a very unfortunate situation, which Rossi was able to sense but not control.

In order not to oversimplify this transatlantic translation, though, we have to mention Alan Colquhoun and his ideas about how it all played out. His article "Typology and Design Method" sheds light on the distinct power that images have on Anglo-Saxon cultures, and how this also casts shadows over the profundity of Rossi's work.[29] In Europe, Rossi produced a dense discussion that left a productive legacy. He contributed to a more profound understanding of the cultural behavior of the European city. This was absent in the Anglo-Saxon world. His legacy became the proliferation of projects with pitched roofs and square windows that looked like Italian beach cabanas in a variety of sizes: small, large, and extra large! In fact, when Rossi participated in the Gallaratese housing complex, which brilliantly speaks to the language of Modern architecture, the project was highly criticized in American circles.

EN Yes, Rossi gave a profundity to the European city that was lost on American audiences, at least initially. His cemetery in Modena really resonates with the Catholic European cemetery. The placement of the various parts demonstrates a sensibility for rituals and conventions that persist in that tradition, deploying pure forms in their service. However, I wonder if, in the end, he abandoned himself to figuration in a pessimistic way.

JS Absolutely. I saw Rossi's cemetery early on, and I was more than impressed; I was moved by it. Not just because of the spatial and iconographic features but also because of how it speaks to the intellect. If you know European Catholic cemetery tradition, which I do because Argentinian cemeteries are a local version of Italian ones, the project transmits something very compelling.

Rossi was incredibly well-versed in history and philosophy. He was also politically active, like many Italians of his generation. He was a Communist, of course, like filmmaker Lucino Visconti, writer Pier Paolo Pasolini, and other poets of that time. With moving pathos, Rossi was able to transmit a deep understanding of and empathy for the civic culture at the core of the European city. And he did this best through thoughts and drawings. In fact, the images he produced were stronger and more seductive than his buildings. I think Peter Eisenman gave one of the sharpest assessments of Rossi's work; he is known for having said something like, "Rossi's buildings are illustrations of his drawings."

Rossi's work failed when it hit the battlefield. There was something very simplistic about it when it was built. I say this with pain in my heart, because I love him, his thinking, his drawings, and, most importantly, the doors he opened for us to look at the relationships between architecture and the city. Toward the end, Rossi was excited about building more work, but I have to agree that he just wasn't all in on the practice. However, despite all of my reservations about Robert Venturi, things went the other way for him precisely because his work was inherently iconographic.

EN I'm glad you highlighted the different ways in which the Rossi effect unfolded on two continents. The American inheritance is the one many of us know today, but there is an entirely other aspect we don't talk about so much.

JS Much like the arrival of Modernism in the US through the 1932 exhibition on International Style at MoMA, the meaning of Rossi's work was inevitably distorted wherever the European city was not the prevailing tradition. Rossi realized this when he came to the US for the first time, years after publishing *The Architecture of the City*.[30] At the

Harvard GSD, we were among the first schools to invite Rossi to the US, and I spent a lot of time speaking with him, since I was one of the few faculty that spoke fluent Italian. Rossi was extremely perceptive, and he really liked certain things about the US. He also went to Argentina in the early '80s, by the way, and he loved Buenos Aires. However, in US cities, he saw big differences from the European city and its ties to Mediterranean urban culture, despite its legacy in the Americas. He was very honest about the fact that when he wrote about the city, he was actually referring to the European city and that his theories were limited in a way that he hadn't foreseen. Sadly, some of his followers did not see it that way. This change of perspective is evident in his later work. Many close to him say that they noticed it. You can tell the difference when you compare *The Architecture of the City* with *A Scientific Autobiography*,[31] which was published after his journey to the Americas. The tone is completely different. The former is affirmative, didactic, and clarifying, and the latter is melancholic, reflective, and grave.

I think the revival of typology at the time had the right spirit, but it left the discussion unsettled. All of the projects that were designed ended up lacking the depth embedded in the typologies to which they alluded. In Rossi, we see clearly this idealization of typologies that allow iconic archetypes to emerge. In Venturi, we see an ironic manipulation of typologies. This begins as a kind of nostalgic mannerism and ends up a tragic parody. They both offer commentaries on typology: Rossi is more metaphorical and Venturi, more cynical. But typology is not actually an instrument for thinking and creating projects. The projects are just images of a type. I think the contributions of others, such as Giulio Carlo Argan and Rafael Moneo, are essential because they help us to overcome this limitation.

EN The tension you set up between Argan and Moneo yields a remarkable reflection on typology in your Sekler lecture. It provides the theoretical grounding for your assessment of the three churches in Palermo and the ways in which they reveal a magnificent hybridity of Catholic, Byzantine, and Islamic architectural configurations. You use this tension as a tool in your argument, and it would be useful to hear you talk about this. You rightly suggest that Argan casts typology as a synthesis of historical processes, whereas Moneo underscores the need to constantly reinvent the term as part of an architect's creative process. Moneo separates the notion of type and typology from historical developments. I felt that you ended up privileging Moneo over Argan in your discussion.

JS You're right, Moneo separates the two and this is important; that is exactly why I think Moneo wrote the last important piece discussing typology on a more robust theoretical level.[32] It is not a surprise for me that such a rich and nuanced perspective was brought up by a practicing architect with a remarkable scholarly mind! When Moneo wrote his piece on typology in the late '70s, it was perfect for that moment. It revealed what we were discussing earlier: typology is a theory in which we take existing architectural evidence, such as ruins, building technologies, precedents, and so on, and redeploy aspects of its logic to generate new architecture—and emphasis should be placed on *new architecture*.

Moneo said something else about typology that leaves me baffled, which is that, for architecture to continue, typology is inevitable; and it probably needs to be destroyed and reinvented by every generation. I don't know exactly what he meant, but as usual, he throws something out there that reopens the whole debate for all of us. I find it productive to take on his challenge and try to translate this destructive necessity into what is going on with architecture today, forty years after his article and after so much has changed in the practice. I think we are now in one of these moments when we feel the need to reinvent typology and even perhaps change the term itself to get rid of some of its baggage. We have experienced some architectural turns of great intensity that might require this reinvention.

EN Moneo's argument about typology as a tradition of reinvention as opposed to synthesis is much more productive for architecture.

JS Argan's understanding of typology as synthesis also has its relevance, of course. It is less deployable for designers, because he is talking about art history, not necessarily architecture, even if Argan is an architectural historian and so many of his examples are buildings. You might know how to better place Argan historiographically, but I think that his idea of synthesis is conceived mostly as an homage to Walter Friedlaender.

EN Yes, this is an interesting connection. We know Argan admired Friedlaender's interpretation of Caravaggio, which he read as he was preparing his own essay on the artist, as well as of the Mannerist and anti-Mannerist movements. This is no doubt why we should reread him.[33] What I admire about Argan is the way he brings other forms of art and visual disciplines into conversation with architecture. His essay on Brunelleschi is a perfect example of this.[34] He is able to convey what it actually means to imagine an architecture that is perspectival.

I see much about Argan's thinking embedded in the way you interpret the three churches in Palermo. You read them as a palimpsest of type, historical precedents, archaeology, and cultural movements. Perhaps you can elaborate on your triangulation of the three

Norman churches you encountered in Sicily. How did you sense that the Cathedral of Cefalù was the original idea, that the Cathedral of Monreale was a spatial mutation, and, finally, that the Cathedral of Palermo was a manifestation of a premodern typological mindset? What were the formal manifestations of this evolution you surmised without, once again, being able to rely on textual sources for an answer? Is it right to posit your deciphering of the three churches as a kind of anthropology of the conceptualization of type?

JS Wow! The anthropology of the conceptualization of type. Whatever you mean, I agree with you! Yes, I would want my take on the three churches to be seen that way! The cathedrals of Palermo, Monreale, and Cefalù are buildings that you see often if you're an architect and you spend some time in Palermo. They are all very close. Monreale and Cefalù are in what might be considered the suburbs of Palermo today. Even when you encounter them today without much understanding of their style or history, you can tell that they are totally different. Yet the more you look at them, the more you begin to connect them. The order in which I arranged them is purely chronological: Cefalù was the original idea because it was the first to be built; Monreale was the second idea and church to be built; and Palermo the last. We need to take into account the architectural learning process that may have been involved, because the players are the same people. They are from just a few generations of Norman nobility, clergy, and artisans and were all working continuously during the brief century and a half that they controlled the region.

The first time I realized that these three churches were secret companions was through a spur-of-the-moment idea at a conference for the eight-hundredth anniversary of the Cathedral of Palermo. It was a huge event, with international scholars and the Italian intelligentsia in attendance. It was held inside the cathedral itself. It was a celebratory event, but it was also organized in support of the efforts by the Archdiocese and the city to initiate major restoration work.

I had prepared a short speech that was modest and supportive of the restoration efforts, because, honestly, what was I going to say about such a monumental cathedral to an international audience of European scholars? Then, during the second day of the conference, I began overhearing conversations that were absolutely unbelievable to me. There were all these "originalists" arguing over what period the restoration should privilege. This is a church that has been worked on for centuries up to the very present. But all these different camps were saying, "We should clean it up and bring it to its original state," with each one claiming a different original version!

The medievalists argued that the church had really blossomed in the late Middle Ages. The Renaissance scholars said that the

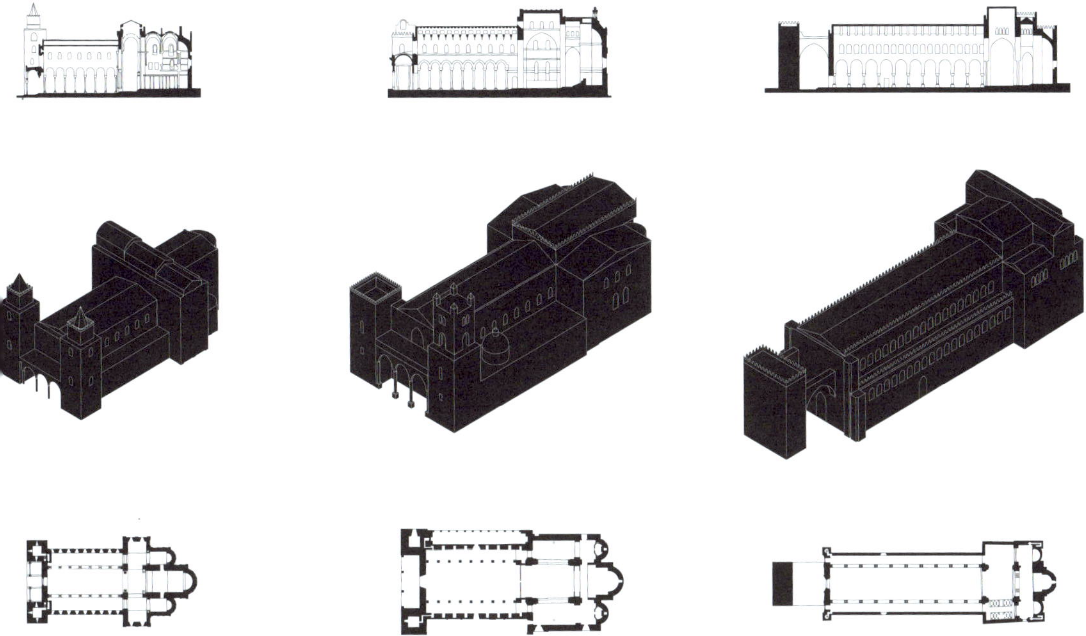

Sections, axonometric perspectives, and plans of the "Three cathedrals." From left to right: Cefalù Cathedral, Monreale Cathedral, and Palermo Cathedral. Drawings by Juan Sala.

A house on the island of Djerba, Tunisia, photographed by Jorge Silvetti in 1971.

Renaissance interventions had really given it its final form and spatial interpretation for the Roman Catholic rite. And then, of course, you had the camp that defended the mature Baroque interventions of Ferdinando Fuga. I'm sorry to say this about your colleagues, but the whole scene at that symposium was just so absurd. All these historians of art and architecture were literally fighting for the enshrinement of the period on which they had written their dissertations! This was bound to be a never-ending debate, so I threw my speech in the garbage at the last minute, went up to the podium, and with all due respect told them they were crazy! I explained to them that what they had in their hands was a completely different kind of problem than determining what style was the "original."

I improvised on the spot an exposition of the three churches, which gave the Palermo Cathedral a more precise and richer meaning. I underlined that they should think about the unique opportunity to present them together as a historical event rarely visible in other places. Because their locations are so close, their historical context remains rather homogenous, which allows you to see with your own eyes the dynamic development of a building type across time in a unique way. Moreover, they were not just dealing with the restoration of an old relic but a living artifact that was in use and had to be kept alive. This is also the case for the other two churches. It was, and still is, a working cathedral, which contains almost nothing of its original interior. In Cefalù, everything remained pretty much in its early Norman state. In Monreale, there was the magnificent invention of mosaic interiors, which are unmatched elsewhere in Europe and transform its meaning into a spectacular visual narrative of the Christian faith. And in Palermo, three or four waves of drastic transformation reveal how the building adjusted to the changing political and cultural fortunes of Sicily. At the time, I didn't know what to do with this reflection, but it gave me great pleasure to deliver it, and it inspired me a lot.

EN What strikes me about this story is that you were thinking relationally, which is a word I really haven't used before when I've thought about this period of your life. You were thinking about history in terms of a set of relations.

JS Absolutely.

EN Looking at the three churches together allowed you to convey a grand archaeological perspective over and against the particulars of any one moment. You are extremely good at identifying these kinds of collisions, which speaks to your complex notion of typology. I think this is where we can agree with Argan that typologies are a synthesis of what emerges from an accumulation of cultural, political, and historical conditions affecting a certain kind of building.

JS Yes. I've always been so surprised when people discover for the first time the supposedly genial idea that changing social and political realities are closely related to architecture. Honestly, since I was young, I've never thought otherwise. Maybe this stemmed from the Marxist understanding of the world that was implicit to the social reality in which I was brought up. Even without being a Marxist myself, I've carried a dialectical and materialist understanding of history and society with me ever since my youth in Argentina. The idea that everything is interconnected, and that our cultural superstructures rest on the foundations of our economic infrastructures, has always opened the door to a profound understanding of these relations.

EN Absolutely. I would say that when you referred to my colleagues, you were talking less about historians with an interest in a thick description of the world and more about people in the field of preservation—which is not history.

JS Well, of course. Yes.

This discussion brings me to the issue of vernacular architecture, which we mentioned briefly earlier and which has become increasingly important to my thinking about typology. I have not followed contemporary discussions on vernacular architecture, but I have a sense that the topic has changed a lot, because students keep asking me questions about it that I don't understand! [*laughs*] So perhaps my idea about the vernacular conflicts with current views, but bear with me.

EN I'm glad you brought up the vernacular. It sounds as though Sicily brought you into contact with things that were outside or on the margins of the written record, right? And the vernacular is deeply tied to this.

JS Exactly. Although maybe I have to go back to my first real encounter with vernacular architecture: the mind-blowing trip to Tunisia I mentioned earlier. This was in the early '70s, and it was not the world that it is today. Tunisia was a very backward country that had just been freed from France's colonial dominance. Yet we were able to go everywhere. We rented a car to explore what we wished, and we actually slept on the beaches during what turned out to be a very hot summer.

This was the first time in my entire life that I really saw vernacular architecture as an outsider. All the vernacular examples I had seen were in Latin America, and especially my home country of Argentina. I had only seen it as belonging to daily life, unnoticeable because it was ubiquitous and belonged to my own set of cultural conventions. This had been my experience even in Europe, but in Tunisia things were different. The architecture was still Mediterranean, but it stood entirely on its own. The colors, the materials, the way the houses were organized, the relationship between architecture and the landscape—all this had a huge impact on me.

Back at UC Berkeley, as I began to work on my dissertation, this question of the vernacular became central, and I spent a lot of time thinking and writing about it. I read, wrote papers, and took courses in anthropology in an attempt to understand the vernacular, which of course paired well with my interest in linguistics. Soon after our return, *Learning from Las Vegas* was published, which tried to put forth a contemporary way of thinking about the American vernacular.[35] And then there was Rossi. All this converged with my inability to separate my interests in the vernacular and architecture with a capital *A*.

One of the most important projects I did was after this trip to Tunisia. While we spent most of the time moving around in Tunisia, we took a real vacation lasting about ten days in the island of Djerba. There was this house on the beach that I later dreamt about. I still have my own original photograph of it. After we came back to the US, it remained an obsession of mine until I resolved to design a response to the vernacular. The house initiated an intense personal argument that I wanted to have with architecture. I could have just bought some books and read more on the topic, but I had to design this house at that moment and, through it, transmit my reflections on the vernacular.

I thought to myself, "Can I do a house that amalgamates architecture with a capital *A* and the Tunisian vernacular?" I responded to the question through design. The project ended up having quite an impact at the time. The house was not a vernacular design. How could it be? It was instead a study of how to grapple with the vernacular. It was very simple. It could have fit the very setting, even if it would have stood out as a bit odd.

EN Maybe what you encountered in Tunisia through the vernacular, as well as in the postmodernist thinking on the American vernacular, was the possibility for hybridity, for choreography, and for improvisation.

JS Yes, and for transformation.

EN Whereas today, I think many students and practitioners think of the vernacular as having some pure and static expression.

JS Yes.

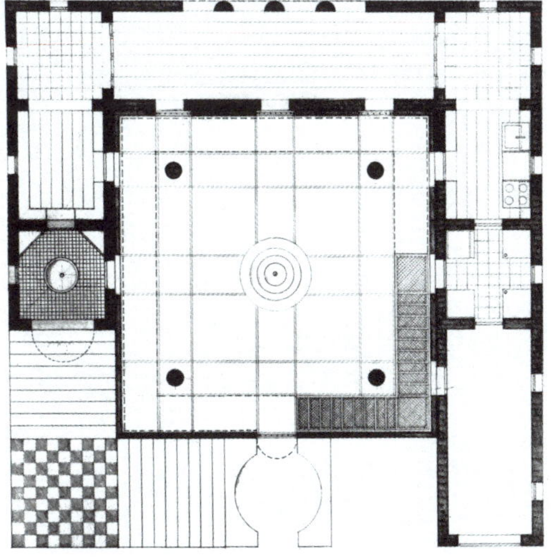
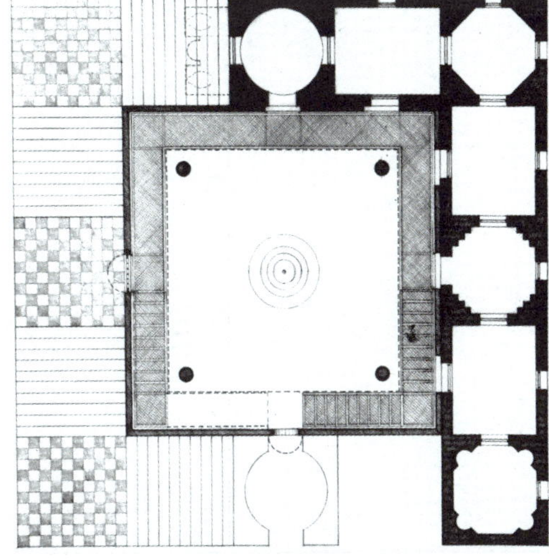
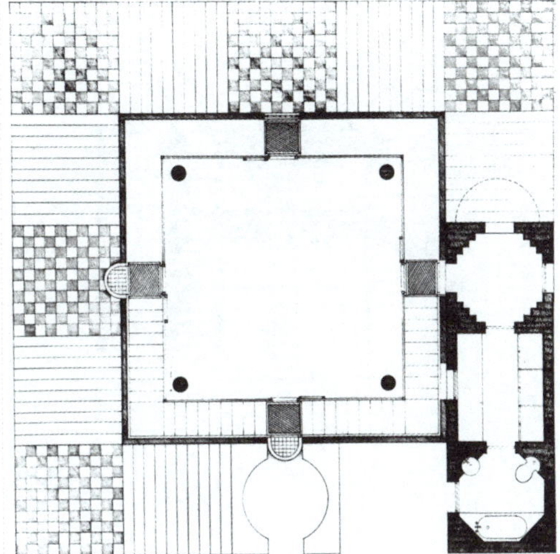
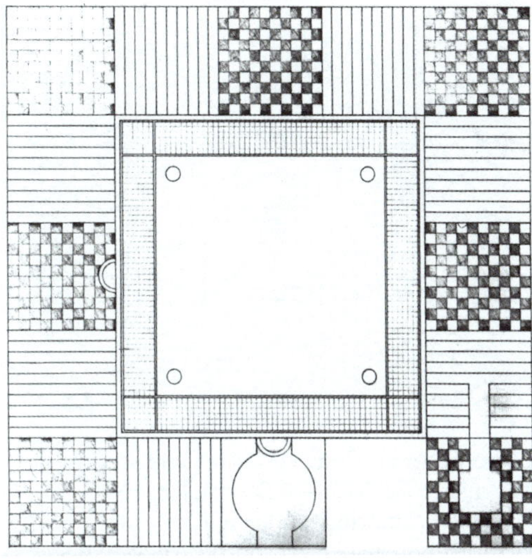

Above: Plans of House in the Island of Djerba, Jorge Silvetti (1976). Drawings are pencil on Strathmore paper.

Wooden model of House in the Island of Djerba, Jorge Silvetti (1976).

Axonometric sections, elevation, and section of House in the Island of Djerba, Jorge Silvetti (1975–1976). Drawings are pencil and color pencil on Strathmore paper, except the axonometric sections, which are on yellow trace. The elevations were drawn and colored by Calvin Tsao.

EN That may be the difference between your understanding of the vernacular and current discussions. This relates to the three churches in Palermo, because there you were confronted with a hybrid manifestation of architecture and the vernacular.

JS Yes, I think that what ties the three churches together has a lot to do with vernacular architecture. I say this because their resulting formal appearance is nothing other than a hybridization of the conventions that the Normans encountered when they landed in that part of the world and the conventions they brought with them. And by "conventions", I mean the social, economic, technological, and cultural norms that converge when you need to create buildings and shape space. I firmly believe that the basis of architecture concerns conventions across these spheres of human life. This is why architecture is a cultural practice.

Wherever you go in the world, you encounter a series of conventions that determine how people live, how they sleep, and how they eat; the way they use the bathroom, how they gather, how they understand the family unit; the ways they make things based on the available material resources, the specific technologies they develop to manipulate them, and so on. Today is no exception. We all live in conventional houses in conventional neighborhoods and conventional cities. To be clear, I don't mean "conventional" in a pejorative way.

NDA Conventions are necessary to the formation of a society; they are the standing consensus on how one thing or another is done.

JS Right. Conventions are the basis of the architectural forms that belong to a certain group of people. These people communicate through these conventions and use them to find a way to live in harmony. By the same token, we live in a society that is obsessed with challenging these same conventions. We are always trying to shock and disrupt, and yet conventions are always there. You can only shock when a convention is there to be transgressed in the first place. The more we talk, the more I'm convinced that this important ingredient is missing from the discussion on typology today. We can't seem to peacefully reason with what the basic conventions through which our society shapes the city according to its spatial necessities might be.

NDA Upholding conventions comes off as wanting to flatten diversity or capitulate to problematic realities, which is not always the case. There is a dogmatic, ideological resistance to exploring what really brings us together as a society, primarily because those that are most critical rarely have a credible proposition. There is diminishing consensus about what a larger "us" means, other than a collection of individuals pursuing their own truth in a radically self-centered, sheltered, and eroded individualist conception, disguised under a lingo that sounds like something entirely else.

JS This is why I think architecture with a capital *A* and the vernacular are inseparable even if distinctly different. No matter what side a building lands on, it is always dealing with conventions. The only difference is that architecture, properly speaking, involves the added conscious effort to elaborate on these existing conventions; to modify them by infusing them with something new or giving them a rhetorical twist.

After being trained as a classical musician, one day, around the time when the Beatles came around and I became entranced by their music, I had this personal awareness that there is no division between popular and classical music that was firmly established in the musical world of the day. Of course there are differences, but in the end it's all the same thing: music, which depends on some adherence to formal principles of syntax and semantics. You can't impose a divide between the genres in a strict way, because even Johann Sebastian Bach and Claude Debussy sourced material from popular music. Think about jazz. Many great jazz composers who influenced popular music were classically trained or attuned, while many twentieth-century classical composers mined the harmonic, rhythmic, and contrapuntal aspects. Igor Stravinsky, Keith Jarrett, Chick Corea, Leonard Bernstein, and Aretha Franklin all come to mind.

My point is that division comes from the need we have in places like academia to clarify the boundaries between disciplines. But I've always felt that the vernacular has never received proper treatment by architects and architectural historians. In the case of the latter, this is because it is not historical in the technical sense of the term. Yet the ways in which we understand the role of the vernacular in regard to the history of architecture are what is important to me. What this implies, of course, is a redefinition of what we understand as the vernacular in contemporary capitalist societies. This is an unresolved question. It is certainly not a collection of localized, premodern building conventions that responded to a given environment and living traditions. What I like about Moneo in this regard is that he raises the question of conventions very strategically, even if I don't know if that is the term he uses exactly.

NDA I think you set up this Argan-Moneo dialectic and frame it as the last relevant moment in the discussion on typology precisely because of this concern for conventions. From Argan, you take the idea that building forms are the result of the conventions of a given time and that historical periods show us how those forms are progressively improved upon to adhere to the specific needs and opportunities of that time. From Moneo, you take the mandate for the architect: to look at these conventions with a critical eye and, while in the process of translating them into buildings, to take advantage of the opportunity they open up as part of the creative moment and tweak them with specific intent. This is why typology is fundamental. Because it's the theory each generation uses to figure out how to understand conventions and to creatively redeploy them in a way that is projective and that participates in shaping the open-ended future to which the building will belong.

EN I agree, and I think what is striking—maybe this is what you are trying to say, Nicolás—is that in Moneo's characterization, there is a clear sense of the creative act. Maybe this sounds straightforward, but it is not. Perhaps we can even describe this approach as somewhat operative. There is an account here about what it means to reflect from a creative standpoint or a characterization of the thought produced by the mind that is concerned primarily with making.

JS I think we need to reignite the discussion of typology if we want to overcome many of the challenges our discipline is facing today, which is the impasse I evoked in my Sekler lecture. I definitely want to clarify aspects of my arguments laid out there. I would have to start where Moneo left off, because there is nothing I would change about his arguments. I just need to use them to reorient debate on the topic that has been meandering for three decades as part of an unfocused theoretical field.

I need to return to the cohabitation of archaeology and typology, which is opening up a new perspective for me. This conversation about the role of ruins in the creative process of architecture and its disappearance from theoretical discourse is full of potential, as well as the reemergence of the ruin, which has finally occurred after two centuries of banishment! As you say, Nicolás, today's ruins are of a different kind, but the search for fragments with generative potential nonetheless remains in place.

Considering typology again over the last few years has led me to think that we should reinsert the concept of the fragment back into architectural discourse. The fragment is a powerful, enigmatic, and ineludible physical entity, which has rarely been conceptualized in theory throughout its long history. The fascination with ruins is perhaps the only exception. I want to reconfigure the corpus that has traditionally been placed under the umbrella of typology and that has been exclusively reserved for types incarnated as formal wholes. By this I mean the idealized compositions intended for a certain kind of building. I want to add another aspect to this category that is a fundamental part of material culture: the fragmentary conditions from which we imagine those formal wholes.

I think that this is the first necessary step to decipher Moneo's last enigmatic words in his discussion of typology.[36] I would say to Moneo, "Yes, Rafael, I agree that we must abide by the ineludible fact that architecture needs typology in order to exist. But to do so, we must also understand how to destroy it too; how to break away from its rules." Another way to say this is to say that a double maneuver becomes necessary. We must maintain the Enlightenment era's foundation for the concept of typology: the symbolic pillar of paradigmatic wholes. But we also need to add a new concept, the allegorical pillar of the ineffable fragment, which unveils another compositional strategy that generates cultural artifacts and has been ignored for so long. This allows typology to be not only about paradigmatic whole forms but also about the relational processes of formal compositions. In both pillars of typology, the amalgamating mortar is vernacular architecture, which is central to a new discourse on typology. The vernacular is a necessary presence with the specific ideological role of keeping architecture consistent with its nature as a cultural practice.

In order to understand the balance between these two forces, I believe we need to go further back into history. We could reassess the ancient Greek world during its peak: Athens in the time of Pericles. This is a period where we can find the foundations of a discussion that blossomed in a particular way during the Enlightenment. That said, it is a period that excluded something that I consider an indispensable protagonist in the discussion about typology today. Thus, the first of my pillars is characterized by the descendants of the Parthenon, and the second, with those of the Erechtheion. This is why the title of my next paper will be "The Acropolis of Athens and Its Consequences." While this is all still in flux, I hope to bring into play all the relevant parts: the whole and the fragment, the symbol and the allegory, the type and the anti-type, architecture and the vernacular.

4. The Architect and the Historian

EN Your comments evoke, for me, the eternal dance between architecture and history—one version of which we saw play out in Caltagirone. How this dance ought to unfold is a profound question, because architects need historians, but historians also need architects! We always think of the historian as the didactic figure who has something to teach to the architect. Yet in your project in Caltagirone, and in many other projects, it was the architect's eye that revealed something to the historian. If the Bridge of San Francesco operated epistemologically in the historian's domain because of extant archival documentation, the Palazzo Sant'Elia operated in the architect's domain because of a specific kind of formal acuity. Without records, it was left to the eye of the designer to figure out what had happened. I realize that this is a bit of a caricature; there are many historians who read buildings with wonderful authority, just as there are many designers who have a profound knowledge of history. Nevertheless, the lack of interest in the palazzo—a kind of misfit left by the wayside in historical records—allowed you to be the one to recognize the design problem it posed and ask why certain decisions were made that led to such a strange result. Through your investigation, you were also forced to proceed from fragmentary conditions and elements as opposed to a typologically coherent entirety. This back-and-forth between the architect and the historian is something in which you are very interested. It brings me to the role of architectural history in design schools.

JS Yes, that's a very good way to discuss what happened in Caltagirone. It's how it felt. This back-and-forth is related to the relationship I had with architectural historian Howard Burns, which was remarkable and didn't reflect my typical experience with historians. Maybe because of my affinity for ruins, I have always felt the need to have a historian by my side. Sometimes I feel uncertain about the robustness of my interpretations, but I certainly have strong feelings and intuitions about certain things!

As you know, history has always been a major interest of mine, and maintaining close relationships with historians has been a defining ingredient of my academic career. Some historians have been my most enjoyable colleagues, and I have also suffered the most with others! [*laughs*] However, these are two sides of the same coin, because I learn so much with them. I enjoy my design colleagues in architecture, and I learn from them too, but in a different way, because we are essentially doing the same thing. History, however, is a discipline outside of my own in which I feel the need to engage. In a sense, this is because I cannot do it by myself.

My relationship with Howard was a gift, because it allowed me to work at an architecture school in the way that I wanted. When he arrived, I continued leading design studios as I had before, but I felt that I had expanded my horizons by having this person next to me doing his own thing. We never interfered with one another. Eventually, this resulted in the fantastic experience of developing the core history/theory course for the MArch program, which we called "Buildings, Texts & Contexts," or BTC.

EN We'll turn to BTC in a moment, but first tell me about the other historian with whom you worked most closely and who must have also had an impact on your thinking: Eduard Sekler. How did you view Eduard's historical approach as opposed to Howard's?

JS I'm not sure that I can articulate this well, but they were certainly different! My relationship with each of them was different too. While I worked extensively with Howard on shared interests and projects, with Sekler I had a more collegial relationship that remained intense and enjoyable. In terms of their differences, I mean, Eduard loved the Gothic, and Howard couldn't look at it! When Howard arrived at the GSD, he brought Andrea Palladio.

The differences you want to explore with regard to these two figures involve a conversation on how history should be taught in a design school. There were real differences between the attitude of a historian like Eduard Sekler in his later years and that of Howard Burns. Sekler was from a different generation than Howard. He was trained in Vienna as an architect, then went to the Warburg Institute to complete his PhD under Rudolf Wittkower. He was very, very . . . I don't know the right term, because I know little about schools of historical thought. But let's say he was very traditional in his training, and he applied this to thinking about Modernism. Team 10 brought him to the last Congrès Internationaux d'Architecture Moderne (CIAM) conference in Otterloo in 1959. He produced the monograph on Josef Hoffmann and was one of the founders of the Department of Visual Arts at the Carpenter Center at Harvard. However, later in life his academic work shifted to conservation, working in Nepal with UNESCO.

As the only historian teaching at the GSD, Sekler played a crucial if traditional role: he taught survey courses. I sat in on some of his classes, and they were what I would imagine a history lesson during the 1930s in Vienna to be like, at their very best! The classes were beautifully organized and structured, with extremely methodical assignments. This was history when I arrived at Harvard.

Sekler was a kind man; he treated me well when I arrived and supported my endeavors when many at the school were suspicious of my ideas. Some even worked to undermine my teaching.[37] Sekler, however, asked permission to sit in on my seminar because he said he was interested in the topic. I called the course something like "Current Topics in Architecture Theory". I don't recall the syllabus, but I am sure it was everything on my mind at the time, and it was directly associated with my doctoral studies at UC Berkeley.[38] Sekler came to every single class and took notes.

EN That's extraordinary.

JS I think he joined the seminar based on the advice of some of the people that were suspicious of me, but he approved of what I was doing. Sekler and the Polish architect Jerzy Sołtan were responsible for containing the resistance and helping me overcome the difficulties.[39] We went on to become good friends. I think something that both Eduard and Howard shared was that they very consciously chose to teach and write from within an architecture school—not unlike yourself, Erika. Sekler was side by side with Josep Lluís Sert during his years as dean of the GSD, and like Howard, he was a historian committed to what he could contribute to an architect's training.

EN This is related to the second half of your lecture dedicated to Sekler, in which you discuss institutions and departments. A key distinction you draw is that art history departments tend to treat the categories of art, architecture, and craft, for example, as isolated objects and images, whereas in architecture schools, these things are not displayed as objects on the wall. Instead, architecture is treated in terms of the problems it addresses, the ways it functions in urban contexts, and the ways in which it is effective at one thing or another. These are different ways of thinking historically. I thought it was interesting that your lecture included a sort of critique of "imagification." I wonder if this was partly directed at art history departments.

JS To say it succinctly, Howard and I were trying to understand how an architect approached a project and executed it. This led to an in-depth study of pertinent historical context surrounding a project, which would be focused on making students think about the design process and the ways in which they would have proceeded in the same situation.

EN Let's discuss "Buildings, Texts & Contexts", which is still taught today as part of the MArch core at the GSD. What was the state of teaching architecture history when you arrived? When Harry Cobb took over as chair of the architecture department?

JS When I came to the GSD in the fall of 1975, it was very different from today. It's hard to believe, but Eduard Sekler was the only historian at the school, and he was only there part-time because he also taught at Harvard College. His office was actually at the Carpenter Center, where he was chair for a period. By comparison, when I left UC Berkeley a few years earlier, Berkeley had three full-time historians: Norma Evenson, Spiro Kostoff, and Stephen Tobriner. When I started my teaching career at Carnegie Mellon University, a smaller undergraduate school, there were two full-time, tenured professors of history. The first big change to the way history was taught at the GSD occurred when we brought Howard Burns on board during the last year of Harry Cobb's chairmanship. You also asked about Cobb, didn't you?

EN Yes.

JS His appointment was a surprise for me as well as others at the school. It was unexpected for many of us because we did not find anything in his curriculum vitae about academic credentials, other than having been an alumnus of the GSD. However, we soon discovered that he was an incredibly well-educated, well-traveled, and sensitive individual. He was enormously interested in what was going on in contemporary architecture practice. And he had a great interest in history as well as a very critical perspective of the GSD, where he had studied. To me, it appeared as if he wanted to include everything in the curriculum that he never got to study as a student at the GSD during the Gropius/Hudnut years! There was still little interest on the part of the status quo to increase the role of history in the curriculum though; older faculty did not think we needed much history to train architects. But Cobb and Gerald McCue, who was the dean and radically transformed the school from its moribund state, thought otherwise—to my delight!

McCue and Cobb moved to create a new position for a historian and insisted that the instructor had to be an Italian Renaissance scholar. This is important, because it gives you an understanding of the times and Cobb's mindset. McCue then structured the position at the senior, tenured level to be filled by a candidate from outside Harvard. He put together a search committee made up of James Ackerman, Neil Levine, Eduard Sekler, Harry Cobb, McCue himself, and me.

We came upon Howard Burns, who we all thought would be a great candidate for the position. He was qualified, so he got the job and started teaching. At first he seemed a bit detached, as if he wasn't comfortable with how we approached the teaching of history. He had to teach the typical courses at the time: required surveys and seminars on selected topics of interest to him. He soon began complaining that he didn't think this was the way to teach history in a graduate architecture school. I kept teaching my own theory courses and Moneo began a series of case-study courses.[40]

All of this brewed slowly until "Buildings, Texts & Contexts" was created. It took form when Mack Scogin became chair in 1990 after Moneo stepped down. At Howard's insistence, Mack entrusted the both of us with rethinking the way history was taught at the GSD. We organized a symposium in 1993 on the subject. This was a true symposium in the ancient sense: closed-door and private, as these things should be if you want to have productive conversations of this kind. From the GSD, we invited Mirka Benes and K. Michael Hays, who were the two other young junior faculty with legitimate credentials as historians. From Harvard's Department of Fine Arts, we included James Ackerman, Neil Levine, and Angelica Zander Rudenstine. Angelica was not on the faculty, but she was a curator and an art historian as well as the wife of Harvard's president at the time, Neil Rudenstine. From outside of Harvard, we invited George Tissot from Princeton as well as Stanford Anderson and David Friedman from MIT.

EN Was Hank Millon there?

JS No, I believe Hank was already in Washington by then. The two-day colloquium allowed us to sit down together in a private setting and openly discuss the ways in which architectural history should be taught to designers. Howard and I already had an idea in mind that was along the lines of what BTC would become. The conversations led to further conceptualization, analysis of existing models of teaching architecture history, and an abstract set of recommendations. These points served as the basis for how to structure and give content to a new mode of teaching, which we called "Buildings, Texts & Contexts." This title that we came up with says a lot.

One of the novel and defining aspects of the course was the decision that it should be taught by a duo: a legitimate historian and a practicing architect with a strong interest in history. The course was structured as a collection of case studies rather than as a survey, although we preserved chronology as an organizational axis. After all, we were teaching architectural history and not the history of single, independent buildings or texts. We also established surveys as requirements for admission into our graduate professional programs, so that students came into the course with a general background in architecture history. This last move was truly transformative in both the way we prepared lectures and the expectations that students would have about them. It was an administrative change that enabled major shifts in the curriculum.

Howard and I were the first to try this out in the fall of 1993. Each week we looked at one case study in class. On Tuesdays, I would present an architectural analysis of the building at hand, trying to articulate how it worked, its relationship to its physical context and contemporary technology, and the possible source of the design decisions. On Thursdays, Howard would amplify this by describing the historical context in which the building was produced only insofar as was necessary to understand it. This meant that we could, together, develop a hypothesis about the design process. We wanted to speculate on how the architect had made design decisions. We discussed this openly with the students throughout the course.

EN Here you are, teaching with a historian. What surprised you? What worked? What didn't?

JS I had a slow start because, honestly, I was not well prepared to deliver weekly hour-and-a-half lectures. I was knowledgeable about buildings and was in possession of solid bibliographies, but I had never really taught their histories. I did catch up quickly, though. It was very intense, a completely new experience. I had to present an architectural description of every case study, which became very interesting for me, and I hope for the students, too. How do you describe in depth, exclusively in architectural terms, a canonical work of architecture like the Pantheon? I forced myself to go into a level of detail that I was not initially prepared for, particularly with cases like Hagia Sophia, which turned out to be among my favorite lectures to deliver.

EN One of your obsessions! Were you also presenting the Mosque-Cathedral of Córdoba as a case study?

JS Yes, another obsession! I brought in Córdoba during the second year of the course, as well as El Escorial. This is when I began to develop the idea of bringing architecture from the margins of the canon into the course, and it was fantastic. We would present Hagia Sophia the week after the Pantheon, so you could see the differences between the buildings based on their different technologies, philosophies, and geographies. We read selections from Procopius of Caesarea and Boethius. We analyzed and compared the use and makeup of mortar in the masonry of ancient Rome and Byzantium. We studied the spectacular jump in geometric knowledge and skill from the simple, Platonic Roman Pantheon to the spectacular configurations of sphere-based intersections that were generated in Byzantine space. We showed the students close-up photographs to compare the brickwork of the Pantheon and Hagia Sophia. It all really worked. The narrative buildup of the course was fantastic, and we reached the high point with Palladio, Howard's forte. We did a great job together.

NDA In surveys, I always walk away with the idea that there is something inevitable about the outcome of any single work of architecture. They instill a sense that context is the driving force that leads designers to make certain decisions. I think the interplay between projection and retrospection, as you defined it, Erika, was really clever in the case of BTC. Looking at buildings from the mindset of the architect immensely opens up the utility of historical references for designers. We get to look at examples in history when complex constraints forced someone to make all sorts of choices in order to ultimately produce a building, which is exactly what we still do.

JS Indeed. Sometimes I feel we overdo the "context" aspect, forgetting that most of the profound contextual conditions surrounding an architectural work are not necessarily pressing in the mind of the architect. Under the same contextual conditions, other architects would have provided different, though equally excellent, responses to the same problems. Context explains a lot and it is indispensable, but it isn't everything. The single creative mind also affects the historical process. This is why we first offered a strict description of the building, and then we provided only as much context as was necessary for understanding it. The context was there only to allow us to hypothesize, in as plausible a way as possible, what was going through the mind of the architect.

EN This is interesting, because if you consider history qua history, as opposed to the history of architecture, original intentions don't matter in the same way.

JS Exactly, they don't. I know that the history of architecture could be conceived in many other ways. But what we were trying to answer was this: "What is an architecture student in graduate school going to take away from a course like this?" We thought the answer involved trying to comprehend what was going on in the mind of someone like Palladio, who was designing villas and palaces for the agricultural landlords of the Veneto region. The context became just another means to understand what that life must have been like back then.

NDA What happened after you both stepped down from teaching BTC?

JS BTC originally involved two teaching teams. Howard and I would teach cases from antiquity to late Baroque in the fall term. K. Michael Hays and Wilfried Wang would then introduce cases from Neoclassicism to Modern architecture in the spring term. A third semester was eventually added to this. BTC was a huge success, and the model was taken up by other architecture schools. That said, in the three decades it has been taught, it has changed drastically for all kinds of reasons.

Howard and I taught the course for about four consecutive years until he left Harvard in 1995, the year I became chair of the Department of Architecture at the GSD. I then continued teaching the fall course jointly with Christine Smith for a few more years. When I stopped teaching BTC, changing circumstances had an effect on the makeup of the course. Moneo, who was back in Madrid, began to take a less active role in the school, and Wilfried left the GSD altogether. The presence of practitioners in BTC diminished almost by natural selection, without much discussion or acknowledgement that this was happening or that this might matter. Later, during my chairmanship, we brought in Antoine Picon to expand the senior teaching team. For a few years, we had the historian and critic Sarah Goldhagen. She accompanied K. Michael Hays, who assumed the role of the architect because, in addition to being a historian and theorist, he also had professional experience. The cohort of historians continued to change and was completed by your arrival, Erika. It is now taught again entirely by historians.

This was all part of an amazing arc of pedagogical transformation at the GSD. The architecture history curriculum has changed radically since the time Sekler was the only part-time instructor. We now have one of the strongest architectural history programs in the country, with a PhD program of international caliber. That said, little trace of the original impetus behind BTC remains, even though at the time it was one of the most inventive pedagogies—at least since Sert's invention of the field of urban design and his establishment of the degree program that coined the term.

These changes have increased the intellectual content and purview of BTC, but I have to say that from my own biased perspective, something has been lost with the disappearance of placing practicing architects on equal footing with historians in the course. There is absolutely nothing wrong with courses evolving and transforming. If they don't, we would be suspicious of them; but I cannot say that I entirely agree with the direction it has taken. That said, there is one other very important ingredient in this story that we have overlooked so far, Erika. As you know, Howard is fascinated by architectural drawing. And this was, above all, what created a strong connection between us from the very start. I have always insisted on the crucial importance of drawing in the design process, because I think it is the locus of the creative moment. This shared interest helped a great deal back then, because he was always going back to drawings in order to explain things. He always engaged students in analytical drawing exercises while he was at the school.

EN One of the things you have repeated to me over the years is that drawing or representing something to yourself is as much an act of projection as it is an exercise in understanding.

Another point you have repeated, which I find extremely moving, is that architecture's history provides no lessons. It is not didactic, but rather it exposes us to the way knowledge was produced.

JS I think that one of the clumsiest errors has been to promote the idea that history provides lessons that nurture future actions: what to do or not to do. This has had lamentable consequences for architectural education. History should not be instrumental in the design process. It is neither a repository from which to pick some lineage or example nor is it a list from which to select design methodologies at a more abstract level.

I also think that the history of architecture that needs to be promoted in design schools should be different from that which is taught in art history departments. Designers need to be given the instruments to engage the creative process and be self-critical. In this sense, learning to understand relevant examples from a historical perspective is very important, because it is a complex matter. Architecture as a building practice is not about solutions. Architecture is about finding positive ways of articulating space and developing iconographies for buildings that help a given society to operate as a true community of interests. The history of architecture allows us to understand how fellow humans, subjected to the cultural demands of their time, managed to produce responses that were appropriate, sometimes spectacular, and on countless occasions, history making.

Notes

1 Jorge Silvetti, "The Bridge and the Palazzo: Urban Interventions and Social Representation," in *Architectural and Urban Environments of Sicily 2: Interactive Realms: The Bridge of San Francesco and the Palazzo Sant'Elia*, ed. Jorge Silvetti (Cambridge, MA: Harvard University Graduate School of Design, 1992), 87–129.

2 The temple was built in the ancient sanctuary at Didyma (8th c. BCE), which was erected on the Ionian Coast (present-day Aydin Province, Turkey). See H. W. Parke, "The Temple of Apollo at Didyma: The Building and Its Function," *The Journal of Hellenic Studies* 106 (1986): 121–131, https://doi.org/10.2307/629647.

3 Giulio Carlo Argan describes Palermo as the "center of Arab culture in Sicily" in his description of the hybridity of the church, which was completed c. 1132. See Giulio Carlo Argan, *L'architettura protocristiana preromanica e romanica* (Bari: Dedalo libri, 1978).

4 See Jorge Silvetti and Alfredo Thiermann, "Architecture: The Question of Method," in this volume, 49–96.

5 *Architectural and Urban Environments of Sicily 1: The First Year of Research by the Harvard Graduate School of Design*, ed. Jorge Silvetti, assistant ed. Thomas Rankin (Cambridge, MA: Harvard University Graduate School of Design, 1989).
Architectural and Urban Environments of Sicily 2: Interactive Realms: The Bridge of San Francesco and the Palazzo Sant'Elia, ed. Jorge Silvetti (Cambridge, MA: Harvard University Graduate School of Design, 1992).

6 It is important to recall the very specific appeal of "cannibalism" which was used literarily by the Brazilian modernist avant-garde painters of the 1920s, when they start to present and explain their "cannibalism" of European Modernity as positive. This was based on the traditions of their local ancestors: the Tupi (a subdivision of the Guarani-Tupi linguistic families), who were cannibals (literally) and transformed the Spanish Catholic imagery and ideology into their own.

7 See *Cattedrale Siracusa: Cronache di un Restauro*, 3 vols., ed. Mariella Muti (Syracuse: Lombardi, 2009).

8 Jorge Silvetti's option studio course was called "Territorio Guaraní III: The Architecture of Living Cultures in Candelaria," whereas Erika Naginski's seminar was called "The Ruin Aesthetic: Episodes in the History of an Architectural Idea."

9 Jorge Silvetti, "The Bridge and the Palazzo."

10 Jorge Silvetti, "Paths, Sounds, Ruins," in *Paths, Sounds, Ruins: Imagining Architecture in Candelaria*, ed. Jennifer Sigler, assistant ed. Marielle Suba (Cambridge, MA: Harvard University Graduate School of Design, 2017), 10–14.

11 Manfredo Tafuri, "*Jugum meum suave est:* Architecture and Myth in the Era of Leo X," in *Interpreting the Renaissance: Princes, Cities, Architects*, trans. Daniel Sherer (New Haven, CT, and London: Yale University Press in association with the Harvard Graduate School of Design, 2006).

12 Claude Lévi-Strauss, *Tristes tropiques*, trans. John Weightman and Doreen Weightman (London: Penguin, 2012), 55–56.

13 Ibid.

14 For an edited transcript of the lecture, see Silvetti, "TYPE: Architecture's Elusive Obsession and the Rituals of an Impasse," in this volume, 427–444.

15 Ibid.

16 Silvetti is referring to one of his many archaeological experiences with Dr. Domenico (Mimmo) Amoroso, a classical scholar, archeologist and Director of the Museo Civico al Carcere Borbonico in Caltagirone. He introduced and familiarized Silvetti with archeological areas, as well as ongoing work in different sites in the southeastern corner of Sicily.

17 Silvetti is referring to Sicilian archaeologist Alba Maria Gabriella Calascibetta. See John K. Papadopoulos, "The Motya Youth: Apollo Karneios, Art, and Tyranny in the Greek West," *The Art Bulletin* 96, no. 4 (2014): 395–423.

18 Giulio Carlo Argan, "On the Typology of Architecture," *Architectural Design* 33, no. 12 (December 1963): 564–564.
Rafael Moneo, "On Typology," *Oppositions*, no. 13 (1978): 23–45.

19 Erwin Panofsky, *Gothic Architecture and Scholasticism* (New York, NY: Meridian Books, 1957).

20 See Rudolf Wittkower, *Architectural Principles in the Age of Humanism* (New York, NY: W. W. Norton, 1971), 70–76. See also James S. Ackerman, *Palladio* (London: Penguin Books, 1991), 36–80.

21 Pierre Bourdieu, "Postface to Erwin Panofsky, *Gothic Architecture and Scholasticism*," in *The Premodern Condition: Medievalism and the Making of Theory*, ed. Bruce Holsinger (Chicago, IL, and London,

University of Chicago Press, 2005), 221–242.
22 See M. Sofia Di Fede, "La festa barocca a Palermo: città, architetture, istituzioni/ Baroque Festival in Palermo: City, Architectures and Institutions," *Espacio, tiempo y forma. Revista de la Facultad de Geografía e Historia,*/ Serie 7, Historia del arte, no. 18/19 (2005/2006): 49–75.
23 See Jorge Silvetti and Elisa Silva, "Architecture: The Purview of the Social," in this volume, 299–339.
24 Jorge Silvetti, "The Bridge and the Palazzo," 128.
25 A Lydian king from the sixth century B.C. renowned for his wealth.
26 Aloïs Riegl, "The Modern Cult of Monuments: Its Character and its Origin," trans. Kurt Forster and Diane Ghirardo, *Oppositions*, no. 25 (Fall 1982): 21–51.
27 Corinne Bélier, Barry Bergdoll, and Marc Le Cœur, *Henri Labrouste: Structure Brought to Light* (New York, NY: Museum of Modern Art, 2012).
28 Aldo Rossi, *The Architecture of the City* (Cambridge, MA: MIT Press, 1982).
29 Alan Colquhoun, "Typology and Design Method," *Perspecta* 12 (1969): 71–74, https://doi.org/10.2307/1566960. See also Jorge Silvetti, "Representation and Creativity in Architecture: The Pregnant Moment," in *Representation and Architecture*, ed. Ömer Akin and Eleanor F. Weinel (Silver Spring, MD: Information Dynamics, Inc., 1982): 159–184.
30 Rossi, *The Architecture of the City*.
31 Aldo Rossi, *A Scientific Autobiography* (Cambridge, MA: MIT Press, 1981).
32 Moneo, "On Typology."
33 See Walter F. Friedlaender, *Caravaggio Studies* (Princeton, NJ: Princeton University Press, 1955) 2: 24–41. See also Giulio Carlo Argan, "Il 'realismo' nella poetica del Caravaggio," in *Scritti di storia dell'arte in onore di Lionello Venturi* (Rome: De Luca, 1956), vol. II, 24–41.
34 Giulio Carlo Argan, "The Architecture of Brunelleschi and the Origins of Perspective Theory in the Fifteenth Century," *Journal of the Warburg and Courtauld Institutes* 9 (1946): 96–121.
35 Robert Venturi, Denise Scott Brown, and Steven Izenour, *Learning from Las Vegas: The Forgotten Symbolism of Architectural Form* (Cambridge, MA: MIT Press, 1977).
36 Moneo, "On Typology".
37 See Jorge Silvetti and Mark Lee, "Architecture: The Emergence of Discourse," in this volume, 117–166.
38 See Silvetti and Thiermann, "Architecture: The Question of Method," 49–96.
39 See Silvetti and Lee, "Architecture: The Emergence of Discourse," 117–166.
40 Ibid.

1

2

Interactive Realms: The Bridge of San Francesco and the Palazzo Sant'Elia

JORGE SILVETTI, 1992

An article by Dr. Domenico Amoroso that appeared in 1987 recounts his archeological discovery of an ancient road, along which a prehistoric necropolis was built[1] in an area known as San Ippolito, outside the city of Caltagirone. The road, he contends, is the oldest in Sicily, dating back to the bronze age, about 1300 B.C. The subject of prehistoric roads sounded so arcane and mysterious, even to people like Professor Howard Burns and myself who are somewhat accustomed to hearing about esoteric sites, that in autumn of 1989 we asked Dr. Amoroso to take us to San Ippolito on one of our regular visits to Caltagirone. Two research assistants, Sam Trimble and Tom Rankin, accompanied us on this memorable tour.

It was a crisp, late November afternoon and we could not help but be moved by the grandeur of both the landscape and the human intervention marking the will to conquer nature, physically and symbolically. The endeavor must have taken tremendous human effort. To sculpt the road, solid bedrock had to be cut and carved vertically and horizontally, an undertaking no doubt demanding great skill considering available instruments. Carved out of the same bedrock as the road are the tombs of the necropolis, which appear as abandoned caves since the lapids or "covering stones" that once closed them were lost. The ensemble is daunting, the carved road without beginning or end lined by the serial caves of the empty tombs, arranged in an open-ended loose grid: a journey to nowhere and gates to the unknown (Figs. 1, 2).

In his article, Dr. Amoroso presents an argument about the historical, cultural, and social meaning of a work of built infrastructure for transportation and its relevance for the archeological studies he is making at the site:

> . . . the existence of built roads, unlike those that are natural, created by animals and men in primitive societies, implies many aspects of social organization, among others: the need of non-episodic contacts of commercial, strategic or religious character; the ability to mobilize society to produce a work of collective (not individual) use, and the ability to physically maintain it.[2]

The dual ensemble of the constructed road and the tombs, also man-made constructions, became dramatically emblematic to me of my preoccupation with Caltagirone, the subject of our survey the preceding summer and, subsequently, this book. This connection was not the consequence of geographical proximity (although it must be pointed out that both phenomena, separated by three thousand years, belong specifically to Caltagirone's culture), bur of an underlying thematic link that extends nor only to our baroque subjects, the bridge and the palazzo, but to my contemporary concern about fundamental urban conditions. Indeed, I had a larger research agenda.

In San Ippolito we find two significant material events, one about physical survival and the other about spiritual survival. Both of them are, literally, carved out of nature at a great

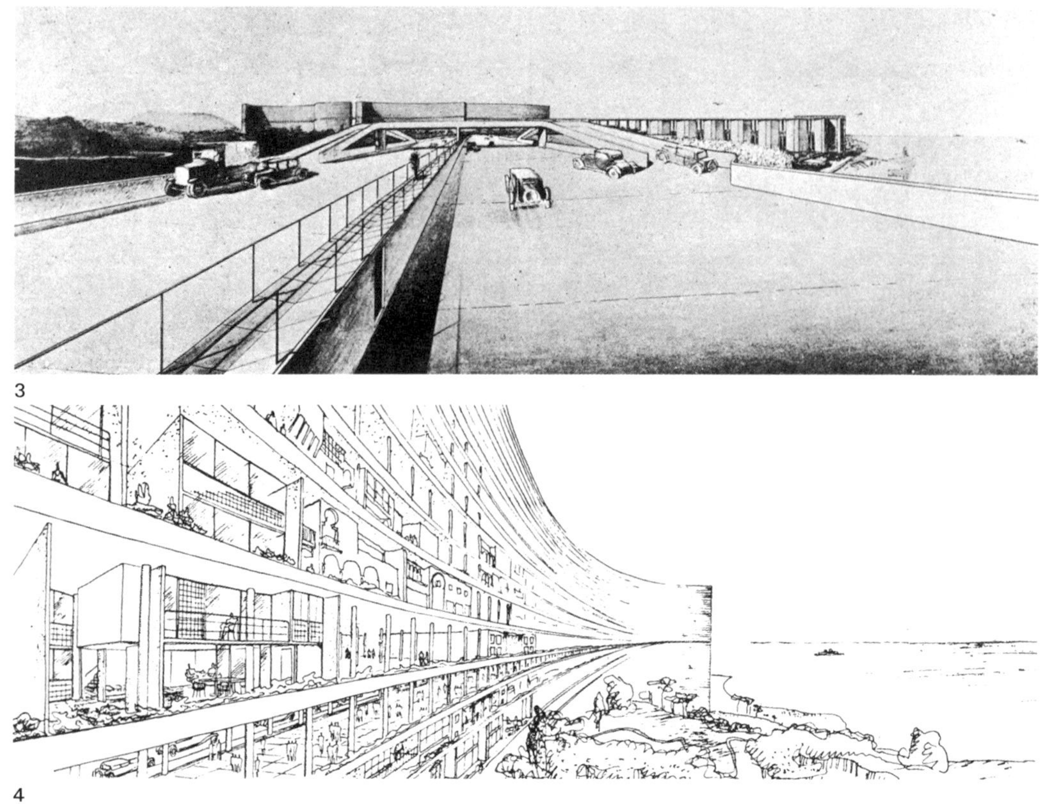

3

4

price in human labor, and their durability and visibility in the landscape makes them inevitably testimonies on the society that produced them. To passers-by, they are a daily reminder of civilization's most enduring marks: a physical, material means of facilitating human movement and a physical, material means of immortalizing the human existence.

In historic times, of course, written documents inform us about the organization of a society more clearly and explicitly than does the physical, built environment. In studying prehistoric times, the lack of written texts and their informational efficiency is offset significantly by the ability of non-literate, physical manifestations to convey sophisticated, subtle, and complex characteristics of culture in synthetic ways comprehensible almost at a glance.

At the risk of sounding too partisan and biased, I would say that even in historic times, documents are not always available, and buildings (monuments, vernacular constructions, and public works) are themselves important texts, often providing the first and most lasting impression of a culture. (This may explain the fascination and empathy architects have for archeology, the only academic endeavor respected as science that looks at objects and makes them speak.)

I believe the study of cities can be approached successfully through a minimal model of two interactive physicalities, public infrastructure and monuments, and that the quality of this interaction indicates in great measure a city's level of civic achievement.

I am not saying these things innocently. As an architect, I have become directly aware of these issues by thinking about the disjunctures that make the image of a contemporary city unmistakable: the division of the city between two incompatible realms, that of the private domain and that of automotive circulation, which seems to cover, as it were, the totality of remaining usable space, or what used to be the public realm (Fig. 6). Awareness of this problem reinforces my conviction that interaction between realms is crucial in properly defining quality in civic life. It also renders more poignant and even tragic the responses that modern architecture offered when significant disjunctures first appeared. I am referring to such examples as Le Corbusier's Algiers proposal (Figs. 3, 4) and various works of Russian Constructivism, which today seem

Figs. 1–2 The road of Necropolis of San Ippolito, 1991.
Fig. 3 Le Corbusier's "Urbanization de la ville d'Algier," 1930. Views of the highway from 100 meters above the ground.
Fig. 4 Le Corbusier's "Urbanization de la ville d'Algier," 1930. View of the housing units below the highway.

both utopian and courageous as well as naive and desperate, as if already aware of the loss of public civic space, but able to respond only in a purely aesthetic or rhetorical manner.

Today, of course, that awareness has made room in some quarters for generalized lament and resignation, as if the divorce between the architecture of transportation and the architecture of habitation, and the resulting disappearance of public space, were inevitable. While in other quarters, awareness has turned to cynicism and renewed faith in purely aesthetic interpretations of the phenomenon, as if representing "discontinuity" in a building were a meritorious obligation of architecture.

In the midst of such preoccupations, I look with awe at the achievements of baroque planning in Sicily, the splendor of its physical beauty, its display of seemingly unlimited skills in resolving particular conditions, and the exuberance of its architectural solutions. But the awe is coupled with the conviction that only a social fabric of tremendous complexity and sophistication could produce such urban environments, a correlation amply proved by our further immersion into the urban history of the Val di Noto. There, we learned that in the aftermath of the tragic Sicilian earthquake of 1693, which left 50 cities destroyed, tens of thousands of people dead, and the fabric of society in shreds, Sicilians mounted a social, political, and ideological effort that resulted in a magnificent rebuilding of the cities in only half a century.[3]

Such enterprise, which became inevitably a point of reference in the diverse studies and projects comprising our research,[4] could take place only if it involved the whole of a society, operating at all levels in a series of complex, conflicting, and at times dangerous relationships, but also with great imagination, expediency, and fervor. The Crown of Spain, which commissioned the reconstruction; local governments; the aristocracy; and the Church, moved by the forceful intervention of religious orders, were the obvious players in this game of power and cities. But the people of those cities who where displaced, hurt, and dispossessed by the cataclysm played a no less crucial role. These were not to be cities built anew for a handful of pioneers or colonizers; these cities would restore a whole urban society deprived of the spatial milieu on which it had worked and lived for thousands of years. And they would restore the daily flow of activities that had in the same span of time woven a rich social fabric. As we illustrate in another document:

> . . . the farmer lost its donkey, nuns reclused behind the protective walls of convents for decades found themselves without roof and protection. The priest did not have his altar to celebrate, the craftsman lost his tools and shops, merchants their places of exchange . . .[5]

Our attempt to study contemporary conditions in these cities, their current problems and future challenges, and to propose an hypothesis for interventions today, as we were charged to do by the City of Caltagirone in 1988,[6] lead us inevitably to historical studies that put us in contact not only with the immense artistic wealth of this urban culture, but also with the society that produced them. The inferences and analogies we draw from the history of these towns, even as we prepare to intervene, are seemingly inevitable and, perhaps, dangerous if not checked carefully. History does not repeat itself, and I have become more and more wary of the notion that there are "lessons" to be extracted from the past, as the meaning of that term has been abused by those using it literally.

As an architect, I do believe in the study of history, not as the repository of "lessons," but as the never-ending process of acquiring knowledge about the production of knowledge. Understanding more and more each day, through continuously rediscovered instances, how rich and intricate is the process of designing and constructing buildings and cities is to understand that those "processual" qualities are the only history that repeats itself. One can only prepare one's imagination and creativity for action in the always-unknown future by achieving some understanding of how others have faced it and acted. In this sense, Volume 2 of this series is less concerned than Volume 1 with recommendations for the future. Instead, Volume 2 seeks to present a long and indirect reflection on an urban event that we believe displays the social, cultural, and artistic richness and intricacy that can help us think about the city of the future.

Humans living together have always had to elaborate and construct systems of service structures that allow them to support their physical and symbolic communication. That a significant part of our preoccupations with cities and their future today still revolves around such issues is then not surprising but reassuring. Looking intelligently at how that perennial condition has been addressed by different cultures at different times and places seems a reasonable proposition. What is sad though, is that history has been so misused in the two current modes of "cultural malaise" I call "literalness," one represented by the unadulterated reproduction of history's physical "lessons," and the other by the misconception that symbolization is a process of "representing" literary metaphors through architectural form.

The experience in Sicily suggests an alternative mode of inquiry by which we can sustain a more fruitful relationship with the complexities of history and its implications for the generation of future ideas. Fortunately, in our work in the Val di Noto we did not have to deal with an event such as that of 1693, with its direct and instant legacy of tragedy and desolation. But the piecemeal and relentless degradation of urban environments in the world at the end of this millennium point to a different type of catastrophe, which could be cumulatively and quantitatively more devastating than an earthquake. Must we wait until then to resist temptation and affirm our faith in the knowledge historical events provide about how to generate ideas for particular conditions of time and place? Must we wait until then to abandon, once and for all, the naive notion that imitating the past or constructing literal metaphors is a magic healing potion?

Two constructions, an urban bridge and a palazzo, caught my attention during my first visit, in 1988, to the City of Caltagirone (Fig. 5). Even at first sight, the strong single image of their contiguous presence seemed to encapsulate the forces of a society at a given time and, further, offered the promise its secrets might unravel if we dared investigate them. The studies so far have not disappointed us. The construction of the bridge and the palazzo is separated by a century, straddling the earthquake of 1693 in a way that gives us, inevitably, a glimpse of life in the Val di Noto at the end of the 17th century.

Our initial approach could not have been simpler, or more "archeological." We started with only a few intuitions, based on the physical evidence and on our own, architect's, taste. Our aims were very modest. We decided to offer a course in the summer and fall of 1989, directed by Professor Kevin Kieran, in which we would attempt only a survey of both structures. With the direct involvement of twelve Harvard students, we proceeded accordingly and, for a while, believed naively that this was all that could be done. After the survey material was translated into accurate drawings that fall, I began to put together a publication in early 1990 and the timid questions that had been simmering unanswered in our minds during those months of mute building observations and drawings began to weigh more and more on our minds as if the promise of hidden treasures had evolved into a demand that they be discovered. It became impossible to write an introduction to the book without including some basic historical information

Fig. 5 The Bridge of San Francesco and the Palazzo Sant'Elia in Caltagirone, 1989.

on the structures themselves. Once that was surfaced, it became impossible not to search for the responsible characters: the architects and patrons.

The concatenation of logical demands and questions continued its natural development and, in due time, more sophisticated hypotheses about the interpretation of some decisions emerged. Initial explications of stylistic inconsistencies and unfinished parts were reconsidered, as was a suspicion, nurtured by layers of different materials, that the two buildings were the result of a tortuous process of construction. In short, the seemingly endless list of questions that any human produce can elicit appeared on the table. The rest is history, no pun intended. The book is "late" by two years because the task of creating it opened up a completely new, and compelling, set of activities to be undertaken and we considered them worthy of effort and the delay.

Of course, the book is very different than the one I first imagined. And, in addition, other preoccupations that appear in my work will show here as well: among them, my interest in incorporating architects and their particular way of thinking and doing into historical research, where I believe they have a lot to contribute. In this particular case, I had an uncomfortable feeling thar the scholarship regarding the two structures we set out to study, precisely because it lacked some of the architect's means of analysis, had settled too easily on obvious explanations and left too many questions and contradictions unexplained. In a way, contrary to the poor effort by architects over the last 20 years to imitate, derive, or justify their work on the basis of historical precedent, I am trying to say that architects can make a significant contribution to the historical process by providing historians with eyes able to see what perhaps is otherwise unseen.

The evolution of the Caltagirone research and its conclusions give weight to this idea. The participation of architects in the research process transformed assumptions about the nature of the inquiry and yielded some unexpected results.

The new, expanded research also increased opportunities to engage local talent, whose contributions were invaluable and which we are happy to include here. I will risk using a worn-out cliché by saying that without them this publication would not have been possible. It cannot be said more simply or strongly. Father Filippo Rotolo's meticulous research on the history of the construction of the bridge of San Francesco, Dr. Domenico Amoroso's brilliant contextualization of the construction of the Palazzo Sant'Elia, and Dr. Vito Dicara's archival contributions all illuminate our understanding of the city and its buildings at that time. All from Sicily, these devoted citizens represent a diffuse class of scholars pervasive throughout the towns and cities of the island. To any foreign scholar attempting to study these locales I offer only one piece of advice and that is to search for these people first. They are always there, some in official civic roles and others almost self-effacingly, openly, or modestly working in their jobs or in their extra time to keep archives or to write little books on their buildings and traditions. All of them in their own way maintain the continuity of their culture and are always eager to help.

Later we discovered an unsuspected contributor among our own. Professor Kevin Kieran produced a personal document that enhances this book's heterogeneous genre. A lively travel journal he kept on the work done "in situ" with the students, the document as abridged by Professor Kieran himself is included, along with student sketches and vignettes, and photographs of the survey.

Finally, I would like to extend special thanks to those who have helped in more than one way, but who are not directly represented in the book. In particular, I want to mention two colleagues at Harvard, professors Howard Burns and Daniel Schodek who have had a direct impact on this project. Dan patiently instructed the students (and "refreshed" Kevin's and my memories) about methods of surveying, with particular emphasis on older structures, prior to our departure in June of 1989. Howard has been, since the beginning, a constant guide in our attempts to understand and to intervene in these cities, and his advice has proven that collaboration between architects, engineers and historians is not only possible, but fruitful and enjoyable. Fortunately, the marginal involvement of Dan and Howard in our "Sicily Project" initially has by now become full-fledged, direct, and more structured. Howard is a key participant in the numerous projects under way, and Dan has started this year to contribute his knowledge about structures in earthquake zones to a specific project. To Dr. Giacomo de Caro, who was the mayor of Caltagirone during the time of the survey, we are indebted for his grace and unqualified support. To all the employees of the Museo Civico, in particular to Francesco Palmiciano who put his seemingly endless local resources at our disposal, our thanks for their disposition and patience.

The Harvard students were twelve and they deserve unqualified recognition for their intellectual as well as physical efforts. Tania Arub, Mathew Berman, Andrew Borges, Eugenia de la Guardia, Douglas W. Dolezal, Sahel El-Ahiri, Greg Etter, Jan Fisher, Caroline Otto, Thomas Rankin, Charles H. Tashima and Lisa Victor all started with enthusiasm and ended with passion about the work and the discoveries. Among them, three deserve special mention: Tom Rankin, the assistant editor of Volume 1, reaffirmed his manifold talents and skills in every instance: during the survey, in consecutive trips to further the investigation on the two structures, and in the initial assembling of the material for this publication and its editing, all of this in addition to being the twenty-four-hours-a-day translator for a group of twelve students and one professor during their three-and-a-half-week stay in Sicily. Charles Tashima contributed to this book his beautiful and gifted photographs, which we are proud to present here; his sensitive work has reconciled me with current architectural photography. Doug Dolezal, who emerged from the group as one of its leading characters, has continuously expanded his role in the project and is now my assistant editor and the main interlocutor in my tribulations about the direction of the research.

And then there is Sam Trimble, whom I acknowledged warmly in our first publication and to whom I feel obliged to reiterate my gratitude and friendship. He joined the group and the course as our teaching assistant and travel guide and he has continued to develop his Sicilian interests in depth and breath after graduation; the following year he returned to Sicily as a Fulbright Fellow to research the contemporary problems of harbor cities in Sicily. We eagerly await his insights.

Back in Boston, and after the drawings were completed in their first version by the students at school, we encountered discrepancies and missing pieces, particularly in the plans of the Palazzo Sant'Elia. This was not unexpected, given the conditions under which the survey of the complex and at times chaotic building was made. Thus, in successive trips we gathered further information, which although still not complete, enabled us to present more consistent graphic information on the palazzo. We also decided to revise many drawings, but alas, a year later the original students were engaged in other more important endeavors, such as working on their thesis, or finding work in other cities after graduation. We were lucky then that Rosa Bolet, an applicant at the time to the school's Urban Design Program and originally from Barcelona, was in Boston and looking for work. Working under the direct supervision of Doug Dolezal, she is the author of the revisions to the technical drawings included in the book.

As editor, I decided in compiling this book to maintain intact, as much as possible, the heterogeneous nature of the material and to reflect that in the graphic design, so brilliantly conceived by Nélida Nassar. My own modest contribution stems from my conviction that by asking "architect's questions" we can also help advance historical knowledge. I attempted to put together a view of the city and the forces that shaped it at a given time, but in trying to understand the reasons, the logic, and the necessity for the appearance of our two idiosyncratic structures, I realized that it was necessary to portray the growth of Caltagirone since prehistoric times until the "settecento." The maps were reconstructed in Boston by Tom Rankin and Doug Dolezal under my supervision.[7] They reflect all of the evidence available to us, plus innumerable checks with Dr. Amoroso and actual visual verification, Yet they do not pretend to describe with precise dimensions and exact form the shape of the city at those times. That is impossible. Rather they should be considered maps of a particular genre belonging to the aesthetics of "realism." They are based on facts, which will always be incomplete, and rendered "verisimil" by an acute faithfulness to what might have been possible, the "realities" we know could have existed. The maps thus give us not the geometric and physical data of a surveyor, but information on how the city must surely have appeared. There is no danger in confusing the reader and scholar about the qualitative nature of these maps. In lieu of exact renditions of the city, which in my view we will never obtain, an "educated" view of what was possible is of great value,

In editing a book containing the contributions of many, the dispersal of responsibilities can lead to confusion. Each author is of course responsible for the content of his own entry. In addition to my own I am accountable for conceiving this research project, this book and its format and content, and for identifying and requesting the contributions. As editor proper, I have only suggested minor adjustments in the articles, although we had to reduce Professor

Fig. 6 Aerial view of Dallas.

Kevin Kieran's journal considerably to focus on aspects directly related to the survey "in situ," and a few anecdotes conveying the flavor of such experience. In selecting the photographs of Charles Tashima, the process of elimination was even more difficult because the images were so compelling, beautiful and informative. However, the next best possible solution was found. A complete collection of his photographs, portraying moments of the trip in Sicily and including more images of Caltagirone, are now in the collection of the Francis Loeb Library at Harvard.

Finally, spending more than two years thinking, wondering, and worrying about these two peculiar buildings established for me an almost personal relationship with them. Buildings are, by all objective measures, considerably big and indisputably inanimate things. But for anyone interested in their history, which may mean simply understanding how humans have impacted them and in turn how they have transformed humans, they begin, inevitably after a while, to acquire vitality and spirit. Reviewing the literature of architecture's lovers, one finds more and more evidence of this seemingly absurd, yet moving belief: Buildings *speak, grow, move, look and welcome you, seduce you*, and so on, for all the imaginable behaviors normally attributed to humans. I must then, being an unashamed lover of buildings, thank the buildings themselves for what they have provided me during these years: an unending intellectual as well as sensory stimulation, and an unabated, persistent longing to see them again.

Cambridge, December 1991

Notes

1 Domenico Amoroso: "Una testimonianza di viabilià preistorica: la strada delle tombe nella necropoli della Montagna di Caltagirone. In *Viabilità Antica in Sicilia*, Atti del Terzo Convegno di Studi (Cattedra di Topografia Antica, Università di Catania, 1987).

2 Translation by the author.

3 For excellent accounts of the cataclysm in specific locations, see Stephen Tobriner, *The Genesis of Noto: An Eighteenth-Century Sicilian City* (Berkeley: University of California Press, 1982) and L. Dufour and H. Raymond, *Dalle Baracche at Barocco - La ricostruzione di Noto - Il caso e la necessità* (Palermo: Arnaldo Lombardi Editore, 1990). See Liliane Dufour, "Dopo il terremoto del 1693: La ricostruzione della Val di Noto," in *Storia d'Italia, Annali 8 - Insediamenti e Territorio* (Torino: Giulio Einaudi Editore, 1985) for a thoughtful overall account of the reconstruction efforts after the earthquake. See also Salvatore Boscarino, *Sicilia Barocca* (Rome: Oficina Edizione, 1981), for a general description of the urbanistic and architectural ideas that played a role in the reconstruction.

4 See Jorge Silvetti, ed., *Architectural and Urban Environments of Sicily* (Cambridge, MA: Harvard Graduate School of Design, Harvard University, 1989), for a description of the general objectives of the research program funded by the city of Caltagirone.

5 *Il Terremoto et la Ricostruzione del Val di Noto in Sicilia, Celebrazione del Tricentenario 1693 – 1993. La Mostra*, brochure published by the O.L.T.U.M. (Osservatorio e Laboratorio sui Tessuti Urbani Mediterranei).

6 Silvetti, *Architectural and Urban Environments of Sicily, op. cit.*

7 See figures 31, 32, 36, 55, and 56 in, "The Bridge and the Palazzo: Urban Interventions and Social Representation," by Jorge Silvetti.

Fig. 1 The Bridge of San Francesco and the Palazzo Sant'Elia.

The Bridge and the Palazzo: Urban Interventions and Social Representation

JORGE SILVETTI, 1992

In Caltagirone, a city full of memorable urbanistic and architectonic events, where the placement of monuments and public spaces follows a scenographic strategy with spectacular results, there is one instance where the pairing of infrastructure and monument assumes for me the same basic and vibrant condition of cultural distillation as that achieved by those prehistoric vestiges, the road and the cemetery of Sant'Ippolito (Figs. 1, 2). I am referring to the Ponte di San Francesco and the Palazzo del Principe di Sant'Elia (Fig. 25).

The presence of an "urban" bridge, a rather extravagant construction unusual in a city of those times (Fig. 27); the compressed proportions of the palazzo's main facade (Fig. 26); the "double ground" of the ensemble that offers two very different visions of the bridge and the palazzo (Fig. 28); and, in particular, the framed view of the palazzo from the lower level, which renders the ensemble very organic and unitary (Fig. 29), makes this pair one of the most memorable sights in Caltagirone or, indeed, anywhere in the Val di Noto. The power of the image was noteworthy enough, I should add, for us to make these structures the subject of a summer surveying course for architecture students at the Graduate School of Design.[1] To discuss the use of perspective methods of representation of space in the process of architectural design today confronts us immediately, and inevitably, with a most substantial and profound (albeit mostly unacknowledged) issue in architectural theory, one that deals with the relationships between techniques of representation on one side, and ideology, creativity and the constraints that such techniques may impose on the language of architecture on the other. In addition, and as with most theoretical issues, it will confront us eventually with the problem of defining the specificity of architecture today, a very promising subject which, however, does not seem to find the echo that it deserves in the field of theory. On the one hand, perspective drawing is trivialized in the current, general debate (which seems to concentrate on the most superficial and banal aspects of contemporary architecture such as "historical styles" vs "modern style") and it becomes yet another stylistic issue. On the other hand, perspective drawing cannot resonate at the level that it deserves in the most serious theoretical debates because the most enthusiastic and productive efforts in theory and criticism in architecture have

Fig. 2 East elevation, the Bridge of San Francesco (view toward the church of Sant'Agata).
Fig. 3 Detail of the bridge showing the two co-existing "grounds"; Via Roma passing over the bridge and Via Infermeria and Via San Pietro crossing below the arch (view from the attic floor balcony of the Palazzo Sant'Elia).

2

3

been devoted almost in their entirety to issues pertaining to the product, its effects and performance, and its relations with other cultural phenomena (such as ideology, language, literature, modernism and avant-gardism, etc.) rather than on an explanation and description of the moment of production of architecture. Besides the inherent difficulties deriving from the nature of the problem that will necessarily include a discussion about "the subject" that designs, it is understandable that the concentration has been on the product, because the habits and tendencies of architectural theory have been heavily influenced by historical research and by theories that are rooted mostly in iconographic or hermeneutic studies, or in theories derived from social studies, psychology or, simply, politics. This ample, rich and fertile tradition from which the ever-incipient architectural theory sprung has ultimately given us, in the best cases, a potent and devastating critique of ideology and a demystification of ideological notions such as "function," "nature," "solution," etc. Or at worst, we might say that we have been distracted by irritating tautologies supported by the kind of statistical trivia which characterize most of the behavioral studies. But whether good or bad, theoretical work has always established uncomfortable relationships with that opaque and seemingly impenetrable instance which is the moment of production and of creativity a problem that has been compounded even more by the tendency inherent in our architectural culture to instrumentalize theory into formulae that presumably would help to produce better buildings.

As mentioned in the introduction to this book, I had intended originally to simply publish the survey drawings, devoting little time and space to the history of either structure, other than to include perfunctory data that would place the buildings in time, space, and historical context. But as the project evolved, it took on its own logic, leading me to change my mind and engaging me and others in historical research and interpretation. This book is the result.

I must stress two important facts about the research at the outset. First, that the individual stories of these two constructions do not coincide chronologically, since the idea for the bridge and what we estimate is the beginning of the idea for the palazzo are separated by about a century. Each construction, therefore, responds to its own particular circumstances and contingencies, although the history of the palazzo, having come later, is inextricably dependent on the vicissitudes of the bridge during the 18th century. Second, that the quality of information available to us regarding the genesis and construction of the bridge and the palazzo differ greatly. The bridge, having been originated by a major religious order and supported in great measure by public funds is well documented. The palazzo, the result of many interventions by an elusive "patron" over an indeterminate length of time, has yielded no written or graphic evidence of any kind so far. My entry into this book is then rather uneven in evidence and interpretations, a fact that undoubtedly reflects not only on the attention devoted to each, but on literary style and tone of discourse.

The duality of this presentation can, however, be taken positively if we modestly accept it as representative of two modes of possible and necessary research today, one based on archival material and the other based on visual inspection and analogical inference. I hope that some day, perhaps in some family archive, more information about the palazzo's ownership and construction will appear. We will continue to search for it. But, for the moment, I would like to report on the status of what we know about this urban event after two years of work. For that, an understanding of Caltagirone's history is necessary in order to explain how these constructions appeared at a given point in time and space and to better understand why they became necessary, or what social and ideological forces converged to promote them.

THE CITY

Located on top of the hills where two geological and orographic systems meet, Caltagirone has existed since prehistoric times as one of many human settlements developed by the "Siculus" people. The particular location of Monte San Giorgio commands the strategic passage that connects the plain of Catania, facing Italy and Europe, with the plain of Gela, facing Tunisia and Africa (Fig. 30). As with most of Sicily, Caltagirone was part of the Greek world and culture as early as the 7th century B.C. Later, it was dominated by the Roman and Byzantine Empires, then the Arabs in the 9th century and the Norman Kingdom in the 11th century, when it acquired extensive privileges and became a demanial city, a status it continued to enjoy and augment until the unification of Italy in the 19th century.[2]

During the period of the Norman Kingdom, Caltagirone consisted of three distinct

Fig. 4 West facade, Palazzo Sant'Elia (view from the arch of the bridge of San Francesco).
Fig. 5 The palazzo framed by the bridge's arch.

4

5

Fig. 6 Map of Sicily depicting passage between the two plains.

Fig. 7 Plan of Caltagirone during the times of the Norman Kingdom (11th and 12th centuries) showing the three distinct settlements around the Church of San Giorgio, the Castle, and the Church of San Giacomo.

Fig. 8 Plan of Caltagirone in the 14th century showing another settlement developed around the Monastery of San Francesco.

7

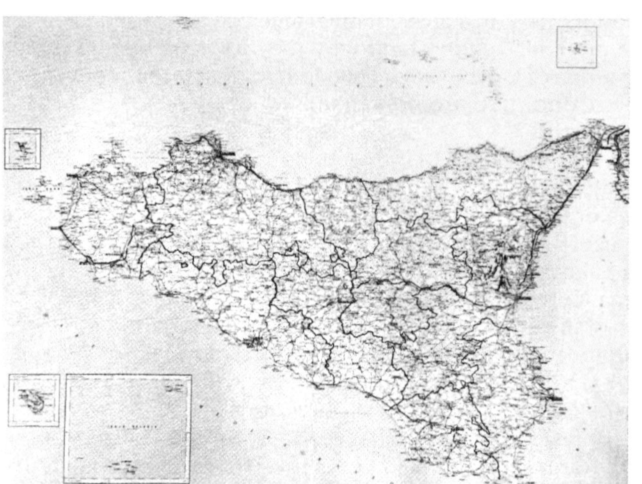

6

8

9

10

Fig. 9 The present-day stair presumed to be in the same location as the original stair that led to the Monastery of San Francesco.

Fig. 10 The Strada Larga alla Matrice (also known as Scalinata di Santa Maria del Monte). Reconstructed in 1953.

settlements organized around a significant building (Fig. 31): the fortified city on the highest hill around the castle, and two conglomerates "fuori le mura," one founded on an adjacent hill to the east by Genoesi merchants (who had a lasting influence on the culture of the city) around the church of their patron saint, San Giorgio, and the other "abitato" a similar village founded by Amalfitanian merchants and located west, near the church of San Giacomo.

A century later, at the time of the Sicilian Vespers (an island-wide revolt against the French house of Anjou that redirected European history and had among its three main instigators one of the nobles of the city, Walter of Caltagirone), new urbanistic developments of great importance cook place. Another major church, San Giuliano, was built on the plain and the Arab and Jewish ghetto grew up around it. To the south, across a narrow ravine on cop of a steep hill, was built the monastery of San Francesco, one of the first erected by the Franciscan order after the death of the Saint, thus creating a new and major center of gravity in the area. As a result of these developments, Caltagirone acquired a definitively polycentric nature that characterizes it still (Fig. 32).

During ensuing centuries the city continued to prosper, acquiring new privileges, including the prestigious title of "Citta Grattissima" granted by King Ferdinand and Queen Isabella. And it is during these early years of Spanish domination (which lasted more than four centuries), that the civic and religious center of Caltagirone moved permanently co the "piano malfitano," at the bottom of the fortified city and monte San Giorgio, which eased a scarcity of space and subsequent growth problems in the hills proper and better served new urbanistic and architectural demands raised by the humanistic and early counter-reformist culture. Important new monuments began to appear: the new City Palace in 1483, the new Jesuit complex initiated with their arrival in 1570, the Hospital established by the Fatebenefratelli in 1591, and the only two important monuments that remain more or less as they were conceived: the 1606 Strada Larga alla Matrice (Fig. 33) and the 1601 Corte Capitaneale (Fig. 34).

THE BRIDGE

It is the Ponte di San Francesco that constitutes the most characteristic, crucial, and decisive intervention in the fabric of the city during this period. Its complex history has

Fig. 11 La Corte Capitaniale (engraving published in the "Le Cento Città d'Italia," Milan, 1895).

Fig. 12 Plan of Caltagirone at the time of the great earthquake of 1693 showing the Bridge of San Francesco complete and the monastery now directly linked to the Church of Sant'Agata and the political center of the city.

Fig. 13 The convergence of via Infermeria (left) and Via San Pietro (right) at the narrow west end of the Palazzo Sant'Elia (view from above the arch of the bridge of San Francesco).

11

13

12

been wonderfully studied and presented to us by Father Rotolo in this book, and I will recall only the salient facts that serve my exploration.

The records of the city and of the reign testify to the desire of the Franciscans to improve accessibility to their church (where the cult of the Immaculate Conception cook place) and monastery for the Feligresy, first by constructing a stair in 1606 (Fig. 35) and then by insistently requesting permission to build a bridge to connect the church of Sant' Agata (a most revered Sicilian virgin saint) with their monastery. The power and persuasive talent of Fray Gerardo Arcolaci led to the city's approval and funding, and an architect was hired in 1626. The architect, Orazio Torriani,[3] completed the design for the bridge one year later, and by 1629 the foundations for a five-arch bridge were under construction, the work commencing near the monastery and moving slowly north towards the city and Sant'Agata. By 1631, however, numerous complaints filed by the Fatebenefratelli, who operated the hospital located at the other end of the bridge, caused construction to stop. The friars claimed the bridge was approaching the city in a straight line and therefore it would inevitably collide with the hospital, or at least, rely on the hospital's foundations for support, thereby threatening their structure.

Only in 1660, after endless litigation between the two religious orders, the city, the Senate and even the King of Spain, did work resume, this time under the direction of architect Father Buenaventura Certo,[4] who is also credited with design modifications. The dispute with the hospital was settled and the bridge was completed and opened for use in 1677.

There was now a new Caltagirone, expanded and inclusive of the settlement around the monastery of San Francesco (Fig. 36). With completion of the bridge, however, a rather unstable new urban condition was produced, full of incoherencies and explosive imbalances (which become very clear in hindsight as, from a purely urban traffic-flow perspective, the bridge is basically an overdesigned grand cul-de-sac justified only by religious needs). It would take another whole century to realize the full potential of this bridge when, by means of a simple addition and distortion in its southern flank, the bridge would accommodate the major traffic route south and out the city, and in so doing would reorient the inexorable growth of Caltagirone for centuries to come, even to the present day.

In the meantime, the imbalance remains. During the previous century, the city had a certain success in directing traffic flow from the center out towards the two southern gates and the countryside beyond by producing connections, however inefficient, through two major roads crossing under the bridge itself. Indeed, the land below the bridge was not entirely marginal or unimportant, as the friars state in their complaints about the difficulties of crossing the valley. It was during the 17th century, for example, that the Landolina, a very important and prominent noble family, bought most of the land comprising the future site of the Palazzo Sant'Elia. The Gancia of the Benedictins was also located nearby in the valley and the streets of the hospital (still named via Infermeria today) and of San Pietro were important primary streets, not only as two of the main arteries in and out of the city, but also as ceremonial thoroughfares for the city's major religious procession route, connecting the major churches of San Francesco di Paola and of Santa Maria del Gesù, both "fuori le mura'" (Fig. 37).

In 1693, Caltagirone was hit by the tragic earthquake, which very seriously affected most of the city's structures, but unlike other urban centers in the Val di Noto, Caltagirone did not suffer the loss of many lives. For all we know, the bridge did not suffer any serious damage either and the city rebuilt itself upon the ruins of the old center. Thus, Caltagirone provides us with one of the best examples of a major city rebuilt on its medieval and antique foundations, but with a new baroque face.[5]

THE PALAZZO

Turning to the other protagonist of our survey, the Palazzo Sant'Elia, it is unfortunate that the vicissitudes of its history are rather obscure, unlike those of the bridge, which are documented abundantly in state archives. Little is known about the early history and the process by which we get such an impressive yet unfinished and problematic building. All is but tentative speculation. Dr. Amoroso provides an excellent interpretation of the milieu in which the palazzo emerged and existed, based on his knowledge of Caltagirone's customs, culture and lore. His piece in this book has contributed enormously to the research, and to the inferences I am offering. What remains problematic is the fact that neither deeds for the transfer of property, nor drawings, nor architects' or builders' construction documents have been found. Nevertheless, it is generally held that the palazzo was designed by Natale Bonaiuto[6] because the ornamental detail is similar to some of his other buildings in

14

15

16

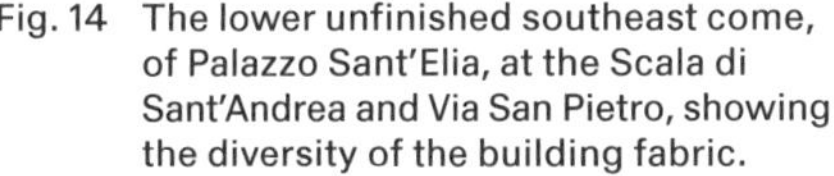

Fig. 14 The lower unfinished southeast come, of Palazzo Sant'Elia, at the Scala di Sant'Andrea and Via San Pietro, showing the diversity of the building fabric.

Fig. 15 "Ponte di San Francesco" (engraving published in "Le Cento Città d'Italia," Milan, 1895).

Fig. 16 Stage set design by Giuseppe Galli Bibiena.

town, and also that his original idea for completion of the palazzo was never fully realized. Its dependence on the bridge for some of the most salient and unique aspects of its architectural configuration had always been unquestioningly assumed because of the proximity of the two structures and because of the imbalance between the dimensions of the facade overlooking the bridge and its elaborate architecture.

The building today is only half occupied and its most stately dependencies are in nearly ruinous condition. The only active and inhabited parts of the palace include some ground-floor shops and some apartments of different epochs scattered throughout what is today a rather chaotic structure. The strict order and detail of the arrestingly narrow facade over the bridge quickly dissipates as it "vanishes" towards its opposite end on the Scala di Sant'Andrea, which is almost its diametrical opposite: a mishmash of windows, levels, materials, and wall heights on an undistinguished city block, seemingly denying any possibility that this site was once conceived of as a unitary entity (Fig. 38).

Yet, we must presume that some kind of plan for the whole had existed, if not in ink on paper, at least in the minds of the owner and architect. The small site has barely the minimum square footage required of a city palazzo for a noble family such as the Landolina and subsequent aristocratic owners.[7] The site's unusual geometry and dimensions dictate that most of the indispensable dependencies for a such a palace be developed on the widest side, with the narrow end considered an anomaly, not unlike the small pavilion on the Ripetta in the Palazzo Borghese in Rome and its awkward site. Of course, one is impressed by the architect's sharp response to the difficulties of the site, turning them into a virtue through a cultivated implementation of current ideas about perspective, scenography and urbanism (Fig. 39). The view of the palazzo seen through

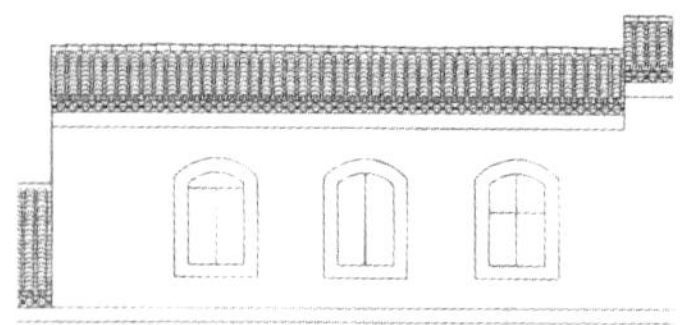

17

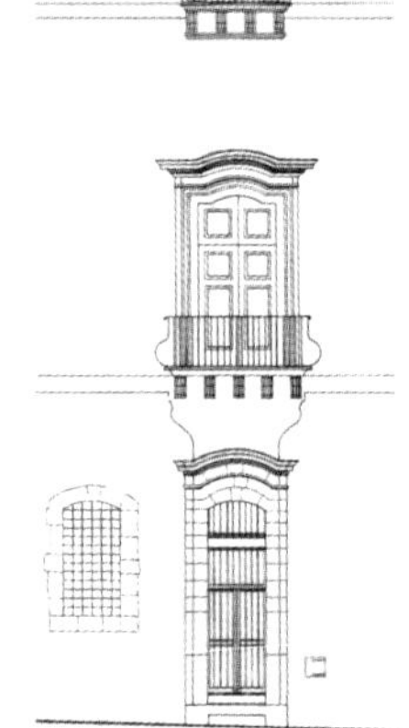

18

Fig. 17 Palazzo Sant'Elia, north facade on Via Infermeria (1989 survey) and detail of the attic story "center body" over the main entrance.

Fig. 18 Typical bay of the generally assumed "three-story-high" Palazzo Sant'Elia.

Figs. 19–20 East and west corner pillars on the north facade.

Fig. 21 Palazzo Sant'Elia, section through the entrance and main staircase, 1989 survey.

Fig. 22 Palazzo Sant'Elia. Hypothetical reconstruction of the south facade on via San Pietro assuming a three-story-high building at the north entrance on Via Infermeria and a continuous height around the entire wedge-shaped block.

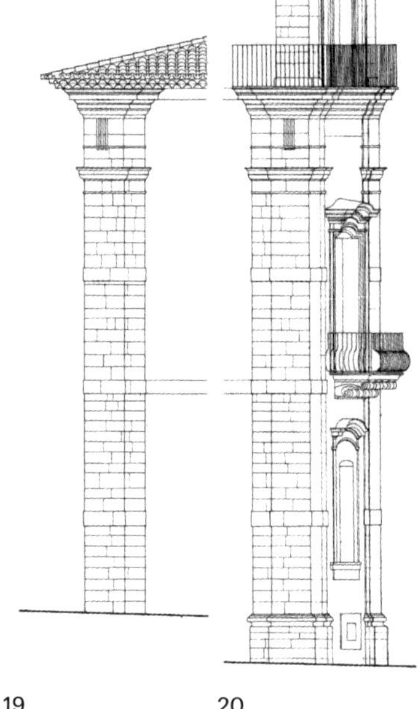

19 20

21

22

23

24

0.0 M
0.0 M
19.5 M
17.0 M
24.0 M

25

Fig. 23 Palazzo Sant'Elia. Interior wall at the northeast corner (via Infermeria and Scala di Sant'Andrea) showing the masonry preparation to continue the main body of the building, turning the corner to the south.

Fig. 24 Axonometric reconstruction of Palazzo Sant'Elia showing the volume of the three-story-high building (as depicted in Fig. 46).

Fig. 25 Detail of the map of 1877 showing parcel divisions for the triangular block of Palazzo Sant'Elia.

the arch of the bridge has become as much an icon of Caltagirone as that of the Scala (Fig. 40). We are struck by the congruence between the two pieces brought together by the architect of the palace, the piece of infrastructure and the civil monument in perfect harmony.

This impressionistic view, while valid for conveying at a glance the breadth of work, effort and sophistication of the urban culture that produced it, does not explain the numerous contradictory moments in the building itself. Persistent and continuous observations made by students, Professors Burns, Kieran and myself of the more chaotic sides of the palazzo began to emphasize inconsistencies within the seemingly obvious inferences that automatically follow appreciation of the view presented by the unfinished ensemble. These discrepancies suggested that a different vision and style may have informed the overall palace configuration.

After the survey drawings were finished at Harvard by the team of students lead by Professor Kieran, I began to probe further into the history of the palazzo. I did not know exactly what to look for, but what I came to hypothesize in fact reinforces the historian's view of the role of the urban palace in baroque times, its inextricable relationship with the street and, in particular, Dr. Amoroso's account of the importance of "la festa" for determining the location and configuration of urban palaces.[8]

The apparent lack of documents regarding the palazzo leaves us with the building itself and a few plans of the city as the only evidence to support an interpretation of what may have happened. If one can agree that the original intention must have been to erect a complete and coherent building on the wedge-shaped site, and that an "image" of sorts must therefore have existed in the owner's and designer's mind and that, furthermore, such an "image" can only be reconstructed by inferring it from the only part of the building assumed complete, namely the facade overlooking the bridge, then specific questions, based on the available evidence, would naturally follow.

But, immediately, this logic created concerns. While everybody had assumed as an unquestionable fact that the facade facing the bridge was the encapsulation of the intended idea for the palazzo, the implications soon proved unsettling. For instance, we noticed that the architecture of the brilliant attic floor overlooking the bridge differs slightly in detail from the architecture of the two lower floors (Fig. 42). We wondered about the "center body" with its three small unadorned windows over the main entrance on via Infermeria and why this piece is slightly lower than the attic floor, creating an inexplicable discontinuity between the two parts (Fig. 41). The comer pillars of the palazzo are only two stories high and have a finished or completed appearance. Was the building to be a three-story palazzo with two orders (a double order for the first two floors and a second single order for the attic) (Figs. 43, 44)? Furthermore, we became troubled by the fact that this urban palace, so grand for Caltagirone, could lack a main stair, so typical of secular baroque architecture in Sicily, that would establish the spatial sequence from the ground floor to the attic (Fig. 45).

We persisted, nonetheless, in efforts to follow the logic of interpretations based only on the "iconic" strengths of the tripartite single bay, but our first attempt only raised more questions. We assumed a standard Italian palazzo, three stories high at its entrance, with shops, or "boteghe," in the ground floor, a "piano nobile" containing the major "appartamenti," and an attic level with living quarters for family, cadets, and service (Fig. 46) and tried to project the presumably "complete" portion of the palazzo around the entire wedge-shaped block. Indeed, we could safely assume that the palazzo was intended to occupy the entire site because from the narrow facade facing the bridge it already continues for a few bays on the south (along via San Pedro) and it was obviously left unfinished at different stages on each of the three floors. To the north (along via Infermeria), only the first two floors are completed in their entirety; the attic is completed for only one third of the overall length of the facade. The intention to use the full block is further corroborated by the two-story finished wing on via Infermeria because there are unmistakable signs of masonry preparation for continuation along the east side (Scala Sant'Andrea) of the palazzo (Fig. 48).

Fig. 26 Detail of the map of 1700 showing the subdivisions of the medieval triangular block prior to the construction of the Palazzo Sant'Elia.
Fig. 27 Present-day ground floor plan highlighting the bearing party walls of the medieval units (depicted in the map of 1700) that may have been reused for the palazzo's structure.
Fig. 28 Present-day south facade highlighting the location of party walls of medieval units (depicted in the map of 1700) and showing the corresponding breaks of rooflines and window alignments.

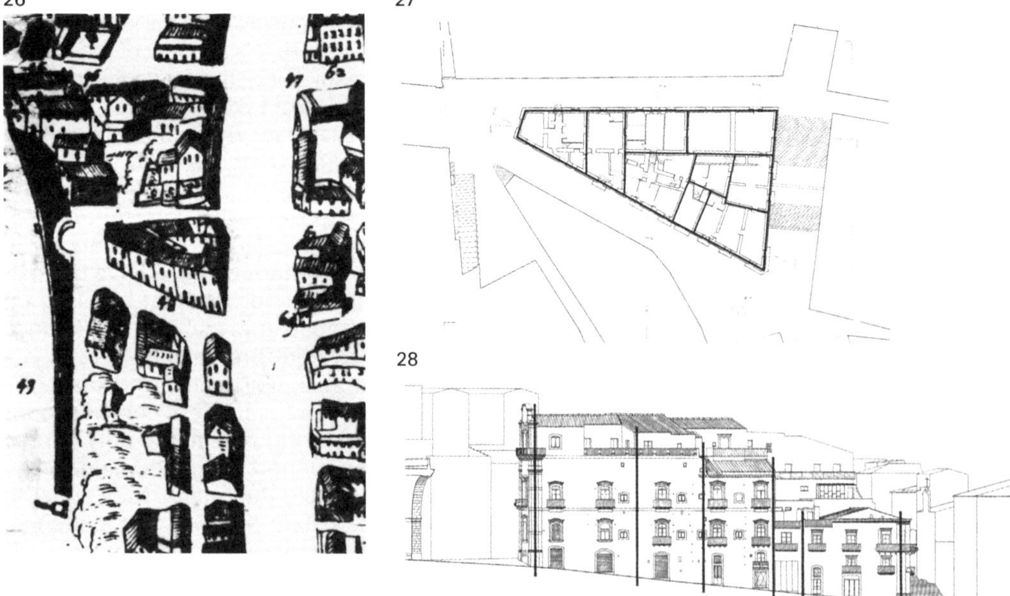

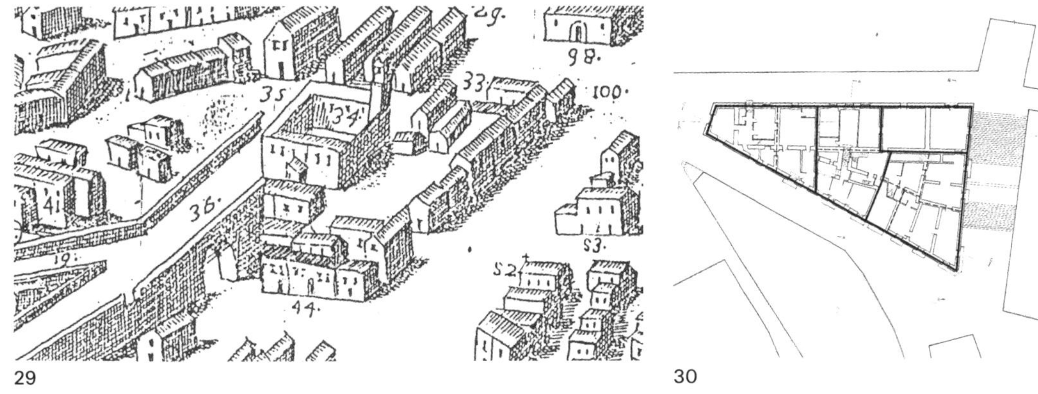

29 30

Fig. 29 Detail of the map of 1774. The Palazzo Sant'Elia (identified by #44) is shown as a two-story building with a center attic over the entrance on Via Infermeria.

Fig. 30 Present-day ground floor plan highlighting the bearing party walls (depicted in the map of 1774) that may have been reused for the palazzo's structure.

Although the argument about the facade continuing around the whole block seems indisputable, I started to reject this initial interpretation of the building after testing the hypothesis against the three-dimensional conditions of the site. The logic of that hypothesis, applied to the actual topography, would have yielded a building of disproportionate dimensions on the lowest southeast corner of the parcel, one seemingly incompatible with an affordable bearing structure for a palazzo of its time (Fig. 47). Furthermore, keeping the "boteghe" always level with the ground means dropping the equivalent of a full floor height (in this case 4.5 meters) between their location on via Infermeria and the lowest corner of the site, creating another atypical condition, that of additional floor space between the shops and the "piano nobile."

The anomalies—dimensional, structural and typological—of the preliminary reconstruction based on the "logic" of the "finished" facade, although not impossible as exceptions to the rule, at least created substantial doubt and led me to the conclusion that no matter how one looks at the problem, no "conventional" solution existed for this site. A simple point, but important because it frees the mind from obvious assumptions. Accepting the "non-conventionality" of the project is the critical first step that opened many doors, some of which we then explored and proposed.

Our own hypothesis about the original idea of the palazzo then differed radically from what had been traditionally accepted or believed. We used as resources three historic plans of Caltagirone (the two earlier ones depicting the city and its buildings three-dimensionally),[9] constructional information, and the partial but suggestive knowledge we had of the history of the site through writings. Without following its chronological sequence, I will present the evidence of our research in an order that may visually clarify the development of the palazzo as well as the logic of our thought.

The plan of 1877 shows that within the boundaries of the triangular site are four parcels and what appears to be a short, public alley opening onto via San Pietro (Fig. 49). However, there is only one number (3601) for the entire wedge-shaped block, signifying only one owner or taxpayer for the entire parcel. Closer inspection reveals that the following numbers, 3602/3/4, are missing and that the sequence jumps from 3601 to 3605. We believe therefore that there were originally four separate parcels (and an alley) and that they were acquired over time and, as the deed was modified to incorporate these changes, the parcel numbers were removed while the original subdivisions lines remained on the map. We corroborated this supposition with the plan of 1700 for a like number of identifiable units in which the medieval dimensions are clearly visible (Fig. 50). This helped to clarify the skeletal structure of the block.

This information was important to our investigation because the subdivision lines on the 1877 map correspond strikingly to major events in the present day building (Fig. 51). We concluded that the subdivisions represent existing bearing walls that may have been reused party walls from earlier buildings and that may have been acquired at different moments. The breaks in the facades and roof lines and the alignment of windows relative to one another support this assumption (Fig. 52). This led us to imagine the south side as three buildings and an alley. (The alley could have been a commonly used entry to shared stables, "magazzini," or storage located at level with via San Pietro.)

Equally as important, it revealed that no matter how whole the image of the Palazzo Sant'Elia in the minds of the owner and architect, the process of achieving it was tedious, complicated and ultimately unsuccessful in erasing the medieval origins of the "isolato." Furthermore, in examining now the building on the site of the palazzo as shown in the map of 1774 (Fig. 53) two revealing facts appear. First, the discontinuities of the roof line on both the north side (on via Infermeria) and on the south side (on via San Pietro) coincide with the original subdivision lines remaining in the map of 1877 (Fig. 54). Second, the block of Palazzo Sant'Elia shows a completely different configuration than the one in the earlier map of 1700, strongly suggesting that construction of the palazzo and consolidation of the block was well under way by the time this map was engraved.

Interpreted this way, the image on the map is startling for its implications. As mentioned earlier, the palazzo is known today for the view it presents as a pavilion overlooking the bridge. This image is the most unusual and original aspect of the design, but I began to suspect that its very strength had so dominated perception of the building that it led inexorably to false assumptions about its origins. Historians had simply assumed that the unprecedented image must have been the fundamental idea for the palazzo and that the remaining building somehow followed. The 1774 plan, however, contradicts this possibility, forcing one to assume either that the "three dimensional" plans of Caltagirone are not accurate in their representation of buildings (a view widely held by others) or that the representations are true, in which case the presumed conditions of origin are indeed false. Therefore, to continue with my hypothesis that we were not dealing with a conventional building, I posed the questions: What if the plans of these surveyors are indeed accurate not only about the general infrastructure and public spaces, but also, as I now believe, about the general configuration and location of buildings? And what if the pavilion over the bridge was not the original intention of the architect but an afterthought, which could never be resolved and which took precedence over a more "serene" and stable original idea?

This logic led to speculation that the attic overlooking the bridge is actually a later addition to the palazzo, and that according to stylistic analysis, it could have been done by another architect, which would make sense of the fact that there are subtle but distinct differences between the architecture of the windows on the attic floor and the architecture on the first two floors. If one accepts for one more moment the logic of this schematic and hypothetical reconstruction, the questions become not if, but when and why.

To try and answer them we needed to reexamine the urbanistic history of the city as it unfolded after the earthquake and, in particular, the transformation of both the bridge in its contradictory condition of "cul-de-sac" and the local culture and traditions of Caltagirone during that period of the 18th century.

THE VIA MARIA CAROLINA

While trying to interpret the complexities of the area immediately adjacent to the palazzo, let us remember that via Infermeria (where the entrance to the palazzo is located despite its marginal location and adjacency to both the hospital and the slaughterhouses) became by necessity, for one block, part of the major procession route for the simulacra of the Patron Saint, leading through the Porta del Vento to the monastery of the Santa Maria del Gesù. It was also, in all likelihood, the route that allowed the procession of the Ceri, from the church of Sant'Aloe (then adjacent to the Porta del Vento) to the basilica of San Giacomo (Fig. 55).[10] As Dr. Amoroso reminded us, the route of the procession and the festivities determined to a great extent the location of the main facades of noble palaces in southern Italy. Via Infermeria was in all probability both uncomfortable and difficult to negotiate, particularly in bad weather, but it was nonetheless an important thoroughfare in and out of the city towards the south. Undoubtedly, we are looking at a neighborhood in an ebullient state of transition during the first part of the 18th century.

The increasing importance of the southern connection led to the appropriation of the bridge, which had been since its inception an over-scaled aberration, as an important piece of public infrastructure. In 1766 via Maria Carolina was opened, starting at the southern end of the bridge at the foot of the monastery and extending southwest as pressure to

31

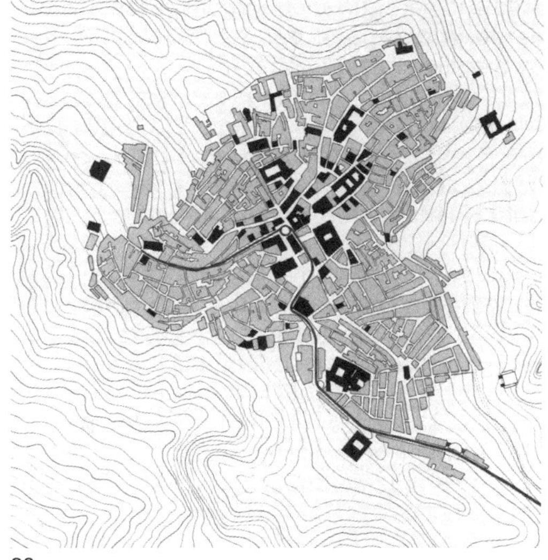
32

Fig. 31 Map showing the procession's route of the patron saint before the opening of via Maria Carolina, passing along Via Infermeria under the bridge and then out through the Porta del Vento towards San Francesco di Paola and Santa Maria di Gesù (see endnote 10 for an alternative route).

Fig. 32 Map showing the route of the procession after the opening of Via Maria Carolina. Re-routed, the procession passes over the bridge now realizing its full functional and symbolic potential.

expand the city could no longer be contained by topographical conditions as restrictive as Caltagirone's, erasing neighboring city walls, the Porta del Vento, and the adjacent church of Sant'Aloe. The transformation allowed the bridge of San Francesco to develop its full potential as a crucial node in the city structure. As a result, the new road caused the procession to be re-routed, passing from the center of town to Sant'Agata, then onto the bridge facing San Francesco, before leading south to the monasteries in the countryside. This created a more logical, decorous, and comfortable ceremonial sequence (Fig. 5 6).

If we look at the map of 1774, Palazzo Sant'Elia is already identified as such, and a building of a certain unity appears on its site. Though unlike the medieval structures visible in the 1770 map, the 1774 building is also very different in appearance from the building we recognize today. And therein the story. It is now obvious to me that the palazzo was built before via Carolina opened, since the map of 1774 was published only eight years after the Senate approved opening the road in 1766. Its main entrance, then as today, was actually on via Infermeria, with the main "balcone" and an ornamental frame above as architectural gestures appropriate to this most important street and procession route. As confirmation, a second closer and confident look at the map of 1774 reveals clearly, in the light of this hypothesis, a two-story-high palazzo with an attic located symmetrically over the entrance on via Infermeria (Fig. 53). A hypothetical reconstruction of the building (Fig. 57) also explains the aforementioned awkward lack of a main staircase to the third floor: the attic over the entrance may have originally been an open loggia, or a "guardaroba alla romana," ascended by a small, secondary service stair.

From all these observations we may infer that when the bridge acquired its new role as the main route out of the city center and its symbolic and functional importance increased, the main facade of the palazzo lost its symbolic importance and representational meaning and an attic space overlooking the bridge became imperative for the prince and his aspirations. That this was done after the face accounts for the awkwardness of the floor plan and the incongruent articulation in relation to the rest of the building. It also explains the importance given to the narrow facade.

This hypothesis is evident in our reconstruction of the famous perspectival icon of Caltagirone, for which we utilized the classic image from the 19th century (Fig. 58).[11] This was very suggestive to me, since the "theatricality" of the ensemble is very convincing. (It includes a "proscenium" defined by the bridge arch and baroque scenography perfectly rendered in two-point perspective established by the street's fork and stressed by the palazzo's walls.) The building is, in fact, perfectly framed and contained within the "palcoscenico" and this is the view that a procession or people arriving through the gates opening onto via Maria Carolina would see.

The view of the three-story palazzo so popularized since the "Cento Città d'Italia" appeared at the end of the 19th century is, with its top floor bearing a coat of arms, cue off by the bridge/proscenium. This is not only unacceptable in itself, but it contradicts the obvious scenographic and representational idea of the whole. It makes sense only when one sees it as an imperfect response to the bridge becoming a major thoroughfare, relieving the lower streets of their importance and forcing a reversal of architectural priorities. By this reversal of meaning and intention, which cultures seem intent on doing over time to confuse us, one of the most emblematic "veduta" of Caltagirone is based on an erroneous interpretation![12]

A two-story palazzo thus conceived would result in a reasonable compromise between the need for a main facade on via Infermeria and a logical height on the lowest corner, which becomes three stories. It is a good compromise for a site that would not allow a conventional palazzo solution, but it permits us to envision a plausible sequence of events during the 18th century, when the contingencies produced by a logical urban development, together with the aspirations of the prince, conspired against this humble yet workable compromise. The whole scheme was subverted by the need to add an attic overlooking the new procession route on the bridge. The narrow facade is well composed, but its proportions cannot be extended around the site without greatly disrupting dimensionally and statically the rest of the building. The problem is unresolvable and so it is left as such, justifying our earlier perplexities.

We are further encouraged in the plausibility of our hypothesis by realizing a small but

Fig. 33 Detail of the Palazzo Sant'Elia and the empty ornamental frame over the main entrance on Via Infermeria and the three hooks where the coat of arms used to hang.

Fig. 34 Hypothetical reconstruction of the famous 19th-century etching of the bridge of San Francesco depicting a two-story Palazzo Sant'Elia perfectly framed by the bridge's arch.

Fig. 35 Hypothetical reconstruction of the north facade along Via Infermeria depicting the center attic over the entrance and a two-story continuous building block.

33

34

35

36

37

Fig. 36 Detail of the west facade of Palazzo Sant'Elia showing the Prince's "movable" coat of arms, now relocated to the attic pediment overlooking the bridge.

Fig. 37 Detail of the west facade of Palazzo Sant'Elia showing a major structural crack in the second floor cornice, possibly due to the extra weight of the attic addition.

crucial detail. While considering these new explications and observing hypnotically and in minute detail from the bridge the abnormally narrow facade, I realized that the coat of arms is really an independent piece, a bas relief "hung" in the beautiful baroque pediment (Fig. 60). A train of thought followed that was logical to one who had been looking at the building in detail for some time.

Recalling the empty frame over the entrance (Fig. 59), I rushed down the bridge, passing in front of Sant'Agata, down the sloping curving street dominated by the house of Bonaiuto, and then under the bridge, stopping finally in front of the entrance to the palazzo on via Infermeria. What I found was worth the running: The form of the shield corresponded to the empty frame at the center of the ornamental figure over the entrance to the palazzo. This supports the hypothesis that at some point the coat of arms was physically removed from the former main facade and reinstalled on the new main facade overlooking the bridge. This is what I suspected when I was still on the bridge as soon as I put together the forms in my mind. What I did not expect to find were the three rusty hooks remaining still in the empty field vacated when the coat of arms was moved. The finding was the perfect confirmation of secrets unraveled.

This modest reconstruction affirms a few important points. It reinforces the view that the "feste" plays a key role in the social organization of urban space in Sicilian cities of the period (as presented by Dr. Amoroso in this book) and, of course, it reinforces the importance of the bridge as a key to understanding the urbanistic, architectonic, social, and cultural history of the city.

It portrays, as an example of the mores and "urbanistic" behavior of the noble class in Sicily, the shifting allegiance of one family, the Sant'Elias, to the street where they located their household and to the architecture of their own "flagship" palazzo. The fickle Palazzo del Principe di Sant'Elia wanted to "appear" where it counted most, first on via Infermeria, and, later, overlooking the Ponte di San Francesco, and its owners wanted to accomplish it with minimum effort and major impact.

Thus a significant move of unprecedented courage took place when the main facade was "relocated." The attic floor was built (now perhaps by Bonaiuto since the dates would be more logical[13]) in such a way that it overlooks the bridge and thus "places" the palazzo on it, and it was done with a crisp and striking baroque pediment that redeploys the family's coat of arms. I am even tempted to hypothesize that the conspicuous and threatening crack in the center of the cornice over the second floor on the narrow facade is the result of the extra weight of the attic addition (Fig. 61) for which the cornice was unprepared.

Problems, however, still remain. We need deeds and transfers of property to confirm our hypothesis and they do not seem to exist, but the drawings describe a lot, and if nothing else, I want to make a case for the old maps and the forgotten surveyors who produced them. These drawings provide invaluable information.

The interplay between buildings, public spaces, and urban infrastructure holds a major key to understanding civic representation. The case of the Ponte di San Francesco and the Palazzo Sant'Elia offers a poignant example of the social forces that move human acts: on the one hand the noble, enterprising, and risky undertakings of a social and religious class struggling for the physical betterment of the city and, on the other, the individual struggle to "appear" at one's best and select the most favorable representation through buildings as monuments and expression of power. The very human balance these two elements of infrastructure and building seem to handle so well in their dialectic relationship appears to have been lost in the typical contemporary city, where the automobile has made that interplay extremely difficult.

Cambridge, November 1991

Notes

1 The course (Architecture GSD 3400) was given in the fall of 1989, with Professor Kevin Kieran as instructor of record. The twelve students, whose names appear in the introduction to this book, were selected after interviews with all the applicants during the spring of 1989. The field trip and survey "in situ," which took place in June, were prerequisites to enroll in the fall course.

2 Most of the historical data on Caltagirone in this brief account comes from *Caltagirone: Lineamenti di Storia ed Arte*, by Antonio Ragona (Caltagirone, 1965); *Caltagirone*, (Palermo: Sellerio Editore, 1977); Umberto Amore, *Caltagirone: con riferimenti e schede sulla storia della Sicilia*, (Catania: Tringale Editore, 1981); Domenico Amoroso, "Caltagirone: a Story of the City," in *Architectural and Urban Environments of Sicily*, ed. Jorge Silvetti (Cambridge, MA: Harvard University Graduate School of Design, 1989). All data on Sicilian history comes from *A History of Sicily*, by M. I. Finley, Denis Mack Smith, and Christopher Duggan (New York, NY: Viking, 1987).

3 See biographic note in Appendices.
To refer to the appendices of the original publication in which this article was published, see Selected Writings at the back of the present volume.

4 See biographic note in Appendices.
To refer to the appendices of the original publication in which this article was published, see Selected Writings at the back of the present volume.

5 Two points of our hypothesis about the bridge and the palazzo concern the decision to rebuild on the city's medieval foundations. According to Vito Librando ("La ricostruzione dopo il terremoto del 1693 e la architettura del Settecento," in *Caltagirone*, 1977), the proposal to move the city to the plain around the convent of Santa Maria di Gesù was rejected because the chapel of the patron saint, San Giacomo, who was deeply venerated, remained intact after the earthquake. This reinforces the importance and desirability of the southern plain where, since the late eighteenth century, the city has indeed expanded. In retrospect, this makes the construction of the bridge even more inevitable and, second, it reinforces the importance we attached to the processional routes (of which the one celebrating the patron saint is the most important).

6 See biographic note in Appendices.
To refer to the appendices of the original publication in which this article was published, see Selected Writings at the back of the present volume.

7 The Landolina family had residences in the triangular block until 1702 when the family surrendered its houses to a knight from the Rizzari family, who lacer yielded the residences to the Strazzieri family. In 1769, the Strazzieri earned the title Princes of Sant'Elia. For more information on the nobility of Caltagirone, see footnote 32 in "The Prince's Dream: Projects and Buildings in Southern Italian Culture Between Mannerism and the Baroque," by Domenico Amoroso.

8 Ibid.

9 The maps are from 1700, 1774, and 1877. The first map is interesting because it concerns the character of the city after the earthquake of 1693. This map, "ristorata dopo la rovina del terremoto del 1693" (literally "restored after the ruinous earthquake of 1693"), confirms the determination to reconstruct on the medieval footprint and depicts a possible reconstruction plan for the city, which in the seven years following the earthquake had not yet been rebuilt. The map of 1774, engraved by Bernardinus Bongiovanni, carries the title of "Citta Grattissima" an old important title from the time of the Emperor Charles V, revived no doubt to reestablish the territorial importance of Caltagirone. See G. Leone, *Il Disegno e la Regola* (Palermo: Flaccovio Editore, 1980).

10 See "La Festa di San Giacomo a Caltagirone - Cenni Storici, Folkloristici ed Artistici" Ass. Beni Culturali. Musei Civici e Pinacoteca "L. Scurzo." Serie Didattica - Mont. I. Caltagirone, 1980.

11 The classic image (figure 40) on which we based our reconstruction appeared in "Cento Città d'Italia," Supplemenco illustrato del Secolo, Lunedi, 25 Marzo, 1895, Milano. Our version involved some modification to the original.

12 Even if processions were to take the other possible route (which followed the sweeping curved slope chat joins the lower areas under the bridge with the Church of Sant' Agata), either as they left town or as they arrived, our hypothesis would be the same because the view of the ensemble would be common to both routes.

13 Natale Bonaiuto moved to Caltagirone in 1769. (See Appendices.)
To refer to the appendices of the original publication in which this article was published, see Selected Writings at the back of the present volume.

* This article was presented at the symposium, "1693—Urban and Architectural Culture in the Baroque Age: The Rebuilding of the Sicilian Cities after the Great Earthquake," held at the Harvard University Graduate School of Design, October 28–v30, 1991, and was sponsored by the Architectural and Urban Environments of Sicily and O.L.T.U.M. All hypothetical reconstruction drawings and maps by Jorge Silvetti and Douglas Dolezal.

Architecture: The Purview of the Social

WITH ELISA SILVA

Previous spread: Extant portal to the Sacristy of the Jesuit mission of San Ignacio Miní near Posadas, Argentina (1696). An excellent example of the work by local Guaraní artisans involved in the construction of the mission and their transformation of the classical architectural orders.

1. Cultural Forces That Invite Architecture

ELISA SILVA I have been reading your writings that will be included in this book, with particular attention to those that correspond to this chapter. But I also came across a book in my library that you gave to me: the book of your introductions to the speakers of public lectures while you were chairman at the GSD.[1] It is signed by you on the front, and it has a CD in the back containing the recording of the lecture, "The Muses Are Not Amused." So not only have I read "The Muses Are Not Amused," I've heard it too.[2] I also found an image in the slides that accompanied the audio recordings.

JORGE SILVETTI I didn't know that was there. I actually never saw everything that was on that CD. It didn't interest me so much! [*laughs*]

ES I also scavenged for my class notes from the GSD. So I have all sorts of material with me from when you taught "Buildings, Texts & Contexts" (BTC). Look, this is the syllabus for the fall of 1998. Going over it, I remembered that you would start teaching the course with the Seven Wonders of the Ancient World.

JS Yes. [*laughs*] There you have it! If you want to conceive an architecture canon—one that is directly connected to society—the Seven Wonders is it. Back then, I thought that it was worth revisiting this historical phenomenon that, today, we learn in a watered-down form that appears to be material for elementary school children. And yet, from antiquity to the late Baroque era, the Seven Wonders continued to be of real interest to artists, scholars, thinkers, and of course the general public. They offer many angles from which to understand the potential for architecture to engage culture at large and the different means through which this engagement can happen.

The Seven Wonders are an incredibly rich topic for an architect or historian to investigate and interpret, in part because they are a canon in capsule form; they include only seven buildings, each with distinctive attributes. These distinctions make comparing the specimens extremely productive, since each one represents a different genre of artifact. There are extremes within the canon, such as a garden and an anthropomorphic figure at an architectural scale, and there are also three "buildings" without interiors.

The Seven Wonders also allow us to discuss the selective criteria of this canon and the reason for its durability. For designers, they have the added attraction that, with the exception of the Pyramids of Giza—which are by nature indestructible—not one of the Seven Wonders has survived. Even though we are certain of their existence, some of them have not even yielded believable traces, let alone ruins. This has made the imagination of designers and historians run wild trying to visualize them based on folklore and written sources.

I included the Seven Wonders as the initial case study in the BTC course as a result of a lecture on the same material that I gave at RISD some years before, in the mid-'80s, although the RISD lecture was focused more on the issue of size versus proportion as a theoretical problem in architecture and monumentality. K. Michael Hays, who was then a very young architecture historian and studio teacher there, loved this lecture and still reminds me of the impact it had on him. I was later encouraged by Christine Smith, who joined the BTC team in 1993, when Howard Burns left Harvard. She had written a very interesting piece devoted to the Seven Wonders, in which she explored their impact on humanist culture in the early Renaissance.[3]

ES Since I took the BTC course, I compulsively feel the need to correct people every time they think they know what the Seven Wonders are! Those lessons stayed with me.

You then taught that whole section on single case studies of architecture, which I had forgotten about. The Pantheon, Hagia Sophia, Speyer Cathedral, Chartres Cathedral, the Ideal City, and so on. I also remember reading *Hypnerotomachia Poliphili*.[4]

JS Yes, although Speyer Cathedral and Chartres Cathedral were in Christine Smith's domain.

ES Then there was El Escorial, which was one of your signatures.

JS Yes, that one and the Mosque-Cathedral of Córdoba. Although El Escorial and the Mosque-Cathedral of Córdoba were introduced to the GSD earlier by Rafael Moneo during his chairmanship. He did this in a novel course, in which he picked a building per session and analyzed it in his inimitable, profound, and inspiring way.[5]

From attending some of Rafael's presentations, I found that the way he unpacked El Escorial and the Mosque-Cathedral of Córdoba was superb, and that these were perfect examples for the course. This is why I decided to take them on myself when I started teaching BTC with Howard in 1993. However, I looked at them from an angle that was skewed more toward a cultural reading. I saw these buildings as "marginal" productions, geographically and in terms of the cultural centers of their times.[6] They were total inventions that amalgamated diverse architectural elements in novel ways.

ES After that you would lead five sessions on the Vatican.

JS That's true! I was working on the Vatican topography back then, do you remember? This is one of the anomalous case studies that I added to the way of dealing with a single moment or architectural event in detail. It is not a building per se but a set of buildings and public spaces that were built over centuries and now make up a single whole in our minds.

I was working on a project using digital modeling technology to reconstruct the whole history of the site. It was quite beautiful. I worked with Geoffrey Taylor, a DDes[7] student who was the TA for the course back then. These were years of intense and rewarding research work, grounded mostly in the topography of the site. Unfortunately, we never properly published it and its products remain in draft papers; reports to the Getty Grants Program, which partially funded the project; a robust bibliography; slides; early 3D digital images; and a very good database that I am sure Geoffrey still maintains.

NICOLÁS DELGADO ALCEGA How did this research come about?

JS It was provoked while I was doing prep work for a lecture on St. Peter's Square for BTC. I was already quite knowledgeable about individual pieces within the Vatican site: the new Basilica of St. Peter, Castel Sant'Angelo, the Borgo, the move of the obelisk, the Cortile del Belvedere, Bernini's transformation of the medieval piazza, and so on. But I learned that Bernini was commissioned by Pope Urban VIII to build the two campaniles that would complete the facade of the basilica. However, during construction the heavy southern tower sank and risked collapsing due to the poor quality of the infill, which led to the abandonment of the project and to a painful stain on Bernini's reputation.

This technical failure brought the conditions of the structures' foundations to my attention and prompted this urge to understand how many architects had managed to build one of the most significant collections of monumental buildings, public spaces, gardens, and urban fabric over the course of fifteen hundred years with a total indifference toward the natural topography of the site. The most interesting thing is that this whole sequence of drastic transformations that would change the city of Rome starts from a purely ideological decision focused, literally, on one point on the map; from the desire to build the Basilica of St. Peter on the very spot where Saint Peter, the first pope and apostle, was believed to be buried.

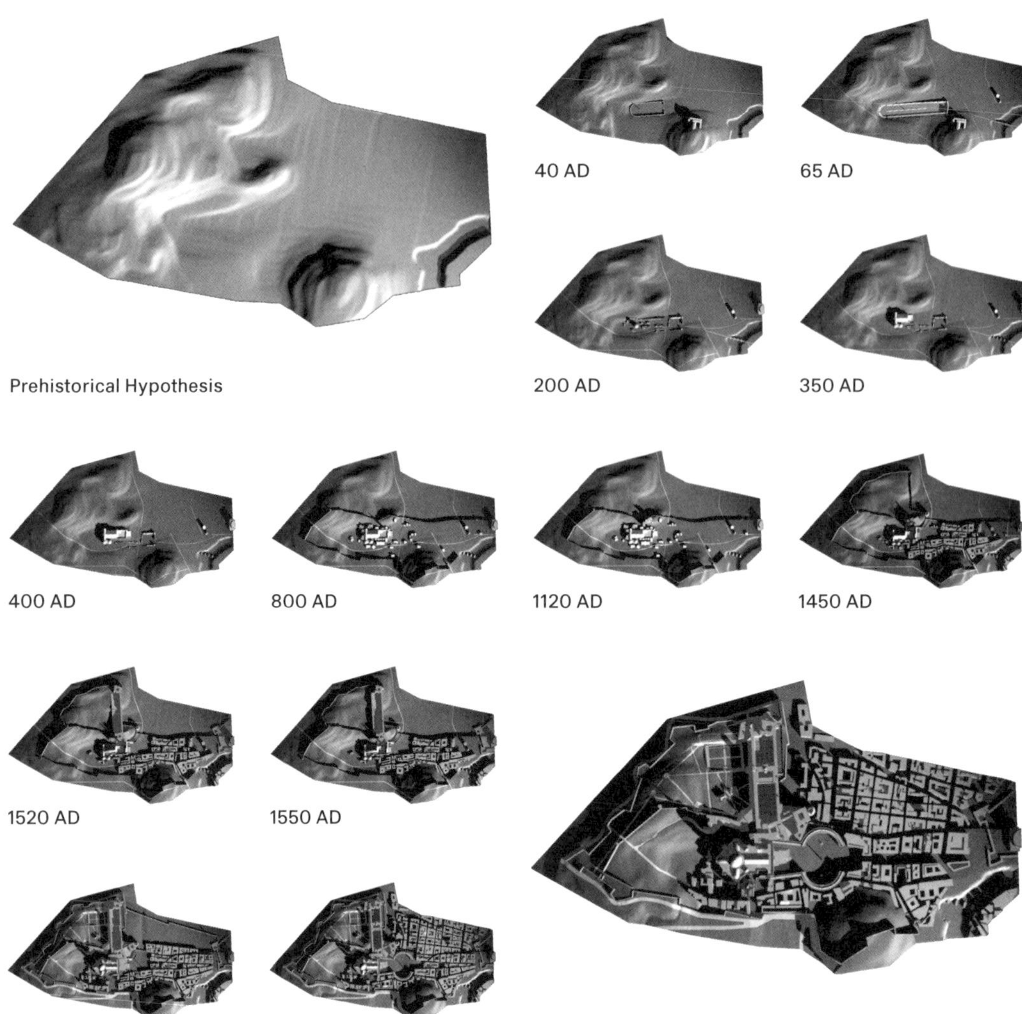

3-D model of the transformation of the Vatican area from prehistory to 1950. These models were created as part of the Vatican Topography research project led by Jorge Silvetti from 1993 to 1998.

This act was a gesture of gratitude by Constantine for the "magic" of this locus, where he had bivouacked with his troops in preparation for the Battle of the Milvian Bridge. On this eve, he had his famous and consequential vision of the Christian cross and decided to carry the cross into the battle against Maxentius. Constantine wins, crosses the Tiber, and enters the city of Rome to become emperor. Let's not forget the Vatican area was *fuori le mura*. Momentously, he then adopts Christianity as the official religion of the Roman Empire and Western civilization takes a defining turn. Constantine's conversion is what inaugurates the sequence of manipulations of the Vatican topography.

The original site sloped naturally toward the Tiber—that is, broadly, from north to south. During early Roman times, the area was occupied by suburban patrician farms. There was the Circus of Nero, which ran parallel to the Tiber, from east to west, as its elongated form required in relation to the slope, and Nero's villa. These buildings were eventually abandoned, and their ruins were turned into a large Christian cemetery, with St. Peter's burial ground among the most venerated tombs. Only soon after Constantine's victory and his decision to build the first major basilica in Rome on that very sacred spot did the site's transformation begin. The basilica was given a main east–west axis that ran counter to the slope toward the Tiber river—a design move that determined everything that followed on the site nonstop until Mussolini's regime!

The ground was progressively flattened so that not a single outwardly visible trace of the original topography is left. I became obsessive about this, because these transformations involved superlative actions in response to issues that individual pieces of architecture within the site needed to address: ideological, symbolic, but also technical demands. It was a large-scale, centuries-long engineering project that involved filling in the site in order to turn its natural axis by ninety degrees and make it horizontal.

ES I remember that. I also recall you invited James Ackerman to give a lecture on the Vatican.

JS Yes, Ackerman had just retired from the Fogg Museum. He was about eighty. He told me he had stepped down due to minor memory lapses. I invited him to give a seminar at the GSD, as well as that presentation on the Vatican to our class. I remember I asked him to talk about the Cortile del Belvedere. Ackerman wrote a piece on it that was never published. I think it is one of the best things ever written about the Cortile del Belvedere.[8] It also fits perfectly with the topography research I was doing. The Cortile del Belvedere deals with the most difficult part of the original topography of the Vatican Hill in such a

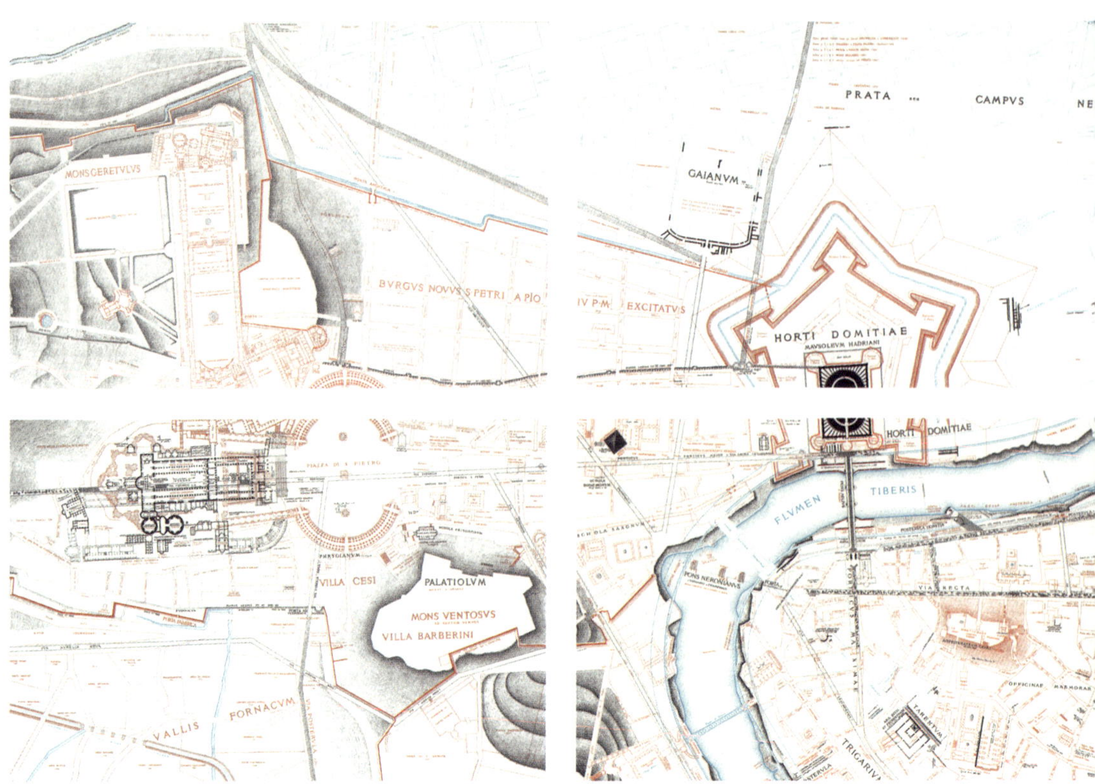

Plates 6, 7, 13, and 14 of *Forma Urbis Romae*, Rodolfo Lanciani (1901). The plates depict, in a single representation, the stratification of major urbanistic, architectural, and infrastructural developments in the Vatican area between antiquity and the date of publication.

creative way. For all practical purposes, Bramante's project concludes the development of the whole area of the Vatican with a bang!

So Ackerman agreed, I gave the students the bibliography, I introduced him in class, and he began to give this magisterial lecture… about the dome of St. Peter's Basilica! [*laughs*] I never told him he gave the wrong lecture, because, among other reasons, even if it was not what I needed for the course, it was a fantastic lecture. Nobody complained about the mistake either. Who cares about lapses of memory if they result in such a feast! It was only a problem for me, because I was supposed to give a lecture on the dome of St. Peter's the following week, and I had no clue what to do in such a short time. What can you add about the dome of St. Peter's after a presentation by Ackerman? [*laughs*]

ES I was in ectasis. I don't know if you remember that I studied art history as an undergraduate student. I had a professor named Sarah McPhee, who was an expert in Renaissance and Baroque architecture, and I had read three or four of Ackerman's books with her. So when this larger-than-life character came along, I just remember telling my classmates, "Do you realize who this person in front of you is?"

Something else that I found in the last couple days were the folders of my thesis investigation, which you asked me about recently. I even have the paper I turned in to you at the end of my preparatory semester. It was full of your markings and notes.

JS [*laughs*] Oh my god, maybe it's better not to tell me what I said!

ES It was a draft where we had already landed on the project *El Camino a Monte Albán*.

JS How beautiful that was! And how fortunate I was to be part of your project. Apart from my interest in working with you, this became a project that fascinated me in itself. I had already been to Monte Albán when we started working on your thesis. I don't recall if I ever told you about my earlier experience on this site?

ES Maybe.

JS I was impressed by the whole path and arrival sequence, but I also had one of those… How do I say it? One of those *mystical* experiences in Monte Albán. I was in Mexico City alone and had decided to go to Oaxaca for a weekend. I went up to Monte Albán in the afternoon, and I was up on the plateau of the acropolis. It was a sublime site, from which you could see everything. The sky was crystalline blue and the temperature was hot.

In the far distance you could see a storm with lightning rays hitting the ground. It was far away and very localized, almost like a dark object within that limpid landscape. But it was moving at a high speed, and in a matter of five minutes the storm swooshed through the landscape and engulfed Monte Albán. I tried to hide under the pyramids, which of course was not possible, because there is no such a thing as "a space under the pyramids!" It was a brutal, short tropical storm with fierce thunder, and on that site it felt apocalyptic. However, within ten minutes, the storm had moved on, and it was clear and sunny once again. At that moment I acquired a primeval awareness of the ways in which one can begin to construct the idea of an omnipotent divinity; how the site could make you think about the forces of the universe manifesting themselves upon human life. It was as if for a minute, as a reminder of how things could have come to be, the world fell on you.

ES Were there a lot of people? Or were you alone?

JS There were people but not a crowd. I don't recall how I got there, but I did not walk the whole route, of course. I didn't even know where I was going.

ES It takes a while to walk it. Today Oaxaca is much more famous, but twenty years ago the city was off the beaten path. When I went to Monte Albán, I said to myself, "That's it. This is my project site." And, as you know, I go to Oaxaca often now for work that evolved from what I started at the GSD a few semesters ago.

JS You were teaching a course about the Mezcal industry, right?

ES Yes, and now with Pablo Perez Ramos, we have a grant from the David Rockefeller Center for Latin American Studies that is allowing us to work there with more intensity.[9]

JS Look at everything that this thesis has produced! Fantastic.

ES I've been thinking about all of these experiences you've revived in our conversation, and it has really made evident your interest in architecture that is not so much referential, but rather tied to society; architecture that emerges from working with cultural phenomena and with people.

JS Yes, I get what you are saying, but there is room for misunderstanding when you describe my interest as "not so much referential." It is, of course, the "so much" that needs clarification. I would say that all architecture is referential at some level, if for no other reason because all material culture needs to associate itself with some meaning that is culturally shared for it to be intelligible to others, regardless of how tenuous this association might be.

I find the referential dimension of architecture to be crucial to the design process and to our ability to interpret existing buildings. At the same time, while we cannot avoid this dimension of architecture, I think architecture should not be exclusively focused on referents. In fact, it does not need to be focused on them at all. Architecture is never autonomous from its contextual conditions, and references themselves are one of these conditions! But there are many other conditioning ingredients, and the users of architecture are among the few inescapable ingredients.

ES I have been teaching in Toronto recently, and I had the magnificent opportunity to get to better know George Baird, who, as a student, I always thought to be terrific. He was at the GSD when you were chairman.

JS Yes, he was the program director while I was chair. I think we made an amazing team! [*laughs*]

ES I never had the opportunity to interact with him back then. But in Toronto, I told him that the way I interpreted his ideas was that everything was apt to be thought of as architecture, be it a shopping mall, a suburb, etc. He told me he had never written that exact phrase anywhere, but yes, this was how he saw it. I proposed an addition to the list by saying, "Well, the informal city can also be thought of as architecture."

JS This is true. When I was just beginning my architectural education in Argentina, we had to read Nikolaus Pevsner's *An Outline of European Architecture*, which, by the way, had an additional chapter in the Spanish translation.[10] This chapter was not by Pevsner, and it was devoted to the architecture of the Iberian Peninsula and Latin America—a condescending gesture toward those readers beyond the Pyrenees! But this aside, the preface to the book by Pevsner sets out to define what makes a building a piece of architecture. It says something like, "while Lincoln Cathedral in England is undoubtedly a piece of architecture, a bicycle shed cannot possibly be!" This is something that many in my generation rejected right away, and we used it in school as an emblematic motto. We would say, "We are architects that do bicycle sheds too." We were in that sense obedient Modernists, expanding the reach of architecture beyond what art history had defined as its disciplinary boundaries. We had the conviction that every building type could be a piece of architecture, even before we knew anything about architecture.

Yes, the informal city can also be a work of architecture, but this does not imply that architecture is possible without architects. This idea requires a special kind of intellectual equipment geared toward the so-called vernacular, which allows us to define it and articulate its role in practice. During your time as a student, the dispute between autonomy and dependence was hot, and the broader "contextual" view was becoming more prevalent among the young. So I was interested in engaging in the discussion. The term *contextual* can be misinterpreted and misleading. It can easily produce a situation in which architecture disappears in the midst of a messy complex of empirical realities, leading to the subsequent invasion of other disciplines into its exclusive realm.

ES When I worked on this thesis with you on the path to Monte Albán, our conversations allowed me to develop a project that was outside of the conventional realm of architecture and perhaps leaned a bit more toward landscape architecture—even though in the moment I would never have thought of the project that way. Landscape architecture as a discipline at the GSD was very different around 2001. The thesis was surely about architecture, but the process allowed me to engage an enormous variety of conditions, issues, and scales that affect architecture—though many others would have discarded them as completely outside the discipline's realm.

JS Your thesis definitely made me think more carefully about architecture and its relationships with multidisciplinarity, which has been a decades-long discussion at the GSD. It never seems to end, and from my perspective, it is generally mismanaged.

ES I liked the approximation we took because it was humble. From the beginning, it was clear that the project was not going to be the protagonist. Monte Albán and all of its dynamics were the protagonists, and what I was going to design was inevitably going to be subservient to that. In retrospect, I don't know if I liked this approach because it was romantic or because I felt safe. But the project without a doubt opened a path of reflection for me that has remained very strong.

There was something similar about the setup of your project at the Getty Villa—a visit that I won't forget, by the way. When I finally went to the Getty Villa, I was there for hours and hours. This incredibly complex project developed around a protagonist that is already there. Its architectural intervention emerged from a very intense engagement with all the realities that gave rise to the project and presented themselves along the way.

Monte Albán photographed by Elisa Silva in 2021.

Model, aerial view of the construction site, and section depicting the public entrance sequence of the New Getty Villa, Machado and Silvetti Associates (1994–2006).

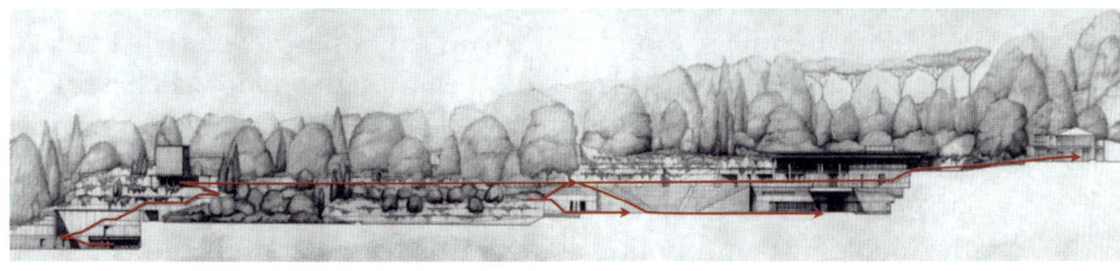

JS I was very interested in your thesis precisely because of the people for whom you were designing. You were finding ways to improve the experience of walking to a place that was an archeological point of interest, but more importantly, it was also an active religious site. It was a place imbued with symbolic value and ritual behavior that is totally ingrained in a segment of the population today. People already had an idea of what this path meant, and they knew how to use it as the protagonists of a ritual. This is a situation from which serious architecture can emerge because there is an active and strong connection between space and the ways a culture has imposed its myths upon it.

NDA This is not unlike your specific interest in the Vatican complex, in which ideology is a driver that pushes us to reshape the built environment in the image we have of ourselves.

JS Right. It is about broad cultural impulses, about human emotions and affects. From the outside, as a designer involved in the production of material culture, I am very interested in these forces, in the religions and myths that truly unite cultures, regardless of whether they are sacred or profane. The faithful that walk this path still believe in the same thing that the—

ES That the Zapotecs believed.

JS Exactly, and of course this is all mixed with the syncretism of Catholicism today. But when people go on that procession, they are propelled by a transformative force, a force that is only activated on that site and through what it represents for them. On Monte Albán, a sudden electric storm reinforces that experience rather than serving merely as a nuisance. My experience on the site was purely based on the site's "form" and its effect on my psyche. But believers also bring *a priori* beliefs about what the site signifies for them.

ES The connection in Monte Albán is very alive.

JS This genuine motor is the most interesting thing about the problem you chose. When you say people really interest me, it is in this sense that they do. I'm fascinated by what moves people and the ways architecture can be a vehicle to trigger that.

Many people respond as if surprised or perplexed that I talk so much about churches and religion even though I'm not a believer myself. [*laughs*] But it is obvious to me that you do not need to profess the faith to understand, say, the Baroque style. From this dispassionate position, you actually have the opportunity to better understand the ideological and political apparatus of the church and the state that generates the tremendous proliferation of the Baroque, first in Italy and then all over Europe and the Spanish empire.

I say "dispassionate" because if you went into this intellectual process with an outsider's prejudice, or a moralistic view of the Counter Reformation, you would not be able to understand the Baroque! You would remain blind to the complete and profound nature of the Baroque style. At most you would get caught up in the formal issues of geometry and the methods that characterize the style. While this is important in scholarly research, it is totally insufficient and empty of meaning if you are trying to understand why and how the Baroque operated in society, where its phenomenal energy comes from, and where its originality is rooted.

More than ever, I am against trends that sustain the idea that someone who makes cultural products, such as an architect, a fashion designer, an actor, or an ethnic-cuisine writer, cannot be the author of a subject matter that stems from another cultural group. This is what some today call "cultural appropriation," describing it as an abusive interference in a particular culture. But no. This is precisely what all cultures are made up of. They are the result of actual interferences, violent clashes, and the cross-fertilization of cultures, ideologies, and ethnic customs that come into contact. This is the true nature and beauty of diversity, as opposed to the false "identitarian" pursuit of purity. Political victims do exist, as we are reminded everyday. But culture is a dynamic, living formation, and its development is not as black-and-white. It must also be said that culture only develops through the interminglings of different people.

From this perspective, I think we have to vindicate the role of the architect. The architect has a role that no one else has. At this point I've been hearing critiques about architecture being secondary or simply an instrument for five decades. But a good architect, one that knows how to think like an architect, has the opportunity to articulate the beliefs and aspirations of a culture through buildings—the large, inert, and permanent solids and voids that turn space into opportunities for diverse actions.

2. The Autonomy of Architecture

ES In "The Muses Are Not Amused," you draw parallels between Conceptual art and Baroque art, and I want to take a moment to talk about this. You have been talking about those who receive the cultural production that we call architecture. You've described the relationship between forms, techniques, and ideas, and the person for whom these will mean something. When you delivered the lecture that led to the article, on the occasion of the conclusion of your chairmanship at the GSD, you tackled a wide variety of architectural trends taking place. You mounted a critique of contemporary architecture, saying it was becoming too automatic, too diagrammatic. And you highlighted how architecture was distancing itself from the receiver of that production, or from the cultural audiences you spoke of earlier.

Something that Conceptual art tries to do in the field of the visual arts is to get people—in this case, the viewers—to ask themselves, "What is this?" Duchamp's *Fountain* is a quintessential example that invites the question "Why is this here? Why is this being presented to me?" The audience is given an opportunity to reflect through the interaction. But I think there is something that gets lost in the objective behind this operation that is typical of Conceptual art; there is not much clarity in its purpose beyond getting people to ask the question.

JS I know what you mean, although I'm not sure the best way to put it is to say that we should try harder to see contemporary architecture from the perspective of the receiver. I think it has more to do with clarity of purpose and trying to steer the discipline toward an architecture derived from the pertinent problems of its contexts, addressing them in the best ways that architecture can. This means making something that resonates with the public. We have to keep in mind that we engage a much broader public than other arts do, and we do so through the sensory opportunities that architecture allows. However, this does not mean that we can make formal design decisions based entirely on what the public wants or believes. Firstly, this is because how can we come to know this? The recent history of architecture is plagued with faux pas because of our naive belief that such knowledge could be ascertained.

We can only approximate this problem by getting a sense of what formal decisions resonate with the collective. This is like overtones in music, those strings that vibrate spontaneously in response to another vibrating sound. To achieve this, we have to equip ourselves with tools that we don't come to the world with.

I think there is no formula. I approached this issue by learning about other cultural processes that have been better studied and then trying to analogously answer questions about what architecture represents in that context. That is, what place does architecture occupy in the larger universe of material culture? Through what mechanisms does it resonate with the broader social reality that it belongs to? It is only after you have some answers to these questions that you can think about how to operate accordingly. This is not easy, but it is what we are all trying to do, whether we are more conscious or more intuitive about it. Ultimately, what is at risk when we design a work of architecture is the degree to which we can trigger a positive connection—some kind of empathy—with the public that we need to engage. This is the real difficulty of architecture, whether we are designing it or teaching it.

Moreover, visually engaging the receiver of architecture is inevitable, but making it analogous to the way the visual arts engage the public is a big mistake. This is because it is hard to narrow down who the receiver is in architecture, with the exception of the rare situation of individual clients. But even in that case, the relationship between an architectural work and a person is only valid through the lifespan of that client, which is a fraction of the life of the building. The aspiration in Conceptual art to encourage a reflection in the viewer through interaction works because of the circumstances under which it occurs: within a gallery or museum that people go to on voluntary terms and where one can definitely challenge an audience willing to participate in the exchange. The audience usually knows or wants to know the work of the artist.

But when a piece of Conceptual art is tested in the public arena, which is the domain of architecture, and takes the willingness of the receiver for granted, its basic premise is put into crisis. Most people fail to engage in the work, or don't take it seriously. Imagine what would happen with a urinal placed upside down on a pedestal in a public park! Conceptual art tends to become an irritable offense in these contexts, and there are plenty of cases where works have had to be taken down due to public outcry! The fiasco of Richard Serra's spectacular *Tilted Arc* in New York is the clearest example.[11] I don't know if we can provide a definitive expiration date for Conceptual art, though I do think it has expired. But we can surely date it to coincide with its inception, around when Duchamp produces works like the *Fountain*. Truly, it was so short-lived!

To your question, I was not really tracing a parallel between Baroque art and Conceptual art. Rather, I brought them together because I think that the basic operation that sustains Conceptual art finds its seeds in the Baroque period. They are planted in a conscious way, and we don't find them before that. This is something I started reflecting on when I delivered that lecture. Baroque art is the first self-aware political art. It has a written program about how art is to be produced that is clearly spelled out in simple but definitive language in the edicts of the Council of Trent.[12] This leads Baroque artists to create the importance that is still given to the concept of a work of art today, or *il concetto* that precedes the work. During the Baroque period, this term translates literally to "the conceit" of the work; the trick or fantastic image; the illusionist *trompe l'oeil*, a technique that expressly connects a textual narrative and a sculpture. Bernini is the master here in his works *The Ecstasy of Saint Teresa, Apollo and Daphne,* or *The Rape of Proserpina* ...

The Baroque conceits transition from clever ideas or ingenious metaphors manifested in forms to written language centuries later, with words themselves incorporated into the work or works that depend on their title to deliver their message. I think this relevance of the written word in visual art occurs in Modernism because it became impossible to give explicit meaning to abstract forms, surfaces, and colors—which do not resonate in the way figurative forms do. Figuration was no longer acceptable, and imitating nature for its own sake was gone. Something else needed to be added to these abstract elements to allow them to signify. So language takes over.

Think of Magritte's pipe. He needed to write "This is not a pipe" on the painting itself for it to become something artistic. I find this particular Magritte brilliant given the time in which it was produced and the fact that the virtues of Conceptual art are time-based. However, a person not interested or familiar with the state of art would simply find it silly. But that does not affect a Conceptual painting: unlike architecture, a painting can operate without concerns about a generalized, anonymous public reaction.

In addition, another difference from Conceptual art is that the Baroque still operates within the norms of a widely shared formal and visual language: the classical. This recognizable, familiar "look" of classical art inevitably engaged the public that tried to interpret the strangeness that Baroque architects presented. This is major. Metaphors inform the production of architecture particularly in this Baroque pursuit to produce the effect of wonder and make something that does not appear explicable by the laws of nature.

For instance, architects start to undulate facades, even though marble and granite are obviously not plastic. However, the technique had a verisimilitude enabled by the classical language employed, which

Detail of *Apollo and Daphne*, Gian Lorenzo Bernini (1622–1625). Galleria Borghese, Rome.

Exterior view of Palazzo Carignano in Turin, designed by Guarino Guarini (begun 1679).

made the works instantly engaging via the effect of wonder. Everybody understood that these were the walls of an important building, that they were made of stone and invested with the classical orders, and then—wow! Now they were undulating. It is the ecstatic Saint Teresa enveloped in wildly agitated fabrics at the moment of penetration, rendered in a gorgeous single piece of carved Carrara marble!

NDA Right, the stone actually undulates like cloth. The metaphor is not an inscription; it leads to something visual and sculptural that people can interpret on their own.

JS For me, the dependence of the visual arts on written language to engage the public is highly problematic. It announces art's own poverty, or at least that the artist has not activated everything that makes a sculpture a sculpture. And yet, we still find ourselves trapped in the wake of this moment. We are still talking about Conceptual art, even though art has continued in other vibrant and diverse directions. Its influence continues to seep into other art forms that frankly cannot be conceptual in the same way, such as music or architecture, while we begin to see contemporary art itself overcome some of these shortcomings. Think of the extraordinary Charles Ray show that was recently put on at the Metropolitan Museum.[13] In these works, the figure is being re-engaged in a clever play between Conceptual and classical art.

To return to what we are concerned with: how "conceptual" can architecture be? Think about it. We are talking about a cultural practice defined by the silent inhabitation of heavy, unmovable, large solids that create an experience of full sensory immersion. Architecture begets objects that resonate with habits, social conventions, precedents, and history. We certainly need words to understand, theorize, and hypothesize about works of architecture. We also need them to teach and criticize, but the existence of the architectural object is still ineffable and impermeable to words *a posteriori*. While artificial and created by humans, architecture enjoys the unique autonomy that its presence, size, materiality, and permanence give to it. This does not prevent architecture or architectural elements from becoming the subjects of Conceptual art, but in that case we aren't really looking at architecture. We are at best looking at an "art installation." In fact, those that insist on treating architecture conceptually belong to a niche that has only been able to survive in the art gallery!

But anyways, I'm not sure if that is where you were going.

ES I was thinking about how this relates to the work of the late '90s, such as the production of Zaha Hadid's office. This work had the ambition to engage with the audience by trying to excite a sense of wonder, or perhaps it's something different. But what happened to Zaha's work was very similar to what happened to abstract and Conceptual art. No questioning or reflection really took place in correspondence with the audience. Instead, the work just became a brand, and I think this is quite sad. Something about the way she thought she could engage her audience actually led to a blind adoption of the work as a fashion.

JS You're right. This also happened with Dada and Surrealism. These movements foreshadow what happens to artistic images that are derived from an "idea," in a moment that still predates the rise of consumer society. These are very prestigious, brilliant, and profound art movements, but all of their imagery and mechanisms ended up simply informing advertising, which is the most banal destiny for an artistic piece one can think of.

ES Exactly!

JS The imagery of Surrealism and the cult of the absurd of Dada are consumed immediately by advertising. This didn't occur with Baroque or even Renaissance art because images were the intermediaries of something that they represented more profoundly, and they served a specific purpose. If images lose symbolic value, they are just discarded.

ES Yes, if we think of an art form like music, it's an entirely different story.

JS In my view, music remains to be the most resistant of all the arts. It is consumed, but it survives the act. Music, and I mean all music—classical, popular, vernacular, folk—continues to have an identity and an integrity as an art form that is almost incorruptible. It always comes back, sometimes vengefully, and surprises us with something original and fresh. What we learn from music is that the nature of the "substance" with which a practice operates is what determines it. Architecture, then, cannot be created as if communicating visually through images, or in a literary way through words! That was a dream we all had in the '60s, but architecture acts on people in different ways, and people judge it more holistically as the unique kind of material culture that it is. Architecture is something that first and foremost has a physical presence that is bigger than the human being, that is inert, that is expected to last longer than a single human life, and that is always assumed to provide some pragmatic utility, even though it contains the promise of an artistic experience. It is large, lasting, and inevitable!

Let's just say I prefer to take on projects like both your theses! When I worked with Nicolás, he was studying these abandoned towns in Italy and these terraced olive groves that had been built for centuries but were now falling apart because of disuse. What was exciting was to start from all of these concrete, simple problems from which fantastic architecture can still emerge; an architecture that can do something for everyone, regardless of the ways in which people happen to engage it.

NDA Much of what we are discussing comes from a broader spiritual and ideological crisis that makes our social reality seem too banal—others would say problematic—to intellectuals. American architects are particularly invested in this role, so there is a lot of cynicism in academic circles. We are at a historical turning point, which means reality isn't responding to the commands or theories of the intellectual elite. Whatever they may say, the intellectual elite are desperately out of touch with the direction of the world. So they relegate themselves to an opposition, to a deep critique of social reality grounded in the belief that little can be done to edify during this age—even if this couldn't be further from the truth. This is the "autonomous" project, and I think it is fundamentally anti-architectural. That is why it only works if you put it on life support within the ascetic, controlled environment of the art gallery. I think architecture fundamentally works to edify a social purpose, not tear it apart. This is why all this cynicism produces such aberrant and historically irrelevant work.

The difference I am referring to is between someone that is trying to design for a processional route, versus someone that is designing just to deliver their jaded personal opinion about the state of high culture.

JS Perfect, Nicolás!

ES Back in the years when I was in school and Jorge was chairman, I think there were two general branches of architectural production. One of them, which relates to our discussion of Conceptual art, liked to follow a sort of recipe. It was like a work by Sol Lewitt. You wrote some instructions and something interesting came out of it every time they were used. Then it was up to the client to see what they did with the result of that recipe, how they made it valuable.

NDA Which means it became advertising.

ES Right. Then there was this other branch, which was based on understanding a context, learning about tradition, doing research, eating in a place, trying to make sense of the economy that has produced a specific set of circumstances, listening to the needs and aspirations of people in an environment, etc. The idea is that this can allow you to produce an architecture that emerges in a resonant way because it engages all of these points is beautiful to me.

So I agree completely with both of your inclinations. This second branch of architectural production involves a much more challenging route in that you don't know where you will arrive from the get-go, but it is also much more rewarding. I think it opens up the possibility for real invention, not in the egotistical sense, but...

JS The possibility to be truly creative.

ES I remember sitting there doing my thesis based on plans that I had found at Harvard. They had been developed by archaeologists, who documented this vast site to the point of having topographical information at one-meter intervals—which was unbelievable back then. That was the level of detail with which I was observing the site, and it was fascinating. It has also informed the work I do today in informal settlements, using drones to map places that have never been mapped in order to work with them carefully.

However, when I graduated in 2002, there was a clear fascination with the other type of architectural production I alluded to, which for some reason didn't resonate with me.

NDA Today "The Muses Are Not Amused" reads like Jorge's attempt to reel architecture back into some sensible relationship with reality amid a chaotic, directionless moment. I know several people who went to the GSD at that time precisely because they wanted to work with you, due to what you represented. But I'm curious to know, what were some of your aims? Looking at some of the initiatives you pursued as chairman, one could interpret you as someone who also embraced this moment of broadening the scope or aim of architecture.

JS Yes, well these were ... complicated years, let's say. And we've been dragging a lot of this confusion through to today. What we're talking about here is, again, whether architecture is an autonomous discipline or not. For me, it has always been so clear: architecture is both! It is autonomous at a certain level and dependent on external forces at another. We all know it well. It is extremely context bound, but then there is a certain disciplinary space within which architecture can engage in its own sort of problems and arguments. Depending on the time period, this space can be larger or smaller. End of discussion.

We live in a moment that, for all the good reasons, is very contextual. We pay a lot of attention to the things that determine the production of architecture. However, it is often only contextual in a very limiting sense. Context takes all the attention and leaves no space for architecture, if I'm allowed the paradox. That core, which is the reason we explore a particular context, disappears. We need to find a

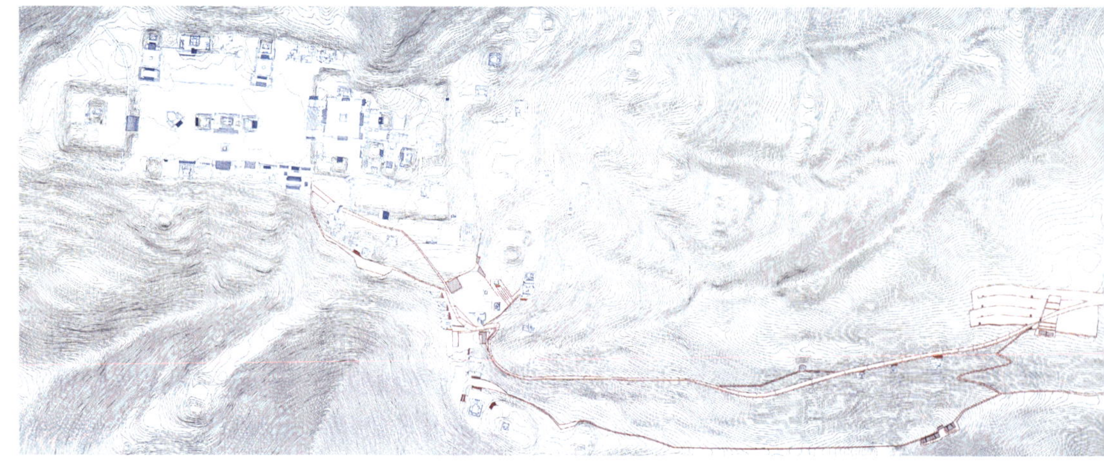

Context plan of *El Camino a Monte Albán*, Elisa Silva's master in architecture thesis project.

The celebration of Harry Cobb's eightieth birthday in Gund Hall, Harvard GSD, 2006. At the head of the table, on the left: Harry Cobb. Around the table, clockwise: Jorge Silvetti, Gerald M. McCue, Guy Nordeson, Peter Eiseman, Mack Scogin, and Rafael Moneo.

new way to look at everything we call context so that it can become an instrument that allows us to produce pieces of architecture that resonate with the social sphere.

Howard Burns and I made clear what we meant by context when we started teaching "Buildings, Texts & Contexts".[14] We centered on the object—the building or the text—and we carefully and strategically moved from it into its external environment. We picked everything that we considered to be lines that connect directly or indirectly with the object. But we extended our investigation only to the degree to which these contexts offered a better understanding of the object and the way the architect made design decisions. This was the ultimate pedagogical goal of this case study method.

Today, architecture is recurrently absent in the discussion. I used to find it paradoxical, but now I just think it is a depressing matter of fact. Most of the interest and excitement in architectural education is focused on considering only that which is peripheral. In very few cases, this contributes in some degree to architectural design, but usually it remains its own foreign and exotic world!

I'll say it again: I think we need to vindicate architecture and the architect. We need to put architecture back where it needs to be in schools: as the centerpiece of pedagogy, academic study, and research. In my last decades of teaching, I got the horrifying sense that some students—and teachers!—were actually trying to avoid studying architecture within an architecture school, avidly diving into any other pool of knowledge.

A growing list of side interests has taken over discourse and silenced architecture itself. This began with "the attack of the form snatchers," the blobs of the turn of this century, which I reacted to in "The Muses Are Not Amused." Then, after they ran their course, this led to the lowest imaginable episode: parametricism. These "styles" were both technical novelties that should have been used to reorient architecture, clarifying and improving the process of design. But they became objectives in themselves. Everyone marveled at the technical and representational results, without ever talking about the architecture itself.

NDA Which for you must have been just a repeat, since you had already seen the same thing happen during your years as a student at UC Berkeley, only with more primitive technologies.[15]

JS Exactly, and that reiteration of a failure is so frustrating. Luckily all of these dominating interests have an expiration date, but unfortunately, they are generally supplanted by yet another peripheral area of concern. In pedagogical terms, the problem is that the period of time when one of these interests dominates everything usually encompasses the whole career of a student. So, you see, here is the problem with architectural education today…

All of these peripheral interests are valid in themselves, and these were particularly important technical novelties. They play a key role in understanding, thinking about, and producing architecture, as you said, Elisa. It is only when they become "isms" that architecture disappears. I am afraid that a lot of what makes up the discourse de rigueur today, under the umbrella of "the social," is just another twist in this story.

Academic discussions about architecture are now focused on the pressing social problems of advanced contemporary societies. But they happen without concurrent, serious research on how, what, where, or when architecture can effectively affect the resolution of social problems positively. The discussion needs to be centered on the attributes or potentials of architecture that we need to know and understand how to articulate in the design process in order to improve the lives of people. However, since this is an arduous intellectual and technical territory to explore, and so far it has shown meager results, the focus usually remains in the more obvious, equally important, pre-design aspects; say, how to provide housing, spatial services, or physical infrastructures that address social or cultural needs. The truth remains, though, that the definition of a social demand, and the appropriate distribution of resources to support and implement it properly, remains purely political in nature. These aspects of design are, to be sure, very important for an architect to know well. But they must take place, always, prior to the specific and unique act of design that the architect is asked to provide. The issues are then explored mostly conceptually rather than through actual design practice.

We need to think seriously about how to help students understand the pertinent, effective tools that produce social change, which are not mainly the products of their design. This belief we are instilling in them that design itself will produce the social change they want will only produce frustration and more of that cynicism you alluded to, Nicolás. It is sad and worrisome for me to see a repetition of what I was already part of in the '70s.

NDA We are sunken in this brand of populism that clouts our ability—or ideological willingness—to understand all the ways in which architecture can be powerful.

JS Architecture can be relevant in its own way. And no one knows more about architecture than architects. If some people don't like the work of architects, that is a different problem. But what architecture as a discipline understands better than any other, through the organization of space and the forms that shape it and allow it to signify, is what gives it a certain autonomy.

NDA Or maybe *leverage* is a better word?

JS Yes, *leverage* is better, because what I am describing is more fragile. There are forces that disrupt architecture and others that make it reconfigure itself, as we were seeing with digitalization back then, and perhaps still see today. But architecture has to look within, because technical or societal changes don't necessarily affect the problems that the architect has historically been best equipped to solve.

3. The Inevitability of Form Giving

ES Nicolás, we can answer your earlier question about how Jorge dealt with this chaotic moment in architecture during his chairmanship by mentioning some of the people he invited to the GSD as chairman. I was an MArch I student back then, and I only had one optional upper-level design studio because I decided to do the exchange program at ETH Zürich for a year, which was a fantastic opportunity the school provided. But from your years, Jorge, I remember Gonzalo Byrne from Portugal, Jürgen Meyer from Germany, and the architect that had done the Whale in the Netherlands.

JS Ah yes, Willem Neutelings; he was so good! I haven't followed him for some time, but he was a very intelligent architect.

ES There was also Sauerbruch Hutton. Who else?

JS I also invited some Latin Americans, as you may remember! [*laughs*]

ES That is where I was going! You invited Alejandro Aravena. That was the one option studio that I took at the GSD, and it was the first studio that Aravena taught. I remember you telling me the story of how you found him. You went to Chile to talk with Matias Klotz...

JS Well, not really to talk to Matias. It was a trip to visit the built work of candidates preselected for the Mies van der Rohe Prize for Latin American Architecture. I was a member of the jury for two years. Matias Klotz had been preselected, so we had to meet him and go see his work in person. However, wherever I was, I would ask around about who were the best young architects. This is also how I discovered Alexia León in Peru, whom I invited to teach at GSD. She had designed a little house on the beach that was absolutely exquisite.

When we were in Chile, I talked to Fernando Pérez Oyarzún, with whom I am very good friends and who was at that time the dean at the Pontificia Universidad Católica de Santiago. I asked him about the best young architects, and he said there was this "arquitecto muy joven," since he was really a young man, who had just done one building I should see. I went to see the building and I loved it. He had also written some very provocative and intelligent pieces that Fernando referred me to, and without even meeting him, I invited him to teach upon my return! He accepted, and one day my secretary at the GSD told me, "Mr. Aravena is here to see you." And there he was, the *joven arquitecto* with unruly hair and penetrating eyes!

Alejandro began to teach, and then he proposed to me this idea that he had come up with working with a Chilean graduate student at the Harvard Kennedy School, an engineer named Andrés Iacobelli. They were trying to figure out how they could use government subsidies that were available in Chile—and improperly used, in their view—to pursue a novel approach to the housing problem. It was very little money, something like $3,500 per house, but enough to jump-start a comprehensive approach to social housing in their context.

They were doing something important at that time, because they were trying to reignite architecture's role in the resolution of the social housing problem. This was a topic that had disappeared from the field. Social housing had been the most potent, signature promise of Modern architecture, but by the end of the twentieth century, it was perceived as its most blatant failure, unfairly in my view. Nonetheless, this was an inevitable conclusion given that the housing problem, as a sociopolitical problem, had never been worse. What was attractive for me about the project was that it attempted to bring architecture back into a playing field where the current players were politics, finance, and ideology. And it all started with what to do with that exiguous amount of money available per household.

It was very appropriate to revive this pursuit at Harvard. Elemental's starting point was a critique of Modern architecture's failures in regard to this topic, and our school is the one that brought all of this to the United States. So we agreed that Alejandro would run a design studio on the matter. This was continued by three consecutive studios in the following years that helped shape the whole Elemental undertaking.[16]

ES That first year that Alejandro taught at the GSD was the year I studied with him. He titled the studio Otherwiseness. It was a very intense year for me. It was the year of the conference on Latin American architecture at the GSD, through which we brought a lot of people, remember? We invited Nieto Sobejano, Enrique Brown, Abraham Zabludovsky—who was still alive—Matias Klotz, and others. It was also the year that I was run over by a van in LA!

JS Yes, that was the year in which, for a few long hours, I took you for dead! Now we can laugh about it but …

ES [*laughs*] Yes. That was … That all happened within one super-intense semester. I learned so much about Latin American architecture thanks to those opportunities. You supported us in everything. Apart from being chairman, you were also advisor to Latin American GSD. And my knowledge was so limited. I had studied chemistry and art history as an undergraduate, so I knew nothing about architecture or Latin American architecture. It was a very beautiful way to get to know Latin America.

Was Pablo Allard also involved with Elemental at the time?

JS Yes, although I think he was still a student in the Department of Urban Design. Alejandro and Andrés had a very strong, attractive idea, which was basically to use the exiguous amount of money that had been deemed useless until that point for a very different design approach. They proposed to spend it on the most basic and determinant urban elements of the city directly associated with housing, namely utilities, circulation, and the basic connections of these features to each building. They would also cover the cost of the kitchen and bathroom. The rest of the "architecture" was left to the recipients.

After laying out the utilities and other infrastructure, they could guide the recipients' interventions through basic design regulations. Owners could expand the units on the assigned sites, following certain formal and dimensional parameters. They thought of the project as a seed because it contained the DNA of a future still unknown. It maintained the idea of providing better, safer housing, while also embracing the reality of self-construction, which seemed inevitable at that point. But this entailed self-construction that was promoted around a structured operation, with regulations and guidelines prepared by architects and technical experts. The individual owner could act upon the design, which history has proven has always happened after occupation in housing projects.

Capital-*A* architecture in the Modern period had failed to address the housing problem partly because it had tried to do so with simplistic and ultimately poor urbanistic ideas that were supposed to change things through architecture itself. Because, as we've discussed, architecture is dependent on so many other forces, it needed to share the responsibility with these other forces. Hence why it was an interesting idea from the beginning to think about the relationships between building fabric, urban space or the overall physical context, and the funding available. They thought about housing differently but still from the perspective of the architecture discipline.

My personal interest in their approach was related to how they wanted to incorporate the material culture of the users to solve the problem at hand. Rather than presuming to correct or replace the habits, conventions, and desires of the users, they sought to strengthen them by providing the lacking layer of infrastructure.

ES I perfectly remember being in Piper Hall listening to the studio lottery during the fall of 2000. Monica Ponce de Leon was right behind me. I'll never forget when Aravena presented his option studio, and Monica said to me, "Elisa, that is super interesting. It would be in your interest to pick that studio." So I did, and it was a very important experience for me. He exposed us to authors from Latin America that I would have never read and Chilean architects, like Pérez Oyarzún or Rodrigo Pérez de Arce. Alejandro had recently published a book with Pérez Oyarzún titled *Los hechos de la arquitectura.*[17]

JS Yes, I have it. A wonderful book! It is the one I was referring to.

ES The whole studio prefigured the attitude of Elemental. The premise was to produce an architecture project that could not be designed another way. You had to pick an emergency where there were limited resources and time and distill an architectural intervention into its most essential form. I picked a major landslide that had just happened near Caracas. It had been a very serious event with a lot of deaths. It defined a before and an after for the city in 1999.

That experience introduced me to the informal city in a way that I had never seen at the GSD before. Then I went to Madrid to work with Rafael Moneo, and the Elemental competition came out. During one of my visits to Venezuela, after my interest in these issues had been sparked, I went to the barrio La Morán in Caracas, which is where I would end up working for several years when I moved to Venezuela. This experience completely informed my proposal for the Elemental competition. However, I remember having mixed feelings about the awarded projects. They didn't seem to coincide with what I had seen in Caracas. I did receive a mention from the jury though, and the whole experience with Alejandro left me with lingering questions and curiosities. It was the seed that helped me make the decision to move to Venezuela after my time in Rome.

JS Getting the competition to happen was its own adventure. Although the idea was very promising, you have to remember that Alejandro and Andrés were very young. Since the Elemental competition would have to involve the Chilean government directly, there was the matter of their proposition's credibility when the time came to actually make it happen. I went with them to Chile and we organized a whole program of lectures and conferences—some of which were given by Hashim Sarkis and me—and we met with all sorts of political figures: the minister of commerce, the minister of the economy, the minister of housing, the president of the university, two or three banks, and of course the church! [*laughs*].

NDA You wouldn't have missed that last one.

JS Yes, there was a Catholic foundation, too. I thought that all those hours I spent reading the proceedings of the Council of Trent to understand how the Baroque artist had to persuade the recipient of the message finally paid off. Only this time the tables were turned; I had to persuade the Church itself!

To these political figures, I represented Harvard's authentication of these young Chileans that were working intelligently on a very noble cause. And it worked! Through that trip they were able to access more than enough money. Along with that, Chilean institutions and Harvard organized the international competition Elemental. I became the president of the jury, and they asked me to put together the rest of the jury. We invited Rafael Moneo, Paulo Mendes da Rocha, Pérez Oyarzún, Enrique Brown, and Jacques Herzog, who unfortunately could not attend and was replaced by Luis Fernandez-Galiano, the editor of *Arquitectura Viva*.

Through a lucky coincidence, this also took place a short time after David Rockefeller decided to fund a center focused on Latin American architecture at Harvard. A few years earlier, Harvard President Neil Rudenstine had called upon me and some others to make the center happen. When Elemental took shape a few years later, I brought the project into the center, which became one of the sponsors of the competition. This was one of their first great international projects.

The competition was impressive. There were about five hundred entries from all over the world, and we had organized a second tier for students who saw the prize as an opportunity to work with the architects that won one of the competition sites. It was a very well-organized project with a clear understanding of how its implementation would play out in the local conditions of Chile. Finally, an example! I can only take the credit for having given them a hand and opening a door here and there, but what they did was theirs, and it was amazing.

What was important about Alejandro and Andrés's proposal was that it began with the premise that architecture, with a capital *A*, or whatever you want to call it, needed to be central if we were to address the issue of social housing again. It implied that architecture should assume the roles and responsibilities it was capable of assuming, leaving the power plays for the politicians, economists, and the other forces that manifest themselves in practice. It stated that we had to place an architecture into the mix that gave a fresh understanding of what the parameters were. There was no other way to do this!

Alejandro was very convincing. I agreed with him that we needed to have a better understanding of the relationship between architecture and broader social issues; we needed to work within the limits of architecture to deploy its power and resources more wisely, precisely, and efficiently within that broader context. Of course, we were all aware that there would be risks involved, and in fact, in the end there were many things that didn't work, but this is not the occasion to go into detail about this.

NDA It was an attempt to deliver the core values of architecture by once more making the architect a proactive social and political actor in his context, a historically relevant role that we often oversee. And yet the result looked very different from what most would associate with capital-*A* architecture.

JS You are right, and in some respects the result was disappointing. But the process took us a step further. We were in another place once the cycle ended, with a better comprehension of the problem and tests of some of the project's successful aspects that we could build upon.

It was a learning experience, particularly for some of us involved in the process. I remember that when we would go to Chile for the Elemental project, we would visit the *barriadas*—large spontaneous settlements on the flanks of the mountains around Santiago. We would talk to community leaders, and it was fantastic; for me it was a lesson in architecture. All they talked about was architecture, even if it did not sound like that at the time. It was in their own language, of course, but the discussion was not only about problems like electric cabling through the streets or figuring out the best way to install gutters—which, by the way, are architectural problems in their own right, too. There was also already a concern and consciousness about how all of it would work together as a whole: as public space, as attractive buildings, and as a collective effort that would make people proud and happy.

The community had already had frustrating experiences in which problems had been solved, but the result was somehow "unsatisfactory." Someone even said ugly! The people building these informal settlements were starting from nothing other than their own experience of living in cities and towns, because no one gave them any assistance. They had taken lands, and they were doing a pretty decent job trying to adapt what they had seen working in other places and adjust them to their current circumstances. They were building the city themselves. They had construction manuals that they referred to, friends that came to lend a hand based on what they knew from their trade, and so on. But they were full of questions and reasoning. They talked about the orientation of streets and whether they should be straight or curved given that they were at the base of a hill. They talked about sidewalks and curbs, not just functionally but in terms of how they could better serve to connect one another and be used as part of the public realm. There was even talk about what a dignified building facade should look like.

Everything was constantly discussed, grounded mainly on the pressing functional and technical problems they encountered. However, everything was at some point connected with issues of representation, form, and beauty. The idea that an architect should be involved in the process was very clear to everyone. But the architect has to know where and how to enter the problem, and where to position himself. All of these opportunities had been left aside because public housing problems were automatically blamed on Modernist architectural design during the first postwar period of housing experiments. This was a blame that architects did not have the arguments to successfully counter. Their naivete, born out of their spectacularly self-centered, avant-garde demeanor, ignored the other factors that played a role in these failures.

ES The Elemental case is very particular to the realities of Chile, but there are so many examples in Latin America of successful, self-built neighborhoods where much of what you are describing becomes evident. There is Ciudad Neza in Mexico City, which has been studied and documented by José Castillo, and also Villa El Salvador in Lima.

NDA I think what the Elemental case shows us is the idea that architecture can meaningfully resolve a series of issues about the built environment that are placed in front of it by other forces in society. It is also an example of what you mentioned earlier, Elisa, about an architecture that is not formally clear from the beginning, but it discovers this important formal definition through the iterative design process that coincides with this deep engagement with a context.

JS Our current discourse has become extremely convoluted, but you know, in the end, architecture is actually not *sooo* difficult. It is complex, for sure, but not complicated.

NDA [*laughs*]

JS I am serious! We have made it very complicated. Of course, one major difficulty of architecture is in how much context it has to deal with because buildings are unavoidable objects. It's in the nature of architecture to be related to many other practices. However, this actually creates many limitations around what architects are capable of addressing, not the other way around. Architecture is not such a mysterious practice in itself. Let me be clear, architecture is also about ideas and the aspirations that touch on politics, art, and pleasure. But at its core, it is always and ever, unavoidably, just a building practice of great power.

ES [*smiles*] Yes, that is very true.

JS I should be careful with my words, but there is a level of common sense in architecture that is lost in all of these discussions we have today. The conversations I had in the *barriadas* in Chile, which were carried out in the most simple of terms, contained ideas that any sensible architect would have thought of if they had to address the same issues. What was very interesting and encouraging in these Chilean communities was that, after having struggled to "make a city" with their own hands, they realized that they needed additional tools and expertise. This was precisely because, as users of the built environment, they were posing the right urban and architectural questions.

ES Yes, absolutely. I think something that we often lose sight of is that in all of these conversations, the architect is the only person that is thinking about the form that can synthesize those concerns. It is so ingrained in us that we believe everyone else thinks that way too.

We go and talk to people, and in our mind, we are giving form to everything they are saying. We give form to each instruction we hear. Other professions don't have that capacity, and I think this is where an architect's agency lies. This is what makes us valuable.

JS Yes! I will never tire of repeating the same thing: architects produce form. That is what they concretely do. Always. You may remember that these were pretty much the first words of "The Muses Are Not Amused," when I delivered it as my chairmanship farewell speech in 2002. The architect's lens is always focused on form, and his only distinctive skill is knowing how to generate and get architectural forms built. Not form in general, but architectural form specifically, which has to do with space, use, scale, and dimension. This is what is distinctive about our discipline. Form can then be studied autonomously and directly applied to practice, can't it? The formal lens is what allows the architect to understand the myriad of complex situations that are presented to him, whether these are anthropological, sociological, economic, aesthetic, technological, or otherwise.

You know, I've never understood this whole debate about the relationship between architecture and society. This is something that I don't even think about, because for me it is so obvious that architecture is tied to the social in everything it does. Architects do not create the need for buildings; they do not finance projects; they do not mix concrete or lay out bricks; they do not participate in the sale and profits of an architectural work. However, architects do depend entirely on all of those external forces—and many more—to do their work. So why do we need so many discussions about the relationships between architecture and "the social"? I think the big issue with this question is that it gets answered, as it has for a while now, by jumping toward an idea of what architecture should do that is completely outside of the bounds of what architecture is best at doing.

NDA Architecture is really effective when it is aligned with the right set of powers that are able to implement the ideas and solutions it generates. This is perhaps less popular or palatable as an answer in the highly politicized cultural climate that we live in. It's easier to say something broad and vague about how architects can single-handedly solve problems that they cannot, or to say they can't do anything at all, which is the opposing claim.

ES Architecture is a profession that I feel is profoundly in crisis. And nonetheless, the possible contribution that architects could make to address urgent topics is huge. There is so much more sensitivity right now toward social issues, but little attention is paid to their spatial dimension, which is such a fundamental part of why social injustices persist. Mechanisms and processes that could facilitate such projects need more attention. I feel like part of the fault falls on us because for many years, we have celebrated the model of the star architect instead of the public-servant architect. We need to explore new roles if we want to advance pertinent architectures, especially in the United States.

Engaging with you on this book has been very helpful in organizing what I've been thinking about myself. I recall Stan Allen's essay "From Object to Field," in which he talks about "field conditions" and the circumstances that shape how we work.[18] I use this essay a lot with my students, because Allen talks about the fact that there is much more out there in the field than we acknowledge, and there are many things that concern space or are the subject of design that are not being taken into consideration. He says the world is full of under-explored domains, which I believe relates to our discussion.

I think we can synthesize the ideas we have been talking about, which are also found in your writings, as follows: There is always a condition from which to think about architecture that, in your case, for example, is the study of how material culture performs across history. This is, without a doubt, a category that produces material for you to think and work within the domain of architecture.

Let's add another example: Alejandro Aravena's study about the architecture that results from a specific economic reality and housing need. Aravena creates something architectural using very real data. Thinking about my work involving *El Camino a Monte Albán*, that condition is an ancestral ritual with an important human force that has physical and spatial demands. There are also the political mandates that lead Baroque architects to communicate certain religious messages through architecture.

But what falls outside the list of appropriate conditions that can be the primary drivers of the creation of architecture? This is the hard question. However, I think it's all of these marginal explorations in the academy, which are looking for a condition within peripheries, that have drifted dangerously far from what it means to produce architecture. To cite some of the things we have already mentioned, this includes the autonomous project, parametricism, the Conceptual approach, or the "blobs" of the digital revolution.

JS The way we can parse out this distinction is to find out whether these external conditions that determine the ways in which we generate a design *actually* affect the making of buildings and cities in a significant way.

ES One phrase that I really liked from your afterword to *Unprecedented Realism* is: "The best and most honest way to change the world is to participate in processes that may lead to architecture."[19]

NDA Yes!

ES That's a great line, and it kind of sums up what you're saying. Since I reread the afterword, I've been reflecting on what motivated you to delve into, for example, the Guaraní culture, or the Getty Villa. I've been asking, How have these things contributed to your act of making architecture? Then of course, I started to ask myself the same questions.

I would position my pedagogical approach in a similar arena. The work I have been doing with neighborhoods starts in a concrete reality determined by context. I often manage to match my thesis students with an existing organization or community so they can rehearse a similar approach. They go to the neighborhood often and engage in conversations with people who are not architects. From there, very real conditions emerge that they start to synthesize into form. The students begin to think as an architect while they listen to all of these issues that determine the shape of space and the city.

JS Right. The force with which reality leads you to produce architecture is interesting. I agree with you that an extreme level of pragmatic reality is very productive for pedagogy at this present moment, in which we are trying to reposition architecture. You can learn architecture and all of its autonomous discourses in a much less questionable way.

I feel tempted to open up another line of discussion by reminding you that at some point in the mid-'80s, Rodolfo [Machado] coined the term "unprecedented realism" to describe our work using this brilliant, paradoxical play on words. But I will not go there. I'll just say that the 1995 monograph of our work that you mentioned can provide a better understanding of where my comments on "the real" and "realism" are anchored.

ES From a pedagogical point of view, I think this approach allows you to get the students to the point much quicker.

JS Many people think that these problems are so challenging and constrained, that they contain very few possibilities. But the truth is quite the opposite: the incontrovertible veracity of facts in your face is what gives you the energy to find the right architectural or urban solution. I would not say that this confrontation with raw reality is indispensable in pedagogy, but I am certainly convinced that it would be greatly therapeutic in architecture schools within the United States at the present time.

ES This approach actually speeds up that induction process a lot. It gives you the opportunity to spend a lot of time at the beginning discussing things that don't rely on subjective interpretation. The student gathers a sufficient amount of criteria and is then able to imagine something and turn this idea into architecture. The answers they find are quite obvious. When they get to the moment of exploring what we call the "domain" of architecture, a very good broth has been created in order to start cooking. Architecture is produced following its own logic and language, but it is produced on a very solid and real foundation.

I am very excited about where the conversation and input goes when I work with my students this way. Many people tell you that this is about expanding the agency of architecture, but I don't agree. I feel that it is a way of focusing on architecture's greatest strength.

JS I agree.

ES I recently came across an interview with Olafur Eliasson in which he talks about what triggers an artist. He says that the trigger is tied to being very interested and curious about the present. This does not exclude investigations of the past, but he explains that we have an additional duty to sniff out what is going on in the present.

I think this is very important, and I would add that this search needs to be done with a temporary suspension of judgment because this is the only way we can identify the opportunities to produce architecture; the only way we can come up with innovative solutions to new problems. This is an interesting way to encourage original architectural thinking today, as opposed to pedagogies that put so much emphasis on referents or typologies. If we are attuned to the changes and the opportunities for the relevance of architecture to be heightened, all these other kinds of knowledge acquire a renewed relevance.

NDA I agree, although part of my concern right now is that, even if there is a lot of commitment to causes that feel urgent, we are discouraged from suspending our judgment in order to read the situation. We are actually pressed to be immediately critical of situations in the present and express ourselves on political terms, even if we don't understand them very well. And I think this is a very different attitude from the one you are describing. Everything right now is about dictating positions on the present rather than trying to understand why certain things are happening. It is one thing to be curious and to want to fill yourself with the present. It's another thing to want to censor right off the bat, pushed by groupthink and the fear of ostracization.

JS The problem is that in the society in which we live today, the present is totally elusive. Architecture is very concrete and its "present" is very long—longer than the span of the "presence" of human beings until now. A piece of architecture remains, and its rate of change is generally very slow. When the rate of change in society was also very slow, it allowed you to produce a built environment that was designed very coherently. The elusiveness of the present is stronger and more evident today than it was for architects in the Renaissance and Baroque periods, or even for those up to the nineteenth century. This makes our work more tentative and riskier today. The conditions that determine this situation are hard to influence. So yes, I think we have to engage the present also because it is the only thing we have. But this puts us in a very fragile situation. This is why history is so important, particularly if we move beyond the study of history as a search for inspiration and use it to understand how the different ways humans have interacted with one another across time impacts material culture.

ES Yes, I understand.

JS Still, we cannot talk about the importance of history and how it relates to a focus on the present—with the intrinsic tensions that it involves—without engaging the third temporal component that is always looming in the mind of the architect: the future!

As architects we cannot escape the complex interactions within this trio that define and problematize what "the present" actually is. Architects simultaneously yearn for and are terrified of the future. They find themselves in this extreme situation of not being able to control the social, cultural, and economic forces that generate the need for architecture. Like any human, they have no capacity to foresee the future. It is always unknown, no matter what planners, economists, and politicians promise. This leaves architects with the present, which they abhor because the present is by definition "what is." In that sense, it is restrictive. Things are what they are in your face, and attempting to change them implies risk, uncertainty, and frustration.

The present is also a constant reminder that what architects do in the moment is only a hopeful representation of a possible future. The importance of what we do is not yet realized at the moment the work of the architect ends. Moreover, all we can do with the present is interpret it, which allows for selective decisions, omissions, preferences, and biases that make it *your version of the present*. At least since postmodernism, we are very aware and self-conscious of this distortion, the relativization of what facts are, even when they are right in front of you. This tends to paralyze, or at least disturb, the creative process. The most we can aspire to is to hope that the future will bring some clarity and comfort. That is what you want, because the product of your work, which is the project, only exists, realized as architecture, in the future, and it is built by other hands.

If a dilemma is a proposition that is very hard and uncomfortable to resolve between two alternatives, I would pose that in this *trilemma*—if you will allow me to use this etymologically correct yet horrendous neologism—the nature of time presented to us is unresolvable. It can only be dealt with by juggling the right kind of unstable equilibrium among its three components. This is something that will be, by necessity, variable depending on ever-changing contexts. An awareness of how this trilemma operates, of its intrinsic instability, can at least give us some peace of mind. This is because it confirms that the present is all we have to work with, and we have to accept that it cannot be disassociated from the unmovable past. The past cannot be changed or ignored, nor can it be validated by a future still becoming.

Notes

1 Jorge Silvetti, *Introductions*, ed. Rodolphe El-Khoury (Cambridge, MA: Harvard Graduate School of Design, 2004).

2 Jorge Silvetti, "The Muses Are Not Amused: Pandemonium in the House of Architecture," *Harvard Design Magazine,* no. 19 (2003): 22–33.

3 Christine Smith, "Foul Enormity or Grandiose Achievement? The Moral Problem of Size," in *Architecture in the Culture of Early Humanism: Ethics, Aesthetics, and Eloquence, 1400–1470* (New York, NY: Oxford University Press, 1992), 40–56.

4 Francesco Colonna, *Hypnerotomachia Poliphili: The Strife of Love in a Dream* (London: Thames and Hudson, 1999).

5 See Jorge Silvetti and Erika Naginski, "Architecture: The Reconception of History," in this volume, 215–271.

6 Ibid.

7 *DDes* stands for the Harvard Graduate School of Design's Doctor of Design Program.

8 See Bates Lowry, review of *The Cortile del Belvere*, by James S. Ackerman, *The Art Bulletin* 39, no. 2 (1957): 159–168, https://doi.org/10.1080/00043079.1957.11408380.

9 The conversation is referring to the course "The Agency of Mezcal in the Oaxaca Valley of Mexico," taught by Elisa Silva in the fall of 2018 at the Harvard Graduate School of Design.

10 Nikolaus Pevsner, *Esquema de la Arquitectura Europea,* trans. Rene Taylor (Buenos Aires: Editorial Infinito, 1957).

11 Michael Brenson, "The Messy Saga of 'Tilted Arc' Is Far from Over," *The New York Times*, April 2, 1989, https://www.nytimes.com/1989/04/02/arts/art-view-the-messy-saga-of-tilted-arc-is-far-from-over.html.

12 The Council of Trent was an ecumenical council that took place between 1545 and 1563 as a reaction to the Protestant Reformation. The discussion about the doctrines of the church that took place determined the direction taken by the Roman Catholic Church throughout the Counter Reformation.

13 Silvetti is referring to the retrospective exhibition of Charles Ray put on at the Metropolitan Museum of Art in 2022, titled *Charles Ray: Figure Ground.*

14 See Silvetti and Naginski, "Architecture: The Reconception of History," 299–339.

15 See Jorge Silvetti and Alfredo Thiermann, "Architecture: The Question of Method," in this volume, 49–96.

16 See Alejandro Aravena and Andrés Iacobelli, *ELEMENTAL—Manuel de Vivienda Incremental y Diseño Participativo* (Ostfildern: Hatje Cantz, 2012).

17 Fernando Pérez Oyarzún, Alejandro Aravena Mori, and José Quintanilla Chala, *Los hechos de la arquitectura* (Santiago de Chile: Ediciones ARQ; Escuela de Arquitectura, Pontificia Universidad Católica de Chile, 1999).

18 Stan Allen, "From Object to Field," *AD Architecture after Geometry*, Profile No. 127 (London: John Wiley & Sons, Ltd., 1997), 24–31.

19 Rodolfo Machado and Jorge Silvetti, afterword to *Unprecedented Realism*, ed. K. Michael Hays (New York, NY: Princeton Architectural Press, 1994), 262.

Afterword to *Unprecedented Realism*

RODOLFO MACHADO AND
JORGE SILVETTI, 1995

We have been asked to write an afterword to this book which, as a genre, would demand our comments on what precedes. Instead we prefer to use this opportunity to supplement the work of these writers who have so generously commented and interpreted our work, and to provide the reader with a brief account of where our thoughts and actions are in our present place and time. Nevertheless, while we wish not to refer specifically to the preceding writings, the fact is worth noticing that their authors' ages span four generations and describe paradigmatically the trajectory of American architectural thought over the last twenty years, into which our work is inextricably inscribed. It is to this intellectual milieu, which has influenced our own thought and actions, that we wish to direct the following comments and criticism.

The architecture perceived as the most advanced in the last twenty years in America has, to a large degree, been determined and dominated by a discourse that, perhaps for the first time, has looked at architecture from its outside and sought to understand it as a cultural and ideological practice. The chief manifestations of this discourse have been two newly reconfigured practices: theory and criticism.

After unquestionable successes, this latest version of theory and criticism has come to a dead end. This was predetermined by the irreconcilable contradiction between its outspoken vocation and its founding principle, which, until recently, have propelled it forward. Its vocation—a moralizing and romantic one (still walking along the fading trail of the neo-avant-garde)—is to insistently seek the most accurate representation of its times—the zeitgeist—and the imperatives it imposes on any cultural enterprise. Its foundation—a theoretical one. still reeling off unrealized and unimaginable consequences—is the devastating awareness (and the belated discovery for architecture) of the arbitrariness of the sign, the structural undecidability of meaning.

Together the vocation and the foundation are untenable. For how can one morally demand that architecture represent its historical-ideological essence, that it illustrate in the singular some particular interpretation of the world (fragmentation, indeterminacy, and difference are favorite examples today), that there be a sure and stable subject "correct" for architectural speculation (all other subjects having been relegated to retrogression) and at the same time, theoretically hold that there can be no authority that guarantees correctness, that there are only differences in the plural, "without a positive term"?

The coexistence and complicity of these two powerful energies, however incompatible they may be, have been and probably still are the dominant characteristic of the most "advanced" architectures of the last two decades. Postmodernism, poststructuralism, and deconstructivism in their diverse guises have tried to summarily settle the question in a single stroke of correct and incorrect, left and right, permissible and impermissible, and provide a noun (a label, a banner) that includes preselected positions as so many modulations or permutations of an imagined exemplary "critical practice."

And so the dominant discourse of architecture has been forced into an intellectual cul-de-sac, paralyzed architecture's ability to engage society, and helped confuse the role of the architect to the point of rendering it irrelevant. As all of this has become evident, so too the current unwillingness to recognize moral fallacies and practical errors has acted as an impediment to a real reformulation of the theory and practice of architecture in the real conditions of the world today. Thus in their retrenchment do the theoretically advanced architectures indeed seem to be among the most paternalistic and reactionary.

The task of repositioning architecture has not yet begun in the theoretical discourse but is nonetheless being decided de facto in the real world. It is with this long overdue repositioning in mind that we offer the following sketch of arguments as a postscript to this book. The arguments—or rather the assertions, polemical as they are—risk being seen as oblique, arrogant critiques of the preceding five contributions. But while we do not deny that we may disagree with some of the assertions made about our work in this book, we offer this outline more as a prefatory sketch for a book we may want to (but never will) write and for which the five contributions would be seen as long footnotes. Our main interest here vis-à-vis architecture at large and the world of theory and criticism in particular is to be as candid, plain, and blunt as possible, so that we may help expose the central myth of what passes as advanced architecture today: to claim that theoretical-political architecture requires one form to the exclusion of others is to claim that there can be no theoretical or political opposition to that claim. Whereas our intention in relation to the present book itself is to transmit the notion that our work is not only about the five aspects herein discussed—epistemology (Colquhoun), technique (el-Khoury), character (Baird), affects (el-Dahdah), and meaning (Hays)—but also about many other things. We must acknowledge also that the following assertions are mostly "arguing" with an exclusive (and narrow) American and American-inspired discourse, the cultural milieu where we act, and not necessarily with the arguments beard in Europe, Latin America, Asia—in short, in the vast "rest of the world."

For us the production of architecture is about the construction of the physical world as the setting of social and cultural life. This is not just one possible mode that architecture assumes alternatively with other modes that are solely about words, drawings, illustrations, and performances. Contrary to what is broadly proposed today, architecture cannot be many different things. To demand "dispersal," to insist on the erosion of disciplinary boundaries as the (paradoxically stable) content of architecture or (what often amounts to the same thing) to collapse architectural production into writing, painting, or graphic design is to foreclose on the more radical difference of architecture as one in a field of social practices. The real of architecture is ultimately constituted by what is built and the process that leads to it—its drawing, writings, thinking, research, negotiations, etc. that aim for and focus on the production of the built world. Along this line we construct our idea of architecture.

We believe that architecture's richness resides in the many "voices" it can speak within these boundaries. In this sense there are indeed many architectures; there are architectures of program, of style, of monumentality, of technology, of ethnicity and cultural identity, of taste, of pleasure and affect, of ostentation, and of simplicity. Diversity in architecture resides not in architecture's substance but in its expression. Within and from an architecture rigorously defined by the matter it manipulates and transforms—including the material of building and the "stuff" of architecture's own history—we can speak the diversity of culture.

We acknowledge that architecture is a constructed social practice that was codified in the Renaissance, constantly transformed thereafter, and that may not be applicable to present historical conditions. Thus the search for a redefinition or repositioning vis-à-vis other social practices seems both necessary and inevitable. With this, at times pressing realization, we understand the many recent attempts at such a redefinition and the many questions about the boundaries that historically have defined the architectural field of operation. And yet today, after observing and exploring those boundaries over the past decades, we feel confident to state that were some new "practice of architecture" to shift its interests to media that exclude building in the last instance (that is, to shift exclusively to cybernetics, virtual reality, drawings, temporary installations, or literature), we would not be interested to practice it. Our practice is concerned with the making of buildings and the physical spaces of public appearance. We are sure that buildings will always have important social, cultural, and economic significance and that somebody will be responsible for imagining them and building them. Repositioning an architecture that insists on buildings as cultural artifacts implies soundly regrounding architecture and staking out its new territory with respect to power, to art, and to scholarship. That is what we do and like to do both in theory and in practice.

Architecture is a weak device for socio-political criticism not only because its mode of expressing such dimensions is weak but, more importantly, because it is inefficient in effecting change when compared to other modes such as literature, painting, film, and, in particular, real political action, an option open to all citizens but rarely used by architects. Above all, this inefficiency is the direct result of the fact that the construction of the physical world is neither initiated nor controlled by architects; they are just part of a process in which they are often in conflict with other agents. It needs to be said without shame: architecture is always and necessarily implicated in the representation of power. The best and most honest way to change the world is to participate in processes that may lead to architecture. As far as criticism is concerned, architecture is only, but importantly, a strong self-critical device, constantly renovating its own mechanisms of production of form. In this respect, we believe in "the magic of architecture" as a metaphor for certain sensual and intellectual possibilities, but not in "architecture as magic," a currently prevalent yet unacknowledged belief in the incantatory powers of architecture, a belief that sees its manifestations (through drawings, models, installations, etc.) as miraculous invocations of philosophical and political ideals, as self-sufficient fulfillments of the "critical" capacities of architecture.

An architecture conceived in our terms does not partake in the alibis provided by the prevailing discourse of architects who avoid engagement with the reality of the problems and only illustrate the problems in their work. So, while we agree that the relationship between form and content is structurally arbitrary, we also know that it is historically and culturally motivated. Moreover, while we agree that architecture cannot change the world or the behavior of people, we do not imply that architecture is devoid of ethics. And furthermore, it is because we recognize that architecture, like any cultural product, has social power that we reject the idea that the architect is free to impose a political agenda on society. These are facts difficult to combine and articulate but, for us, they are inescapable. For this reason, we believe that the genesis of architectural form cannot be whimsical or indifferent to social and cultural conventions; for instance, architecture cannot be generated by an author's penciled scrawls on a piece of paper resulting from uncontrolled, nervous, and vibrant wrist movements, which are later geometrized and/or "architecturalized," or by pretending to erase the author by interposing mediating or "mechanical" generative systems, or by simply declaring it to be architecture. In short, an architecture engaged with society cannot be the result of conscious absurdity. All of this implies that just because the structure of the sign is arbitrary, the author is not therefore free to arbitrarily constitute the architectural sign.

How can architecture be proclaimed as "political" and at the same time all reference, all content, be declared "infinitely deferred"? There is no point in moralizing about "bad" precise representations versus "good" open-ended creations. We cannot cleanse the stigma of representation by washing our hands in the pool of pluralism. There is no longer an ideological advantage in declaring the author dead and the reader-in-process a new creator. Authorship is a responsibility, rhetoric is unavoidable. The only possibility to move out of the deadlock produced by the contradictory demands for a simultaneous expression of the zeitgeist and a formal pluralism is to accept representation (it is inevitable in architecture) and to effect it without moralizing intent but rather with technical skill—with the specifically architectural techniques, technologies, and paradigms. The locus for ethics is in the professional conduct and integrity of the architect, not in the forms produced.

While an idea of "process" has been emphasized lately as the proper modality of architecture in a simplistic opposition to the idea of "product," we suspect that its emphasis has been strategic—that is, devised in order to bypass the inevitable fact that architecture must always commit itself to a product, that architects must commit themselves in each instance to a form and to an expression. In architecture, something always has to be designed, detailed, "spec'ed," bid, built, and paid for—something that is concrete and finite, whether or not the object "looks" indefinite, fragmentary, or unfinished, or whatever rhetorical "trope" it wishes to deploy. A product is necessary and, if architecture is to address and deal with socio-cultural and political problems, a product must be the ultimate goal of architectural theory and practice.

Architecture cannot move one more step forward without putting back on the table the issue of popular culture, so much repressed by the current elite, this time as an integral part of the true process of design.

Taste and beauty are anathema to current theory. There are good reasons for having questioned their authority and their politics up to this point, but it is undeniable that in their absence have rushed in untenable and short-lived banalities. The void remains. Collective memories and myths, desire and pleasure—these are good candidates for renaming the perennial forces that are at the bottom of ideological constructs such as beauty and taste. Among them, the collective socio-cultural yearning for the monumental and the colossal and the exaltation of the individual sensory experience of space (not just visual, but tactile and acoustic), today so repressed by the advanced architectures, are anthropologically, psychologically, and artistically correct issues to repropose to fill the void.

To the extent that the basic knowledge of an architect is no longer technique and theory but exclusively theory and criticism, and to the extent that theory and criticism have not been normative but rather have suspended or negated all norms, it is not surprising that architects professing such "theoretical knowledge" today have nothing concrete or socially valuable to offer as architects, and that, inevitably, they lose or give away their social and professional power. In architecture, concrete knowledge about architecture is empowering, rather than knowledge about power itself. But there is ignorance in architecture today: ignorance of architecture's own history, of its constitutive technologies and languages, of its real processes. The self-denial of the reasons for this weakening, hidden behind a conscious "avant-garde" decision to abandon the mainstream of the profession, has led architects to propose models of "marginality" as alternative critical practices. But marginality can be only a personal, individual choice, grounded in knowledge about architecture, and not a program of action for a profession, a normative theory, or a system of education. Marginality offered as a solution to the current problems of architecture is profoundly escapist.

The old dichotomy between form and function had been broken, we thought, with the reformulation of a richer and more complex idea of typology as a cultural phenomenon. Type abandons metaphysics, as history has doubly demonstrated: by its diachronic indifference to function and detachment from style on the one hand, and by its synchronic dependence (at the concrete and opportune moment of its appearance) on the programmatic demand on the other. Thus the opposition between "formalism" and "programmatics"—the controversy that is being revived these days in advanced circles under different guises as to whether architecture is formally "autonomous" or programmatically generated—is reductive and retrograde, as most revivals are.

Theory can no longer be separated from practice. Both the structuralist and poststructuralist moments of theory have run their respective courses. While theorizing the structural conditions within which architecture produces itself did help to articulate the complex mechanisms of production, and while theorizing the ideological dimensions of architecture did reveal the inescapably political nature of all architecture, most structuralist and poststructuralist positions have come to regard theory as separate, distant, and detached from the act of making—in fact indifferent and even antithetical to any instrumental or operational role. On the other hand, much of the would-be-progressive architectural profession has confiscated the more fashionable aspects of theory in a deplorable way, distorting theory's undeniable contributions. Ultimately, the necessary distance that theory took from its object of study became its undoing, producing the high-flown and self-fulfilling concerns of a detached elite that evolved into a self-perpetuating, self-congratulating group of experts. *In order to reposition architecture in the field of social practices it ought to develop a theory that inhabits practice itself.* Toward this, we believe that we can commence with certain strategic technico-artistic moves that allow and call for calculated action. "Unprecedented realism," however elusive this term still is for us, serves to articulate such action.

Fig. 1 John Stuart Gibson (American, b. 1958). *Bright Green Rings and Balls*, 1989. Oil on linen, approx. 46" x 67".

Figs. 1–5 MVRDV, Stack Attack.

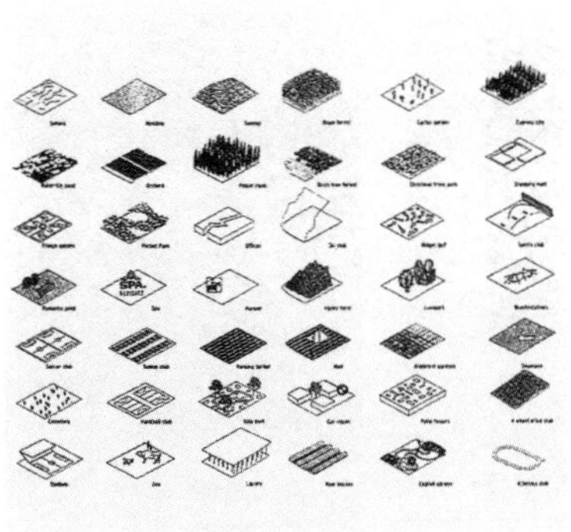

1

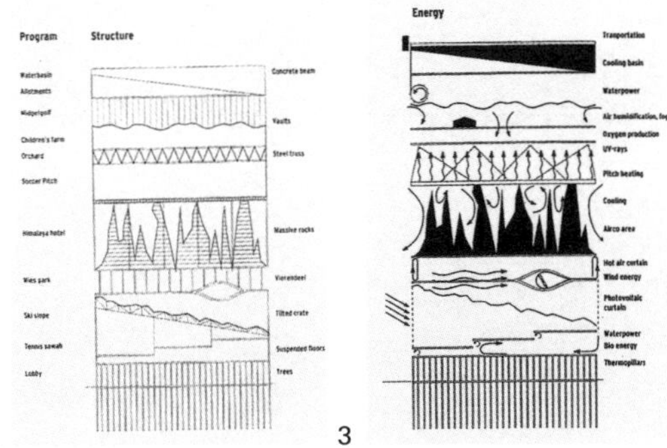

2 3

The Muses Are Not Amused: Pandemonium in the House of Architecture

JORGE SILVETTI, 2003

This essay was first presented as the Gropius Lecture at Harvard Graduate School of Design in April 2002, on the occasion of the School's honoring Professor Silvetti for his seven years as chairman of the Department of Architecture. The lecture was propelled by almost 200 images, only a fraction of which can be reproduced here; the text therefore required appropriate modification. In the spring of 2003, Professor Silvetti added a postscript outlining possible implications of his talk.

If there is one consistent trait that propels my intellectual and artistic pursuits, it is a desire to explore, explain, and experiment with all the forces that converge in the conception, imagination, and proposition of architectural form, ultimately to produce it and have it perform. The fundamental and specific thing that we architects do is imagine and produce architectural form. The "form" I am talking about is not just concerned with a priori elaborated aesthetic stances or received vocabularies. Rather, it is architectural form that involves all the forces that converge in the final result, be they cultural, social, economic, or ideological as well as technical or methodological. Thus language, buildings, topography, art, fashion, TV and movies, new and old materials—just to name some of all that is form and begets form—have been and still are the flora and fauna that inhabit and nourish and topography of my intellectual path. Moreover, in the cases that interest me, that effort of producing form happens because the architect has a will to produce this form, to author it, be it by necessity, interest, or irrepressible desire.

This introductory self-profile is necessary because it helps explain why I am distraught about what I perceive to be a progressive dissipation of the centrality of our mission as educators to teach and learn rigorously and vigorously about form-making and its consequences, a process that is becoming secondary and peripheral. I consider this ever-increasing neglect, which I see in design school reviews, in writings, and in discussions, as nothing less than suicidal for a profession whose creativity and standing depends ultimately on its absolute command of this unique and difficult task. The conditions under which this progressive loss takes place are doubly unfortunate because they occur under the deceiving euphoria of a proliferation of different modes, approaches, and techniques of form-production that purport to have eased and multiplied our abilities to generate form. Yet, as I see it, they instead are turning the architect into a dazed observer of seductive wonders.

Nevertheless, during this past decade that serves as the somewhat arbitrary period

Figs. 4–5 MVRDV, Stack Attack.

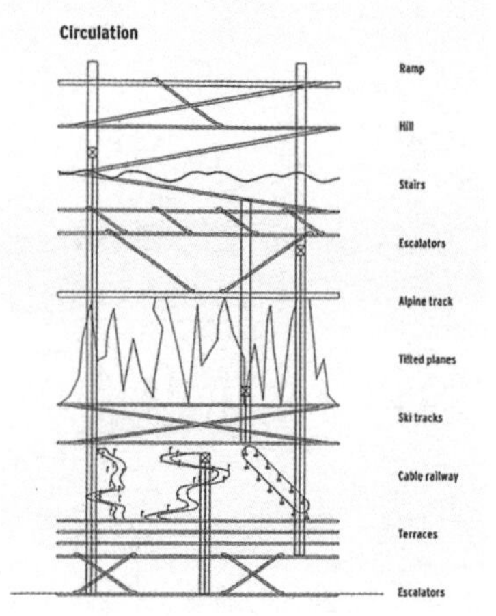

4

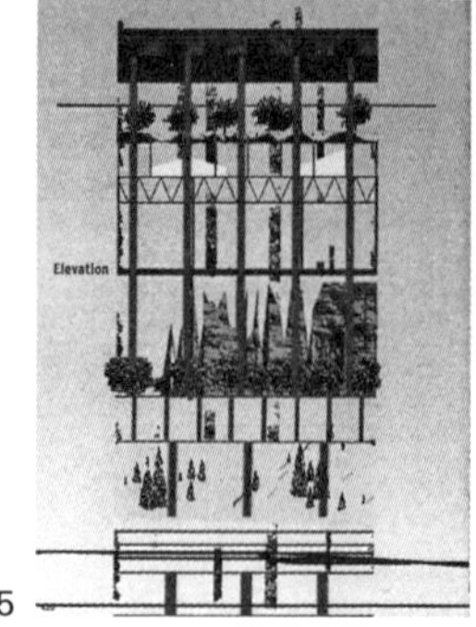

5

that provides my cases, we have had evidence that architecture matters, and that it is through its forms that it impresses us. Such evidence is the result of an accumulation of events that have been moving and enlightening both in joyful and painful ways for architecture and in particular architecture's physical presence in the city. And since I want to focus not on specific building and architects, but instead on design strategies and techniques that produce architectural form, and the ideas and ideologies behind them, suffice it to say that the period and corpus I am looking at could be bracketed by the exultant irruption in the world and in our imagination of the Guggenheim Bilbao and by the wound to our affects left by the physical consequences of the September 11 attack, the disappearance of two buildings we did not know we would miss so much.

Today, I will focus mainly on the issues involved in the production of form and the designer's will to produce it within academia. In this context, the theoretical underpinnings reflect my continuing preoccupation with understanding how ideas are represented and imbedded in architecture and how to teach this aspect of the process of design. I have chosen four cases that I believe present a wide spectrum of that aspect of the creative process. Of course there have been many others things of importance going on in the past decade that affect this process and that would certainly be worth discussing, mostly in technology and building construction, and in sustainability and the environment. But in my view these are ultimately dependent for their success on the ability with which architects transcend their purely technical achievements and give them intentional and adequate form.

My victims today are: first, a much discussed trend (or method?) for which we have no official name and meager literature but which one of my colleagues has called "Programism"[1]; second, a widespread mode of production of architecture that has hit schools at a high intellectual level, mostly as a topic for analysis, and which the architectural and general media has called "Thematization"; third, "Blobs"; and fourth "Literalism" in architectural representation. This is an odd grouping of heterogenous "architectures" that nevertheless share common traits. Ultimately they will help me open up the discussion to the larger issue of what the task of Architectural Theory could be in the coming years.

PROGRAMISM

First "Programism," the current trend that derives from an over-enthusiastic embrace of the otherwise healthy revisitation of the idea of "program" (as opposed to "function") as the generator of architecture, program understood as a protocol of complex nonlinear conglomerates of information that animates, inspires, impacts, grounds, influences, and colors a design, a building, or any physical condition for habitation. The vagueness in trying to define it is part of its attraction and peril.

"Programism" is the extreme development of a tendency to accumulate and manipulate information that, by the sheer power of

Fig. 6 Hameau de la Reine, Versailles, France.
Fig. 7 New York, New York Hotel, Las Vegas.

its quantity, uncritical method of being gathered, apparent authority as "neutral data," and compelling graphic representation becomes, with little transformation, the very form of the architecture proposed or its figurative inspiration (Figs. 1–5). This bizarre development belongs more to the realm of primitive magic than of design, since it relies on sympathies between diverse media that seem to act interchangeably as cause-and-effects agents—the "form" of the data matrixes or charts producing the form of the architecture, and in turn, the "form" of such architecture supposedly inducing the "actions" promoted by the program.

We can take this as a first example of a process that potentially exonerates the architect from his or her creative role. But behind this surrender also lies a suspect methodological operation that assumes that an arbitrary graphic rearrangement of data, coordination of figures, and composition of data in charts automatically provide the solution to the very problems they contain. Crass empiricism, tautological doctrine of inference, this poverty of imagination is not too far from the ideological structure of the well-established, worn out, and discredited methodological doctrines of the recent past, such as those of the Pattern Language or General Systems theories. In all this we relive the Sixties naiveté about the creative process, and it is not surprising that "the program" was also first elevated to primacy then.

I am not ready to discard entirely what is still an in-process development based on an unimpeachable initial consideration of program, but as one witnesses the steady spread of this idea as a mindless method of design based on graphic mimesis, one's uneasiness over the resulting undermining of our abilities grows.

To be convincing and useful, Programism would have to be intellectually more serious about how to assess the quality of data it uses and how to articulate intelligently the passage from data to form, which is not more or less that the quintessential and minimum ability that an architect ought to display, but which would require, as always, hard work, knowledge about architecture's own history, rigor, imagination, and the cultivation of the creative talents, rather than the automatisms that so far typify its moves.

THEMATIZATION

"Thematization" is, surprisingly as we will see, a mirror image of "Programism," operating as the latter's simile or analogue.[2] "Thematization" was not coined specifically to define this mode of operation in architecture and planning, but rather (and significantly) it was borrowed from marketing and advertising, which coined it to identify very particular developments called "theme parks." The reasons are clear.

The idea is simple but powerful and implies that architectural design is guided by the goal of exerting total control on all forms of an environment, not only on its physical vocabulary and its syntax, but also on its messages themselves, which means that an appropriate rhetoric is required within well-

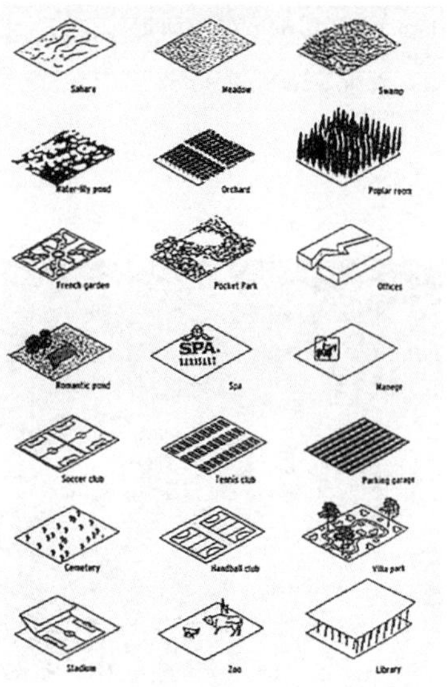

8

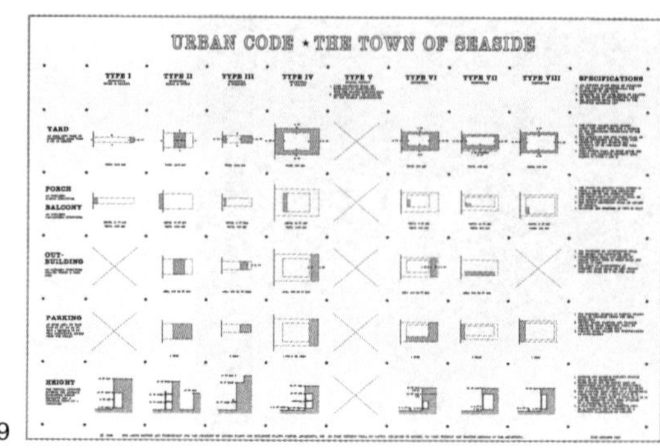

9

Fig. 8 MVRDV, Stack Attack.
Fig. 9 Andrés Duany and Elizabeth Plater-Zyberk (DPZ), Urban Code, The Town of Seaside.

defined physical precincts. Importantly, whether its general sources of referents come from either historical precedents or popular culture, its vehicle is always architecture itself. Its aim is to conjure up something that cannot be present, either because it exists only in the past, in memory, or in literary fiction, or because, while contemporaneous, it exists in some exotic, far-off, or inaccessible place.

With these goals as guides, Thematization's formal operations are kept to a minimum, since it seeks to shorten the distance between the model used as referent and the architecture produced to invoke it, and aims to elicit in the beholder either the pleasure of a momentary, playful, and contrived enactment or the delusion of the restitution of a whole way of life and its values. The difference between these two effects is fundamental enough to warrant an attempt to define them as distinct models of Thematization. And for that, good old rhetoric serves us best to sort it out, since it provides us with the figures of *parody* and *mimesis* to circumscribe with some precision a typology of this rather complex set of phenomena and their correspondent ideological consequences.

Here a bit of history would help. Alluding to a preexisting or contiguous architecture is not new in architecture. We could go back to Imperial Rome and interpret some of Hadrian's efforts at Tivoli intended to evoke his favorite spots in his Mediterranean domains, but indeed Hadrian's is too sophisticated, erudite, and subtle an operation for my current purposes. Marie Antoinette's *hameau* at Versailles is the classic example, and it is more directly related to Thematization (Fig. 6). It was the outpost retreat of the Queen, where she and her guests could relieve their boredom and indulge in the silly game of acting like peasants.

It has come all the way to us reincarnated in the modern theme park, of which the supreme example is Las Vegas (Fig. 7)—not just a theme park, but a whole city whose success relies on the extravagant idea of creating a heterogeneous conglomerate of adjacent "theme" experiences. Unlike Marie Antoinette's *hameau*, which was private entertainment by means of mimesis, we have now mass entertainment by means of parody.

On the other side of these two examples driven by the forces of "Thematization for entertainment" is a more troubling instance that I would call "Thematization for living," and that, with humorlessness, pomposity, and unbearable earnestness, attempts to occupy, by right, the title of architecture. Although it has been around for some time, it has only recently been catapulted to the fore because of its sudden, uneasy, double fame of being both the most contemporary example of Thematization and successful real estate development.

Now on the one hand, in the two previous cases of Las Vegas and Versailles, the fakery of thematic architecture is not only overt but also actually underlined by the way in which it is deployed, always within well-confined boundaries that provide the necessary thresholds to promote and effectively induce the suspension of disbelief that makes them palatable.

Fig. 10 Oosterhuis, Saltwater Pavilion, Neeltje Jans, Netherlands, 1998.
Fig. 11 UN Studio, Pavilion Triennial, Milan, 1996.

10

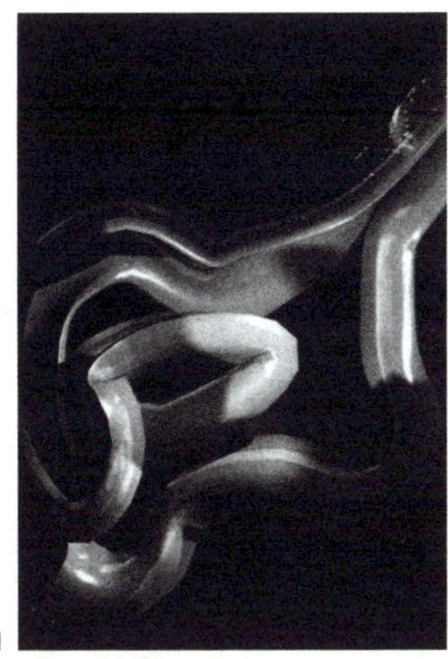

11

"Thematization for living," on the other hand, implied a double fakery: the formal operation of mimicking a well-known architecture and the promise that such architecture will deliver a predetermined, good way of life. Or to put it in another way, the attempt at mimesis is total—not just of forms but also of actions and contents. "Thematization for living" not only suppresses disbelief but also posits amnesia as the necessary condition to permit moralistic prescription of the way of life it wants to enforce (Fig. 8).

The two best examples, which have been gestating for at least two decades but which have come into full being in the past few years, are the extreme contextualism that has acquired legal status in many cities and the most recalcitrant excesses of New Urbanism.

And it is both amusing and disturbing to verify, briefly, how much "Programism" shares with "Thematization," in spite of their radically divergent aesthetic and stylistic proclivities. While on the one hand "Programism" attempts to avoid associations with any preestablished referent by spreading in front of us overwhelming arrays of apparently exhaustive, neutral information that conveys a sense of coolness, indifference, and objectivity about "reality out there" and, contrarily, on the other hand, thematized projects, like some promoted by New Urbanism, prescribe only one solution based on one precedent (Fig. 9), in both cases their uncritical reliance on carefully selected empirical evidence of the whole "as is" serves to validate their formulation. The two ideological positions are wrapped by different rhetorical ploys, in the former one of indifference inclusiveness, in the latter one of exclusive moral example. Aesthetically they are archenemies, but at the more profound philosophical and ideological levels they are siblings in their passive ratification of the status quo.

But now on to an entirely different story of formal production that swept the academic scene, magazines, exhibitions, and biennials in the past few years, although few exemplary actual buildings exist.

BLOBS

For some of us involved directly with working for the progress of architecture, the sudden outburst appeared strange, a few years ago, of shapeless creatures, seemingly from outer space (Fig. 10) or some bad intestinal condition (Fig. 11). On the other hand, for those more involved with technical developments in digital technology and its applications, particularly in academia, this outburst could be seen as the logical result of the fast development of that technology in three-dimensional representation. What happened in this past decade was an exhilarating and exciting evolution of a technology that not only sped up the process of describing and representing complex form, enhanced the accuracy of its representation, and multiplied the architect's ability to manipulate it as if it were actually plastic matter, but also allowed production of actual 3-D prototypes directly from the screen at the push of a button.

What a feast this offered! What tremendous repercussions these developments had

Fig. 12 Greg Lynn, blob forms, ca. 1998.
Fig. 13 Reiser+Umemoto, West Side Proposal, New York City, 1999.

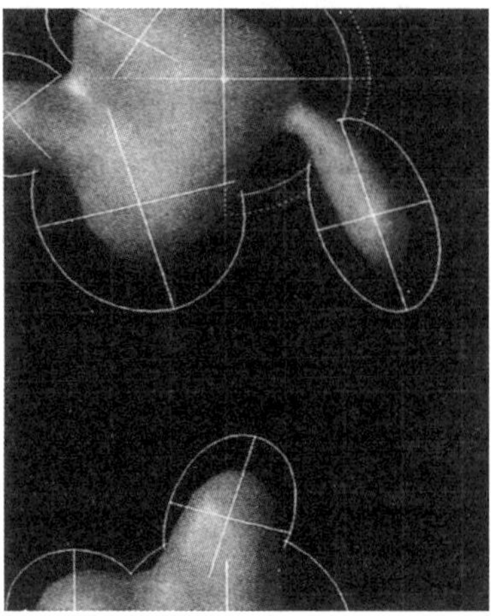

12 13

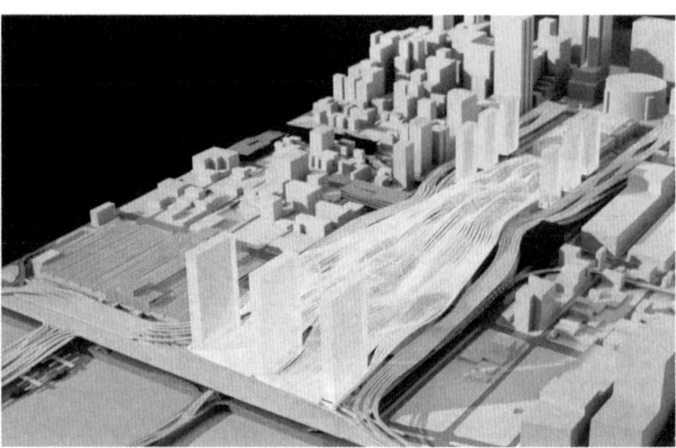

and are still having in the transition of architectural processes, from design to construction to the profession itself, without an end in sight!

And what a sudden, frightening abyss it opened up in front of us as the computer certainly intimated that it could produce forms that not only do not have precedent, but more perplexing, may not even have referents! Freedom from semantics, history, and culture was perhaps made possible for the first time in civilization.

My reaction upon this realization was then, as it is today, "So what?" Who wants that? My only interest in producing architecture is because it is a practice within cultural practices (in the anthropological sense), which is to say that the play with referents is not only of interest to me, but also inherent in the very idea of architecture. To be sure I do not want to reproduce such referents, but instead appropriate and use them in some fashion in order to engage people, to criticize ideas, to transform them into other things, to debunk or to enhance, to undermine or to sanction, to produce beauty and pleasure.

However that does not seem to have been the reaction of many who could not resist the temptation or generating certain forms *just because they could*—because of the sheer fascination of this seemingly God-like power bestowed suddenly on the ever power-deprived profession of architecture.

We make Blobs because we can, that was, for a while, sufficient reason. Both their proliferation and quick fall into benign indifference today (by 2002 the whole thing had subsided in both magazines and schools) speaks clearly about their fascinating but somewhat misguided pursuit. Yet I would like to emphasize their valid promise of more substantial achievements, which must be pursued, since the technology has become a natural part of our doings.

Blobs have also exposed an important element of our current Zeitgeist: a nostalgia for the future, a position almost predetermined as the inevitable swing of the pendulum of trends reversed itself in the '90s from the nostalgia for the past that dominated the '70s and '80s, as it finally became asphyxiating, and we ran out of decades to revive. It is only a matter of time before out nostalgia for the future will become just as ridiculous and debilitating.

But I am not done with Blobs yet, since they afford a unique opportunity to explore our architectural culture. Why did the emergence of the possibility of producing form without a referent elicit such an enthusiastic response, and how did architecture proceed to attempt this? The "why" is clear. Highly sought after by maverick thinkers, envisioned as a chimerical possibility in literary fiction, the idea of producing form without meaning seemed irresistible and has always deserved a Promethean try.

But what did we actually do with this "thing" that appeared on our computer screen? Very quickly, we stuffed it with meaning. Since as creatures that may wish to produce a form without meaning also harbor the even more compelling and contrary impulse to be

Fig. 14 Coop Himmelblau, Skyline, Hamburg, 1985.
Fig. 15 UN Studio, Yokohama Port Terminal, Japan, 1994.
Fig. 16 Johnson Burgee, AT&T Building, New York, 1984.

14

15

16

repulsed by that which we cannot name or understand, we began to invest Blobs with the meaning of whatever we could associate with them. We proceeded to see Blobs as representative of many conditions, as vehicles of more esoteric referents, so there was resurgence of organic, biological analogues to architecture, followed by processes, informational flows, then more abstract manifestations such as statistical data, in short, all those "formless" things that perhaps, given our sudden acquired power to produce them, could supplant other more traditional, simpler, historical, some would say conservative generative forces of architecture.

Thus the deliberate assigning of meaning to Blobs has produced a new generation of more evolved creatures that, while having the same source in digital representation, have acquired both a higher architectural status and identity of their own, which I would like to describe, conceptually, as the phenomenon of literal representation, our fourth category of cases.

LITERALISM

"Literalism" is the defining attribute of a more evolved and difficult-to-name species of creatures, more purposeful and meaningful, since it interprets and invests formlessness with concrete physical attributes. For example: a meaningless blob (Fig. 12), when seen as liquid, suggests a flow; when seen as viscose, suggests adaptability; and when seen as a malleable solid, suggests flexibility. And more: indeterminacy (they have no center), process (they seem to "evolve," to be alive), parasitism (they seem to stick), etc.—all physical properties that may suggest architectural properties, if what these forms, with their continuity and smoothness, evoke can be used to illustrate an architectural idea. All we need to do is label them. And since adaptability, flexibility, flow, indeterminacy, process, malleability, etc. are general descriptive terms favored today (some for very good reasons) to describe certain conditions of either the contemporary city or contemporary life in general, they have become useful metaphors for speaking about those conditions in architectural design.

What has been tremendously disappointing, however, is the mindless embracing of such tempting liquid-viscous-plastic formal intimations as the actual formal architectural solutions to those urban or social conditions considered as problems to be resolved. Such an attempt can only be result of an impoverished imagination reenacting the worst nightmares of postmodernism. And that is because if an aspect of a complex activity can be described. insightfully, as "a flow," it does not follow that architecture and urbanism can address it by making it look like, well, a flow (Fig. 13). Yet, even though we thought by now we knew better, we are still being subjected to the same insufferable process of illustration of ideas that gave us, a decade earlier, deconstructed (Fig. 14), folded (Fig. 15), and historicist (Fig. 16) projects and buildings. To no avail do we know that buildings are not really organic things, even though we can use organic metaphors to describe them. Yet there

Fig. 17 Church of Montevergine, Noto, Italy.
Fig. 18 Church of S. Domingo, Noto, Italy.
Fig. 19 Borromini, San Carlo alla Quattro Fontane, Rome, Italy, 1667.

17

18

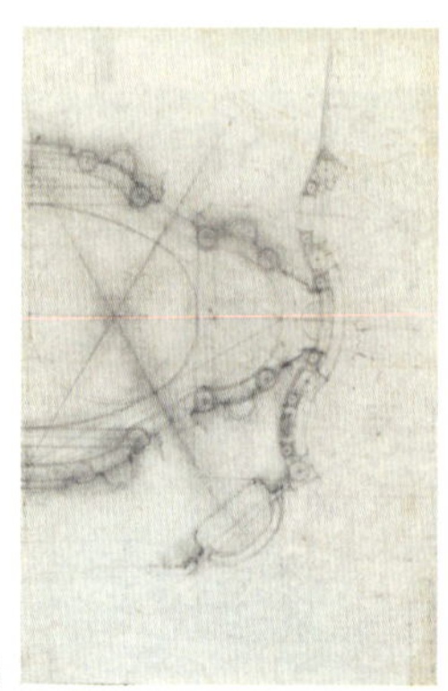
19

is continuous insistence in making them look as if they were. Nor has there ever been any good real reason to build a building that looks broken simply because its creator adheres to deconstruction as a philosophy, nor, of course, buildings that flow, fold, or are old if they really do not or are not. Buildings cannot be "flexible" or "indeterminate" either. They are hard and immobile no matter what (although they may, with some effort, alter and adapt their forms to particular purposes).

Perhaps it is time to accept that metaphor in architecture is useful as a sparkle, as a starter, as a guide, or as a shadow, but that it becomes a dangerous game every time it leaves its comfortable abode in language and poetry for excursions into other media, a fact that we know well at least since baroque times, when it was widely used, under control, but always treading on dangerous borderlines between the sublime and the ridiculous.

Just to make sure the point I am trying to make is not missed, what I suggest is that the use of metaphor in architecture, as in any practice, should be looked at as an enrichment of meaning and not as a replacement for the thing itself.[3] Metaphor is most useful when either we find no words to explain something on its own terms and we need an analogy to draw an insight, or as an inspiration for properties that cannot be described better than with analogy. As such, metaphor will always be indispensable for the advancement of knowledge.

By and large, "Literalism" is the most weakening formal development of the last twenty years of architecture. Yet, not surprisingly, it is the one with widespread acceptance because of its easy consumption, since it is the domain par excellence of the one-liner.

And as if closing a circle, I am one thought away from connecting Literalism with Programism, which would allow me to make Literalism the general condition of architectural representation today in all the cases we've covered and the real target of this essay as the dominant design strategy and method in the academy. I leave such sweeping speculation aside for the time being, since I would like to advance the argument in another direction.

TEMPORARY CONCLUSION

What perhaps is evident by now is the fact that, disparate as these four strategies for the generation of form may seem, they all share a weakening of the designer's indispensable volition to create it. Perhaps seduced by the possibility of minimizing efforts and costs with the help of preexisting models and machines, the architect is inadvertently minimizing also the quality of the intellectual work that the architectural imagination requires, as he or she steps aside from the role of the knowing, willing, acting agent in the creation of architectural form.

Let there be no mistake: these developments are all honest and well-intentioned attempts to produce form, in some cases born from genuine and positive criticism of existing conditions, to be sure, since they want to generate good architecture and address issues and problems.[4] But nobody involved in these attempts seems to want to be responsible

Fig. 20 Bernini, St. Peter's Square, Vatican City, 1667.
Fig. 21 Guarino Guarini, Santa Sindone, Turin, Italy.
Fig. 22 Bernini, *David*, 1624.

20

21

22

for the outcome and its authorship insofar as *form* is concerned. Interestingly, for all their superficial ideological differences, they all relegate the architect to the role of intermediary—the midwife, as Colin Rowe would have said—in the delivery of form that somehow is understood as the product of the marriage of other agents, external and independent of the architect. The architect, a lonely, aseptic figure, then remains chaste and pure.

It will not be useful to belabor further the sterile consequences of Thematization, contextualism, and new urbanisms, in short all those literal resorts to architectural precedents, since they have been evident to all of us for a while. Yet, on the other wise of this landscape, as we see these examples of literalism (Blobs, flows, flexibility, etc.) and Programism marching together as the bearers of the torch that illuminates the heroic path towards an architecture presumably without representation, without historical precedent, without shadows of itself, unbeknownst to them we also notice that such a path leads to an inevitable *cul de sac* where the representation of all the things *other than architecture* reign free, available, and predatory. And since, from any serious cultural perspective, we know that representation is unavoidable, in this trapped condition architecture would be condemned to wear costumes that do not suit it.

BAROQUE

I would like to first bring in a historical analogy that would permit the advancement of the argument to a point where we may see where all this comes from and then to conclude.

Let me affirm, as an apparent paradox, that most of the salient conditions under which this contemporary condition of form-giving denials operate resonate as analogues with the operations that controlled the exuberant formal production during the baroque period—a paradox indeed, since the baroque is associated with an excess of consciously controlled form production based on a precedent, namely the classical language of architecture. And yet just about all the characteristics that we described in the contemporary scene can be found in the aesthetics of baroque architecture.

From the perspective of our discussion today, there has never been a period so similar to ours in which: the art of rhetoric was so close to the art of architecture; the roles of entertainment and popular art were so dominant; the boundaries among the traditional art forms were so much probed and violated, challenged, eroded, and transgressed; the role of metaphor was so active; and within the latter, the widespread use of the literal representation of movement in architecture was so prevalent. Indeed, preferred among the metaphors for the baroque is that of movement.

And let's start with that. One could say that architecture, being such a physically heavy and inert art, has an innate longing for movement, that the baroque period was the time when such predisposition was the dominant formal impulse, and that today we reencounter such longing expressed in many an undulating surface. There is nothing

Fig. 23 Mary Miss, *Field Rotation*, 1981.
Fig. 24 Rachel Whiteread, *House*, 1994.
Fig. 25 György Ligeti, *Continuum*, 1968, selection.

23

24

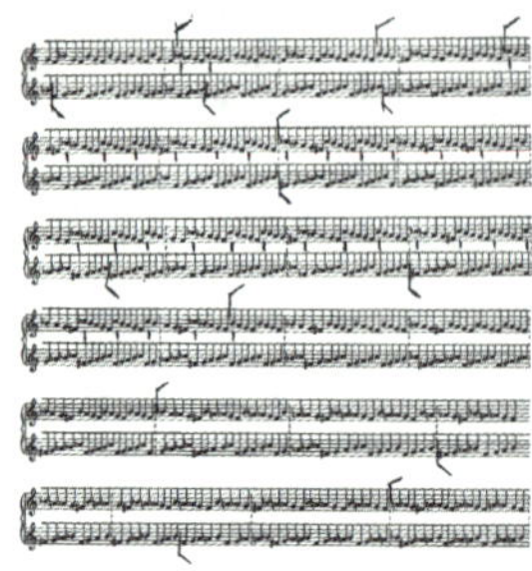
25

wrong with the "formal desires" of an epoch. Anybody walking around Rome or any major Italian city from the end of the 17th century to the middle of the 18th would have felt a bit dizzy about the undulating walls, about alternatively imploding (Fig. 17) and exploding (Fig. 18) facades. Anybody walking around the studios of architecture schools in the last few years would have felt that such forms were about to return to our streets. But to understand the fundamental difference between the baroque metaphor of movement and that of current explorations that represent movement in architecture beyond what is undoubtedly a similar formal proposition is to grasp that there is a sense of "performance," theatricality, and self-consciousness about what such conceit in baroque architecture that we don't find in the literal, naïve representations of these principles of flow and dynamism today.

On the one hand, the support provided by the classical language of architecture, by then two thousand years old and still thriving in myriad incarnations, gave both a recognizable vocabulary and a resounding proof of its very artificiality. Metaphor was just a poetic maneuver in search of an effect. On the other hand, there is the baroque effect itself, which has the concrete aim of producing *wonder*. Wonder is baroque's effect, clear and simple. In all of it, the suspension of disbelief that the baroque work of art expects from the beholder is no more that a generalized complicit strategy about the role and possibilities of the arts and of the gentile and entertaining game that they proposed. While awed by the dexterity, virtuosity (but we architects know about the hard work and intellectual rigor that this smoothness required—see Fig. 19), and seemingly magic power of these representations, nobody ever really believed that buildings moved, facades undulated, basilicas could embrace (Fig. 20), or domes could eat you alive (Fig. 21).

Of course I am not bringing this up because I think this baroque operation is what we need to revive. History does not repeat itself (this is the only "lesson" of history) and a look at the baroque for similarities now could only help us distinguish better the differences with our times and possibilities. So here there are two other seemingly similar characteristics that the baroque could share with the current moment, whose true nature and understanding would help us push this discussion to its tentative conclusion.

In baroque visual arts, the first one is the recourse to a "conceit," usually a literary theme, as the operative force, and the second is the dissolution of the traditional boundaries among the arts. The conceit, usually a climatic moment in narrative, most often involved the representation of an instant in which movement was frozen (Fig. 22). As for the dissolution of boundaries, it was found mostly in the seemingly indifferent and highly effective transgression of boundaries among architecture, sculpture, painting, through the subtle and ambiguous manipulation of color, materials, and natural light. These two constitutive characteristics of the baroque correspond directly, in my view, to two defining conditions of contemporary Art, namely: the primacy of

Fig. 26 Stockhausen, Refrain.
Fig. 27 Johann Zoffany (1734–1810), *The Minuet*.

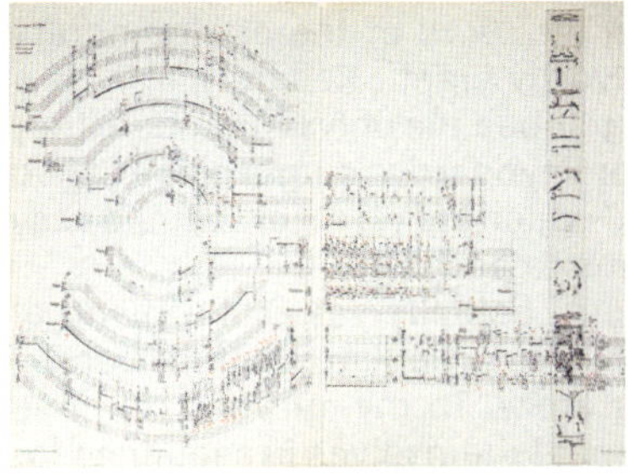

26

27

the Concept and its logical sequel, the loss of medium specificity of works of art.

I would argue that, in the passage from a world where "the arts" reigned, each one easily associated and defined by aspects of a medium (sound, color, flatness, matter, actions, stories, etc.), into another, our own world, where more and more the arts have collapsed into a single idea of "Art," where the specificity of the medium no longer has validity, somehow architecture got confused by being defined by two clear but incompatible conditions.

It is either *Architecture as Art* or remains *the art of architecture*.[5]

Just to make sure that we can ground this, let me bring in one of architecture's favorite art critics, Rosalind Krauss, who, throughout her writing confirms the advent of the termination of the individual arts as medium specific and the supreme reign of Conceptual Art.[6] She has convincingly asserted that art has finally freed itself from attachments to specific media, which is to say, conversely, that any medium can serve as the vehicle for Art. But of course this now Art with a capital A, the one and only one, not any "specific" art like those that were once associated with specific media, such as painting, sculpture, music, drama, and architecture, each one with its own Muse. In this contemporary condition, which I believe exists, Conceptual Art occupies the triumphant center—Conceptual Art with its privileging of the Big Idea and its necessary indifference to medium.

This, in retrospect, seemingly inevitable denouement of the history of Western art is the undeniable achievement of the modern art's avant-garde, whose successful and brilliant debunking of the notion of medium specificity commenced almost at the moment when art theory was founded by Gotthold Lessing in 1766 by the very act of identifying the artistic medium as the indispensable condition to define the specificity of each art, an effort that, by the way, could be seen as the Enlightenment's critique of the baroque.[7] Of course, the latter's demise was prematurely celebrated then.

It is fairly obvious to me that the relatively recently acquired possibility of architecture to maneuver so freely outside of its traditional formal and material boundaries, opting instead for unconventional referents for its forms as well as media for its expression, has a direct, perhaps even sole, source in this atmosphere of debunking the specificity of the medium in the arts.[8] It is also clear to me that such ease has been facilitated by Architectural Theory's equal softening and drifting away from a core of conventional architectural substances during the same period to become exclusively dependent on, if not subservient to, the overall discourse of Art Theory of which it is today, in fact, a chapter.

It is actually spectacularly good for Art that Architecture has become a medium readily available to it, the vehicle for some of its Big Ideas, and that, as such, it can have a protagonist's role in performing many of its different manifestations, such as earth art installations (Fig. 23), happenings, and other forms in which it is either content or container. In fact, some truly remarkable moments in contemporary art have architecture as their vehicle (Fig. 24), and I relish them as much as I relish good buildings.

Yet to the extent that the real contents of all these media-unspecific instances of Art are concepts and ideas, sometimes quite honestly represented by words themselves, the processes by which they are generated are not necessarily reversible so as to warrant an inversion of the equation that would claim that *any medium can be architecture*, which is, I am afraid the basis of many of our confusions today.

Architecture as Art is an instance of the most advanced condition of Art today. Art as Architecture is a travesty.

We have heard in writings, symposia, reviews, and courses that "architecture" can now be many things, even words, and perhaps Mark Wigley at Columbia University would still disagree with me in the friendly feud we started eight years ago in New Orleans as to whether he is an architect simply because he writes and thinks about architecture. If so, I would continue to say he is not, even as he continues to write about architecture so intelligently and lucidly. And for me this is not a play of words or definitions. The difference is real and vital and almost a matter of survival.

What we have now is a phenomenal confusion, mostly prevalent in academia, journalism, and museums, between two conditions in which architecture finds itself performing absolutely legitimate but absolutely different roles, one as the support of artistic ideas and another as the inspiration for buildings, but most of the time without realizing on what stage it is actually standing.

Let's just spell it out clearly, because it is simpler than it seems: on the one hand, as the vehicle of the Big Idea, architecture is standing in the grand proscenium of Art. On the other, as the proper vehicle for human actions, it is standing, naked as a building, in the social arena where real life takes place. Both are legitimate and inspiring. However, they are different and not interchangeable and very rarely concurrent. The way we maneuver, sort through, and get out of this confusion is at the heart of the future of architectural education, and ultimately of architecture itself. This is the challenge that I would like Architectural Theory to take earnestly in order to re-energize what I perceive is its languid state as an appendage of Art Theory.

EPILOGUE, THE MUSIC ANALOGY

To conclude let me turn to a totally different field, music, where visuality is not dominant and the interaction (and confusion) between creator and performer place it in an entirely different conceptual and material realm from architecture and the visual arts. As an amateur pianist, I marvel at music's staunch resistance to dissolve itself into Art; it is one of the last traditional arts that is incorruptible and able to hold its own in terms of specificity of medium—not without attempts to the contrary. In the past year or so, I became more interested in the work of the contemporary composer Gyorgy Ligeti. Recently, at a New York shop, I grabbed the only Ligeti score they could find for keyboard, a single piece called "Continuum," which at first sight seemed easy enough for me to perform.

But when I actually sat at the piano at home and tried to articulate the first bars, it was another story. To my surprise, the two notes that repeat themselves in sequence for the first few bars are exactly the same for both hands but are played alternatively. So as the middle right finger depressed B-flat in conjunction with the middle left finger depressing G, the following move requires a reversal, as the right thumb depresses G while the left one does the same with B-flat—a difficult and uncomfortable proposition. If to such an inconvenient physical state we add the particular dynamics that the author prescribes for the piece—"prestissimo," extremely fast, with absolute continuity of sound—the result is that the movements cancel each other out and (surprise, surprise) no sound is produced.

What a bummer if you really wanted to play and hear some music! But this is not all. As I became more familiar with the score and unfolded its pages, I began to realize that perhaps actually really this piece is not about the sound, melody, or any of those old-fashioned things that we found in music—perhaps it is about pattern-making, about graphic design, about visual narrative, a pictorial metamorphosis, a visual form that by the way would also produce some sound. Perhaps (Fig. 25).

I was both fascinated and troubled by this frustrating smart trick.[9] As it turned out, I was wrong in my initial reading of the score: I found out later that it is intended for a two keyboard instrument (harpsichord), and its first bars can be played and will produce sound. So why do I use this wrong example? In a funny way, my misguided disappointment is nonetheless historically validated by a condition under which my own artistic judgement operates. For one, the very idea that I could accept as possible the fact that Ligeti wanted to produce, through the act of performance, a piece of music that denied its very nature by producing silence describes the state of mind in which we all now think about art. But more importantly, such instances have already been produced, as with John Cage's famous piece "4'33" of 1952, in which the musicians, on stage and ready to play, remained silent, and the concert was in effect whatever were the sounds in the environment where the "concert" took place, or less radically as with his "Music of Changes," in which musical decisions are made by "chance operations" decided by coin-tossing procedures (hence the typical "language" pun of Conceptual Art), and in general as with all the avant-garde music of the second half of the 20th century that starts with an idea outside music itself, with a "concept" if you wish, and then applies it to the medium of sound, such as Stockhausen's "Refrain" of 1959 for piano, celesta, and percussion, in which the "refrain" is printed on a transparent strip that can be rotated to different positions for different performances (Fig. 26). Not surprisingly, these attempts to align music with Conceptual Art's ideas have resulted in these pieces surviving only in textbooks, rather than in concert halls, where they have rarely returned after their first "performances." The point was some Big Idea, somewhere. This is Music as Art. OK. It is smart. It is intelligent. It is interesting, isn't it?

But next to this score on my piano was the score of Bach's *French Suites*, with its well-established form, a sequence of dances rendered totally anew. And suddenly I could not contain the flow of thinking that this juxtaposition produced. Because, here in Bach's creation I had an undisputed work of art that aimed at something fairly precise yet humble. *No Big Idea here.* It tried only to exist within the confines of "the art of music." As such, this particular genre of suites was intended for home playing and dancing. But as one hears it even today, it is possible to experience its exuberant richness and power to evoke or suggest to our imagination all the things it represented and engaged: the *petit bourgeoisie* interior décor of a German house (Fig. 27), its gentle, imperfect acoustics, the discoveries by the adolescent dancers of their bodies with their rhythms, their temperatures, their contacts and incipient eroticism, the melodies alluding to a foreign land, the sound of garments touching furniture, shoes scratching the floor, and a great sense of pleasure, of intimate fun. All the while the art of music is being well served and advanced as probably never before.

Today of course we would pay a lot of money to hear some of the greatest keyboard soloists play Bach's *French Suites* at a large concert hall, even though Bach never conceived them to be played that way. He was just a composer and player, a music maker who made money as best as he could, publishing dances and keyboard exercises, and playing and composing for the local church.

Well, too bad if music today were not able to look at the life of people and nourish itself directly from it, to get inspiration, to transform itself and advance its own traditions. Yet as a music lover, I do not despair, since the world of sound seems to find other venues outside Art that continue to make us happy.

Music, whatever realm it is relegated to, never stops.

POSTSCRIPT, A YEAR AFTER THE GROPIUS LECTURE

For those familiar with the developments of Architectural Theory in the last decades, it would appear that the whole line of reasoning I presented is full of traps, some potentially fatal. But I feel nonetheless prepared to confront and avoid these traps, since I am too aware that accepting such warnings and changing directions would play into the arms of those mutually exclusive extremes that result from that pervasive yet silent and lethal pendulum that regulates so much of the Zeitgeist, the pendulum that swings between conservative and avant-garde, reactionary and progressive, classic and modern, past and future.

One thing I learned after the pendulum had already swung from extreme to extreme a few times during my professional life (and in doing so deprived both theory and architecture itself of any richness and accumulated wisdom) was to ignore the opposites as such and work with what I think is good from both. That is why I have identified a few topics that are currently repressed by Theory, topics that insinuate themselves throughout all my arguments and that appear to me, for all their dangers, necessary to bring back to the fore without throwing out what we have gained in the recent past, even if Theory has cast each as anathema to the other.

A threat of creative paralysis might be inferred from my assertion that once we accept representation in architecture is inevitable, its referents must come from architecture itself. This could be read as reopening the door to stifling historicism. Yet we are now at a stage, thanks to theory and history, in which we understand "architecture itself" not to mean exclusively its received figurative repository. Today it means, rather, that architecture *as the sole source of architecture* could look at anything as formal inspiration, *but from its inside out*, keeping its footings in its building core, anchoring its imagination in a programmatic research beyond literal formal translations, and continuing in the flow of its own cultural trajectory, both responsive to and critical of its conventions, which does not imply the literal figurative use of referents. Thus the most promising developments of Blobs are not those resulting from a metaphorical reading of their formal properties but from the logical integration of advanced computer technologies with tectonic consciousness and an historical/anthropological knowledge of the discipline.[10]

As a corollary of this, it seems inevitable that a reconsideration and reformulation of the heated issue of disciplinary "autonomy" must be undertaken without denying the "intertextuality" and cultural "contamination" that we so much appreciate now in architecture. It seems to me that, for instance, a judicious, unbiased reading of Rossi's most important writing and ideas always reveals such rich understanding of architecture and the city, understanding that is not irreconcilable with some of the most advanced aesthetic and formal notions of, for example, Herzog and de Meuron.

It also seems urgent, even imperative, to renew and promote a discussion seriously focused on popular culture, not as a figurative source for architecture but as the operative cultural mechanism with which architecture cannot avoid interaction. It seems that carefully selected ideas from Venturi and Scott Brown's iconographic theory of architecture, some of Gehry's artful yet seductive and persuasive tricks to manipulate emotions, and Koolhaas's understanding of cultural phenomena (reformulated after a serious critique of his suspect silence with respect to the political implications of some of his stands) should be able to propel and circumscribe the territory of architecture in novel and more fruitful ways.

And I also believe that we must overcome definitively the avant-garde clichés of inflated and unrealistic portrayals of the power of architecture to "criticize" and subvert society.

Which brings me back to the polemic about "Architecture as Art" and "Art as Architecture."

The Muses may very well be unamused by the current state of architecture. But frankly, who cares? Erato, Clio, Euterpe, Melpomene, and the rest are old ladies who long ago lost their credibility as art changed and they were left playing, idle or irrelevant, with the worn attributes of dead art forms. And of course we could not think of reestablishing the orderly world of Bach.

But the pandemonium in the house of architecture is real, in my view, and an effort to understand what the Muses represent, namely, that there is a territory and a certain specificity that a *métier* such as architecture could claim as its own, is worthy of exploration, particularly in good schools of architecture, where we are concerned, above all, with education and the advancement of knowledge.

ACKNOWLEDGMENTS
I would like to thank GSD Professor Scott Cohen, Assistant Professor Gary Rohrbacher at the School of Architecture, University of Texas, Austin, and Mark Pasnik, Associate, Machado and Silvetti Associates, for their comments and encouragements as I worked on this version of the Gropius Lecture.

Notes

1 The culprit is Preston Scott Cohen, who coined the term during the GSD's thesis reviews season of 2000.

2 This symmetry is already noticeable in the fact that while Programism is prevalent and even rampant in school, Thematization is much more "triumphant" in the fields of design practice and the real estate industries.

3 When Frank Lloyd Wright's architecture was referred to as "organic," it was not because it looked like an organism, but because its characteristic suggested the attributes, the analogue characteristics of an organic phenomenon: it was neither confused with a natural living organism nor dressed up to look like one.

4 I am alluding to many good and encouraging example that experiment with and use the technology and principles of these recent developments such as the work of Foreign Office in Japan.

5 I owe much of the thinking implied in this dichotomy to the writings of Spanish writer and philosopher Félix de Azúa, particularly his *Diccionario de las Artes* (Barcelona: Editorial Planeta, S.A., 1999).

6 See Rosalind Krauss, *A Voyage on the North Sea*: *Art in the Post-Medium Condition* (London: Thames & Hudson, 2000.)

7 Gotthold Ephraim Lessing, *Laocoön: An Essay on the Limits of Painting and Poetry* (Baltimore: The Johns Hopkins University Press, 1962, originally published in 1766.)

8 Unlike the formally analogous, intermittent, and intrinsically different "expressionist" outbursts during the 20th century, such as Mendelsohn's, Scharoun's, Utzon's, and even Gehry's, all highly individualistic and still rooted in an idea of the architect as an artist that is alien to the phenomena I am addressing. Yet despite the fundamental changes that separate "expressionism" from the developments I am addressing, such lineage is often alluded to and invoked as legitimizing provenance by the promoters of the latter.

9 This paragraph was added after the original Gropius Lecture as a necessary clarification and correction to a wrong assumption I made regarding Ligeti's "Continuum." In turn, as the mistake reinforces rather than changes or modifies the argument presented in the Epilogue, it was important to keep it within the original text.

10 This is a line of thinking and research that I am proud to see flourishing at the GSD at all levels, see, for instance *Immaterial/Ultramaterial: Architecture, Design and Materials*, ed. Toshiko Mori (Cambridge, MA: Harvard Design School in association with George Braziller, 2002).

Block That Metaphor!

JORGE SILVETTI, 2014

My chapter finds itself unwittingly, if usefully, framed by the last part of this volume on nature and architecture, and I should say something about this. I always worry that discussions about architecture and sustainability prompt too much talking about Nature and not enough about Architecture—because the problem we have is Architecture*: Nature is; it exists. Architecture we must make.*

This brings me to one of my favorite topics: what architecture looks like these days, and what that tells us about the state of the art as well as the state of architectural education more generally. If we consider the architecture currently on offer in magazines, competitions and graduate theses, then it admittedly looks very much like "Nature." The polemical position I would like to introduce to the discussion, in a nutshell, is this: Architecture should not look like what it is not—a statement that can only be understood in the context of broader reflections on the "Nature of Architecture" and what this means historically as well as currently. I shall address the issue somewhat obliquely by focusing on a few relevant examples of how Nature has entered into the equation of Architecture.

By the same token, and since I am taking my lead from titles, I would like briefly to mention the source of my own. For those not familiar with the expression "Block That Metaphor!," this is the heading for a minuscule and delicious occasional feature published in *The New Yorker*. It showcases independent snippets serving as humorous graphic fillers at the end of full-length articles in which are quoted a host of mixed metaphors and unintended meanings picked up from newspapers, magazines and advertisements—a litany of figures of speech gone wrong. If I appropriate *The New Yorker*'s title, this is because, on the one hand, my essay is only a snippet of a much larger debate on the "Nature of Architecture" and, on the other, we must block not one but many metaphors. For while any moderately educated reader can readily pick up on mixed metaphors or incongruous comparisons in a piece of writing, the task of unlocking such mechanisms of misfired meaning in architecture is not so easy—especially when a confounding literalism seems to be at work. The issue of understanding the efforts of literal bio-mimicry in creating human environments remains a great challenge, since these efforts should arguably be conceived instead to help us *differentiate* our acts from those of nature and, in so doing, to protect us from it. Highlighting this inherent cultural perversion strikes as a way to remind ourselves that even the oft-cited Vitruvian myth of primitive shelter insists on the transition from the human "imitation of the nests of swallows" to building better dwellings by virtue of "the powers of thought and understanding."[1] Literal biomimicry, therefore, opens a myriad of doors of inquiry as to what such recourse to natural imagery stands for at this particular moment.[2]

Out of all this, it is the process of architectural creativity on which I want specifically to focus. Let us not despair at the surprising recurrence of literalism, for its formal repertoire and image sources per se do not really threaten architecture. Mostly, the repertoire points to naïveté, as such visual operations bring the design process and architectural efficiency lamentably close to the role of magic in early human societies. These were societies in which formal similarities, say, the visual affinity between a garlic clove and a human tooth—a forceful example of the "going together" of things that Claude Lévi-Strauss identified as the intellectual basis of magic—imparts to the garlic clove the power to cure a tooth in pain.[3] Naturally, this curative power was due to its chemical composition and not its form (which is why Hippocrates, for one, prescribed garlic as a cure for any number of ailments).

Such "sympathy" between analogous forms is not what worries me—think of Leonardo da Vinci's drawing juxtaposing the layers of an onion with the dissected human brain—although its recurrence today points to intellectual poverty rather than to scientific discovery.[4] As with all formal trends to which we inevitably fall victim to some degree, their longevity is necessarily curtailed and, indeed, we are already witnessing the fading away of naive naturalism. But if the latter is fading, just as the invasion of blobs receded almost a decade ago, what they threaten to leave in their wake is an invisible and insidious metaphorical transformation—insofar as their ostensive claim to being "natural" is transposed from palpable images and transformed into intangible processes.

THE NATURAL PROCESS

Forms, like metaphors, are never innocent. Their appearances have consequences—particularly if they lie—and while one may tire of

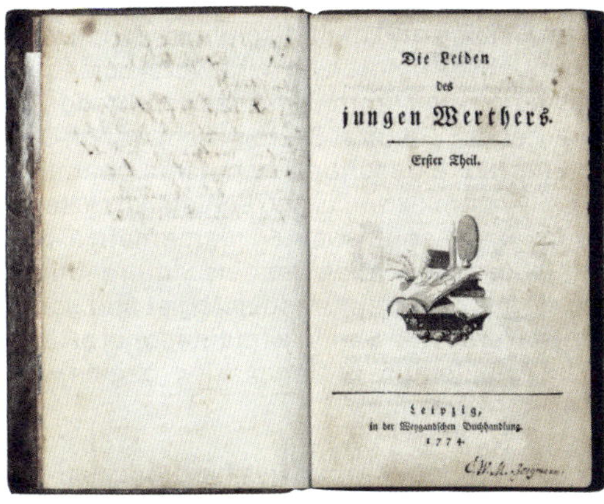

Die Leiden
des
jungen Werthers.
Erster Theil.
Leipzig,
in der Weygandschen Buchhandlung.
1774.

1

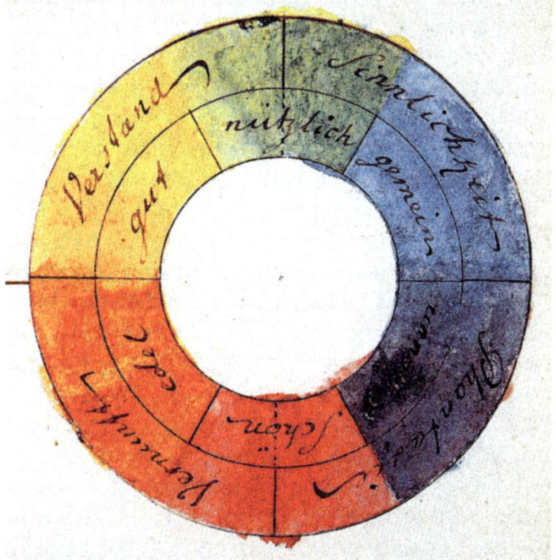

2

3

4

Fig. 1 Johann Wolfgang von Goethe, title page vignette, *The Sorrows of Young Werther*, Part I (Leipzig, 1774) .

Fig. 2 Johann Wolfgang von Goethe, sketch of the "color circle," 1809.

Fig. 3 William Chevalier after Theodor M. von Holst, "Frankenstein and His Monster," frontispiece steel engraving for the revised 1831 edition of Mary Shelley's *Frankenstein, or the Modern Prometheus*.

Fig. 4 Tesla Coil Sparks 4KVA with Corona on Wire, March 15, 2007.

naturalized aesthetics, the literal message of "Architecture as Nature" seems to have emerged with increasing efficiency as it has migrated from the visual analogue to the less tangible domain of beliefs. In other words, the exercise of producing the visual metaphor of nature in architecture has resulted in a silent, undetected reverse transfer of what these sympathetic forms suggest: namely that in addition to looking like nature, they are seen as being the result of a "natural" process of production, the very process of design.

Hence at the moment when the forms themselves are gradually being discarded, they are not falling into oblivion without leaving their mark. All to the contrary, they are leaving behind their baggage—transferring their meaning, so to speak, by following a process typical of a contemporary culture prone to peripatetic semantics: from one practice to another, from one medium to another, from forms and images to processes of making. As Kenneth Burke once wrote, such slipperiness is constitutive of the metaphor, "a device for seeing something in terms of something else. It brings out the thisness of a that, or the thatness of a this."[5] By the same token, metamorphic slipperiness is what some of the most exciting digital techniques of computation, in their ability to manipulate, coordinate and relate multiple variables and parameters, have enabled. The mesmerizing, almost sublime and confusing sight of printers spitting hitherto sleek and unimagined images, as well as 3-D models of a representation of an architecture that looks like nature, seduces the mind. It induces us to believe that a process of creation in which seemingly so little human intervention occurs is also natural, with this frightening corollary: that the state of mind that has allowed architecture to think about itself as the result of a "natural" process so precise—so seemingly outside our hands, so abandoned to invisible controls—cannot help but see the results (formal, organizational, structural, etc.) not only as inevitable but, worse yet, as a manifestation of *truth*. And if the whole process produces truth—here is the real problem—there is no need to assess the resulting form. Judging form is no longer important. Critical thinking has become moot.

Small wonder, then, that what has seemingly vanished is the discourse of ideas, which good architectural form had always conveyed to us and by means of which it had always provoked us. Instead, there are conversations about how and what scripting programs were used, and to what purpose, or what the appropriate algorithmic relationships of parameters were—as if sorting out programs, verifying algorithms and counting constraints were akin to checking with the technical crew at an airport to make sure that all controls are in working order before a departure for a successful trip.

THE RELATIONSHIP BETWEEN ARCHITECTURE AND NATURE

Revivals may be retrograde, but when they are intentional, at least their purposes can be argued. Yet if they are the product of lamentable ignorance or the wholesale dismissal of their own history, then conditions for disaster abound. Current discourses that claim possession of the keys to an unimpeachably legitimizing process, that consider the status of architectural form as insignificant and irrelevant, and that emphasize presumably measurable performance parameters, are all commonplaces we've visited before—in fact, quite recently.

Personally, I have already been through one such fallacious condition of which I was a willing victim. In the 1970s, when I was working on my Master's of Architecture at the University of California, Berkeley, one thing that was all the rage (besides Christopher Alexander's pattern language, which fortunately never seduced me) was General Systems Theory: a totalizing, synthesizing and multidisciplinary undertaking mostly promoted by behavioral scientists but happily and enthusiastically embraced by architects.[6] General Systems Theory or GST attempted to describe and put into operation deeply complex social and ecological systems by means of sophisticated mathematical and statistical simulation models. Interestingly, the cognitive scientist, sociologist and economist Herbert A. Simon's foundational article, "The Architecture of Complexity," begins with a word of warning:

> A number of proposals have been advanced in recent years for the development of "general systems theory" which, abstracting from properties peculiar to physical, biological, or social systems, would be applicable to all of them. We might feel that, while the goal is laudable, systems of such diverse kinds could hardly be expected to have nontrivial properties in common. Metaphor and analogy can be helpful, or they can be misleading. All depends on whether the similarities the metaphor captures are significant or superficial.[7]

Needless to say, when applied to architecture and design, these models cum metaphors simply fell apart in the face of the intrinsic resistance of any cultural practice to yield to technocratic manipulation—and I found myself, after having written a rather boring thesis in that vein, forever inoculated against all the viruses of Nature (if it can be believed, me, writing about my findings based on a statistical regression model that analyzed social networks in an urban area alongside the moose populations of the Lake Michigan islands).

Soon architecture fought back with productive vengeance, giving us simultaneously the best theory and design that we had experienced in generations and the worst excesses of Postmodernism. At its best, the critique acted as an inspiration stemming from cultural studies, literary criticism, history, anthropology; in short, all the humanities and sciences came to architecture as well-formulated perspectives whose imports could prompt the creation of new architectural products. At its worst, architecture was used to illustrate concepts from those fields without any transformative effect whatsoever; that is, we were left with another form of literalism.

We do not yet know where we stand in the life cycle of these current trends, but it is beginning to be apparent that there are just too many illusions and mirages, too much magical thinking, too much infantilism around to be sustainable. So if there exists a willingness to learn from history, recent and less recent, then a serious attempt to alter course would be desirable and, even, imperative.

THE PERFECT STORM

Here is a brief sketch of the script on how we got here. At least three conditions, all valuable and positive in their own right, have converged to produce an "atmosphere" prone to producing wreckage: first, the environmental crisis and its consequences for architecture introduced the reign of sustainability; second, the availability of sophisticated computational techniques allowed hitherto impossible formal explorations to be generated; and third, the lack of clear formal norms, patterns and standards in architecture resulted in the liberating and energizing sense that all was possible in the ensuing torrent of formal possibilities.

Taken individually, each of these significant ingredients is good and welcome. However their commingling has emerged as toxic and devastating. The confluence of digital technology and formal liberation encouraged experimentation and, conversely, created an immense vacuum in architectural discourse; as the architect was confronted with an infinite number of unexpected formal possibilities, there was not much to say about them. How to discourse about forms that are coming from scripted programs? That was the failure of the first wave of blobs as nobody, save for Greg Lynn who originated the idea with great eloquence in 1995, knew what to say about them. Then, the entrance made by, on the one hand, sustainability, which carried with it the unshakable authority of "Nature" (as if this were some sort of a priori truth and not a changing political and cultural construct), and, on the other, the ineffable and acute ability of architects to analogize forms and construct metaphors: the passage from those mute, smooth and rounded blobs with no story to tell yet imploring us for meaning—the passage from those suggestive, yearning silences—to loud metaphors screaming "I am nature!" was seamless. Now, these metaphors can everywhere be seen as bones, muscles, trees, glands or geographies assuming the authority with which their condition endows them. Next step: the belief that they can perform the task implied by means of their metaphorical forms "naturally," with the requisite verbs attached to them for describing the actions performed. We act as if the process by which such forms were generated is not simply "like" a natural process, but actually *is* one—and because of this, can claim definitive and objective authority. End of discussion. End of Architecture.

ROMANTIC EXEMPLARS

I would like to end on a more optimistic note by turning to history—this in order to give a few examples of the productive, positive and immensely creative relations between the arts, sciences and nature or, more specifically, the *knowledge of nature*—the format in which nature should be brought into architecture (as opposed to as trees, waves, clouds, knolls, tentacles, glands or mollusks). These examples stem from the notably effervescent decades around the turn of the nineteenth century, which witnessed the passage from the Enlightenment to Romanticism. This period could be thought to be, if not similar to our own, at least comparable, presenting us with characteristics resembling some current predicaments and sensibilities (as the literary critic Edward Larrissy says, "the persistence of Romanticism in the present").[8] This was an era "when the arts were increasingly turning away from the frigid idea of Enlightenment aesthetics and towards a new stress on imagination and feeling."[9] This was also an era of major discoveries in which the emergent discipline of science (in the modern sense) referred to the activities of its practitioners as "experimental philosophy"—a characterization falling much closer to the idea of the "knowledge of nature" to which I alluded earlier. According to the historian of science Elizabeth Garber, "natural philosophy and philosophy could not be separated. This was partly because of the belief that the study of experimental phenomena could uncover the actual workings and structures of nature. The findings of experimental philosophers and interpretations of the meanings of their results contained within them metaphysical and philosophical implications no philosopher could ignore."[10]

It is interesting that in such productive decades, both artists and experimental philosophers enjoyed intense personal and professional relationships with each other, a guarantor of the interaction between their respective disciplines. Thus the founder of modern astronomy, Friedrich Wilhelm Herschel was a first-class musician, performer and composer of some 24 symphonies who went on to devote his life to the major discoveries that would change our understanding of the nature of the universe, shatter theological tenets and illustrate the philosophical concept of the infinite and the sublime.[11] Thus Johann Wolfgang van Goethe could navigate between writing paradigmatic Romantic novels and plays such as *The Sorrows of Young Werther* (1774) and *Faust* (a life-long project), studying botany, and developing a theory of color, which not only served as basis for Arthur Schopenhauer's *On Vision and Color* (1816) but also prompted a complex response in the painted works of the English painter J. M. W. Turner (Fig. 1, 2);[12] all the while, he absorbed the art and architecture of the ancients during his Grand Tour of Italy, over the course of which he collected stone samples, investigated the formation of clouds and experienced on Vesuvius "a hill of ash which had been recently thrown up and was emitting fumes everywhere."[13] And thus Sir Humphry Davy, one of the founders of modern chemistry, penned some of his discoveries in verse because he was a gifted amateur poet encouraged by his close friend Samuel Taylor Coleridge.[14] In all these cases and countless others, the knowledge of nature was central to the dialogue between the sciences and the arts. As Robert J. Richards reminds us, Goethe, in an essay penned in 1789 and entitled "Simple Imitation of Nature, Manner, Style," distinguished between moderate talents "who would imitate nature very precisely in their simple compositions, from those of greater talent, who would discover within themselves a language, a manner, by which to express more complex subjects."[15]

Now to turn to two non-architectural examples in which such expression emerges: The first involves the great Austrian composer Joseph Haydn, the inventor of the "Symphony" form and a man of the Enlightenment living the last chapter of his life by straddling the century. Over the course of his travels to England in the early 1790s—he had accepted the invitation made by the German impresario Johann Peter Salomon to produce and conduct new symphonies in London—he took it upon himself to visit none other than Herschel in his observatory in Slough. Herschel gave him a demonstration of his extraordinary telescope, 40 feet long and 5 inches in diameter, which struck Haydn, so he noted in his travel notebooks, as "so ingenious that a single man can put it in motion with the greatest ease."[16] That glimpse of the universe, and the idea that the cosmos could have evolved out of chaos, undoubtedly came to mark his monumental oratorio *The Creation*, which premiered at the Schwarzenberg Palace in Vienna in 1798.[17] This was Haydn's first attempt at composing in a genre known for centuries in England. And in the musical introduction, subtitled "The Representation of Chaos," he played with receding and assertive tonalities in unprecedented ways in order to convey how, as Richard Taruskin puts it, "inchoate matter strives . . . toward shape and differentiation."[18]

The second example involves the English novelist Mary Shelley: that a woman in that period should have been interested in writing was already somewhat unusual; that she should have been, in addition, seriously interested in "experimental philosoph" was almost unconceivable. Yet, she religiously attended Sir Humphry Davy's lectures on chemistry at the Royal Society, read his *Discourse, Introductory to a Course of Lectures on Chemistry* (1802) and corresponded with scientists of the day. She was especially interested in the discovery of electricity and associated phenomena (something comparable with our excitement with things digital), which had been observed but still largely unexplained. All of this helped her to shape *Frankenstein, or the Modem Prometheus* (1818), which was unmistakably founded on the scientific and philosophical discourses of the time.[19] Her interest in electricity, which at the time was thought potentially to hold the definitive explanation of the origins of life, sits at the core of her disquisition about the nature of man, his ambitions and his conflicted desire to know and to produce (Figs. 3, 4).

My point, in closing, is perhaps not as apparent as one might think; these artists were serious about learning about nature. If they went through the pains of acquiring a substantive knowledge of nature, when they came back to produce, they did so with the tools of their *métier* (which they never confused for the things they had learned). Mary Shelley wrote the consummate Romantic novel, created a new genre—that of science fiction—and thereby not only reaffirmed her vocation but advanced its capacities. She directed her knowledge of chemistry, electricity, voltaic arcs, etc. at the construction of a story about scientific hubris. *She had a literary idea not an electrical idea*. For his part, Haydn did the same. He encountered theories about the formation of the universe, then sought out a musical form—the oratory—that would allow him to narrate a sublime story by means of an acoustic marvel evoking the creation of space. However exciting or foreboding, scientific

5

6

knowledge never kept them away from their respective crafts nor did they ever confuse nature with what they were making: no naive magic here, instead intellectual rigor and artistic integrity. *We should regain that dominion of our own doings, the nature of what we do, i.e. the Nature of Architecture, before we venture to bring nature into the equation.*

To end on a high note (no pun intended), imagine yourself listening to Haydn's *The Creation*, all the while picturing the galaxies alongside the manuscript page containing the notations of what you are hearing: image–music–text (*pace* Roland Barthes). These would be three representations of the same thing in different media: the photographic image; the sound of the music itself; and the sheet of paper whose vertical axis represents the space of the orchestra and whose horizontal axis indicates the rhythmic passage of time (Fig. 5, 6). They all address spatial infinity within their own substance and without betraying their own nature. No mixing, no blurring, no subsuming, no confusion.

Fig. 5 Joseph Haydn, score, "The Representation of Chaos" from *The Creation* 1797–1798.

Fig. 6 Portrait of Barnard's Galaxy, October 15, 2009, taken using the Wide Field Imager attached to the 2.2-meter MPG/ESO telescope at ESO's La Silla Observatory, Chile.

POSTSCRIPT: NEW RULES FOR ARCHITECTURE

Rule #1: Architectural projects should not resemble natural forms, irrespective of whether they are good natural forms (such as fruits, flowers, pandas, etc.) or bad-natured natural forms (such as rotten eggs, tumors, arthrosis, swarming killer bees, etc.). Any forms that recall matter in a smelly state of decomposition should be banished.

Rule #2: Discourse on architecture should never refer to the design process as if it were a digestive, meteorological or oceanographic phenomenon. It is not. It is an architectural process. Learn the differences. Starting now, there will be a five-year moratorium on the following terms: propagate, intestate, parasitic, embryonic, harvested, mining, grafting, and so on.

Rule #3: Presentations should not imply that nature is good and architecture is bad. Be an educated person and learn, once and for all, that architecture was invented to protect us from nature. *Nature can kill you.*

Rule #4: Be serious and learn from history. Marc-Antoine Laugier's representation of the primitive hut does not offer historical proof that architecture is the result of a natural process because it shows the natural source of some of its structural components. This is a record of precisely the opposite: the moment at which architecture emerges and distances itself from nature by transforming organic matter into architectural matter.

Notes

1 Vitruvius, *The Ten Books of Architecture*, trans. Morris Hicky Morgan (New York, NY: Dover Publications, 1960), 35, 37. As William A. McClung, *The Architecture of Paradise: Survivals of Eden and Jerusalem* (Berkeley and Los Angeles: University of California Press, 1983), 93, has noted: "It is less in the identification of architecture with nature . . . than in the redefinition of nature itself that Vitruvius laid the basis for the Renaissance glory of the craft."

2 So often at issue is the gloss of scientific authority that references to nature in architecture seemingly want to evoke. As Esa Väliverronen, who has considered the simultaneously communicative and obfuscatory power of metaphor in the environmental sciences in "Biodiversity and the Power of Metaphor in Environmental Discourse," *Science Studies* 11/1 (June 1998), 19–34, emphasizes: "[B]iodiversity is not just a normal scientific concept. It is often used as an all-encompassing term, a 'scientized synonym for nature'. . . . Biodiversity is about almost anything that is good and under threat in our natural environment. The power of biodiversity as a metaphor in semiprofessional and popular discourses is linked to its origin as a scientific concept" (31).

3 Claude Lévi-Strauss, *The Savage Mind* (French ed. 1962; Chicago, IL: University of Chicago Press, 1966), 9.

4 Leonardo da Vinci, *Leonardo on the Human Body* (New York, NY: Dover Publications, 1983), 330.

5 Kenneth Burke, *A Grammar of Motives* (Berkeley and Los Angeles: University of California Press, 1969), 503.

6 See, for instance, Ludwig von Bertalanffy, *General System Theory: Foundations, Development, Applications* (New York, NY: George Braziller, 1969).

7 Herbert A. Simon, "The Architecture of Complexity," *Proceedings of the American Philosophical Society* 106/6 (Dec. 1962), 467.

8 Edward Larrissy, ed., *Romanticism and Postmodernism* (Cambridge, MA: Cambridge University Press, 1999), 1.

9 Andreas Friesenhagen, "Let there be light," liner notes for the Harmonia Mundi HMC 992039 recording of Joseph Haydn's "Die Schöpfung," performed by the Freiburger Barockorchester directed by René Jacobs (2009).

10 Elizabeth Garber, *The Language of Physics: The Calculus and the Development of Theoretical Physics in Europe, 1750–1914* (Boston, MA: Birkhäuser, 1999), 140.

11 For a recent history of Romantic science in England organized around the biographies of prominent scientists and artists of the period, see Richard Holmes, *The Age of Wonder: How the Romantic Generation Discovered the Beauty and Terror of Science* (New York, NY: Pantheon Books, 2008).

12 On this, see for example Gerald Finley, "Pigment into Light: Turner, and Goethe's 'Theory of Colours'," in Frederick Burwick, Jurgen Klein, eds., *The Romantic Imagination: Literature and Art in England and Germany* (Amsterdam: Rodopi B.V., 1996) 357–376.

13 Johann Wolfgang von Goethe, *Italian Journey, 1786–1788*, trans. W. H. Auden and Elizabeth Mayer (London: Penguin Classics, 1970), 189. See David Seamon, Arthur Zajonc, eds., *Goethe's Way of Science: A Phenomenology of Nature* (Albany: SUNY Press, 1998).

14 Roger Sharrock, "The Chemist and the Poet: Sir Humphry Davy and the Preface to Lyrical Ballads," *Notes and Records of the Royal Society of London* 17/1 (May 1962): 57–76.

15 Robert J. Richards, *The Romantic Conception of Life: Science and Philosophy in the Age of Goethe* (Chicago, IL: University of Chicago Press, 2002), 402.

16 Norman Lebrecht, ed., *The Book of Musical Anecdotes* (New York: Simon & Schuster, 1985), 51.

17 Karl Geiringer, *Haydn: A Creative Life in Music* (Berkeley and Los Angeles: University of California Press, 1982), 356.

18 Richard Taruskin, *Oxford History of Western Music* (Oxford: Oxford University Press, 2009), ex. 11–10a.

19 I find it interesting that the feminist interpretation likewise pushes back against the metaphor. Anne K. Mellor, *Mary Shelley: Her Life, Her Fictions, Her Monsters* (London: Routledge, 1988), 89, writes: "The explanatory models of science, like the plots of literary works, depend on linguistic structures which are shaped by metaphor and image. When Francis Bacon announced, 'I am come in very truth leading to you Nature with all her children to bind her to your service and make her your slave,' he identified the pursuit of modern science with the practice of sexual politics: the aggressive, virile male scientist legitimately captures and enslaves a fertile but passive female nature. Mary Shelley was one of the first to comprehend and illustrate the dangers inherent in the use of such gendered metaphors in the seventeenth-century scientific revolution."

Boston

Architecture: The Making of a Practice

WITH NADER TEHRANI

Previous spread: A partial view of the "New" Getty Villa, showing the convergence of many elements and types of intervention in this twelve-year-long project. To the left is the northern corner of the restored original Museum Building's entrance portico and terrace. At the center and to the right are some of the most notable new architectural components by Machado Silvetti: the main entrance plaza, including a corner of the new outdoor theater; the bookstore and visitor services; and the public dining facilities above. In the foreground, and below the entrance plaza, is the courtyard of the education facilities.

1. The Emergence of a Cultural Practice

NADER TEHRANI Jorge, your education in Buenos Aires established a certain relationship to practice, if not because of its ideological underpinnings, then simply because students graduated from the university as licensed architects. There was a natural relationship between education and practice.

JORGE SILVETTI Yes, and let me add that every single one of our professors was a practitioner. It was inconceivable that someone who didn't practice would teach. I'm not saying this is the only way, but that's how it was. The best architects in Argentina taught, and they were respected as architects. As students, we wanted our professors to be people whose design work we admired. We were not attracted to them for their theory, their writing, or their pedagogy. We had no idea what pedagogy was!

NT Still, I get the sense that you and Rodolfo [Machado] fostered a latent critique of this model of practice. The two of you left Argentina almost immediately after graduation. Beyond the political reasons for doing so, you had a vision of how practice could be redefined. This led you to Berkeley and Rodolfo to Paris.

Can you describe what prompted your departure to other lands?

JS Rodolfo would probably agree that we weren't interested in exploring other forms of practice abroad. We never thought there could be other ways of practicing architecture than what we knew from Buenos Aires, either in school or in the field, nor did we see a need to change this. Somehow architects got projects, whether from clients or by submitting entries to open competitions. If they got the commissions—and they were lucky—they got to build the projects.

At that time, we were more concerned with understanding how to design an architecture that was more responsive to the reality we experienced. There was a widespread feeling at the school that this reality felt misaligned with the one modernism was still promoting. Most design studios were pursuing a great diversity of approaches. We were part of a circle at the school that wanted to pursue new ideas about architecture that dealt with social, intellectual, and aesthetic issues, which we felt needed to be retooled. That said, we were more focused on developing ourselves intellectually than on problematizing practice. So we looked for places where we thought there were the best opportunities to do so.

There was a moment of change brewing, but it was mostly happening in places other than Buenos Aires. Rodolfo got a fellowship to study urbanism and planning at the École Pratique des Hautes Études in Paris, and I went to UC Berkeley to study design methodology, the systems approach, and cybernetics. In time, however, we both ended up focusing on understanding architecture through the lenses of very different disciplines. But that's another story.[1]

You know, even when I came to Berkeley with some time to kill before starting graduate school, I had the same experience with practice as I did in Buenos Aires. I was working in Donald Olsen's one-man office, doing competitions and helping him finish a beautiful modern house in the Berkeley Hills. So even American practice at that point felt very much in line with my previous experience in Argentina.

NT But why does it seem like you were intent on pursuing an expanded definition of practice—something that goes beyond the conventional notion of professional practice—from the beginning? Your practice has taken you over the years from design to writing, from architectural theory to historical research, and from leadership within the academy to curatorial support for cultural institutions. These are all involvements through which you have pursued a definition of *the architect* that has more cultural latitude than the model you grew up with. Perhaps you did not plan this path from the beginning, but it is certainly the result of very specific investments over time.

What opportunities prompted this expansion, and at what point did you realize that the conventional practice was outdated in terms of its ability to provide the discipline of architecture with the agency you desired?

JS However we broadened the definition of practice, it was simply the result of our conviction to pursue a broader understanding of how architecture works as a whole. This conviction was rooted in a widespread feeling during the late '60s: that modern architecture had failed to address some of its most distinctive goals. I think it's worth revisiting this moment of dissatisfaction and comparing it to some of our own dissatisfactions today. It was our generation's understanding that modern architecture sought to address a new society that had changed radically by focusing intensely on social issues—in many ways, they were much more focused on that goal than we are today. But at the time, our explicit critique of modern architecture was that its formal, programmatic, and aesthetic proposals had failed the social agenda they had set themselves up to address, which we still thought was a valid objective. So in those early years of our career, we thought that what needed to be done was to renew that same social agenda of modern architecture, but our concern was focused on the creative process of design, not on the production and execution process. This was why we thought that we needed to better understand how architecture worked in relation to society—to real life.

We did not have a polemical stance toward the foundations of modernism, although attempts to challenge the official history of modern architecture were already underway. The first attempts at scholarly criticism were beginning to create a climate in which we could question the knowledge we had received from modernism. For example, we were very impressed by the early work of Reyner Banham. He was pursuing very serious scholarly work through which he demonstrated in a convincing way the solid links that modern architecture had with the French Beaux-Arts tradition. It was shocking and revelatory at that moment to see these links in how buildings were conceived, represented, classified, and designed. This was the opposite of the narrative we were all accustomed to: that modernism had signified a radical departure from the Beaux-Arts tradition.

Already in Buenos Aires, we were aware of the contemporary discussions about "design methodology" and its potential to improve the design process by drawing on knowledge from other disciplines. Some of us were excited about Christopher Alexander's recently published *Notes on the Synthesis of Form*.[2] UC Berkeley, where Alexander taught, was at the time focused on a quasi-scientific attempt to methodically relate architecture to social issues. There was also a lot of discussion about emerging fields of knowledge, such as cybernetics and the systems approach to design. These were seen as promising techniques to understand complex natural and social systems in relation to the creative process.

The curiosity of "the computer" was slowly making inroads here and there in the social sciences, and it was predicted that it would soon enter the world of design! From a purely intellectual point of view, all participants in these discussions were obsessed with optimizing and quantifying, rather than imagining or proposing alternative solutions to design problems. Today, these qualifications betray the clear positivist, empirical, and pseudoscientific roots of what was going on and how cultural factors were basically left out of the conversation. But it was a necessary impulse that helped break through some of the stunted scaffolding that was still haphazardly supporting modernism.

NT So, your notion of social engagement was already distinct in its recognition of what architecture could do through its own mechanisms? And by that I also mean what it could not do.

JS Well, that would attribute to me a clairvoyance that I certainly didn't have at the time. The architecture systems approach at Berkeley was full of flaws, since it was based on a total misunderstanding of architecture. However, what it did give me was a more solid understanding of how architecture is inextricably linked to other aspects of life and reality. I realized how simplistically modernist architects had summarized their own contemporary condition.

My first year at Berkeley was one of happy discoveries. I realized that we needed to have a much broader understanding of the complex constellation of forces with which architecture comes into contact in society. However, Rodolfo's arrival from Paris after that first year led me to abandon the mechanistic approach that Berkeley had encouraged, as he had been exposed to the continental view of culture and its relationship to architecture. Rodolfo saw the two ways we had approached the same problem as complementary, but my exposure to the ideas he brought from Europe undermined the whole construct of the Berkeley way in my mind. It was the biggest intellectual leap I ever made, from a systems approach to architecture to a cultural approach![3]

It wasn't until after that turn that I more consciously became *an architect*. We immersed ourselves in all these other disciplines in the sciences and humanities, and these perspectives helped us understand architecture, even if architecture was neither a science nor a humanity in itself. Linguistics and literary criticism, for example, became some of the most useful fields for us. But as tempting or necessary as it was to think that architecture worked in an analogous way to language, we began to sort out the ways in which architecture was different and to figure out what was actually useful to take from those fields.

We also eagerly participated in the world of literature, poetry, film, theater, and other fields that operate through highly articulated linguistic and visual narratives. My generation, at least in Argentina, was addicted to film. I still am—as you are, Nader—and it was reinforced during my experiences abroad. Rodolfo always says that in addition to his work at the École Pratique des Hautes Études, he went to the Cinémathèque Française every night during his year in Paris. When he came to Berkeley, we did the same at the Berkeley Repertory Theatre on Telegraph Avenue, two blocks from where we lived.

We slowly came to the conclusion that what all these arts have in common is that their power to affect human experience depends first and foremost on the production of form, be it literary, cinematic, or architectural. All of these arts also produce total visions that are deliberately conceived by an author. But these years also allowed us to see that the political or social power that each of these cultural practices can muster is different from the others.

I think it's only when you can see what these fields do and do not have in common that you can assess the degree to which each can have an impact on people's lives. This is very important from an intellectual and methodological point of view. When we are readers, moviegoers, or users of space, we allow ourselves to be affected in different ways. Navigating between all these practices back then allowed us to clearly identify the specific field of architecture. I think something that was generally undermined when we started our careers in the United States was that architecture does not produce a sequential linguistic narrative that unfolds over time like a film or a book and that this quality makes its behavior as a cultural product very different. Architecture does not have a card announcing *The End* or a final page. Its outcome is much more open-ended and uncertain.

You can see that we were trying to understand the practice of architecture, if you want to call it that, conceptually first. We thought that this would allow us to become better architects, who would apply this knowledge to our design work. We learned very slowly that this would require a different way of practicing, because we were very naive about practice. It took a *really* long time after we started practicing for us to acquire an understanding of the American practice and to realize that we were working in a peculiar way in that context. We never saw the separation between teaching and practicing, for example, simply because all our professors did both. We came to the United States and just carried on. That is how we always thought of ourselves.

Many students still ask me how they might emulate what we did back then, and I don't really know what to say. It wasn't something calculated.

NT Obviously I inherited some of that naiveness!

JS [*laughs*]

NT I have to say that all the ignorance I have about actual American practice …

JS You owe it to me!

NT Yes, I do! [*laughs*]

JS Yes, it's not so much ignorance as it is … a lack of interest in practice as a topic in itself. American professional practice is something I didn't participate in very actively. Of course I played the game when it was necessary, but I never really bought into the idea that it was fundamental to be part of that sphere. With respect and dedication, I did what I had to do to keep the practice moving effectively but without getting involved in the broader issues of practice itself.

NT Yes, I completely understand that. What I find interesting—perhaps because of my own experience in your office—is that you have nevertheless created a "North American" professional practice. Just one that looks nothing like the experience of other offices.

JS That may be, but if we did, it was surely unintentional. We always felt that we were pursuing the only possible route to keep doing the same thing we had always done.

NT One of the arenas that make up this expanded field of practice that you have cultivated is your focus on urbanism. You've focused on it not only in your design work but also in your research since the '70s. The presence of the city is visible everywhere: in the the Steps of Providence, in the research in Caltagirone, in the intervention in Leonforte, or in the master plan for the Getty Villa. In all of these cases, the city is not just a backdrop; it is another protagonist incorporated into the project as a cultural factor. The city is what positions architecture as one voice among many others, what allows your work to address cultural politics and larger social issues that make up urban life.

Can you talk about how urbanism has influenced your idea of an architectural practice? As we see in *Buildings for Cities*, the first monograph of your work with Rodolfo, urbanism was a defining aspect of the office's identity early on.

JS The city permeates all of our work, our thinking, and our lives. So I agree that it is one of the defining characteristics of our understanding of architecture. Our work is inseparable from the city to which it belongs, whether it's the actual city or the way we imagine the city through the project. Today, of course, this is an almost de rigueur tenet held by designers. However, I am not sure that we all mean the same thing when we talk about the city. For us, it is more of a cultural compact than a feature of scale or strictly functional complexity. It is a solid whole made up of all of those forces that shape architecture. We're trying to go beyond the broad idea of the city as context, which doesn't mean much anymore.

By the time we left Argentina, Rodolfo and I were both adherents of Team 10's critical positions on the reductive understanding of the city that characterized orthodox modernism. But we found that these were things that were not so widespread in the American academic world when we arrived. My thesis project in Argentina had been a large urban complex in Liniers, a peripheral and densely populated working-class neighborhood of Buenos Aires. As a team, we designed

Model of Cumbernauld Town Centre (Phase 1 in Scotland, U.K., designed by Leslie Hugh Wilson, Dudley Roberts Leaker, Geoffrey Copcutt, Philip Aitken, and Neil Dadge (1963–1967).

Model of Jorge Silvetti's undergraduate thesis project at the Universidad de Buenos Aires (1964, team work), which received the Premio Taller for the best work in the Taller Odilia Suárez.

a very large urban center and transportation exchange. It brought together commuter rail and surface transit and commercial, residential, institutional, and recreational programs. It was a multilevel, sectional design, modeled after the recently completed Cumbernauld town center project in Scotland.[4]

The Cumbernauld project was a sectionally extruded megastructure of urban scale. To us, it represented the most advanced thinking and work being done at the time, and in many ways it was, even if it was short-lived and posed some insurmountable challenges. The project boldly addressed some of the inherent problems that the city of modern architecture had created, like the disruption of the social fabric of the traditional city through repetitiveness, a lack of programmatic variety, a loss of local identity, and a destructive indifference to historic centers and the landscape.

The Cumbernauld proposal embraced the inherent verticality of the twentieth-century city, but not through the stacking up of a repetitive floor plan. It organized the life of the city through the layering of different programs, avoiding the disconnection and monotony that the Ville Radieuse had inspired and produced. The project introduced a much stronger understanding of how social groups behave and interact in space. It embodied a new awareness of how societies evolve and enrich themselves as they construct elaborate physical environments. The discussions it generated were incredibly productive.

Although it soon became clear that such megastructures posed other problems, some of them seemingly insurmountable, the discussions they generated were fertile and inspiring. There was even a strong critical stance in the project toward the megastructures that the Metabolists were proposing in Japan, which was their own second-generation critique of modernism. The utopianism of the Metabolists was a very important part of the discussion during those years, and we should keep it in mind as we assess the formalist utopias of parametric megastructures that haunt us to this day.

Here was a reform of modernism coming out of its own tradition. The work being produced demonstrated a concerted effort to go beyond its failures and limitations of models like the Ville Radieuse. Whether you look at the Smithsons in England or Ernesto N. Rogers and the *Casabella* circle in Italy in the '50s, modern architecture had evolved rapidly without breaking as an intellectual project, and we saw ourselves as the new generation continuing this critical work.

NICOLÁS DELGADO ALCEGA Some of the projects Nader mentioned, like the Steps of Providence, demonstrate your interest in architecture's relationship to the city, but they also manifest an urban ambition that operates at the scale of architecture. This combination becomes an early characteristic of your office's work. I see a parallel between this

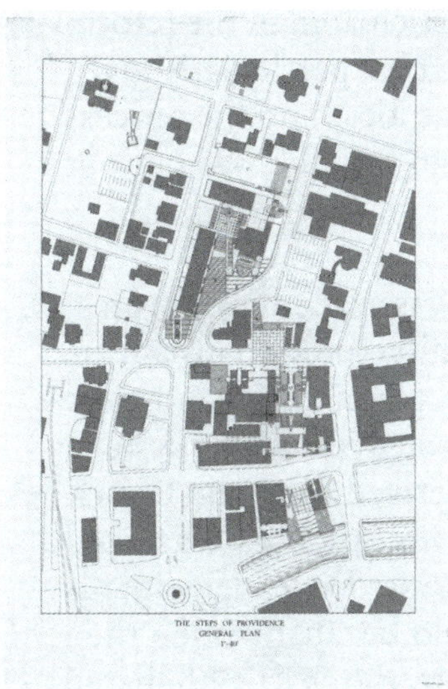

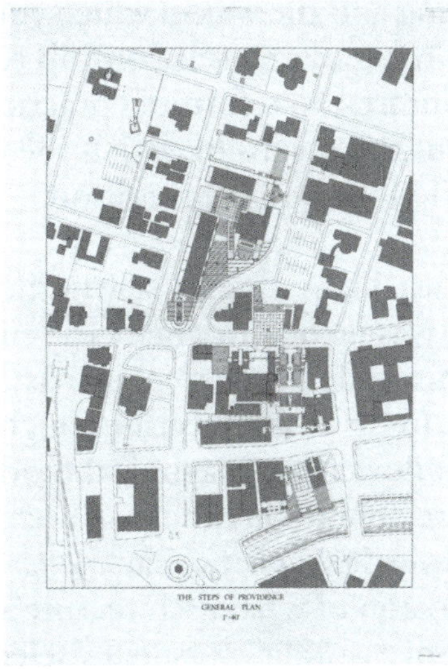

Drawings of the Steps of Providence, Rodolfo Machado and Jorge Silvetti (1977–1979).

Before and after depictions of the overall plan for the Rhode Island Schoolof Design.

Before and after depictions of the Memorial Steps and Plaza area.

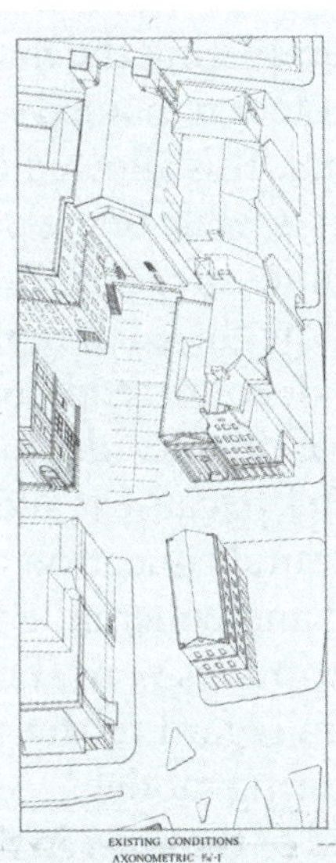

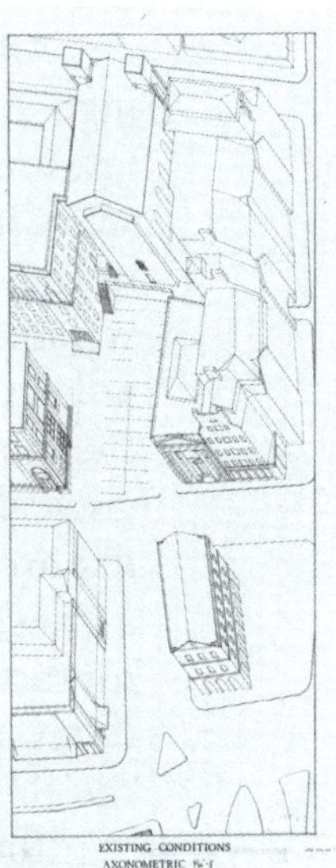

Longitudinal section of the proposal for the Memorial Steps and Plaza area.

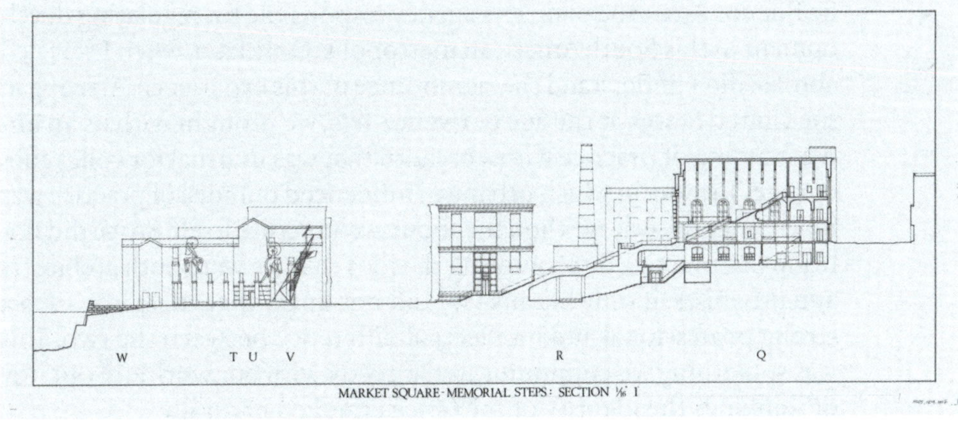

urban thinking and the way in which you participated in the reform of modern architecture's relationship to the city, particularly given you had no interest in reforming practice. The ideas and the process were new, but the means by which the design product was put out into the world followed the tradition.

JS In the work we did in Argentina, whether it was academic or professional, there was no distinction between architecture and urbanism. There were no academic degrees in urbanism, planning, or landscape architecture. It was all architecture, taught through the atelier system, which still followed a pedagogical model derived from the Beaux-Arts. We were about five thousand architecture students organized in a series of vertical *talleres*.[5] Each *taller* had a strong leader with his or her own vision of what architecture should be. That person then had a cohort of assistants personally selected by the chair, who shared their views.

After completing the first two years of basic architectural training, each student remained with the *taller* of his or her choice for the last four years. This allowed us to follow a distinctive pedagogy and set of interests while being part of a larger community that exposed us to other lines of study. The school was a sort of conglomerate of schools of thought, each represented by one of the two dozen or so *talleres*. We all coexisted in one building but dedicated ourselves to the pursuit of distinct ideologies. In fact, it was a truly diverse pedagogical model, because it allowed for a diversity of thought, but, unlike architectural education now, it also allowed students to receive a structured and coherent education within a single field of inquiry for four continuous years. I think we can learn something from this today, also in regard to the advantages of mass education vis-à-vis the elite tutoring model.

The head of the *taller* in which I did my design work was the leading architect and urbanist in Argentina at the time, Odilia Suárez. She was a full professor and the director of El Plan Regulador de la Ciudad de Buenos Aires, the main city agency responsible for regulating development in this South American metropolis. Only later, when I traveled abroad, did I understand the significance of this experience. Arriving in the United States at the age of twenty-five, we brought with us an understanding of practice with a breadth that was unusual for colleagues our age. The way in which urbanism influenced our idea of practice was inherent in the way we thought about architecture itself. So we did not begin our practice by promoting the idea that we were both architects and urbanists, if only because we did not know that there was such a strong professional and intellectual difference between the two. This was something we communicated directly with our work and our way of thinking. The identity of the office emerged naturally.

With the long view that five decades in American higher education gives me, I cannot be more appreciative of the solid, deep, and broad foundation with which the Universidad de Buenos Aires prepared me for this moment that now belongs to the history of architecture. It was six years of intense study that integrated an incipient critical theory, technology, and architectural composition into the studio format. The result was an understanding of the city as the natural and indisputable protagonist of the architect's work.

By the time we left Buenos Aires, Rodolfo and I had worked with our "partners"—in an arrangement we called Arquitectos Asociados—on competitions, some of which involved very large urban projects. We did a couple of projects, for the Berisso town center and El Frutillar, for which we won awards. Soon after, a former classmate called Jorge Lestard and I were hired by the City of Buenos Aires as lead designers of a team working on two very large social housing complexes in the outskirts of Buenos Aires: Villa Lugano 1 and 2.[6] We brought with us these new ideas, developed in the United Kingdom, of separating urban circulation systems by level and vertically layering different programs. In the end, however, the scale and ambition of the architecture was undermined by political realities, and the complex was very poorly realized.

The complex still stands on the way to the airport, where I see it every time I go to Argentina. It is the largest residential urban design project in Argentina, and was the largest in Latin America at the time. It is also the largest project that I have ever designed, and it was my first, at the age of twenty-three! Every time I see it, I mourn for what it could have been. I must add that all those frustrations at the end of the project led Lestard and me to resign and slam the door as we left. What a way to start a practice!

NT Meanwhile, other architects in Europe and North America were also revisiting the status of the city, as well as the way meaning is produced in architecture through a system of thinking. To what degree was your intellectual journey impacted by this? Otherwise, to what degree did you anticipate these changes in the air?

JS When Rossi and Venturi and Scott Brown began to circulate ideas about the city in the American architectural culture of the 1970s—when *the city* finally found its place in academia and practice—we were fortunate to be very well-prepared to participate in this broad shift. Rossi's introduction of the dialectic between urban morphology and architectural typology on the one hand and Venturi's focus on iconography and symbolism on the other were transformative. These were distinctive, sometimes incompatible ways of thinking about architecture that we received contemporaneously and interpreted as

From left to right: Tito Varas, Miguel Baudizzone, Rodolfo Machado, and Jorge Silvetti displaying a panel from their winning entry for the national architectural competition El Frutillar, Buenos Aires (1966).

Mannequins for Portantina designed by Jorge Silvetti and plan of the Porta Meridionale di Palermo entry for the 1986 Triennale di Milano exhibition at the American Academy in Rome end-of-the-year exhibit (1986).

one. They complemented, corrected and amplified the ideas of Team 10, of Rogers's *Casabella*, and other conversations in Italian journals.

The way in which some architects of our generation were able to put together these contributions produced something closer to a break with the recent past than the previous generation of late modernists. The arrival of the ideas best exemplified by Venturi and Rossi definitively laid the groundwork for us to begin to conceive of architecture as a "cultural practice." We had a mature understanding of architecture's relationship to the field of urbanism and, thanks to our experiences in Buenos Aires, had developed real, solid design skills to address problems across scales.

NT Your relationship to the city reminds me that you are as invested in the design of interiors and furniture as you are in the urban landscape. You've often described the dialogue you see between each of these arenas and how they come together to create this expanded form of practice that we alluded to earlier. Many architects assume this multiplicity of scales as part of their practice, but most simply apply the same assumptions and ideas across scales. They don't take the time to develop a framework that allows them to articulate their thoughts in relation to the possibilities associated with each scale. Your practice has found ways to develop discourses that are quite specific when dealing with these different scales yet remain consistent with your overall intellectual project. Can you provide some examples that demonstrate this confluence and departure across the scales that you've engaged with?

JS Are you referring to Rodolfo's designs for rugs, chaise longues, and lamp-shades? I think it's important to mention that if there's one of us who was leading the way with what you refer to as an expanded field that pays attention to furniture as much as it does to cities, it's Rodolfo. We didn't see clearly this differentiated correlation between all the scales that make up our lived environment early on. However, our intuition and the guidance of certain thinkers at the forefront of the design world led us in this direction of cultural and critical studies, which had an important impact on our personal sensibilities. Rodolfo was always ahead of me in this respect, marking the path, finding the milestones, and interpreting the messages that came our way. This attitude has stayed with Rodolfo to this day, and he still has one of the best libraries on interior design that I know of, built all the while he was chair of Harvard's Department of Urban Planning and Design!

NT That is such perfect irony!

JS Perfect and revelatory at the same time. Once you understand the practice of architecture as a cultural practice, most of the conventional categories into which our society classifies or divides the work of architects fall apart. They may be necessary from a professional and operational perspective, but from an intellectual point of view, they are all made of the same stuff. Regardless of the scales at which we intervene, everything that is built around us belongs to the realm of material culture.

What we do as architects is to intentionally design the elements of material culture that make up the environments in which we live. The scale at which we operate determines the resources at our disposal and the appropriate technologies to be used. For us, thinking about the city and thinking about a chair were two different things that came out of two very different kinds of practice. But at the same time, they belonged to a system, to a universe in which all its components were highly interconnected and in which one could move comfortably—a universe of designed objects. I think this is nothing other than the collection of images—what we can call the formal manifestations—of a culture that secretes them in space. It is a system constituted by forms and the inconstant meanings we ascribe to them, whether actual, circumstantial, accumulated over time, or temporary. These meanings inhabit and activate these forms so that they resonate with distinctive vibrancy at a given point.

NT My own early work on furniture was, in some way, an attempt to address the undue ascription of superficiality—or lack of discipline—in interior design, decoration, and iconography. These are all things that Rodolfo and you have very strong opinions about, but schools of architecture have proven to be too ideologically straight to take them seriously. I suspect that your focus on language has allowed you to reveal the discursive continuities that exist between the interior and the body of architecture as a whole.

JS This idea that an interior and the city are both fundamentally forms of material culture is a very important aspect of our work, and it is why I keep referring to our practice as a cultural practice. We think our job is to develop knowledge about how these forms of material culture work so that we are best equipped to produce potent versions of them ourselves.

Architecture as an extended field, to use your term, is not a new concept. It exists in the long history of architecture, going back to Vitruvius, who described the domains of architecture quite broadly. Since the Renaissance, architects have not only painted but also designed magnificent interiors, household artifacts, furniture, gardens, waterworks, cities, and infrastructure. However, being aware of the

Rodolfo Machado on the terrace of the Institute for Architecture and Urban Studies in New York City, holding a model of the Roosevelt Island Competition entry, designed with Jorge Silvetti, Diana Agrest, and Mario Gandelsonas (1975).

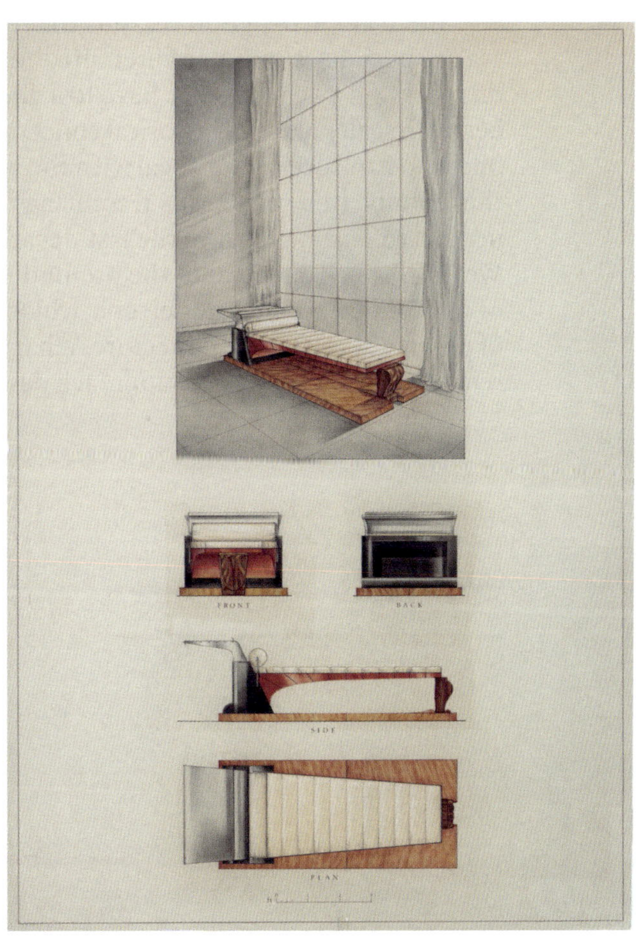

Drawing of L.A. Borghese chaise longue, designed by Rodolfo Machado (1981).

commonalities between these still requires us to understand the particular conditions of each scale and function. For example, a teapot is not the same as a building. I've seen dozens of teapots designed by famous architects that are total failures!

If we look closer to our time, the Bauhaus is another pristine example of this lineage. It is more reductionist in fashion, but it still tends to make every part of life a subject of design. As modernism wore out, failing to produce better cities, we lost this ambition and ended up with many new professions, each more precisely focused on a specific scale and its corresponding building technologies. Modernism was not reductive in terms of the number of practices it tried to encompass. Its failure was more in the philosophical and ideological foundation on which it based its reformulation of architecture's field of action. The brilliance and weakness of the modernist proposition came from the same places. On the political level, it's modernism's alignment with one of its favorite myths: the zeitgeist. On the technical level, it's the clumsy, mechanical borrowing from an aesthetic revolution taking place in the visual arts and in industry, such as cubism or the cult of the machine.

There are many good reasons that can explain this shift toward scalar specialization in architecture, but I still think it is a tremendous loss on two levels: we have lost the dynamic interrelationship between scales and the historical conception of the designer as someone who can successfully deal with the complexity and richness that this entails. In a sense, this fracturing is what we began to feel we needed to react against in the last decades of the twentieth century. We didn't need a revival of the premodern creative world that many of our contemporaries undertook, which derailed the best intentions of postmodernism in architecture. What we needed was a preliminary refoundation of the way we approach design practices in their totality.

2. A Theory That Inhabits Practice

NDA I think that what you mean by "cultural practice" is a way of working that is not determined by a specific scale but rather the ability to design objects and spaces in a way that is very intentional about how these could perform as material culture in the built environment. This clarifies the link between architecture, anthropology, and literary criticism in your understanding: Anthropology allows you to understand architecture as material culture. Architecture gives you the problem of designing pieces of material culture. Literary criticism then allows you to assess instances of architecture and the degree to which they are successful formal manifestations of a set of cultural conditions.

Correct me if I'm wrong, but I think that being a designer who uses the analytical frameworks of the humanities is what defines the first generation of people like yourself, who were involved in what we call "architectural theory." It is also what distinguishes them from the second generation of theorists, the generation of Jeffrey Kipnis or Sanford Kwinter, who perhaps existed more in opposition to the world of practitioners. This latter generation came directly from the humanities, and in architecture they found an interesting academic subject. This is the opposite orientation of designers.

JS First, you are correct in your characterization of the drastic difference between the two generations that participated in the formation of architectural theory during the last decades of the twentieth century. However, we shouldn't characterize the second generation of architectural theorists as existing in opposition to practice. I think that would be giving them too much credit! It would imply that they understood practice, when I think they were more indifferent to it than anything else. They existed in a parallel world, but they thought they knew the practice, and that's the problem. They thought that because they were part of the discipline of architecture—since they undoubtedly were protagonists in the formation of its "discourse"—they were somehow doing the same thing as everybody else, which was not true.

Up until the '70s, the theory of architecture that we inherited from the Beaux-Arts tradition of the nineteenth century was still very operative as a mode of structuring pedagogy, which later determined how architects approached, discussed, and evaluated the project. Much of what was considered theory was a good description of specific architectural events. Precise and clear descriptions of the object being theorized are always an important aspect of theory. In the case of my generation, we were trained by the modernists to think about the relationship between architecture and technology, one line of which came from the architectural historian Auguste Choisy. He built up the grammar of a style based on the different ways you could make a wall or an opening or a roof. Of course, the question of beauty was also present in these architectural theories but was mostly implied and not necessarily explicit in an aesthetic position.

I'm very biased, but I think that when some in our generation began to understand architecture as one of the most important cultural practices of any society, we started to look beneath the surface of it all for the first time. It required us to take some distance and bring in other perspectives to interpret what architecture itself is. That is when many of us took those steps out of the discipline. In our case, Rodolfo and I went to French structuralism, through Claude Leví-Strauss, Roland Barthes, Louis Althusser, and others. But everybody at that time came up with slightly different answers to how architecture works as a cultural practice in society.

NDA This is somehow the underlying thread that we come across every time we look at an instance of your work, teaching, or writing: an obsessive search to understand how architecture works. Why does it come into being? How is it made? And how does it function in relation to culture and society?

JS You're right, yes. I'm still obsessed with understanding how architecture functions in society. It seems like the main preoccupation of my life has been to try to understand that! Not just technically but culturally. And that is what I think architectural theory should do. It should produce that knowledge.

I'm curious about your views on this, Nader? How *does* theory fit into practice today? We have questioned some of the second-generation theorists, but we are way past them at this point. I'm not sure that there is really such a thing as a consistent field of architectural theory like there was in the '70s and '80s, even though there are a lot of people working on theoretical issues.

Was the second generation of theorists led down a blind alley? Maybe that was the fate of theory all along. I'm not going to sit here and say that we were on the right track and they weren't. All I know is that at the time we felt like we were moving in a productive direction, but perhaps that was meant to be short-lived. I don't know. What I do know is that Rodolfo and I began moving away from the direction that cultural theory was taking in the early '90s. We could see and feel the inadequate ways in which it was taking a turn toward a purely critical model based on the philosophical approach of deconstruction.

When people tried to apply deconstruction to architecture, the limits of the analogy between the practice of architecture and language, or *la langue, l'ecriture*, became resoundingly clear. Deconstruction requires a great deal of self-consciousness about the author's fragility and his limited ability to control underlying cultural forces that affect his work. This is a tremendously productive approach when *deconstructing* texts philosophically and aesthetically. However, it just doesn't work for a practice that produces material culture.

While Rodolfo and I still marvel at Stéphane Mallarmé's genius, his poetic revolution is simply not applicable to architecture. By virtue of their most basic qualities, works of architecture cannot operate permanently as critiques of themselves. They can do so only in minor and ephemeral ways, which is apparent if we put them in the context of the greater life of a building. I think awareness about this condition of architecture remains a truly critical issue in architecture today. In my case, it took me until the early '90s to put the whole picture together. However, by the time I wrote my first article, "The Beauty of Shadows," I had begun to assemble the pieces that led me to this conclusion, which is that the defining characteristic of architecture as a cultural practice is that the building must exist in an energizing contradiction of two forces: it has to criticize, but it also has to mythify.[7]

NT The afterword in K. Michael Hays's *Unprecedented Realism* addresses this question in a direct way.[8] It was an explicit challenge to the direction that theory had taken by the mid-'90s.

NDA Reading it with some distance, it feels strangely sharp and refreshing! Even in relation to some of what is going on right now.

NT And yet, it's been almost thirty years since it was written. Much has changed, so it would be interesting to know how you would update or revise those positions, Jorge, given what we have seen unfold.

Let me remind you that many theorists today describe their work as a form of architectural practice. They are also attuned to an idea of expanded forms of practice, but I suspect that this is still far from what you describe as cultural practice. I think we need to be more precise about what practice is, especially when we talk about it in the academy. Part of this is about language, but it is also about arenas within the academy that are contested by different groups.

JS Well, if anything has become clearer to me after fifty years of working on this, it is that theorizing about architecture is not a way of practicing architecture. But that does not mean that we have to come full circle to get back to where it all began. As a discipline, we have arrived at a different place than the "new theory" that crystallized in the '70s.

The study of architectural theory should lead us to the practice of architecture, not away from it. It shouldn't presume to flourish in parallel. It should inform the creative moment of design and work in concert with the design methods at architects' disposal. It's been my experience that theory for its own sake only leads us to the wrong places. In this regard, I must correct some of what I believed when I began my forays into that new theory. At that time I was implicitly sure that we should abandon the old theory because it was prescriptive. I still believe theory shouldn't be as normative as it was before, but it should help us clarify the process of design, in both its technical and symbolic dimensions.

NDA So what can a practice informed by architectural theory look like today? What is the next iteration of this lineage that we can experiment with right now? I'm quite tired of intellectually sophisticated practices that can only produce drawings because of their inept relationship with reality *and* aesthetically sophisticated practices that are cynical about the relevance of their built work. In my view these are both unprincipled ways of practicing that are content to simply sell their value to the highest bidder, whether elite universities or clients that designers neither know nor really want anything to do with. Both evince how unhinged architecture has become from a broader social purpose.

JS I think this is a question that Nader and you have to answer! Each from your own relative positions. I have to deal with those aspects of my own experience that are worth articulating and preserving in the interest of your newer searches, those reformulations of a lineage that I think is worth continuing.

I *would* say, however, that I think we can rephrase your question. When we were writing the afterword in 1994, Hays suggested that the relationship between theory and practice in our work is one in which theory *inhabits* practice. This is a felicitous term that Michael coined at the time and that I have since adopted. Although he used it to describe our practice, I think it can be generalized. It represents the proper place that architectural theory should occupy. Michael's phrase captures very well what we have been doing all these years and what I think you are alluding to. There are forms of practice that can actually embody theoretical lessons.

NT The idea of theory inhabiting practice is as relevant today as it was then. In part, this is because the expansion of the definition of practice has given way to a laissez-faire moment. Anything qualifies as theory and anything qualifies as practice, even though neither is necessarily committed to the social engagement that an architect must participate in to make buildings and shape the built environment.

This reminds me of an episode from when I worked with you on the Gateway to Venice competition. Until then, our engagement was limited to school reviews, that is, discussions and debates that were certainly theoretical. They were an arm's length away from the kind of commitment that only drawings and models can bring to an architectural idea. Until that moment, I had also never seen you draw.

For Venice, I had done a series of random sketches revealing that the road to our site, Piazzale Roma, was exactly ninety degrees to the Grand Canal, which is, of course, the main channel for the *vaporetti*. Although I recognized it to be of urbanistic consequence, the discovery did not give me any ideas; I merely mentioned it to you as an architectural curiosity. When I arrived the next day, you called me over to show me a drawing you had made in response. It was an amazing composite plan and section drawn on tracing paper, with the ninety-degree figure extruded to reveal a half-open book held by the Lion of Saint Mark, depicted in an essentially unorthodox manner. It was inscribed with the words *PAX TIBI MARCE EVANGELISTA MEUS,* the legend of Venice.

As the creative process goes, it was one of those moments when the geometric alignment of an urban diagram coalesces with the semantic figure of an architectural icon in a surreptitious slippage. Though entirely arbitrary to each other, their confluence could be said to bring together a moment where theory *inhabits* practice, as you put it. That is, theory inhabits the act of drawing. We can talk about concepts all we want, but architectural ideas emerge when they are embodied, that is, when they are represented by formal, spatial, or material means, not just developed and communicated in narratives. After that drawing, I knew we had arrived; the drawing capped the project in a gesture that seemed so inevitable that it was impossible to retract. The process was an epiphany for me.

Even though architects generally declare that architectural ideas are born through drawing, something considered universal to the discipline, the way you draw is a particularly important aspect of your practice. I think this is something we should discuss further. When you draw, you are thinking through different levels of cultural affiliation and at the same time producing a new form of knowledge. In this case of Gateway to Venice, it had to do with the circumstantial overlap of geometry and a set of different icons present in the city. These were the opportunities: the Lion of Saint Mark as a cultural symbol, the figure of a book as a hinge, and the *campanili* of Venice as urban markers within the city, just to name a few.

NDA What do you mean by "a new form of knowledge"?

NT I mean something beyond the resolution of practical considerations that also contributes to culture in broader terms, the ability to discover new relationships between the city, its civic structures, and the iconographies that make them legible. These constitute a lexicon that has the capacity not only to enable communication between people with a common set of cultural conventions but also to transform the meaning of symbols, producing new kinds of knowledge through the architectural drawing itself.

JS The role of drawing in our work is fundamental. This may sound dramatic, but it is one of the reasons why it has become so difficult for me to practice anymore. It has become impossible for me to draw. I don't even have a drafting table in the office.

NDA Why is that? Having recently seen the exhibition of your archive at the GSD, I can say that this statement is tragic.

JS For me, drawings are the fundamental means of establishing a dialogue in the design process. The story you told about the Gateway to Venice *is* the way I know how to work with other people. But I find that drawings don't evoke reactions from people in the same way anymore. Everything has to be communicated in words and then mechanically translated into a drawing.

The other thing that has made drawing increasingly difficult for me is that the design process has become so mechanical with the computer. For all the usefulness of digital drawing, it makes it very difficult to translate ideas into a spatial investigation quickly and iteratively. It is very rare to find people who are digitally native but at the same time able to explore ideas with a few lines; to convince themselves of something before entering the reductive, tedious process of mechanically producing a chosen iteration.

NT The computerized drawing or model certainly has its own protocols, and managing them is a critical part of how many practices have adapted their design process to new technologies. But even on the computer, the iterative process remains as important as ever, only that its potential has been expanded exponentially.

JS Yes, but there is still a paradoxically disturbing aspect of the computer's iterative process: its economy. Iteration is extremely important in

Nader Tehrani (seated) and Jorge Silvetti at work in the Boston offices of Machado and Silvetti Associates (ca. 1991).

Wood and brass model of Gateway to Venice, the competition entry for the 1991 Biennale di Architettura di Venezia, Machado and Silvetti Associates.

the design process, and it is extremely time-consuming and tedious when drawing by hand, so it necessarily requires an editing process that has been strategically considered. Most of the time it is consciously directed toward a goal, but with the computer you can generate formal alternatives for free, *unintentionally*, in minutes. Then you choose the one you like without having generated a real idea by thinking seriously about the problem at hand. These kinds of "solutions" tend to have no conceptual basis—there is no architectural idea, even if there might be an alluring formal novelty that gets confused for one!

This is all so boring. But worse than that, it paralyzes creativity, which, I might add, is also different from novelty. I simply cannot take part in this process that is everywhere today.

NT The offices that have done better with these issues are perhaps those that have a process where making study models is very important. But models have played a slightly different role in your practice, wouldn't you say?

JS As you know very well, Rodolfo and I don't make models! We never did, not even as students. It was just something I never needed in my work. I am all about plans, sections, and perspectives and how they activate the imagination. I am a drawing person, as I think you are too. Maybe it sounds arrogant to those who do not draw, but in the drawings, I see everything I need to understand the architecture I want to make. I see all its dimensions. I do not need a model in the creative moment. This does not mean that I disagree with all of those architects from my generation who used models that way. I can see why they can be useful.

Nevertheless, we have many models in our office. I remember you supervised the model of the wall fragment for the Gateway to Venice, which was something! You brought a student of yours from RISD who cut every single tile for the floor and glued it all together! Whether it is that model or the one for the garden folly—for which we had someone cut every single brick into the facade—we felt these objects were so precious.

A lot of the projects we never built, but we clearly built them as models anyway!

NT I've never thought of your models as just representational. I think they simulate the process of construction, anticipating the means and methods of fabrication long before they actually happen. They are almost mock-ups. In that sense, I interpreted these models as aspiring to the logic of their making. They are objects that manifest not only what things look like but, more importantly, how they work.

JS That's interesting. People see these models today and they don't believe them, even though you could probably replicate them quite easily with a 3D printer. The fact that they were done by hand was important.

NT I don't want to get stuck, but I would like to continue talking about the way in which the act of drawing remains for you a central precondition of architectural thinking. You have developed a series of drawings that do not fit neatly into canonical formats. They are what I like to call "catalytic drawings," because they challenge representational conventions to force us to think differently.

Could you talk about some of these drawings and the role they play in your practice? I'm thinking of drawings like the plan of the Fountain House or the manifesto for the 1980 Venice Biennale.

JS Drawings are the paradigm of representation in architecture, and representation is the most fundamental component that defines all the phases that go into the creation of architecture. As I said long ago, architects do not build buildings, they draw them. Drawings are the technical enablers that allow the realization of the subject—say, the building—that they represent. But in representing the subject, they also register the creative act of designing it. In this sense, then, drawings represent twice: they represent their subject, and they represent the designer's process of arriving at its final form.

Like in all systems of representation, there is always a "loss" in the transfer from reality or imagination into representation. Especially in the case of drawings, there is a loss of one dimension. Claude Lévi-Strauss discussed this very well when he analyzed an oil painting to suggest that systems of representation are reduced models of reality.[9] But he added that the loss of what does not make it into the representation is compensated for by the expanded understanding we gain of some aspect of reality that may not be apparent or even present in actual experience. Although it may seem paradoxical, drawings, paintings, theatrical performances, and any other act of representation are attempts to strategically distance ourselves from reality in order to better understand it. That is why we resort to them.

The drawing you mentioned from the Venice Biennale is the result of stepping outside the conventional modes of architectural drawing and exploring the gaps between them. It is an ambiguous game of slippages. A drawing that morphs from plan, to elevation, to section, to perspective and from line, to shade, to color. The lines of the orthogonal projections become perspectival and disappear! And in the end, all that's left is a conventional, two-dimensional drawing.

One of the four versions of this drawing has gone missing, though I still hope it will turn up someday as we work to inventory our archive

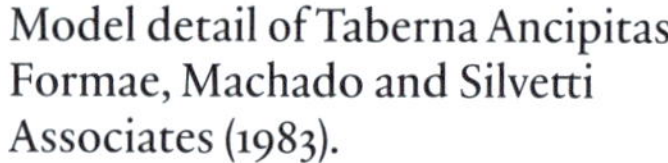

Model detail of Taberna Ancipitas Formae, Machado and Silvetti Associates (1983).

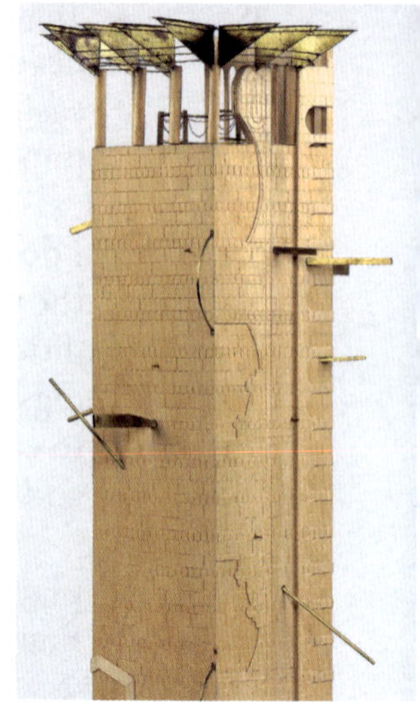

Detail of wood and brass model of the Tower of Leonforte, Machado and Silvetti Associates (1983).

The Production of Meaning in Architecture, graphite on paper, Rodolfo Machado and Jorge Silvetti (1980).

Plan of Fountain House, Rodolfo Machado and Jorge Silvetti (1975), diazo copy of original ink on mylar.

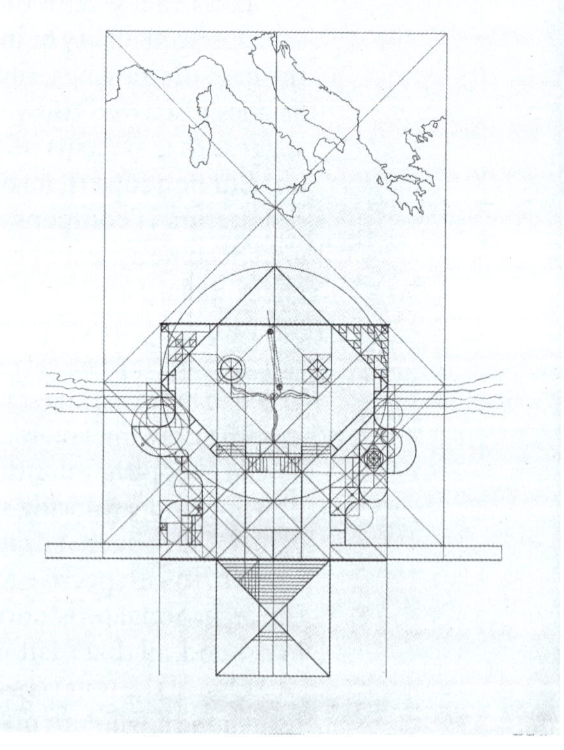

at Harvard. It's the very first pencil drawing I did on tracing paper at the same scale as the three other versions. After this, Peter Lofgren transferred the line drawing I made onto Mylar as a clean, second version under my supervision. Then, the third moment came when we decided to render a black-and-white version in pencil, adding shadows and three-dimensionalizing the line drawing, which Peter executed brilliantly. In the fourth drawing, made without consulting me, he added color. He was on a roll!

But it is the earlier version that captures the moment when I realized I could take the drawing in an unexpected direction. This drawing was meant to summarize all of our design work to accompany a manifesto-like text of our thoughts on the theme of the Biennale: the presence of the past. So the drawing was supposed to be a representation of projects that only existed as representations. At that point, we had designed a lot but built almost nothing.

The initial vague idea for the drawing was to make an updated version of Thomas Cole's *The Architect's Dream*. I started by drawing a frontal facade, and then I used that to develop a Chinese or Hedjuk-like axonometric, as we liked to call these three-dimensional drawings. At one point, when I was drawing a line with my pencil that was part of the axonometric, it began to vibrate as if it wanted to disappear, as if it could not remain faithful to Euclidean principles. It had a mind of its own and wanted to converge with its parallel siblings! Suddenly the drawing became a treasure trove of discoveries. It was the closest thing I had experienced to what some writers describe as "the text taking over and writing itself"!

Drawing is one of the activities I have enjoyed most in my life, but this was an amazing, joyful, and playful experience I had never had before. Looking at that drawing still makes me very happy. It has a certain mystery that continues to fascinate and delight me. Drawings are wicked, much more so than paintings, and I think this is because they are made of lines. For me, lines are much more powerful than color and volume.

The other drawing you mentioned, the line drawing of the Fountain House, is also a kind of summary from which I learned another important lesson in drawing. It was a drawing that Rodolfo and I discussed and produced together in ink on mylar in the summer of 1974. Unlike the drawing for the Venice Biennale, this was a drawing of a project that had already been completed, so it was more than generative, it was a graphic summary.

Here, the sole protagonist is a line, a single type of line that barely changes in weight. Everything is flattened and equalized: walls, stairs, water, the map of Italy, construction lines, geometries, floor textures, and so on. Everything that is a whole is transformed by the gliding of lines that swirl over each other like fancy calligraphy. Lines that represent one thing become another; they cross intellectual realms. There is a point at which the line is alive and truly leading the way. As we took turns drawing, I experienced the feeling that Paul Klee had so poignantly expressed about drawing: "A line is a dot that went for a walk"!

If I believed in magic, I would say that the synthetic drawing of the Fountain House also contains a hidden premonition. The geographical center, marked by the two diagonals of the upper square—an inevitable mechanical operation of drawing—meets in Sicily around the Valley of the Temples. This is a place in the universe that, a decade later, would become the site of a professionally and intellectually life-changing experience for us!

3. Sensibility and Authorial History

NT You've mentioned your collaboration with Rodolfo several times in our conversation, but let's talk about collaboration in a broader sense. Your practice has certain idiosyncrasies within the larger realm of American practice. In a way, you have brought some aspects of the academic model into your practice: the critique format, a certain speculative looseness, and perhaps even a certain stubbornness about the primacy of ideas. From my years in the office, I felt that you were willing to delay other professional priorities in order to let the architectural resolution simmer before you put it out there.

JS Yes, indeed! "The primacy of ideas" is a good way of putting it.

NT These qualities have led to a shared authorship within the office that includes not only you and Rodolfo but also many of your collaborators over the years. I suppose the office culture I experienced was a direct extension of academic models. Many of the same conversations flowed seamlessly into the professional environment, which allowed their speculative nature to become concrete as they were translated into the specifications for each project.

This environment is generally very difficult to replicate, especially for those outside of academia. Even more so with the added pressure of democratizing the workplace, or with collaborative models that need to consider participatory processes with clients and consultants. It is simply harder to create an office environment where shared sensibilities, research, and methods can be internalized with the same ease. More dramatically, what has been lost in the equation perhaps is the possibility of what you call architecture as a cultural practice.

JS I think this is a very important topic for us to discuss today. Everyone agrees that architecture is the result of a collaboration among many people; not just architects but people of all trades involved in making buildings. All offices today say that they operate with a collaborative ethos for this reason. Some even say that there should be no such thing as authorship in architecture, which I disagree with. But "collaboration" has become a bit of a catch-all term. It is useful for everyone who uses it to describe their practice, which means it is mostly lip service.

One of the things I enjoyed most about our practice in the years you were there, Nader, was how dynamic the relationships within the team were. Everyone was so enthusiastic and eager to participate in generating ideas, in solving design problems for their own sake. It wasn't something we even discussed. The environment was created by the people who were there at one time or another. This is what I would call the root of the collaborative ethos of our practice. People wanted to be there, and there was space for their talent and energy to find its way into the work of the office.

However, that didn't mean that what happened in the office was the result of a "democratic" system of participation. In the current climate, there's a push to politicize everything. There is talk of democratizing the design process in offices and democratizing the education process at the university. But this is absurd! These are organizations that are not democratic by nature. This does not mean that they are bad or oppressive. They simply cannot be "democratic" in the most common, serious, and widespread sense of the word.

Democracy is a system for regulating the way issues of power affect the lives of individuals in a society. It is based on individuals agreeing to organize themselves as a group with equal rights and responsibilities. However, it is a system of government that works in the interest of establishing basic conditions under which a citizenry lives. It is not perfect, but I believe it is the best system we humans have come up with.

The way we produce and disseminate knowledge, or the way we provide services, is a very different affair from regulating everyday life. There are certain hierarchies that are necessary for them to work. It's not that universities, for example, are somewhat undemocratic institutions. University systems are antithetical to democracy, even if they play an important role within our democratic society. They are necessarily hierarchical systems that at their best function as meritocracies.

In our practice, there was always collaboration within the team, and that in some ways influenced the projects that came out of it, but this is not what I think of as the authorship of the office. Everyone was there because there was a certain consistency in what Rodolfo and I were doing. This is an old and recognized condition of teamwork in artistic and scientific practices that require many individuals to work together. Think, for example, of the workshops of Raffaello Sanzio or Gian Lorenzo Bernini, which are well documented. We understand that Raphael's rooms in the Vatican are the result of a collective effort. But we also understand without a doubt that they are the sole authorship of Raffaello.

Some extraordinary artists worked with Raffaello, among them Giulio Romano. However, there is no confusion about his subordinate role in the process. Giulio Romano is only recognizable as the author of his own work when he takes the lead later in the century.

Romano's paintings become unmistakable precisely because they are neither those of Raffaello nor those of his students.

In our case, the people who worked with us had similar aspirations. They wanted to develop within a structure that would provide all the intellectual, ideological, and aesthetic frameworks to allow them to participate in the flow of the process. Once they became part of the journey, they began to propose, discuss, and reflect on the work, and in that sense they became active parts of the process.

I'm curious to hear your thoughts on this, Nader.

NT I suppose one of my preoccupations revolves around the balance of control and collaboration, which is another way to put what you have aptly touched on above. On the one hand, specificity is entirely about control. On the other hand, collaboration, when it goes well, is all about the ways shared sensibilities can bring more diversity of ideas to a common cause.

Beyond the productive complexity that you and Rodolfo brought to questions of authorship, especially when working together on projects, my question is about the culture you produced within the practice. I am less concerned about questions of style, imagery, or iconography associated with practices. I am more concerned with the way of working; the themes that migrate from one project to another; the connection between certain techniques and ideas; and how the two sometimes work together in critical ways, at the service of the intellectual project at large. I am thinking of your personal preoccupation with perspective as a drawing technique, the writing you have done on the subject, and the many projects this has produced. When seen in tandem, this exemplifies what I would consider to be a characteristic of a cultural practice.

JS I think that in our cultural history, authorship was never determined by a stylistic signature. The negation of the stylistic aspect of creativity is something I am very happy that Rodolfo and I discovered early on. I think overcoming this is essential for contemporary cultural practice. Authorship today is *not* form per se and not even formal technique. Authorship is a way of working, of making sense of things. It is activated by ideas. These ideas, in turn, are activated by a universe of inevitable personal affinities that determine the author's field of action: the ways of working, expressing, and signifying that are available to him or her.

NT Let's delve deeper into this question. How can we characterize your work then?

Beyond the intellectual challenges you take on, I think your practice also revolves around certain sensibilities, perhaps what you call "personal affinities." Again, avoiding a strict adherence to a style, the authorship of your work comes from a developed culture of associations. However constructed, they are a series of shared histories, artifacts, and prejudices. Knowing some of the protagonists in your constellation of collaborators, I have little doubt that these references form a shared set of footnotes for all of you. But they also derive from an ideological standpoint that explains your agreement on aesthetic issues, whether in relation to the classical, the anomalous, or the strange in architecture.

JS Authorship is not found in a particular kind of architectural move or iconic project. It is a sensibility informed by a way of working and a backpack full of all the experiences and ideas that we accumulate throughout our creative lives. Authorship is found in the cumulative result built up along a path as we incessantly, distractedly, or selectively pick and choose different pieces of evidence. The result is a compact of images, experiences, techniques, and even the stockpile of our own design production.

NDA What one identifies as the authorship of the work is more so an accumulation of your authorial history.

JS Exactly! Authorship is a path made up of stops each time a new design challenge presents itself, requiring the activation of some of the contents in our backpack. It is not an "innovative" formal twist or the surprising formal output of an algorithm but something that becomes evident over the long span of a lifetime's work. In our case, we can also say that authorship is the perfecting of a way of working together through a shared sensibility and a family of evidence that animates it.

For instance, when we worked on the long project of the Getty Villa, we employed two ways of accessing our imagination equally. The first was to tap into all of that compact that we had constructed until that moment. This was the theoretical and aesthetic sensibility that served as scaffolding to support all of our design operations. The second was more specific to the project and involved mainly myself. It was all of the new historical and aesthetic research that I immersed myself in intensely in order to address the difficult problem we had at hand: how should we, conceptually and formally, frame a replica of a Roman building from antiquity with our new design?

This is different from the last major project that I designed and built, twenty years later. When I did the expansion and restoration of the Denver Art Museum, which was completed in 2019, I really researched nothing. It was a project where Rodolfo was not directly involved, and in which I relied almost entirely on my labyrinth of affinities, a term that came up in a conversation I did for a journal to describe what my own architect's mind looks like.[10]

This meant letting components of that networked stockpile pop up and play freely in order to generate a new piece that amalgamated memories, images, and sympathies among "old friends." For example, in this project's urban concept there are clear resonances with the Prato della Valle in Padova, which Colin Rowe had introduced us to in the late '70s and so impressed me; of Bernini's sketches for the design of St. Peter's Square, which reverberate often in my mind; and then many early modern still lives, a painting genre that corresponded to the way I metaphorically conceptualized the heterogeneous ensemble of buildings that conformed the physical urban context of the project. Still, hovering insessantly above all of this, there was an image of a very specific piece of architecture that I had seen and stumbled upon so often in the Greek ruins of Sicily, particularly at Selinunte: a single Doric drum in stone. This stirring image was a recurrent apparition over the years that I never imagined I would activate as a protagonist in a project of mine. But this time it came to stay. Without much hesitation I used it, reincarnated in glass and deformed into an oval drum—as in Prato della Valle—to give form to the fluted glass pavilion that condensed, as it were, all the complex programmatic requirements for the new public areas established by the client, as well as the architectural and urbanistic goals that I had established for this project.[11]

I agree, then, that "sensibility" is a good term to describe what binds my partnership with Rodolfo and what has characterized the culture of our office. It is a common path that allows for individual forays into other paths from time to time. We've seen many intelligent and talented architects come and go through our office, but the ones who have really made a difference are those who, for one reason or another, share this sensibility.

NT As students, we were initially perplexed by the term "unprecedented realism," but as we developed our own projects through the studio process, we also came to realize the degree to which many of your ideas were built on cultural conventions, known ways of working, and particular ways that knowledge is transmitted in different regions of the world. Moreover, we also came to understand that much of your work is invested in the mutability of these conventions, with the act of transformation being an architect's key contribution. Might you expand on this?

JS I would say that another way to characterize our work is through a thread that has always been present: a fascination with the conventions of life. For example, since giving the Sekler lecture in 2017, I've been working on rethinking my understanding of typology. Because I am coming more and more to understand architectural typology as a group of conventions, as a subset of all the cultural conventions that make up a society, which materialize in a formal arrangement that is best suited to answer a problem of that society.[12] I now think that what the Enlightenment thinkers did with typology—formalizing it and rooting it in classical language—was logical and inescapable at the time. But this rigidity needs to be shaken up today. We need to take note of what still stands and move beyond the rest with an understanding of how the creative process works in relation to social conventions.

I wouldn't say that I'm in the same group as Christopher Alexander, because in the end he effectively played down the way culture operates in the creation of the material world, in order to create his ideal, universalized manual for architecture. But I do think that a concern with the conventions that make up the life of a society has definitely been at the core of our work. That is a big part of what it means to me to run a cultural practice. Thinking about how people use a bathroom or a sidewalk but also the ideological principles by which they live. It's about understanding the extent to which we can transform a convention, or even subvert it when the time is right, and how to do it.

NT I'd like to talk about what all of this looks like within the larger arc of your career. An architect's work inevitably evolves over decades. In some cases, it also changes in response to the contingencies and externalities of the world, to history, and to evolving building technologies. But a few architects actually drive these evolutionary changes through their thinking itself. As you move from the '60s to the '80s to the twenty-first century, are there some key thematic phases that we can identify in your work? Was there a sequence of periods that were concerned with particular aspects of these unifying threads that created this cultural practice of yours?

JS That is an incredibly difficult question to answer.

I often think of architects or writers who have these incredible shifts in their production throughout their lives. That is certainly a sign that their creativity is alive and well! I always remember, because I was in school at the time, when Le Corbusier did the Philips Pavilion with Iannis Xenakis. We thought he had gone mad. And Le Corbusier came out and said that he had not changed his principles or his approach in any way. The same thing happened when he did Ronchamp chapel, or even earlier, when he designed the vernacular-inspired Maisons Jaoul.

Le Corbusier never acknowledged that he had changed or that there were distinctly formal or even stylistic periods in his work. I'm sure he was being disingenuous, because he was not a naive person when it came to managing his public image. But I think part of it comes from the fact that it is really hard to analyze yourself in that way. It happens to a lot of musicians. It's hard to see what is an obvious and natural continuum—your own life—as something that has these kinds of clear breaks. I could try to identify some of them, but I'd actually be more curious to hear how you see them, as someone who knows me well but is also an outsider to my experience.

NT I have some ideas, but I'm more interested in what these moments mean to you. Perhaps there are some projects we could discuss that have changed the course of your practice? Projects that have catalyzed a change in your creative and professional work.

JS Okay, let's try ... I have to say that most of the projects I have worked on seemed to me at the time to be a new kind of problem, one that challenged and motivated me. Maybe I'm just lucky, because I've never had to work on a project that didn't excite me. I have always found something challenging in the work in front of me, no matter how small the project. However, there are some projects that stand out as clearly catalytic; projects that have opened new doors of inquiry and redirected my work.

The mother of all these projects was the Getty Villa. This is a project that created a new universe of work for us at all levels of design—intellectual, scalar, thematic, and technical. It involved both of us at the office in a new way, especially me, since I was the partner in charge on a day-to-day basis, working with our formidable client, the Getty Trust, for twelve years.

The project touched me deeply. As soon as I saw what was in front of us, I felt I had to go back to the books and understand what all of this architectural material that we had to work with was. For the first time, I was reading the history of architecture with a clear design purpose. It was a different exercise from what I had done before, both as a student and as a practicing architect. I made a serious attempt to understand the classical in depth, in its most pristine and dense moments: the classical antiquity of the Greeks and Romans. I entered it with a very concrete object of study: the *domus romana*. Then I felt the need to branch out even further, as philosophical and ethical issues emerged the deeper we got into the project. The overarching question was what to do with a replica of a first-century Roman villa in Campania, built in California in the late twentieth century.

NDA This was a project that combined architectural research and theory with practice in an almost didactic way.

JS Yes, because this research was not only based on the history of the architectural periods relevant to the original villa. It was also based on aesthetic, philosophical, and literary practices that shed light on the ways in which these histories have been reconceived over time. This project influenced my teaching, my pedagogy, and my approach to the theory and history of architecture. Sometimes I wonder whether the GSD is aware of its debt to the Getty!

The Getty Villa project was also a huge leap for our office in terms of the sheer scope of the work. It was far beyond anything we had done before. More importantly, it was an experience with an institutional client unlike any other in the world in terms of mission, ambition, resources, clout, and expectations. The pressure was immense, the excitement exhilarating, and the intensity of the work extreme.

The project also touched me on a personal and emotional level. Our project became the unintended backdrop for the tragic controversy over the illegal trade of antiquities. This scandal erupted just as we were reopening the Villa in 2006. After more than a decade of work, the Getty Trust became the main protagonist in this scandal, which played out in the international press and in the courts. It was something that completely overshadowed the completion of the project and affected many of those we had worked closely with over the years and with whom we are still close friends. A complete lesson in architecture's relationship with power.

NDA I think the Getty Villa is a great project for discussing this idea that your practice is characterized by a certain sensibility. It takes me back to a conversation we had with Mark Lee, who was trying to explain why he thought you were perhaps better suited to do that project than some of the other runner-ups in the competition, like Alvaro Siza.

JS Well, that's a big question I still have! [*laughs*]

NDA His theory was that you were the right person to go on that journey with the client. Rodolfo and yourself were positioned to have a certain kind of conversation with an institution like the Getty Trust and navigate all of the cultural complexities that came with the project in a collaborative and intellectually stimulating way. Your strength was not in offering a measurable product based on iconographic authorship, even of the most sophisticated sort, like in the case of Siza. It was in having the right sensibility to engage the kind of interlocutors that made up the Getty and working your way toward a design proposal that was coherent with that intellectual engagement.

JS Maybe, maybe. It sounds nice!

NDA I think this also relates to some points you have made in the past about working for universities and cultural institutions. You've said that a lot of the most satisfactory work you have done has come from working with clients that want to have a debate about architecture and culture because to some degree they are already concerned with it.

JS Yes, this is true. And this also has to do with conventions. These have all been patrons that we share a language with, the most basic of human conventions. Even in front of the toughest board of trustees or university presidents, I've always felt incredibly comfortable. Even if I don't know what the outcome will be, I know how to manage myself because I share so many things with the people in that room, and this instills a certain kind of confidence. This is irrespective of whether they are good clients or bad ones, whether they are good listeners and challengers, or whether in the end they do not really understand what we do as architects. I had all of those types of clients. Still, I never felt that I could not communicate with them.

I'm always terrified, on the other hand, when I have to sit with a developer! I'm just totally lost in those situations.

NT [*laughs*]

JS Really! I mean, sometimes it's just the pure fear of not knowing how to behave in front of them, you know? They belong to a totally different world.

NT [*laughs*] Please don't lose this passage.

NDA Architects need to participate in cultural projects that they commune with. They need to put themselves at the service of something and someone who they can sincerely work in the interest of so that the outcome can be powerful and authentic. And those circumstances are always out there. We are surrounded by people that are cynical about this possibility or the means through which it can be achieved. But these are just people that are really out of touch with reality—because they can be—or that pay lip service to grand ideals without any actual commitment to the work implied in bringing them about in the world. I think if we have less dogmatic and intellectualized ideas about what a proper practice is, focusing first on finding where those real problems we can solve are, and who to solve them for, we can strike a healthy balance in which theory actually *inhabits* practice once more.

NT Jorge, knowing you and your work so intimately would make one think that, as an interlocutor, I am simply here to unlock what I already

This dried acanthus leaf grew last year among the ruins of a Greek archeological site in Morgantina, Sicily. I picked it on January 9 of this year 1993 and kept it, treasured, within the pages of my sketchbook, where it slowly and imperceptibly changed its nature and outlook.
Today, confronting the problem of how to start this other sketchbook, we thought the leaf would – with its serene classical reference and its contradictory reality of being both a dead fragment of nature and yet a real and lively cultural icon – make a most appropriate frontispiece for it... Announcing some choices and some processes of thought and of formal transformation.
1

One of the most memorable sites we have ever seen ... and a very didactic one, too: about materials (and their passage from nature to culture), about technology, about landscape art, and about power.
food for thought, as they say...

an idea for a stone garden

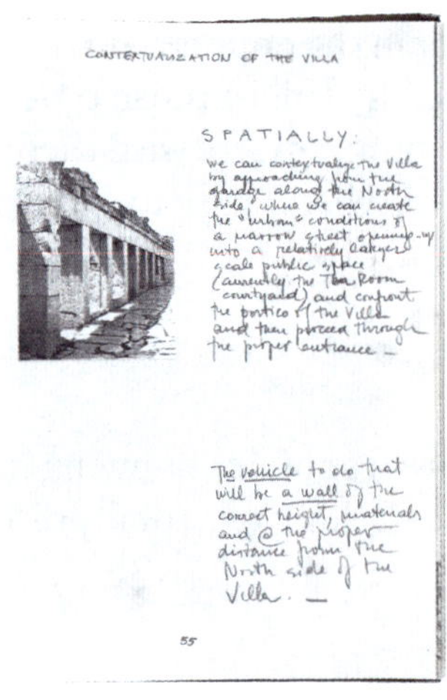
CONTEXTUALIZATION OF THE VILLA
SPATIALLY:
we can contextualize the Villa by approaching from the garage along the North side, where we can create the "urban" conditions of a narrow street opening up into a relatively larger scale public space (currently the Tea Room courtyard) and confront the portico of the Villa and then proceed through the proper entrance –
The vehicle to do that will be a wall of the correct height, materials and @ the proper distance from the North side of the Villa. –
55

"CONTEXTUALIZING" THE VILLA

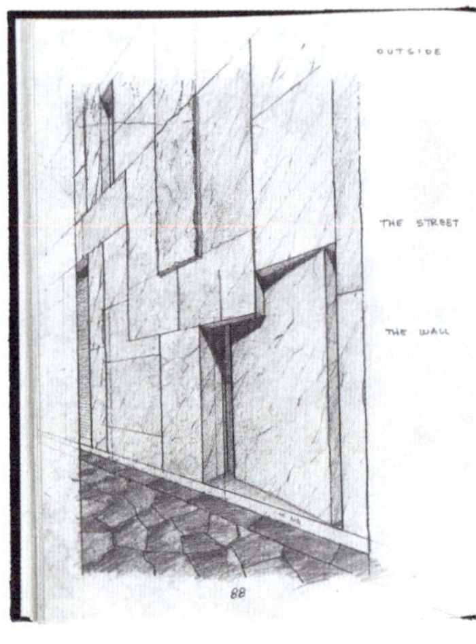
OUTSIDE
THE STREET
THE WALL
88

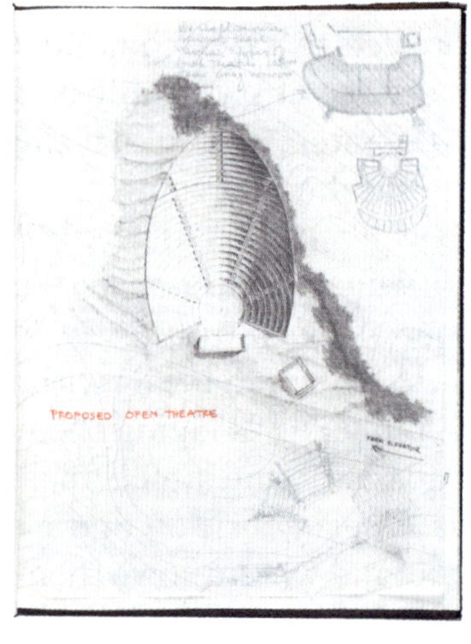
PROPOSED OPEN THEATRE

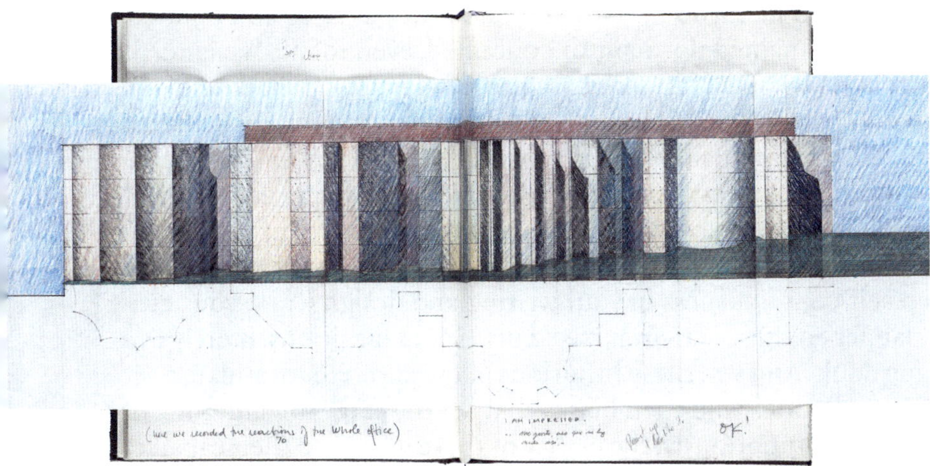

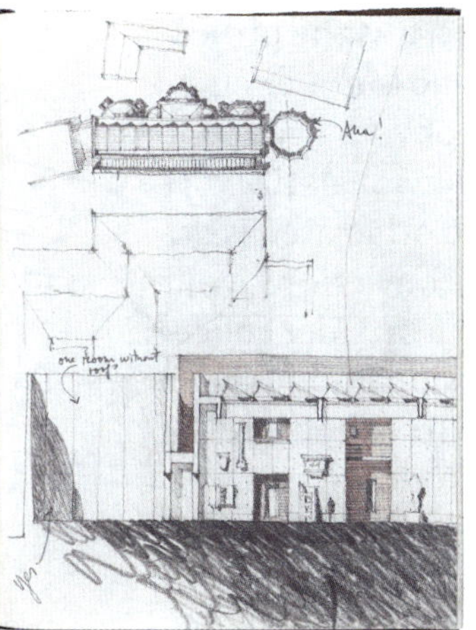

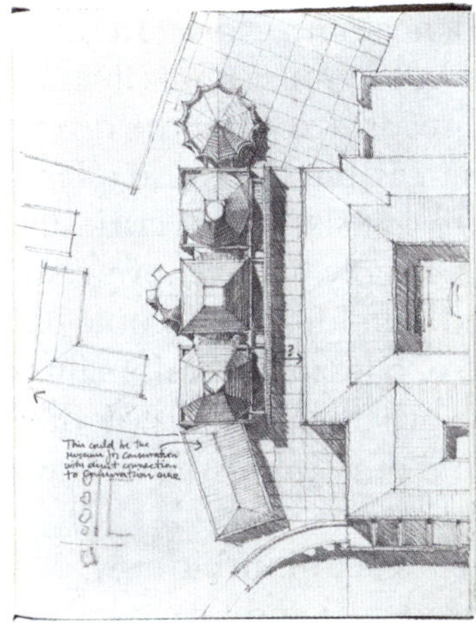

Selected pages from the Design Competition Sketchbook for the Getty Villa Renovation, Machado & Silvetti Associates. The selection follows the evolution of thinking from the opening page through different topics and modes of design. Also pictured: the variety of graphic media utilized for the two different phases of development: the preliminary research and the final exploration of design ideas. Institutional Archives, The Getty Research Institute, Los Angeles (2005.IA.07). © J. Paul Getty Trust.

know. But, in fact, you have opened up new passages and connections that remained dormant or concealed, even to me. We entered this conversation talking about architectural practice, alluding to the activities you undertake outside of school. But, in fact, the richness of this discussion has revolved around the intricacy of "practices," the cultural practices, that lend themselves to a unique definition of what an architect may do.

You also revealed great humility in this conversation; despite a deep self-consciousness in your writing and design work, you actually launched these activities based on a set of intuitions, merely as a young adult. And yet, these intuitions allowed you to formulate a set of ideas, theories, and even biases that set the stage for a lifetime of work. More importantly, the clarity of these ideas and their capacity to be pedagogical has allowed for several generations of architects, myself included, to benefit and evolve. In this sense, it is the projective capacity of your work I must underline. Its value is not circumscribed by the red threads that bind the diversity of your academic and professional practices, but it has also offered individuals like myself the opportunity to translate them critically into other arenas decades later. At once a deeply held set of personal convictions, your pedagogy has allowed your ideas to become part of a broader collective lexicon, a way to debate in other domains outside of our circle, and a way to imagine other worlds not yet drawn. To me, this is the richness of the cultural practice you've built with Rodolfo.

JS I thank you for saying "a set of intuitions," because intuition is not a welcome word in academia and I have become accustomed to repressing it. However, I'm convinced our intuition has guided every move we've made. This may not be a good note to end on in a discussion about practice. It may even be disappointing to some, but what you say is true. However, it is true only if we understand intuitions as punctual, epiphanic pulsations that occur alongside the creative process, animated and fueled by an active life of observation, study, and reflection upon what life presents to us everyday. These actions are inseparable from our intuitions. They imply a continuous involvement with the study of our discipline and with its history. They also imply a deep involvement with society and all the cultural practices that make up society. All of these factors can establish a sound foundation for the emergence of productive intuitions, and only then should we feel very confident about letting them lead the way.

The Sie Welcome Center at the Denver Art Museum, Machado and Silvetti Associates in association with Fentress Architects (2019). With Jorge Silvetti as designer in charge, the project involved the restoration, renovation, and expansion of the museum.

Doric column drum, Temple of Artemis (6th century B.C.), Sardis, Turkey.

Notes

1 See Jorge Silvetti and Alfredo Thiermann, "Architecture: The Question of Method," in this volume, 49–96.
2 Christopher Alexander and N. Dadge, *Notes on the Synthesis of Form* (Cambridge, MA: Harvard University Press, 1964). See Silvetti and Thiermann, "Architecture: The Question of Method," 49–96.
3 Ibid.
4 Cumbernauld Town Center, 1963–1967. Belgate Estates-Glasgow. Architects: L. H. Wilson, D. R. Leaker, G. Copcutt, P. Aitken, N. Dadge. Contractor: Cumbernauld Development Corporation. Designed in the 1950s. Opened in 1967.
5 *Taller*: atelier.
6 Lugano I and Lugano II (today Conjunto Urbano General Savio), is a residential complex of 6,640 two- or three-bedroom units as part of the "Centro Urbano Integrado" (the largest housing projects undertaken in the city of Buenos Aires). The complex was built in Parque Almirante Brown, a large 1,474-hectare (3,642 acres) site of recently drained swamps in the southwestern corner of the city. The project was designed by the Comisión Municipal de la Vivienda and financed by the Inter-American Development Bank (IDB).
7 Jorge Silvetti, "The Beauty of Shadows," *Oppositions*, no. 9 (1977): 43–61.
8 Rodolfo Machado and Jorge Silvetti, afterword to *Unprecedented Realism*, ed. K. Michael Hays (New York, NY: Princeton Architectural Press, 1994).
9 See Claude Lévi-Strauss, *The Savage Mind* (London: Weidenfeld and Nicolson, 1972).
10 Jorge Silvetti and Nicolás Delgado Alcega, "Labyrinth of Affinities: On Perspective, Anamorphosis, and Repositionings," *Pairs*, no. 2 (2021): 119–132.
11 Jorge Silvetti, "The Ponti Question," in *The Lanny and Sharon Martin Building* (Denver, CO: Denver Art Museum, 2021), 81–100.
12 See Jorge Silvetti and Erika Naginski, "Architecture: The Reconception of History," in this volume, 215–271.

Vestiges of Cities Without Evil: The Case of the Territorio Guaraní

GRACIELA SILVESTRI AND
JORGE SILVETTI, 2014

The center of gravity of the vast Río de la Plata basin resides in a territory whose physical and cultural characteristics are so particular that they defy the most stable convictions of those who study spatial phenomena. This territory is divided today between Argentina, Brazil, Paraguay, and Uruguay, but these political frontiers have not erased the common accents that allow us to approach this as a "territory," that is, as a system—and palimpsest of traces of past and future projects that overlap, crisscross, and intertwine with each other in unpredictable ways.[1] This *territorio Guaraní* in all its sensible dimensions is our subject of study.

Realizing the great amplitude of the work that we are proposing, we decided to begin by focusing our efforts on four paradigmatic moments in the construction of the Guaraní territory: a) the *avá-Guaraní* period prior to the Conquest; b) the fifteen decades of developing Jesuit missions; c) the period after political partition of the territory with the emergence of the modern nations in the nineteenth and twentieth centuries; and d) the contemporary and unfolding period characterized by the challenges of sustainable development policies.

From this large mosaic we extract here the second moment: the experience of the Jesuit missions. The case of the *treinta pueblos jesuiticos* confronts us with an interpretive dilemma because of its radical duplicity: these "jesuits cities" in the *territorio Guaraní* can be interpreted simultaneously as isolated fragments of paradise in a violent planet, or as machines of perfect domination. However, before we delve into this extraordinary and complex episode, we need to understand the region in which it took place.

It is water, in all of its different manifestations, which continues to define the destiny of the *territorio Guaraní*. But it would be reductive to define such territory by one natural element: if, as we believe, territory implies both physical and mental conditions, then what defines its character would be not only a natural portent, but also its social and symbolic dimensions.

Consider as an example the area where the impressive hydroelectric dam of *Yaciretá* was built, at the heart of our territory. Its location takes advantage of the rapids of *Apipé* (which in Guaraní means "land of many hills"), on the Paraná river (from the Guaraní's "relative of the sea") and whose name, *Jaci-retá*, comes from one of the three islands that have disappeared under the reservoir, and means "island where the moon shines," a sacred and strategic island for the communities that inhabited the region. We are therefore entering the field of toponymy, which is of crucial importance for the understanding of the historic structure of this region. We can then notice that the frequency of Guaraní names assigned to cities, towns, and counties is less notable. Such listing points instead towards two other important historical moments as name sources: one is the period of the *treinta pueblos* in the Jesuit Province of Paraguay (with names such as *Santa Ana*, *San Ignacio*, *Apóstoles*, *San Cosme y San Damián*, *Trinidad*, *Jesús*, *Encarnación*, *Corpus Christi*, etc); and the other moment with names that correspond to the period of nationalization in the nineteenth and twentieth centuries, alluding to patriotic ephemerides or national heroes (*25 de mayo, General San Martín, General Belgrano, Berón de Astrada*, etc.).[2]

Such reading of the names allows a study of their different logics: in contrast with the ecological repertoire that characterizes the names of the Guaraní language, those blatantly Catholic names given by the Jesuits are destined to a veritable rosary of towns which define a porous and ambiguous area that crosses the large rivers (Paraná and Uruguay) as if they did not exist. Then, those names referring to national histories demarcate well-defined areas, bounded by frontiers that eventually coincide with rivers or watercourses. Along these there are also other maps, without political or legal value, which nonetheless connect popular social practices with spatial phenomena—for example, the roads of the *promeseros* which tie together places visited by pilgrims who have made promises to the saints that protect the land in exchange for favors or miracles. Compared with these maps of devotional practice, the secular map of the modern nations appears diluted under the torrent of sacred connotations, myths, and fantastic stories evoked by those names attached to physical events.

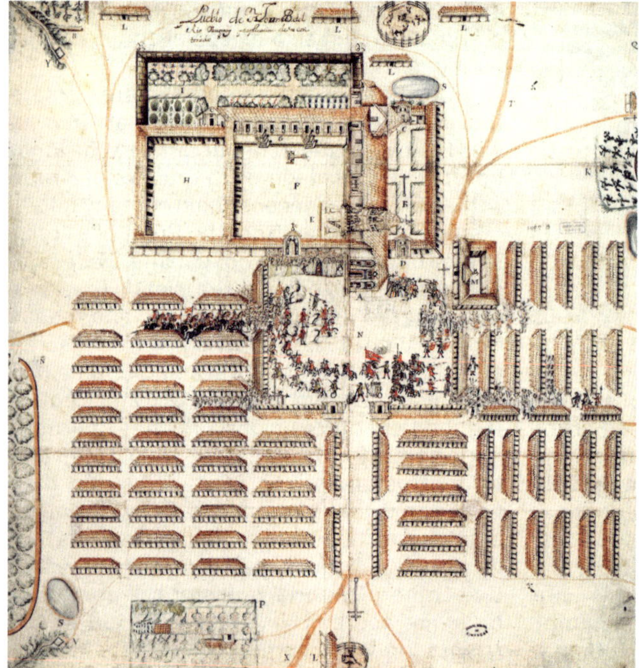

1

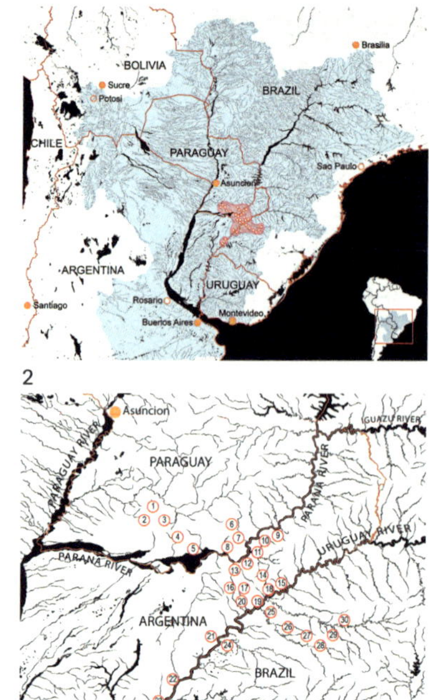

2

3

Following this interpretive key, we may propose a new map that would correspond with this palimpsest, and define other meanings attributed to the regional landscape that would then connect interpretations of pre-Columbian cosmologies with Christian faith, with ecological conditions, and with political debates. One such case might be the identification of the *Acuífero Guaraní* with the *Tierra sin Mal* of the *Avá* people, the mythical territory of the Guaraní that was later likened with the Christian Paradise.[3] Thus, this aquatic territory will acquire new meanings within the framework of current political ecologism whose religious undertones cannot be discarded. This character could not be more different from other regions of the same Río de la Plata basin, such as the lower Paraná that shelters large city harbors such as Buenos Aires, Rosario, and Montevideo, of which it could be said that their secular character is due to their later metropolitan nature.

For all this, as we look for keys to understand this *territorio Guaraní*, we return to the foundational moment of the encounter between the Guaraníes and the Jesuits, who represent two ways of understanding the world which could not be more contrasting, but which nevertheless form together an exceptional syncretic experience whose consequences are still palpable today.

Fig. 1 Plan of the San Juan Bautista Mission. This remarkable plan from the eighteenth century clearly shows the presence of the jungle around the mission, as well the orthogonal organization of the core of the mission. In the plaza, a procession of sorts is being shown, with musicians and a crowd. Around the core, paths emerge and lead to the surrounding areas of work such as orchards and stables, and eventually to the surrounding jungle.

Fig. 2 *Los treinta pueblos*. This map highlights the vast area of the fluvial system of the Río de La Plata basin (in light blue), and marks the major cities and the five countries it engages. The area where the *treinta pueblos jesuíticos* are located (in red) show the spread of the mission in the SE–NW direction, perpendicular to the rivers.

Fig. 3 *Los treinta pueblos*. The names of the missions are all based on Catholic events and saints of the religious calendar.

Fig. 4 *In tutto amare e servire.* Poster published by the Jesuit Order in 1998, commemorating the five-hundredth anniversary of the birth of its founder, S. Ignatius Loyola.

It is not surprising that these hundred and fifty years of missionary life called the attention of Europeans early on: a theocracy apparently without fissures; a form of communism with early Christian airs; a successful economic model; cities as "perfect" as Thomas More imagined them; a *mestizo* art of incredible creativity, and all this in the midst of the *paranaense* forest.

Contemporary historians, trying to evade the moral judgments that color the classic readings of this experience, emphasize the socio-political conditions that made possible such an extraordinary undertaking. But such narratives barely confront the environmental aspects that exceed the realms of "politics" or of "society" as we understand them in Western culture. For centuries, Christianity focused on the spirit and the corruptible—completely negating the body and the environment.[4] The Jesuit Missions of Paraguay stand out in this complicated panorama not only because they help us think through a particular territory, but because they allow us to reflect on the forms that space adopts when confronting the tension between the visible and the invisible, the sacred and the profane.

1. THE EVANGELICAL GLOBE

In his work on the genealogy of the Earth, Denis Cosgrove assigns a prominent place to the Jesuit order, approved by Pope Paul III in 1540, and serving as a central apparatus of the Church during the high times of Counter-Reformation. With great success, the Jesuits put into practice the Church's ecumenical will to evangelize, opening paths to others in expanding the frontiers of knowledge, especially those in the disciplines related to the description of space. For these men, the world was already global.[5]

Cosgrove returns to the Jesuits at the end of his study, as he analyzes a poster produced by the order in 1998, commemorating the fifth centennial of the birth of its founder, Saint Ignacio de Loyola. The Saint's full image appears over a background displaying NASA's familiar Apollo 17 image of the blue marble planet that we today associate with an early moment of "globalization"—an image that is the result of both the most daring expedition and the most advanced technology of the day, suggesting an analogy with the Jesuit undertakings on behalf of the Catholic counter-offensive in the sixteenth century.

Others went even further, arguing that the roots of our conception of one, homogenous earthly space exists in Christianity from its inception. Massimo Cacciari makes the case of how scorn for the body, together with the idea of celestial citizenship in—a fatherland located in a transcendental future—radically distanced the Christian world from pagan antiquity, and especially from the primitive Greek conception of city rooted in a place (to the *ethos* that houses a *gens*). Thus, the very emergence of our ways to inhabit the world can be found in this eschatological break.[6]

Aside from these hermeneutical debates, current historical readings that try to sidestep both European ethnocentricity and the rhetoric of alterity have stressed the permeability between human societies and the ever-active contact among civilizations. Thus a more convincing initial moment of a global, modern world could be located in the sixteenth century thanks to the almost instantaneous dissemination of a marvelous finding: America. This "discovery," as well as the institutions and foundations that assured its colonization, are closely associated with the ecclesiastic power and the missionary orders that extended the divine message while buttressing the earthly power of European monarchies. Among these orders the Jesuits stand out for their unique strategies of participation. Men of action destined to submit even more indomitable societies, they were at the same time natural philosophers and historians who contributed to the serious knowledge of American space. Their probabilistic philosophy and their contact with other cultures distanced them from the doctrinaire tendencies of the Church, favoring a strategy of adaptability that assured evangelization by means other than armed violence.

Within this larger history, what attracted the attention of those engaged with spatial operations has been the development of the Jesuit Province of Paraguay, in particular during the period of establishment and consolidation of the *treinta pueblos* from 1640 to 1768. These missions stand out from the many other Jesuit enterprises in the world because of their remarkable level of independence from Spanish institutions, a fact strongly underlined by the physical autonomy of their location in a territory difficult to access and administer. As one result, these missions, structured as closed, ordered, and regulated spaces even in their most miniscule details, have inversely mirrored both their contemporary Spanish new cities and the Portuguese *factorias* in America. In this context, the *treinta pueblos* can be seen as idyllic and manipulative, benign and dominating, liberating and oppressive.

2. AQUATIC TERRITORY: LIMIT AND FRONTIER

The Jesuit settlements were far from presenting the a-temporal perfection which their crisp planimetric layouts seem to suggest. In fact, the supposed autonomy of the Jesuit-Guaraní territory that such a formalist reading may suggest was relative: for the Spanish crown they functioned as a buffer zone against the advance of the Portuguese *bandeiras*,[7] which implied the eventual militarization of the indigenous Guaraní population and their participation in the defense not only of the mission's land, but of other distant Spanish territories. From this perspective, the missions supported a mobile and spatial version of "frontier" that is very contemporary; one that challenges the prevalent legalistic version of frontier as a one-dimensional line. For architectural culture, these debates are essential as they put into question one of the fundamental attributes of form: the limit, the measurable contour line that allows differentiation at all scales of planning and design.

Therefore, in the vast areas where the *treinta pueblos* were established, a question emerges about the complex relationship between form and aquatic territory. These areas, crossed by voluminous fast flowing rivers such as the Paraná, Paraguay, and Uruguay, and by their innumerable tributaries, springs, swamps, and marshes were the context in which the Jesuits, following the indigenous experience, delimited their territory by strategically locating themselves in relation to natural aquatic occurrences (rapids, falls, marshes, etc.) so as to establish a realm almost invulnerable to the feared Portuguese invasions.

But then, how does one define a territorial form in an aquatic territory subjected to constant change? In the Aristotelian version, later adapted by St. Thomas, *forma* results in a generating principle precisely because of its *permanence*—the essence of a thing, the Soul in humans; the intangible Unmoved Mover, the Idea, God. The ancient argument was committed to reason, movement, and change, and at the same time to finding something fixed, unmovable, that could defy the terrible destiny of human bodies as the corollary of change: death. Thus, geometrical figures determined by the lines of their contour, such as circles and squares, had represented for centuries the type of perfection that had to be achieved, becoming in turn models in architecture and urban design.

Yet, water is all about change. Slowly but inexorably, it erodes and blurs all differentiation, all limits, hindering any temporal stability. Water has the prestige of being "the origin of life," but never acquires the quality of those elements associated with permanent forms—roots in the earth, millenary stones, metal objects crafted with fire. That's why, perhaps, its essence seems to be "feminine": soft and plastic, in eternal movement, without the fixed bounds of classic geometry.[8]

So we ask ourselves in the territory of the great rivers whether or not water should have a central role in the comprehension of cultures. Historically, the Paraná and its tributaries are part of a larger interconnected system that includes the Amazonas and the Oricono—a fact that facilitated the migration of the *Tupí-Guaraní* groups from the heart of South America to the Rio de la Plata.[9] For some groups (such as the *payaguás* or the *Guaraníes* of the Delta islands) the major part of their daily life happened in canoes rather than on *terra firma*. Moreover, all of these groups classified as "nomadic" or "seminomadic," revealed their familiarity with water in their

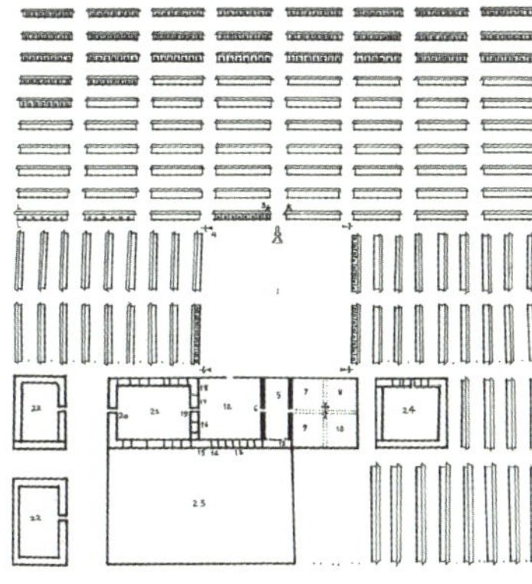

Fig. 5 A Jesuit city plan in the Guaraní territory. This plan, drawn by a twentieth-century scholar, contains inaccuracies of interpretation.

Fig. 6 Aerial view of the ruins of the Trinidad Mission, Paraguay.

forms of inhabitation, their utensils, and their myths. We believe that is the case because of a basic difference that was established from the beginning of the European conquest between the Andean cultures and those of "the jungle." The Andean peoples left their marks in stone, in forms of permanence, while the products of the hunters and gatherers dissolved and disappeared. Of these products, "the city" (or the settlements that the Occident homologizes with cities) is the most striking and indelible legacy of the Andean peoples—those who, together with Mesoamerican societies, occupy the place of prestige in Western scholarly and scientific narratives. On the contrary, and in spite of the fact that the recently discovered geoglyphs and other footprints proved the "urban" complexity of many non-Andean settlements, the nations of the rain forests and the pampas continue to be considered as noble savages immersed in pure nature.

Indeed, for the populations of the cities of Posadas and Encarnación—new cities built on the traces of old Jesuit missions—the presence of the rivers and their occurrences determined both their initial locations and livelihoods as well as the recent radical transformations produced by the impact of the construction of the international hydroelectric dam of Yacyretá, itself a result of the same topographical conditions.

3. ORIENTATION SCHEMES

The *territorio Guaraní* brings back to life other dormant questions about the general organization of an aquatic territory. We know, thanks to recent archaeological studies, that in the sixteenth century the *Tupí* occupied the middle and lower part of the Amazonas, together with its principal tributaries of the right margin and the Atlantic coastal areas up to the Cananea island (State of São Paulo). The *Guaraní*, for their part, extended their realm from the Tieté River (a Paraná tributary that crosses São Paulo) until Rio Grande do Sul, penetrating along the Paraná until its confluence with the Paraguay.[10] The direction of the lines of constant movement of these groups proposed by the archaeologists are directly related with the movement of fluvial currents and the boundary with the Atlantic: the migrations move South along the Paraguay, Paraná, and de la Plata rivers, and East in the direction of the Atlantic.

In their first missionary assignment in 1568, the Jesuits departed from Asunción towards the vast area of the *Paraquaria* province. In 1609, at the request of the governor of Asunción, they were given the right to spiritually conquer this large region whose heart would be established a few decades later between the rivers Tibicuary, the *esteros* of *Ñeembucú*, *Santa Lucia* and *Iberá*; and the mountains of *Tapé*—a territory that is cut by the Paraná and Uruguay rivers. The disposition of the Jesuit settlements in this region is transversal to these rivers in a clear Northwest to Southeast direction, always locating the pueblos near tributaries and never on the main rivers. Where the Spaniards, in their expeditions and campaigns, founded their major cities along the banks of the main rivers, the Jesuits followed a completely different orientation in the organization and conquest of the *territorio Guaraní*. By conceiving their domains in those areas in which major rivers became centers of gravity rather than lines of circulation or political borders or the loci of major harbors, they re-imagined anew a vast area of South America.

This new territorial cardinal orientation can be explained by understanding the role of the missionary area as a frontier intended to halt the *bandeiras'* penetrations. We can observe now how the current Argentinian province of Misiones (where most of the thirty *pueblos* were situated) is divided from Southwest–Northeast by the central mountains that create the watershed with slopes towards the Paraná and the Uruguay. Looking Southwest, the mountains and woodlands give way to ample fields that allow for agriculture and cattle raising, and thus the locations of most of the *pueblos*. The combination of jungle, woodlands, and fluvial occurrences protect the settlement and its productive areas from the threat of incursions. Of course, the Jesuits could not understand the structure of this territory without the help of those who really knew it: the Guaraní people.[11]

Thirty years after the Jesuits' expulsion, with the *pueblos* now being administered either by the Franciscans or by the secular civil administration, only half of the original Guaraní population (which during the most prosperous times had reached over 200,000 souls), remained in place. Some had left for the cities as qualified labor force (especially those who were trained as artisans); it is probable that others, who were skilled in rodeo, became the forerunners of the legendary *gaucho* in the north of Uruguay and the adjacent Argentinian provinces. In both cases, those Guaraníes mixed with the *Criollos* (creoles) and with former colonists—miscegenation that had not been allowed within the missions. Yet many others "returned" to the jungle, perhaps occupying traditional settlements: they were called *Cainguá*, people of the forest.[12] These migrations complicate our possible interpretations as of the ways in which native people once understood what we call "space."

But there is still another paradox: as the nineteenth-century division of the territory into national portions restored the grand rivers' axes as a general spatial orientation, the rivers became hard frontiers totally alien to the native and the Jesuits' orientation. But recently, we witness an inversion that reestablished the Jesuit Northwest–Southeast direction, due to the construction of the bi-national hydroelectric plant of Yacyretá across the Paraná at the point of Ituzaingó. This enterprise, with its subsequent ecological, urban, and infrastructural remediation works have re-articulated the spatial conception which the Jesuits had once imposed in these lands, linking towns, settlements, and agricultural fields on both sides of the rivers.[13]

This surprising parallel poses some interesting questions: is it possible to find similarities in the modes of spatial articulation effected in a territory, between such disparate landscapes and systems and cultures, between past and present? The same physical organization of the territory can result from very different proposals, but at the same time points out to recurrent morphological configurations. Perhaps we have to return to the problems that Carlo Ginzburg spelled out several years ago: the formal similarity between territorial designs, products, and even myths, in contrast with the fluency of times and history—the diversity of meanings that the same forms present now and then.[14]

4. CITY

In the case of the encounter between the Jesuits and the Guaraní people, the contrasts regarding the cultural mechanisms of spatial organization (the modes of fixing coordinates, orientation, demarcation, ways of moving and crossing space, etc.) could not be more noticeable. Above all, the Jesuits' intervention fixed the pueblos in a precise site. Let us remember that the original Guaraní groups, after a period that oscillated between five and ten years, abandoned their settlements—they considered them only as provisional stations in a continuous path without a fixed destination—and moved on. They were searching (it is said) for the *land without evil*. Many *Tupí-Guaraní* groups resisted the evangelization, but those who stayed with the Jesuits were transformed by the experience of the city—the particular Jesuit city that stands in contrast with the Spanish and Portuguese settlements. Could these be interpreted as a *land without evil*?[15]

The literature on the Jesuit experience emphasizes the final form of its "cities" or, more precisely, their "ideal form" as registered in plans or deciphered today from the magnificent extant ruins. Such evidence is based on current modes of preservation of Jesuit cultural heritage which are almost exclusively focused on the walls and foundations of extant buildings, and as such is limited to the nuclear space of the mission

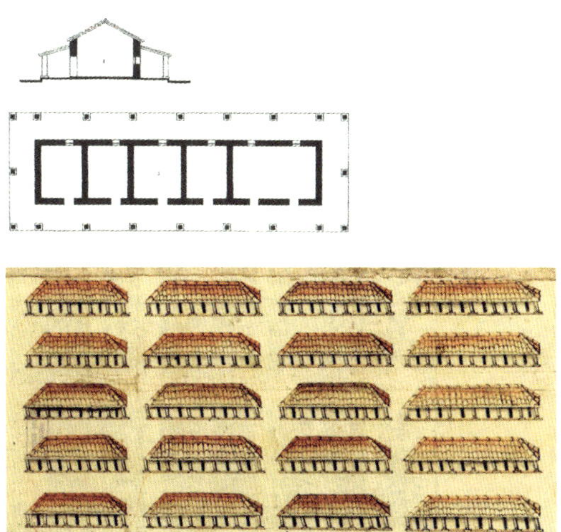

Fig. 7 A typical mission house, plan, and section.

Fig. 8 A Guaraní village. This 1557 illustration shows a Tupí-Guaraní village, from Hans Staden, *Warhaftige Historia und beschreibung eyner Landtschafft der Wilden Nacketen, Grimmigen Menschfresser-Leuthen in der Newenwelt America gelegen* (True Story and Description of a Country of Wild, Naked, Grim, Man-eating People in the New World, America).

settlement. In this way, we tend to think of each mission as a perfect, immovable fragment of space: a perfect land.

Very few research projects study in detail the modalities in which the Jesuits' *pueblos* were dependent upon an environment that could not be ruled in the same way as the City itself.[16] As with any city, the *pueblos* were dependent upon the productive role of adjacent lands—in this case, the agricultural fields and particularly those of the original *yerba mate*—the distinctive regional crop of a tea-like infusion that to this day continues to be one of the most important crops in the territory's economy, and the *estancias*—the Jesuit sites dedicated to livestock breeding. The commerce resulting from the artisanal crafts (textiles, musical instruments, religious figures, etc.) produced in the missions' workshops was secondary within this larger productive landscape. However, traditional research tended to misrepresent this reality by focusing exclusively on the still extant stone architecture and its associated crafts.

The available secondary sources also underline another characteristic of the city design that is difficult to ascertain: adaptability. Franciscans in Paraguay earlier attempted the practice of adapting indigenous motives and customs in order to make evangelization more effective. But, it was in the Jesuit missions where it was established as *the norm*, sustained over time, and proved successful in introducing cultural modifications. Unlike the rigorist philosophers of the Church, and the military practices of the conquerors, the Jesuits understood early on that the introduction of a new religion required flexibility. This flexibility can be read in the organization of the whole Jesuit territory.

When visiting the ruins of the missions today, one is struck by the proximity of the forest that closes the immediate horizon in all directions. The Jesuits seem to have understood and learned from the organization of the *Tupí-Guaraní's tekohá*, a complex that combined house, farm, and forest. At the same time, the Jesuit "city" also introduced systems of irrigation and drainage canals, of running water and sewage, the adaptation of dams for fishing and control of natural springs, and even bathrooms and toilets—indeed a very *modern* infrastructural system when compared with the practices in Western cities of the time, including those in Europe.[17]

The same negotiation between old local practices and moral impositions can be found in the residential typology, a fundamental element in the plan of the mission. Essentially, it was based on the scheme of the *Guaraní*

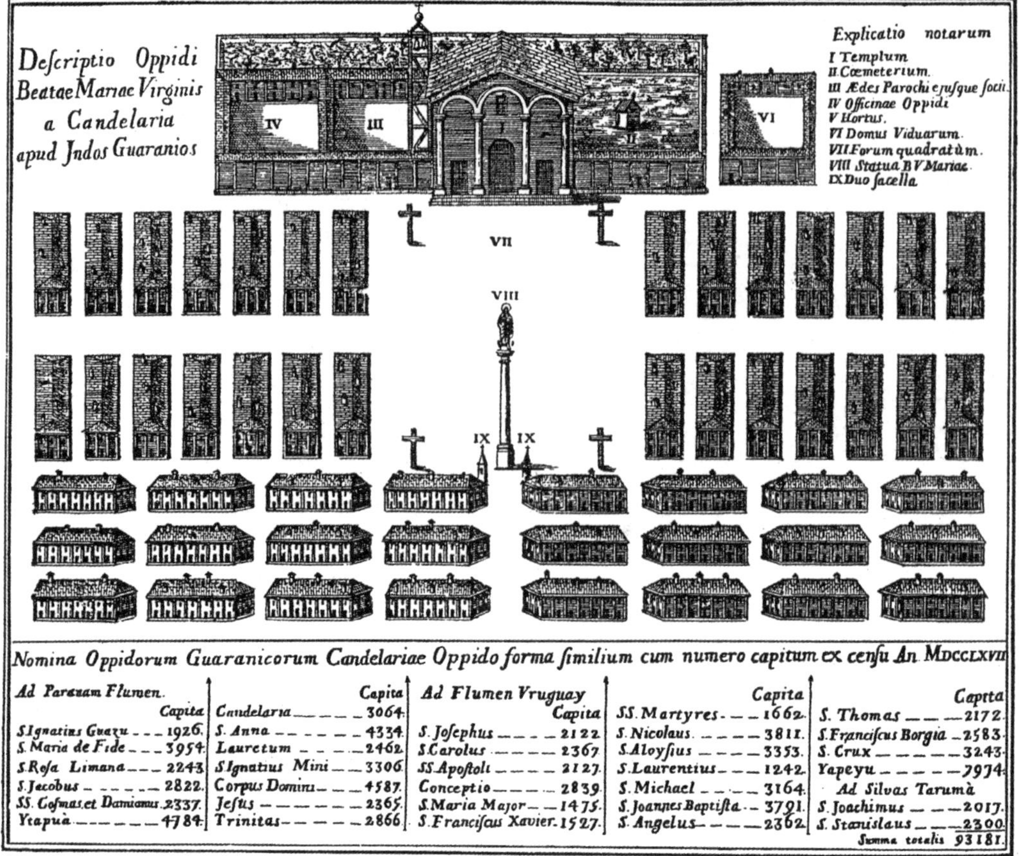

9

communal housing, reinterpreted as pavilion. In the earliest missions, many families populated each of these houses, which could reach fifty meters in length by five meters in width.[18] But the Jesuits could not tolerate the legendary lust of the Guaraní men; they had to use incentives in order to slowly convince the principal men not to take more than one wife. This fact explains in part the "evolution" of the residential unit as it shrinks in size over time.[19]

The contradictions between the adaptation of certain local forms and the introduction of new technologies or moral conventions can be found at the very heart of the *pueblos*. The standard design of these settlements cannot be attributed so far to any author or clear precedent, but we know that it was not an immediate invention. While the earliest missions were modeled after Spanish colonial cities, we see a brisk process of urbanistic invention that takes only three decades to crystallize—a process that arrives finally at the formula that we all acknowledge as the *ciudad jesuítica*.

Fig. 9 In this iconographic plan from the seventeenth century of the mission of Candelaria, the Guaraníes' residential units, based on the traditional Guaraní communal housing typology, are clearly represented, but they would shrink over time as the incentives to eliminate polygamy succeeded in reducing the family compounds. Notice also how, as part of the enforcement of this promotion of monogamy, single, widowed, or orphan women were moved from the generic residential units into the single courtyard unit on the upper right, marked in the key as "VI: DOMUS VIDUARUM" ("house of widows" in Latin).

This design reveals the ways in which the evangelizing goal becomes tightly intertwined with a spatial order that does not make a distinction between space and time, or between tangible and intangible. Two axes that cross at right angles structure the overall layout. The major axis cuts through the center of the plaza and culminates at the church, while the other axis demarcates the church, *colegio*, and workshops complex from the area allocated for the Guaraníes' residential units. This organization inscribed a strict hierarchy that had little to do with the traditional *Tupí-Guaraní* settlements, which were normally circular precincts without hierarchical differentiation. At the same time, unlike the Spanish colonial cities, there was not an abstract grid system of city blocks and streets that could potentially extend infinitely. As such, the Jesuit scheme is alien to the separation of public from private space. While these "cities" deployed *recovas* (porticoed sidewalks), "streets," and plazas as epitomes of the public realm, this is somewhat misleading, as their constitutive charter did not allow for outsiders to remain within a mission for more than two or three days. After all, it was a theocratic system in which everything important belonged to God, to "Tupá." This was reflected in the preference, noted by critics of the Order, to invest surplus commercial income in the elements of religious representation, rather than in any form of communal works.

Somewhat as in our own world, the idea of *representation* was central in the high baroque Jesuit's culture. The central plaza embodied the importance of this notion within the spatial and symbolic organization of the mission. Let us imagine these plazas with the immediate horizon dominated by the Church's façade, whose dimensions and ornamental richness are perceived concurrently with the homologous exuberant sumptuousness of the forest's backdrop that emerges at a short distance: a "natural" stage set where daily life was ritualized by the minute. The Palladian stage pales in comparison: this theatrical representation has evacuated the interior stage in order to colonize real life. And all of this was used, built, and adorned by a people that only some decades ago lacked tangible figurative representation.

How did those natives who encountered the first Jesuits see and interpret the crosses, the stoles and habits, the sacred figures on the banners that the missionaries proudly carried as they opened their way through the jungle playing the violin and singing hymns? How is it that in a few decades, these "innocent" societies adapted costumes, refined their artistry, and created a *mestizo* art so original that it is difficult to categorize even today? Much has been written about the art of the *pueblos*, attempting to understand the unusual characters that emerge from the friezes, sculptures, or devotional pieces.[20] But what was put under debate is our strong association between religion and symbolic representation, in the sense of *presenting again* something absent through an autonomous medium. Representation, thus understood, imposes a distance between object and subject. This distance would eventually imply the autonomy of objects, originally of cult, and their entrance in the world of "art."

"They believe in something that resembles a squash," said some of the first European eyewitnesses about the Tupí-Guaraní people.[21] The "squash" will appear later in wonderful friezes like that of the musician angels in the form of sacred *maracas*, a rattle profusely used in pre-Columbian times and incorporated in the missions in Christian religious musical performances. But it was true that there were very few objects of cult, and no known mimetic representations. The seminomad Guaraníes travelled light: objects could not be accumulated and carried along, and thus lacked the "value" ascribed by Western cultures.

The Guaraní people also lacked written music, written language, and tangible figurative representation. But the Jesuits soon recognized their language as an authentic treasure: they transcribed it, formalized its grammar, as well as organized its lexicon. And thus Guaraní became a *lengua general*, a generalized common language, something like an indigenous Latin of the broad *territorio Guaraní*.[22] Among the Guaraní language treasures, the hymns recovered by León Cadogan in 1959 tell us that language was created by the great father *Ñamandú*, before he created the earth.[23] In this way, we can say that in the Guaraní cosmology, language precedes the physical order of the World. We can speculate that the scenic plaza, while hierarchic and European in form and concept, could have reconfigured for the Guaraníes the central open space of the *tekohá*, the locus of ceremonies where they articulated, through music and words incarnated in bodies, their mediation with the invisible world.

In fact, Christian processions and the Way of the Cross with its stations could well be interpreted as a representation of pre-Columbian

10

Fig. 10 Guaraní "baroque pathos" and the Musical Angels Frieze. Trinidad Mission, Paraguay, 1706. Historians have attempted in vain to establish a periodization in the evolution of what they have called the *barroco jesuitíco-guaraní* style. For them, the clear "alterations" of the canonic baroque forms in this art were perceived in the early interpretations as indigenous mistakes, failures, or clumsiness in the process of copying the original models. More seriously, Guaraní images lacked baroque pathos: martyr saints, archangels crushing demons, virgins in pain appeared serene and even smiling instead. Beyond nineteenth-century prejudice, the idea of an evolution of successive stylistic periods does not concur with the evidence, which shows overlaps of diverse manners, a variety of products and presumed "anachronisms" in the repetition of "primitive forms" towards the end of the missionary period, so well represented by the "return" to frontality and corporeal weight in the famous freeze of the Angels Musicians in the late church of the Trinidad Mission. This freeze is an extraordinary artistic occurrence whose interpretation and implications have received great scrutiny and produced an intense, brilliant, and still-open debate.

Guaraní migrations. Today, the well-established *caminos de los promeseros* in this territory constitute a network that exceeds the political boundaries between countries and provinces—as the local "saints" that inspired them exceed the Christian pantheon. In other words, we can read in these hybrid territorial practices the footprints of an old cosmology.

The colorful Christian procession, accompanied with Guaraní lyrics in the eighteenth century or the *promeseros* marching with banners and musical instruments towards sacred sites today, lead us then to the foundational myth of the Guaraní cosmology, that of the Land without Evil (*la Tierra sin Mal* in Jesuit's texts; *Yvy Marane'y* in Guaraní), that sustained the migrations before and during the Missions era. This figure illuminates not only the ways in which cultural elements are renovated and intermixed with external influences, but also, and more precisely, the forms of inhabitation of the *territorio Guaraní*.

5. THE LAND WITHOUT EVIL

When the *Treatise of Madrid* (1750), attempting once more to settle the boundaries of the American domains between Spain and Portugal, decreed the swap of territories, among which the Portuguese harbor of Colonia do Sacramento (on the left side of the Río de La Plata just across from Buenos Aires) was to go to Spain in exchange for the seven Jesuit missions on the eastern side of the Uruguay river, it was necessary to move and relocate the populations involved in Spanish territory. At first the transfer was not resisted, as migrations were part of the way of being of the Guaraní, always roving the *Land without Evil*. However, this time, conditions and context were different: the transfer did not emerge from internal needs or custom; both the Jesuits and the natives involved considered the time given for the move as insufficient, and their requests for a postponement were ignored. To complicate things, they did not seem to find the proper sites to establish new settlements. Considering the situation, the seven *pueblos* decided to resist the ordinance to relocate—a decision that triggered one of the bloodiest wars in missionary history: *la guerra guaranítica* (the Guaranític war 1754–56). Soon after, in 1767, the Jesuits were expelled from all Spanish colonial territories.[24] The detailed narratives of this war can be read as testimonies of the intimate and sophisticated relationships that had evolved between these missionary societies and the territories they did not want to abandon. It is evident that after a century and a half of being part of the missions' system, these Guaraníes were already at a far distance from identifying themselves with the original Amazonian *avá* nations that moved continuously. Even so, the idea of the Land without Evil was far from forgotten.

In recent decades, the suggestive name of a "Guaraní paradise" has been used in multiple forms—in travel books, in political speeches, and in anthropological research, just to name a few. Paraguayan writer Augusto Roa Bastos, who in 1998 published a drama called *La Tierra sin Mal* (Land without Evil), provided many keys to interpret and understand the reasons for this widespread use. In principle, he points out the different conceptions of this Guaraní myth and the paradise of the Jesuits to which it had been assimilated: in the original myth, the virgin land, not spoiled by sin, exists in this world, while the Jesuit conception offered a "land without evil" only in the *next* world. Concurrently, and in a breathtaking move that shifts the time scale of the discussion, Roa Bastos also proposes a parallel between the Guaraní journey and the political exile that so many South Americans suffered during the various military dictatorships, thus accounting for the political tone of many current interpretations: if, paraphrasing the famous verse attributed to Paul Éluard, "there is another world but it is in this one," the Land without Evil of the Latin American

Left seems to find and recreate a not-modern past, a kind of primeval harmony, whose echoes resonate in the indigenous struggles for rights.

The Jesuit Ruiz de Montoya, the linguist who codified the Guaraní, was the first to register the term *Tierra sin Mal* in 1639, giving it an ecological meaning: a virgin land still unworked. Let's remember that the Guaraníes worked the land with the *roza* method (slash and burn), which exhausted the area's resources for subsistence at least for the immediate generations. At the same time, living in an aquatic territory, without the means to confront water's whims, must have reinforced their tendency to frequently migrate. Bartolomeu Meliá, a contemporary Jesuit linguist, tells us that the Guaraní cosmology is consubstantial with an acute consciousness towards the fragility and instability of this land, and for which the ritual practice of *ñembó'e* (a prayer that is still sung and danced) reestablishes the equilibrium.[25] It is indeed a very different conception than that which holds Western remedies for the fragility and errors of human affairs, immortality achieved by means of cities, art, books, and things. Perhaps today, in this highly unstable world that exhausts all seemingly permanent forms, we are better equipped to understand this aspect of Guaraní culture. However, what still separates us from it is our lack of "material imagination,"[26] a deficit in sensitivity that does not allow us to see into the depths of the concrete things of the world. We keep seeing just H_2O in rivers rather than the "book of secrets" Mark Twain saw in the surface of the Mississippi when writing: "The face of the water, became a wonderful book—a book that was a dead language to the uneducated passenger, but which told its mind to me without reserve, delivering its most cherished secrets as clear as if it uttered them with a voice. And it was not a book to be read once and thrown aside, for it had a new story to tell every day."[27]

Notes

1 See the authors' "Shaping the Guaraní Territory," introduction to the special Spring 2015 issue of *ReVista: Harvard Review of Latin America*, which they co-edited and whose content, presented in twenty articles, reflects the palimpsest-like character of the concept of "territory" advanced here. Among those of special interest is Carlos Reboratti's "Territories and Territories: The Shifting Guaraní Space."

2 The Spanish conquerors also named the cities of the larger area after Christian saints or episodes; in the interest of brevity we only contrast these two historical moments.

3 See, for example, the militant article of Bartolomeu Meliá, S.J., one of the principal ethnolinguists in Paraguay: "Y marane'ỹ rekávo. En busca del agua sin males," *Accion*, 263 (2006): 31–32.

4 It's only in the last years, under the suggestion of new trends in geography and anthropology, that environmental issues (and more generally, non-human life) began to occupy a productive place in scholarly works of Hispanic South America.

5 Denis Cosgrove, *Apollo's Eye: A Cartographic Genealogy of the Earth in the Western Imagination* (Baltimore, MD: Johns Hopkins University Press, 2001).

6 Massimo Cacciari, *La città* (Venice: Pazzini editore, 2004).

7 The "bandeiras" (from the Portuguese "flags or banners") were expeditions led by fortune hunters that moved South and West from the area of São Paulo, pushing the limits between Spain and Portugal. The most important loot at the time was in capturing natives and forcing them into slavery. In doing so, the *bandeiras* expanded the borders of the future Brazilian nation.

8 The classic text about the relationship between water and human productions—in particular literature and arts—is: Gaston Bachelard, *Water and Dreams. An Essay on the Imagination of Matter*, (Dallas, TX: Dallas Institute of Humanities and Culture, 1983). There is also an interesting reflection about water and classical architecture in Indra Kagis McEwan, *Vitruvius: Writing the Body of Architecture* (Cambridge, MA: MIT Press, 2003).

9 The migration of the Tupí-Guaraní (a major linguistic family, rather than an ethnic group) is traced from the Amazon Basin to the Río de la Plata. One group went to the Brazilian Litoral; the other traveled down along the tributaries of the Amazon River (the Xingu and the Madeira Rivers), and continued along the northern tributaries of the Paraguay River, and from there they continued south until they came out onto the Paraguayan and Southern Brazilian forests. At the time of the Conquest, some groups arrived to the Delta of the Paraná. The classic articles about these migrations are those of Alfred Metraux (1948), Pierre Clastres (1973), and Branislava Susnik (1975).

10 Hélène Clastres, *The Land-Without-Evil: Tupí-Guaraní Prophetism*, trans. Jacqueline Grenez Brovender (Urbana: University of Illinois Press, 1995).

11 Esteban Angel Snihur, *El universo misionero Guaraní. Un territorio y un patrimonio* (Buenos Aires: Golden Company, Gobierno de Misiones, Argentina, 2007).

12 According to Hélène Clastres, from these *cainguá* descend the three existing groups of *mbyá*, *chiripá* and *pa'i*, that could still be detected by their ancestral costumes when recorded by the Jesuits.

13 Together with urban infrastructure works, the binational entity is obliged to contribute to the care of the natural reserves (the swamps of *Iberá* and the remains of the *selva paranaense*) as well as that of the cultural patrimony embodied in the remains of the Jesuit missions, which are now one of the aspects of the region that is attracting more and more international tourism.

14 Carlo Ginzburg, *Miti, emblemi, spie. Morfologia e Storia* (Milan: Piccola Biblioteca Einaudi, 2000).

15 Michel Foucault, *Of Other Spaces: Heterotopias*, translated from the French article published in *Architecture, Mouvement, Continuité*, 5 (October 1984): 46–49, http://foucault.info/documents/heterotopia/foucault. heterotopia.en.html This very condition of real space yet radically different from the habitual ones, this palpable challenge to the confusion and disorder of the profane cities, is what made Michel Foucault use them as the key example of *heterotopia* (spaces which, as different from utopias, are precisely located, formally limited and tangible). In any event, as with ships ("pieces of floating space without place") the missions open up multiple dimensions to help us think modern space and its relations with the spatialization of Capital—and also they provide, says Foucault, a "major source of imagination."

16 One example of such new, more comprehensive visions of the missions as part of the *territorio Guaraní* can be found in Noberto Levinton, *La arquitectura jesuítico-guaraní: una experiencia de interacción cultural* (Buenos Aires: Editorial SB, 2008).

17 Ibid.

18 They were built in wood, tacuara cane, and wicker roof (presumably in the shape of continuous vaults). The Jesuits maintained the structure, but later they replaced the ephemeral materials with *adobe*, stone, or bricks, and gabled roofs were covered with tiles. In some cases, the roof was extended to form the covered walks or recovas. R. Gutiérrrez, *Estructura socio-política, sistema productivo y resultante especial en las Misiones Jesuiticas del Paraguay durante el siglo XVIII* (Chaco: Departamento de Historia de la Arquitectura, Facultad de Arquitectura, Resistencia, 1974).

19 The Jesuits, were flexible on many moral fronts, such as their accommodating efforts to modify polygamy, to integrate within the Christian cosmology the myths of the Land without Evil, to convert Tupa in God, and to tolerate the parallels between shamans and angels. However, they could not allow for ritual cannibalism. This uncompromising prohibition profited the first of São Paulo's artistic avant-gardes centuries later, when they searched for sources to invent and build their identity. Among those who got closer and more provocatively to the subject of anthropophagy was Brazilian poet Oswald de Andrade in his *Manifesto Antropófago* (Cannibal Manifesto)

of 1928. Anthropophagy is transformed in the essential character of a culture that "devours everything"—and because of that, it doubles the ante of the open, dissolving, and critical character of modernity, playing it against European post-colonial domination. While other Latin American modernist "pro-indian" currents of those times turned to illustrious and firmly-established pasts such as those of the Andean cultures, the Paulist nucleus of artists, essayists, and polemicists had no doubt in grafting cuisine and sex with fragments of European high culture; airplanes and *fútbol* with indigenous foundational myths. This mode of articulating their interests and critiques may be the key, perhaps, for us to understand this territory and to draw a new map of its evolving culture that would also reflect its always unstable (and because of this, inevitably modern) liquid form which never could respond to the idea of an original heart that would determine its future, nor to the utopic will of establishing the perfect city in this world.

20 The different perspectives about the mission's art can be understood comparing an erudite work from the traditional point of view of an art historian, Bozidar Darko Sustercic, *Imágenes Guaraní-jesuiticas*, Centro de artes visuals (Asunción: Museo del Barro, 2010), and the innovative recent book of Horacio Bollini, *El barroco jesutico-guaraní. Estética y atavismo* (Buenos Aires: Las cuarenta, 2013).

21 Cf. Clastres H. *op. cit.*, 20.

22 Today's Guaraní is the only language of pre-Columbian roots spoken not exclusively by an ethnic group. Widely spoken (estimated about 5 million people), it became one of the official languages of Paraguay, of the province of Corrientes, Argentina; and of the Mercosur. A map of the Guaraní language, that coincides with our territory of study, can be found in A. Guasch and D. Ortiz, *Diccionario Guaraní-castellano y castellano-Guaraní sintactico-fraseologico-ideológico*, 13º edicion (Asunción: Centro de Estudios Paraguayos Antonio Guasch, 1996).

23 León Cadogan, *AYVU RAPYTA (el Fundamento de la Palabra) Textos míticos de los Mbyá-Guaraní del Guairá* (São Paulo: Universidade de São Paulo, Facultade de Filosofía, Ciencias e Letras, Boletim 227, Antropología no 5, 1959).

24 Lía Quarleri, *Rebelión y guerra em als fronteras Del Plata. Guaraníes, jesuítas e impérios coloniales* (Fondo de Cultura econômica, Buenos Aires, 2009).

25 See Bartolomeu Meliá, "A terra sem mal dos Guaranís: economia e profecia," *Revista de Antropologia* 33 (1990): 33–46. Meliá, one of the principal ethno-linguistics of Paraguay, also published and prefaced the *Tesoro de la lengua guaraní* (1639) of Ruiz de Montoya.

26 We use the term material imagination paraphrasing the idea of Gaston Bachelard in *Water and Dreams*, *op. cit.*, 6.

27 Mark Twain, *Life on the Mississippi* (Boston: James R. Osgood and Company, 1883).

TYPE: Architecture's Elusive Obsession and the Rituals of an Impasse

JORGE SILVETTI, 2017

This text is an edited transcript of Jorge Silvetti's Eduard Sekler Memorial Lecture, *delivered at Harvard Graduate School of Design on November 7, 2017. The lecture transcript has been published for the first time here given the repeated references made to it throughout the conversations prepared for this volume. It should be noted that the contents of the lecture were not originally conceived for publication, and that the text that follows is just intended to register the contents of the aforementioned public event.*

Good evening and thanks for being here tonight to honor the memory and the legacy of Eduard Sekler, who for more than fifty years at Harvard promoted tenaciously the virtues of a continuous interaction between the teaching and research of the history of architecture and the learning and practicing of the métier of the architect. He was a dear friend, a colleague, a mentor, and an extraordinary neighbor. For decades, he was two doors away from my office in this building, and our frequent casual encounters in the corridor or the mail room would invariably end up in memorable conversations about architecture and life, some of them among the most precious moments I would retain of my collegial life at this institution.

It is precisely because of Eduard's unique profile as both a trained architect and an architectural historian that when confronted with the honor I received to represent the School in this event together with the responsibility of honoring someone of his stature, I decided that the best and most honest way to go about it was to attempt to transmit through a series of thoughts, illustrations, and hypotheses, how architectural history actively and creatively works in the mind of a designer.

I hope I can rise to the occasion—one that is full of emotions and anticipation for me—as I felt all along in preparing it that I was and am truly presenting this to Eduard for his consideration, critique, and advice as I did many times with my work and my ideas. In that sense, this is also my very personal tribute.

It is, interestingly, a good moment to bring the discussion of the dynamics of architecture history and architecture practice into the School as we are in the midst of the unfolding of the second Chicago Architecture Biennial, which is titled *Make New History*, and which defines as its objective, ". . . to understand the channels through which history moves and is shaped in architecture today."[1] One of the main impetuses inspiring its curators, Sharon Johnson and Mark Lee, is to re-propose the discussion of the connection between history and practice as it quickly unfolds in the exhibits into a series of issues, questions, and problems that help make us think again and anew about this interaction. It is not surprising that a call to reconsider the relationships between the practice of design (which from now on I will call the Project) and the history of architecture would put back on the table, almost immediately, the concepts of type and typology: "Typological problems are necessarily, like language, collectively derived, maintained, and extended . . . To study a building's typology requires the understanding that forms cross and break historical periodization."[2] And, it is not surprising either that, in re-proposing this topic, it resorts to both the seemingly inevitable analogy with language and to the reminder that typology works across historical periods, styles, and geographies.

I would like to focus on this reappearance, but with the reminder that history does not repeat itself, and that if we hear words and thoughts that resonate with a not-so-distant past, it is an intellectual obligation to understand and flesh out, as quickly as possible, what is different, new, and unique that distinguishes its re usage and meaning at this moment. I would like only to sketch out this fresh situation, as I see it, and to stake out the intellectual territory that it occupies and in which it acts so that we could explore this relationship of the history of architecture and the Project today without falling into false continuities.

It helps me to start by recalling a very important moment when, similarly, the world of architecture was reminded of the relevance of the concept of type in a famous article by Giulio Carlo Argan of the early sixties:

> [A type] is never formulated *a priori* but always deduced from a series of instances . . . The birth of a "type" is

> therefore dependent on the existence of a series of buildings having between them an obvious formal and functional analogy. In other words, when a "type" is determined in the practice or theory of architecture, it already has an existence as an answer to a complex of ideological, religious, or practical demands which arise in a given historical condition of whatever culture.[3]

This passage is important for many reasons. For what it says and for what is doesn't, and for its appearance in the field of architectural practice (for which it was not originally intended), in a reprint by the now legendary *Architectural Design Magazine* of Monica Pidgeon, at a time that, for many, it was feeling as the twilight days of a languishing Modernism.

From this, architecture needed only a decade and a half to see a subsequent flurry of active—architectural minds working around it both in terms of the Project and of theory. Both the "Anglo-Saxon" as well as the "continental" view reflected a renewed interest in the foundational role of the history of architecture in the Project—the use of precedent and type, and the indisputable protagonistic role of the city in the speculation and theorization about urbanism, architecture, and their relationships to culture. But they did not share the same understanding of the nature of type, and certainly a different view of what "city" they were referring to.

At the height of this intense period of theoretical and design production, a landmark contribution to and pivotal point in this profound debate was Rafael Moneo's article in *Oppositions* 13, 1978, that clarified not only our understanding of typology's role in the Project, but, just as importantly, with lucidity and succinctness, it historicized the diverse incarnations of the concept of type and typology in the history of architectural thinking.

Let me recall its memorable opening statement, "To raise the question of typology in architecture is to raise the question of the nature of architecture itself." Immediately followed by yet another in which he relativizes the very unity of the concept of type and typology by establishing the dialectics at play:

1

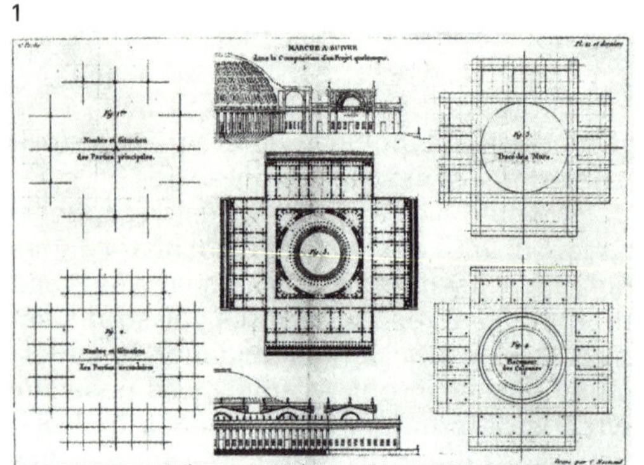

2

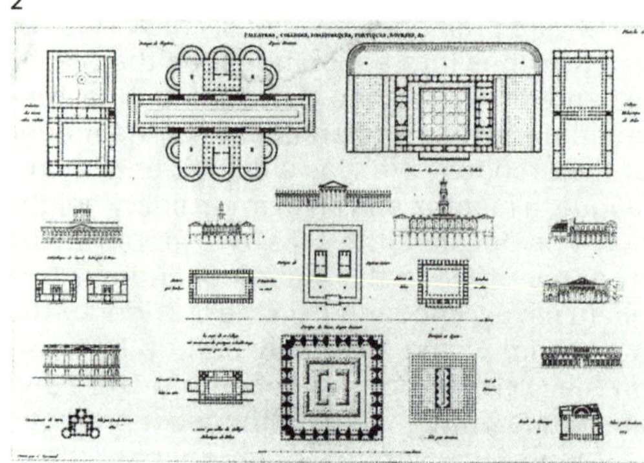

3

Figs. 1–2 Diagrams from Jean-Nicolas-Louis Durand's *Graphic Portion* of the *Précis of the Lectures on Architecture* (1821). Fig. 1: Procedure to be followed in the composition of any project. Fig. 2: Gymnasia, colleges, libraries, porticos, commodity exchanges, and so on.

Fig. 3 View of the Palermo Cathedral (12th–19th century).

> ... To answer it means, for each generation, a redefinition of the essence of architecture and an explanation of all its attendant problems. This in turn requires the establishment of a theory, whose first question must be, what kind of object is a work of architecture? This question ultimately has to return to the concept of type.[4]

This is a powerful conceptual capsule which he then proceeds to develop systematically in its historical, theoretical, and operative dimensions. I take now from Moneo's argument the complex dialectics of the nature of typology: on the one hand, the implicit unifying idea that typology and type are constitutive parts of what architecture is, but also, and on the other, that, as such, they are not immutable, but rather they are variables that, in the process of design, occupy different positions and partake in different roles, depending on the historical circumstances and opportunities and perhaps, yes, even on the spirit of the times.

At this point I need to state perhaps the obvious, but sometimes forgotten, condition of the existence of this concept: that for all the temptation to analogize it to the natural sciences, from where it borrows its vocabulary, architectural typology is not a scientific category but an ideological construct, one that exists in culture like any narrative literary structure that organizes, explains, and enacts its cultural practices. As such, its position within the Project has been historically variable.

It is the accumulation of these different positionings that I want to review first tonight, starting with the semi-conscious awareness that maybe there are buildings that share formal properties, something that was certainly evident to an observer at the time of Vitruvius and became clearer later within the tangible reality of the cities of the Renaissance, when buildings could be perceived and understood as belonging to "classes of buildings." To this, Serlio stepped up with a first proto-classification that created a framework around which a discourse about the still unnamed concept of type could evolve and emerge.

The next conceptual breakthrough would need to wait for the fertile seventeenth to eighteenth century, particularly in France with Perrault, Laugier, and Quatremère de Quincy, who saw type as a vehicle for ideation, up to the end of the eighteenth with Boullée and Ledoux, who proposed substantial, serious theoretical content to those observable "classes of buildings," by coining the term that defines a new concept, "character," which for them was that which makes buildings communicate what they are for, and thus elevates type from mere relations to building to the category of architecture and begins to insinuate the concept as an operational one and not just as a historical category of analysis. It is soon after, when their student Jean-Nicolas-Louis Durand truly swerves the course of this conceptual evolution, transforming "character" into "genre," and moving from discourse to methodology. In this vision, the grid, the axis, and the operation of the composition of elements based on a limited repertoire of forms are the interactive elements of a method that could produce any building (Fig. 1–2). These are also the emblems of the typological birthmark, no more nor less, of formal architectural education— of which we are all inheritors.

We have then discourse first, and method after, installed in our consciousness as significant moments for our analysis:

> *Conscious*
> Discourse – theory and description
> Method – analysis, process, composition, and synthesis

Here, a word perhaps is needed to register the ambiguous relationship of modernism towards type and typology. Within the diversity of incarnations of Modernism, it is possible to find consistent and recurrent ideas of type directly tied to the Beaux-Arts tradition of methodologies of composition, as many historians and theorists, Reyner Banham notably, have pointed out, but noticing that, while they all remain ambivalent, if not antagonistic, to the role that historical precedent may play in the process of design, they do so while displaying all along a constant adherence to the rationale that it was indeed very modern to classify certain formal classes of buildings, and even offer them in the format of catalogs, as long as they were types of modern invention. One of Modernism's most defining topics being function, of which housing typologies is its paradigm.

It is this oscillating path of changing positions that makes us, or at least me, ask, on the occasion of this call to restart the discourse on typology, what today are our theoretical and operational relationships to these past positions? I don't think I can get those answers tonight, but I can sense that we can describe the field, stake out the conceptual territory,

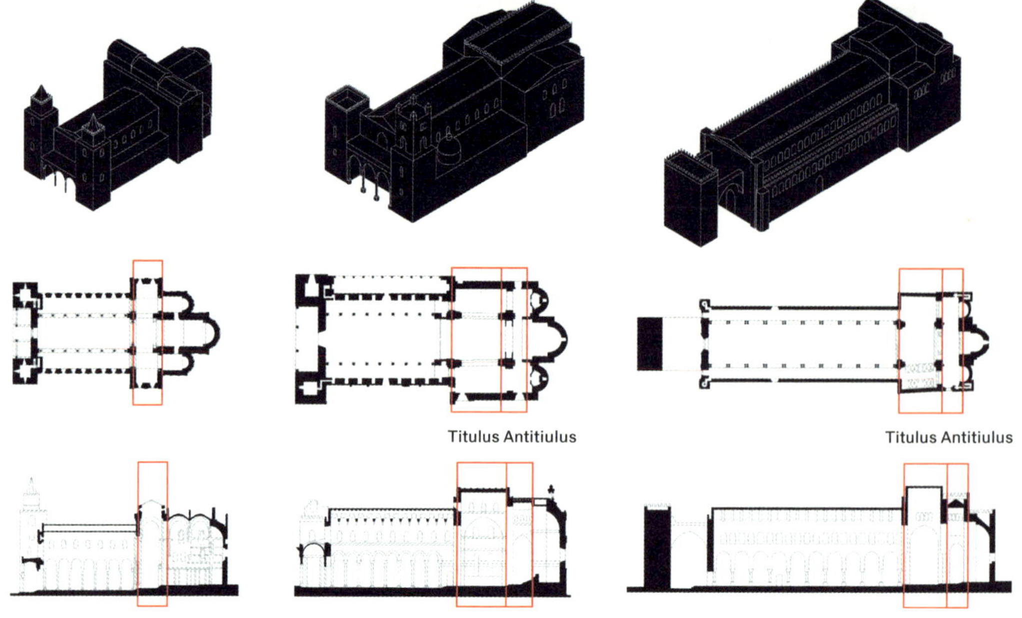

Figs. 4–12 From left to right: Axonometric, plan, and sections of Cefalù Cathedral (1131), Monreale Cathedral (1170), and Palermo Cathedral (1185).

and take a calculated position so as to then begin that task.

And, for that I propose an exercise of analysis that I found revelatory. Let's say, for lack of a better word, that we are going to "psychoanalyze" the "typological mind" by going to its "unconscious" origins, observing the material and factual basis on which it is founded and how it acts, that is, on the pre-discursive moment when typology did not exist as a consciousness, a method or a conceptual apparatus, when we only had the facts of buildings. This is important because, if acting as historians (and for good reasons) we rely on historical evidence based on written material, on discourse, then the Renaissance is our only possible starting point for understanding typology. What I am proposing is to complete the scope of our understanding by attempting to describe the full arch of typology's presence as it accompanies architecture from its very beginnings in the act of making at the times when, while architecture is indisputably present in the life of men, the intellectual awareness of any typological structure, theorization, and further methodological proposition was not. We will then perhaps get a glimpse at the infancy of the typological mind at its moment of innocence. In short, let's try a sort of anthropology of the concept of typology. After that we can complete such an arch by considering the question as to where we are today.

For tonight and as a first step, let's just move only a little further back in time from the Renaissance and place ourselves in the High Middle Ages and at a remarkable place, Sicily. Why here? Too make a very long a story short, it is sufficient to say, Sicily is a very important and formative part of my life as an architect, one that provides me with rich resources to get to what I want to explore tonight, one in which Dean Gerald McCue, present tonight, had a direct and decisive involvement in the role the GSD played in it.

First an event: in 1988, I was invited to participate in an international symposium in Palermo to celebrate the eight hundredth anniversary of the consecration of its cathedral. It was organized as a gathering of scholars and practitioners with the aim to obtain informed and consensual strategies about how to approach the restoration and conservation of this unique and complex monument.

The cathedral today (Fig. 3) shows in its architectural magnificence the record and wealth of the different civilizing moments of its history, with major modifying interventions during the Renaissance, Baroque, and Neoclassical periods, as well as displaying the visible vestiges of all its earlier Norman foundational stages in the twelfth century.

To my surprise, three days of deliberations by scholars in the fields of history, history of art, history of architecture, archaeology, paleography, and architectural conservation yielded no insights or serious advice to help the imminent decisions to proceed with conservation and restoration measures in the monument.

What it did produce, though, was a partisan war between factions defending a certain historical or stylistic "period" and promoting selective erasures of some in favor of others, and all of this in the name of "authenticity."

I surprised myself with my response to a forum where I had arrived, humbly, as an outsider hoping to learn from learned colleagues about respect and care for the monument. I discarded my prepared speech in favor of an improvised, ardent rejoinder, based on the very important aesthetic as well as intellectual experience I had had with this building that I saw as part of a larger, extensive experience of the unique architecture of this island. After eight years of work and having had traveled constantly from one end to the other of the confines of Sicily, I had always delighted at one particular, felicitous historical coincidence in the region of Palermo.

In parallel to its cathedral there are two other ones that were erected concurrently in the last decades of the twelfth century, all promoted by the same patron, the Norman King, and driven by the same goal, to become the mother cathedral of the recently established Norman Kingdom of Sicily. Needless to say, in the context of our conversation, the three shared identical architectural typological origins.

Starting with the earliest, Cefalù, and followed by Monreale almost concurrently with the Cathedral of Palermo (Figs. 4–12), these three competing, magnificent monumental works provide a perfect laboratory for a comparative exploration of how a "preconscious" typological mind would imagine and create three buildings, dealing with the same programmatic requirements and specific site, social, political, and material conditions, but which over time evolve along their own individual trajectories to produce highly singular architectures. Let me cut through details and summarize this rich story by saying that what prompted my reaction at the symposium was my awareness of those startling differences among them, singularities that these three buildings present precisely as the tangible historical and artistic lessons that they propose, one next to the other and capable of being experienced in a single day's journey, about the multiple possibilities that an identical initial defining formal starting point offered for their diverging itineraries, which make each one of them become a unique and extraordinary piece of architecture.

Cefalù is where we can test and experience the original idea almost intact, and the pains of its typological struggles; Monreale is where we observe to an unmatched spatial mutation that alters the building experience as it becomes a literal canvas for the propagation of the faith that unfolds over the interior walls an iconographic program that leaves not a square inch uncovered; Palermo, instead,

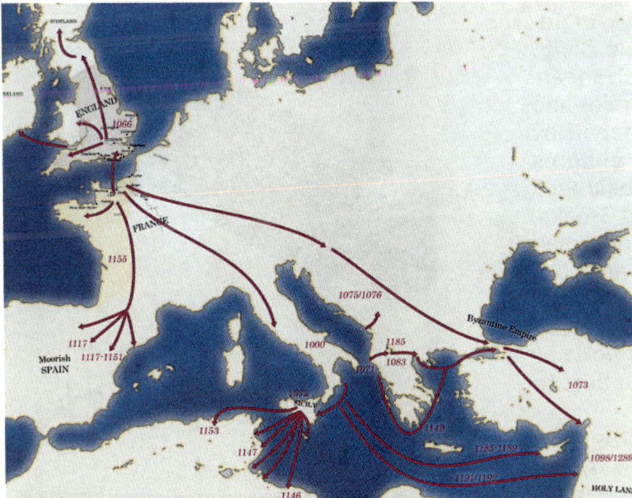

Fig. 13 Map of the Norman expansion in Europe and the Mediterranean during the Middle Ages.

registers the animated, intense, and at times violent architectural history of this particular society, its ideology, its politics, and its struggles over seven centuries. Thus, for me at the symposium, to favor one "period" over another as "authentic" was denying Palermo precisely its authenticity of having been protagonist of a very different history than its two nearby siblings.

These three buildings look, typologically speaking, pretty much the same at first. But on closer look, they begin to show some dissimilarities that are significant for this discussion. Cefalù, the one most chronologically isolated of the group, clearly reflects a divergent format from what would become normative of what is known as Sicilian-Norman architecture. The marked difference in plan—the addition of an extra component in the sanctuary—is supported by the political mutation of Sicily in that period—the functional, ritualistic requirements in the late twelfth century to accommodate in the cathedral both the thrones and the burial sites of the kings' families and those of the archbishops. Hence the doubling up of what appears to be the crossing, or in the liturgical language, the addition of the unusual Antititulus to the Titulus, whose absence in Cefalù eliminates it immediately as a contender—it just came too early.

Such an expansion is easy to understand for functional reasons, but it is also and already a red flag: what are the Titulus and Antititulus? We need just a parenthesis for a bit of straight history here:

The adventurous Normans conquered Sicily in 1060 (Fig. 13) after a sweeping spread throughout the confines of the continent with final stops in two of their major islands. But, while upon their arrival in Britain they found and conquered a marginal, Anglo-Saxon European Christian domain, in Sicily, itself the central point in the Mediterranean, they confronted a centuries-old complex and well-organized society that was shaped by the accumulated sediment of the cultures that had inhabited this land at the crossroads of the Mediterranean—Phoenicians, Greeks, Romans, Byzantines, and Arabs. Indeed, when the Normans arrived what they found and conquered was a society where the prevalent political-social-cultural makeup was that of a fresh, cultivated, and inspiring Islamic society that had spread from the Middle East to Spain through Northern Africa.

To make things more complex, this well-organized and evolved society ruled by the Fatimid Dynasty was a politically and administratively tolerant society that allowed Christianity to exist and even flourish, but, and this is important, it was not the Christianity that the Normans would bring in, Roman Latin Christianity, but the "oriental," Greco-Byzantine, and this displacement presented for the conquering Normans a double adversary to be dominated both politically and ideologically, as the Eastern Christian Church was already a rebel to the Roman papacy and in the early days of the definitive schism of 1054.

This cultural and ideological panorama as a context, together with what will be a continuous, clear political strategy of the Normans to be flexible and accommodating to circumstance and locality begins to give us an important clue to understand these and other transformative cycles of established architectural precedents. If we look very closely at the plans, we begin to notice very strange things (Figs. 4–12).

These plans are not, as we thought first, basilical Latin plans after all—although they did want to be. What we have here is an unprecedented, in fact unimaginable, conflation of plans of both rival rites: half a Latin Basilica and half a Byzantine centralized cross plan—a recognition that while coming with the blessing of the Roman Pope, the reality in the field obliged the Normans to address and include the Byzantine rites of the local Christian flock. The consequences are enormous, and there are new and for a while uncertain and unresolved relationships between nave and sanctuary. The most evident and never resolved being the contradiction between the desired Latin transept and the

14

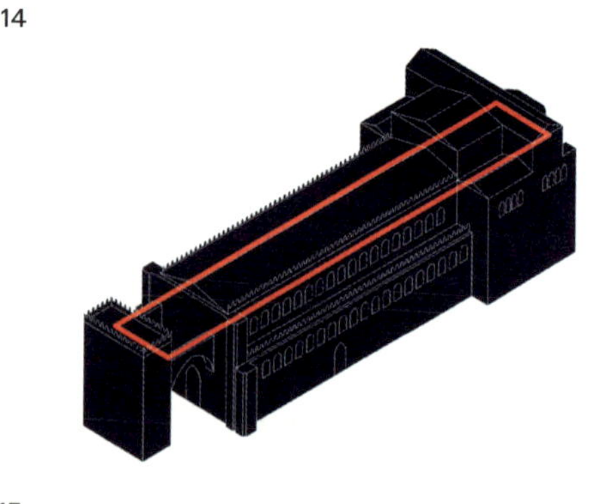

15

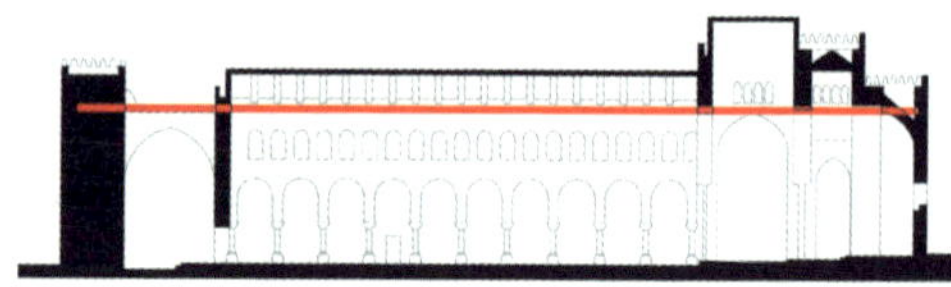

16

17

18

19

Figs. 14–15 Axonometric and section of the Palermo Cathedral (12th–19th century).
Fig. 16 View of the Cefalù Cathedral (12th–15th century).
Fig. 15 View of the Monreale Cathedral (12th–16th century).
Figs. 18–19 The Norman castles of Castello di Cefalà and Castello di Adrano (11th century).

centralized crossing, which is so clearly visible in Cefalù and only smoothed out, though not really resolved either, in this minor church of a few decades later in Palermo.

Moreover, the campanile, which was a somewhat free flowing element in Western Europe—sometimes extant, sometimes on one side, others at the center or in the back, but a prevalent feature of the Roman Romanesque Churches—here is perfunctorily located, in Cefalù and Monreale, as a robust, disproportionately broad flanking pair in the facade, disguising what in reality they were, military defensive structures. (Figs. 16, 17) The defensive motivation becomes explicit in the most striking move of the later one, the Cathedral of Palermo, when the defensive tower emerges as a distinctive compositional element in its own right and without precedent in the whole history of church building. It is a massive, single tower, located precisely on axis with the nave of the church in front of the facade with which it shares its width.

From a military standpoint this amplifies the visual reach and defensive efficiency of the cathodral that doubles now as a fortress with an unusual and very efficient continuous circulation loop that requires the construction of two supportive arches in the main facade to bridge the street and complete the circuit (Figs. 14–15).

Staying and focusing on these towers as purely formal elements helps us change yet again our direction of inquiry to reveal another dimension of this story of intense formal cross-fertilizations and transformations. These massive prismatic volumes are part of a material, technological, and formal vocabulary that populated the island by the twelfth century, Arab defensive square-point towers. (Figs. 18, 19) Indeed, the Norman dynasty of the Hautevilles did not come to Sicily carrying in

20

21

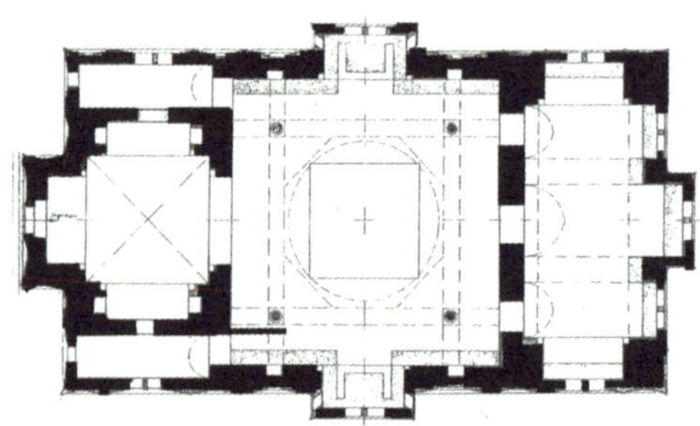
22

23

their Viking-via-Normandy luggage a complete kit of architectural, artistic, technical, and ideological ready-mades; they brought, instead, memories of buildings and of experiences as well as practical knowledge that they were forced to adapt, complement, or change under local conditions. And the local conditions were those of a well-organized and advanced society with its own architecture, engineering, and skilled labor well above the practical knowledge that these Nordic adventurers could deploy.

There was a local Arab aesthetic so peculiarly consistent and widespread throughout Sicily during the almost four centuries of Arab dominance, a type of masonry construction and precision labor (Fig. 20) that produced this massive, prismatic and crisp, chiseled-detail and carved-in architecture with filigree geometric decoration and elaborate structural motifs that continues to appear long after the Normans are settled and in control—particularly when we moved from religious architecture into noble domestic architecture where freedom from traditions, rituals, and symbols is more possible. (Figs. 21, 22) It seems unbelievable that these are the palaces of Norman kings and nobles only a few generations separated from their origins in northwest France and even earlier roots in Scandinavia!

Finally, a decisive touch we find in the interiors of this so-called Norman-Arab architecture (Fig. 23)—which are neither Norman nor Arab but of a different artistic practice derived from another cultural and technological source—gives this architecture its complex identity: unsurpassed mosaics of Byzantine pedigree, attesting to a prior civilization that just remained, after their political demise, in the hands and eyes of their building trades.

We are at a point we can take some stock of all this. What we see in this intense and short-lived episode of architectural experimentation is the productive dynamics of an unchecked typological force in action—what I labeled earlier a *preconscious* moment when typology is just an operative force fed by the accumulated experience of a culture and propelled by the particular demands of place and time that need to be articulated into forms, all without the pause and consideration required by theory and conceptual frameworks.

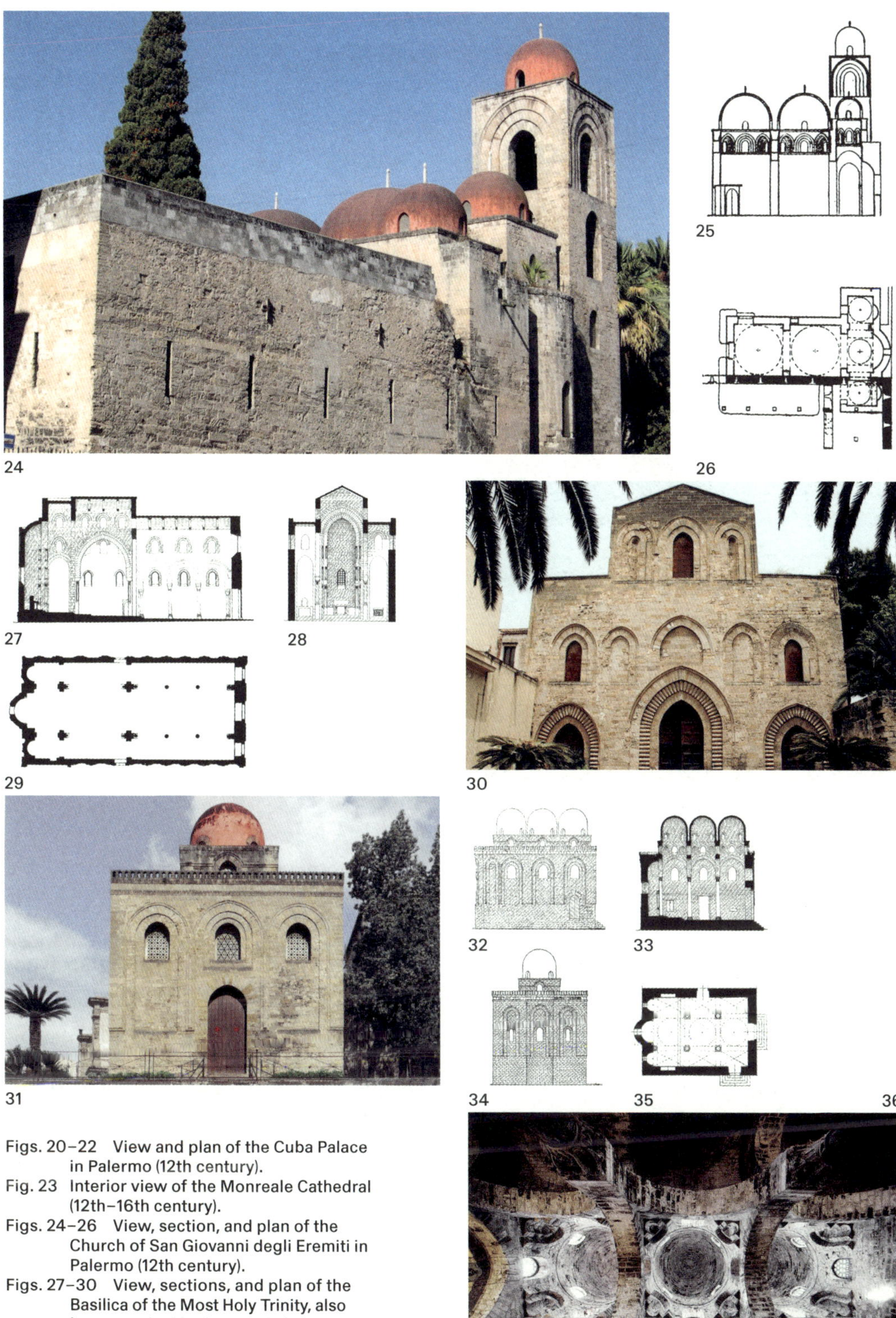

Figs. 20–22 View and plan of the Cuba Palace in Palermo (12th century).
Fig. 23 Interior view of the Monreale Cathedral (12th–16th century).
Figs. 24–26 View, section, and plan of the Church of San Giovanni degli Eremiti in Palermo (12th century).
Figs. 27–30 View, sections, and plan of the Basilica of the Most Holy Trinity, also known as La Magione, in Palermo (12th century).
Figs. 31–36 View, interior view, sections and elevations of the Church of San Cataldo in Palermo (12th century).

37

40

41

38

39

Figs. 37–39 Collages depicting the Cathedral of Palermo as it would have appeared in 1801, 1781 and 1185. Drawings: Juan Sala.
Figs. 40–41 Detail view of a column at Oberlin College, designed by Venturi, Scott Brown and Associates, Inc. (1976), and another at the Gallaratese Quarter, designed by Aldo Rossi (1967).
Fig. 42 Interior view of the Church of Santa Maria dell'Ammiraglio, also known as La Martorana, in Palermo (12th century).

This preconscious moment is characterized by or inhabited by techne:

Preconscious
Techne – craft and necessity

Conscious
Discourse – theory and description
Method – analysis, process, composition, and synthesis

It is remarkable to see the ease with which opposite ideas and symbols, and the forces of function, ideology, politics, technology, and craftsmanship harmonize and express in each case a strong sense of determination to move ahead and to create, yes, new architecture. Because what is ultimately even more impressive is the resulting feast of creativity, inventiveness, and formal as well as ideological freedom all this has on the occasions when it needs to work out design problems; how the confrontation of rival, adversarial, contradictory, or presumably irreconcilable and antithetical ideas and elements mix, blend, copulate, and create the new, the ineffable, the pleasurable. It confirms the loose connection that formal play has with typological rigor but, at the same time, its dependence on the permanence of some formal cues and relationships that assure intelligibility, continuity, and communication. Taking a sample of some of the contemporary buildings that appear around Palermo verifies this (Figs. 24–36).

I want to take note, without further elaboration, for everyone to just think and ponder, that typology, in whatever degree of consciousness it acts in the mind and hands of the designer, certainly demonstrates in these architectural examples the power it possesses and the central role it assumes in the articulation of the complex variables and issues related to the expression of cultural identity and to the integration of cultural diversity at the level of the conception of new works, and in the formulations of strategies for the conservation of old works—themes that, I need not to stress much to this audience, are pressing and inescapable today in the practice of architecture, a practice of cultural significance par excellence—which will be a topic that I would very much like to elaborate on further in the future. Furthermore, the parallelism of these similar yet different architectural occurrences call into question, inevitably, conventional definitions of "authenticity."

But there is one more very important attribute of type in the way we have come to understand its relations to visuality and the imagination that I would like to extract from these examples. If we look again at the Cathedral of Palermo now in reverse historical sequence, understanding that what we are seeing today (Figs. 37–39) is the result of a series a continuous changes, not only in ornamentation and décor but also on the overall spatial configuration and image of the building, starting with the radical, yet expert, transformation in the hands of the Florentine Neoclassical architect Ferdinando Fuga at the end of the eighteenth century—which finally manages to transform the still odd Norman-Arab-Byzantine hybrid into a veritable Roman Catholic, Latin-cross basilical artifact with its dome and its unifying interior organization—not a change easy to swallow for us, regardless of its intrinsic and skillful merits. Let's look in reverse time through the different stages of design transformations to understand what the cathedral looked like in its original state—a hypothetical reconstruction that I believe is quite accurate based on all the archaeological, historiographic, and stylistic evidence. This last image is the original cathedral/fort! (Fig. 39) What is stunning is that the ease with which the image of the building disassociates itself from the typology that its corresponding immutable plan type produced, underlines the non-necessity of a strict, or even logical, let alone necessary, relationship between an abstract or generic notion of type and that of its image.

It was on this, let's call it, mutual indifference between type and image, that much of the initial energy of Postmodernism rested on and played with. I focus on that because, while today this may seem obvious, it was not the most prevalent notion, neither in the history of architecture nor the Project, how type operated until late in the twentieth century. This brings our discussion, somewhat abruptly, to the other end of the chronological arc and to our days.

We can take a deep breath and now look at the two exemplar protagonists of that moment of awareness, Robert Venturi and Aldo Rossi (Figs. 40, 41), both of whom relied on the possibility (and need) to disconnect an abstract, generic form from a concrete image for the explorations of their concerns in the Project, although in opposite ways.

42

43

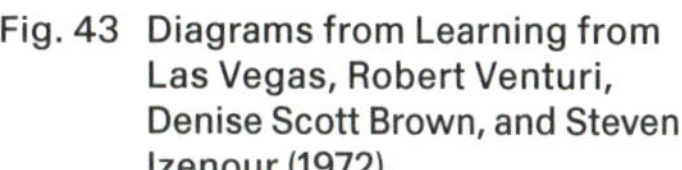

Fig. 43 Diagrams from Learning from Las Vegas, Robert Venturi, Denise Scott Brown, and Steven Izenour (1972).

Fig. 44 Model for National College Football Hall of Fame Competition, designed by Venturi, Scott Brown and Associates, Inc. (1967).

44

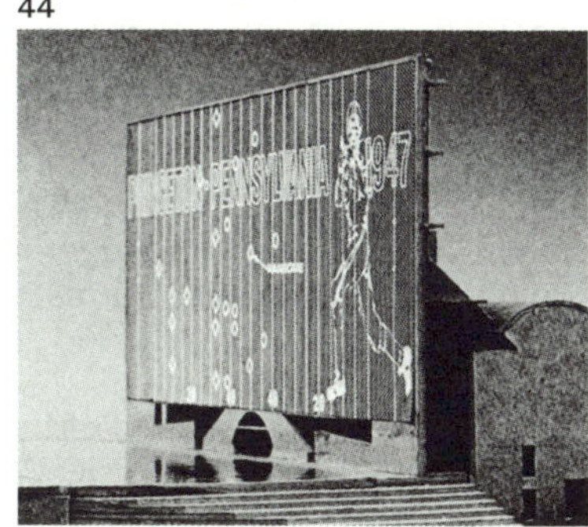

45

47

46

Fig. 45 Drawing of San Cataldo Cemetery in Modena, Aldo Rossi (1971–1978).

Fig. 46 Teatrino Scientifico, Aldo Rossi (1978).

Fig. 47 *Dieses Ist lange Her / Ora questo è perduto*, Aldo Rossi (1975).

In Venturi's case, the complex relationship between typology, history, and image was inherent in the way he conceived of architecture. He sought solid sustenance in the history of western art and architecture as source of precedent and knowledge, but having detected early on the possibility of a separation of image from type (interestingly enough using the example of Norman-Arab Palermo's mosaics as applied to building as a continuous malleable surface (Fig. 42), he offers not just an explanation as to how image works, at least in the American urban landscape, but also proposes a methodology of work that would permit and give validity to the image's free play in his projects. What is the decorated shed (Figs. 43–44)—a concept worked together with D. S. Brown—but a powerful demonstration of that principle, which they followed religiously in all their work.

Rossi, on the other end of the spectrum, struggled with a counter force. While declaring early on that type is indifferent to function, he was then silent about such indifference between type and image. For his purposes, he needed a stable image. He was in a deep search for an ultimate and inexpugnable principle that would anchor the elusive type into the larger and more solid matrix of the city. And, in proving his thesis, he succumbed inexorably to image, as architecture always does when it wants to persuade but is not yet present in the world. It needs a drawing, a model, a miniature that can synthesize and convey the principle. (Figs. 45–46) In his attempt to represent and condense an abstract, complex, and expansive conceptual model that puts in motion the dynamics of the trio of architectural typology, urban morphology, and collective memory, Rossi demanded the impossible: to find a synthetic visual illustration that could embody such complexity. Such an image, a drawing, could not be specific but must be abstract, but this is, of course, an impossibility.

Even if the task weren't impossible, it was

further complicated by his own reductive and personal views as to what are the constitutive elements of his complex vision. His own words, in this beautiful paragraph full of images, are nevertheless the equivalent of the closing of the door to the possibilities of typology in action:

> Now it seems to me that everything has already been seen; when I design I repeat, and in the observation of things there is also the observation of memory. I design my projects with a discrete sense of affection for each one, but I reduce them to things that surround me; country houses, smokestacks, monuments and objects, as if everything arose from and was founded in time; in this beginnings and endings are confounded.[5] (Fig. 47)

Peter Eisenman's caustic but incisive characterization of Rossi's buildings as "representations of his drawings" (Figs. 48–49) put the finger in the wound, showing the potential

48

49

50

51

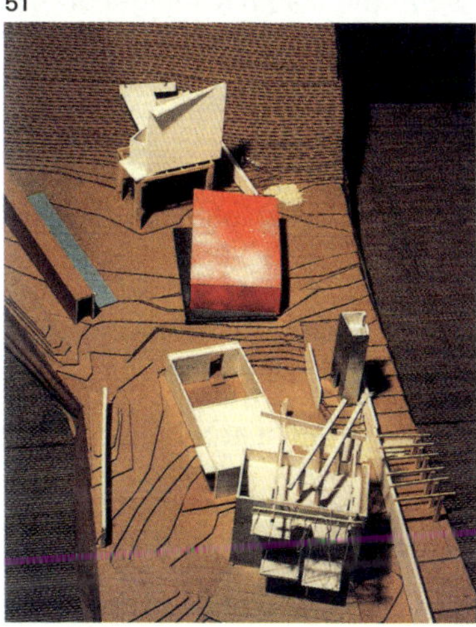

52

53

Fig. 48 View of Centro Direzionale di Fontivegge in Perugia, designed by Aldo Rossi (1983).
Fig. 49 Città analoga, Aldo Rossi (1975).
Fig. 50 Un'altra estate, Aldo Rossi (1979).
Fig. 51 Model of Frank Gehry's John Whitney House, also known as House for a Filmmaker (1981).
Fig. 52 Model of Frank Gehry's Loyola University Law School (1979).
Fig. 53 View of the Nationale-Nederlanden building, designed by Frank Gehry (1992–1996).

of Rossi's extraordinary propositions being capable of causing their own undoing and demise. In fact, there is something purely circumstantial about the way in which the tremendous impact of Rossi's ideas lead to their instantaneous mass consumption as a result of a dissemination that was effected mostly by means of the powerful images of his drawings—a process my generation witnessed with awe that was fast and widespread and which reduced all the richness of his thinking to the power of a few condensed images (Fig. 50), which in turn ended by being synthesized in a single one, the lonely cabin.

For all its profound intellectual intensity, Rossi's typology, enshrined in mesmerizing drawings and less convincing buildings, with all their simplicity, impacting communicability, and resonating references to primeval, elementary architectures. The primitive hut of old became reduced in its dissemination to the innocent cabin, and as such, to a universal icon.

Both the reductionist precipice opened by Rossi's type and the open-ended ability of Venturi's type to play freely with images—both undertakings intellectually profound and visually provocative—undermined the very efficacy of typology which is based on its capacity to harmonize principle and expression with motivation, or abstract formal clarity with inspired visual articulation, in order to express an idea or a concept. Rossi and Venturi worked at the extremes of the possibilities of the Project: one obsessively offering type as a transcendental, quasi-tragic icon, the other as an elusive, dizzying carrousel of fantasies.

If in the panorama of how type inhabits the practice of architecture since its prehistory, we can now represent the saga of typology in this high period of Postmodernism as associated with the evolution of *conscious* to *self-conscious* and defined by the activity of *criticism*:

Preconscious
Techne – craft and necessity

Conscious
Discourse – theory and description
Method – analysis, process, composition, and synthesis

Self-Conscious
Criticism – deconstruction of discourse

And further, I would like to complete this working model with what defines the way typology is operating uninterruptedly since then, decisively and almost exclusively, in the realm of image itself:

Self-Conscious
Criticism – deconstruction of discourse
Image – reduction to the sensible

In view of this, and for the past two decades, many had predicted the death of type and typology in any of its modalities, and for a while the flurry of enthralling, smooth a-typological images that the contemporary impact of digital technology and computation ceaselessly produced, seemed to prove that type would never recover its hold.

Rightly, it was easy to see that the degradation produced by Postmodernism was attributable to the effects of too much image and too little substance as the condition in which typology survived—and that all that was possible to expect from it was a final fall into historical pastiche.

But not so fast. After Rossi and Venturi, it could be said that type, reduced to an icon, became instead a persistent and indestructible representation of a kind of typology-in-waiting itself: the cabin's image or the undifferentiated housing block in different renditions became the refuge of an idea of architecture at an impasse that is showing signs of ending.

How long the condition of no method, no discourse, no self-analysis, plus the exhaustion of theory, produced a stalemate where type waits, as an actor on the sidelines, for the right moment to enter the scene and recover protagonism. In fact, and startlingly, if we look closely, we can trace it in the work of some of the most representative architects of this post-Postmodern period, starting with an unsuspected fellow, Frank Gehry, who in my view is the most consistent typologist of all.

Looking deeply and carefully through his oeuvre, in between the folds of the formal bravura, there is a clear and constant dialogue between his formal experimentation with type at its most basic, almost Rossian version, and a conscious engagement, from the outset to the final product, with a typological presence (in the occurrence of the image of type) in almost all his projects. These are just some examples from all the different periods of his work:

(Fig. 51) The early "House for a Filmmaker" dismantles the conventional suburban house but deploys all its Durandian elements—living room, patio, corridor—as if waiting for a new

54

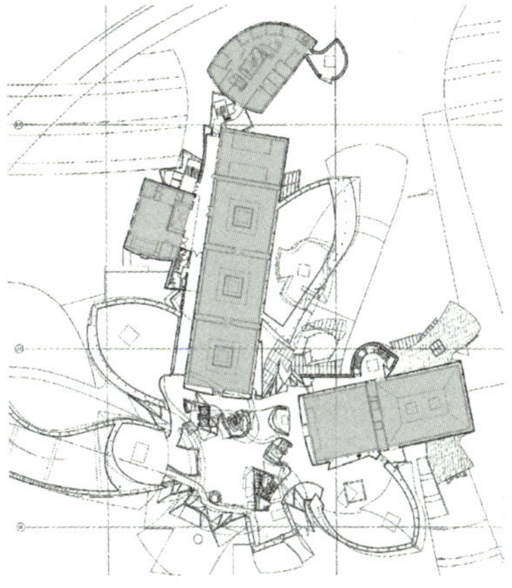

55

56

57

Figs. 54–55 View and plan of the Guggenheim Museum in Bilbao, designed by Frank Gehry (1997).
Figs. 56–57 Exterior and interior views of the DZ Bank Building at Pariser Platz 3 in Berlin, designed by Frank Gehry (1998–2000).

method of composition. This cutting up of the domestic typological elements, caught up at the expectant moment of waiting for the editor to splice them into a new whole, defines well this Gehry moment as a preamble to the following stages of his production.

(Fig. 52) Loyola, where competing icons of types—the chapel, the temple, the urban housing bar—are deployed in a fragmentary arrangement and where, from its most Rossian element, the long rectilinear bar dotted with equal rectangular basic windows, bursts out the uncontrolled rolling stair. This move of contrasting formal opposites will later become his signature. It seems that Gehry's always need to have the immutable city of Rossi in the vicinity!

(Fig. 53) Prague is the proof! The whole architectural idea depends on a borrowed Baroque metaphor of movement to affect a contextual approach to the historical city by deforming the monotonous, dominant infill housing typology.

And Bilbao, when even under the most extreme formal exuberance there remains, silent but persistent, the Rossian urban types that would connect it to the eighteenth-century city. (Figs. 54–55) Finally, Berlin, in my view his most distilled and elegant rendition of these ideas, where the enforcement of urban design rules in the historic center imposes on the project the calm discipline and order of the European city, and where "the Gehry effect" is thus reserved for the interior, where we find the jewel (Figs. 56–57) as being offered in an exquisite wooden coffer.

We can check Koolhaas on this too. Not a denier of typology himself, in his love affair with the skyscraper (Fig. 58), his defining favorite type, he seemed for a while unsettled with it in his many trials that oscillate between, on the one hand, his breathtaking CCTV (Fig. 59), a daring annihilation of the formal, functional, and symbolic characteristics of the skyscraper (Is it now an "earth-scraper"?), and on the other his notable, immediate retraction soon

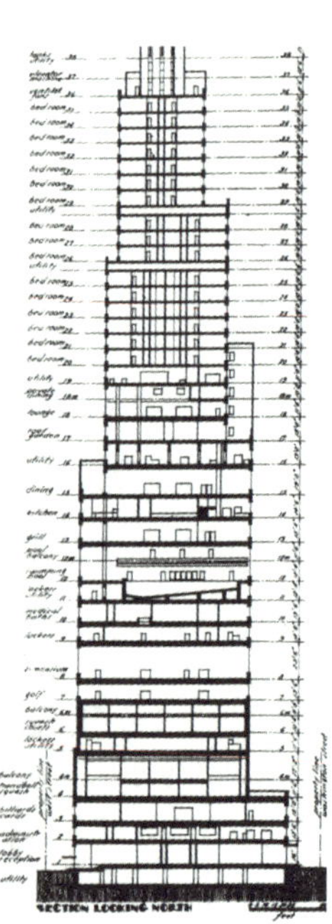

58

59

60

61

after in a quasi-penitent act of *mea culpa* with the irrefutable, typologically triumphant set in De Rotterdam (Fig. 60).

Perhaps today the most poignant and persistent example of this typological presence can be found in the work of Herzog and de Meuron with their insistence on a single image (Fig. 61) that recurs ritualistically at regular intervals as in a litany of typological reaffirmations—as if to say that in their hearts the Rossian cabin will always be present and that it needs to be "sacrificed" periodically as an act of purification, which is also to acknowledge in these periodic homages, as they do openly, their debt to their teacher.

This act of seemingly eternally recurrent reincarnation, which sometimes has the feeling of a requiem (Fig. 62), has reached a moment of mutation that I observe with great interest as it announces a reversal of this religious tone, when the emblematic cabin, imaginatively altered, becomes the generator of one of their most extraordinarily vigorous and complex interventions, where everything is the same but also all is changed. The Feltrinelli Foundation in Milan where the gabled section becomes urban morphology/building typology/memory, which paradoxically, given its historical references, produces a tremendous novelty in this vibrantly modern European city. (Figs. 63–66) Type has even become indifferent to a corresponding urban morphology as this gabled section has nothing to do with the city of Milan, with this

Fig. 58 Section of the Downtown Athletic Club building in New York City (1930).

Fig. 59 View of the CCTV Headquarters building in Beijing, designed by the Office for Metropolitan Architecture (2002–2012).

Fig. 60 View of the De Rotterdam complex, designed by the Office for Metropolitan Architecture (1997–2013).

Fig. 61 View of Blue House in Oberwil, designed by Herzog & de Meuron (1980).

Fig. 62 Elevations of Herzog & deMeuron projects that use shed roofs, from left to right: Blue House (1980), House for Art Collector (1986), House in Leyman (1997), Schaulager (2003), Prada Aoyama (2003), St. Jakob Tower (2005), VitraHaus (2010), Parrish Art Museum (2012), and Fondazione Feltrinelli (2016).

Figs. 63–66 Views, site plan, and site section of the Fondazione Feltrinelli Building in Milan, designed by Herzog & de Meuron (2016).

particular neighborhood, nor with the buildings (fortifications walls and city gates) that used to occupy the site. Changed in scale, it is now a gigantic cabin, recast in glass, and reincarnated as a horizontal skyscraper that reinvigorates and probably shows an aperture to a new direction of a free image in search of a type. Multiple displacements and inversions—conceptual, formal, scalar, material, and figurative—confuse origins but proceed with typological clarity to reconfigure the city. A lot to be expected from this!

Where do I find my thinking about architecture and typology at this moment? I think first, Moneo is still right and we will have to answer the challenge he posed, now to us as to each generation:

> . . . To answer it means, for each generation, a redefinition of the essence of architecture and an explanation of all its attendant problems. This in turn requires the establishment of a theory, whose first question must be, what kind of object is a work of architecture? This question ultimately has to return to the concept of type.[6]

Second, what this impasse has given us is the time to understand better not only what was going on in parallel in architecture and to sustain with composure and patience the end of the exhausting parade of somewhat sterile but necessary formal experimentation that the arrival of digital technologies of representation produced as these tests needed to run their course.

Moreover, we have calmly absorbed the realization that architecture is standing in a new playing ground, and that it is playing with old but also new protagonists, conditions, and rules that need a welcome consideration. But I am also suggesting that, indeed, we should consider likely that the questions we ask ourselves today may require, as I believe always had, that we return to the concept of type. It seems that we cannot evict it from the creative process and that indeed type inhabits

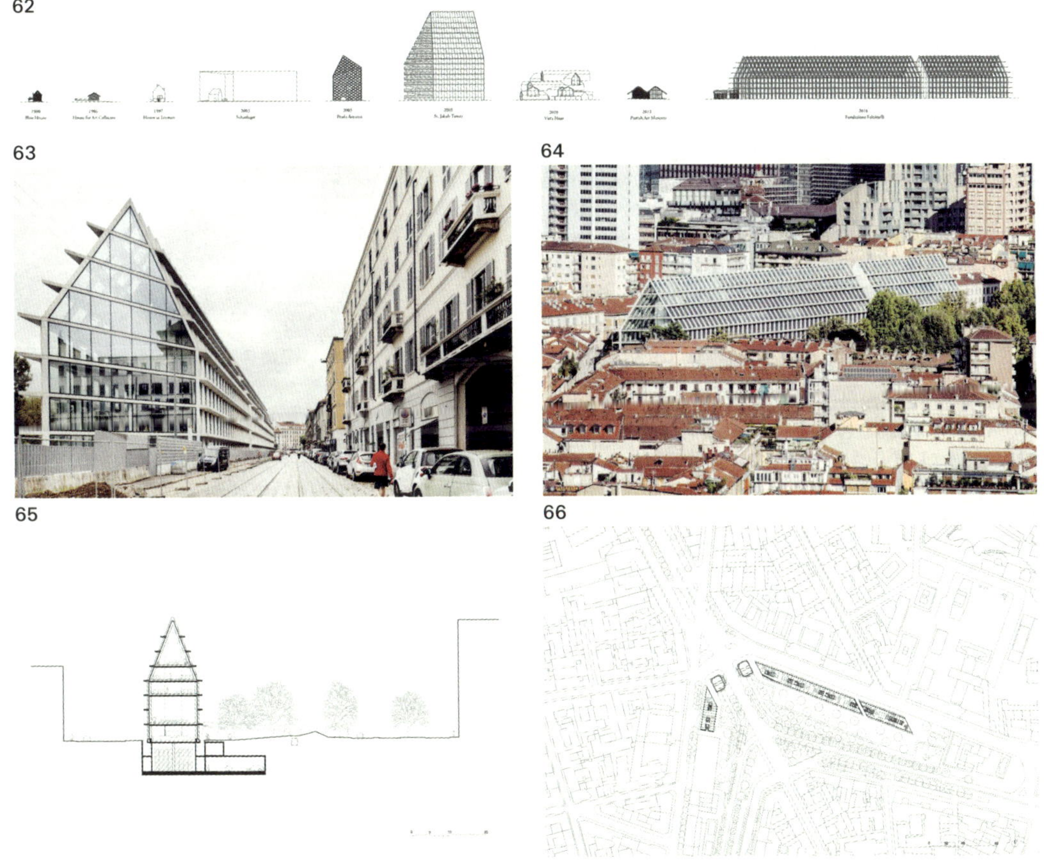

the project as a permanent tenant. It should also be welcomed back.

Under what guise it will show up is unclear. Throughout its history we've seen it at times to appear as *idea*, at others as a *method*, a *discourse*, as *image* and *icon*. Should we not consider the possibility that image may be by now totally independent of iconographic associations and perhaps be considered as free form within which may still resonate its original typological pedigree and with which we might play intelligently, judiciously, and architecturally as Jacques and Pierre seem to be doing here?

As intimated earlier, we must also awaken to the new demands of both modes of conservation, environmental and cultural, with their associated polemics and cultural wars, to the marvels of digital technology, computation, and their associated cultural dominance of the world of images, and, in short, to all the technological advances in materials, structures, social formations, and to the crises of politics and institutions. Such a panoply of riches that we are offered should also propel us to try to conceive new possibilities of types, so while accepting Rafael's challenge, I am tempted to take exception to G. C. Argan's narrower view of his understanding of the genesis of type as only a result of a synthesis of past occurrences:

> The birth of a "type" is therefore dependent on the existence of a series of buildings having between them an obvious formal and functional analogy. In other words, when a "type" is determined in the practice or theory of architecture, it already has an existence as an answer to a complex of ideological, religious, or practical demands which arise in a given historical condition of whatever culture.[7]

I truly believe that when we move from the field of scholarship into the world of design, into the Project, a type can indeed be invented—but not out of nothing as some designers had hoped in the recent past as they relinquished their responsibility to making decisions about form to the control of algorithms—but out of architecture itself. That means a close, intelligent relationship between the history of architecture and the Project.

Sorry, we cannot dream of returning to our infancy even as we may yearn for the mythical times when the builder could play freely with types, words, and forms and still be surprised by them. But we can see how the powerful combination of history and the Project, can propel the imagination to yet unimagined results.

Notes

1 Mark Lee, Sharon Johnston, Sarah Hearne, and Letizia Garzoli, *Make New History: 2017 Chicago Architecture Biennial* (Chicago, IL: Chicago Architecture Biennial; Baden: Lars Müller Publishers, 2017).

2 Ibid.

3 Giulio Carlo Argan, "On the Typology of Architecture," trans. Joseph Rykwert, *Architectural Design* 33, no. 12 (December 1963): 564–565.

4 Moneo, "On Typology."

5 Aldo Rossi, introduction to *Aldo Rossi in America: 1976 to 1979*, ed. Kenneth Frampton (New York: Institute for Architecture and Urban Studies, 1976).

6 Ibid.

7 Ibid.

On Perspective, Anamorphosis, and Repositionings

JORGE SILVETTI AND
NICOLÁS DELGADO ALCEGA, 2021

The following conversation developed through a periodic set of exchanges that took place between September 2020 and March 2021.[1] *As a series of social events unfolded—at the GSD, in the United States, and around the world—the authors opened up a discussion that began with a set of personal notes that Jorge Silvetti had collected in the months prior. Alarming current events catalyzed a slow discussion, one in which personal experiences, disciplinary issues, and large cultural processes constantly intertwined through an exchange of words and images, one through which the authors, both raised surrounded by a degree of social unrest, sought to make sense of what they saw around them.*

This conversation took place amid Silvetti's retirement from the GSD after forty-six years of involvement in the school. It accompanied the donation process of the Machado & Silvetti archive[2] *to the Frances Loeb Library and paralleled a seminar at the GSD in which related issues were engaged through a different mode. It precedes a retrospective exhibition of the work of Machado & Silvetti and has been a sounding board for a new course that Silvetti will teach as a research professor in the coming years. It is a conversation between two South Americans from opposite ends of the continent and on opposite ends of their professional careers, who are both curious, concerned, and stimulated by this moment in the history of architectural culture.*

NICOLÁS DELGADO ALCEGA In preparation for our conversation, I have been going over your office's three monographs,[3] because I wanted to have a discussion with you about your long-standing interest in the history of architecture. To that end, the projects in the monographs that you and Rodolfo produced in Sicily over the years struck me as a good place to start.

How did you get to Sicily? And why did it capture your professional and intellectual attention for so many years?

JORGE SILVETTI Before I answer your question, let me first say that I was chiefly educated within the context of the Western tradition but from a distinctly *marginal location*. I was raised in Buenos Aires, a city at the bottom of the Western world, in the southernmost tip of the continent. At the 34th parallel south, I was not only literally at the geographic bottom of the world but also on the fringes of the history of Western society. When I say marginal then, I mean simply that I was in a position[4] at an edge farthest away from the centers of cultural dominance.

From Buenos Aires everything was far, particularly those centers of power and their histories. This was amplified by the fact that, back then, people didn't travel that often to Europe. To do so affordably meant a month-long journey by boat, and even that option was not available to middle-class families.

Nonetheless, everything I was learning in school—music, history, art—was invariably founded on the Western tradition. It was assumed that everything you were learning was the way it was supposed to be, which I suppose today means "canonical." But I grew up feeling that whatever my reality was, it was upended from that "normality." So, my understanding of the canonical was always inevitably skewed by the particular angle from where I had been positioned by fate, where distant traditions were intertwined with other local cultural ingredients that fed my mind and imagination. In marginal positions, local cultural pressures are inescapably very active. This is particularly true in the arts, language, and daily customs, whether it's classical or pop music, painting, literature, cuisine, or local jargon.

All these elements that were bound by location coalesced into my individual cultural profile. They contaminated my understanding and regard[5] for the "canon"—my way of seeing it—and importantly influenced and inspired my creative and intellectual work. I think this all points to my particular, seemingly deviant predilections and interests among the canonical expressions of Western architecture, which are generally found in places that are far from the accepted "center," be it Athens, Rome, or Paris. Even though the Hagia Sophia or El Escorial were presented as part of the canon, I was always inclined to interpret them as marginal. I found them to be anomalies, deviations, or even perversions by which I was fascinated.

However, these conditions not only determined my interest in certain cases on the edge of the canon, they also influenced my reading of works squarely in line with the canon. At one point, I even convinced myself that the whole Palladian oeuvre was a peculiar, provincial oddity of the Roman Renaissance. Although I used to be somewhat embarrassed of myself for holding these positions—keeping most to myself—today I am convinced that we can and should present Palladio's work first and foremost as such. Certainly at least the corpus of his domestic architecture around Vicenza! Those sober, restrained, stuccoed villas qua farms screaming their classical pedigree yet speaking a "dialect" far from Rome and Florence, to which they allude. I think today they become clearer and more powerful when seen this way. It makes them more productive and meaningful in the context of our current concerns. Ultimately, it shows convincingly that the canon is an ever changing, layered, and shifting body of models and ideals. Seen this way, Palladio's work moves quickly from being marginal to becoming central to the canon, not only in Italy but all over Europe and eventually North America.

This way of seeing is, really, the indelible mark that this "position"—physical, historical, cultural—left on my persona and the perspective[6] from which I look at the world. And today it explains to me—even if it's too late for my mother of Tuscan origins to understand!—why I became so enchanted and involved with Sicilian architecture and its intensely hybrid and exuberant artistic pedigree.

NDA You're suggesting Sicily has a similar condition to that of Buenos Aires? Of being at the edge of a culturally dominant center that it is in contact with?

JS In some ways, say in relation to Rome, Florence, or Venice during classical periods, yes. Sicily is a place where this phenomenon is very much a part of the island's cultural condition and history. When viewed from the position of dominant cultural centers, it is a culture that has been marginal to other centralities for millennia: to the Phoenicians, the ancient Greeks, the Romans, the Byzantines, the Normans, the Spanish, and so on.

So, Sicily is a place where all major cultures converged, but for which Sicily was never a particular center.[7] And yet, when you see things *from* Sicily, the island prompts its own form of centrality. This duality is inevitable in Sicily. On a map, we can see it as an ineludible roadblock in the *Mare Nostrum* upon which all Mediterranean cultures stumbled and "accidentally" left their marks. But conversely, we can also see it as a "center" of Mediterranean culture, which collected the tolls particular cultural makeup. The deep layers of cultural stratification caused by this geographical, cultural condition have produced something unique in Sicily that is still palpable today.[8]

Nowhere is this clearer than in Sicilian Baroque architecture, a local strain of what was otherwise a Roman cultural epiphenomenon. In Sicily, the Roman Baroque is appropriated and completely reinvented. Its exaggeration, ebullience, and luxuriance goes far beyond Rome's, and its urban ambition is much more comprehensively realized. The architectural and urban planning experiments of the Val di Noto, as well as the codevelopment of sculpture, ornament, and stucco in Palermo have few parallels elsewhere during this time.

The same can be said of the so-called "Norman architecture," a short period in the late eleventh and most of the twelfth century, where an original architecture was created by the fusion and coalescence of Byzantine, Islamic, and Norman architectural streams.

NDA For how long were you actually involved with research and projects in Sicily?

JS It was about eleven years. We would spend every moment we didn't have to be in Boston in Sicily. And when we were in Boston, there was usually ongoing work for Sicily at the office. It was undoubtedly one of the most formative experiences of my life, professionally and intellectually. I don't think I learned more about architecture in any other place. Sicily is a place where I understood so much about how cultures are put in motion and transformed.

NDA In a way, your journeys to Sicily sound like the more canonical pilgrimage to Rome, but instead of offering the "definitive" references of antiquity or the Baroque, Sicily offered uniquely "derivative" ones.

JS Well, firstly I would never call what Sicily produced a "derivative" type of work, which has a derogatory connotation. This is architecture that I would call original, fresh, and powerful. As to your other point about an alternative canonical pilgrimage, I'm not so sure about that. I knew Rome well before I went to work in Sicily. However, by the time I got to the American Academy in 1986, I had been involved in Sicily for four or five years. So at that point, it was in fact Sicily that tainted a posteriori my mature understanding of the Rome I thought I knew well and not the other way around.

NDA We normally judge what is "on the edge" by contrasting it with what is at the center, with the canonical reference. I think this idea of reading things the other way around, as you are describing, is interesting. Looking back at the reference or origin point from what you've learned at the edge.

I guess if you think about it, it's the only way. We are always seeing from our point of view, with all of the baggage that this implies.

JS Absolutely. This is actually at the core of what the so-called "Western tradition" truly is, or at least, that is how I have come to understand it. I think this is the way we should always position ourselves to look at any cultural practice.

Now that I have been relieved of most of my academic responsibilities, I've been working on a seminar that tries to reframe what we understand by the Western tradition and leaves behind this notion of "canon," which I don't believe is really a solid, homogeneous, and compact cultural phenomenon. It is an attempt to reposition[9] my thinking around the topics that have occupied my mind as a teacher and practitioner, which has been fueled and energized with great impetus in the past year, since we have all felt the need to move at a different pace with sharper focus and new objectives.

My main intent is to dismantle the idea that the Western tradition is a monolithic, static, and intrinsically problematic thing, as it has become customary to describe it. While this is not a particularly original idea—scholars like Salvatore Settis have dealt with this idea in great depth already—I think we have much to gain by restating this fact. I believe we should try to further understand the ways in which this tradition is an ever changing, highly heterogeneous, macrocultural formation that has been around for thousands of years. The Western tradition is a cultural phenomenon that has had quite a few dominant strains at different times and has always been fueled, energized, and transformed by the internal dynamics of its intrinsic diversity, by the interplay of its component parts.

What I hope to achieve with the course is to take this tradition and see how once "marginal" or "dominated" component strains of its diversity have at times advanced to become dominant themselves—Palladio, again . . . For me, cases of this kind are evidence that the attempts we are undertaking to respond to today's issues require—or better, deserve—reconsideration. I think that by repositioning our strategic intellectual perspective in order to productively work from within this collective of cultural strains—instead of taking on an approach of rejection—our capacity to amplify certain strains is much higher.

I'm actually of the opinion that going as far back as the Acropolis of Athens—two and a half millennia behind us—gives us incredible opportunities to study strains that deal with issues that are at the forefront of our concern right now, whether related to identity, diversity, inclusion, or justice. In fact, the course may be called "The Acropolis of Athens and Its Consequences."

NDA It's exciting to think that architecture can play a role in these changing balances of power. But can it actually operate at the speed necessary for it to be proactive in these processes?

JS I think we have to understand architecture as part of the constellation of cultural products that define a moment. In academia, we lately tend to fall under the temptation of making architecture overreach into other domains of society and culture in which other practices are more effective and powerful. But if we look at cases in a nuanced way, I believe we can see many of these forces at play in the making of architecture.

A lot of the interests I will be exploring in the seminar began developing years ago in some option studios I taught at the GSD. In the courses, we would deal directly with the profound and tense issues of cultural identity and diversity that characterize our age through many cases, including, for instance, the Indigenous Guaraní cultural territory, a place that exists at the intersection of several South American nation-states.

We took as a starting point the physical remains of the *Misiones jesuíticas*: a century-and-a-half-long colonial cultural project that spanned the seventeenth and eighteenth centuries. The *misiones* were the result of interactions between European architectural culture and local practices.[10] The combination of these two traditions under the extreme environmental conditions of this area produced a form of heritage that differed greatly from the better-known, typical outcomes of the

Spanish colonial sociopolitical models prevalent at the time.

There was clearly at play here a power dynamic in which one of the parties was still under the control of another. And yet, the remains of the architecture that we still see there are the result of an act of cultural negotiation, one which had ultimately produced something altogether new, distinct, and extraordinary from either perspective. The architecture did not vindicate any specific individual or wholeheartedly upend a power balance; the outcome was not black, white, or gray. But I do believe that what it manifested was a swerve in the direction of an altogether new cultural construct.

Something that I've learned from all of these experiences is that we are always influenced and determined by a dominant way of seeing things. But to be critical of this dominance within a specific practice, which is what most of us always want to do anyway, we need to do so from within as practitioners of such practice. We can't just stand there, reflecting on it passively or taking an outsider's perspective; you cannot really walk away from the cultural constructs you are embedded into, no matter how much you disagree with them.

NDA I'm curious how you dealt with all these questions in the studio format, where you must move beyond analysis and critique into specific design proposals.

JS We did what studios are best suited to do: respond to intellectual demands through design by engaging a specific set of circumstances and needs. The "design mode" of research and pedagogy gives us a unique perspective and understanding of society: its history, its present, and its possible futures. In all these studios I made sure that we amplified and diversified the students' perspectives on all the areas of knowledge, art, and politics that converged in relation to our problem at hand. But I also made it so that they had no alternative to confronting their proposed interventions other than by addressing these issues through *exclusively architectural* means.

I think that broadening our understanding should not be confused with studio formats prevalent today in which architecture is just a support scaffolding to principally address topics provided by the field of technology or the politics of the humanities. I believe that making architecture the *inescapable protagonist* of an architectural education is today an ethical imperative. All these other topics should be a part of the questions we ask ourselves in the studio but not the ultimate goal.

NDA In a recent conversation with Sarah Whiting for *Pairs* 01, she pointed out that design teaching was essentially about dialogue because discourse advances through conversation, regardless of the form it takes. When I reflect on some of the theory seminars that you have taught recently, I remember them as exactly that: agglomerations of concepts, ideas, and references in the process of finding shape; propositions, questions, and observations more than definitive answers. Perhaps what was most refreshing about the experience was seeing how we can revisit the history of our discipline and, by virtue of the way we compose and connect its parts, find new and useful ways of learning from it. It is perhaps the closest approach to Aby Warburg's methodology that I encountered in my years as a student.

Maybe because you are not a historian but rather a designer with a passion for history, you are constantly trying to understand why a given architect made certain decisions. I think more than ever this is a worthy undertaking. It enables us to look at the history of our discipline as a set of exercises performed by people trying to make the right choice given their priorities amid complicated and often contradictory constraints. And it gives us the hindsight to evaluate the consequences or impact of these decisions in time. With so many anti–status quo priorities implicit in discussions in schools of architecture today, this feels incredibly useful.

JS Yes, that's the way teaching the history of architecture should be approached in a school of architecture! One of the pedagogical contributions that I am most proud of is the work that Howard Burns and I did at the GSD to create the course "Buildings, Texts, & Contexts" (BTC), which was then amplified by the contributions of K. Michael Hays and Wilfried Wang at the turn of the millennium. We essentially broke away from the idea of the survey course as a way to teach architectural history at the graduate level, since we thought it was unnecessary, in favor of the approach you are describing.

We imposed surveys as a prerequisite to admission to the program and developed a way to teach history that was specifically conceived and designed for graduate architecture programs. Until that point, history in architecture schools was taught in the same way as in fine arts schools. We thought this was not the best approach because the courses were too distant from the studios and lost all relation to the design process, which is ultimately one of the chief concerns of our education.

Howard and I argued that the history of architecture in a professional school had to be taught jointly and on an equal level by one architect and one historian. We were the first to try this out, and the result was fantastic. Though we started it at the GSD, I think it did have some repercussions in other graduate programs across the country.

Each week we taught a case, usually a single building, and every once in a while a text. On Tuesday, I would start off by looking at the building in itself. On Thursday, Howard would then bring in more of the historical context. But he would do so by extending out from the piece of architecture (or text) under scrutiny and going only as far as necessary to hypothesize what the actual process of design had been. So, we would look at the building from the inside out, trying to reconstruct, in a somewhat speculative way, what was going through the mind of the architect in the creative process. This, by the way, is another example of how one can position oneself within what one is studying, analyzing, or interpreting.

It was a total success because it really made the cases useful and accessible to us as architects tasked with our own creative endeavors, with our own need to respond to the myriad of conditions in our context in order to give shape to a specific building or space.

NDA Did your interest in the "marginal" expressions of Western architecture percolate into the list of cases?

JS Of course! One of the first things we did was incorporate cases like El Escorial or the Mosque of Córdoba as breakthrough dislocations within Western culture. These were buildings that were discussed in conventional courses but always in passing. Much of what I've shared with you today was less clear to me back then, but this urge to push these cases toward the center was there, I guess.

By placing these types of buildings in equal position among canonical exemplars, we make them act as moments of epiphany in our understanding of the cultural dynamics of architecture. The mosque was a building done entirely with Roman technology and Roman architectural component pieces, and yet, a complete invention for an emerging religious and political power. It was a type of building that had never been seen anywhere else. It was also a building that underwent expansions and modifications across centuries, adapting itself to rituals and a religious culture in evolution. Its later history is actually its transformation from mosque to cathedral, which I think is an extraordinary cultural phenomenon to witness and which deals with many issues that are resurfacing in our contemporary concerns.

NDA I think our generation feels an urgency to reinvent many of the conventions that we take for granted in order to respond to new conditions that we are alarmed by. And I think this holds true whether we talk about the way we build, practice, foster community, or govern.

To me, the events that unfolded around the issue of police brutality in the US last year are a very clear example of this. But they also showed that the desire to dismantle and reassemble anew or to radically restructure something is very complex and nuanced. It is ultimately an act of negotiation between a new set of aspirations and an establishment that it is often at odds with.

Do you think there are tangible ways to use the sort of scholarship we have discussed today to seriously deal with issues like the representation of cultural minorities or marginalized segments of society in our fields?

JS Well, I'd like to first say that the culture of minorities and marginalized groups—in any society—are strains that are as much a part of that culture as the dominant strains are. They may be distorted, diminished, subjugated, or repressed, as they usually are. They may also enjoy uncontrollable success, as they do in some exceptional cases. But they are an inextricable component in the larger cultural pot.

I think that the most productive way to effect positive change is to understand from within how all these strains exist within the larger whole. In what conditions and degrees of dependency, freedom, and repression do they operate and interact with one another?

By understanding these mechanisms, we can put them at our service to transform the processes of change in positive ways. Can we build a cultural condition in which the dominance of one strain is transformed into the collective interaction of many diverse strains? I believe this is an aspiration that we can only hope to achieve by better understanding what has brought us to where we are today.

Fig. 1 Labyrinth of Affinities

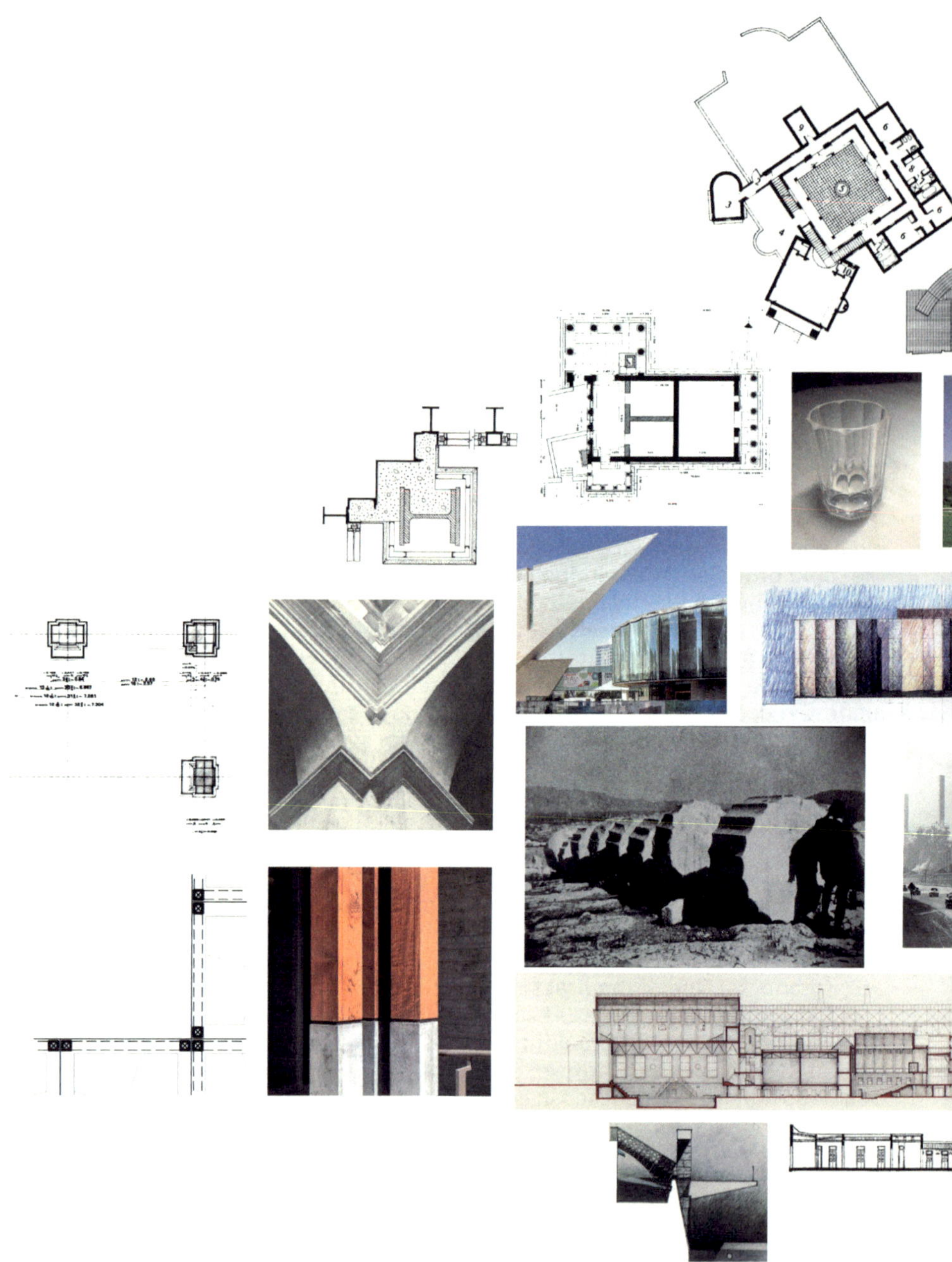

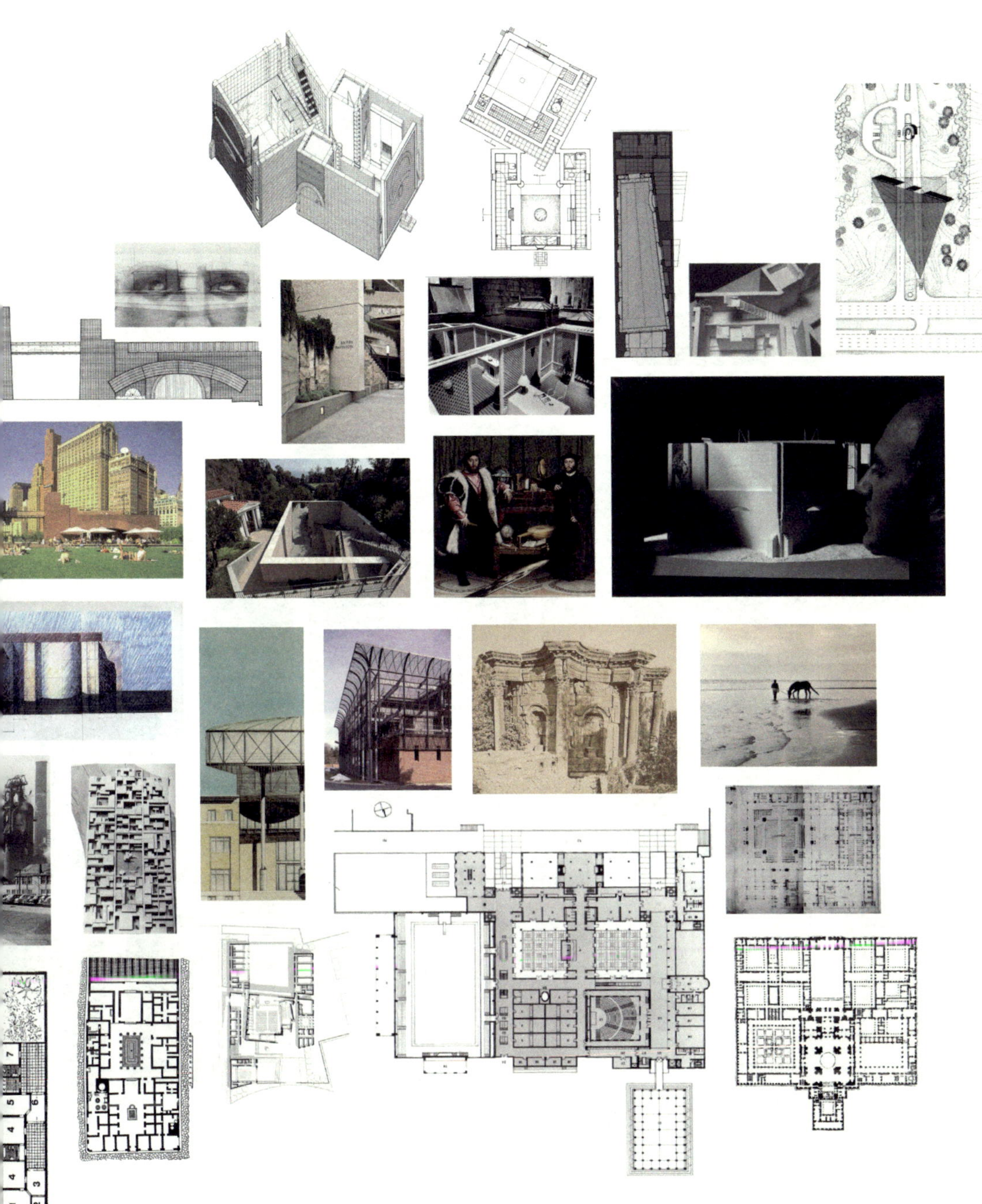

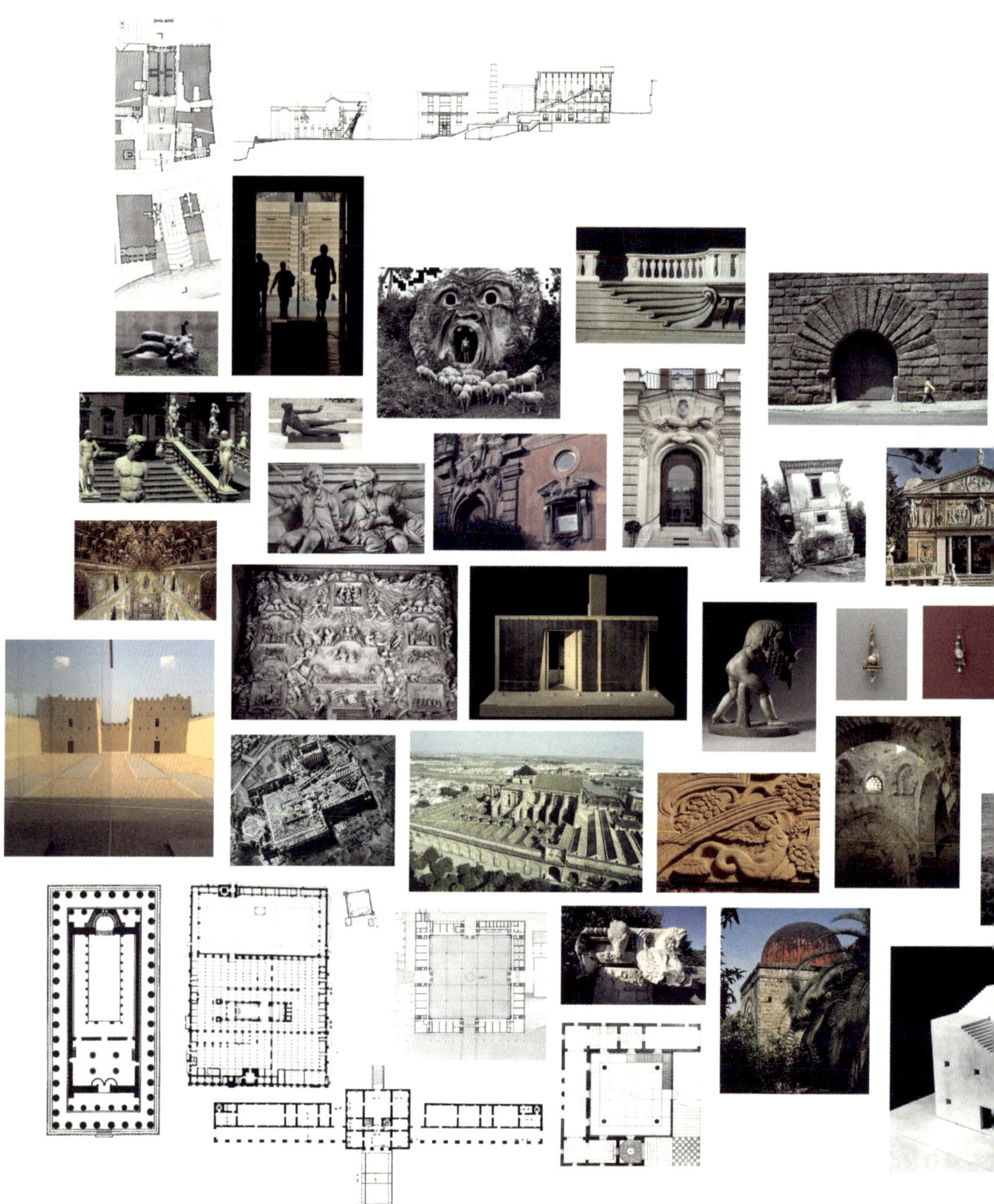

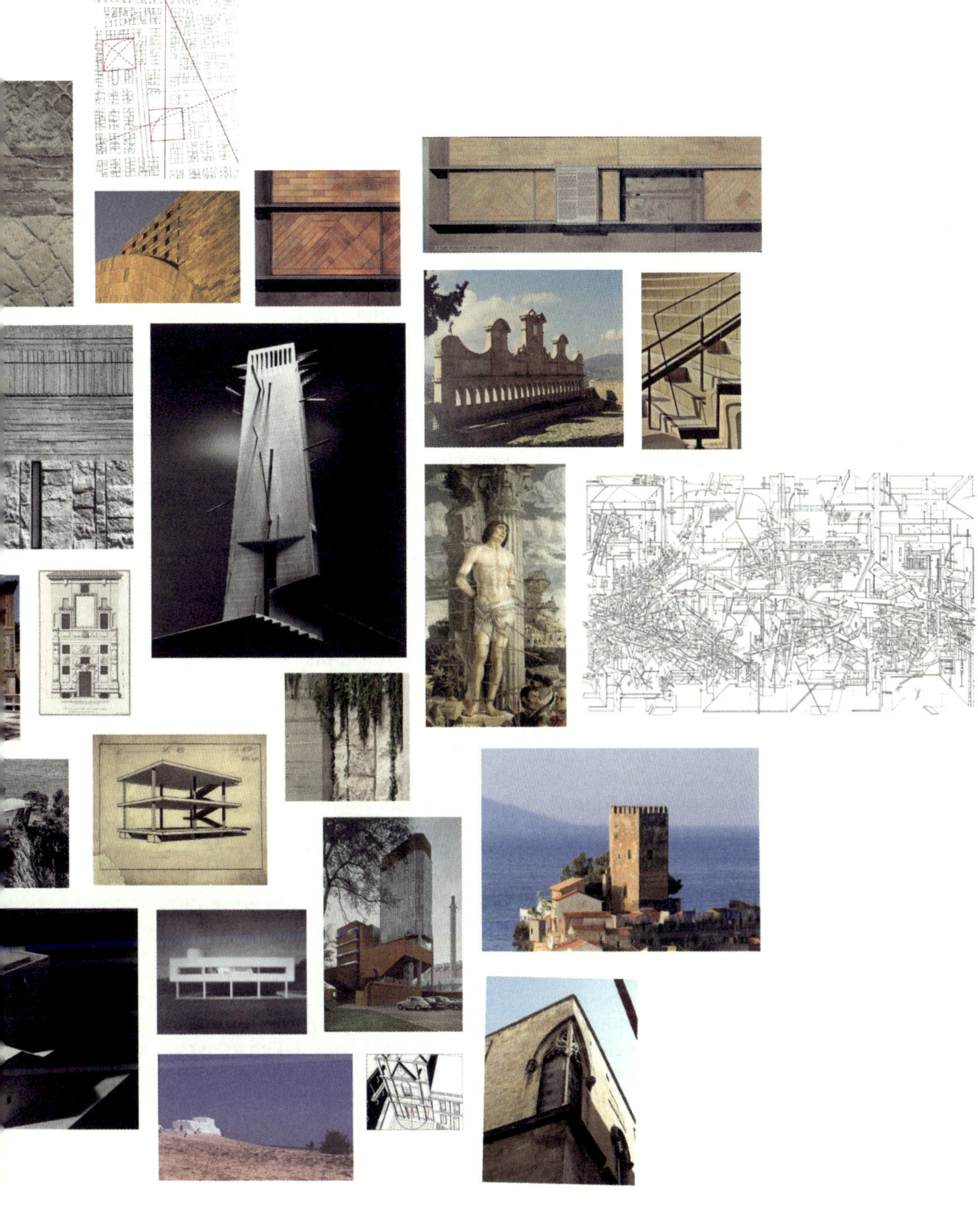

To answer your question, I think we can look at cases that help us better understand these processes. We can look at how marginalized strains within a dominant culture have been able to operate with diverse efficiencies and degrees of success. For instance, I am currently trying to spell out the difference between architecture and music for my course.

Why that pair? Because I want us to assess in my upcoming seminar why Black culture in the US has registered such a meager impact in one—architecture—versus such extraordinary influence in the other.

These are two fundamental and universal cultural practices. Each of them has distinctive modes of production based on basic and inescapable scientific and natural phenomena: gravity, sound waves, the human need for shelter, the urge to symbolize, to communicate emotionally, etc. They also have specific relations to material infrastructure and modes of transmission.

So, why is it that jazz became the most extraordinary and truly original American cultural product? Can we gain something from reading it as a synthesis of multiple strains, sources, and directions, whether they came from minority or canonical histories? I think that by discerning between the particular combinations of factors that come together to create music and architecture, we can better understand how power operates in these different practices. With what intensity do dominant forms of power register in each one of these cultural practices, and what does that tell us about the different ways in which we can affect American culture through them?

This is a great case, because we have the last century and a half to look into. And I do think it can help us develop feasible, grounded strategies through which to address many of the issues that surfaced in 2020 in our discipline over the next decade.

NDA I'd like to end with a question about the changing role of history in our discipline. You came up in a period when history was being truly rediscovered for architecture as modernism met its demise. I'm curious what you think about the discussions being had about history today among designers in schools of architecture? There seems to be a renewed interest in talking about architecture and history, in unpacking and problematizing certain histories with all their political and social implications for the present.

JS What we were doing in the mid-1960s and 1970s was really rediscovering history for architecture, which had been buried by modernism for decades. But it was a very conceptual search, deeply rooted in philosophy, anthropology, and other domains. We were trying to explain to ourselves how architecture really worked, culturally and socially. And I think that was the best contribution that postmodernism made to our discipline. Through analogies with language, we tried to explain how signification and meaning works in our discipline and how you can structure them into the creative process.

In a way, it was the first pass at this return to history, and I think it achieved a base level understanding of these concepts that today is quite mainstream. But that return to history was trivialized by interpreting it literally in an operative way, by actually returning to a classical vocabulary.[11] And when this made it to the scene, it caught on like wildfire, reigniting the pendulum of fashion. It soon led us to encounters with the equally reactionary and fragmentary discourse of Deconstructivism, which became dissipated through the later fascination with new technologies, materials, and digital tools. All in all, architecture disappeared as a central topic for almost two decades in our discipline.

I think it's interesting and exciting that we are in fact seeing renewed interest in talking about architecture itself and in engaging the topic of history. I think what is new about this moment is not really the social and political dimension of architecture. This was something we were already heatedly discussing in the 1960s. Rodolfo and I were pursuing our master's degrees at UC Berkeley back then, so there was no escaping this!

What is truly new is the determination—the need—to treat this not just at a conceptual level, but at an operational one. That is what I perceive we have relative consensus about right now: the desire to get our hands into it and make architecture change. Reflecting upon the topic and understanding it better isn't enough anymore. Your generation seems to want to take these understandings of history and change everything. It's about action now.

¿A ti qué te parece, Nicolás?

Notes

1 "The worst labyrinth is not that intricate form that can entrap us forever, but a single and precise straight line." —Jorge Luis Borges, *Labyrinths*, 1962.

2 ar·chive
/ 'är ˌkīv /
Noun
1. a collection of historical documents or records providing information about a place, institution, or group of people;
2. the place where historical documents or records are kept

Verb
1. place or store (something) in an archive

3 K. Michael Hays, *Unprecedented Realism: The Architecture of Machado and Silvetti* (Princeton, NJ: Princeton Architectural Press, 1995). Rodolfo Machado, Jorge Silvetti, Peter G. Rowe, and Gabriel Feld, *Rodolfo Machado and Jorge Silvetti: Buildings for Cities* (Cambridge, MA: Harvard University Graduate School of Design, 1989). Javier Cenicacelaya, Ínigo Saloña, and Nader Tehrani, *The Work of Machado & Silvetti* (San Francisco Bay Area: Oro Editions, 2018).

4 po·si·tion
/ pə'ziSH(ə)n /
Noun
1. a place where something is located
2. a particular way in which something is placed or arranged
3. a situation or set of circumstances that affect one's power to act
4. a person's point of view or attitude toward something

Verb
1. put or arrange something in a particular place or way
2. promote a product
3. portray or regard someone as a particular type of person

5 re·gard
/ rə'gärd /
Noun
1. attention to
2. best wishes

Verb
1. consider (something) in a specified way
2. gaze at steadily in a specified fashion

6 per·spec·tive
/ pər'spektiv /
Noun
1. the art of drawing solid objects on a two-dimensional surface so as to give the correct impression of their height, width, depth, and position in relation to each other when viewed from a particular point
2. particular attitude toward or way of regarding something; a point of view
3. gaze at steadily in a specified fashion

7 anamorphic
/ ' ˌanə'môrfk /
Adjective
1. denoting or relating to projection or drawing distorted by anamorphosis

8 an·a·mor·pho·sis
/ ' ˌanə'môrfəsəs /
Noun
1. a distorted projection or drawing which ap pears normal when viewed from a particular point or with a suitable mirror or lens
2. the process by which anamorphic images are produced

9 re·po·si·tion
/ ˌrēpə'ziSHən /
Verb
1. place in a different position
2. adjust or alter the position of

10 "There are those who want a text (an art, a painting) without a shadow, without the 'dominant ideology'; but this is to want a text without fecundity, without productivity, a sterile text . . . The text needs its shadows; this shadow is a bit of ideology, a bit of representation, a bit of subject: ghosts, pockets, traces, necessary clouds: subversion must produce its own chiaroscuro." —Roland Barthes, *The Pleasure of the Text*, 1975.

11 "Better than recognizing things I hadn't thought of in years or remembering those I hadn't entirely forgotten, I wanted to imagine them, keep stepping back till I saw what was inside me, not what was out there. As if in order to experience this thing called the past, I needed distance, temperance, tact, an inflection of sloth and humor even—because memory, like revenge, is best served chilled." —André Aciman, *Harvard Square: A Novel*, 2013.

This timeline is designed to help the reader contextualize events and experiences mentioned in this book, overcoming the limitations of typical bullet-style timelines. It remains succinct and factual, while also providing depth and breadth. Organized into three thematic columns—year and place, personal life, and academic and professional—it allows the reader to follow the chronological (vertical) and synchronic (horizontal) unfolding of events in my life. Some broader global events are also integrated in italics across columns. This format is the closest I've come to writing an autobiography, concisely collecting and describing the significant facts of my lived experience. This should make it easier to understand the relationships between those different aspects that have made up my life.

After extended periods of meditation, I carefully selected these events and experiences based on their importance, influence, lasting impact, and transformative power on me. I am aware that some globally significant events are absent. This is because, while I acknowledge their importance, I do not consider them pivotal in shaping my intellectual and artistic identity. In contrast, localized events like a military coup in a South American country in 1973—which profoundly impacted my political understanding and approach—have a significant place in this timeline, because they revealed to me the harsh and deceitful nature of the political reality of my world.

Jorge Silvetti

Year	Location	*Global* Personal	Academic & Professional
1941		*December 7: The Japanese attack Pearl Harbor.* *December 8: The United States declares war on Japan, extending WWII to the Pacific.*	
	Buenos Aires	My family moves from the Argentinian town of Villa Cañás (Santa Fe) to Buenos Aires. I am born on December 31 at home during an emergency procedure performed by my grandmother Rosa Maria Ramacciotti de Malanca.	
1942		Due to difficulties reporting my emergency birth during the holidays, I am registered as officially born on January 5 in Buenos Aires to Catalina Rosa Malanca de Silvetti and Samuel Lareano Silvetti.	
1945		*World War II ends with the defeat of Germany and Japan.*	
1946		*J. D. Perón is elected president of Argentina after popular and military upheaval.*	
		My family moves to a *casa chorizo* in the Barrio Sur of Buenos Aires.	I attend La Virgen Niña, a kindergarten run by nuns.
1948		My family begins vacationing in Mar del Plata during the summer, a yearly move that will last until 1959.	I attend a co-ed elementary school associated with the Escuela Normal de Maestras #8, Julio Argentino Roca.
1950			I begin piano and music-theory studies in the Conservatorio de Música de Buenos Aires.
1952		*July 26: Eva Perón dies.*	
			I transfer to Escuela Gervasio Posadas, a boys school. I give my first student piano recital. I continue to do recitals every year until 1959.
1954			I enroll in high school (*bachillerato*) at Colegio Nacional Nº 5, Bartolomé Mitre (el Shule Mitre).
1955		*J. D. Perón is deposed by a military coup. He is exiled in Paraguay and later Spain.* *The government becomes ruled by a military junta.*	
1958		*Arturo Frondizi is democratically elected president of Argentina.* *A major political dispute breaks out in defense of public, laic education in response to governmental promotion of private confessional schools in Argentina.*	
			I graduate from high school. I graduate from the musical conservatory with honors.
1959			I enter the Universidad de Buenos Aires, Facultad de Arquitectura y Urbanismo (UBA-FAU).
1960		My family moves to a modern Rationalist apartment from the 1930s. I spend the summer camping with college classmates in Lake Futalaufquen (Chubut) in the Patagonian Andes.	

Year	Location	*Global* Personal	Academic & Professional
1961		I spend the summer camping with college classmates in the National Parks of Los Alerces (Chubut) and the Nahuel Huapí (Rio Negro) in the Patagonian Andes	I start working as part-time draftsman in the office of Bell and Ladizesky in Florida and Paraguay, Buenos Aires. I enroll in the Taller Wladimiro Acosta, UBA-FAU.
1962		*President Arturo Frondizi is deposed by a military coup, leading to a decade of continuous armed military strife and general political upheaval.*	
			I enroll in the Taller Odilia Suárez for the remainder of my studies. I met my teacher and mentor Horacio Baliero. Together with other classmates I begin to help Horacio Baliero and Carmen Cordoba Iturburu in their professional work at Organización de Arquitectura Moderna (OAM).
1963		*Dr. Arturo Illia is democratically elected president of Argentina.*	
			Invited by the International Union of Architects (UIA), I attend their world congress devoted to "Architecture in Developing Countries" in Havana, Cuba, as part of a large group of international advanced architecture students from all over the world. I have a gripping, memorable experience in their company in parallel with a disconcerting direct contact with the early years of the Cuban Revolution.
1964		*American military forces are deployed to Vietnam.* *The Gulf of Tonkin incident triggers the Vietnam War.*	
		I am drafted into military service in the Army Corp of Engineers at Campo de Mayo and the Ministry of War, and later transferred to the Army's Cavalry, in an agricultural and horse breeding military estate.	I successfully conclude my coursework at the UBA-FAU. I join (*ad honorem*) the team working in the Plan Urbanistico Particularizado Zona Centro Ciudad de Buenos Aires, under the direction of architect Oscar Fisch.
1965		My mandatory military service ends in April at the Army's agricultural estate in Tandil (BA). I meet Rodolfo Machado at the office of architect Jorge Erbin in Buenos Aires when I join a team working on a competition for a new civic center in the town of Berisso.	I begin to take the final exams at UBA-FAU. I am appointed assistant to the Taller Soto-Winograd at the Universidad de La Plata, Facultad de Arquitectura. I am appointed as a designer in the City of Buenos Aires Housing Authority. I meet Rafael Viñoly at UBA-FAU and we become close friends.

Year	Location	*Global* Personal	Academic & Professional
1966		*June 28: Dr. Arturo Illia is deposed by a military coup and is replaced by a military junta. July 29: La Noche de los Bastones Largos. The Universidad de Buenos Aires is closed by the military government.*	
		In January, I take a month-long trip with Jorge Lestard, visiting central Chile's major natural sites and cities, crossing the Andes from Puerto Montt to San Carlos de Bariloche (Argentina), where we join Rodolfo.	I am appointed assistant to the Taller of Manolo Borthagaray at the UBA-FAU through a public competition. I graduate from UBA–FAU with the title of Arquitecto and a professional license on September 20. I conclude my work at the Housing Authority with the end of the Lugano I and II projects. With Nucho Petchersky we work as construction supervisors for a pavilion at the National Rural Fair, designed by T. Diaz and J. Erbin. With a few classmates and two young faculty members we establish Arquitectos Associados. I work for an engineering firm on construction documents for the new Santa Fe–Paraná Bridge.
1967	 Berkeley	I depart for San Francisco, CA, on September 6. I live temporarily with friends in Albany, CA. I move to the International House on the UC Berkeley campus.	I work at Francisco Bullrich y Alicia Cazzaniga (OAM) on construction documents for a new guest house in the province of Buenos Aires until my departure to California. I work at Donald Olsen's architecture office in Berkeley. I apply and am accepted to the Master Degree Program of the College of Environmental Design at UC Berkeley (CED-UCB).
1968		*May 1968: Civil unrest events in France unfold.*	
		I move out of campus to an apartment in Berkeley's Northside. Rodolfo arrives in Berkeley on June 26.	I begin my graduate studies in January at the CED-UCB. I do freelance work for the summer residence of Mr. and Mrs. Sabouni in Sea Ranch, CA, as well as the remodeling of their house in Russian River, CA.
1969		*May 15: Bloody Sunday. A major violent confrontation between UC Berkeley students and police erupts over the People's Park controversy, leaving one person dead and over one hundred hospitalized.*	
	Oakland	I return to Argentina after graduation for a visit. I travel extensively throughout Mexico during the summer with Rodolfo. We move to an apartment in Oakland, CA.	I graduate with a Master of Architecture during the spring quarter. I am appointed as an associate at the CED-UCB.
1970		*In Chile, Salvador Allende is the first democratically elected Marxist president in the world, rekindling the hopes and aspirations of the Latin America's political left after their disillusion with the experience with the Cuban Revolution.*	
	Berkeley	We move back to Berkeley's Southside.	I begin the course of studies for the PhD Program in Architecture at the CED-UCB. I am appointed Associate in Architecture and teach studio sections in the undergraduate architecture program at the CED-UCB.

Year	Location	*Global* Personal	Academic & Professional
1971		Rodolfo and I undertake a three-month Grand European/Mediterranean Tour throughout the summer (UK, France, and Italy). In Rome, we are joined by Diana Agrest and Mario Gandelsonas for a final tour of Sicily and Tunisia.	I meet two freshmen at CED-UCB, Tarek Ashkar and Calvin Tsao, who became two of our closest friends and colleagues to this day.
1972	San Francisco	We move to San Francisco in July. We attend the San Francisco premiere of John Waters' *Pink Flamingos* at the Palace movie theater in Chinatown.	I successfully pass my PhD qualifying exams at the CED-UCB. I am appointed as a lecturer at the CED-UCB. Rodolfo and I do freelance architecture design work for a commercial center in San Francisco.
1973		*After the electoral triumph of the Peronist Party, J. D. Perón returns from exile and assumes the presidency of Argentina.* *Salvador Allende is deposed by a bloody military coup on September 11, and commits suicide at the Palacio de La Moneda, in Santiango. The sinister sixteen-year-long period of General Augusto Pinochet's dictatorship begins.* *The first global oil crisis and economic recession since the end of WWII unfolds, ending a period of prosperity in the West.*	
	Pittsburgh	We move to Pittsburgh in August. We travel in Spain and Portugal during the summer.	I receive offers to join the architecture departments at Cornell University and Carnegie Mellon University (CMU) during the spring. I join the College of Fine Arts at CMU in the fall.
1974		*July 1: J. D. Perón dies in Buenos Aires. He is succeeded by vice president Isabel Martinez de Perón, his third wife.*	
		I travel across the Veneto and Emilia Romagna regions with Tito Serebrinsky.	I deliver a lecture at Princeton University's School of Architecture as part of the series "Practice, Theory and Politics in Architecture," organized by Diana Agrest. I later transcribed and edited the lecture, which become the article "The Beauty of Shadows." We make the acquaintance of Colin Rowe. I attend a Conference on semiology in Milano.
1975		*April 30: The Fall of Saigon puts an end to the Vietnam War.*	
	Cambridge	I move to Cambridge, MA, in August	I am appointed assistant professor at the Department of Architecture at the Harvard Graduate School of Design (DA-GSD) in the fall.
1976		*March 24: The armed forces seize power in Argentina, deposing Isabel Perón and establishing a military junta.* *A five year period of systematic state terror known as "The Dirty War" begins in Argentina.*	
	Boston	I move to Boston in May. Rodolfo is appointed to the faculty of the Department of Architecture at the Rhode Island School of Design (RISD) and moves to Boston.	Gerald M. McCue is appointed chair of the DA-GSD. Rodolfo and I establish our professional office. We win a Progressive Architecture (P.A.) Award for Fountain House, a project we designed in 1974–1975 while in Pittsburgh (unbuilt).

Year	Location	*Global* Personal	Academic & Professional
1977			I organize and lead a group of DA-GSD students during a six-week visit to Rome and the Veneto region. My first published article, "The Beauty of Shadows", appears in *Oppositions* 9. I receive a P.A. Award for the project House in the Island of Djerba, on which I have worked for the past few years (unbuilt).
1978		We acquire a Victorian townhouse in Boston's Back Bay, where we live and set up the first Machado & Silvetti architecture and urban design office.	I am promoted to the rank of associate professor at the DA-GSD. RM is appointed Head of the Department of Architecture at RISD.
1980			Gerald McCue is appointed dean of the GSD. Harry Cobb is appointed chair of the DA-GSD. I am invited to teach as a guest professor at the Eidgenössische Technische Hochschule – Zürich in the spring. We win the P.A. First Award for the Steps of Providence, a project initiated in 1977 (unbuilt).
1982		*The Guerra de Las Malvinas (Falklands War) is fought in the South Atlantic between Argentina and the UK. After defeat, the governing Argentinian military junta calls for free elections.*	I am invited to teach as a guest professor at the Universitá degli Studi di Palermo in Sicily (May–July). I remain a seasonal visitor and teacher there for the next three years.
1983		*Raul Alfonsin assumes the presidency of Argentina, restoring the democratic system of government that has continued unaltered until the present.*	I am appointed professor of architecture and design theory with tenure at Harvard University. Our project Taberna Ancipites Formae is presented in the exhibition *Follies: Architecture for the Late Twentieth Century Landscape* at Leo Castelli Art Gallery, NY.
1984			I receive three P.A. Awards, (all for work done in Sicily), becoming the first recipient of P.A. Awards in all of its categories: in architecture for the House in the Lake Pergusa, in urban design for Four Public Squares in Leonforte, and in research for the work on "The Architecture and Urban Environments of Sicily" project that I conduct at Harvard.
1985			Our office, Machado & Silvetti Associates (MSA) is incorporated. Howard Burns is appointed professor of architectural history with tenure at GSD. Rafael Moneo is appointed chair of the DA-GSD.

Year Location	*Global* Personal	Academic & Professional
1986 Boston and Rome		We move the offices of MSA to the South End of Boston. I receive the 1986 Rome Prize (mid-career) and reside at the American Academy in Rome from January to August. Rodolfo steps down as Head of the DA, RISD. Portantina store, designed by RM and I, opens in New York City.
1988 Boston		I begin work as principal investigator in the five-year research program "The Architecture and Urban Environments of Sicily," a collaboration between the DA-GSD and the municipalities of the Val di Noto in Sicily. The program is jointly conceived by Gerald McCue and myself.
1989	*November 9: The Berlin Wall falls.* We acquire a cottage in Wellfleet, Cape Cod, MA. It will become our year-round working and leisure retreat.	We win the first prize in the international competition for the new Piazza Dante in Genoa (unbuilt).
1990		I am appointed Nelson Robinson, Jr. Professor of Architecture Chair at DA-GSD. Mack Scogin is appointed chair of the DA-GSD.
1991	*December 26: The Soviet Union is dissolved.*	Rodolfo and I lead a team of intenational students working on the Nordbahnhofgelände project in Vienna, Austria. MSA wins the second prize of the international competition by the Biennale di Venezia, *Una porta per Venezia*. MSA wins the competition for the Cranbrook Academy New North Entrance (unbuilt).
1992		Peter Rowe is appointed dean of the GSD. MSA's Princeton University Parking Garage opens.
1993		MSA is one of the six firms selected among forty other international firms to compete for the Expansion and Master Plan of the Getty Villa in Malibu, CA. The first edition of the required course "Buildings, Texts & Contexts," taught jointly by Howard Burns and myself, is delivered in the fall.
1994		MSA wins the competition for the expansion of the Getty Villa in California (built).
1995		I am appointed chair of the DA-GSD. I lead a design studio at the DA-GSD on the Roman archeological area of La Manzana de San Pedro in the city of Cordóba, Spain.

Year	Location	*Global* Personal	Academic & Professional
1997			I am appointed juror of the Pritzker Architecture Prize and will remain on the jury until 2004. Rodolfo and I travel with the Getty to visit major archeological sites and museums of antiquities in Italy and France. MSA's Robert Wagner, Jr. Park opens in Battery Park City, NY.
1998			MSA wins the master plan project for the UC Mission Bay New Campus in San Francisco (implemented). Rodolfo and I travel with the Getty to visit important museums of antiquities in Denmark, Germany, and Switzerland.
1999		I visit Athens, Delos, and Paros in Greece with Rodolfo.	
2000		I travel extensively with Rodolfo in Jordan and visit Jerusalem in Israel.	My appointment as chair of the DA-GSD is extended for two more years. MSA's Utah Museum of Fine Arts at the University of Utah campus opens in Salt Lake City.
2001		*September 11: Al Qaeda's attacks on the United States take place.* I visit Beirut, Byblos, Tripoli, and Baalbek in Lebanon and Damascus in Syria.	MSA's Honan-Allston Branch Library, for which I am designer in charge, opens in June in Allston, Boston.
2002			I step down from the chairmanship of the DA-GSD. MSA's master plan for the Isabella Stewart Gardner Museum, for which I am designer in charge, is approved and implemented.
2003			MSA's One Western Ave Graduate Residential Complex at Harvard University opens in Allston, Boston. I travel with the Getty Villa Council to visit antiquities and art museums in Germany.
2004	Boston and Buenos Aires	RM and I purchase and restore an apartment in the 1934 Minner Building in Buenos Aires by Jorge Kalnay, a notable early modernist building in the city. We establish a second residence in Buenos Aires.	I end my third and last three-year term as jury member for the Pritzker Architecture Prize. MSA's Rockefeller Stone Barns Center for Conservation and Promotion of Agriculture and Food, for which I am designer in charge, opens in Pocantico Hills, NY.
2005			Construction work begins on Citadel Square, in Beirut, Lebanon, a project I lead as designer in charge. This is an urban archeological park and public plaza on the site of the original citadel promontory of prehistoric origins. Construction is later abandoned by the government. I travel with the Getty Villa Council and co-guide a visit to archeological sites and museums in Spain.

Year	Location	*Global*	Personal	Academic & Professional
2006				I begin a research and teaching program on the Copan archeological site in Honduras, in collaboration with the Department of Archeology at Harvard University. I will lead design studios on the topic over the following three years. MSA's new Getty Villa opens in January. MSA's Provincetown Art Association and Museum expansion, for which I am designer in charge, opens in Provincetown, MA.
2007		*The subprime mortgage crisis and Great Recession begins.*		MSA's expansion and restoration of Bowdoin College Museum of Art in Brunswick, ME, for which I am designer in charge, opens in October. I am designer in charge of MSA's project for the Church and Parish facilities of Madre Teresa di Calcutta in Rome for the Vatican's Office for the Propagation of the Faith and the Provision of New Churches (unbuilt).
2008			We acquire and restore a unit within the notable 1937 modernist building by Sanchez, Lagos y de la Torre in Buenos Aires.	We open a branch office of MSA in Buenos Aires, in one of the Ateliers in Tres Sargentos by Sanchez, Lagos y de la Torre, that we had recently acquired and restored.
2010				I lead MSA's master plan for the Cultural Quarter Complex and Conservation of the Al Ain Oasis in Abu Dhabi that receives UNESCO World Heritage Site status in 2011.
2011				MSA wins the Porto Olímpico Competition in Rio de Janeiro, Brazil (in association with Jorge Jáuregui, local architect), for which I am designer in charge (unbuilt).
2012				MSA's Black Family Visual Arts Center, for which I am designer in charge, opens in September at Dartmouth College, NH.
2013			I travel to Posadas, Argentina, and visit all the Jesuit Mission ruins on both the Argentinian and Paraguayan sides of the Paraná River.	I conceive and begin a three-year research project sponsored by the Entidad Binacional Yaciretà (EBY) of Argentina and Paraguay. I travel to Lima to participate in an international symposium and visit the Machu Picchu site, as well as other archeological monuments in the region.

Year	Location	*Global* Personal	Academic & Professional
2015			Together with professor Graciela Silvestri, I organize and host a week-long international seminar on the Territorio Guaraní in Posadas, Argentina. MSA's New Museum and Gardens, in conjunction with the restoration of the existing Al Muwaiji Fort in Al Ain, Abu Dhabi, of which I am designer in charge (with Imad Gemayel as landscape architect), opens to the public. MSA's New Museo del Territorio Guaraní, for which I am designer in charge, is presented to the Provincial Government of Misiones. The project is sponsored by the EBY (unbuilt). MSA expands its leadership with new principals and adopts MACHADO SILVETTI as the new name for the firm.
2017			I am invited as a guest professor by the University of Miami's School of Architecture Rome Program to conduct an in situ history of architecture from antiquity to the late Baroque period in the city of Rome.
2018			I am awarded the 2018 AIA-ACSA Topaz Medallion for Architectural Education Award. I reduce my teaching at Harvard for the remaining four years before my retirement and begin a series of specially conceived seminars. I teach the first of two editions of both the the seminar "Bramante is Better than Alberti" and "Selected Current (and Recurrent) Topics in Architecture and Design Practice." I will teach the second editions of these seminars in 2019–20.
2019			MACHADO SILVETTI's leadership is restructured with Rodolfo Machado and Jorge Silvetti as founding partners and Jeffry Burchard and Stephanie Randazzo Dwyer as partners.
2020		*November: The first outbreak of COVID-19 infection is discovered in Wuhan, China.*	
	Boston and Wellfleet	We move to our Wellfleet cottage for the duration of the COVID-19 pandemic.	I begin individual studies on musical theory, harmony, and counterpoint remotely with professor J. M. Miceli in Berlin, Germany. Nicolás Delgado Alcega edits a conversation with me, published in *Pairs* 02 (2021), that emerges from several months of remote exchange during the COVID-19 lockdown.

Year	Location	*Global*	Personal	Academic & Professional
2021				I teach my last two seminars at Harvard, "Regarding an Archive" (spring) and "Interpreting an Archive" (fall). After preparing my preliminary outline for this book with Kyle Winston, Nicolás and I conceive the idea for this book. We begin recording our conversations with the five interlocutors in November and start to edit the book. Rodolfo and I donate our professional and academic archives to the Special Collections of the Frances Loeb Library at Harvard University. MSA's new Benton Art Museum, for which I am designer in charge, opens in September at Pomona College, Claremont, CA. MSA's new building expansion and the restoration of the Gio Ponti structure at the Denver Art Museum, for which I am designer in charge, opens in October in Denver, CO.
2022	Boston and Buenos Aires		We begin to alternate residence between Buenos Aires and Boston.	I retire from Harvard and become the Nelson Robinson, Jr. Professor of Architecture Emeritus. A comprehensive exhibition of MSA's work opens at Harvard University's Drucker Gallery in Gund Hall with drawings, models, and documents from the MSA archive. MSA's new gallery and headquarters for Fundación Lariviere—a project I worked on in association with Mariano Clusellas, local architect—opens in November in La Boca, Buenos Aires.
2023			In May–June I visit Athens and Rome with Rodolfo. I spend extensive time with Prof. Manolis Korris at the Athenian Acropolis, inspecting and learning about the Erechtheion's history, architecture, and current archeological work.	I begin collecting my notes for the essay "The Acropolis of Athens and Its Consequences" (tentative title). Nicolás and I submit the *Large, Lasting, & Inevitable* manuscript to Park Books in Zürich, Switzerland.

The following list of writings by Jorge Silvetti does not include subsequent editions in other languages for texts originally published in English. The texts are organized chronologically.

Silvetti, Jorge. "The Beauty of Shadows." *Oppositions*, no. 9 (1977): 43–61.

Silvetti, Jorge. "On Realism in Architecture." *The Harvard Architecture Review*, no. 1 (1978): 9–31.

Machado, Rodolfo, and Jorge Silvetti. "325. 'A theory of production of Architecture': Collage of projects by Machado and Silvetti from 1972 to 1979." In *Architecture, 1980: The Presence of the Past*, edited by Gabriella Borsano. New York, NY: Rizzoli, 1980.

Machado, Rodolfo, and Jorge Silvetti. "Machado-Silvetti: The Steps of Providence, 1979." *Design Quarterly*, no. 113/114 (1980): 52–53. https://doi.org/10.2307/4091042.

Silvetti, Jorge. "Representation and Creativity in Architecture: The Pregnant Moment." In *Representation and Architecture*, edited by Ömer Akin and Eleanor F. Weinel, 159–184. Silver Spring, MD: Information Dynamics, Inc., 1982.

Silvetti, Jorge. "Perspective and the Envious Longing for the Renaissance." *Daidalos*, no. 11 (1984): 10–21.

Silvetti, Jorge. "Four Public Squares in the City of Leonforte, Sicily." *Assemblage*, no. 1 (1986): 55–71. https://doi.org/10.2307/3171054.

Silvetti, Jorge. "Aires de la Pampa." In *Amancio Williams*, edited by Jorge Silvetti and Gabriel Feld (project assistant), 5–9. New York, NY: Rizzoli; Cambridge, MA: Harvard University, Graduate School of Design, 1987.

Silvetti, Jorge. "The Poetics of Counterpoint." In *Mario Campi-Franco Pessina, Architects*, edited by Kenneth Frampton. New York, NY: Rizzoli, 1987.

Machado, Rodolfo, and Jorge Silvetti. "Note on the Project Texts." In *Rodolfo Machado and Jorge Silvetti: Buildings for Cities*, edited by Peter G. Rowe. New York, NY: Rizzoli, 1989.

Silvetti, Jorge. Introduction to *Architectural and Urban Environments of Sicily 1: The First Year of Research by the Harvard Graduate School of Design*, edited by Jorge Silvetti, assistant editor Thomas Rankin, 10–24. Cambridge, MA: Harvard University Graduate School of Design, 1989.

Silvetti, Jorge. "The Architecture of the Late Twentieth Century American City." In *Papers Delivered at the Conference: Harvard University. Graduate School of Design 1989 Seminar in Tokyo, Japan*. Cambridge, MA: Harvard University Graduate School of Design, 1989.

Silvetti, Jorge. Introduction to *Architectural and Urban Environments of Sicily 2: Interactive Realms, The Bridge of San Francesco and the Palazzo Sant'Elia*, edited by Jorge Silvetti, 1–22. Cambridge, MA: Harvard University Graduate School of Design, 1992.

Silvetti, Jorge. "The Bridge and the Palazzo: Urban Interventions and Social Representation." In *Architectural and Urban Environments of Sicily 2: Interactive Realms, The Bridge of San Francesco and the Palazzo Sant'Elia*, edited by Jorge Silvetti, 87–129. Cambridge, MA: Harvard University Graduate School of Design, 1992.

Silvetti, Jorge. "The Symptoms of Malaise." *Progressive Architecture* 73, no. 3 (1992): 108. http://search.proquest.com.ezp-prod1.hul.harvard.edu/trade-journals/symptoms-malaise/docview/197296100/se-2.

Machado, Rodolfo, and Jorge Silvetti. "Banffire." In *Queues Rendezvous Riots: Questioning the Public in Art and Architecture*, edited by George Baird and Mark Lewis, 19–27. Banff, Alberta: The Banff Centre for the Arts, 1994.

Machado, Rodolfo, and Jorge Silvetti. Afterword to *Unprecedented Realism*, edited by K. Michael Hays, 259–265. New York, NY: Princeton Architectural Press, 1994.

Robbins, Edward, and Jorge Silvetti. "Jorge Silvetti: Machado & Silvetti Associates." In *Why Architects Draw*, edited by Edward Robbins, 103–124. Cambridge, MA: MIT Press, 1994.

Silvetti, Jorge. "After Words." *Assemblage*, no. 27 (1995): 75–79. https://doi.org/10.2307/3171432.

Silvetti, Jorge, Mark Wigley, and Catherine Ingraham. "Assembly 3." *Assemblage*, no. 27 (1995): 99–105.

https://doi.org/10.2307/3171435.
Silvetti, Jorge. "Juan Navarro Baldeweg: Architecture's Outside." *Assemblage*, no. 34 (1997): 31–55.
Silvetti, Jorge. "Introduction." In "Design Arts and Architecture," edited by Jorge Silvetti (guest editor) and William Saunders. Special issue, *Harvard Design Magazine*, no. 5 (1998): 2–5.
Silvetti, Jorge. "Citation." In *Philippe Starck: The 1997 Excellence in Design Award*, edited by Brooke Hodge, 8–17. Cambridge, MA: Harvard University Graduate School of Design, 2000.
Silvetti, Jorge. "Citation." In *Robert Wilson: The 1998 Excellence in Design Award*, edited by Brooke Hodge, 8–18. Cambridge, MA: Harvard University Graduate School of Design, 2000.
Silvetti, Jorge. "Prólogo." In *Buenos Aires natural + artificial : exploraciones sobre el espacio urbano, la arquitectura y el paisaje*, edited by Alberto Varas, 5. Buenos Aires: Universidad de Palermo; Cambridge, MA: Universidad de Harvard; Buenos Aires: Universidad de Buenos Aires, 2000.
Silvetti, Jorge. "Preface: Millennium Matters." In *Before and After the End of Time: Architecture and the Year 1000*, edited by Christine Smith, vii–ix. Cambridge, MA: Harvard Design School in association with George Braziller, 2001.
Silvetti, Jorge. Preface to *Richard Neutra's Windshield House*, edited by Dietrich Neumann, viii–xi. Cambridge, MA: Harvard University Graduate School of Design; Cambridge, MA: Harvard Art Museums; New Haven, CT: Yale University Press, 2001.
Silvetti, Jorge. "Citation." In *Rei Kawakubo, Comme des Garçons: The 2000 Excellence in Design Award*, edited by Brooke Hodge, 8–19. Cambridge, MA: Harvard University Graduate School of Design, 2002.
Silvetti, Jorge. "The Muses Are Not Amused: Pandemonium in the House of Architecture." *Harvard Design Magazine*, no. 19 (2003): 22–33.
Silvetti, Jorge. Foreword to *Enrique Norten: A House in the City*, edited by Brooke Hodge, 9–11. Cambridge, MA: Harvard Design School, 2003.
Silvetti, Jorge. *Superquadras, Projections and Pilotis: Design Experiments on the Preservation of Brasilia's Architectural Heritage*. Cambridge, MA: Harvard Graduate School of Design, 2004.
Silvetti, Jorge. "Jorge Silvetti's response to the letter about his HDM 19 article by Jeff Kipnis and Sanford Kwinter in HDM 20." *Harvard Design Magazine*, no. 21 (2004): 112–113.
Silvetti, Jorge. *Introductions: Jorge Silvetti*. Edited by Rodolphe El-Khoury. Cambridge, MA: Harvard Design School, 2004.
Silvetti, Jorge. "The Getty Villa Reimagined." In *The Getty Villa*, by Marion True and Jorge Silvetti, 97–211. Los Angeles, CA: Getty Publications, 2005.
Silvetti, Jorge. *Puntižela: Touristic Development in the Istrian Peninsula*. Cambridge, MA: Harvard University Graduate School of Design, Department of Architecture, 2005.
Campbell, Robert, Jorge Silvetti, Jerry Podany, and James Wood. "The Art and Science of Conservation." *Bulletin of the American Academy of Arts and Sciences* 61, no. 4 (2008): 11–17. http://www.jstor.org/stable/40481189.
Silvetti, Jorge. Foreword to *Beyond Surface Appeal: Literalism, Sensibilities, and Constituencies in the Work of James Carpenter*, edited by Sarah M. Whiting. Cambridge, MA: Harvard University Graduate School of Design; Chichester: John Wiley, 2010.
Silvetti, Jorge, and Felipe Correa. *Invention/Transformation: Strategies for the Qattara/Jimi Oases in Al Ain*. Cambridge, MA: Harvard University Graduate School of Design; Abu Dhabi: Abu Dhabi Authority for Culture & Heritage (ADACH), 2010.
Silvetti, Jorge. "Collaborations Between a School and a Continent." *Harvard Design Magazine*, no. 34 (2011): 200–241.
Silvetti, Jorge. "Buenos Aires: A Tale of Two Cities?" In *In the Life of Cities*, edited by Mohsen Mostafavi, 138–151. Cambridge, MA: Harvard University Graduate School of Design; Zürich: Lars Müller, 2012.
Silvetti, Jorge. "Effective Affinities." In *Interdisciplinary Design: New Lessons from Architecture and Engineering*, edited by Hanif Kara and Andreas Georgoulias, 4–9. Barcelona: Actar; Cambridge, MA: Harvard University Graduate School of Design, 2012.
Silvetti, Jorge, and Conrad Ello. *La Nueva*

Villa Getty. Valencia: General de Ediciones de Arquitectura (Biblioteca TC), 2013.

Silvestri, Graciela, and Jorge Silvetti. "Vestiges of Cities without Evil: The Case of the Territorio Guaraní," edited by Anthony Acciavatti, Justin Fowler and Dan Handel. *Manifest*, no. 2 (2014): Kingdoms of God, 24–39.

Silvetti, Jorge. "Block That Metaphor!" In *The Return of Nature: Sustaining Architecture in the Face of Sustainability*, edited by Preston Scott Cohen and Erika Naginski, 197–209. New York, NY: Routledge, 2014.

Silvetti, Jorge, and Matías Imbern. "Conversación con Jorge Silvetti." *A&P Continuidad*. 1, no. 1 (2014): 86–95.

Silvestri, Graciela, and Jorge Silvetti. "Shaping the Guaraní Territory," edited by Graciela Silvestri and Jorge Silvetti. *ReVista* vol. 14, no. 3 (2015): 2–6.

Silvetti, Jorge. "Paths, Sounds, Ruins." In *Paths, Sounds, Ruins: Imagining Architecture in Candelaria*, edited by Jennifer Sigler, assistant editor Marielle Suba, 10–14. Cambridge, MA: Harvard University Graduate School of Design, 2017.

Silvetti, Jorge. "Territorio Guaraní." In *Paths, Sounds, Ruins: Imagining Architecture in Candelaria*, edited by Jennifer Sigler, assistant editor Marielle Suba, 10–115. Cambridge, MA: Harvard University Graduate School of Design, 2017.

Silvetti, Jorge. "TYPE: Architecture's Elusive Obsession and the Rituals of an Impasse; Eduard Sekler Memorial Lecture." Lecture presented at Harvard Graduate School of Design, Cambridge, MA, November 7, 2017.[1]

Silvetti, Jorge, and Nicolás Delgado Alcega. "Labyrinth of Affinities: On Perspective, Anamorphosis, and Repositionings." *Pairs*, no. 2 (2021): 119–132.

Silvetti, Jorge. "An Architect's Reflection on Expanding the Denver Art Museum." In *Gio Ponti in the American West*, edited by Taisto H. Mäkelä, 116–127. Denver, CO: Denver Art Museum; New York, NY: Rizzoli Electa, 2020.

Silvetti, Jorge. "The Ponti Question." In *The Lanny and Sharon Martin Building*, 81–100. Denver, CO: Denver Art Museum, 2021.

Machado, Rodolfo, and Jorge Silvetti. "Rafael Viñoly (1944–2023)." *Architectural Record* 211, no. 4 (04, 2023): 25-26. http://search.proquest.com.ezp-prod1.hul.harvard.edu/trade-journals/raf-el-viñoly-1944-2023/docview/2794913179/se-2.

Silvetti, Jorge, Mark Lee, Nicolás Delgado Alcega, Erika Naginski, Elisa Silva, Nader Tehrani, and Alfredo Thiermann. *Large, Lasting & Inevitable: Jorge Silvetti in Dialogues and Writings on Architecture as a Cultural Practice*. Edited by Nicolás Delgado Alcega. Zürich: Park Books, 2025.[2]

1. An edited transcript of this lecture has been published for the first time in the present volume.
2. Refers to the present volume.

NICOLÁS DELGADO ALCEGA

Nicolás Delgado Alcega is the Vice President of Liminal, an organization that supports action research initiatives in Italian territories struggling with depopulation and disinvestment. He is based in Rome, where he is a principal of the architecture practice Alliata/Alcega.

Delgado Alcega holds a Master in Architecture from Harvard University and received his Bachelor of Architecture from the University of Miami. He teaches a seminar at the University of Miami on city-country dynamics in the Papal States during the Italian Renaissance. Before editing this book, he founded and edited the design journal *Pairs* (Harvard University Press).

MARK LEE

Mark Lee is a Professor in Practice at the Harvard Graduate School of Design and its former Chair of the Department of Architecture. He is also a founding partner of the award-winning architecture firm Johnston Marklee, based in Los Angeles.

Lee was one of the Artistic Directors of the 2017 Chicago Architecture Biennale, and his work has been widely published. He has also taught at Princeton University; the University of California, Los Angeles; the Technical University of Berlin; ETH Zürich; Rice University; and the University of Toronto.

ERIKA NAGINSKI

Erika Naginski is the Robert P. Hubbard Professor of Architectural History at the Harvard Graduate School of Design. Her research interests include seventeenth- and eighteenth-century architecture, theories of public space, and aesthetic philosophy.

Naginski's books and edited volumes include *The Return of Nature* (2014), *Sculpture and Enlightenment* (2009), and *Polemical Objects* (2004). Before joining the GSD faculty, she taught at MIT and the University of Michigan. She has been awarded fellowships from the John Simon Guggenheim Memorial Foundation, the Radcliffe Institute for Advanced Study, the Clark Art Institute, and the Harvard Society of Fellows.

ELISA SILVA

Elisa Silva is the director and founder of Enlace Arquitectura and the Enlace Foundation. Her practice and research challenge prejudiced narratives that support spatial inequality and mine resources to improve livelihoods and environments in territories such as Latin American self-built neighborhoods, the Guaire River in Caracas, Little Haiti in Miami, and the rural landscapes of Oaxaca.

Silva's writings and work have been widely published and exhibited. She was a Rome Prize recipient and teaches at Florida International University, Harvard University, and the Universidad Central de Venezuela. She has also taught at Princeton University, University of Toronto, and the Universidad Simón Bolívar.

NADER TEHRANI

Nader Tehrani is a professor at the Irwin S. Chanin School of Architecture of the Cooper Union and its former Dean. He is also Principal of NADAAA, a multidisciplinary practice with projects in architecture, urbanism, and planning.

Tehrani has been the recipient of multiple prizes, including the 2020 Arnold W. Brunner Memorial Prize of the American Academy of Arts and Letters, the 2022 Design Visionary Award from Cooper Hewitt, Smithsonian Museum of Design, and recently the election to the American Academy of Arts and Sciences. He also served as the 2017–2018 William A. Bernoudy Architect in Residence at the American Academy in Rome.

ALFREDO THIERMANN

Alfredo Thiermann is an architect and Assistant Professor for History and Theory of Architecture at the École polytechnique fédérale in Lausanne. Through his practice and theoretical research, he explores the intersection between architecture and different media, from sound installations and film scenography to single family houses, public buildings, and large-scale infrastructures.

Thiermann is the recipient of multiple fellowships and prizes, including the Rome Prize of the German Academy in Rome. He has taught and lectured at Harvard University, Pontificia Universidad Católica de Chile, and other institutions.

IMAGE CREDITS

Some of the drawings by Machado Silvetti in this book were created by collaborators or employees of the studio. Although a complete list of these collaborations is not yet available, efforts are underway to document them in The Rodolfo Machado & Jorge Silvetti Collection, donated in 2021 to the Frances Loeb Library, Harvard University Graduate School of Design. While some collaborators have been identified, others remain unconfirmed. Due to the incompleteness of the list, the authors have chosen not to include a partial list and instead direct readers to consult Special Collections at the Frances Loeb Library.

ENDPAPERS

1, 480 Permission of Paul Maguire, Shutterstock.

PROLOGUE

14 Esmeralda esquina Arroyo, Horacio Coppola, 1936. Permission of Galería Jorge Mara - La Ruche. © Archivo Horacio Coppola.
19, 20, 31 (top), 32, 38, 39, 41 Courtesy of Jorge Silvetti.
21 (top) Courtesy of Congrégation de Notre-Dame de Sion.
21 (bottom) Courtesy of Rodolfo2901, Tripadvisor.
22 (top) Source could not be determined.
22 (bottom) Courtesy of Cruce's Hotel Boutique.
23 (top) Olivos; la ribera del Río de la Plata, Horacio Coppola. Permission of Galería Jorge Mara - La Ruche. © Archivo Horacio Coppola.
23 (bottom) Courtesy of Archivo de Imágenes Digitales, FADU–UNBA. Taller Tony Díaz, Relevamientos, 1984–1985.
25 Courtesy of Argentoria. Photographer: Alfred Eisenstaedt for *Life* Magazine.
26 (left) Courtesy of Andrzej Otrębski, Wikimedia Commons.
26 (right) Courtesy of La Nación. Photographer: Claudio Larrea Brando.
27 Courtesy of Monoambiente.
28 Courtesy of Archivo General de la Nación, Wikimedia Commons.
30 Permission of Fondo Alejandro Bustillo, Archivo Di Tella Arquitectura, EAEU–UTDT.
31 (bottom) Courtesy of Rodolfo Machado.
34 Courtesy of Digital Images and Slides Collection, Fine Arts Library, Harvard University.
36 Courtesy of Canadian Centre for Architecture. James Stirling/Michael Wilford fonds. Collection Centre Canadien d'Architecture/Canadian Centre for Architecture, Montréal. Photographer: Richard Einzig.
37 Provided by Secretaría de Cultura de la Nación Argentina.
43 Permission of Eduardo Comesaña, Alamy Stock Photo.

DIALOGUES

48 Courtesy of the Library of Congress.
62 Group carrying "Free Speech" banner through Sather Gate, ca. 1965. Provided by UC Berkeley, The Bancroft Library.
67 Courtesy of Raptproductions, Flickr. Photographer: Scott Runyon.
70 (top) Courtesy of *San Francisco Chronicle*. Photographer: Bill Owens for Associated Press.
70 (bottom) Permission of Getty Images (Bettmann Collection).
78 Provided by ARTSTOR (Visual Arts Legacy Collection, University of California, San Diego).
87 (top) Courtesy of Dustin McGrew.
87 (bottom), 242, 251 (bottom), 255 (top), 256 (top left), 256 (top right), 256 (bottom right), 298, 304, 311 (bottom), 322 (bottom), 377 (bottom), 382 (top), 385 (top), 393 (top), 411 (top) Courtesy of Jorge Silvetti.
90 (top) Unknown American, Carnegie Institute: Hall of Architecture, no earlier than 1906. Courtesy of Carnegie Museum of Art, Gift of the Carnegie Library of Pittsburgh.
90 (bottom) Courtesy of Bruce Coleman, Flickr. The Rodolfo Machado & Jorge Silvetti Collection. Gift of Rodolfo Machado and Jorge Silvetti, 2019.
92 BB006; 132 D001_002_0006;
255 (bottom) D002_001_0007;
256 (bottom left) A004_004_0001;
379 (top left) A005_005_0001;
379 (top right) A005_005_0002;
379 (center left) A005_004_0001;
379 (center right) A005_004_0003;
379 (bottom) A005_004_0007;
382 (bottom) A017_005_0001;
385 (bottom) A011_002;
393 (bottom) D007_001_0009;
396 (top left) D003_001_0006;
396 (top right) D004_001_0009;
396 (bottom left) A007_005_0001;

396 (bottom right) A002_003_0009. Courtesy of the Frances Loeb Library, Harvard University Graduate School of Design.
116 Permission of Ralph Lieberman.
121 (top) Courtesy of Schlesinger Library, Harvard Radcliffe Institute.
121 (bottom) Permission of Ezra Stoller/ Esto.
124 (top) Courtesy of Harvard Alumni Magazine.
124 (bottom) Bennett Jones, Courtesy of Schlesinger Library, Harvard Radcliffe Institute.
127 (top) Courtesy of Nicolás Delgado Alcega.
127 (bottom) Section, studio trays. George Gund Hall. Drawings. Harvard University, Cambridge, Massachusetts. Courtesy of Harvard University Graduate School of Design Frances Loeb Library, Visual Collections (132911).
138 Courtesy of Jorge Silvetti Photographer: Diana Agrest.
214 Courtesy of Trolvag, Wikimedia Commons.
219 Tuchelt, Klaus, Branchidai-Didyma: Geschichte und Ausgrabung eines antiken Heiligtums, Mainz am Rhein: P. von Zabern, 1992, p. 13, fig. 17. Courtesy of Digital Images and Slides Collection, Fine Arts Library, Harvard University.
220 (top), 238 The Jorge Silvetti Research Collection Sicily. Courtesy of the Frances Loeb Library, Harvard University Graduate School of Design.
220 (bottom) Permission of Gacro74, Alamy Stock Photo.
234 (top) Courtesy of Ministero per i Beni e le Attività Culturali (Codice di Catalogo Nazionale 1500219946).
234 (bottom) Permission of Universal Images Group North America LLC, Alamy Stock Photo.
251 (top) Courtesy of Jorge Silvetti. Drawing: Juan Sala.
306 Courtesy of David Rumsey Historical Map Collection.
311 (top), 322 (top) Courtesy of Elisa Silva.
317 (top) Photo Scala, Florence – courtesy of the Ministero Beni e Att. Culturali e del Turismo.
317 (bottom) Courtesy of Fulvio Spada, Wikimedia Commons.
368 Courtesy Jorge Silvetti. Photographer: Facundo de Zuviria.
377 (top) Courtesy of North Lanarkshire Archives.
408–409 Permission of Institutional Archives, The Getty Research Institute, Los Angeles (2005.IA.07). © J. Paul Getty Trust.
411 (bottom) Courtesy of Anita Gould, Flickr.

REPRINTS

All image credits for republished material in this volume have been sourced from the original essays and articles. Where credits were not originally available, they have not been provided. Where the works presented make use of images that substitute those originally published, appropriate credits have been provided.

97 (Fig. 1), 111 (Fig. 16) Courtesy of Google Art Project, Wikimedia Commons.
99 (Fig. 2), 167 (Fig. 1) Courtesy of Wikimedia Commons.
99 (Fig. 3) Courtesy of Parsifall, Wikimedia Commons.
99 (Fig. 4), 201 (Fig. 12), 352 (Fig. 17) Courtesy of Sailko, Wikimedia Commons.
102 (Fig. 5), 104 (Figs. 9, 11–13), 206 (Fig. 1), 207 (Fig. 2), 210 (Fig. 8), 211 (Fig. 9), 212 (Figs. 10–11), 344 (Fig. 1), 414 (Figs. 2–3), (Figs. 4–12), 431 (Fig. 13), 432 (Figs. 14–15), 436 (37–39). Courtesy of Jorge Silvetti.
102 (Fig. 6) Reprinted from *Oppositions* 3, May 1974.
102 (Fig. 7) Courtesy of Griffin Turnbull Haesloop Architects. Photograph by Morley Baer.
102 (Fig. 8) Photograph by Rollin R. La France.
104 (Fig. 10) Courtesy of Julian Weyer, Wikimedia Commons.
108 (Fig. 14) Courtesy of Michael Graves.
108 (Fig. 15) Photograph by Chris Richie. Model built by Richard Cordts.
167 (Fig. 2) Courtesy of Cliff, Wikimedia Commons.
168 (Fig. 3) Courtesy of Museum Boijmans Van Beuningen.
168 (Fig. 4) © 2015 The Pollock-Krasner Foundation / Artists Rights Society (ARS), New York.
169 (Fig. 5) Courtesy of Swann Auction Galleries.
170 (Fig. 6) Courtesy of Architectural Design.
170 (Fig. 7) Casa alle Zattere by Gardella, host of the 2016 Unfolding Pavilion. Photo Giorgio Casali, 1958. © Archivio Gardella, CSAC Parma/Fondo Casali, IUAV Venezia.

174 (Figs. 12–13), 175 (Fig. 14) From Ezio Bonfanti, Marco Porta, Città, museo e architettura, Firenze, 1973.
175 (Fig. 15) Courtesy of ArchDaily.
178 (Figs. 18–19), 179 (Fig. 20) From *Urban Space*, by Rob Krier, 1975.
181 (Fig. 24) From *Masterpieces of Architectural Drawing*, ed. Helen Powell and David Leatherbarrow, 1983.
182 (Fig. 25) Courtesy of 7szz, Wikimedia Commons.
182 (Fig. 26) Courtesy of Andy Warhol Foundation.
184 (Fig. 29) Courtesy of Architizer.
186 (Fig. 33), 437 (Fig. 42) From *Learning from Las Vegas*, by Robert Venturi, Denise Scott Brown, and Stephen Izenour, 1972.
186 (Fig. 34) Courtesy of Canadian Centre for Architecture. © Eredi Aldo Rossi/ Fondazione Aldo Rossi, Collection Centre Canadien d'Architecture/Canadian Centre for Architecture, Montréal. The Rodolfo Machado & Jorge Silvetti Collection. Gift of Rodolfo Machado and Jorge Silvetti, 2019.
190 (Fig. 1) A007_005_0001; 191 (Fig. 2) A005_005_0002; 192 (Fig. 3) A005_003_0005; 192 (Fig. 4) A005_004_0007; 192 (Fig. 5) A005_003_0001; 193 (Fig. 6) A005_001_0001; 193 (Fig. 7) A005_001_0002; 193 (Fig. 8) A005_003_0007; 208 (Fig. 3) A005_005_0002; 208 (Fig. 4) A005_003_0004; 209 (Fig. 5) A005_003_0007; 209 (Fig. 6) A005_001_0002; 209 (Fig. 7) A005_001_0001. Courtesy of the Frances Loeb Library, Harvard University Graduate School of Design.
194 (Fig. 1) Courtesy of Lafit86, Wikimedia Commons.
194 (Fig. 2) From *Callas, The Art and the Life*, by John Ardoin.
195 (Fig. 4) Courtesy of Musée du Louvre, Wikimedia Commons.
195 (Fig. 5) Courtesy of The Yorck Project, Wikimedia Commons.
197 (Fig. 6) Dover Publications, reprint edition.
198 (Fig. 7) Courtesy of National Gallery, London, Wikimedia Commons.
198 (Fig. 8) Courtesy of Jan Arkesteijn, Wikimedia Commons.
199 (Fig. 9) From Dover Publications, reprint edition, 1964.
199 (Fig. 10) From *Hidden Images,* by Fred Leeman.
199 (Fig. 11) Courtesy of Canadian Centre for Architecture. Collection Centre Canadien d'Architecture/Canadian Centre for Architecture, Montréal.
201 (Fig. 13) From *Oeuvre Complete, 1929–1934*.
201 (Fig. 14) Courtesy of Marcok, Wikimedia Commons.
202 (Fig. 15) Courtesy of Wiley Online Library.
287 (Fig. 16) Courtesy of Ministero per i Beni e le Attività Culturali (Codice di Catalogo Nazionale 1500313019).
347 (Fig. 6) Courtesy of Daderot, Wikimedia Commons.
347 (Fig. 7) Courtesy of Ronnie McDonald, Wikimedia Commons.
348 (Fig. 9) Courtesy of Congress for the New Urbanism.
351 (Fig. 16) Courtesy of David Shankbone, Wikimedia Commons.
352 (Fig. 18) Courtesy of Poudou99, Wikimedia Commons.
353 (Fig. 21) Courtesy of Giuseppe Marino, Wikimedia Commons.
353 (Fig. 22) Courtesy of Jk1677, Wikimedia Commons.
354 (Fig. 24) Courtesy of Ian Goodrick/ Alamy.
355 (Fig. 27) Courtesy of Glasgow Life Museums.
361 (Fig. 1) Courtesy of H.-P. Haack, Wikimedia Commons.
361 (Fig. 2) Courtesy of Berlin/Frankfurter GoetheHaus/Art Resource, NY.
361 (Fig. 3) Courtesy of Getty Images, The Bridgman Art Collection #80584504.
361 (Fig. 4) Courtesy of Arne Groh, Wikimedia Commons.
365 (Fig. 5) Courtesy of Music Division, The New York Public Library for the Performing Arts, Astor, Lenox and Tilden Foundation
365 (Fig. 6) Courtesy of Originalwana, Wikimedia Commons. Photograph by the European Southern Observatory.
428 (Figs. 1–2) From *Precís on the Lectures on Architecture*, by Jean-Nicholas-Louis Durand, The Getty Research Institute, 2000.
428 (Fig. 3) Courtesy of costagar51, Flickr.
433 (Fig. 16), 435 (Fig. 30) Courtesy of Matthias Süßen, Wikimedia Commons.
433 (Fig. 18), 435 (Fig. 36) Courtesy of Barbaria1995, Wikimedia Commons.
433 (Fig. 19) Courtesy of Clemensfranz, Wikimedia Commons.
434 (Fig. 23) Courtesy of Regione Sicilia.

436 (Fig. 41), 438 (Fig. 45, 47), 439 (Figs. 49–50) © Eredi Aldo Rossi. Courtesy Fondazione Aldo Rossi.
438 (Fig. 46) Aldo Rossi with Gianni Braghieri and Roberto Freno, *Teatrino Scientifico*, 198. Private collection. © Eredi Aldo Rossi. Courtesy Fondazione Aldo Rossi.
439 (Figs. 51–53), 441 (54–55) From *Frank O. Gehry: The Complete Works*, by Francesco Dal Co and Kurt Forster, 1997.
441 (Fig. 56) Courtesy of Wolf, Flickr.
441 (Fig. 57) Courtesy of Wolfgang Neeb.
442 (Fig. 58) Courtesy of Canadian Centre for Architecture. Abalos & Herreros fonds. Collection Centre Canadien d'Architecture/Canadian Centre for Architecture, Montréal; Don de Iñaki Ábalos et Juan Herreros/Gift of Iñaki Ábalos and Juan Herreros.
442 (Fig. 61) Courtesy of Tatsuya Krause, Flickr.
443 (Fig. 62) Courtesy of Jorge Silvetti. Drawing Juan Sala.
443 (Figs. 63–64) Courtesy of Divisare. Photograph by Filippo Romano.
443 (Figs. 65–66) Courtesy of Herzog & deMeuron.
450–453 (Fig. 1) Courtesy of Nicolás Delgado Alcega and Jorge Silvetti.

The editor and the author thank Miranda Goldschmidt, Juan Martin Miceli, Mary Maxwell, Eugenio Monjeau and Graciela Silvestri, who graciously agreed to read portions of the manuscript for this book. They also thank Kyle Winston and Inés Zalduendo, whose commitment to this project throughout large swaths of the process played a crucial role. The editor would also like to thank Ginevra D'Agostino for her unwavering support throughout the making of this book.

Editor: Nicolás Delgado Alcega
Assistant Editor: Kyle Winston
Proofreading: Arts Editing Services, Eugenio Monjeau, and Stacey Wujcik
Design: Konst & Teknik
Image processing: Dexter Pre-Media
Printing and binding: Printer Trento, Italy
Production: Sophie Kullmann

Park Books AG
Niederdorfstrasse 54
8001 Zürich
Switzerland
+41 44 262 16 62
info@park-books.com
www.park-books.com

Product Safety:
Responsible person according to EU regulation 2023/988 (GPSR):
GVA Gemeinsame Verlagsauslieferung Göttingen GmbH & Co. KG
P.O. Box 2021
37010 Göttingen
Germany
+49 551 384 200 0
info@gva-verlage.de

Park Books is supported by the Federal Office of Culture with a general subsidy for the years 2021–2025.

ISBN 978-3-03860-374-0